The United Nations
in the Balance

The United Nations in the Balance

Accomplishments and Prospects

EDITED BY

NORMAN J. PADELFORD

AND

LELAND M. GOODRICH

FREDERICK A. PRAEGER, Publishers

New York · Washington · London

FREDERICK A. PRAEGER, PUBLISHERS
111 Fourth Avenue, New York, N.Y. 10003, U.S.A.
77–79 Charlotte Street, London W.1, England

Published in the United States of America in 1965
by Frederick A. Praeger, Inc., Publishers

The essays in this volume originally appeared in a
special issue of *International Organization* entitled
"The United Nations: Accomplishments and Prospects," Vol. XIX, No. 3 (Summer, 1965).

Second printing, 1966

Library of Congress Catalog Card Number: 65-24725

Printed in the United States of America

Introduction

THE twentieth anniversary of the United Nations is a milestone meriting special recognition.

That the Organization has come thus far is a tribute to the vision of those who drew the founding plans, a testimonial to the soundness of the guiding principles upon which it was built.

The task of the United Nations has been encumbered almost from the start by great-power conflicts. Its efforts to promote social progress have been hampered by discord and strife. It has been called upon to keep peace where there has been no peace in the hearts of men. It has been buffeted by the winds of racism and nationalism as the peoples of the former colonial lands have moved to rule themselves in freedom and to assert their right to speak, and act, as equals in the forum of the nations. It has been beset by financial and constitutional crises threatening to bring its operations to a standstill and ultimately to tear it apart.

Franklin D. Roosevelt, whose breath was stilled before the United Nations was formed but whose indomitable spirit infused the proceedings at San Francisco, spoke a truth when he said that the structure of world peace "cannot be a peace of large nations or of small nations. It must be a peace which rests on the cooperative efforts of the whole world."

Impelled by mutual interest to create a structure to safeguard peace, the Conference that gathered by the Golden Gate in April 1945 took as its aim the establishment of an organization "adequately prepared to meet every challenge."

For a moment in time, the conflicting forces activating the relationships of the powers were channeled into a constructive effort to improve upon the model of the League of Nations. The founders sought to form an agency that would encompass in the fullness of time the community of peoples, an institution that would serve both great and small alike, the downtrodden as well as the elite, those aspiring to nationhood and those mature from long experience. They aimed to create an instrument flexible enough to accommodate the interests of many powers while fashioning a new order founded upon precepts of equity and justice. This was to be no closed society. Rather, it was to be open to all nations prepared to live in peace with one another and to practice tolerance toward others.

The Charter of the United Nations was conceived to be a living thing, adjustable to changing circumstances, able to meet the tests of political struggle, strong enough to help mankind in its search for "better standards of life in larger freedom," designed to grow by usage and amendment.

It is not surprising that the Organization has become enmeshed in the conflicts of power politics. This was expected. For, as President Harry S. Truman said:

> Differences between men, and between nations, will always remain. In fact, if held within reasonable limits, such disagreements are actually wholesome. All progress begins with differences of opinion and moves onward as the differences are adjusted through reason and mutual understanding.

The task as the founders saw it was to provide workable machinery for the accommodation of these differences and the advancement of common interests.

The object of this volume is to appraise the results of what was fashioned at San Francisco in the light of what has happened in the past twenty years and to weigh the prospects of the institution as it moves into its third decade.

Looking back over twenty years and weighing the steps taken, one is reminded of the spirit evoked by that great rhetorician of our age Sir Winston Churchill, when he wrote that "History with its flickering lamp stumbles along the trail of the past, trying to reconstruct its scenes, to revive its echoes, and kindle with pale gleams the passion of former days."

The papers written for this volume afford a comprehensive overview of the main problems that have been encountered in the functioning of the United Nations, the difficulties that have arisen in implementing the Charter, the objectives Member states have sought in relation to one another, and the concerns they have brought to bear upon issues as these have come before the Organization.

Taken together, these efforts to weigh the accomplishments and prospects of the institution arrive at a consensus that the United Nations is still far from having achieved its goals. Shortcomings exist in nearly every facet of its operations. It has been gravely hampered by the Cold War, conflicts of interests, lack of adequate funds, and unbridgable differences. And yet its contributions to peace and security have not been negligible. No major contest at arms has found it unable to innovate some constructive move to restore quietude. It has not achieved as much as many would desire in the realm of human rights. Yet it is not standing still in this or any other realm. It has witnessed an unprecedented transition, largely in peace, from colonialism to self-government and independence in the underdeveloped areas of the world. It has registered a willingness on the part of most nations to see their unsettled disputes go before its forum for discussion and recommendation. It has mobilized substantial resources for assisting the progress of the peoples of the less developed lands. On the whole, it has served the interests of its Members reasonably well.

It cannot be overlooked, however, that the Organization is in trouble. It faces unsolved issues that could be as difficult or more so than those of the past. It is not clear where it is headed. Nor can one be certain what its future is. One can only say there is a need for an organization of this kind—an instrumentality that can help promote stability, ease tensions, accommodate differences, and encourage cooperation. When one looks back over the twenty years, it becomes clear that the United Nations will be no less, and can be no better, than its membership makes it in the context of its times.

The Organization cannot prevent a nuclear war from engulfing mankind if nations become bent upon this. It cannot compel great powers to do its bidding or to follow its recommendations. It is not a world government and was never intended to be such. It is essentially a commitment to basic purposes and principles that affect the policies and attitudes of its Members. It offers a forum in which the representatives of states can reason together, if they will. It can make available procedures of preventive diplomacy, of conciliation, and of peace-keeping to help settle disputes and to maintain international peace and security. But states must be prepared to accept and use these or the efforts will be stillborn.

As the United Nations looks forward from the present crossroads in history, an observation of Lord Halifax at the concluding session in San Francisco springs to mind:

We cannot claim that our work is perfect or that we have created an unbreakable guaranty of peace. For ours is no enchanted palace to "spring into sight at once" by magic touch or hidden power. But we have, I am convinced, forged an instrument by which, if men are serious in wanting peace and are ready to make sacrifices for it, they may find means to win it.

Improvements are still needed, as in the representation of the newer nations of Africa and Asia on the elective organs. These will come. But as the infant learns to walk by taking one step at a time, so it is with this instrumentality of the nations. Having come over the rough path of the first twenty years and having ushered in the large company of newly created states, it must now move on to become a more effective center for "harmonizing the actions of nations" in the attainment of common ends and the forging of a stronger world community.

It is still true, as the late President John F. Kennedy remarked in 1961, that:

Never have the nations of the world had so much to lose—or so much to gain. Together we shall save our planet, or together we shall perish in its flames. Save it we can—and save it we must—and then shall we earn the eternal thanks of mankind and, as peacemakers, the eternal blessing of God.

It is our hope that the present volume may make a timely contribution to public thought concerning the United Nations and afford some useful insights into its progress and prospects for the future.

We wish to express our sincere appreciation to those who have contributed to the present appraisal. Each is an expert in his own field. Many were at San Francisco. All have followed developments since then with a sense of immediate concern. The writing of each of our associates is his own responsibility and does not reflect the views of any institution with which he may be connected.

All the chapters in this volume appeared originally in a special anniversary number of the quarterly journal *International Organization,* published by the World Peace Foundation in Boston, Mass., in the Summer of 1965. As the principal periodical concerned primarily with the activities and problems of intergovernmental agencies and regularly containing critical articles by experts, factual summaries of UN activities, and other materials relating to contemporary international affairs, this seemed an appropriate channel for reaching those deeply concerned with the United Nations. We are grateful to the journal and to the World Peace Foundation for permission to publish these contributions in book form for the general reader.

We are also indebted to the Carnegie Endowment for International Peace, the Institute for International Order, and the Trustees of the World Peace Foundation for grants of financial assistance that made this undertaking possible. And we wish to record our appreciation for the editorial assistance rendered by the staff of *International Organization.*

News of the sudden death of Ambassador Adlai E. Stevenson has come as these pages are being written. The passing of this devoted public servant, who so ably represented U.S. interests at the United Nations and who so eloquently voiced the spirit of those who hoped for a better world order, may indeed mark another of those milestones on what he himself termed that "long, wearisome, erratic, quarrelsome but relentless journey toward that lighter and brighter community which is the central thread of the human story." In a world in which all of mankind is now bound up in a common fate of peace or of destruction, there is no more worthy task than that of working for a decent human order on which a reasonable, effective peace can be built—a peace founded upon cooperation and mutual respect, upon law and justice, and dedicated to human progress in larger freedom. It is as a small contribution toward the ultimate attainment of this goal that this volume has been prepared.

NORMAN J. PADELFORD
Massachusetts Institute of Technology
LELAND M. GOODRICH
Columbia University

July, 1965

TABLE OF CONTENTS

IV. Looking to the Future

I. The Evolving Institution

The United Nations: Then and Now

Lawrence S. Finkelstein

"We do not want to entrust to five great Powers or to two great Powers the task of deciding . . . what our common destiny will be. . . . "

To anyone who attended the great assemblage gathered at San Francisco in 1945 to write the Charter for the United Nations, these words have a familiar ring. Indeed, they might have been uttered (and no doubt were *ad nauseam*) by small-power representatives during the seemingly interminable debates over the rule of unanimity—the veto—in the Security Council. In fact, these words were spoken in February 1965 by the Mauritanian delegate explaining, on the final day of the "abortive" nineteenth session of the General Assembly, why he voted with Albania in protest against the "basis of consensus" which had governed the session.[1]

The role of great and small powers in the Organization is by no means the only issue in the crisis over the financing of UN peacekeeping operations. Yet, there is no doubt that the relationship between the Security Council, in which the Great Powers can cast a veto, and the General Assembly, in which a majority rules, lies close to the heart of the matter. Secretary-General U Thant recently put it this way:

> We are now witnessing the beginning of the great debate—whether the big powers in unison, through the agency of the Security Council, should take exclusive responsibility for maintaining international peace and security while the General Assembly functions as a glorified debating society in political matters, or whether an attempt should be made to secure a fair, equitable, and clearly defined distribution of functions of the two principal organs. . . . [2]

Lawrence S. Finkelstein, a member of the Board of Editors of *International Organization*, is Vice President of the Carnegie Endowment for International Peace. The author wishes to thank Eva Popper for her research help, especially in compiling the table on pp. 13–16.

[1] UN Document A/PV. 1330, February 18, 1965, p. 47.

[2] Text of the Secretary-General's address to the Pacem in Terris Convocation, February 20, 1965 ("The UNITED NATIONS in a Changing World," *UN Monthly Chronicle*, March 1965 [Vol. 2, No. 3], p. 46).

The Secretary-General was wrong only in failing to recognize that "the great debate" is not beginning but has been going on since 1945.

The current crisis, in fact, mirrors the crisis of 1945 which came close to frustrating the effort to create the United Nations. Then, the majority, which resented the discrimination represented by the Great Powers' insistence that they should have the power to block decisions in the Security Council, had to accept what the Great Powers wished when the latter were able to agree among themselves. Today, great-power agreement remains to be achieved. It does not seem unlikely, however, that if the Great Powers, more particularly the United States and the Soviet Union, can agree on guidelines for the future handling of UN peacekeeping functions, the majority will again find that their interest lies in accepting that agreement. The speech of the Mauritanian delegate referred to above suggests that some at least may do so resentfully. Thus it was in 1945.

The crises of 1945 and 1965 are parallel in another respect. Then, as now, the Soviet Union and the United States disagreed, not over the principle that the Great Powers should have a veto but over the extent of its application. In 1945 the question was whether the Yalta formula meant that a veto could be employed to block discussion in the Security Council. This issue, on which the United Nations Conference on International Organization in San Francisco nearly came to grief, was resolved only as a result of Harry Hopkins' dramatic mission to Stalin on behalf of President Truman. In 1965, the question is whether only the Security Council is empowered to authorize UN peacekeeping measures even when great-power forces are to be excluded, or whether there should be a door open to the General Assembly when decision is blocked by exercise of the veto in the Security Council. Then, as now, the Soviet Union has sought to fortify its veto power in the Security Council. In both cases, the United States believed that this power should not be unlimited and it acted as a surrogate for the majority which had an interest in keeping the veto power within limits and in supporting the role of the General Assembly.

It is striking that, as the preceding paragraphs suggest, the United Nations has come full circle on this issue in twenty years. Surely, the Organization has confronted no more serious crises than the one which attended its birth and the one which dominated the year leading to its twentieth anniversary. It is not accidental that the theme of the two crises should have been the same.

To leave the matter here, however, is to give the impression—which is certainly erroneous—that the twenty years since the San Francisco Conference have left no mark on the Organization. In fact, of course, the United Nations today would be hardly recognizable to those such as Field Marshal Jan Smuts (South Africa), Prime Minister William Lyon Mackenzie King (Canada), Foreign Minister Jan Masaryk (Czechoslovakia), Prime Minister Peter Fraser

(New Zealand), United States Secretary of State Edward R. Stettinius, and Senator Arthur Vandenberg (United States) who played significant roles in the Conference but who did not survive[3] to watch the Organization mature. Those leading figures who are still with us, some of them still active in the affairs of the Organization, such as the United Kingdom's Sir Anthony Eden (now Lord Avon), V. M. Molotov and Andrei Gromyko (Soviet Union), Alberto Lleras Camargo (Colombia), Herbert V. Evatt (Australia), Eelco van Kleffens (Netherlands), and Carlos Romulo (Philippines), must be surprised when they view it today against their images of what they thought they were creating in 1945.

It is the tension between the institutional constancies and historical parallels, on the one hand, and the vast changes in the Organization and its setting, on the other, that poses the UN's most central dilemmas and which in part immobilize it today and will comprise its most urgent future agenda. In the following pages an attempt will be made to describe these changes. Obviously, due to the confines of space, only the broadest outline will be possible.

The Environment of 1945

The San Francisco stage had World War II as its backdrop. The Conference was convened as an act of faith in the future and of remorse for the past even as the allied armies were driving through a bleeding and prostrate Germany to their fateful meeting in the heart of Europe. In fact, it was on April 25, 1945, the day the Conference convened, that United States troops of the First Army and the vanguard of the First Ukrainian Army Group made contact on the Elbe.[4] Germany's surrender came on May 8. The victorious end of fighting in the Pacific, already assured, did not come until months later, on August 14.

Thus, the Conference was in a very real sense dominated by the war then in progress, the events that led to that war, and the hope that that war could not recur. The participants in the Conference were the states which had participated in the war effort of the United Nations or had at least acceded to the Declaration by United Nations of January 1, 1942. The Organization, at the outset at least, was to be "an association of nations of like mind."[5] The decision to use the name "the United Nations" for the new organization was

---

[3] In his address in the General Assembly's special International Cooperation Year (ICY) series, Alberto Lleras Camargo, himself a leading figure in the 1945 Conference, commented on the passing of many of "the men of San Francisco." ("International Cooperation: Twenty Years After the San Francisco Conference," *UN Monthly Chronicle,* February 1965 [Vol. 2, No. 2], pp. 63–73.) It is, for example, striking that of the eight members of the United States delegation to the Conference only two, Harold Stassen and Virginia Gildersleeve, survive.

[4] Omar N. Bradley, *A Soldier's Story* (New York: Holt & Co., 1951), p. 546.

[5] Testimony of Dr. Leo Pasvolsky in U.S. Congress, Senate, Committee on Foreign Relations, *Hearings, The Charter of the United Nations,* 79th Congress, 1st session, 1945, p. 230.

clearly understood at the time to reflect the wartime origins of the postwar association and to imply continuity between the wartime and postwar manifestations. It was well understood, for example, that the wartime enemies would have to work their way back to respectability and acceptability as Members of the Organization. (For reasons that were not then anticipated, Germany has not yet become a Member.) Indeed, there were articles in the Charter providing specifically for the postwar control of the former enemies by the members of the wartime alliance (Article 107 and Article 53).

It might thus be said that the dominant figures in the Conference were four world leaders who were not actually present: the three leaders of the UN coalition, Winston Churchill, Joseph Stalin, and Franklin D. Roosevelt (who had died less than two weeks before the Conference was scheduled to convene);[6] and Adolf Hitler, who represented the archevil the Conference was intended to prevent from recurring. The Conference was held because the three United Nations leaders had agreed that the wartime partnership of the nations they led should be institutionalized in a postwar general international organization. The main thrust of the Conference—the limits set on it and the guidelines it largely followed—was predetermined by their agreement. The Organization's chance of achieving success in its principal task of peacekeeping depended on the degree to which the cooperation achieved in war could in fact be preserved in peace. In this respect, the last meeting the three statesmen had held (in the Crimea in February 1945) was none too promising because the understandings reached there had already given rise to dissension. Poland was not represented in San Francisco, for example, because the three powers could not agree on how to implement the Yalta Agreement concerning the constitution of a Polish government.

Finally, although one should not overstate the point, it was probably true that Adolf Hitler was the model the three UN leaders had in mind in designing a system to deal with threats to the peace in the future. U Thant was probably correct when he recently said:

> Chapter VII, for instance . . . plainly stems from the experience of the aggressions of the Axis powers in the thirties. . . . Some provisions of the Charter . . . were framed with an eye on the potential re-emergence of the Axis powers as a threat to international peace and security. Memories of the war and the ruthlessness of its perpetrators were still very fresh in the minds of the founding fathers of the United Nations when they met in San Francisco.[7]

It is difficult to see how it could have been otherwise. The lessons of collective security had been hard-learned ones. It was entirely natural that the wartime leaders should have entered the future looking over their shoulders.

---

[6] Alberto Lleras Camargo recently observed that despite Roosevelt's passing, "nevertheless, the San Francisco Conference was still dominated by his extraordinary personality." (*UN Monthly Chronicle*, Vol. 2, No. 2, p. 64.)

[7] *UN Monthly Chronicle*, Vol. 2, No. 3, pp. 43–44.

Besides, the outlines of the future were extraordinarily murky. No one could foresee what arrangement would fill the vacuum created by the extirpation of Nazi power in the center of Europe. The peace settlements had not been reached or even agreed upon in broad outline by the victorious powers. With the Versailles experience in mind, it was in fact deliberately decided that the San Francisco Conference should be held before peace was negotiated so that the Organization would not appear linked to the maintenance of any particular status quo. Moreover, the Conference was to avoid the substance of contemporary and future international problems and concentrate instead on the machinery with which to handle them. In a certain sense then, the Conference was an exercise abstracted from the environment in which the UN would have to operate. With the future undecipherable, the Conference looked largely to the past.

Great-Power Unanimity

The mystique of great-power unanimity deserves a further word. Obviously, the leading United Nations powers had not fought the war in complete harmony. There had been all manner of disagreements, over goals, strategy, allocation of resources, personalities, and prestige. Yet, throughout, great emphasis had been placed on the necessity of finding accommodations for these differences in order to avoid giving comfort to the enemy and to concert joint effort for the common goal of victory. This habit of thought had become deeply ingrained. "I wish to make it absolutely clear," said Secretary of State Stettinius,

> that the primary objective of the United States' foreign policy is to continue and strengthen in the period of peace that wartime solidarity which has made possible the defeat of Germany.[8]

Moreover, it appeared to the leaders that their major postwar problems would be either with the wartime enemies or with each other in areas of the world in which great-power interests would be directly engaged. During the late stages of the war, an important preoccupation of both political and military leaders on the Western side, for example, was how to conclude the war without incurring excessive risks of military conflict with the Soviet forces slicing westward through Germany and Austria or occupying parts of Korea.

Thus, it was entirely natural that postwar organization and, for that matter, the peace settlements were seen primarily as great-power problems. The Dumbarton Oaks Conversations in the summer of 1944 were a great-power rehearsal for San Francisco. The critical decisions were taken then and in the Yalta Conference in February 1945. The great-power consultations, it should not be forgotten, were continued during the San Francisco meeting itself. The

---

[8] "Report on the San Francisco Conference," Department of State *Bulletin*, June 3, 1945 (Vol. 12, No. 310), p. 1007.

San Francisco drama offered a play within a play: The public saw the open sessions of 50 delegations; simultaneously, however, the five leading powers[9] were meeting frequently in secret session in the Fairmont Hotel. Throughout the Conference and with very few exceptions, the Big Five, as they were called, strove to maintain unanimity. When they could not agree on important matters, as on the veto question, the Conference had to mark time until they were ready. The Big Five sat in judgment on the proposals of other delegations to amend the draft which had emerged from Dumbarton Oaks. Often, a Great Power which was willing to accede to a small-power proposal abstained from doing so in the interest of great-power unanimity. And, when the Great Powers were in agreement in the political and security field, they could be voted down only on questions none of them thought especially important.

The fear of regional military coalitions led by the Great Powers had considerable influence on the view taken by the Great Powers, the United States particularly, regarding the relation between the UN and regional agencies in the field of peace and security. In the planning phases there had been a good deal of interest in regional bases for postwar peace and security organizations. The Dumbarton Oaks Proposals reflected the decision to place the emphasis on global machinery and procedures with carefully limited exceptions for regional initiative. Thereafter, however, the United States was subjected to great pressure from Latin American countries which wanted assurance that the inter-American system would not be submerged by the new global organization. At San Francisco it was apparent that the Arab states and Australia and New Zealand also were interested in maintaining some scope for autonomous regional arrangements. Moreover, the whole matter became entangled with the interest of France and the Soviet Union in maintaining the freedom of the principal allies to police the former enemy states and in preserving the effectiveness of mutual assistance agreements which might not qualify as regional arrangements. Furthermore, there was concern over the effect the veto might have—the UN might be prevented from acting and regional agencies might be limited by the requirements of the Dumbarton Oaks draft. As a result, concessions were made at San Francisco to the pressures for exceptions to the principle of global responsibility. The compromises are to be found in Chapter VIII and in Article 51, the famous "individual or collective self-defense" clause.[10] However, the concessions were limited by the conviction that it was important to require the Great Powers to try to act in harmony via the Security Council rather than risk having them pursue divergent paths through strong regional agencies.

[9] See pp. 9–10 below.

[10] Ruth B. Russell, *A History of the United Nations Charter: The Role of the United States, 1940–1945* (Washington, D.C.: Brookings Institution, 1958), especially Chapter 27.

This background is important because of its bearing on the expectations concerning the Great Powers' role once the Organization was in being. Briefly, no one seriously entertained the belief that the Organization could be effective in preserving peace in the absence of great-power unanimity. Their combined strength could ensure peace, but if they disagreed, peace could not be ensured. It was recognized that such unanimity might not be forthcoming. Indeed, there was already ominous evidence that the Great Powers might find themselves in basic disagreement. The point was not that they would necesssarily agree but rather that without such agreement the UN security system could not work. In such circumstances, Members might find it necessary to resort to other means to defend their interests, such as "the inherent right of individual or collective self-defense" in case of "armed attack." The system, in such a case, would have broken down or at least failed to work. No one suggested in 1945 that there might be a substitute for great-power unanimity in the peacekeeping field. The idea that the small powers might concert to pacify a situation in which peace was threatened in order to keep the Great Powers from becoming involved would have been considered too ridiculous to deserve a hearing.

Of course, among the Big Five, some were, as George Orwell might have said, bigger than others. Generally, there was little disposition to quarrel with the assertion that the Soviet Union, the United Kingdom, and the United States were in a class by themselves when it came to the qualities that make for preeminence in international affairs. Among the three, the United States, having developed and demonstrated its economic strength and military muscle during the war and having emerged entirely unscathed except for its losses in the field, was clearly the foremost. The Soviet Union, despite the heavy human and economic losses it had suffered, was no doubt a power to be reckoned with. In 1945 the United Kingdom, still the leader of a vast empire, about to emerge victorious from the extended ordeal which had tested to the very limit but had not shattered British courage and will, and shining with the luster of its incomparable leader Winston Churchill, had not yet begun to display the evidences of weakness which within a very short time after the war would reduce it to the second rank of leadership.

There was less certainty, however, about the other two "permanent members" of the Security Council. The Republic of China was included, largely on the United States' urging, not only in order to recognize its dogged wartime resistance to Japan but also to give stimulus to China's progress toward fulfillment of its great-power potential. There was in the United States' position a conscious element of self-fulfilling prophecy—"we can help it to be so by behaving as if it were so."[11] France, a loser in the war, ended up on the winning side and was rescued from total national disgrace owing to the

[11] There were other reasons as well. On this question, see *ibid.*, especially pp. 106, 129–130.

extraordinary leadership of General Charles de Gaulle. Although the British insisted strongly that France be accepted as one of the Great Powers and the United States ultimately agreed, despite the difficulties President Roosevelt had in getting along with General de Gaulle, while the Soviet Union acquiesced, it was apparent that France did not and could not rank as a Great Power with the Soviet Union and the United States.

Uncertainties about the great-power status of China and France gave rise to suggestions that the Charter provide for future change in the "permanent" membership of the Security Council. When such moves failed, the issue strengthened the pressures to include arrangements to facilitate general revision of the Charter and thus had something to do with the adoption of Article 109. In some quarters it was even thought that if a "permanent member" which proved to be no longer a Great Power sought to stultify the Organization by "abusing" the veto, the remedy would be for all the others formally to form a new organization from which that power would be excluded or in which its status would be altered.

Economic and Social Role

Part of the backdrop was the statement of war aims which took form first as the Atlantic Charter and then as the Declaration by United Nations. These statements of goals made it inevitable that the allies would want the "general international organization" to pursue economic and social as well as political and security objectives. The Atlantic Charter, particularly, had included the following goal in its fifth clause:

> the fullest collaboration between all nations in the economic field with the object of securing, for all, improved labor standards, economic advancement and social security.

From this humble beginning developed what became Chapters IX and X of the UN Charter.

As they met, the delegates at San Francisco were inescapably aware of the panorama of misery, destruction, and chaos which dominated the war zones. Moreover, there was wide understanding that, as Walter Lippmann has recently said, the UN could "not live by peace alone"[12] but must be concerned, in the words of its Preamble, with "social progress and better standards of life in larger freedom." While it was expected that relief and reconstruction operations and the economic and social functions generally would be dealt with by other organizations—such as the UN Relief and Rehabilitation Administration (UNRRA), the International Bank for Reconstruction and Development (IBRD), the Food and Agriculture Organization (FAO), and other "specialized agencies" which might later be established—the Conference

---

[12] "The Great Revolution," *UN Monthly Chronicle*, April 1965 (Vol. 2, No. 4), p. 72.

provided a forum for the formulation of broad economic, social, and humanitarian goals for the postwar period and for the shaping of the Organization's functions as formulator, recommender, and coordinator of programs in these spheres.

Although they had opened the way for consideration of these questions by including economic and social clauses in the Dumbarton Oaks draft, the Great Powers were by and large fairly conservative about the role the Organization might have with respect to economic and social matters. The United States, for example, had a tradition of concern for states' rights in its federal system and a race relations problem in the South. These considerations, coupled with memories of what a fractious Senate had done in 1919–1920, led the United States to resist any notions, such as those implicit in positions advanced by Herbert Evatt, that the Organization should have powers going beyond the hortatory. It was with some satisfaction that the chairman of the United States delegation was able to report to the President that "the Economic and Social Council was not to have any coercive powers. . . . Its tools and procedures are those of study, discussion, report, and recommendation. . . . "[13] There was no hint that the new economic and social machinery would have any operating responsibilities. The limited character of the Organization's role was seemingly doubly assured by the expedient of moving the "domestic jurisdiction" clause to its present position as Article 2, paragraph 7, where it is applicable to the entire Charter rather than merely to the section dealing with pacific settlement of international disputes as it had been in the Dumbarton Oaks draft. Moreover, the relevant committee approved a statement for the permanent record making it clear that nothing in Chapter IX authorized the Organization "to intervene in the domestic affairs of member states."[14]

Colonialism

In 1945 colonialism was a burning issue. Over half a billion people had lived in non-self-governing territories before the war.[15] The United States, inspired by traditional sympathy for colonial peoples, had made clear its hope that the postwar era would bring rapid change looking toward full liberty for all peoples who, as Secretary of State Hull had said in July 1942, are "prepared and willing" to accept its responsibilities.[16] While there was a growing recognition among the colonial powers that it was necessary to hold out hope

[13] *Charter of the United Nations: Report to the President on the Results of the San Francisco Conference by the Chairman of the United States Delegation, the Secretary of State, June 26, 1945* (Department of State Publication 2349, Conference Series 71) (Washington, D.C.: U.S. Government Printing Office, 1945), p. 111.

[14] Report of the Rapporteur of Committee II/3 (General Assembly, Economic and Social Cooperation) in *Documents of the United Nations Conference on International Organization, San Francisco, 1945* (New York: United Nations Information Organization, 1945), Vol. 10, pp. 271–272.

[15] Emil J. Sady, *The United Nations and Dependent Peoples* (Washington, D.C.: Brookings Institution, 1956), p. 3.

[16] Department of State *Bulletin*, July 25, 1942 (Vol. 7, No. 161), p. 642.

that the colonial peoples could share equitably in the benefits of the postwar era, there was also much anxiety as to how evolving relationships would affect continuing material and strategic interests. Australia, New Zealand, and the United States, for example, all had reasons, learned in the Pacific war, to be concerned about the status of Pacific island territories. The metropolitan powers also felt a sense of responsibility toward the peoples under colonial rule. Many, led by such figures as Carlos Romulo, Peter Fraser, and Herbert Evatt, demanded that the Charter include a charter of colonial progress acknowledging the international character of the colonial problem, establishing standards to be pursued, and providing machinery to supervise the performance of the colonial powers.

The result of this blend of widespread support for the general principle of progress toward colonial liberation, national commitments to the institutions of colonialism, and national self-interest was a compromise. The Conference adopted and included in the Charter as Chapter XI the first general binding statement of principles governing the administration of all non-self-governing territories. However, the Organization was given no powers of supervision with respect to such territories although the colonial powers accepted a limited obligation to report on them for "information purposes." After much hard bargaining in the Conference committee, which was intently followed around the world, the political goal of colonial administration was, according to this Chapter, to be the development of "self-government . . . according to the particular circumstances of each territory and its peoples and their varying stages of advancement." It was, however, clearly understood that "self-government" comprehended "independence."

For a limited group of territories, those which might be placed under trusteeship principally because they had been mandated territories under the League of Nations, a more rigorous system was established. As set forth in Chapter XII, such territories would have as their goal

> progressive development towards self-government or independence as may be appropriate to the particular circumstances of each territory and its peoples and the freely expressed wishes of the peoples concerned. . . .

The trusteeship system set forth in Chapters XII and XIII of the Charter provided for fairly rigorous supervision by the Trusteeship Council of the administration of trust territories.

Not only were the goals carefully formulated and the powers of the Organization carefully spelled out and delimited, but the structure also ensured that a special weight was given to the administering powers in the Trusteeship Council. The compromise included recognition of a special category of strategic trust territories for which the Security Council would be responsible. With respect to other territories, the Trusteeship Council was under the authority of the General Assembly.

This carefully designed set of compromise solutions represented all the agreement that was possible at San Francisco. It was widely hailed as representing a considerable advance over any previous system—as indeed it was. It was also expected to prove more or less adequate to cope with, indeed to anticipate, the orderly and progressive development of non-self-governing territories toward full self-government or independence. While few would have ventured to predict how long the process of colonial emancipation would require, the general expectation would have involved scores of years. President Roosevelt is reported to have believed that the Southeast Asian territories might need twenty years to be ready for self-government.[17]

The United Nations Today

How does the UN today resemble and differ from the expectations of 1945?

Membership

The most striking difference is the transformation of membership. The following table tells the story.

UN MEMBERSHIP, 1945–1965

Country[a]	Date of Admission	Date of Independence (Where Applicable)
WESTERN AND SOUTHERN EUROPE		
Belgium		
Denmark		
France		
Greece		
Luxembourg		
Netherlands		
Norway		
United Kingdom		
Austria	December 14, 1955	State Treaty Ratified July 27, 1955
Finland	December 14, 1955	
Iceland	November 19, 1946	
Ireland	December 14, 1955	
Italy	December 14, 1955	
Malta	December 1, 1964	May 31, 1964
Portugal	December 14, 1955	
Spain	December 14, 1955	
Sweden	November 19, 1946	

a Countries listed in italics were original Members of the United Nations.

[17] Robert E. Sherwood, *Roosevelt and Hopkins: An Intimate History* (New York: Harper & Row, 1948), p. 573.

Country	Date of Admission	Date of Independence (Where Applicable)
EASTERN EUROPE		
Byelorussian Soviet Socialist Republic		
Czechoslovakia		
Poland[b]		
Soviet Union		
Ukrainian Soviet Socialist Republic		
Yugoslavia		
Albania	December 14, 1955	
Bulgaria	December 14, 1955	
Hungary	December 14, 1955	
Rumania	December 14, 1955	
MIDDLE EAST		
Egypt[c]		
Iran		
Iraq		
Lebanon		
Saudi Arabia		
Syria[c]		
Turkey		
Cyprus	September 20, 1960	August 16, 1960
Israel	May 11, 1949	May 14, 1948
Jordan	December 14, 1955	March 22, 1946
Kuwait	May 14, 1963	June 19, 1961
Libya	December 14, 1955	December 24, 1951
Yemen	September 30, 1947	
SOUTH ASIA		
India		
Afghanistan	November 19, 1946	
Burma	April 19, 1948	January 4, 1948
Ceylon	December 14, 1955	February 4, 1948
Nepal	December 14, 1955	
Pakistan	September 30, 1947	August 14, 1947
FAR EAST AND SOUTHEAST ASIA		
Australia		
China		
New Zealand		
Philippines		

[b] Poland did not attend the San Francisco Conference because the composition of its new government was not announced until June 28—too late for the Conference. A space, however, was left for the signature of Poland as one of the original signatories of the Declaration of the United Nations. Poland signed the Charter on October 15, 1945.

[c] In February 1958 Egypt and Syria united to form the United Arab Republic with a single membership in the United Nations. Following dissolution of the union, the Syrian Arab Republic on October 8, 1961, notified the United Nations that it had resumed its status as an independent state. In the absence of any opposition, Syria resumed its seat in the General Assembly on October 31, 1961.

Country	Date of Admission	Date of Independence (Where Applicable)
Cambodia	December 14, 1955	August 17, 1953
Indonesia^d	September 28, 1950	September 28, 1949
Japan	December 18, 1956	
Laos	December 14, 1955	May 11, 1949
Malaysia^e	September 17, 1957	August 31, 1957
Mongolia	October 27, 1961	January 5, 1946
Thailand	December 16, 1946	

AFRICA^f

Country	Date of Admission	Date of Independence (Where Applicable)
Ethiopia		
Liberia		
South Africa		
Algeria	October 8, 1962	July 3, 1962
Burundi	September 18, 1962	July 1, 1962
Cameroun	September 20, 1960	October 1, 1961
Central African Republic	September 20, 1960	August 13, 1960
Chad	September 20, 1960	August 11, 1960
Congo (Brazzaville)	September 20, 1960	August 15, 1960
Congo (Leopoldville)	September 20, 1960	June 30, 1960
Dahomey	September 20, 1960	August 1, 1960
Gabon	September 20, 1960	August 17, 1960
Ghana	March 8, 1957	March 6, 1957
Guinea	December 12, 1958	October 2, 1958
Ivory Coast	September 20, 1960	August 7, 1960
Kenya	December 16, 1963	December 12, 1963
Madagascar	September 20, 1960	June 26, 1960
Malawi	December 1, 1964	July 6, 1964
Mali	September 28, 1960	September 22, 1960
Mauritania	October 27, 1961	November 28, 1960
Morocco	November 12, 1956	March 3, 1956
Niger	September 20, 1960	August 3, 1960
Nigeria	October 7, 1960	October 1, 1960
Rwanda	September 18, 1962	July 1, 1962
Senegal	September 28, 1960	August 20, 1960
Sierra Leone	September 27, 1961	April 27, 1961
Somalia	September 20, 1960	July 1, 1960
Sudan	November 12, 1956	January 1, 1956
Tanganyika^g	December 14, 1961	May 1, 1961
Togo	September 20, 1960	April 27, 1960

^d Indonesia formally declared its withdrawal from the United Nations on January 7, 1965, effective March 1, 1965.

^e The Federation of Malaya became part of the Federation of Malaysia on September 16, 1963, and it is the latter which is now the Member of the United Nations.

^f In addition to the Members listed, Gambia seems likely to be admitted before long. Gambia attained independence on February 18, 1965. The Security Council recommended admission on March 15, 1965. Presumably, the General Assembly will complete the process of admission when it next meets.

^g Tanganyika and Zanzibar formed the United Republic of Tanzania on April 26, 1964, and now have only one membership in the United Nations.

Country	Date of Admission	Date of Independence (Where Applicable)
Tunisia	November 12, 1956	March 20, 1956
Uganda	October 25, 1962	October 9, 1962
Upper Volta	September 20, 1960	August 5, 1960
Zambia	December 1, 1964	October 24, 1964
Zanzibar[8]	December 16, 1963	December 9, 1963

THE AMERICAS

Argentina		
Bolivia		
Brazil		
Canada		
Chile		
Colombia		
Costa Rica		
Cuba		
Dominican Republic		
Ecuador		
El Salvador		
Guatemala		
Haiti		
Honduras		
Mexico		
Nicaragua		
Panama		
Paraguay		
Peru		
United States		
Uruguay		
Venezuela		
Jamaica	September 18, 1962	August 6, 1962
Trinidad and Tobago	September 18, 1962	August 31, 1962

Fifty-one original Members have grown to 114. Only in its twentieth year has the UN lost a Member through deliberate withdrawal. In this respect, the contrast with the League of Nations is striking.

The balance of the Organization has, of course, drastically shifted. Whereas the majority of the original Members were European and American, the majority now are African and Asian. This has brought in its train a shift in the concerns and in the character of the Organization, which will be described in subsequent sections.

The membership of the United Nations now approaches universality. The gaps in participation are of four kinds. There are a few states that have not wanted to join: Switzerland because of its unwillingness to compromise traditional neutrality; Western Samoa because it did not want to bear the material and human burdens of UN membership; and other small states which have not considered applying. There are the three divided countries—Korea, Vietnam, and Germany—which are not Members because neither the non-Communist nor the Communist halves can be admitted without the other and neither side is prepared to agree to such an arrangement. Thirdly, there is Indonesia which withdrew from membership over the Malaysian issue. Finally, there is the large gap because of the failure thus far to find a solution to the problem of the representation of China.

With these exceptions, the UN can be said to represent today all currents of thought and interest in the contemporary world. The General Assembly has indeed become, in Senator Vandenberg's phrase, the "Town Meeting of the World."

This representative quality carries with it certain difficulties. The first is mechanical and procedural. The UN is pressing against the physical limits of its Headquarters facilities. A body of 114 sovereign states is too large to be fully effective. The widespread insistence on literal interpretation of the "sovereign equality" of Members, however, has made it difficult to work through smaller bodies. When such an effort is made, as in the newly formed 33-member Special Committee on Peacekeeping Operations, the need to make it broadly representative of the membership results in groups which are still too large to be effective instruments of negotiation and decision.

Another problem is that the membership now represents great diversity of experience and perspective which makes it increasingly difficult for the UN to serve as "a center for harmonizing the actions of nations." For one thing, 47 Members did not exist as states when the Organization was created. They do not bring to the Organization the perspective of those older nations which either as participants or as onlookers shared the experience on which the Organization was founded. The generations also differ in the priorities they attach to the several purposes of the Organization.

Disharmony thus often exists and accommodation is not facilitated by the tendency, which has a long history in the Organization, to regard voting as a solvent for disagreement. The negotiating process in the corridors often works to narrow areas of disagreement and to identify the bases of consensus. On some issues, however, efforts to deal with differences by mobilizing voting pressures against the minority whose interests are at stake serves only to harden rather than resolve the disagreements. Moreover, the correlation between voting strength and capacity to effect results is not always precise. It is obviously at best misleading and it can be harmful to permit decisions to be taken which the majority are unable or, in some cases, unwilling to carry out.

It is both a virtue and a shortcoming of the new nations that they are by and large indifferent to the ideological, ethical, and political concerns of the competing forces in the Cold War. It is a virtue because their indifference

serves to cushion the controversy in the UN. It is a liability because their indifference tends to become institutionalized. The new nations sometimes permit the fact that an issue is in dispute between a Communist and a Western
nation to deter them from examining into the rights and wrongs, the legali-
ties and the illegalities, and the peace-promoting or peace-defeating factors
that are involved.

The Role of the Great Powers

It did not take long for the San Francisco hopes of great-power unity to
fade. Bitter disillusionment rapidly replaced the cautious optimism of the
spring of 1945. Irreconcilable conflict over the German settlement, harsh disagreement over the other peace treaties, the clash of interests over Trieste,
guerrilla war in Greece, and the continuance of Soviet forces in Iran beyond
the agreed deadline rapidly produced an atmosphere of distrust and hostility.
In the UN itself, the Security Council was the scene of bitter clashes and
within a year after San Francisco the Soviet Union had cast several vetoes
and had staged the famous walkout over the Iranian affair. As early as February 1946, Winston Churchill had both reflected the deteriorating situation and
given stimulus to it in his famous "Iron Curtain" speech in Fulton, Missouri.
In September, United States Secretary of State James F. Byrnes signaled the
end of East-West cooperation and a new departure vis-à-vis the German enemy in his Stuttgart speech.

The crippling of the UN's intended peace and security functions as a result
of great-power conflict led to a search for alternative security measures. These
were found in regional arrangements. In the Atlantic area, the North Atlantic
Treaty was signed in 1949 after the narrower Brussels Treaty of 1947 between
the Western European powers. The Western European Union (WEU),
which, among other things, ended the occupation of West Germany, came
into effect in 1955. The inter-American system was strengthened in the Inter-
American Treaty of Reciprocal Assistance (Rio Treaty) of 1947. The Arab
League had been formed in 1945. On the Soviet side, various forms of cooperation culminated in the signature of the Treaty of Friendship, Cooperation, and Mutual Assistance (Warsaw Treaty) in 1955. The regional road is
marked by such acronyms as ANZUS, MEDO, and SEATO.[18]

By and large, the patterns established in the UN in the early days have
prevailed. In general, the Security Council, for example, has not functioned
as was intended. The conflicting interests of the Great Powers in all corners
of the globe have meant that the veto has often operated to preclude a role
for the Security Council. In fact, it is hard to believe that the use of the veto
to prevent Security Council action with respect to situations far removed from

---

[18] The Australia, New Zealand, United States Tripartite Security Pact, the Middle East Defense Organization, and the Southeast Asia Treaty Organization, respectively.

vital concerns of the permanent members conforms with what was intended or anticipated in 1945.

However, exceptions to this pattern should be noted because of their possible relevance to the future. For one thing, the impact of the veto was early softened by the development of the practice that an abstention was not to be counted as a veto despite the Charter requirement that Security Council decisions on important matters required the "concurring votes" of the permanent members. Secondly, as the Soviet Union and the United States in view of their nuclear arsenals became concerned over the risks of direct confrontations, evidence developed that they might have a minimum consensus enabling the UN to intervene in order to quiet situations that threatened peace in parts of the world in which their vital interests were not directly at stake. Thus, the Soviet Union seemed to acquiesce in the General Assembly's action setting up the United Nations Emergency Force (UNEF) in the Middle East although it would not go so far as to pay its share of UNEF's costs. More striking still was the Soviet vote in the Security Council in favor of the UN action in the Congo (Leopoldville). In this case, however, whatever minimum agreement may have existed between the Soviet Union and other members which voted in favor of the UN Operation in the Congo (ONUC) was soon overwhelmed by disagreement over the objectives and conduct of ONUC.

There is disturbing evidence that the Soviet Union's position, perhaps under pressures generated by its dispute with Communist China, may be shifting so that it is no longer willing to acquiesce in UN peacekeeping operations in pursuit of objectives with which it does not wholly agree. If UN peacekeeping roles are not possible in future crises in Africa and Asia, there is some danger, difficult to assess in the abstract, that the two Great Powers might be drawn into direct confrontation if only to prevent each other from gaining competitive benefit out of such situations. The hazards are magnified by the danger that other nations may follow the example set by France and Communist China in acquiring independent nuclear-weapons capabilities. That the picture is not entirely black is suggested by the fact that the Soviet Union joined in a unanimous vote in the Security Council in March 1964 to set up the UN Peacekeeping Force in Cyprus (UNFICYP).[19] However, the disclosure in March 1965 that Soviet-made tanks and antiaircraft missiles were appearing on Cyprus was alarming.

There is one ground for a degree of satisfaction about the relations between the Great Powers. For a number of reasons, among them the hazards of nuclear confrontation in an area of vital interest, the European situation has been reasonably stable since the Berlin crisis of 1948–1949. However, the new tendencies toward polycentrism on both sides of the Trieste-Stettin line, aggravated on the Eastern side by the Soviet-Chinese split, may introduce new

---

[19] UN Document S/5575.

unsettling factors. While there is reason for some satisfaction over the situation, there is no ground for complacency. Although it is not very likely that issues which might arise in Europe, such as the reunification of Germany or border rectifications in Eastern Europe, can be dealt with centrally by the United Nations, the reactivation of such questions might seriously affect great-power relations with important consequences for their collaboration or conflict over other issues before the UN.

Throughout much of the UN's history, the United States has been content to introduce issues in the General Assembly or to see them dealt with there when introduced by others. In this respect, the United States has been more permissive than France, for example, which has often resisted UN claims to jurisdiction over colonial questions and which resisted a UN role in the Congo (Leopoldville). It is often said, particularly by Communist Bloc delegations, that the United States has been able to count on an "automatic voting majority" in the General Assembly. It might be said with greater justice that the Soviet Union has pursued policies or taken positions which isolated it from the views of most of the Members. Whichever way the point is formulated, however, there is current reason to wonder whether the old assumptions will necessarily continue to prevail.

The point is that the influx of new Members, most of them inclined toward positions of "nonalignment" between the Communist and Western blocs, may have brought about a basic shift in the voting situation. The recent record suggests that whatever automaticity of response there may have been in the past to the positions of the United States and the Soviet Union may no longer exist. The Mauritanian speech quoted above suggests a "plague on both your houses" approach. The important thing is that the majority, if it is neutral vis-à-vis any pair of governments or blocs, should not be neutral as to the purposes of the Organization, the application of the rules of the Charter, or the Organization's capacity to grow. The record of the crisis over peacekeeping financing is not without ambiguity in this connection, but it is surely not terribly reassuring as to the membership's ability to arrive at consensus on goals and priorities which can serve as a platform to support the Organization's essential functions. In the light of these uncertainties it is of course difficult to forecast what roles the Great Powers may play in the Organization in the future.

The Place of the General Assembly

Perhaps the most remarkable development in the UN's brief career has been the place assumed by the General Assembly, at least until the uncertainties introduced during the nineteenth session.

Clearly, the original expectation was correct that there could be no substitute for great-power cooperation in the peace and security field. And the

General Assembly has not been able to perform the functions for which the Security Council was created. Particularly, it has no power of decision comparable to the Security Council's powers under Chapter VII, matched by the Members' obligation in Article 25 to comply. However, beginning very early in the Organization's history, the General Assembly has resorted to its powers to recommend. A sign of the direction to be followed was to be found in a January 1946 article by Herbert Evatt in which he noted the evidence that "some of the major Powers will be tempted to paralyze the Security Council. . . . " The remedy, not surprising for one who had fought at San Francisco for extended powers for the General Assembly, was "a determined use" of the powers of that organ "to redress any unfair exercise of power." "The lesser powers," Mr. Evatt urged, "should take the initiative in the field of security as in the field of welfare."[20] By the time of the second session of the General Assembly in 1947, the staff of the Carnegie Endowment for International Peace could call attention to "the steadily growing importance of the General Assembly."[21]

It is important to recognize that the Uniting for Peace Resolution of November 3, 1950, added nothing to the powers which the General Assembly already possessed under the Charter. As early as the second part of the first session of the General Assembly in 1946, the first real working session, it had on its agenda the Spanish question, specially dropped for the purpose from the Security Council's agenda to avoid conflict with Article 12, paragraph 1, of the Charter. The question of the treatment of Indians in South Africa was placed before the General Assembly, not the Security Council. By April 1947 the question of Palestine was before the General Assembly at the request of the United Kingdom. The Uniting for Peace Resolution dramatized the General Assembly's role and provided a new procedure for rapidly convening the Assembly in emergency session, but it did not add to its Charter-given powers of study, discussion, consideration, and recommendation. In fact, by tying its procedures to a veto in the Security Council, that resolution may have slightly narrowed the existing scope of the General Assembly.

The development of the General Assembly's role in this sphere is recounted elsewhere in this symposium.[22] At this point it is necessary only to observe that while the power of recommendation to which the General Assembly has resorted was in the Charter from the beginning, the uses to which it has been put represent a development which was entirely unanticipated at San Francisco. The General Assembly's role, for example, in serving as a forum for negotiation of the armistice terms for the Korean War, its authorization and

[20] "Risks of a Big-Power Peace," *Foreign Affairs,* January 1946 (Vol. 24, No. 2), pp. 2, 4, 5.

[21] "The United Nations General Assembly: Its Expanding Role and the Issues Before the Second Session," *International Conciliation,* September 1947 (No. 433), p. 479.

[22] See later in this volume, Ruth B. Russell, "Changing Patterns of Constitutional Development"; and Leland M. Goodrich, "The Maintenance of International Peace and Security."

guidance of UNEF, and its guidance of the Congo operation after consensus had broken down in the Security Council are examples of advanced functions in the field of peace and security which it was not believed the UN could perform in the absence of great-power unanimity. It is too soon to be certain whether the lesson of the financing crisis will prove to have been that, for the future, the 1945 expectation was the correct one.[23]

In other spheres as well, the General Assembly has shown unanticipated vitality. It has been, in some respects, the world's conscience in the field of disarmament[24] and was able at critical moments to press the Great Powers into negotiations they were reluctant to undertake. While the General Assembly has not recently been the forum for the negotiations that have been going on, it was the setting for the promulgation of the resolution banning the orbiting of weapons of mass destruction in outer space.

The Secretary-General

The combination of the Great Powers' failure to agree among themselves and the belief of UN majorities that it was necessary that the UN should intervene to prevent the deterioration of crisis situations in the Middle East and the Congo when more far-reaching consensus did not exist resulted in a devolution of substantial political and administrative responsibilities on the Secretary-General. This trend, which came to its apex under Secretary-General Dag Hammarskjöld, has now been arrested as a result of the controversy over the Congo and the financing of peacekeeping activities.[25] It was always an unsatisfactory substitute for the arrangements contemplated by the Charter. It was, however, remarkable evidence of the UN's ability to improvise at least the minimum arrangements that would serve the need of the moment.

Basically, the UN Secretary-General is endowed with greater constitutional power than was his predecessor in the League of Nations. Article 98 of the Charter gives him broad authority to "perform . . . functions entrusted to him" by the other UN organs. (The Secretariat is a "principal organ.") Article 99 authorizes him to "bring to the attention of the Security Council any matter which in his opinion may threaten the maintenance of international peace and security." Mr. Hammarskjöld used to refer to his peacekeeping role, for example, in UNEF and ONUC, as deriving from Article 98½, by which he meant that he was exercising powers implied by the broad functions entrusted to him by the appropriate organs which were unable to agree on any more precise instructions.

Of all the developments in the UN's history, this one was perhaps the most surprising. While the Secretary-General's power in these situations was limited

[23] See later in this volume, Norman J. Padelford, "Financing Peacekeeping: Politics and Crisis."

[24] See later in this volume, Daniel S. Cheever, "The UN and Disarmament."

[25] Hans Morgenthau has dramatized the point in an article entitled "The U.N. of Dag Hammarskjold is Dead," *The New York Times Magazine*, March 14, 1965, pp. 32, 37-40.

by the terms of his mandate, broad as they might be, and by the vigorous defense of their interests by the various parties concerned, he had considerable room for maneuver and initiative in bending the limits of consensus or redirecting them slightly. And, most astonishing of all, the Secretary-General was the commander in chief of a UN army composed of national contingents that totaled around twenty thousand men in the Congo, with an air force, signals, transport, and all the rest. Surely, that was the high-water mark of international authority in the peacekeeping field.

Colonial Questions

From the outset the General Assembly has played a vigorous role with respect to colonial questions. Particularly as the Organization absorbed new Members from the ranks of recently independent countries, their passionate concern for self-determination came to dominate the proceedings. The climax came with the adoption in 1960 of the Declaration on the Granting of Independence to Colonial Countries and Peoples,[26] an advanced statement of revulsion with colonialism which stands in stark contrast to the measured phrases of the 1945 compromises. In 1946 it had been considered a breakthrough when the General Assembly decided to set up an *ad hoc* committee to review the information submitted by the colonial powers under Article 73 (e).[27] That sixteen-member committee was equally balanced between colonial powers and others elected by the Assembly. Colonial questions are now dealt with by the Special Committee on the Situation with Regard to the Implementation of the Declaration on the Granting of Independence to Colonial Countries and Peoples among whose 24 members there are only three with responsibility for administering non-self-governing territories, i.e., Australia, the United Kingdom, and the United States.[28] The new majority, in which African and Asian states have joined forces with Communist Bloc countries and the Latin American countries, has succeeded in isolating the colonial powers and in establishing the principle that "immediate steps shall be taken . . . to transfer all powers to the peoples of . . . territories, without any conditions or reservations. . . ."[29]

Human Rights

In the field of human rights too, the pace has been quickened as a result of the influx of new Members. In 1963 the General Assembly adopted a strong

[26] General Assembly Resolution 1514 (XV), December 14, 1960.
[27] "The United Nations and Non-Self-Governing Territories," *International Conciliation,* November 1947 (No. 435), p. 714.
[28] For the complete list in 1963, see Carnegie Endowment for International Peace, "Issues Before the Nineteenth General Assembly," *International Conciliation,* November 1964 (No. 550), p. 64.
[29] For a more detailed discussion of this question, see later in this volume, Rupert Emerson, "Colonialism, Political Development, and the UN."

Declaration on the Elimination of All Forms of Racial Discrimination.[30] And in recent years the General Assembly has been utilized as a forum for the condemnation of *apartheid* in South Africa. Between August 1963 and June 1964 the General Assembly adopted two resolutions on the subject and the Security Council four.[31] Special attention is being given to the possibility of coercive measures to induce South Africa to alter its racial policies. The issues may come to a critical head in connection with South West Africa, the mandated territory administered by South Africa, when the International Court of Justice hands down its decision later this year in a contentious proceeding initiated by Liberia and Ethiopia. If the Court should rule against South Africa and if South Africa should refuse to comply with the Court's judgment, then the possibility would exist of invoking Article 94, paragraph 2, of the Charter which gives the Security Council, on the request of a party to the case, authority "if it deems necessary" to "make recommendations or decide upon measures to be taken to give effect to the judgment" of the Court.

Economic and Social Questions

In many respects the General Assembly and indeed the UN as a whole have functioned more or less as anticipated with respect to the broad subjects covered by Chapters IX and X of the Charter. The UN has discussed the principles that should govern in various fields, conducted or sponsored studies, convened conferences, issued declarations, and drafted conventions for adoption by the Members. It has stimulated efforts leading to the creation of new specialized or affiliated agencies, beginning with the UN Children's Fund (UNICEF) and the World Health Organization (WHO). It issued the Universal Declaration of Human Rights in December 1948 and has been struggling ever since to complete the covenants which were intended to provide the obligatory complement to the hortatory Declaration. It has proclaimed the Development Decade, and special years such as International Refugee Year and an International Year for Human Rights.

Perhaps the one surprise has been the extent to which the UN through the General Assembly and the Economic and Social Council (ECOSOC) has undertaken direct operations. Refugee problems, for example, have given rise to the Office of the United Nations High Commissioner for Refugees (UNHCR) and the United Nations Relief and Works Agency for Palestine Refugees in the Near East (UNRWA). The UN has sponsored regional development institutes in Latin America, Africa, and Southeast Asia which serve as centers for research and training with respect to development problems of these areas. They are affiliated with the regional economic commissions set up for those areas, a development under the auspices of ECOSOC not entirely

---

[30] General Assembly Resolution 1904 (XVIII), November 20, 1963.
[31] "Issues Before the Nineteenth General Assembly," *International Conciliation,* No. 550, p. 103.

anticipated in 1945 although they are not essentially or legally different from the functional commissions which were contemplated. Then there are, of course, the Expanded Program of Technical Assistance (EPTA) and the UN Special Fund, both offering services and resources directly to governments. The UN has created an Industrial Development Center. The UN Institute for Training and Research has been inaugurated and has begun work in its Rockefeller-Foundation-donated premises across the street from UN Headquarters. Thus, the UN has spawned a sizable family of agencies conducting direct relief or assistance functions or providing training and research facilities.

One recurrent theme which has been given new impetus by the surge of new Members has been the pressure of less developed countries for measures to narrow the gap in living standards between themselves and the richer countries.

Statistics work against the developing countries. There are the statistics of population growth[32] which mean that before there can be a net gain in per capita income there must first be an increase in production and gross national income to provide for increases in population. Secondly, even if the rates of growth in developing countries are greater than the growth rates of the developed countries, the gap may not narrow absolutely, because of the greater productive base from which the latter begin.[33]

Under such pressures, the developing countries have sought to use the UN as a political forum in which to voice their grievances over trade arrangements which they claim are unfavorable, to try to influence the development-aid policies of the richer countries, and to create new machinery in which their numbers can be felt in the determination of policies to be followed. In short, they are trying to join in a global dialogue in which the stake is a measure of direct control over the distribution of the world's wealth. This dialogue is not new in the United Nations. It is often forgotten that the plans for an International Trade Organization (ITO) came to grief in the years 1948–1950 in considerable measure over the infant industry issue, the demand of developing countries that they be allowed an exception to the general rules of non-discrimination in trade in favor of new industries. The issues then foreshadowed have grown more acute with the swelling voice of the developing countries and the growing acknowledgment that their problems are real and urgent and their demands deserving of response.

The consequences of this engagement have been many. One, perhaps the

[32] See the general description of this problem in "Long-Range Programme of Work in the Fields of Population (Proposals of the Secretary-General to the Thirteenth Session of the Population Commission)" (UN Document E/CN.9/196).

[33] If country A has a gross national product (GNP) of $100 million and increases at 2 percent per annum while country B has a GNP of $10 million and increases at 5 percent per annum, the production gap between the two will increase by $1.5 million per annum. Country B would have to achieve a growth rate of 20 percent to keep the gap from growing.

climactic one to date, was the UN Conference on Trade and Development (UNCTAD) which grappled with a broad range of contentious issues and produced agreement that the UN should have new machinery in this realm to supplement the General Agreement on Tariffs and Trade (GATT) which the developing countries claimed was too much influenced by the interests of the developed countries. Another consequence has been the growth of new international agencies, the International Finance Corporation (IFC) and the International Development Association (IDA), both affiliated with the International Bank, and the UN's own Expanded Program of Technical Assistance and Special Fund. It is abundantly clear that the UN has become a forum for a continuing active effort to deal with trade and development issues at the level of broad policy direction and, perhaps more surprisingly, through a direct technical assistance program of growing significance and resources.

THE ISSUES TODAY

If the financing crisis had somehow been delayed until after the UN's twentieth birthday, the temptation would have been great to contrast the vigor of the United Nations and the state of the world twenty years after San Francisco with the sad condition of both the League of Nations and the world in 1939. That comparison may still be relevant although with the situation what it is, one is impelled to approach the task a bit more soberly than otherwise.

In fact, both the UN and the world are in far better shape today than were their counterparts in 1939. In 1939 the League was dead, although interment was delayed until after the war. The world was plunged in that twentieth year into the holocaust of World War II and had already clearly failed to solve the dilemmas it had inherited from World War I. The world today, on the contrary, while it has not solved all its legacies from World War II, has nevertheless learned by and large to live with them. Europe, as has been noted, is remarkably stable for a continent that has undergone so great a succession of shocks in the past 50 years and more particularly in the ten years from 1939 to 1949. It would be unwise to take too much comfort from this fact as long as the central European issue, the German peace, is not finally settled. Walter Lippmann wisely warned us recently that before we can reach what he termed the "universal society" we must first have "a basic situation that is acceptable to all who might have the power to disturb it."[34]

The UN, over its twenty years of existence, has demonstrated its usefulness to the point where it would be difficult to visualize a world which did not have a UN. The UN's attraction for new Members has on balance been a healthy indicator. To be sure, the Organization has never been able to overcome the limitations which result from the lack of great-power consensus.

[34] *UN Monthly Chronicle*, Vol. 2, No. 4, p. 68.

Thus, many problems in which the Great Powers have been directly concerned—issues arising out of the European peace settlement, for example—have remained beyond the UN's realm of effective influence. Nevertheless, over virtually the entire life of the Organization, the UN has proved that it has a contribution to make in situations which threaten peace. The UN's ledger bears entries such as Iran, Kashmir, Palestine, Irian, and Cyprus, all of which represent situations which might have resulted in serious hostilities had the UN been unable to intervene.

In the sphere of economics, social and humanitarian affairs, colonial matters, and the development of international law, the UN has been carving out a role of growing utility. In short, the UN clearly has been a vigorous, growing organism, a dependent organism to be sure, responding moderately well to its challenges, operating for the most part with necessary restraint, but responding flexibly by a process of organic interpretation and growth to opportunities which came its way.

Now, however, the UN is confronted with a crisis, not with respect to all its functions, but primarily with respect to those in the peacekeeping sphere. The dilemma arises out of the UN's effort to fill with small-power participation the relative vacuum resulting from limits on the Great Powers' ability to perform, in a nuclear world, the policing functions in Africa and Asia that might otherwise be theirs. This effort has taken place at a moment in history when the Organization itself has been undergoing its most fundamental changes. The UN thus has not yet satisfactorily solved the issues posed in a new world for an organization which is in some respects new.

For example, the very facts of stability in Europe and of nuclear deterrence have served to divert the competition between Communist and Western countries into other areas. This has been taking place during that period in history when the colonial revolution and its immediate consequences have been in full spate and when mainland China has chosen to emphasize its independent and militant role. Clearly, the UN has not worked out programmatic or institutional responses to the problems of new countries simultaneously seeking to build new societies and to fend off the unwanted external interference that comes with desired external assistance. It has not been deemed able to cope with the serious dilemma posed when a country responds, as the United States has done in Vietnam or the United Kingdom in Malaysia, to the request of the government of another state for assistance against externally supported insurrection or externally based guerrilla invasion. If the Great Powers intervene on both sides in such a situation, one side legitimately in terms of existing international law and the other side surreptitiously and illegally, can the UN act to contain the clash? Is it possible to conceive of ground rules to govern such situations? Is it appropriate that there should be a financial or any other kind of veto to stop UN intervention aimed at preventing the Great Powers from clashing in areas far removed from any legitimate conception of their vital interests? How should the disinterested majority behave to protect its interest in the peaceful resolution and stabilization of such situations?

In the spirit of Walter Lippmann's observation about acceptable situations, it is worthy of comment that the UN by and large has been unable to bring about settlements of situations it has been able to stabilize. In Kashmir, the Middle East, Korea, Cyprus, and other places, the UN has been able to bring hostilities to an end but not to resolve the issues that led to the hostilities in the first place. Is it possible for the UN to insist on a greater willingness than has existed in the past on the part of contesting parties to accept the settlement proposals of third parties?

The continued existence of such unsettled, often emotion-laden, issues has given rise to much frustration. This frustration has given impetus to a trend which had other origins—toward experimentation with regional forms of organization as alternatives or supplements to the global United Nations. With respect to political and security matters, trade and development, and the performance of various technical functions, regional solutions are increasingly being sought and sometimes found. A major pervasive issue for the United Nations is how this trend toward regionalism can be accommodated to the needs of an effective global association.

Another problem the UN has not solved is the difficulty of achieving meaningful consensus among a membership as diverse as that of today's UN. Are there procedural devices—delegation of authority to smaller representative groupings or employment of rapporteurs to narrow differences and propose solutions are but two examples—that might enhance the possibilities of reaching agreement? Can governments do better than they have done in subordinating individual interests which diverge from the consensus to their own unmistakable larger interest in allowing the UN to deal successfully with threats to peace? In this respect, the Indonesian example is not encouraging. That precedent—that a nation withdraws from the UN when it cannot have its way—is the path to dissolution and chaos. Fortunately, there is little evidence that the Indonesian action is regarded with favor or that others are disposed to emulate it.[35]

Another problem which has begun to show itself but which may grow more serious with time is the political relationship in the Organization between the haves and the have-nots, the discontented and the satisfied. The influx of new Members has already accelerated the pace at which pressures are being applied against noxious racial practices in South Africa. Older Members, which also dislike *apartheid,* have been carried along reluctantly, partly in some cases because they have interests at stake but partly also because they

---

[35] However, see Arthur Lall in this symposium who underscores the potential seriousness of the Indonesian action.

are troubled by the implications for the constitutional balances of the Organization. Surely, it is right and proper that the more impatient Members should exert pressure to hurry along their slower partners. But at what point does too much impatience, no matter how justified the objective, jeopardize the basic understandings on which any structure of cooperation must rest?

Similarly, it may well be inevitable that the UN should become, far more than it has been, a forum in which there is political argument about the ways and means to give expression to the common interest in improving the welfare of the less privileged members of the community. From the point of view of the developing countries, every moment of delay in channeling effective assistance to them is obviously too long in terms of real and urgent problems that they face. From the point of view of the developed countries, it may not be easy to win politically necessary domestic acceptance of the view that their interest requires that they acquiesce in international political procedures which result in pressures to share their wealth with less privileged countries. In working through to mutually adequate solutions it is the degree of tension that is all important. Too little, and nothing or not enough happens. Too much, and the binding ties may snap to the disadvantage of all.

These issues suggest that more attention needs to be paid to the institutional and procedural responses to the new balances of interest, of numbers, of strength, and of resources that now exist in the Organization. In an organization of 50 Members, it was possible to ensure rough equity by the patterns of representation that were established in subordinate organs and in the balances which existed between these organs and the General Assembly. Now, those balances are no longer adequate. They neither sufficiently reflect in the subordinate organs the numerical preponderance of the countries of Africa and Asia nor adequately protect in the General Assembly the interests of the various minorities. The constitutional problems confronting those seeking to provide equitable and effective institutions and procedures which would reflect differences of population, power, and wealth and to accommodate the numerous, often crosscutting, interests that require representation, have never been easy. Yet there is no more important task, whether it takes the form of ventures in formal constitutional change and procedural innovation or the less formal routes to adjustment through the normal processes of political friction.

The future vitality of the UN and its ability to serve the essential needs of its community will depend on the responses which are found to these and similar questions. As of today, one might well conclude that the UN's problems are basically problems of growth and adjustment and not signs of a decline.

The New Diplomacy and the Quest for Peace

KENNETH W. THOMPSON

PARLIAMENTARY diplomacy in international organization has its roots in the movement toward "diplomacy by conference." As early as 1928, Frederick S. Dunn could assert:

> The rapidity with which the conference method has come to the forefront in the conduct of international intercourse is one of the most striking developments in the present era of world affairs. Within the space of a very few years, this method has almost entirely supplanted bilateral diplomatic negotiation in matters of interest to more than two or three nations.[1]

EVOLUTION AND CHARACTER OF PARLIAMENTARY DIPLOMACY

If parliamentary diplomacy has its roots in modern conference diplomacy, its evolution has taken place along significantly different lines. The most persistent distinction emphasized in the literature is that between diplomatic conferences or congresses made up of representatives of independent states and quasi-parliamentary assemblies organized along the lines of legislative bodies. The evolution of parliamentary diplomacy and its departure from the forms of international conferences become evident in the distinctions that arise in certain fundamental procedural practices. Diplomacy by conference as viewed by the text writers is primarily a question of voluntary agreement. The burden of proof is on those who propose a conference. Meetings at specified intervals, however, are normally provided for in the charters or procedural rules of international organizations or parliamentary bodies. Some established machinery is provided to cope with preparatory work. In the mid-

KENNETH W. THOMPSON, a member of the Board of Editors of *International Organization*, is Vice President of The Rockefeller Foundation.

[1] Frederick Sherwood Dunn, *The Practice and Procedure of International Conferences* (Baltimore, Md: The Johns Hopkins Press, 1929), p. v.

twentieth century the network of regional and worldwide interests is sufficient to limit the full independence of states to participate or not, and the existence of an international organization further obviates the reluctance of member states to join in discussions. The power to initiate passes to an international body.

Moreover, a similar distinction is possible for invitations to conferences. States that initiate *ad hoc* conferences retain the power to pick and choose participants. The watchword is to invite all states whose concurrence is essential to a given result. By contrast, the membership of parliamentary bodies is fixed. Votes and the location of authority are defined. While change is the law of international bodies no less than it is of life outside them, it is change within a given framework. The deliberative group is wider than that of the parties most immediately concerned with a problem.

Again, the agenda of a particular conference is outlined in relationship to its specific purposes. The debate on the agenda before and during the conference determines whether it will be held and whether it succeeds. States attend or refuse to attend a conference because of the agenda, as the postwar negotiations between the Soviet Union and the United States make clear. For parliamentary bodies, the procedures for fixing the agenda are commonly set forth at least in broad outline in the covenant or charter. They are also the product of continuous custom and practice, standing orders or rules of order, and certain resolutions of the parliamentary body.

The rules for the choice of the presiding officer also differ between conference and parliamentary diplomacy. In conference diplomacy, the foreign minister or principal delegate of the host country customarily presides. As the number of participants grows, the influence of the president in turn grows and can become determining. The role of United States Secretary of State Dean Acheson at the San Francisco Conference for the Conclusion and Signature of a Treaty of Peace with Japan and that of Secretary of State Charles Evan Hughes at the Washington Conference on the Limitation of Armaments illustrate the point. For parliamentary organizations such as the General Assembly, the president is more likely to be drawn from the smaller and ostensibly more disinterested states.

Finally, the practices of conference and parliamentary diplomacy diverge on parliamentary procedures and records. Writers on the subject distinguish between bargaining and so-called legislative conferences. The former fits its procedures to the needs and demands of the negotiators. The latter follows more closely the time-honored procedures of legislative or quasi-legislative bodies throughout the world. The records of conferences are likely to take the form of "protocols," *procès-verbal* or minutes, verbatim records *(comptes rendus)* including agreements, and supplementary protocols distributed after each session. Results are embodied in treaties and conventions which must be signed and ratified with or without reservations, declarations or joint statements of principles of law or policy, and sometimes general or final acts as with the Hague Conferences. If these records are compared with the recommendations of the General Assembly or the resolutions of the Security Council of the United Nations, another difference is illustrated.

Parliamentary diplomacy, therefore, both shares characteristics of conference diplomacy and partakes of its own peculiar qualities and features. The term has come to be used in the broad sense to describe the practice of intergovernmental negotiations and discussions carried on under fixed rules of procedure in bodies like the League of Nations and the United Nations. United States Secretary of State Dean Rusk prior to his appointment to that high office provided the following working definition:

> What might be called parliamentary diplomacy is a type of multilateral negotiation which involves at least four factors: First, a continuing organization with interest and responsibilities which are broader than the specific items that happen to appear upon the agenda at any particular time—in other words, more than a traditional international conference called to cover specific agenda. Second, regular public debate exposed to the media of mass communication and in touch, therefore, with public opinions around the globe. Third, rules of procedure which govern the process of debate and which are themselves subject to tactical manipulation to advance or oppose a point of view. And lastly, formal conclusions, ordinarily expressed in resolution, which are reached by majority votes of some description, on a simple or two-thirds majority or based upon a financial contribution or economic stake—some with and some without a veto. Typically, we are talking about the United Nations and its related organizations, although not exclusively so, because the same type of organization is growing up in other parts of the international scene.[2]

PRACTICE AND METHODS OF CONTEMPORARY PARLIAMENTARY DIPLOMACY

The United Nations by now is a continuing organization with 114 Members including—in contrast to its predecessor, the League of Nations—all but a handful of the most important nation-states. Its existence dictates that a majority of foreign offices conduct a significant fraction of their international business within the United Nations framework. The smallest of the new states may in fact at particular moments have as many officials at work in United Nations organs and agencies as serve their governments in foreign ministries at home. Beyond this, countries like the United States annually participate in some 350–400 international conferences with delegates instructed by their governments on a long list of agenda items. In the setting of international conferences, the representative must practice the arts of both the negotiator and the

[2] Dean Rusk, "Parliamentary Diplomacy—Debate vs. Negotiation," *World Affairs Interpreter*, Summer 1955 (Vol. 26, No. 2), pp. 121–122.

parliamentarian. The necessity of combining them has forced states to reconsider the qualities of their diplomats. For the Greeks, the gift of rhetoric was included among the attributes of the ideal diplomat, but with modern history this requirement largely disappeared. With the birth of parliamentary diplomacy, it resumed, in Sir Harold Nicolson's tart phrase, "its clumsy place among the arts of negotiation."[3]

With respect to public diplomacy, three distinctions must be made. First, if by rhetoric we mean "fine language without a conviction," Nicolson's stricture is doubtless controlling. Yet are there not times when a diplomat by the clarity of his remarks and his evident sincerity moves fellow negotiators to accept his viewpoint? Surely we can point to such instances in "quiet" diplomacy as in Judge Philip C. Jessup's example:

> I have witnessed a Secretary of State of the United States in most confidential session with a large cabinet group of a friendly power thus turn antagonism into friendliness and misunderstanding into accord.[4]

John Foster Dulles observed:

> The United States delegation has almost always modified its initial position after hearing the point of view of other delegations. The same can be said of most delegations.[5]

Since the aim of negotiations is to harmonize the varied interests of states, evidently this requires logic and precision of thought if the reciprocal advantages of the parties are to be established. Yet threats, menaces, invective, and provocation will rarely serve this goal and the public spokesman is all too readily the victim of those techniques. Today, no less than in the days of Jules Cambon, "the best instrument at the disposal of a Government wishing to persuade another Government will always remain the spoken words of a decent man."[6]

Second, the strident and raucous exchange that often marks the debate between Communist and other diplomats within international forums may excite patriotism without providing a reasonable alternative to diplomacy. Communists approach international negotiations with the grand assurance of men carried along by the dialectic of history. The open forum of the United Nations becomes a sounding board for missions and crusades. Their affirmations of faith may be more fervent in the halls of international conferences than in the suite of a rival negotiator. Of the Communists, Nicolson writes: "Their activity in foreign countries or at international conferences is formidable, disturbing, compulsive."[7] No one can afford to underestimate Commu-

---

[3] Harold Nicolson, *The Evolution of Diplomatic Method* (New York: Macmillan, 1954), p. 65.
[4] Philip C. Jessup, "Parliamentary Diplomacy," *Recueil des Cours de l'Académie de Droit International*, 1956 (Vol. 89, No. 1), p. 235.
[5] *Vital Speeches of the Day*, May 15, 1949 (Vol. 15, No. 15), p. 465.
[6] Quoted in Nicolson, p. 84.
[7] *Ibid.*, p. 90.

nism's potency or danger. But neither should it be confused with diplomacy, as Premier Nikita Khrushchev learned to his dismay.

Third, those who mistake forensic propaganda for the sum total of United Nations diplomacy are in error. Parliamentary shenanigans conceal more than meets the eye. Today's international parliamentarians include men who are genuinely professional in debate and maneuver; they have mastered the rules of procedure to serve diplomatic ends. Moreover, it is broadly true that the majority of delegates are capable of distinguishing between sincerity and bombast, devotion to the Charter and pure opportunism. Leadership in multilateral diplomacy comes to the top; character is not extinguished even in harsh international debate. The general debate and the days that follow it are a time for placing before the world community the issues of greatest concern to the national interest. Painful and protracted as these statements may seem and oftentimes tailored to the world press or an audience back home, they are the tribute men pay to their prime loyalty to the sovereign state. Yet, however responsive national leaders must be to their parochial interests, they have found that "you cannot secure the sympathetic support of the General Assembly by ignoring moral values."[8] No responsible delegate is likely to mock the high principles of the United Nations within its walls—and if he does, like the Asian diplomat who spoke of the Charter as a mass of words, he will probably amend his statement the following day.

The parliamentary forms and continuing organization of the United Nations have led to another hopeful and important development. The moral and political consensus which linked the rulers of eighteenth century states has been gravely weakened in our day. The moral cleavage between East and West or North and South is a fact with which we must learn to live. Only the naïve expect these profound differences to erode overnight, and yet we may each of us help to remove those that rest on myth and illusion. Massive and glacial movements are after all the result of countless small shifts of particles, whether of mind or matter.

One major criticism of the itinerant international congresses of the twentieth century has been that continuous, confidential, and informed negotiations were impossible. By contrast, the traditional ambassador in a foreign capital enjoyed numerous local assets. He knew the people with whom he was expected to negotiate; he was able to assess local interests, personalities, and events; he could confer with the host country's foreign minister on a courteous, routine, and undramatic basis; and he felt secure in interrupting and then resuming discussions without thereby dashing popular hopes or arousing public clamor. In negotiations, the inevitable stages of disappointment and delay mixed with progress and understanding seldom if ever became matters of public controversy. The results and not the stages were the

[8] Jessup, *Recueil des Cours de l'Académie de Droit International*, Vol. 89, No. 1, p. 56.

object of public scrutiny. Envoys had faith that confidence would not be betrayed or indiscretions committed. Negotiations were a process, not an episode, conducted by a corps of professionals who shared common values, standards, and rules of the game.

The United Nations family has within limits become a latter-day approximation of this earlier corps of diplomatists. The family is, of course, divided within itself. Yet its solidarity exists despite a pervasive disunity made tolerable by the principles of the Charter. This clash between the forces of unity and disunity is seemingly endless. Thus, if the philosophy of the Charter pays tribute to freedom, respect for individual rights, and the consent of the governed, many of the peoples living under it are drawn to authoritarianism, submission to native tyrants, and the achievement of mass security and rapid economic development by means of drastically thoroughgoing state controls. New states find they require a firmer social and political discipline if they are to avoid economic and social disintegration. The problem is broader than Communism. For some, anti-Americanism is the strongest unifying tie—stronger even than the Charter with its happy identity of Articles 1 and 2 and the United States' Declaration of Independence. Yet no matter how profound and divisive the forces of national antagonism and of conflicting political philosophies, the common interest of members of national delegations, the Secretariat, and top-ranking visitors also exists. At the opening of each session of the General Assembly, ties of camaraderie unite "old friends, old enemies, all old colleagues." The bonds are not those of an ancient diplomatic elite—common language, class, and purpose—but for that reason perhaps more in keeping with the present age.

Yet if moral solidarity is enhanced by parliamentary diplomacy, other forces that lead to disunity and disarray persist. Peacekeeping assumes the conditions of peace mutually established and ratified in peaceful settlements. As Walter Lippmann has observed:

> The universal society must have a foundation, and that foundation can be made up only of peace settlements which are accepted by all the nations capable of overthrowing the settlement.[9]

Yet around the world, whether in Southeast Asia or Central Europe, not peace but at best tenuous armistice lines separate contending groups and movements. Sources of disorder exist in the disappearance of old regimes and of the hierarchical international order of the eighteenth and nineteenth centuries, the legacies of World Wars I and II, and the birth pangs of a newly emergent system of nation-states founded not on tradition but on the consent of the governed. The great historical process which began with the liquidation of an ancestral order continues in the struggle for a new international order. The

[9] Walter Lippmann, "The Great Revolution," *UN Monthly Chronicle,* April 1965 (Vol. 2, No. 4), p. 68.

changes through which we are living involve far-reaching and fundamental differences separating East and West and North and South over the shape and character of the new order. The United Nations, created to preserve the peace, has been called upon to establish the conditions of peace, to bridge the gap between the old and the new, and to help build situations of cohesiveness and stability where none exist. Ironically, as historians and publicists have long maintained, the task is one that an international organization could not, by itself, accomplish or control although it might assist and encourage. In Lippmann's words:

> The failure of the League of Nations has much to teach us today. The primary and supreme lesson is that it failed because it could not make peace and nobody else was able to make peace.[10]

Diplomacy and the Quest for Peaceful Settlement

United Nations practice is more varied and fruitful in preventing war and limiting conflict than in drawing up terms of peace. The two World Wars have not yet been settled and concluded by either the United Nations or the Great Powers. By contrast, in Suez and Gaza, Lebanon and Jordan, Laos and the Congo (Leopoldville), parliamentary diplomacy proceeded along the lines of limiting the conflict and preventing its extension. Its initiative, in the words of the late Secretary-General Dag Hammarskjöld, was "to forestall developments which might draw the specific conflict, openly or actively, into the sphere of power bloc differences."[11] In all these areas, violence has continued and who can say that any great-power treaty concluding the World Wars would have eliminated these conflicts? The wars confronting parliamentary diplomacy have not involved the attrition of conscript armies nor the bombing of civilians with fire bombs and nuclear weapons. Today's wars are revolutionary wars fought by bands of guerrillas with terrorism and propaganda. Parliamentary diplomacy seeks to prevent little wars, isolate and contain them when they break out, and draw a circle around the combatants and neutralize them against the encroachments of Great Powers. If this task is reminiscent of traditional diplomacy, this is not accidental. It tells us something of the recurrent nature of political conflicts and the measures by which a half-organized world is destined to cope with them.

Practice has shown that parliamentary diplomacy must be attuned to the circumstances of conflict. Its methods are a means to an end. Its purpose may involve, alternately or in combination, encouraging the parties to negotiate their differences, to bring them before the world forum, to buy time and re-

---

[10] *Ibid.*

[11] *Introduction to the Annual Report of the Secretary-General on the Work of the Organization, 16 June 1959–15 June 1960* (General Assembly *Official Records* [15th session], Supplement No. 1A), p. 4.

duce passions, or to reestablish a more favorable balance of forces less inimical to peace. The founders were clear that before the United Nations became seized with a problem, states had a prior obligation. In Article 33, they provided:

> The parties to any dispute, the continuance of which is likely to endanger the maintenance of international peace and security, shall, first of all, seek a solution by negotiation, enquiry, mediation, conciliation, arbitration, judicial settlement, resort to regional agencies of arrangements, or other peaceful means of their own choice.

In Dean Rusk's thoughtful phrase,

> a solemn warning is written into the Charter itself that the processes of debate are to be considered a serious matter, that they are drastic medicine to be used where less dangerous therapy has failed.[12]

Nevertheless, the trend has been to overload the agenda, to throw issues onto the floor before other remedies have been exhausted, or, in more recent years, to call on the Secretary-General—"let Dag do it."

There are of course other circumstances when preventive diplomacy is served by exposing an issue to the international community. Debate may bring an issue to the attention of a largely disinterested community of states. "It provides a testing of policy by the standards of the Charter, an expression of a decent respect to the opinions of mankind."[13] Every Member State in moments of crisis endeavors to show that its policies are in harmony with the Charter and its adversary's in conflict with it. "The continual pressure of the Charter upon debate in the presence of a world community is a powerful political fact not to be disregarded."[14] Nations like individuals before the bar of justice are given incentives to bring their conduct into line with commonly accepted standards. Yet open debate carries risks and dangers. Pressures are ever present to appeal to powerful passions of national pride and ambition. It remains true that

> debate is a substitute for *more* violent means and not a substitute for *less* dangerous techniques. It is a substitute, or the last chance if you like, before self-help or organized sanctions.[15]

THE IMPORTANCE OF QUIET NEGOTIATION

The test of the parliamentary approach internationally differs significantly from the measure of its success nationally. Within an organized national society, the test is lawmaking and legislation; on the world stage, the purpose

---

[12] Rusk, *World Affairs Interpreter*, Vol. 26, No. 2, p. 125.
[13] *Ibid.*, p. 126.
[14] *Ibid.*
[15] *Ibid.*, pp. 126–127.

is peacemaking. To assert this detracts not a whit from the search for orderly rules of procedure that are binding on the members. An international body that is more than a collection of negotiators takes on a corporate character. It resolves important questions concerning voting procedures, the role of its presiding officer, and acceptable techniques for the handling of disputes. Agreement on the rules may reduce the impact of powerful national emotions and keep to a minimum unnecessary disagreements.

The constitutional practice of the United Nations and its rules of the game are probably at a crucial phase of growth or decline when the limits of majority action are unclear and the habit of majority decision still comparatively new. Parliamentary procedures

> should be calculated to promote a maximum of negotiation and agreement in international discussions as contrasted with a sterile majority vote achieved by parliamentary maneuver but ineffective in practice. . . . [16]

The late Secretary-General Dag Hammarskjöld sensed this more keenly than many of his contemporaries. In a speech at Ohio University in 1958 he explained:

> Since the "legislative" processes of the United Nations do not lead to legislation, and the power of decision remains in the hands of the national governments, the value of public debate in the United Nations can be measured only by the degree to which it contributes to the winning of agreement by the processes of diplomacy. If public debate contributes to winning consent either immediately or in the long run, it serves the purpose of peace-making. If it does not so contribute, then it may be a useless or even harmful exercise.[17]

If public debate sometimes serves the cause of peacemaking, it can as readily be slanted for home consumption or for waging the propaganda war. A parliamentary triumph in a national legislature leads to decisions that carry the force of law. A voting victory in the United Nations leads at best to recommendations without the force of law and at worst to a steadily declining consensus between the powers opposing one another in parliamentary debate. Dean Rusk has noted:

> Success in the conduct of our foreign affairs is to be measured not in tally sheets, but by issues satisfactorily resolved, friendships consolidated, rivalries reduced or circumscribed.[18]

"It is diplomacy, not speeches and votes, that continues to have the last word in the process of peace-making."[19] In 1954, provisional settlements were

---

[16] C. Wilfred Jenks, "Craftsmanship in International Law," *The American Journal of International Law*, January 1956 (Vol. 50, No. 1), p. 54.

[17] "The Element of Privacy in Peace-Making: Text of an address by Secretary-General Dag Hammarskjold at Ohio University, Athens, Ohio," *United Nations Review*, March 1958 (Vol. 4, No. 9), p. 12.

[18] Rusk, *World Affairs Interpreter*, Vol. 26, No. 2, p. 137.

[19] "The Element of Privacy in Peace-Making," *United Nations Review*, Vol. 4, No. 9, p. 11.

reached on the Iranian, Suez, and Trieste problems, and at some stage along the way the United Nations was involved in all three. Is it crucial that the United Nations was not in on the final stages? This standard may lead to new uses of parliamentary machinery not envisaged by its framers. It calls to mind the skillful use of committees of rapporteurs under the League of Nations and the functions of the Council of Four at the Paris Peace Conference. In the late Secretary-General's words:

> I think the experiences of the past twelve years have demonstrated that there is need to redress the balance between public and private procedures of the United Nations. . . . [20]

Perhaps historians will find that Mr. Hammarskjöld's most enduring efforts were as innovator blending the two procedures. In this he reflected the Charter which requires prior obligation to pursue other means before bringing an issue before the United Nations (Article 33, paragraph 1). It was he who gave dignity to "quiet diplomacy" within a United Nations framework and practiced it himself with consummate skill. He preferred confidential dealings with leaders and would have accepted Dean Rusk's pungent phrase: "There is a utility in tedium, and I suspect that we could use more of it in the conduct of our foreign policy."[21]

Among public officials, Secretary-General Hammarskjöld had the courage to proclaim to those who viewed open diplomacy too simply:

> The best results of negotiation between two parties cannot be achieved in international life, any more than in our private worlds, in the full glare of publicity with current public debate of all moves, unavoidable misunderstandings, inescapable freezing of position due to considerations of prestige, and the temptation to utilize public opinion as an element integrated in the negotiation itself.[22]

What is called for is a proper perspective between secrecy in deliberations and publicity in results. It is essential that debate and voting follow careful advance preparation through available channels of negotiations. Without this it may be unproductive and even dangerous. Open diplomacy is often the last phase of negotiations.

THE PLACE OF THE SECRETARY-GENERAL AND HIS ADVISERS

The Secretary-General as the symbol of an international body preserving objectivity and neutrality in the great struggle is peculiarly well qualified for quiet diplomacy. In Mr. Hammarskjöld's words,

> He is in a position of trust vis-à-vis all the Member governments. He speaks for

---

[20] *Ibid.*
[21] Rusk, *World Affairs Interpreter*, Vol. 26, No. 2, p. 137.
[22] "The Element of Privacy in Peace-Making," *United Nations Review*, Vol. 4, No. 9, p. 11.

no government. . . . He can never give away what must be considered the property of the government with whom he is working.[23]

He has at his command subtle resources of power and prestige deriving in
part from past successes in implementing UN resolutions. He and his staff
keep watch over the peace 365 days of the year. He consults with permanent
missions when major UN organs are not in session and is more continually
on hand than others who serve the Organization. By deft reporting or a helpful remark, he can guide the negotiations of others, for, as Mr. Hammarskjöld
once remarked, "A car can often be driven by only a light touch of the
wheel."

The deep conflicts and the limits of consensus within the United Nations
not infrequently impel the chief bodies of the Organization to pass broad and
general resolutions calling on the Secretary-General to act but providing him
with few guidelines for action. The vagueness of his directives may reflect
the lowest common denominator of agreement attainable for states torn by
dissension or at times the bypassing of a broad area in which compromise had
proven impossible. Sometimes Member States prefer to escape responsibility
and other times they prefer to provide the UN executive with the authority
for urgent and necessary action.

From the standpoint of diplomatic techniques, the Secretary-General seeks
to respond through a variety of techniques. Particularly noteworthy are the
advisory committees whose members meet with him in private, contributing
day-by-day advice on delicate problems in which they possess a vital stake
and helping him to carry out his mandate. No votes are taken, but while the
committee members reflect their governments' views, they show independence
in discussing practical issues of the moment. Members remain in touch with
their governments on details of the meetings and thus provide the Secretary-
General with a more secure sense that his policy is "on the rails." The Secretary-General as the presiding officer guides the discussions and rallies the
judgments of participating states. The UN Scientific Advisory Committee is
a body of seven outstanding nuclear scientists sitting as government representatives of the three major atomic powers, the Soviet Union, the United
Kingdom, and the United States. Its work has paved the way for constructive
agreements despite barriers of the Cold War. Of the Advisory Committee on
the United Nations Emergency Force (UNEF) in the Middle East, made up
of smaller Member States most of which had supplied troops to UNEF, Mr.
Hammarskjöld wrote:

> Its work is an example of the practical value in the United Nations of a formal
> instrument of private diplomacy in carrying forward action once the main policy
> lines have been laid down by a decision of the General Assembly. That decision,

[23] *Ibid.*, p. 12.

in turn, was made by the General Assembly in the public proceedings of parliamentary diplomacy only after the informal procedures of private classical diplomacy had done their work. Thus, this case is also an example of a kind of three-stage operation which is natural in the United Nations and which is capable of yielding constructive results . . . private diplomacy preceding public debate and then employed again to follow through.[24]

The Advisory Committee on the Congo met with the Secretary-General on more than 50 occasions for discussions lasting on the average of three hours. In a series of complicated and difficult meetings following the Security Council resolution of February 21, 1961, representatives of Member governments who were deeply divided on the issues, nevertheless, through discussion enabled Mr. Hammarskjöld to formulate a consensus of views, to which Members might dissent, that furnished a basis for his policy in the Congo (Leopoldville). An earlier advisory committee of foreign ministers concerned in October 1956 with the impending Suez crisis succeeded through informal and private negotiations in reaching unanimous agreement on the six principles essential to any settlement of the Suez crisis—principles that proved their worth even after fighting had broken out.

Taken together, the work of these advisory committees illustrates the resources for private diplomacy that exist in the United Nations. Their success underlies the proposal of a wise UN diplomatist:

> Classical diplomacy continues to be usefully practiced in the old tradition on a bilateral basis. But more of it is needed now in the practices of the United Nations if we are to develop to the full the capacity of the Organization. . . . [25]

Beyond this, the UN may provide from time to time the one common meeting place for ambassadors and foreign ministers from more than 100 countries. The opening of the General Assembly may even allow heads of state to contact one another for private, off-the-record talks. Their physical presence in New York gives a unique opportunity for the continuing exercise of private diplomacy without the fanfare of public diplomacy or the formal procedures of "summit" diplomacy. The presence of Soviet Foreign Minister Andrei Gromyko in New York in the autumn of 1961 enabled Secretary of State Dean Rusk and President John F. Kennedy to engage him in exploratory talks on the Berlin crisis—an approach that was wholly consistent with Mr. Hammarskjöld's view of parliamentary diplomacy.

THE FUTURE: WEIGHING SITUATIONS AND TACTICS

Former United States Ambassador Charles Dawes is quoted as saying "diplomacy is hell on the feet," to which a colleague replied, "It all depends

[24] *Ibid.*
[25] *Ibid.*

on whether one uses one's feet—or one's head." Parliamentary diplomacy puts a still greater premium on using one's head as well as one's feet.

For Demosthenes the first duty in politics was to be "in control of occasions." There is a time to act and a time to wait but the question is always which is it. There is a time to debate and a time to negotiate, a time for firmness and a time for conciliation. If states are willing, the world forum can be used for national propaganda.

> When the foreign minister of a great country mounts the . . . world platform and when he states a position in the name of his country . . . when he attacks . . . the position of other countries, and when the dispute touches upon the very basis of the political regimes to which he finds himself opposed . . . it is rather difficult . . . the next day to say "I was mistaken."[26]

Often when a delegation is unwilling to negotiate in confidence, it may employ an international assembly as a sounding board. In 1954 the Soviet Union showed its hand at the Berlin Conference on the prospects for an Austrian treaty and German reunification by launching a propaganda broadside against the West. Large international congresses are as subject as the UN to such abuses. Reviewing the early years of the United Nations, Paul-Henri Spaak (Belgium) declared:

> I have often wondered . . . whether we have not pushed open diplomacy a little too far and have not sometimes made it more difficult to arrive at a solution by making public everything that we said and did within the diplomatic framework.[27]

The rise of the newly independent states has magnified the prospect that the United Nations will be used as a sounding board. Nations that are emerging with the breakup of the British, French, Belgian, Dutch, Portuguese, and Spanish empires have thus found a ready-made instrument for speeding the liquidation of colonialism. The once secure majority of the United States and its European and Latin American friends in the General Assembly has ended.

With the tide running against the United States, it is tempting to suggest a curtailing of the use of the worldwide forum. Sober thought leads to the opposite conclusion, however, if the goal is to bridge the gulf between old societies and new or between the Atlantic Community and the developing world. To ignore a tumultuous parliament on the theory that "he who is not my ally must be my enemy" would be to resign world leadership in the vast reaches of Africa and Asia to the Soviet Union if not to Communist China.

Nevertheless, if the situation does not call for an abandonment of parliamentary diplomacy, the friends of the United Nations have a duty to face the problem of how a multitude of governments can be saved from becoming a sometimes irresponsible mob. In this task, "the dogmas of the quiet past are

[26] Paul-Henri Spaak, "The Role of the General Assembly," *International Conciliation*, November 1948 (No. 445), p. 613.
[27] *Ibid*.

inadequate to the stormy present." Sydney Bailey has well said that the trouble with parliamentary diplomacy is that it has become "more and more parliamentary, and less and less diplomatic."[28] Debate has come to be viewed as an end in itself. It is forgotten that "the chief purpose of parliamentary diplomacy . . . is to cause a reassessment of national interests in the light of the national interests of others."[29]

There are situations where mere discussion may prove useful as in the General Assembly's handling of the Syrian-Turkish conflict in 1957 and the Security Council's treatment of the Sudan-Egyptian border dispute in 1958. Talk can serve as a poultice drawing the infection from a conflict. Yet the facts of a situation may call for more than this. There may be times when the findings of an international body must be supported by the power and prestige of a United Nations presence. Diplomacy historically has been validated by national power. Parliamentary diplomacy acquires force from the more subtle and intangible power of the international community.

> A government may refuse to comply with a decision of a policy-making organ but would think twice before taking action which would bring it into direct, on-the-spot conflict with representatives of the international community.[30]

To challenge a United Nations presence can be seen as an affront not to the power of a national society but to the full authority of the international society.

It is also true that parliamentary diplomacy suffers from a certain unwieldiness. It may not always respond swiftly to a crisis. Writing of national assemblies, Walter Lippmann observed: "The reason why we trust one man, rather than many, is because one man can negotiate and many men can't."[31] He added:

> One diplomat may see what is in the other diplomat's mind, and time his utterance accordingly; a whole people cannot see quickly into another people's mind and its utterance is inevitably crude. The very qualities which are needed for negotiation—quickness of mind, direct contact, adaptiveness, invention, the right proportion of give and take—are the very qualities which masses of people do not possess.[32]

Nations including those in Asia and Africa are not oblivious to this fact. In 1957 as tension mounted between Thailand and Cambodia, they turned not to the General Assembly or the Security Council but to the Secretary-General. Then, and again in 1962, they asked for a personal representative of the Secretary-General who might work with them in resolving their dispute. In taking

[28] Sydney D. Bailey, *The Secretariat of the United Nations* (Rev. ed.; New York: Frederick A. Praeger, 1964), p. 42.
[29] *Ibid.*
[30] *Ibid.*, p. 43.
[31] Walter Lippmann, *The Stakes of Diplomacy* (New York: Macmillan, 1915), p. 26.
[32] *Ibid.*, p. 29.

action with the knowledge but not the approval of the Security Council, Dag Hammarskjöld explained that: "Such actions . . . fall within the competence of his Office and are . . . in other respects also in strict accordance with the Charter, when they serve its purpose." This philosophy undergirded the Secretary-General's visit to Laos in 1959 and his successor's appointment of a temporary executive for West Irian in 1962, the dispatch of United Nations observers to Yemen in 1963, and the mission appointed "to ascertain the wishes" of Sabah and Sarawak in 1963.

Another situation which impairs successful negotiation is the illusion that the United Nations is strengthened by throwing on its table a maximum of international business. Overloading the agenda may have the opposite effect. Negotiation takes time and agreement is often a dividend of patience. The impression grows apace that the General Assembly in particular now tries to do more than it can do well. It has infrequently found a way of dispensing with "the old reliables" like South West Africa, universal disarmament, and colonialism. Serious students urge greater discrimination to avoid what some would call "irrelevance or tedious repetition." There are limitations in public debate, and once the parties have made initial statements in public session, efforts to narrow differences should go on in private. The Secretary-General has appointed a committee to consider whether the General Assembly might not delegate some of its powers, especially in peacekeeping, to a small representative committee. The League of Nations went further than the United Nations in the use of special rapporteurs capable of elucidating the issues and examining possible solutions. Individuals are frequently able to succeed where committees fail, whether as Secretary-General or as the chosen instrument of an organ of the United Nations.

Parliamentary diplomacy can also help to keep open the channels between rival powers in world politics. The leaders of the Great Powers may in speeches, press conferences, or interviews give the signal they are prepared to negotiate. Then, within or outside the United Nations, alert diplomats move to explore the prospects of agreement. The classic case is of course the settlement of the Berlin blockade in 1948–1949 when United States Ambassador Philip C. Jessup successfully explored with his Soviet colleague at the UN the meaning of a conciliatory statement by Soviet Premier Joseph Stalin. Thus far, diplomacy in the conference rooms and anterooms of the United Nations has filled in the gaps in contacts between adversaries in the Cold War. Is it too farfetched to ask whether the United Nations may in the future provide opportunities for unobtrusive diplomatic contacts for countries separated by conflicts not between East and West but between North and South?

United Nations spokesmen have given appropriate emphasis to the strengthening of machinery for collective security, to developing a police force, and to marshaling support for UNEF. Winston Churchill's apt phrase has relevance here: "When wolves are about, the shepherd must guard his flock even if he does not himself care for mutton." If by its power the United Nations has not deterred many wars, it has helped to shorten at least four of them: in Indonesia in 1949, between Arabs and Jews in 1949, at Suez in 1956, and in the Congo (Leopoldville) from 1960–1964. The mid-twentieth century has witnessed less the establishment of peace than a "general truce" in the Cold War and, in particular, in conflicts such as the Arab-Israeli dispute and the war in Korea.

Vattel, in describing such a state of affairs, wrote:

> It [a general truce] scarcely differs from a treaty of peace, except that it leaves undecided the dispute which gave rise to the war. When the nations are weary of fighting, and yet can not arrive at a settlement upon the question at issue, they have recourse to an agreement of this character. It is thus that between the Christians and the Turks, instead of treaties of peace, truces for long periods are generally made. This is due sometimes to a false spirit of religion and at other times to the fact that neither side is willing to recognize the other as lawful master of their respective possessions.[33]

Instruments of peaceful change and accommodation must be adapted to the circumstances of a "general truce." They must function in a world divided by "a false spirit of religion" and recurrent disputes over the status quo. The United Nations is probably incapable of establishing peace but it has won its spurs in the limitation of conflict. And lest this achievement be undervalued or its price counted too high, we do well to recall with Churchill that

> a war postponed may be a war averted. Circumstances change, combinations change, new groupings arise, old interests are superseded by new. Many quarrels that might have led to war have been adjusted.

In such a world, a parliamentary forum must be the meeting place where any nation can talk with its neighbors in the world, where talks are never finally broken off, where issues, however insoluble, are never pressed beyond the point where civilization is threatened. It must remain the scene of quiet talks between the world's leaders no less than of lengthy prepared statements whether of hatred and mistrust or mutuality and goodwill.

It has been said that

> though the U.N. cannot alter the international distribution of power, nor even guarantee the weak against the determined depredations of the strong, it can mobilize and maximize the forces which in any given situation favour just or peaceful action, and can put at their disposal for this purpose the most extensive armoury of diplomatic and parliamentary devices so far known.[34]

In this sense, parliamentary diplomacy carries hope for the future.

[33] Emmerich de Vattel, *The Law of Nations, Or, Principles of the Law of Nature Applied to the Conduct and Affairs of Nations and Sovereigns* (first published in French in 1758), Book III, Chapter XVI, section 235.

[34] Herbert G. Nicholas, *The United Nations as a Political Institution* (London: Oxford University Press, 1959), p. 179.

Changing Patterns of Constitutional Development

RUTH B. RUSSELL

AT the end of its twentieth year the United Nations is in the midst of a constitutional crisis the outcome of which is still in doubt. During its lifetime it has survived other profound changes, some no less constitution shaking than the present one. Other developments were absorbed chiefly through a process of informal Charter interpretation and institutional adaptation; whereas the current financial crisis was allowed to reach the stage where formal confrontation of conflicting Charter interpretations could be avoided only by adopting a procedural device to evade decision that, unfortunately, also brought the Assembly to a halt.

Such devices have been used before now to avoid pushing a bitterly divisive issue to formal decision, as on the Chinese representation question. The present case, however, involves the Members in their capacity as Assembly participants so that the price of avoiding decision on whether to apply Article 19 to Members in arrears on peacekeeping assessments is the paralysis of that organ. In the constitutional arguments over the financing issue, the major actors on both sides—the Soviet Union, France, and the United States—all contend that the basic need is to "return" to the Charter, inconsistent as that may seem.

FORCES AFFECTING CHARTER INTERPRETATION

"That we now have this Charter at all is a great wonder," President Harry S. Truman reminded the final session of the United Nations Conference on International Organization in June 1945.[1] The sessions at San Francisco had

RUTH B. RUSSELL is a senior staff member of the Foreign Policy Studies Division of The Brookings Institution, Washington, D.C.

[1] *Documents of the United Nations Conference on International Organization, San Francisco, 1945* (New York: United Nations Information Organization, 1945), Vol. 1, p. 715.

been marked by differences so strong that more than once they almost halted the negotiations. The will to establish a successor to the League of Nations had finally proved stronger than those substantive differences, but only at a cost in consensus.

The outcome was a Charter committing its signers to act in pursuance of purposes and in conformity with principles that they understood in widely varying ways. It had to serve, moreover, as the constitutional basis of an institution dedicated to the promotion of international cooperation but born into a world of revolutionary conflict. One group of its Members saw their destiny in violent opposition to another, and many were not wholly averse to the occasional use of "a little bit of" force as an instrument of national policy, despite the Charter undertakings to the contrary.

The tie between political context and constitutional issue is always present in some degree. It is exceptionally strong in the UN which, as a voluntary international agency, is not an independent center of political power. It rather reflects the confluence of power factors in other political arenas of the world it seeks to organize. The constitutional development of the UN has consequently been shaped by political disputes outside the Organization as well as by the nature of its Charter.

Controversial issues at San Francisco were often resolved not in favor of one extreme or the other but by "fuzzing over" the controversy at the lowest common denominator of agreement and in language that was inevitably vague if not confusing. Strictly speaking, all that the Conference decided was the form of words that went into the Charter's provisions and into certain official interpretations.

The linguistic puzzle was further complicated by the lack of provision for authoritative interpretation. This left matters to the daily decisions necessary in the work of each organ and to procedures for resolving differences within or between organs.[2] But if such interpretations were not "generally acceptable," the Conference considered that they would not be binding and that Charter amendment might be required.[3]

A proposed amendment can be blocked by any permanent member of the Security Council failing to ratify it (Article 108), leaving matters quite inflexible when there is a serious difference among the major powers—as in the

[2] Various delegations favored making the Court or the Assembly (as the plenary body) authoritative in matters of interpretation. But neither time nor disposition permitted accord on this. See Ruth B. Russell, *A History of the United Nations Charter: The Role of the United States, 1940–1945* (Washington, D.C: Brookings Institution, 1958), especially pp. 925–927.

[3] See the report of Committee IV/2 (Judicial Organization, Legal Problems) in *Documents of the United Nations Conference on International Organization, San Francisco, 1945* (New York: United Nations Information Organization, 1945), Vol. 13, pp. 709–710; see also, Oscar Schachter, "The Relations of Law, Politics and Action in the United Nations," *Recueil des Cours de l'Académie de Droit International*, 1963 (Vol. 96, No. 2), pp. 185–190, 196–198.

present crisis.[4] The difficult amendment procedure has meant that, despite numerous constitutional disputes since 1945, the first amendments were officially proposed only in December 1963 to enlarge both the Security Council and the Economic and Social Council (ECOSOC)—changes widely desired for many years but never voted because of Soviet opposition to any structural change while Peking did not occupy China's seat in the Organization.[5] A special "review conference," callable any time after ten years, was also provided for (Article 109) to mollify delegations that were dissatisfied with various provisions. No strong sentiment for convening such a conference has ever arisen, however, due to the continuing differences among the powers.

Had the UN achieved effective consensus on either a "strict" or a "liberal" construction of the Charter, it could have developed peacefully as either the "static conference machinery" or the "dynamic instrument of governments" which Secretary-General Dag Hammarskjöld described as its future alternatives in his final *Annual Report*.[6] The kind of Charter interpretation that would have become customary under the second alternative was shown early in 1946 when the Soviet representative announced he was abstaining from voting on, but not vetoing, a Security Council resolution. This became accepted practice in spite of the literal meaning of the requirement in Article 27(3) that decisions must receive "the concurring votes" of all permanent Council members. A more recent pragmatic adaptation, also generally accepted, has been to split the two-year terms of elected Council members between two contestants when neither could command the requisite majority. That device not only resolved certain election difficulties but it also permitted more states to participate as Security Council members, which partly compensated for the inability to enlarge that organ after the UN's membership had increased so greatly.[7]

In the years since 1945 the UN, without such consensus, has in practice had to "flesh out" the Charter skeleton of authority and principle, of machinery and procedures, for the attainment of its declared objectives. The record, while not consistent and steady, has on balance been "dynamic." Constitutional developments have also displayed a variety of patterns in the areas symbolized by the three Councils which reflect partly the changing world outside the

---

[4] The Assembly "accepted" an advisory opinion of the International Court of Justice by a majority of 76 in favor, 17 opposed, with 8 abstentions (General Assembly Resolution 1854 A [XVII], December 19, 1962), but there is a question whether an Assembly vote constitutes a "generally acceptable" interpretation.

[5] Under General Assembly Resolution 1991 A and B (XVIII), December 17, 1963, the Security Council would be increased to fifteen members (all new members to be elected ones) and ECOSOC to 27.

[6] *Introduction to the Annual Report of the Secretary-General on the Work of the Organization, 16 June 1960-15 June 1961* (General Assembly *Official Records* [16th session], Supplement No. 1A), p. 1.

[7] The origins of the practice are traced in Norman J. Padelford, "Politics and Change in the Security Council," *International Organization*, Summer 1960 (Vol. 14, No. 3), pp. 381-401.

UN, partly the inconsistency of Members within it, and partly the continuation of fundamental conflicts of interest that made it difficult to negotiate the Charter in the first place.

ACTION, REACTION, AND STALEMATE IN THE SECURITY FIELD

At Dumbarton Oaks, the Soviet Union initially favored a postwar organization limited to security functions; even when it accepted the broader institution proposed by the United States and the United Kingdom, it wanted the Assembly confined to discussing only those matters referred from the Security Council. At San Francisco, a deadlock over this question of the Assembly's competence was only broken by an appeal to Moscow.[8] The Assembly ultimately received the broad authority contained in Articles 10–12 and 14, which have always been interpreted by the vast majority of Members so as to allow them to discuss and recommend on practically anything they consider "international."

Although the Soviet Union has protested that any recommendatory "action" by the Assembly in matters of peace and security is illegal (thus interpreting Article 12 to fit its original desire), it has often gone along, on the basis of abstention, with the majority view; and it has sometimes promoted the use of the Assembly when the Security Council was prevented by a veto from acting. The first such shift to the Assembly was in fact initiated by Poland, in 1946, on the Spanish question.[9] This practice was extended in 1947, on Western initiative, after a Soviet veto of further Council action in the Greek border case. In 1956 the Soviet Union voted in favor of invoking an emergency session of the Assembly after Anglo-French vetoes in the Security Council had prevented decision there on the Suez invasion.

The Assembly early established the use of subsidiary organs for field operations. Thus, in 1947 it set up a UN Special Committee on the Balkans (UNSCOB) to observe and report on Greek border violations, a UN Temporary Commission on Korea (UNTCOK) to observe proposed elections intended to unify the country; a UN Special Committee on Palestine (UNSCOP) to investigate the situation and make recommendations concerning its future government; and subsequently the UN Palestine Commission to implement the Assembly's plan for partition.

The utilization of military officers as field observers also began with the early operations: by UNSCOB in Greece and by the Security Council's Consular Committee in Indonesia (1947) to report on a cease-fire; by a similar consular Truce Commission for Palestine (1948); and by more elaborate and

[8] See Russell, Chapter 10, especially pp. 761–764, 770–775.

[9] The Byelorussian Soviet Socialist Republic even urged (unsuccessfully) that the Assembly recommendation that Members terminate diplomatic relations with Spain be broadened to cover economic relations as well.

continuing truce observation machinery set up in Kashmir (1948) and Palestine (1949). A significant change also occurred in the composition of such groups. Initially made up of government representatives, with minimum services by the Secretariat, their personnel gradually came under the Secretary-General's authority, either as part of the regular Secretariat (e.g., the UN Field Service) or as seconded national officials, including military officers.[10]

There was thus a considerable body of experience with field operations authorized on a recommendatory basis by the time Korea exploded while the Soviet representative was boycotting the Security Council. Abstention was already accepted as not equivalent to a veto, and now the other Council members extended the doctrine to cover absence as well.[11] Since Soviet–United States differences had prevented conclusion of any agreements to make armed forces available to the Council (Article 43), that body simply recommended that all Members come to the aid of South Korea. It improvised a UN Unified Command, asking the United States to take charge as the only practical method in the circumstances.

When the Soviet representative returned to his seat and vetoed further action on Korea, the question was shifted to the Assembly, then opening in September 1950.[12] It passed the Uniting for Peace Resolution[13] in an effort to rectify Council inability to act by providing formally for Assembly supervision of enforcement action under its recommendatory authority. It included a procedural change to speed the transfer of a question from Council to Assembly and established a standing Peace Observation Commission, thus seeking to institutionalize that recognized type of field machinery. It also recommended that Members earmark units of their armed forces to be maintained in readiness for future use under either Council or Assembly resolutions (equivalent to Article 43 obligations); authorized a panel of military experts (equivalent to the Military Staff Committee) to advise governments on the

[10] See Ruth B. Russell, *United Nations Experience with Military Forces: Political and Legal Aspects* (Washington, D.C: Brookings Institution, 1964), pp. 49–50; Brian E. Urquhart, "United Nations Peace Forces and the Changing United Nations: An Institutional Perspective," *International Organization,* Spring 1963 (Vol. 17, No. 2), pp. 340–341; and Schachter, *Recueil des Cours de l'Académie de Droit International,* Vol. 96, No. 2, pp. 206–207.

[11] For contemporary arguments pro and con this extension, see Leo Gross, "Voting in the Security Council: Abstention from Voting and Absence from Meetings," *Yale Law Journal,* February 1951 (Vol. 60, No. 2), pp. 209–257; Myres S. McDougal and Richard N. Gardner, "The Veto and the Charter," *ibid.,* pp. 258–292; and Norman Kogan, "U.N.—Agent of Collective Security," *Yale Law Journal,* January 1952 (Vol. 61, No. 1), pp. 1–13.

[12] Had action been so vetoed in June, with the Assembly not in session, convening an emergency session might have seemed too slow in the circumstances, and the United States might have sought to rally collective support for Korea under Article 51. In effect, the Korean operation was a collective self-defense action but carried on within the UN framework rather than outside it, as originally anticipated. See, for example, the explanation of the United Kingdom representative in Security Council *Official Records* (2nd year), 140th meeting, June 10, 1947, pp. 994–995.

[13] General Assembly Resolution 377 (V), November 3, 1950.

technical aspects of doing that; and a Collective Measures Committee to recommend further steps to improve UN ability to meet future aggression. This attempt to provide the elements of a sanctions force in readiness was destined to have no more success in practice than the Charter provisions for achieving the same end.[14] Thus, the constitutional changes often attributed to the Uniting for Peace Resolution seem much overrated; although the objective may have been to enhance the Assembly's powers—"showing the way to an enforceable rule of law," as United States Secretary of State Dean Acheson put it at the time[15]—it did not in fact result in any such institutionalization of earlier practice beyond the procedural change. The former view has nonetheless persisted so strongly that the current crisis has been widely and erroneously described as in effect nullifying the Uniting for Peace Resolution.[16]

Similar jumping to conclusions was indulged in when the Suez case in 1956 was shifted from a vetoed Security Council to the Assembly, which authorized the establishment of the UN Emergency Force (UNEF) by the Secretary-General. The sheer novelty of seeing an international armed force, in the name and under the flag of the UN and commanded by Secretariat officials under Assembly direction, was so great that its relationship to the earlier and smaller—but politically and functionally similar—field operations noted above was largely overlooked, although General Burns (its first Commander) and his initial staff were drawn directly from the Palestine armistice team. As with the earlier groups, UNEF's functions were essentially the same nonfighting type of impartial, pacific-settlement activity, carried out with the consent of the parties in conflict and for the purpose of assisting them to comply with their undertakings to suspend violence. Those basic characteristics have applied to all subsequent peacekeeping operations in spite of their varying sizes, mandates, and details of organization. Even the highly contentious Congo operation got into trouble primarily because in rapidly changing and often chaotic circumstances it was unable to make effective those same guidelines as laid down by the Secretary-General and accepted by the Security Council.[17]

The tendency to see these nonsanctions peacekeeping forces as a means of

[14] The Peace Observation Commission was requested by the Assembly in 1951 to set up a Balkan Subcommission and send military observers to Greece to replace the discontinued UNSCOB. It was never utilized again. See Russell, *United Nations Experience with Military Forces*, pp. 19–23.

[15] Department of State *Bulletin*, October 2, 1950 (Vol. 23, No. 587), p. 524. For other views, see Joseph Johnson, "The Uniting for Peace Resolution" in Clyde Eagleton (ed.), *Annual Review of United Nations Affairs, 1951* (New York: New York University Press, 1952), pp. 239–247; and A. H. Feller, *United Nations & World Community* (Boston: Little, Brown and Company, 1952), pp. 36–39.

[16] See, for example, Thomas J. Hamilton in *The New York Times*, February 22, 1965.

[17] See Russell, *United Nations Experience with Military Forces*, pp. 86–123. Mssrs. Hammarskjöld and U Thant both emphasized the limitations on peacekeeping forces; see especially, "Summary Study of Experience Derived from the Establishment and Operation of the Force (UNEF): Report of the Secretary-General" (UN Document A/3943); and U Thant, "A United Nations Standby Peace Force," Address at Harvard University, UN Press Release SG/1520, June 12, 1963. See later in this volume, Leland M. Goodrich, "The Maintenance of International Peace and Security."

achieving more than they reasonably can also results in part from the constitutional arguments about them. Despite the antecedent operations and their nature as pacific-settlement machinery, the Soviet Union insists that *any* international military operation is illegal unless it is both organized and operated under the Security Council, including its financial arrangements.[18] Consequently, it refuses to pay a share of the costs as assessed by the Assembly or to contribute voluntarily to support the peacekeeping operations. The French, on the other hand, argue that voluntary operations must be paid for by governments supporting them or at least not opposing them. In both cases, if those particular assessments were not included in calculating their arrears, Article 19 would not be in question.

The United States, on the other hand, has advocated "strengthening" the "operational capability" of the UN to undertake peacekeeping ventures, including more institutionalized arrangements for standby peace forces and has done so at times in language that seems to exaggerate their potential or even to imply they might become an incipient sanctions force. United States insistence on the legal authority of the Assembly in financial matters has also added to the political confusion.

The argument for the Assembly's right to assess the budgetary expenses of the Organization under Article 17 can be accepted without necessarily concluding that all the costs of UNEF and the UN Operation in the Congo (ONUC) which were so budgeted and assessed had to be handled in that way. In the technical assistance field, only a minor part is charged to the UN budget, the rest being regularly left to voluntary pledging. And peacekeeping operations since the Organization got into financial straits (in West Irian, Yemen, and Cyprus) have been wholly financed outside the UN.[19] The widespread willingness of Members to accept the principle of collective responsibility for financing peacekeeping—even if not its full price—evidently misled the United States into pushing a good legal case to a poor diplomatic conclusion. In a situation where there is no "sheriff" to seize the Kremlin or the Quai d'Orsai to meet overdue debts, the result is that the Assembly is in desuetude, the UN wholly dependent on voluntary financing, and all security action under Council control—where it will probably remain until another serious crisis, as in 1956, creates enough political consensus to bring the Assembly back into action.

---

[18] In July 1964 the Soviet Union made its own proposal for establishing UN forces under Security Council control. While maintaining that "aggressor states" should pay for any measures necessitated by their aggression, the Soviet proposal recognized that emergency conditions might necessitate collective defraying of expenses, in which it would be prepared to participate when international forces are established in "strict compliance with" the Charter (UN Document A/5721).

[19] See below in this volume, Norman J. Padelford, "Financing Peacekeeping: Politics and Crisis."

Evolutionary Progress in the Economic and Social Field

In the economic and social field the UN has also developed along very different lines than anticipated in 1945 but with a remarkably high degree of accord.

In the great-power negotiating period before San Francisco, with Moscow uninterested, Washington and London established the basis for the economic and social provisions of the Charter, agreeing that activities in this sphere must expand beyond their level under the League. The concept they developed was centered around the objective of an expanding world economy. International cooperation, briefly, was to focus on an effort to stabilize the international effects of cyclical fluctuations of boom and depression, which had marked the interwar years, by maintaining national "full employment" and rising standards of living. In terms of postwar organization, they visualized a series of global technical agencies coordinated by a central economic organ which would also functionally harmonize the national actions of Members to maintain employment.[20]

The Charter accordingly authorized the UN to promote cooperation in the solution of "international problems of an economic, social, cultural, and humanitarian character"; established the Economic and Social Council as the organ to carry out these responsibilities and to bring the specialized agencies "into relationship" with the Organization. The overwhelming needs of the war-devastated areas had before 1945 led to the establishment of the UN Relief and Rehabilitation Administration (UNRRA) whose experience influenced the inclusion of authority for ECOSOC to "perform services at the request of" Members or of the agencies and to arrange for several new technical agencies in the fields of agricultural, monetary, and capital investment problems. "Temporary" regional Economic Commissions for Europe and Asia and the Far East (ECE and ECAFE) were early formed, later followed by the Economic Commission for Latin America (ECLA)—all made permanent in 1951—in addition to the functional economic, social, and human rights commissions specifically provided for in the Charter.[21] Paralleling the Economic and Employment Commission as the main ECOSOC subsidiary in view of its contemplated coordinating function, the group of specialized agencies was to be rounded out with a wide-ranging International Trade Organization (ITO) aimed to clear the channels of restrictive international practices in the related fields of trade, commodities, cartels, employment, investment, and development. Agreements on these matters were finally signed at a major

[20] The general concept was outlined in a 1943 "Memorandum concerning the Washington Meeting between British and American Economic Experts," in *Postwar Foreign Policy Preparation, 1939–1945* (Department of State Publication 3580) (Washington, D.C: U.S. Government Printing Office, 1950), pp. 562–564. See also, Russell, *A History of the United Nations Charter*, pp. 72–74.

[21] The Charter authorized ECOSOC to establish, in addition to the particular functional commissions, "such other commissions" as it required. (Article 68.)

UN Conference on Trade and Employment held in Havana in 1948. But ITO never came into being,[22] nor were the hoped-for liberal international economic policies generally adopted by governments.

What happened instead was epitomized in the title of the Organization's second great trade meeting, held in Geneva in 1964: the UN Conference on Trade and Development (UNCTAD). In the intervening years, UN emphasis over the whole range of economic and social activities became centered on economic development of the underdeveloped areas as the international coordinating theme for UN policies. Fulfillment of the "revolutions of rising expectations" took the spotlight from the maintenance of full employment. The importance given the subject is indicated by one of the few accomplishments of the nineteenth Assembly—the establishment of the continuing machinery proposed by UNCTAD by unanimous consent since voting was impermissible.[23]

Development was always, of course, the chief concern of the economically less advanced countries which from the start stressed the Charter's provisions on promoting "economic and social progress and development." This, however, called less for accord on harmonizing separate national policies than for direct assistance in meeting the lack of technical skills and capital that accounted for much of the underdevelopment. The Assembly in 1946 ventured into this then uncharted field by calling on ECOSOC to study ways of extending such expert advice about the requirements of economic development, and it unwittingly began the operational programs that have become the UN hallmark in this area when (with UNRRA about to be liquidated) it also authorized the Secretary-General to continue the urgent advisory functions of UNRRA in the social welfare field.[24] These became the supposedly short-term "Advisory Social Welfare Services," which still continue. From this beginning[25] the UN's program of technical assistance evolved into the well-publicized Expanded Program of Technical Assistance (EPTA) in 1949[26] and, a decade later, it was greatly extended by the UN Special Fund.[27]

[22] Although ITO never came into existence, many of its commercial policy and commodity provisions have been applied through the General Agreement on Tariffs and Trade (GATT) and the Interim Coordinating Committee for International Commodity Arrangements (ICCICA). See Robert E. Asher and others, *The UN and Promotion of the General Welfare* (Washington, D.C: Brookings Institution, 1957), pp. 240–265.

[23] General Assembly Resolution 1995 (XIX), December 30, 1964, established the UN Conference on Trade and Development as an organ of the Assembly and approved a 55-member Trade and Development Board and subsidiary organs. See Richard N. Gardner, "GATT and the United Nations Conference on Trade and Development," *International Organization*, Autumn 1964 (Vol. 18, No. 4), pp. 685–704; and, below in this volume, Roy Blough, "The Furtherance of Economic Development."

[24] General Assembly Resolutions 57 (I) and 58 (I), December 14, 1946.

[25] ECOSOC Resolution 51 (IV), March 28, 1947, and General Assembly Resolution 200 (III), December 4, 1948.

[26] ECOSOC Resolution 180 (VIII), March 4, 1949.

[27] General Assembly Resolution 1240 (XIII), October 14, 1958. In the interests of efficiency, ECOSOC on August 11, 1964, recommended the consolidation of the Special Fund and EPTA as the UN Development Program (ECOSOC Resolution 1020 [XXXVII]).

The similar activities of the many specialized agencies have combined with these two programs to result in a great extension of field activities by international Secretariat personnel. These reflect a quiet revolution of the past twenty years in the degree to which governments covering a wide spectrum of political shadings now accept action by international institutions with, and even within, national states. The UN Resident Representative, who may advise on country programming, and OPEX officials who actually fill government posts while training replacements, are only the most dramatic illustrations of how these activities have practically obliterated the traditional distinctions in the economic and social field between "domestic" and "international" jurisdictions.[28] The very success of the assistance program—at first castigated by Communist spokesmen as an economic sheepskin on the imperialist wolf—in time even brought about a diminution of their polemics and some limited participation, often disruptive, by Communist Members.[29]

The decentralization of ECOSOC, unforeseen at San Francisco, was further increased when the Economic Commission for Africa (ECA) was set up in 1958. The regional economic commissions have also had a greater flexibility than ECOSOC, permitting the participation of certain non-Members of the UN and some non-self-governing territories. Meanwhile, also reflecting the change of emphasis in ECOSOC's work, the Economic and Employment Commission after several metamorphoses was allowed to expire, and there is now no strictly economic commission under the Council.

REVOLUTIONARY CHANGE IN DEVELOPING LANDS

Radical change has likewise marked the expanding relationships of the UN to dependent territories and peoples, but it has been accompanied by continuous conflict over the Organization's jurisdiction, in contrast to the economic and social field, and has resulted in clear victory for one side rather than the stalemate that prevails in the security field. The nature of the substantive conflict underlying the constitutional developments has, moreover, brought about another, and wholly unexpected, revolution in the nature of the human rights problems in the UN.

The viewpoints in conflict since 1945 were already in evidence before then. President Franklin D. Roosevelt and other United States leaders were convinced that the emerging nationalist demands of colonial peoples would be a major political factor in the postwar world. Their somewhat vague vision of an international trusteeship system was a projection of United States policy in

[28] OPEX officials are recruited under the program for the provision of Operational, Executive, and Administrative Personnel. See Schachter, *Recueil des Cours de l'Académie de Droit International,* Vol. 96, No. 2, pp. 237–238, 242–245.

[29] See below in this volume, Walter R. Sharp, "The Administration of United Nations Operational Programs," for some of the problems of coordination and administration involved in these activities.

the Philippines, the theme of which was training for self-government with target dates for independence. But neither during nor after the war were they successful in persuading the chief European imperial powers to "go and do likewise" in the interests of peaceful, evolutionary decolonization. By the time of San Francisco, the United States' position was somewhat ambivalent as a result of military insistence on retaining the Japanese-mandated islands for security reasons.[30] At the Conference, the other major powers divided on this issue along lines that later became so familiar: The United Kingdom and France opposed any significant extension in the UN role beyond that of the League in the mandate system, while the Soviet Union and China favored much stronger international activity.

Underlying these positions on constitutional issues of function and authority lay conflicting political judgments on the strength of the rising nationalist movement. The European colonial powers, as time showed, woefully underestimated the effects of war and wartime promises; even those accepting the inevitability of political evolution in their dependencies misread the clock. The result, in oversimplified terms, was continual conflict between defenders of the status quo and those in accord with United States Undersecretary of State Sumner Welles who announced in 1942 that: "The age of imperialism is ended."[31] The rhetoric of that conservative diplomat and the doctrine of the Communists were in accord on this—and their judgment was to be vindicated by the sweep of decolonization that within a decade began to transform the UN.

In 1945, however, since the provisions of the Charter had to be voluntarily accepted, the colonial powers by threatening to reject *any* trusteeship provisions successfully opposed proposals to put all colonies in trust if not to declare their imminent independence.[32] To forestall more drastic provisions, they accepted the Declaration Regarding Non-Self-Governing Territories (Chapter XI of the Charter). They praised its uniqueness as a joint statement of colonial policy principles but insisted on its form as a "Declaration" supposedly not binding them beyond responsibility to promote the well-being of dependent peoples and voluntarily to transmit technical data ("for information purposes" only) on dependencies of their own choosing. That eight states promptly listed 74 territories as in this class indicated their evident self-confidence

---

[30] See Russell, *A History of the United Nations Charter,* Chapters 4 and 23.

[31] Department of State *Bulletin,* May 30, 1942 (Vol. 6, No. 153), p. 488.

[32] Not all colonial powers were equally resistant. Australia and New Zealand, in fact, favored Assembly authority to

> specify territories in respect of which it shall be the duty of the states responsible for their administration to furnish annual reports to the United Nations upon the economic, social, and political development of the territories concerned.

See *Report by the Australian Delegates on the UN Conference* (Australian Cmd. Paper, No. 24, Group E-F.4311) (1945), pp. 10, 22–24, 97.

that the Charter contained adequate safeguards from their point of view.[33]

The trusteeship provisions were even more permissive. This system depended on the sovereign states voluntarily placing territories under UN trusteeship on their terms although it was understood that former mandates and any "detached" enemy territories would be included. The membership of the Trusteeship Council, moreover, was evenly divided between "administering" and "nonadministering" governments, thereby compensating for the former's numerical inferiority in the UN even in 1945 by practically guaranteeing a deadlock over contentious issues. The potentials of the Charter for the development of a wide-ranging trusteeship system along Rooseveltian lines could only be realized through the initiative of the imperial powers—which was not forthcoming. In fact, only ten of the former mandates (all but South West Africa) and the former Italian colony of Somaliland were made trust territories.[34] By 1965 the Trusteeship Council had about "withered away," as eight of its territories, all but New Guinea and Nauru (Australia) and the Pacific Islands Trust Territory (United States), had become independent. This left a curious situation. The Council can only be constituted in nominal accord with the terms of Article 86 by including New Zealand and the United Kingdom as "administering authorities" although Australia alone administers Nauru on their behalf.[35]

The Charter also contained a time bomb, little recognized in 1945, in the "principle of equal rights and self-determination of peoples" as the basis of "friendly relations among nations." (Article 1[2].) No one was prepared to oppose the principle which was first suggested by the Soviet Union but neither was there agreement on its meaning; the rights of revolution and secession were both debated but the result was one of the fuzziest terms in the Charter.[36] By 1960, however, it had been "defined" in practice and embodied in an

[33] See Russell, *A History of the United Nations Charter*, pp. 813–824. The unusual Declaration in the midst of a treaty was aimed at placating France in particular which did not want any general statement of principles and which entered a formal reservation of its right to resort to the domestic jurisdiction clause in connection with this Chapter. For a list of territories, see *Everyman's United Nations* (7th ed.; United Nations: Office of Public Information, 1964), pp. 344–346.

[34] Special arrangements were also made through the Assembly, by request of the major allied powers in 1949, for the other Italian colonies: Libya was to become independent with a UN commissioner helping to establish its government; and Eritrea, after investigation by a field commission and the assistance of another UN commissioner, was to become an autonomous unit federated with Ethiopia. (*Ibid.*, pp. 134–136.)

[35] This arrangement, with the United States also an administering authority, gives the Trusteeship Council four members of that class. With three permanent Security Council members as automatic nonadministering members, this has left one state to be elected to give a balanced total of eight. If Australia and the United States only were counted as administering states, then the need to include all nonadministering permanent Security Council members would make it impossible to have an evenly divided Trusteeship Council.

[36] *Documents of the United Nations Conference on International Organization, San Francisco, 1945* (New York: United Nations Information Organization, 1945), Vol. 6, p. 455. After "self-determination" was added to Article 1, the Soviet delegate left no doubt where Moscow stood on its meaning. The goals of "equality and self-determination of nations" in the Charter, he said at a press conference, would help dependent peoples to realize them sooner. "We must first of all see to it that dependent countries are enabled as soon as possible to take the path of national independence." (*The New York Times*, May 8, 1945, p. 15.)

Assembly resolution as the right of colonial peoples to be freed from imperial rule. As newly independent states, however, they adopted the almost universal view of governments of whatever age in refusing a right of secession to any domestic group.[37]

These developments were more the result than the cause of the historical decolonization movement. But the world spotlight on the UN stage has misled many to credit the Organization with more authority than it can in fact exert. However, the Assembly early established its right to set up a Committee on Information to consider the "technical data" transmitted on the non-self-governing territories, and it pressed increasingly into the political field as well. One committee has succeeded another until the present Special Committee on the Situation with Regard to the Implementation of the Declaration on the Granting of Independence to Colonial Countries and Peoples (Special Committee of Twenty-Four).[38]

Every step increasing the Assembly's area of concern has been resisted by the colonial powers under the claim that the subject was *ultra vires*—a position still adhered to by Portugal and South Africa. Even today, the Assembly's actions may be pragmatically accepted by the more liberal colonial states while its competence is formally denied, as when a UN representative was authorized to supervise elections in the Cook Islands at New Zealand's request.[39] The Assembly has nonetheless established its right to determine which territories fall under Article 73 (Portugal's resistance notwithstanding),[40] and the Special Committee of Twenty-Four now receives petitions, hears individuals, makes field investigations in relation to dependent areas, and somewhat resembles liberal hopes of 1945 for the Trusteeship Council.

In the course of this transformation the issue of national self-determination became inextricably mixed with that of racial discrimination, a prevalent characteristic of colonialism. The legal approach to human rights as a field of UN activity began with the relatively rapid achievement of the Universal

---

[37] See later in this volume, Rupert Emerson, "Colonialism, Political Development, and the UN," and writings cited therein.

[38] For an account of the *ad hoc* Committee on Information's evolution into a continuing committee of the Assembly, see Emil J. Sady, "The United Nations and Dependent Peoples" in Asher, pp. 878-888. The Special Committee of Twenty-Four began in 1961 as a seventeen-member committee (General Assembly Resolutions 1654 [XVI], November 27, 1961, and 1810 [XVII], December 17, 1962). This Special Committee has taken over the functions of the Committee on Information, the Special Committee on South West Africa, and the Special Committee on Portuguese Territories.

[39] General Assembly Resolution 2005 (XIX), February 18, 1965. The New Zealand request is in UN Document A/5880; the Secretary-General's memorandum in UN Document A/5882; a Soviet letter to the President of the Assembly "not supporting" the proposal for a UN observer without "due consideration" by the Assembly in UN Document A/5885; and, in UN Documents A/5893-5895, letters from the representatives of Australia, the United Kingdom, and the United States in which they solemnly reserved their governments' positions by stating that the action did not constitute a precedent or create any obligation of "general applicability."

[40] Schachter, *Recueil des Cours de l'Académie de Droit International*, Vol. 96, No. 2, p. 187.

Declaration of Human Rights of 1948,[41] but then the intended development of covenants specifying those rights in detail and making them binding never passed the drafting stage. However, a political approach to the issue also appeared in 1946 when India complained against discriminatory treatment of Indians by South Africa. In 1952 the general problem of *apartheid* was added to the particular case with the charge that race conflict also threatened the peace. The idea that racism could be such a threat, even though an internal issue, was recognized in 1945, as the horrors of Nazi concentration camps were being revealed. At San Francisco, for example, France proposed that the domestic jurisdiction reservation should not apply if serious violation of human rights became a threat to the peace. Article 2(7) was phrased so as to make that or any other internal source of international disorder subject to the enforcement authority of the Security Council.[42]

By 1960 the Declaration on the Granting of Independence to Colonial Countries and Peoples pronounced colonialism a "denial of fundamental human rights," incorporated the right of self-determination as defined in the pending human rights covenants, and admonished all states also to observe the Human Rights Declaration and the Charter.[43] Since then the denial of both self-determination and racial equality have been ever more strongly condemned as threats to the peace. The Assembly and the Security Council have even recommended that Members apply diplomatic and economic sanctions and an arms embargo against South Africa. Pressures mount for even stronger mandatory sanctions but no general consensus has yet developed on the criteria for determining when, in the French terms of 1945, "the clear violation of essential liberties and human rights constitutes in itself a threat capable of compromising the peace."[44]

As long as these two group rights—self-determination and racial equality—remain far from universal realization, pressures for their achievement will certainly continue to take priority over any significant expansion of UN activity in other human rights areas. Indeed, the end of both colonialism and racism might not mean much greater UN concern with the rights of individuals. For those touch upon sensitive domestic policies of *all* countries, not

[41] General Assembly Resolution 217 (III), December 10, 1948, which was adopted by 48 in favor, none opposed, with 8 abstentions (Byelorussian Soviet Socialist Republic, Czechoslovakia, Poland, Saudi Arabia, South Africa, Soviet Union, Ukrainian Soviet Socialist Republic, Yugoslavia), and two absences (Honduras, Yemen).

[42] Russell, *A History of the United Nations Charter,* pp. 900–910.

[43] In view of the stubborn adherence to domestic jurisdiction claims by the colonial states generally, it is curious that not one of them voted against the Declaration, which was passed by 90 in favor, none opposed, with 9 abstentions (Australia, Belgium, Dominican Republic, France, Portugal, Spain, South Africa, United Kingdom, United States). A similar reluctance to declare public opposition was seen in 1948 when the Communist Bloc states abstained in the vote on the Universal Declaration of Human Rights.

[44] *Documents of the United Nations Conference on International Organization, San Francisco, 1945* (New York: United Nations Information Organization, 1945), Vol. 3, p. 386.

just of a small minority of the Assembly—and few governments are yet prepared to be as liberal about their own policies as about others', as the Soviet
Union demonstrates when pressing for UN intervention in other dependent
areas generally while remaining silent on its own policies in the Kuriles.

CONCLUSION

The foregoing sketch of developments since 1945, incomplete as it is, demonstrates how constitutional adaptation to change in the international scene
in a period of serious political conflict tends to be made through informal
interpretation and usage rather than through formal interpretation and
amendment. The political conflict itself reflects the fact that we live in a tran-
sitional world where old norms of international law are no longer so widely
accepted while new ones are still being painfully forged on the anvil of contemporary political experience. The International Court of Justice has consequently been less utilized than was the Permanent Court of International
Justice under the League of Nations. Given the flexible terms of the Charter
and effective consensus of the Members, however, the doctrine of implied
powers has provided adequate rationale for rather liberal constitutional adaptation. The controlling factor in the future will continue to be the "effectiveness" of that consensus which must include, in the positive consent of the required majority, those states with means to implement the decision in question and, additionally, at least the "negative consent" of abstinence on the
part of those in the minority with power to prevent implementing action.
The current crisis demonstrates that such power—either to prevent or to implement—may be psychological and political as well as financial or military.

The lack of common accord on the standards of peace to be enforced
through Security Council action continues to prevent the constructive use of
that body as originally planned in the Charter. It has been partially compensated for in times of crisis by the development of enough consensus to support action through the Organization to contain outbreaks of violence. In
such circumstances, operations by the Secretariat have expanded into the vacuum left by the Security Council's inability to act through its own machinery.
The role of the Secretary-General has developed in answer to the demand
created by the difficulties of operating under the original division of constitutional functions. In the field of economic and social development, the role
of the Secretariat has likewise expanded beyond the 1945 concepts to fit the
changing nature of the problem as perceived in the Organization and to the
extent of the willingness of Members to support its operations. Since the near
future promises no rapid change for the better in the degree of international
cooperation likely to be practiced, there is also little reason to anticipate much
change either in the prevalent mode of constitutional development in the
foreseeable future.

The degree of national commitment to action through international organization is still weak, especially when it involves giving rather than getting on the part of Member States. This is true in specific instances even of states that are generally strong supporters of the United Nations. In part, this results from the relative novelty of multilateral activity; for governments, like individuals, tend to be suspicious of the new. Even when willing to engage in collective action, moreover, they are novices in utilizing the potentialities of the permanent organizations. Yet the League was only a pale foreshadowing of what the United Nations has become under far from optimum conditions of growth; given the normal slowness of social evolution, the range of concern of the Organization has expanded remarkably in the past twenty years. In that perspective, we may look to the next twenty years with more optimism than the immediate situation seems to warrant.

II. Cooperation and Conflict

The Maintenance of International Peace and Security

LELAND M. GOODRICH

IT is a truism that the text of the Charter gives a quite misleading picture of the United Nations as it is today. In no respect is this more true than in the working of the Organization in the maintenance of international peace and security. Those provisions of the Charter which were claimed by its authors to provide the new Organization with teeth that the League of Nations did not have either have never been used or have in practice been of little importance. New emphases and new methods have been developed through the liberal interpretation of Charter provisions. These have not always been equally acceptable to all Members, however. The process of adaptation and development continues, with great present uncertainty as to what the future has in store.

THE SYSTEM ENVISIONED AT SAN FRANCISCO

According to its Charter, the United Nations, like the League before it, has as its primary purpose the maintenance of international peace. Those who were responsible for the drafting of the Charter sought to profit from the League experience and to incorporate in the Organization features that would enable it more successfully to accomplish its major purpose than the League had been able to do. Central to the thought of the drafters of the Charter was the belief that an international peace organization, to be successful, must be based on the active cooperation of the major military powers. This in a sense involved a return to the Concert of Europe idea and amounted to a substantial modification of the system of collective security provided for in the Covenant of the League. Those who drafted the Charter believed that all

LELAND M. GOODRICH, a member of the Board of Editors of *International Organization*, is Professor of International Organization and Administration, Columbia University.

states, great and small, should be committed to basic purposes and principles, including a prohibition of the use or threat of force going beyond the corresponding ban of the Covenant. They nevertheless concluded from the League experience that the application of collective measures, including military, against a major military power or without the cooperation of all such powers, was not likely to be successful and might in fact be disastrous.

Under the terms of the Charter, Members confer upon the Security Council "primary responsibility for the maintenance of international peace and security." While the Charter provisions are not free of all ambiguity on the division of powers and responsibilities between the Security Council and the General Assembly, they explicitly state that the General Assembly is not to make recommendations while the Security Council is discharging its responsibilities. Furthermore, the clear inference is that the General Assembly is the organ that is primarily concerned with the development of general principles of cooperation and with handling those situations that are not of such a nature as to be likely to endanger international peace and security.

By placing this responsibility on the Security Council and by providing that no substantive decision of the Council can be taken except with the concurrence of the permanent members, the authors of the Charter went far toward assuring that no collective measures would be taken against a permanent member or without its consent. This could be expected to mean that Members enjoying the protection of a permanent member would be exempt as well.

Guarantees that the permanent members would themselves, in the language of Article 2, paragraph 4, "refrain in their international relations from the threat or use of force," were not to be found therefore in provisions of Chapters V and VII but rather in the willingness of these states "in good faith" to respect their obligations under the Charter. If a permanent member of the Council failed to do this, other Members would have no choice but to fall back on their own resources for defense and to take such countermeasures in protection of their vital interests as might be deemed necessary. Thus, the UN peace and security system not only was premised on the willingness of the major powers—the permanent members of the Security Council—to cooperate but also assumed their ability and willingness to take such measures as might be necessary for their own defense if one or more of them disregarded basic commitments under the Charter to refrain from the use of force. Thus, as its core, the Charter system of peace and security rested upon a condition of balance in relations between the major powers as well as upon a willingness of these powers to cooperate for common ends.[1]

For the maintenance of peace generally, primarily in situations outside the relations between the major powers themselves, the Charter provides a variety

[1] See Inis L. Claude, Jr., "The United Nations and the Use of Force," *International Conciliation*, March 1961 (No. 532).

of means to be used by the Members in their relations with each other or by organs so constituted as most effectively to discharge the responsibilities placed upon them. The explicit emphasis of the Charter is upon the use by states of means of their own choice to settle their differences. In case of failure, appeal may be made either to the Security Council or the General Assembly. It is the Security Council, however, that not only is given "primary responsibility" for maintaining international peace and security but also is under specific instructions as to how it may and should proceed in discharging this responsibility. It should, first of all, except in a case of actual breach of the peace, seek to get the parties to agree on the methods or terms of settlement. In case of a threat to the peace or breach of the peace, it may also, depending upon its evaluation of the circumstances, call upon the parties to adopt provisional measures to prevent a worsening of the situation. When faced with a situation of great seriousness, it may order Members to take collective measures of an economic, political, or military nature. The obligation of states to carry out military measures, however, is conditioned on their having entered into special agreements with the Security Council by which they place forces and facilities at the Council's disposal. Furthermore, in the preparation and execution of plans for the use of military measures, the Security Council is assisted by a Military Staff Committee consisting of the Chiefs of Staff of the permanent members or their representatives. The authors of the Charter apparently had in mind that the major powers themselves would be the chief contributors of forces to be placed at the disposal of the Council.

From this brief review of the Charter provisions for the maintenance of international peace and security, the conclusion can easily be drawn that the principal architects of the system were influenced not only by the League experience, particularly in the years immediately preceding the outbreak of World War II, but also by the war experience itself and the preoccupations that naturally came with the prosecution of such a momentous struggle to a successful military conclusion. It was hoped that the powers engaged at the time in a common military effort against the Axis powers would continue this cooperation after the war. More specifically, it was hoped that these powers would be able to agree upon the terms of peace settlements which would constitute a substantial part of the new legal order on which the maintenance of international peace and security in the postwar years would be based. Certainly the principal challenge to this order was expected to come from the losers in the then current struggle. The UN, then, like the League before it, was in a real sense to be the guarantor of a peace settlement imposed by the victors against future efforts to change it by force. This was to be an important part of its total responsibility for the maintenance of peace and security.

THE IMPACT OF THE COLD WAR

Even before the first meetings of the Security Council and the General Assembly in January 1946, it was becoming apparent that major difficulties would be encountered after the conclusion of hostilities in maintaining even that limited measure of cooperation that had been achieved when the war was still in progress. At Moscow in December 1945 the Foreign Ministers of the Soviet Union, the United Kingdom, and the United States had been able to agree on the procedures to be followed in the conclusion of the peace treaties, but this appearance of cooperation was possible only because important areas of potential conflict and disagreement were not seriously explored. Though the major victors were able to reach agreement during 1946 on the terms of peace treaties with Italy, Bulgaria, Hungary, Rumania, and Finland, they found themselves in increasing conflict and disagreement over the terms of settlement with the two major Axis powers—Germany and Japan. Furthermore, in the Balkans and the Middle East, Soviet interests clashed with those of the United States and the United Kingdom. It was in this area, in support of the Greek government, that President Harry S. Truman in his message to the United States Congress on March 12, 1947, first proclaimed the policy of assisting "free peoples to maintain their free institutions and their national integrity against aggressive movements that seek to impose upon them totalitarian regimes,"[2] a policy that was to be followed by the United States in ensuing years to curb alleged Communist expansionism and that set the tone of the ensuing "Cold War" as far as the West was concerned.

The confrontation that developed between East and West—essentially between the Soviet Union and the United States and the United Kingdom—was hardly conducive to the full implementation and carrying out of the Charter provisions for keeping the peace. On questions such as the claim of Soviet intervention in Iran, alleged aid to Greek guerrilla forces by Greece's northern neighbors, and the presence of British and French forces in Syria and Lebanon, the Soviet Union found itself consistently in a minority position and used its "veto" to prevent decisions being taken which did not meet with its full approval. The frequent exercise of the "veto" by the Soviet Union was technically consistent with Charter provisions but was claimed by the West to be an "abuse" since, according to the Four-Power Statement at San Francisco,[3] it was not to be "assumed—that the permanent members, any more than the non-permanent members, would use their 'veto' power wilfully to obstruct the operation of the Council."[4] The acrimonious exchange

[2] *U.S. Congressional Record*, 80th Congress, 1st Session, 1947, Vol. 93, p. 1999 (Daily edition, March 12, 1947).

[3] See "Statement by the Delegations of the Four Sponsoring Governments on Voting Procedure in the Security Council" in Leland M. Goodrich and Edvard Hambro, *Charter of the United Nations: Commentary and Documents* (2nd ed.; Boston: World Peace Foundation, 1949), pp. 216–218.

[4] *Ibid.*, p. 218.

which developed over the frequent exercise of the "veto" by the Soviet Union was one aspect of the Cold War. While this use of the "veto" could with justification be regarded as a violation of the promise made by the Great Powers at San Francisco that the "veto" would be used sparingly, it could also be contended in support of the Soviet position that the principle of majority rule was accepted only with an important qualification, namely, that the permanent members must be in agreement and that, contrary to the original San Francisco understanding, formal voting and establishing a record of vetoes came to be emphasized at the expense of reaching agreement.

The confrontation of East and West in ideological and political conflict not only made it impossible for the Security Council to take decisions on many questions brought before it but also prevented the Council from equipping itself to exercise the full powers given it by the Charter. In February 1946 the Security Council directed the Military Staff Committee to examine the provisions of Article 43 from the military point of view. However, having decided that it should formulate basic principles to govern the organization of forces to be made available to the Council under this Article, the Committee was unable to agree on important questions such as the size and composition of forces and their location and employment.[5] As a consequence, no agreements under Article 43 have been concluded and most of Chapter VII has remained a dead letter.

Notwithstanding the Cold War and the consequent failure of the permanent members of the Security Council to agree on many questions, the Council has been able to discharge its responsibilities with considerable effectiveness in a number of matters. In the course of doing so, it developed and utilized techniques that were to prove of great value at a later time. In the Indonesian case, the Council by its resolution of August 1, 1947, requested the Dutch and the Indonesians to cease hostilities immediately and settle their differences by arbitration or other peaceful means. Subsequently, after the parties had issued cease-fire orders, the Council requested that consular officers of Members in Indonesia report on its observance, and it later established a Committee of Good Offices which assisted in the implementation of the cease-fire and the reaching of agreement on principles to provide the basis for a political settlement. Following the failure of political negotiations between the parties and the resumption of military action by the Dutch, the Council, through the United Nations Commission for Indonesia, played a more aggressive role in bringing the hostilities to an end and assisted in achieving the political settlement that resulted from The Hague Round Table Conference of 1949.[6] It is significant to note that there was sufficient agreement among

[5] For a summary of its report, see Leland M. Goodrich and Anne P. Simons, *The United Nations and the Maintenance of International Peace and Security* (Washington, D.C: Brookings Institution, 1955), pp. 398-405.

[6] For an excellent analysis of the UN role in Indonesia, see Alastair M. Taylor, *Indonesian Independence and the United Nations* (Ithaca, N.Y: Cornell University Press, 1960).

the permanent members to permit key decisions to be taken, though this was achieved as the result of treating abstentions as not negating the necessary concurrence. In this case there was sufficient common interest in the elimination of instability and possible threats to major-power interests by the termination of hostilities and the satisfaction of Indonesian demands for independence to make cooperation appear desirable in spite of differences of specific national interests and objectives.

Another example of Security Council effectiveness was the handling of the Palestine question. After having refused to accept the General Assembly's invitation to assist in the implementation of its recommendations of November 30, 1947, for the settlement of the Palestine question, the Security Council by a series of progressively insistent requests contributed to inducing Israel and the Arab states to accept a cease-fire and, with the assistance of a UN mediator, to conclude armistice agreements. By a decision of the Council the United Nations Truce Supervision Organization (UNTSO) was established with a corps of UN observers, thus providing a precedent and experienced personnel for the United Nations Emergency Force (UNEF) which was established in 1956. UNTSO, in close collaboration with the four Mixed Armistice Commissions established by agreement of the parties, has provided procedures for continuous observation and the orderly consideration of complaints of violation of the armistice terms, initially by the Commissions and then by the Security Council on appeal.[7] These initial arrangements, reinforced at a later time by UNEF, have succeeded well in keeping violence under control. Success in the early years especially was due largely to the common interest of the major powers in preventing the situation from getting out of hand if for no other reason than to avoid giving a rival power an excuse to intervene militarily in the area.

Success in controlling the use of violence in Palestine was not accompanied by a corresponding measure of success in achieving the settlement of basic issues in the conflict between Israel and the Arab states. At an early stage it was concluded that the work of the Acting Mediator in assisting the parties in the conclusion of armistice agreements was compromised by the exercise of mediatory functions in the political dispute. Consequently, the function of peaceful settlement was given to the UN Conciliation Commission for Palestine established by the General Assembly in December 1948. All efforts of the Commission to achieve agreed settlement of the issues separating the parties have been marked by failure.

The dispute between India and Pakistan over Jammu and Kashmir provided another example of United Nations success in controlling the use of force accompanied by failure to achieve peaceful settlement. In this instance

---

[7] See J. C. Hurewitz, "The Israeli-Syrian Crisis in the Light of the Arab-Israeli Armistice System," *International Organization*, August 1951 (Vol. 5, No. 3), pp. 459–479.

the Security Council, through the UN Commission on India and Pakistan (UNCIP), assisted in arranging a cease-fire and, by establishing a system of military observers, helped to obtain continuing respect for the cease-fire and the amicable adjustment of incidents.[8] However, all efforts to achieve a peaceful settlement through the Commission and through specially designated UN Representatives have failed. The dispute has been considerably narrowed in scope, but agreement has never been possible on the conditions for holding a plebiscite.

The successes of the Security Council have been in matters where the permanent members do not regard their more important interests as being directly involved and where they have a common interest in keeping violence under control. Where there has been a more direct conflict of vital interests, as, for example, in Central Europe, the Balkans, and the Far East, discussions have generally been kept outside the United Nations altogether or, as in the case of Greece and Korea, appeal has been made to the General Assembly. In fact, during the Organization's first five years, largely on the initiative of the United States, considerable use was made of the General Assembly as an instrument of United Nations action. By this means the possibility of the Soviet Union's using its veto to prevent a decision contrary to its interests was circumvented. To be sure, the General Assembly could only discuss and recommend. However, an Assembly resolution supported by a substantial majority of the total membership of the Organization had certain advantages for purposes of psychological warfare, political pressure, and legitimization.

The formal development of the Assembly's role reached its apex in the Uniting for Peace Resolution of November 3, 1950.[9] Though it had been possible to initiate collective measures in support of South Korea by Security Council resolution in June 1950 due to the absence of the Soviet representative, there was little likelihood that any permanent member would again allow this to happen.[10] The United States' initiative, leading to the adoption of the Uniting for Peace Resolution, was clearly prompted by a desire to be able to use the General Assembly, in the manner in which the Security Council had been used, as a means of initiating or bringing under UN sponsorship collective measures to contain Communist expansion. On the assumption that future aggression would likely be Communist or Communist inspired, the United States sought to get away from the original United Nations system for keeping the peace, dependent for its effectiveness on great-power agreement, and to introduce in its place something more closely resembling the League system with the General Assembly, the organ in which influence

---

[8] See Sylvain Lourié, "The United Nations Military Observer Group in India and Pakistan," *International Organization,* February 1955 (Vol. 9, No. 1), pp. 19–31.

[9] General Assembly Resolution 377 (V).

[10] On collective measures in Korea, see Goodrich and Simons, Chapters 17–18; and D. W. Bowett, *United Nations Forces: A Legal Study* (New York: Frederick A. Praeger, 1964), Chapter 3.

of the United States had up to then been generally decisive, acting as stimulator and coordinator.

From the Soviet point of view the provisions of the Uniting for Peace Resolution, which authorized the General Assembly to determine the existence of a threat to the peace, breach of the peace, or act of aggression and to recommend that collective measures be taken, and which invited Members to maintain trained and equipped military elements for service on recommendation of the Assembly, were completely contrary to Charter provisions giving the Security Council the primary responsibility for the maintenance of international peace and security and the power to make use of military forces for that purpose. It is interesting to note that, notwithstanding their approval by a large majority of the General Assembly, the provisions relating to the use of military forces for enforcement action have not in practice been implemented even by the states that gave them most enthusiastic support. The experience with the General Assembly's handling of Communist Chinese military intervention in Korea proved that the majority of Members, and not the "neutralist" states alone, have little stomach for measures against a major military power that may escalate into another world war.[11] Members for the most part showed great reluctance to make units of their armed forces available in advance for the kind of operations envisaged in the resolution. Furthermore, the recommendations of the Collective Measures Committee,[12] established under the terms of the resolution, have remained a dead letter, and the Peace Observation Commission established by the resolution has been used only once. Even the United States soon lost its ardor for using the General Assembly as a means of initiating and organizing collective measures against aggression.

New Trends in Peacekeeping

The decade of the 1950's saw a new trend in thought and practice regarding the role of the United Nations in keeping the peace. This change was due to many factors no one of which was by itself decisive. The total impact of the Korean experience and the ineffectual efforts to implement certain provisions of the Uniting for Peace Resolution were disillusioning. The balance of atomic terror came to be recognized as the effective deterrent of major power aggression while, with the death of Joseph Stalin, Nikita Khrushchev's emphasis on "peaceful coexistence" seemed to offer some reasonable prospect that the Soviet Union would find it in its interest to avoid war. The breaking of the membership deadlock in 1955, the consequent large increase in the total membership of the Organization, and, more particularly, the increase in the

---

[11] See Leland M. Goodrich, *Korea: A Study of U.S. Policy in the United Nations* (New York: Council on Foreign Relations, 1956).

[12] General Assembly *Official Records* (6th session), Supplement No. 13.

number of Asian and African states committed to "neutralism" in the Cold War struggle made it necessary to find a role for the United Nations which was consistent with the policies and aspirations of the new Members.[13] Finally, and this perhaps proved to be the most important factor, Dag Hammarskjöld's appointment as Secretary-General in 1953 brought to that office a person who soon demonstrated a capacity for performance that won for him the confidence of governments and led to their vesting unprecedented responsibilities in him.

The new approach to peacekeeping—new in the sense of contrast to the emphasis of the preceding decade, though embodying elements of earlier practice—can best be described in the words of Mr. Hammarskjöld. In a press conference on February 27, 1956, the Secretary-General was asked to tell what kind of "preventive action" the UN might be able to take in an area where war threatened or was "right on the verge of breaking out." After explaining his view in some detail in relation to the current situation along the Israeli-Arab border, he generalized as follows:

> In other words, the two lines of preventive action which I think are obviously indicated are, first, to stabilize the situation in the field on a day-to-day basis and to avoid the incidents which may lead to major friction, and, secondly, to be— you will excuse me for using the word—*quietly* helpful by being a third party with which the two conflicting parties can discuss matters and which may help them to bridge the gulf not by formal mediation but by working out a maximum of understanding which, I think, will increase as time goes on if the operation is wisely run.[14]

That these techniques were not new is obvious. In previous cases, the UN had sought to "stabilize the situation" by getting the parties in conflict to agree to a cease-fire, to withdraw forces from dispute areas, and to accept UN observation and report as a means of assuring respect for armistice or cease-fire agreements. Furthermore, the use of "quiet diplomacy" to achieve wider agreement had been practiced, though customarily through formal arrangements involving the appointment of a committee of good offices, a mediator, or a UN representative. The novelty of preventive diplomacy, as conceived and practiced by Dag Hammarskjöld, lay rather in the contrast to previous emphasis on methods of coercion and in the fact that he proposed to exercise or to accept personal responsibility as Secretary-General for initiating and for carrying out such preventive measures.

In the Middle East crisis of 1956, after Mr. Hammarskjöld's efforts to mediate the Suez and Israeli-Egyptian conflicts had been cut short by appeals to violence and after the Security Council had been prevented from taking deci-

[13] See John Karefa-Smart, "Africa and the United Nations," later in this volume; and Laurence W. Martin (ed.), *Neutralism and Nonalignment: The New States in World Affairs* (New York: Frederick A. Praeger, 1962).
[14] Wilder Foote (ed.), *Dag Hammarskjöld: Servant of Peace* (New York: Harper & Row, 1963).

sions by the British and French vetoes, the General Assembly authorized the Secretary-General to organize a UN force "to secure and supervise the cessation of hostilities." The UN Emergency Force, in accordance with the Secretary-General's proposals, approved by the Assembly, was to be composed of contingents voluntarily contributed by Members, was to enter Egyptian territory only with the consent of the host state, was not to use force except in self-defense, and was to be under the executive direction of the Secretary-General. Furthermore, the permanent members of the Security Council were not asked to contribute military contingents. It was made clear by the Secretary-General that the Force was not to be used in any way to influence the political settlement which was to be the responsibility of the parties with such assistance as they might accept from the UN.[15]

Two years later, when the government of Lebanon complained of intervention in its political affairs by the United Arab Republic, the Secretary-General was authorized to dispatch an "observation group" to insure that there was no "illegal infiltration" of personnel or supplies of arms across the Lebanese frontier. While the UN Observation Group in Lebanon (UNOGIL) was not able to satisfy the United States in regard to the extent of infiltration and thus to forestall United States military intervention at the request of President Camille Chamoun, it did contribute to the eventual stabilization of political power in Lebanon. Furthermore, in this instance the Secretary-General established the important precedent that such a UN group should not interfere in the domestic politics of the host state.[16]

This technique of introducing the UN presence and seeking through it to stabilize the situation and assist the parties in reaching wider agreement received its most vigorous test in the Congo (Leopoldville). In this instance the Secretary-General used his powers under Article 99 of the Charter to bring the situation resulting from the collapse of law and order and the Belgian military intervention to the attention of the Security Council. His motive in part was, by interjecting the UN into the situation, to prevent what might be regarded as a power vacuum from being filled by the major contestants in the Cold War. By its resolution of July 14, 1960, the Security Council authorized the Secretary-General to provide the Congolese government with military assistance necessary to enable the national security forces to perform their tasks. The Secretary-General made it clear that he intended to follow the UNEF guidelines in the organization and conduct of the force. The Congo situation turned out, however, to be much more difficult to handle by techniques of preventive diplomacy than the Middle East or Lebanese situations since the UN Operation in the Congo (ONUC) had to contend not

[15] See Gabriella Rosner, *The United Nations Emergency Force* (New York: Columbia University Press, 1963); and Bowett, *United Nations Forces.*

[16] See Gerald L. Curtis, "The United Nations Observation Group in Lebanon," *International Organization,* Autumn 1964 (Vol. 18, No. 4), pp. 738–765.

only with the unwanted Belgian and foreign presences but also with the disintegration of the recognized government and the attempted Katangese secession, aided and abetted by foreign influences. In the course of discharging his responsibilities under Security Council and General Assembly resolutions and the Charter of the UN, Mr. Hammarskjöld came under criticism from Congolese authorities for failure to give sufficient support to their political objectives, from the Soviet Union for failure to act with sufficient force to expel the Belgians and other foreigners, and from certain Western powers for excessive interference in the internal affairs of the Congo. Though Mr. Hammarskjöld's successor, U Thant, equipped with more adequate authority to use force, was able to bring the Katanga secessionist movement to an end, the financial crisis caused by the refusal of certain Members, especially the Soviet Union and France, to contribute to the expenses of the military operation made necessary its premature ending with the initial mission of the force still unfinished.[17]

Other peacekeeping operations since 1960 have been undertaken and arranged under the shadow of the financial crisis that the Congo engendered, with the Secretary-General adopting a more cautious attitude regarding the assumption of responsibilities, more particularly insisting that there be reasonable assurance in advance that funds will be forthcoming to cover the costs. In West Irian in 1962, through the United Nations Temporary Executive Authority (UNTEA), the United Nations provided a face-saving device under which the control of the disputed territory could be transferred from the Netherlands to Indonesia.[18] The mission of the UN Authority was determined by agreement of the parties, subsequently approved by the General Assembly. The Authority was supported by a military contingent of 1,500 men provided by the government of Pakistan, and costs were shared equally by Indonesia and the Netherlands. In 1963 the United Nations Yemen Observation Mission (UNYOM) was established by agreement of the United Arab Republic and Saudi Arabia to observe compliance with a disengagement agreement these two countries had entered into with respect to their military interventions in Yemen. The Mission was handicapped from the beginning by failure to get the full cooperation of the parties and the difficult physical conditions of its work. In this instance also, the parties directly concerned agreed to pay the costs.[19]

The most recent United Nations peacekeeping operation has been the UN Peacekeeping Force in Cyprus (UNFICYP) which is still in process. By

---

[17] For good discussions of the Congo military operation, see Arthur Lee Burns and Nina Heathcote, *Peace-Keeping by U.N. Forces: From Suez to the Congo* (New York: Frederick A. Praeger [for the Center of International Studies, Princeton University], 1963); and Bowett, Chapter 6.

[18] For a critical account see Paul W. van der Veur, "The United Nations in West Irian: A Critique," *International Organization,* Winter 1964 (Vol. 18, No. 1), pp. 53-73.

[19] See *Annual Report of the Secretary-General on the Work of the Organization, 16 June 1962-15 June 1963* (General Assembly *Official Records* [18th session], Supplement No. 1).

its resolution of March 4, 1964, the Security Council called upon Member States to refrain from action that would "worsen the situation" in Cyprus and recommended the creation of a peacekeeping force

> to use its best efforts to prevent a recurrence of fighting and, as necessary, to contribute to the maintenance and restoration of law and order and a return to normal conditions.

It also recommended that the Secretary-General designate a mediator to promote "a peaceful solution and an agreed settlement" of the Cyprus problem. Certain features of the Cyprus operation differentiate it from the UNEF and ONUC operations. A permanent member of the Security Council is a major contributor to the Force, the mandate runs for limited periods of time (three months), extension requires explicit action by the Security Council, and costs have been covered by voluntary pledges. It is too early to say what the success of the Cyprus operation will be; thus far it has succeeded in maintaining an uneasy peace with some difficulty.[20]

LESSONS FOR THE FUTURE

UN experience with peacekeeping to date suggests that the detailed prescriptions of the Charter have in many respects proved to be completely unsuited to postwar conditions, that adaptations that have been developed by Member governments and the Organization in dealing with postwar situations have had some success but have encountered serious difficulties, and that the future is uncertain with various possibilities of future development now open.

Experience on the whole has shown that the emphasis of the Charter on peace enforcement was unrealistic; at least in the conditions that have prevailed since 1945, peace enforcement of the kind that was thought to give "teeth" to the Organization has only been possible, and then in highly modified form, in one case—Korea—and there with only limited success. But while peace enforcement has not been practiced, there has been ample demonstration that the assumption of the Charter-makers that peace enforcement requires concurrence of the Council's permanent members, especially the United States and the Soviet Union, and that such measures are not likely to be effective against a major military power is sound.

It has been possible, however, for the United Nations to play a somewhat more restricted role with considerable success. In a number of instances, with the agreement of the permanent members of the Security Council, or at least in the absence of positive disagreement, the United Nations has been able to achieve agreement of the parties in conflict to the cessation of hostilities, either

---

[20] For the text of the resolution establishing UNFICYP, see UN Document S/5575. See also the periodic reports by the Secretary-General on the United Nations operation in Cyprus.

through a cease-fire or a formal armistice agreement. Furthermore, the UN has assisted in securing the observance of such arrangements through various forms of UN presence, thus providing opportunities for observing, reporting, mediating, and exercising a restraining influence. The possibility of the Organization's playing a limited role of this nature was anticipated in Article 40 of the Charter but has been developed beyond the limits of purely provisional measures. It is important to note that many of the basic techniques that have been utilized in recent peacekeeping operations were developed and utilized early in the Organization's life, for example, in Indonesia and Palestine. Furthermore, Trygve Lie's proposal, which was not accepted, of a United Nations Guard envisaged the establishment of a UN military body with limited police functions.[21]

Limiting the role of the UN in the control of violence to the arrangement and supervision of cease-fires and armistices and to the performance of mediatory functions does not of course eliminate the possibility of UN activities having important political implications and effects. Sponsoring a cease-fire or being willing to assist in implementing one and assuming responsibility for the establishment of internal order and stability, as in the Congo, involve taking decisions that are bound to affect the development of situations in which many states, including Great Powers, have serious interests. The discharge of such responsibilities must consequently be based on an adequate consensus of Members. The need of such consensus cannot be avoided by delegating authority to an international official pledged to impartialty and to placing the purposes and principles of the Organization ahead of national interest. To be more specific, the conclusion can fairly be drawn, from the Congo experience in particular, that vesting discretionary power in a Secretary-General who has demonstrated outstanding qualities as a public servant is not an adequate substitute for agreement of the major powers on critical issues.

In the light of experience, many questions arise with regard to the organization and direction of peacekeeping operations. We have had instances of such operations being initiated by decision of the Security Council, on the recommendation of the General Assembly, with the parties themselves sometimes making the initial request, and with the Secretary-General in some cases taking important initiatives. If the consensus of the major powers is considered important to the success of the operation, obviously the Security Council is in the best position to assure this agreement. Up to the present, there has been no permanent international force available for peacekeeping operations and there is little likelihood that such an international force will be established in the near future. Dag Hammarskjöld was of the opinion in 1958 that peacekeeping forces should be organized on an *ad hoc* basis because

---

21 UN Document A/656, September 28, 1948.

of the uniqueness of each situation.[22] Other studies that have been undertaken suggest that the establishment of an international police force with enforcement powers, such as has been envisaged in plans for a disarmed world, are far in the future.[23] In an address at Harvard University on June 13, 1963, Secretary-General U Thant gave a number of reasons why it seemed to him that "a permanent United Nations force would be premature at the present time."[24] These judgments appear sound. Nevertheless, there are obvious possibilities of advanced planning that would assure smoother and more efficient operations once the need for peacekeeping arises. These include the establishment of a planning staff and the assumption of advanced commitments to make properly trained and equipped units available when needed.[25] It should not be assumed on the basis of limited experience to date that the major military powers should necessarily be excluded from contributing military contingents to peacekeeping forces. The special considerations that dictated exclusion of major power contingents in the Middle East and the Congo will not necessarily be decisive in other situations where the UN is called upon to perform a "peacekeeping" function as Cyprus has already demonstrated. However, since the essence of the UN's task is likely to be that of persuading the major powers to stand aside rather than become more involved in a given situation, it can reasonably be anticipated that the practical requirements of preventive diplomacy in the future will be more commonly met by excluding the military contingents of major powers and using the forces of relatively uncommitted states to represent and implement the general interest in stabilizing many situations.

The measure of success that the UN has achieved to date in discouraging and controlling the use of armed force has not been accompanied by equal success in bringing about accommodation of the conflicting interests and demands that are the source of tension. Since the war we have had a progressive accumulation of situations in which serious tension and the danger of open violence continue to exist after initial outbreaks of violence have been brought under control. What is particularly significant is that old areas of tension tend to remain as new ones are created. The failure of the UN in its efforts to promote settlement or adjustment is in all likelihood due to a number of considerations. The major cause may well be the failure thus far to

[22] See *United Nations Emergency Force. Summary Study of the Experience Derived from the Establishment and Operation of the Force* (UN Document A/3943, October 9, 1958).

[23] See William R. Frye, *A United Nations Peace Force* (Dobbs Ferry, N.Y: Oceana Publications, 1957); Lincoln P. Bloomfield and others, *International Military Forces: The Question of Peacekeeping in an Armed and Disarming World* (Boston: Little, Brown and Company, 1964); and Bowett, *United Nations Forces.*

[24] *United Nations Review,* July 1963 (Vol. 10, No. 7), p. 56.

[25] Canada and the Scandinavian countries have shown interest in these possibilities and the readiness to act. See Per Frydenberg, *Peace-Keeping: Experience and Evaluation* (Oslo: Norwegian Institute of International Affairs, 1965); and Lester B. Pearson, "Keeping the Peace," in Andrew W. Cordier and Wilder Foote (ed.), *The Quest for Peace: The Dag Hammarskjöld Memorial Lectures* (New York: Columbia University Press, 1965), pp. 99–118.

harness the influence and authority of the major powers in support of reasonable accommodations of conflicting interests. Efforts to achieve equitable settlements through the organs and procedures of the UN have thus far had limited success because the proposals of UN organs for peaceful settlement and accommodation have not as a rule been supported by necessary agreement among the Great Powers. Too often these powers have seen it to their advantage to give encouragement to one side or the other as a means of gaining advantages in their own power struggles or at least have so distrusted each other's motives as to be unwilling to join in promoting a result which each might otherwise consider desirable. Thus, in 1948, while both the United States and the Soviet Union supported the General Assembly's recommendation for the settlement of the Palestine question, they could not agree on using the Security Council as an instrument to implement that recommendation. Furthermore, the Cold War confrontation has permitted the parties in conflict to exploit the situation by playing one side against the other.

It is often maintained that the agreement of the permanent members of the Security Council is not as important to the exercise of its mediatory and conciliatory functions as to the discharge of its responsibilities under Chapter VII. The General Assembly has in fact recommended that permanent members refrain from claiming the right of veto in such cases. While there is much to be said for this point of view, it must be recognized that any UN recommendation that has the support of all the major powers is more likely to be accepted than one that might have the support of only a majority of them. Furthermore, it is clear that if the permanent members use disputes or situations before the UN for airing their own propaganda claims and introducing a major-power confrontation, the result cannot fail to be negative so far as the promotion of settlement is concerned.

The experience of the UN during the past twenty years suggests that those who wrote the Charter were not too far off the mark when they emphasized the need of agreement among the major powers if the Organization was to succeed in performing its peacekeeping function. New techniques have been developed, but these too depend for their effectiveness, as the current financial crisis demonstrates, on agreement among the Great Powers. The authors of the Charter recognized that in an international organization of sovereign states for keeping the peace, while there must be recognition of the interests and possible contribution of each Member, large or small, there must also be recognition of the special position that the major powers must occupy in any system based upon voluntary cooperation. Recognition of this truth may result in limiting the activities of the United Nations in the maintenance of peace but it will assure a more substantial success in what it undertakes.

Financing Peacekeeping: Politics and Crisis

NORMAN J. PADELFORD

THE differences which have been building up within the United Nations in recent years over the financing of peacekeeping have reached a point where strenuous measures are needed to rescue the Organization from its divisions and paralysis.

The roots of this crisis lie in the disagreements between the powers over the right of the General Assembly to call for international forces and to apportion the expenses of peacekeeping activities, and the obligations of states to pay the apportionments. The crisis is in part financial. But surrounding this is a more serious political and constitutional dispute over powers and responsibilities under the Charter.

THE FINANCIAL SITUATION

The financial difficulty can be summed up in the fact that the Organization had unpaid commitments amounting to $129.7 million at the end of 1964 and was short $145.3 million in unpaid assessments. These amounts were chiefly related to the peacekeeping operations undertaken in the Near East and in the Congo (Leopoldville).

Maintaining the UN Emergency Force (UNEF) of 5,000 men in the Gaza Strip and Sinai Peninsula cost the United Nations on the average $20 million a year from 1957 to 1963. In 1964 the cost was cut to $17,750,000 and is being held at that in 1965.

At the height of the Congo military operation, when the force there was at a level of 20,000 men, the expenses for this undertaking ran as high as $114 million. For the 1960–1963 period they averaged $100 million a year. In the final six months before the force was withdrawn, the costs amounted to $19 million.

NORMAN J. PADELFORD, Professor of Political Science, Massachusetts Institute of Technology, is Chairman of the Board of Editors of *International Organization*.

80

It is these activities and the assessments voted to cover them and the refusal of some states to pay their assessments that have led to the main difficulties. The normal running expenses covered by the regular budget have for the most part produced few problems. Payments on these have normally worked out at about 98 percent of the amounts assessed.[1] But at the time of the nineteenth session of the General Assembly no less than 62 Member States were in arrears on one or both of the special peacekeeping accounts.[2] This tide of arrearages reflected a good deal of feeling in the low-income countries that these expenses had been imposing heavy and unjust burdens upon them. Although extensive concessions were made to these states in the form of rebates, voluntary contributions by the more advanced countries, and the UN bond issue in lieu of assessments,[3] they did not alleviate the complaints or stay the tide of arrears. Numbers of these states have paid enough from time to time to keep themselves within the two-year arrearage line. And not a few would undoubtedly pay up if the dispute between the larger powers were resolved.

The crux of the financial dispute was reached when the Secretary-General reported in early 1965 that sixteen countries including France and the Soviet Union were in arrears "in excess of the amounts of their assessed contributions for the preceding two full years."[4] This raised the question of their right to vote in the General Assembly under Article 19. Thus, joined to the financial problem was the political and constitutional question of whether Article 19 is applicable to arrears on peacekeeping assessments or only to those on the regular budget.

Although some difficulties have arisen in connection with the financing of other peacekeeping forces, particularly the UN Peacekeeping Force in Cyprus (UNFICYP), these have been essentially of a financial rather than a political nature and relate to shortages of voluntary contributions instead of failures to pay assessments. Furthermore, these have not produced cleavages comparable to those arising out of the UNEF and Congo operations.

[1] On the financial problem of the UN generally, see John G. Stoessinger and others, *Financing the United Nations System* (Washington, D.C: Brookings Institution, 1964); and Norman J. Padelford, "Financial Crisis and the Future of the United Nations," *World Politics,* July 1963 (Vol. 15, No. 4), pp. 531–568. Data on the financial situation at the end of 1964 was taken from a personal letter of the Deputy Controller of the UN to the author.

[2] See *Collection of Contributions as at 30 November 1964: Report of the Secretary-General* (UN Document A/5822), Table II.

[3] The rebate arrangements will be found in General Assembly Resolutions 1732 (XVI) and 1733 (XVI), December 20, 1961; and Resolutions 1835 (XVIII), October 18, 1963, and 1983 (XVIII), December 17, 1963. The resolution authorizing the bonds is General Assembly Resolution 1739 (XVI), December 20, 1961; bonds amounting to $168.7 million of the $200 million authorized were sold. Payments on the interest and principal were made charges on the regular budget. The Soviet Union and France have refused to pay their apportionments for these.

[4] *Collection of Contributions as at 17 January 1965: Report of the Secretary-General* (UN Document A/5847).

Two Concepts of the Charter

The fundamental disagreement within the United Nations relates to the interpretation of the Charter.

There are, on the one hand, those who believe the Charter must be construed strictly. The advocates of this view believe that the Charter, being a treaty between sovereign states, should be read as conferring only those powers upon UN organs which are explicitly stated. Moves which appear designed to extend the powers of organs beyond those explicitly given to them by the Charter are resisted as being illegal as long as they are not formally approved by all parties. The United Nations is deemed to have only those powers which are expressly granted to it by the contracting parties. Its organs must remain strictly within the bounds imposed by the written agreement. Powers beyond those expressly granted are reserved to the Member States and can be exercised by the UN only with their express consent.[5]

The strict constructionists, which number the Soviet Union and France among their leaders on the present issue, are likewise opposed to allowing the Secretary-General to move beyond the bounds drawn for him by the Charter. These countries viewed the actions of Dag Hammarskjöld in directing the UN Operation in the Congo (ONUC) as not only running counter to their interests but also as taking liberties with the office. They saw in his choices of manpower and in the ways in which the force was used a calculated effort to transform the office of the Secretary-General from that of an administrative officer carrying out the policies of the other major organs to a chief executive with powers of leadership and initiative of his own.[6]

Those who take these positions deny that the General Assembly has authority to apportion peacekeeping costs as binding assessments without a decision of the Security Council on which, of course, the Great Powers can exercise the veto. This organ, they contend, has not only "primary responsibility" for all matters relating to the use of armed forces but also, by inference, the power to decide how the use of such forces should be financed. Thus, the Soviets argue that Assembly actions "usurp" the powers of the Security Council, are "attempts to circumvent" the Council, and are an "inadmissible violation" of the Charter. Consequently, they argue that they have no obligation to pay and

---

[5] The positions of the various parties on the main issues are conveniently summarized in *Financing of United Nations Peace-Keeping Operations: Report of the Working Group on the Examination of the Administrative and Budgetary Procedures of the United Nations* (UN Document A/5407, March 29, 1963).

[6] The *Introduction to the Annual Report of the Secretary-General on the Work of the Organization, 16 June 1960–15 June 1961* in which Mr. Hammarskjöld set out two differing views of the United Nations added fuel to these apprehensions. For the text of the *Introduction*, see General Assembly *Official Records* (16th session), Supplement No. 1A; or *United Nations Review*, September 1961 (Vol. 8, No. 9), pp. 12–17, 34–35.

that it is "impossible to speak of arrears" which Members must reimburse.[7]

Politically speaking, the Soviet position is directed toward an undercutting of the Uniting for Peace Resolution of 1950 which they would like to see nullified, thereby reducing the Assembly to a debating forum. They are uncomfortable in an organ whose voting majorities include many new, inexperienced, small states whose stands cannot be controlled and whose activities in the world forum they fear.

At the other end of the spectrum are the United States and those who have joined in defending the right of the General Assembly to call for forces in an emergency, particularly if the Security Council has been prevented from doing so by the use of the veto, and to apportion expenses of all peacekeeping operations whether established by the General Assembly or Security Council and who have asserted the collective responsibility of Members to pay for these apportionments.

Those who have made common cause on this front do not deny the right of the Security Council to initiate peacekeeping operations or to make recommendations on financing them if it so desires. Indeed, they recognize the "primary responsibility" of this organ and have supported the Council in calling for international forces whenever it has been asked to do so and its members have been able to agree—as in the Congo, West Irian, Yemen, and Cyprus cases. They have turned to the Assembly only when in grave circumstances it has been found impossible to get a decision from the Security Council on a peacekeeping force.

On the other hand, these states do support the right of the General Assembly to apportion peacekeeping expenses with or without a Security Council recommendation, on the ground that the Charter itself gives the Assembly the explicit power to apportion the expenses of the United Nations. They also believe that Article 17, paragraph 2, calls for collective responsibility in paying apportionments once they are voted.[8]

In turning to the General Assembly for initiating peacekeeping operations in an emergency under the Uniting for Peace formula when the Security Council has become blocked by the veto, these powers have in a sense adopted something like a common law approach to constitutional law, namely, that the original Charter commitments can be developed through practice, the passage of declarations and resolutions, as well as by formal amendment of the document itself.

[7] The statement of Nikolai Fedorenko at the final meeting of the Assembly's fourth special session (General Assembly *Official Records* [4th special session], pp. 19–21) contains a strong assertion of the Soviet case. A later affirmation of the Soviet position will be found in the statement of Soviet delegate Victor Ulanchev in September 1964 before the Working Group on the Examination of the Administrative and Budgetary Procedures of the UN (Working Group of Twenty-One) as reported in *UN Monthly Chronicle*, October 1964 (Vol. 1, No. 5), pp. 48–50, together with the United States reply.

[8] See the statements of the Australian, Brazilian, Italian, Japanese, Mexican, and Netherlands representatives before the Working Group of Twenty-One (*ibid.*, pp. 50–56).

DISPUTE OVER FISCAL POWERS OF ASSEMBLY AND SECURITY COUNCIL

The issue which has threatened to tear the Organization apart has been the refusal of the Soviet Union to budge from its stand on the right of the Assembly to apportion certain expenses and its own obligation to pay peace-keeping assessments.

In denying the Assembly the right to call for forces in the absence of a recommendation from the Security Council, Moscow is not only seeking to wipe out the Uniting for Peace Resolution but more fundamentally is bringing into question the language accepted at San Francisco giving the General Assembly the right to consider, discuss, and make recommendations upon

> any questions or any matters within the scope of the present Charter or relating to the powers and functions of any organs provided for in the present Charter . . .

as stated in Articles 10–14. What the Soviet Union would in effect like to do would be to return to the Dumbarton Oaks design where the Great Powers acting through the Security Council were accorded an undivided measure of authority.

In arguing for a limitation in the rights and powers of the Assembly, the Soviet Union overlooks the Dumbarton Oaks Proposals which gave the Assembly the power to apportion the expenses of the Organization.[9] These were not touched in this respect by the San Francisco conferees.

Notwithstanding the advisory opinion of the International Court of Justice supported by the majority of the judges,[10] the acceptance of this by the General Assembly,[11] and the resolution entitled "General Principles to serve as guidelines for the sharing of the costs of future peace-keeping operations involving heavy expenditures" which was adopted by an overwhelming majority of the General Assembly,[12] the Soviet Union has continued to insist that these interpretations are "incorrect and incompatible with the Charter" and create no "obligations of any kind for states."

It must be acknowledged that there is nothing in the Charter which gives the General Assembly the authority by a majority vote to make a conclusive interpretation of the Charter as far as individual Member States are concerned. The report of Committee IV/2 (Judicial Organization, Legal Problems) at San Francisco, approved by the Conference, contains the essence of the prin-

[9] Chapter V, Section B (5). The United Nations Conference on International Organization at San Francisco did amend the Proposals to add what ultimately became Article 19 of the Charter.

[10] *Certain Expenses of the United Nations (Article 17, paragraph 2, of the Charter), Advisory Opinion of 20 July 1962: I.C.J. Reports 1962,* pp. 151–308. For a discussion of the opinion, see Leo Gross, "Expenses of the United Nations for Peace-Keeping Operations: The Advisory Opinion of the International Court of Justice," *International Organization,* Winter 1963 (Vol. 17, No. 1), pp. 1–35.

[11] General Assembly Resolution 1854 (XVII), December 19, 1962, which was approved by a vote of 76 in favor, 17 opposed, with 8 abstentions.

[12] General Assembly Resolution 1874 (S-IV), June 27, 1963, which was adopted by a vote of 92 in favor, 11 opposed, with 3 abstentions.

ciple applicable here. "It is to be understood," the report said, "that if an interpretation made by any organ of the Organization or by a committee of justices is not generally acceptable, it will be without binding force."[13]

The government of France, while agreeing to the establishment of UNEF and paying its assessments for this, abstained when the Security Council voted to send UN forces into the Congo (Leopoldville), subsequently opposed apportionment of the costs by the General Assembly, and has refused to pay the assessments.[14] Ambassador Roger Seydoux has repeatedly stressed that the General Assembly can only make "recommendations" which become binding "only on the responsibility of the states that would have accepted them."[15]

States may be penalized for refusing to pay assessments. But there is no way by which they can be compelled to pay against their will unless the Organization is to become a superpower. In this sense the language of Article 17 is more vocative than imperative. The institution must have funds in order to fulfill its assigned tasks. These can be supplied only by the Member States. It was quite natural that the function of apportionment should be given to the organ representing the entire membership. It does not give the Organization the attributes of a world government to compel states to pay if they do not see fit to do so.

THE APPLICABILITY OF ARTICLE 19

The focal point of attention at the nineteenth session of the General Assembly was the question of whether Article 19 would be invoked against the Soviet Union, France, and other states that had become more than two years in arrears in the payment of peacekeeping assessments for UNEF and ONUC. Notwithstanding repeated warnings by the United States that the penalty article must be applied before the Assembly could be allowed to proceed to any formal transaction of business, and Soviet counterwarnings that it would walk out if its vote was denied, many Member States clearly wished to avoid a showdown fight ending in a vote upon this question. Even the United States indicated its reluctance to have matters reach this point but professed to see no alternative but to press for the fulfillment of the Charter stipulation. Accordingly, much of the maneuvering at this session was directed first toward trying to extract some payment from the members of the Soviet bloc and France, then at trying to impress upon the smaller powers the need to put pressure upon these states if they wished to avoid the showdown vote, and finally toward finding a pathway of retreat that would preserve some semblance of face and still allow the parties to continue to negotiate.

[13] *Documents of the United Nations Conference on International Organization, San Francisco, 1945* (New York: United Nations Information Organization, 1945), Vol. 13, pp. 709–710.

[14] It may be noted that the Soviet Union voted in the General Assembly in 1956 in favor of establishing UNEF but has refused to pay any assessments for this.

[15] General Assembly *Official Records . . . Fifth Committee* (4th special session), pp. 79–81.

Article 19 was inserted in the Charter in the light of the troubles that the League of Nations had had with states failing to pay their dues in the 1930's. The object of the provision, which was added at San Francisco, was to give the United Nations a means of prodding those who might fail to keep up their payments to the new Organization.

Denial of the right to vote in the General Assembly was thought to be the minimal penalty that could be applied in such a circumstance although a state threatened with the loss of its vote might view the matter quite differently, as the Soviets professed to do. No provision was made for graduated increases in the severity of the penalty if the arrearages continued. And no restriction was placed upon the right of a state to maintain either its seat or its voting rights in other organs.

In drafting Article 19, the San Francisco conferees omitted to say how it should be brought into force. And they did not indicate whether it is applicable to anything more than arrearages on assessments for the routine running expenses of the Organization. The interpretation of the simple language was left entirely in the hands of the General Assembly to work out in practice.

It has been argued that application of Article 19 is mandatory and automatic once the President of the Assembly has been informed that a state has passed the two-year grace period.[16] This is approximately the way in which it was handled in 1963 by President Sir Muhammad Zafrullah Khan (Pakistan) when Haiti had fallen more than two full years behind in its payments, except that in this instance the President withheld any announcement until after Haiti had paid enough to bring it out of danger inasmuch as no vote was taken in the interim.[17]

Others have argued that the Assembly must first determine that a state is in fact more than two full years in arrears and then vote formally to apply the Article. Those who take this point of view believe this is too important a matter to leave to administrative procedures. Under this interpretation a two-thirds vote of those present and voting would be needed to apply the penalty. On the larger question it has been argued by the Soviet Union that since the Assembly cannot make apportionments for peacekeeping expenses binding upon states, Article 19 does not apply to those who refuse to pay such apportionments.

Some of the smaller states caught in the middle have contended that since the Assembly has recognized that the UNEF and ONUC expenses were "extraordinary expenses" which were "essentially different in nature" from others, there is no "basis for grouping together unpaid contributions to the regular

---

[16] See *Article 19 of the Charter of the United Nations: A Memorandum of Law* (prepared by the Office of the Legal Adviser) (Washington, D.C: United States Department of State, 1964).

[17] *The New York Times,* May 22, 1963.

budgets and payments due for such emergency operations." Accordingly, they too have argued that Article 19 is not applicable.[18] The Charter, however, makes no such distinction. Nor does the record of the San Francisco debates sustain it. It is left to the Assembly to work out whatever interpretations and limits it will.

The failure of the nineteenth session of the Assembly to take action on this issue when the votes seemingly were available at the outset may have been a lamentable act of retreat.[19] Unquestionably there were many who wished to avoid a major blowup and not a few who feared that this could lead to a Soviet walkout, to an even deeper, sharper cleavage between the nations, and possibly to the downfall of the United Nations itself.

The test having been skirted, there is no way of telling whether the Soviet Union and others would have paid on their arrearages had a roll-call vote been called on the main question. Despite frontal appearances of firmness, a turnaround could have occurred. This would not have been the first time in United Nations history. As it was, the retreat was made instead by the United States when on the next to the last day the Albanian delegate moved that the Assembly return to its normal voting procedure in place of the no-voting consensus technique devised by Secretary-General U Thant and President Alex Quaison-Sackey (Ghana).[20] In asking the Assembly to treat the action required on this as a "procedural vote," Ambassador Adlai E. Stevenson announced that the United States would not demand that any Member be denied its right to vote on that question.[21] Thereupon, the Assembly witnessed the spectacle of the United States and the Soviet Union voting together to defeat the Albanian motion.[22] Seldom has a more surprising outcome been witnessed at the United Nations.

Reflection on the United States refusal to allow itself or the Assembly to be pushed by Albania into invoking Article 19 against the Soviet Union suggests that this was a calculated political act, not merely a tactical maneuver. The United States could hardly wish to see itself or the Assembly forced into a major clash with the Soviet Union by Albania, whether acting alone or at Communist China's urging. A recriminatory confrontation at this point could have cut off whatever possibility of accommodation there may be between Moscow and Washington for a long time to come. It could perhaps have ended by driving Moscow into Communist China's arms in a new conflict with the West.

But the other side of the picture cannot be ignored either as far as the fu-

---

[18] Positions summarized in the *Annual Report of the Secretary-General on the Work of the Organization, 16 June 1962–15 June 1963* (General Assembly *Official Records* [Supplement No. 1]), p. 141.

[19] See Arthur Krock in *The New York Times*, February 21, 1965.

[20] UN Document A/PV.1329, February 16, 1965.

[21] UN Document A/PV.1330, February 18, 1965, pp. 28–33.

[22] *Ibid.*, pp. 33–34. The vote was 97 in favor, 2 opposed, with 13 abstentions, including France.

ture of the United Nations is concerned, for the net effect of the failure to test the applicability of Article 19 to states two years in arrears on the peacekeeping assessments when these became due may be to give a negative interpretation to its applicability. It will be difficult to apply the penalty henceforth when it has been withheld from so many states at this time.

The UN must now look to other ways of replenishing its treasury and to relying more upon voluntary cooperation among its Members. The hope, of course, is that the atmosphere may have been cleared enough by keeping silent on Article 19 so that some motion can be gotten into talks between the powers on the issues that have been dividing them. But it cannot be overlooked that the Organization may have merely piled up more trouble for itself in the future by evasion.

In authorizing President Quaison-Sackey to appoint a new committee to undertake a comprehensive review of the whole question of peacekeeping operations in all of their aspects, including financing, the Assembly Members testified to their desire to make a fresh start on these questions.[23] Furthermore, in agreeing to the Secretary-General's plea to continue expenditures at the 1964 rate and the appeal to Members to contribute at least up to 80 percent of the previous apportionments,[24] the membership signaled its desire to keep the Organization going and its recognition that some states object to paying for UNEF, the servicing of the UN bonds, and some other items and that they will not be held responsible for them. These added concessions may be helpful in further lowering the tension levels. But they do leave serious questions about the future of the Organization.

If no agreement is reached and no payments are forthcoming, a move can still be made to invoke Article 19. But it is by no means certain that a majority can be found to apply it. If delegates continue to avoid the issue, there may be no alternative to admitting that in fact the Charter has been undermined by its very supporters as well as by those who have been opposed to the peacekeeping activities. Formulas might then preserve the conference aspects of the institution's functioning. But it could hardly be expected that the Charter would command the same respect which it has had in the past.

The reluctance of the United States and the nonaligned countries to press for a showdown on the question of arrearages suggests that these states are desirous of finding compromise on the problem. The proposals introduced by Francis T. P. Plimpton in September 1964 suggest that the United States is prepared to make another try to have the Security Council function, provided the door can be kept ajar to return to the Assembly if the Council becomes completely blocked again by the use of the veto.[25] The sharp criticism

---

[23] General Assembly Resolution 2006 (XIX), February 18, 1965.

[24] General Assembly Resolution 2004 (XIX), February 18, 1965.

[25] A digest of these proposals appears in *UN Monthly Chronicle*, Vol. 1, No. 5, pp. 47–48. A report on an earlier United States–United Kingdom compromise proposal is given in a dispatch of Thomas J. Hamilton, "U.N.'s Fiscal Plight," *The New York Times*, March 22, 1964.

of the United States rescue operation in the Congo (Leopoldville) as well as the rising crescendo of voices pressing for the admission of Communist China with all of the complications which this would bring in its train have no doubt contributed to the reappraisal of the relative advantages and disadvantages of the Assembly and Security Council as well as the desire to keep an open line to both Paris and Moscow.

Writing in *The New York Times* shortly after the close of the Assembly, Thomas J. Hamilton remarked that

> having steered away from the Scylla of an Assembly dominated by the African-Asian members, the United States is still threatened with the Charybdis of a Security Council that can be paralysed at any time by a Soviet veto.

But, he noted, "at the worst, the United States will at least be able to use the veto to prevent actions in the Council that it considers unacceptable."[26] Whether this may be an advantage or merely a return to the days of stalemate can only be determined in the fullness of time.

Meantime, there is a substantial group of smaller powers standing midway between the Great Powers that are eager to keep the Assembly an effective instrumentality. Their influence will unquestionably be cast in the direction of retrieving whatever can be salvaged from the failure to take action on Article 19 and the inclination of the larger powers to turn toward the Security Council.[27]

ALTERNATIVES FOR THE FUTURE

There is no simple solution to the bundle of questions wrapped up in the UN's financial-political problem. Important elements are not prepared to accept majority rule where this touches vital interests. Decisions cannot be imposed upon these states against their will. The registering of world opinion may serve useful purposes at certain points. But on vital matters attempts to override opposition by voting majorities can lead only to toughened resistance, blockage, and whatever other tactics a party may be able to employ. In such circumstances negotiation offers the only way out, however laborious this may be.

The financial needs of the United Nations for peacekeeping operations can be met in essentially only three ways: by payment of assessed contributions; by voluntary contributions; or by some combination of these. Money in the amounts needed cannot be raised out of present-day independent sources of income such as from the business of the gift shop, documents service, or philatelic office.[28] The Organization has no authority to print money.

---

[26] *The New York Times,* February 22, 1965.

[27] See statement of the Argentine representative speaking at the Working Group of Twenty-One on behalf of a group of Afro-Asian and Latin American states in *UN Monthly Chronicle*, Vol. 1, No. 5, pp. 50–51. The Swedish representatives have taken a similar stand.

[28] See Stoessinger, Chapter 11.

Deficit financing may be feasible in extreme emergencies, but this is hardly desirable as a normal practice in an institution that has no means of creating capital.

Funds on the order of magnitude needed cannot be raised out of levies or surcharges upon such items as tourist traffic, passports, foreign postage, international freight, or profits realized from extraction of gas or petroleum from suboceanic beds without the concurrence of Member States. There is little indication that the more advanced countries are prepared to approve such extensions of UN jurisdiction save in limited situations like the surcharges imposed on transiting vessels after the Suez crisis to reimburse the cost of clearing the Canal. People are apprehensive that any general inauguration of levies might open a door for the UN to disregard the wishes of Member States or pave the way to its acquiring independent power.[29]

POSSIBILITIES OF ASSESSMENT

It is not altogether foreclosed that some peacekeeping may be supported by apportionment and assessment. The record of practice in this respect has been a slender one. It is possible that the limits have not yet been fully established within which states will agree to apportioning peacekeeping expenditures and beyond which they will not go. Had, for example, the military forces been recruited for the Congo in a somewhat different way, and had they been employed more consistently in accordance with the wishes of the principal states, possibly some would have paid who have refused to do so.

It may be suggested that like the supreme law of the United States, the bounds of permissibility will become clear only after tests in a long sequence of cases have "pricked out" the lines of demarcation.

Speaking before the Working Group of Twenty-One in September 1964, Victor Ulanchev of the Soviet Union stated that if an operation were authorized by the Security Council in "strict compliance" with the Charter, his country would be "prepared to take part with other member states in defraying the expenditure involved in the maintenance of those forces."[30] Several loopholes were left by the statement through which exceptions could be taken. But there was an affirmation that under what the Soviet Union might consider to be compliance with the Charter it would support peacekeeping forces. The statements of the delegate of France as well as the actions of his country on UNEF have testified that payments may under some circumstances be forthcoming from France.

[29] Norman J. Padelford, *Some European Attitudes Toward United Nations Financing* (Cambridge, Mass: Center for International Studies, Massachusetts Institute of Technology, November 1964).

[30] *UN Monthly Chronicle*, Vol. 1, No. 5, p. 49. See also, *Memorandum of the Government of the USSR Regarding Certain Measures to Strengthen the Effectiveness of the United Nations in the Safeguarding of International Peace and Security* (UN Document A/5721, July 10, 1964).

Thus, not all recourse to apportionment is necessarily foredoomed by what has happened. But this method must be approached cautiously. It must not be pressed beyond the bounds of active opposition or it will collapse as it has for UNEF and ONUC. The nature of the international scene at the time and the interplay of domestic forces as well must be taken into account in each instance in determining whether to try to finance a given peacekeeping mission by assessment of the whole or a part of the membership or by some more limited voluntary means.

SEARCHING FOR CONSENSUS

The practical aspect of the problem is to find the area within which sufficient consensus can be developed to allow the Organization to proceed in given instances.[31] In searching for this area one can start from the assumption that it still is in the interests of most states to preserve the United Nations, at least in a minimal role. Stated in oversimplified terms, the majority of the Members wish to have a United Nations that is capable of promoting peace while at the same time being able to evoke commitment for support. As practice has developed, it appears that the more voluntary an operation is, the more support it will derive politically within the UN. As the costs rise or appear likely to rise, willingness to support decreases. Small states become

FIGURE I. GREAT-POWER CONSENSUS

Nature of Consensus	United Nations Control	Financing	Example
I. Great-Power Agreement	A. Security Council (Support)	Assessed All Normal Scale	Kashmir
	B. Security Council (No Veto)	Assessment and/ or Voluntary	Early Congo, Cyprus
II. Limited Great-Power Opposition (or Acquiescence)	Veto in Security Council; Assembly Action	Assessment plus Voluntary	UNEF
III. Great-Power Opposition on a Vital Interest Basis	No Force Authorized by Council or Assembly	None	Hungary

[31] I am indebted to a group of graduate students including Dana G. Mead, Gordon S. Smith, Paul L. Gurnee, Randolph T. Major, Robert L. Fischer, Aaron Seidman, and Mrs. Loretta M. Sicat for suggestions relating to the problem of finding consensus.

reluctant to assume indeterminate financial burdens. Major powers become doubtful about supporting operations that may threaten their interests or what might be their interests under some circumstances. The problem then becomes one of finding a level of mandatory financing acceptable to the largest majority.

Great-power consensus can generally be visualized as falling into one of three categories as outlined in Figure 1. Past experience indicates that where there is great-power agreement there is the largest likelihood of consensus on financing peacekeeping operations. At the other extreme, where there is active opposition, as in the case of the Hungarian uprising, any proposal is fraught with danger to the Organization. No force will normally be approved by the Security Council or recommended by the General Assembly. It is in the in-between areas where there is either passive or limited great-power opposition that the principal difficulties lie with respect both to the composition of the force, its mandate, and its financing.

The "Peacekeeping Model" suggested in Figure 2 is an attempt to schematize the responses of Member States to a wide range of different situations and various types of peacekeeping operations. States inclined to take minimalist positions are aligned along the left-hand vertical axis; those in favor of more far-reaching activities along the right-hand axis. The location of individual states will depend upon circumstances. Stretched along the horizontal axis is a range of different possible types of peacekeeping operations extending from the smallest, least expensive, functionally narrow observation groups to the most far-reaching, expensive, and theoretical UN independent forces. The Korean action is regarded as a unique instance, hence separated.

The area marked by the S-shaped curve (which should be visualized as a caterpillar-like curve with hairy edges rather than fixed lines) suggests a spectrum of attitudes and their natures which the UN Members comprising the two elements might display at particular times and circumstances to varying types of peacekeeping activities. The relative density of a plot out of a large number of operations, extrapolated from present limited experience, would appear approximately as suggested. Minimalists would tend to range in their responses from passive acquiescence to active obstruction; liberalists from a minimum of tacit consent to enthusiastic support. In general, the resistance of minimalists will rise as more advanced forms of peacekeeping operations are proposed and as they encroach upon or appear to threaten areas of vital interest. Contrariwise, liberalist support will tend to rise as the probable effectiveness of peacekeeping efforts increases or holds promise of doing so, to the point that the costs in terms of manpower requested or financing discourage individual states or activities appear to threaten their interests.

The object here is merely to *suggest* that in a region designated as the "Negotiating Area" there can be conceptualized the area in which posi-

FIGURE 2. PEACEKEEPING MODEL

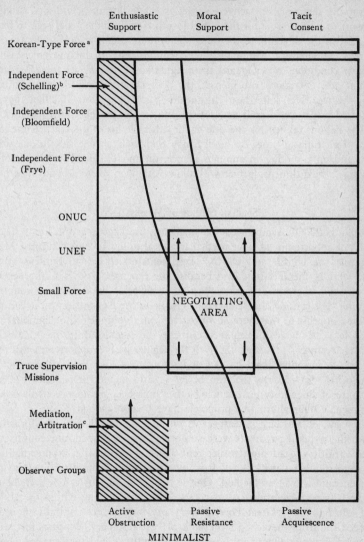

a Korean-type actions are of such a special nature as to belong in a separate category.
b Under certain conditions of cost, size, and political control even the most liberal would object to UN action.
c Area in which a minimalist may feel that smallest UN presence is a threat to a vital interest.

tions tend to have the largest measure of flexibility. Neither side is at the low-est point in support or highest in opposition. Minimalists will tend to refrain in varying degrees from active obstruction while liberalists will give stronger support to a larger role for the UN. Liberalists will undoubtedly seek to move the UN in the direction of the functionally more extensive operations as crises increase in intensity. Minimalists will tend to restrain this movement or to impose conditions to safeguard their rights and interests. As these pressures mount and operations rise in cost, the poorer nations are likely to demand that the wealthier states bear the greater part of the costs and that they be required to pay very small amounts to support the peacekeeping activities.

The nations ranged on one side or the other of this conceptual scheme may vary from time to time. A country may find itself on one side in one situa-tion and on the other in another. Hence, the model should be visualized as having a third dimension that will allow nations to rotate around these posi-tions.

Special Scales of Assessment

Among the ideas advanced for financing peacekeeping operations special scales of apportionment have particular appeal to low-income countries. Many felt that the UNEF and ONUC assessments added serious burdens to the costs of UN membership. And because the expenses of ONUC skyrocketed as they did, the pressures for reductions in favor of the developing countries became very considerable. Concessions made to these countries in the form of rebates, appeals to the more advanced for extra voluntary contributions, and the sale of UN bonds in lieu of assessments did establish differential financing arrangements for peacekeeping from the regular budget apportionments. And the rebate formulas voted in 1961 and 1963 did in effect set up special scales. These have set patterns that can be reverted to in the future if there is any measure of unanimity on financing other peacekeeping operations by appor-tionment. Other alternative proposals have been suggested.[32]

In view of the large measure of withholding which has been practiced since the reduced payments were authorized for the low-income countries, it seems fruitless to attempt further refinement of the existing arrangements or to suggest other bases of special scales until there is more readiness to pay for operations by this method. One is bound to take note, however, of the rather considerable and persistent ground swell of feeling within the UN to the effect that the Great Powers or at any rate the economically more ad-vanced countries should bear the bulk of "extraordinary" expenses for peace-keeping activities. One may suspect that this attitude will continue for a fairly long period of time and must be reckoned with whenever it is proposed from now on in the General Assembly that such expenses be apportioned. The fact

[32] See Stoessinger, Chapters 7 and 12.

that the majority of the more advanced states have accepted and paid at the higher rate and made voluntary contributions over and above their apportionments does not obscure the fact that some of the Members have been altogether opposed to apportionment in the first instance and refused to pay. All of which brings one back again to the proposition that the United Nations system as it is now constituted cannot force Members who are opposed to paying for an operation to do so against their will.

Voluntarily Accepted Assessment

One possibility that might be considered in future situations would be what might be termed a voluntary assessment scheme. This would allow a country to "opt out" of paying for an operation. On a vote to apportion the expenses of a peacekeeping operation, all states voting for or abstaining on the apportionment resolution might be assessed with the understanding that Article 19 would become applicable unless the General Assembly voted to excuse states falling into arrears. Those voting against the operation might also be assessed unless they notified the Secretary-General within a brief period that they wished to be excused.

Such an arrangement would meet the principle of collective responsibility but would concede to political feasibility by allowing states who so wished to disassociate themselves from the action. By allowing states to vote against an apportionment, this would permit a state to be excused from paying without necessarily opposing peacekeeping as such.

In this connection, an upper limit might be set on the dollar size of the operation. If it were continued beyond this limit, a new resolution would be required. If this were not forthcoming, the force would be withdrawn unless it could be supported by completely voluntary means. By establishing such a limit, states would know in advance how much the total obligation might be.

Financing by Voluntary Support

Practice has revealed in several instances that those inclined to take a minimalist stand may be willing to allow a particular operation to proceed provided others will raise the necessary funds. A number of courses of action are open in this event. Contestants can be asked to agree in advance to share the costs, as was done for the UN Temporary Executive Authority (UNTEA), and the UN Yemen Observation Mission (UNYOM). Or, a larger circle of interested states can be asked to pledge enough to cover the expenses for a stated time, as was done when UNFICYP was authorized. In this instance the Soviet Union was willing to vote for the Force but not to pay for it. Since it was apparent that the costs would exceed what Cyprus, Greece, and Turkey would pay, the Force was formed only after others had agreed to pay enough to cover the first three months of operation. No state that was unwilling to share the burden was required to do so.[33]

Such a procedure may avoid the critical problems that arose over UNEF and ONUC financing. But as U Thant remarked later:

> The method of financing the Cyprus Force . . . is most unsatisfactory. Since funds are available only through voluntary contributions, there is a large degree of uncertainty about what will actually be available, and therefore the planning and advance arrangements essential to an efficient and economical arrangement are sorely hampered.[34]

Reporting to the Council at the end of six months by which time the costs of UNFICYP had mounted to $12,800,000 and shortages had begun to appear, the Secretary-General criticized the "flimsy" and "inadequate" financing and the "notable absences on the list of states making voluntary contributions."[35] Efforts to obtain agreement to charging overages to other UN revenues failed. Consequently, he concluded that if funds were not forthcoming, there would be no alternative but to inform the Council and withdraw the Force. It was continued but amid disquieting signs of remaining financial shortages.

An alternative to the case-by-case method of voluntary financing would be to establish a permanent peace fund. This could be contributed to by those who might desire to do so. And it might even be open to private contributions. Such an idea was put forward by Cyprus, Ghana, the Ivory Coast, and Nigeria in 1963.[36] Although this was objected to at the time by the Soviet Union and France on the ground that it would facilitate further bypassing of the Security Council and unwarrantably increase the powers of the Secretary-General, the Assembly voted for a study of the idea by a margin of 91 in favor, 12 opposed, with 2 abstentions.[37] A first charge upon such a fund, if established, might be the clearing up of the present debts. Once these were removed, the fund might then be devoted to underwriting a modest amount of training exercises or staff planning or both for standby reserve units and for defraying the initial costs of future approved operations.[38] It should be possible to surround the use of such a fund with sufficient safeguards to prevent abuse.

The British suggestion of offering permanent logistic support for a given

[33] UN Document S/5575, March 4, 1964. The debate is summarized in the *United Nations Review,* April 1964 (Vol. 11, No. 4), pp. 5-15, 35-36.
[34] UN Document S/5764, June 16, 1964, p. 40.
[35] *Report by the Secretary-General on the United Nations Operation in Cyprus* (UN Document S/5950), p. 67.
[36] General Assembly Resolution 1879 (S-IV), June 27, 1963.
[37] *Ibid.*
[38] See Stoessinger, pp. 158–162.

size of detachment is another possible alternative for handling the costs of peacekeeping. If a number of states were willing to finance the costs of their own or other standby reserve units and to provide them with transportation, supplies, or other needs, this might go quite a way toward covering the expenses of at least some peacekeeping activities. This would lend confidence that ends could be met and might accelerate the response to crises.[39]

No voluntary contribution system can altogether overcome the fact that Member States who refrain from contributing thereby escape the moral responsibility of supporting collective security efforts. But if there is no other alternative, it may be better to have the limited possibilities that can be handled by voluntary arrangements than none at all.

CLEARING UP THE EXISTING DEBTS

Among the steps that will need to be taken sooner or later will be a clearing up of the unpaid commitments of the UN to those who made advances of transportation, supplies, or troop wages for UNEF and ONUC. Suggestions have been made for a rescue fund or something like that to raise funds to settle these debts. This could be done on a voluntary basis with the proceeds being equitably divided among the creditors. Should this fail to produce enough to pay off all of the commitments, the UN might then ask those who made advances to forego reimbursement of the remainder. This could probably be absorbed by most of the creditors without undue sacrifice although it might lead to economic and political reactions. Should some of the principal nonpayers decline to contribute, this would be regrettable and would violate the spirit of collective responsibility upon which the Organization was founded. Conceivably, this might deter others from cooperating in the future. But removal of the indebtedness would be desirable, however, from the point of view of clearing the air in order to move ahead.

CONCLUSION

Dark as the outlook appeared following the nineteenth session of the Assembly, there may still be much that can be salvaged. The Organization has succeeded in assembling peacekeeping forces or missions of one kind or another on no less than nine occasions. These have on the whole discharged their missions in a useful manner. Ways and means have been found to finance the larger part of the costs. Useful experience has been gained. Serious as the financial crisis has been, it is not insuperable. It could be quickly alleviated if this became essential and will be when agreement is reached on the

[39] See Lincoln P. Bloomfield and others, *International Military Forces: The Question of Peacekeeping in an Armed and Disarming World* (Boston: Little, Brown and Company, 1964), especially Chapter 7.

future handling of peacekeeping activities. No irreparable harm has yet been done to the institution.

Reflection coupled with determination to make a fresh try to reach agreement may yet yield constructive ends. If some accord can be reached on the political and constitutional problems and the present debt removed, it is conceivable that the Organization may be able to regain its position in world affairs. Agreement upon these questions might then pave the way for a more comprehensive review of the Charter and enable the United Nations to become once more what it was designed to be: a center for harmonizing the relations among nations.

The UN and Disarmament

DANIEL S. CHEEVER

IN 1964 Secretary-General U Thant asserted
that more significant progress in achieving some measures of disarmament has
taken place since the summer of 1963 than in all the years since the founding of
the United Nations.[1]

The evidence cited included five achievements: 1) the coming into force in
October 1963 of the Moscow Treaty, a partial test-ban treaty banning nuclear-
weapons tests in the atmosphere, in outer space, and under water to which
more than 100 states had subscribed by 1965; 2) the establishment of the direct
communications link between Moscow and Washington; 3) the resolution of
the General Assembly to ban nuclear and other weapons of mass destruction
from outer space;[2] 4) the unilateral reductions of the military budgets of the
Soviet Union and the United States; and 5) the mutual cutbacks in production of fissionable material for military purposes by these two countries and
the United Kingdom.

Our inquiry here will have a threefold objective: to evaluate the Secretary-
General's unguarded optimism in the perspective of twenty years' experience
in disarmament negotiations, to examine the role assigned to the United Nations in major disarmament proposals, and to analyze the use and influence
of the Organization as a disarmament forum. The term "disarmament" will
be used throughout except in cases where the use of a more analytically precise term such as "arms control" becomes necessary. It is our thesis that disarmament negotiations in the United Nations have made progress to the ex-

DANIEL S. CHEEVER is Associate Professor of International Affairs in the Graduate School of Public
and International Affairs at the University of Pittsburgh and a member of the Board of Editors of
International Organization. The author makes acknowledgment of assistance in the preparation of this
contribution to Gary Wamsley, Graduate Assistant in the Graduate School of Public and International
Affairs at the University of Pittsburgh.

[1] "Introduction to the Annual Report of the Secretary-General on the Work of the Organization,"
UN Monthly Chronicle, December 1964 (Vol. 1, No. 7), p. 44.

[2] General Assembly Resolution 1962 (XVIII), December 13, 1963. Also see General Assembly Resolution 1963 (XVIII), December 13, 1963.

tent that they have followed the principles of the Charter. Taking disarmament and peacekeeping experience together, there is some evidence that with the partial test ban and the impasse on the financing of peacekeeping operations, developments in the United Nations have come nearly full circle in twenty years. There has been a progression from the initial premise in the Charter that the management of force in international relations requires the consent and collaboration of the major powers, through an unmapped land of near utopian proposals and enforcement actions by the General Assembly designed to obligate great and small powers alike, back to a grudging acceptance of the Security Council and the rule of big-power unanimity. This is not to say that all the major powers are agreed on disarmament matters. France and Communist China not only have refused to subscribe to the partial test-ban treaty but remain apart as well from the Conference of the Eighteen-Nation Committee on Disarmament, facts that by themselves outweigh the "achievements" noted by Secretary-General U Thant.

Whether this record reflects any real progress toward disarmament is at best a moot question. Perhaps the most that can be said for the Secretary-General's statement is that it is factual. The partial test-ban treaty is the first tangible fruit of post-World War II disarmament negotiations, and its realization *may* have been hastened by General Assembly resolutions. It was nourished, however, in the soil of mutual confidence between the major nuclear powers which was established when seismic technology enabled each to "inspect" the other for limited purposes without recourse to international or supranational control mechanisms. This limited confidence is sustained further by the defense strategies of both the Soviet Union and the United States which have been designed both to slow down or prevent the proliferation of nuclear weapons and to decrease their importance.

To say that the UN is moving full circle back to the starting point of big-power collaboration, however, is not to say that the circle has been followed without deviation. If the partial test-ban treaty, the unilateral reductions of military budgets, and the mutual cutbacks in fissionable-material production of 1963 were limited confidence-building steps that did not envisage enforcement action against major powers, the United States–Soviet Union Joint Statement of Agreed Principles for Disarmament Negotiations of 1961 paradoxically seemed to envisage world control mechanisms and international forces to enforce community peace and law against all states, both great and small. More will be said on this below. It is enough to note for the moment that peacekeeping efforts designed to circumvent the big-power veto by substituting the General Assembly for a deadlocked Security Council and the political initiative of the Secretary-General for major-power intervention in Africa gave rise to the "troika" and to strains on the Organization's purse strings as countermoves, and that the differing conceptions of international organization which marked these controversies have plagued disarmament proposals as well. Before examining the latter, it seems relevant to analyze the extent to which the achievements noted by the Secretary-General have braked the arms race.

THE ARMS RACE 1945–1965

Plus ça change plus c'est la même chose. In 1945 the Soviet Union had already embarked on, or was about to embark on, a desperate race to overcome or narrow the United States' lead in nuclear weapons. By the time the Cold War had become a limited war in Korea, the United States and its North Atlantic Treaty Organization (NATO) allies were seeking in turn to counterbalance the Soviet Union's superiority in ground forces. The Soviet Union startled the West by exploding an atomic device as early as 1949 and in 1953 was hardly a year behind the United States in detonating a H-bomb. During the Korean War the United States began to rearm as hastily as it had disarmed after World War II and initiated a series of steps that were designed to enable West Germany to rearm as a NATO partner short of an independent nuclear capacity. In 1965 the arms race continued and could be likened to a track meet with several events taking place at once. While the Soviet Union and the United States had completed their heats in atmospheric nuclear testing, France and Communist China were still running, though far in the rear. Although the Soviet Union and the United States were agreed that there should be no arms competition in outer space, they continued to compete indirectly in the Congo (Leopoldville) and elsewhere, supplying military equipment to rival factions.

Nonetheless, the Secretary-General's contention that progress toward disarmament had been made had some justification. The arms race between the two nuclear giants appeared to have slackened appreciably under circumstances in which each could detect whether the other was living up to the partial test-ban agreement. This treaty, in short, had codified a self-enforcing, arms control agreement which gave rise to a limited degree of mutual confidence and tended to focus attention on the interpretation of events that might be treaty violations rather than on the question of violation itself. An episode on January 19, 1965, gave some indication of this self-enforcing mechanism in operation. The United States Atomic Energy Commission reported that through seismic signals a Soviet underground test had been detected with a yield in the intermediate range. "A certain amount of venting" was reported to have taken place, but the amount of measured radioactivity was described as too low to "produce measurable exposures to persons." The Soviet Union, in turn, confirmed that a nuclear explosion had been carried out underground. While some radioactive debris leaked into the atmosphere, the amount was said to be so insignificant that the Soviet Union excluded the possibility of a violation of the limited test-ban treaty. The United States reported that it was "continuing its own evaluation of the facts involved."[3]

Although the armaments race continues, it does so in the full recognition that new weapons of mass destruction are dangerous to great and small powers alike and particularly to the great since they are the more likely candidates for nuclear destruction. It is the mutual fear shared by nuclear powers that appears to have brought a note of realism and restraint into recent disarmament negotiations despite the fact that little progress has been made to provide means of change without resort to force and violence through the establishment of an international legal order. Moreover, from the very first meeting of the General Assembly, the major powers have either felt compelled to or have chosen to justify their armaments policy in the United Nations presumably because disarmament is a matter of first concern, judging from the attention paid to it even when compared with economic development.[4] To sustain the thesis that present-day disarmament discussions and proposals show at least some sign of returning to the Charter's principles, the role assigned to disarmament in the original concept of the United Nations should be recalled.

Disarmament and the Charter

Disarmament is not featured prominently in the UN Charter. What would have been specified had the framers been aware of nuclear war will never be known. As it was, most of the United Nations planners of all the governments concerned were ignorant of the weapon being forged in the United States' Manhattan Project, and the handful of leaders at the pinnacle of government in the United States, the United Kingdom, and Canada who knew of World War II's most important secret thought almost exclusively in military terms as they planned the use of A-bombs against Japan. Thus it was that atomic energy was unleashed in June 1945, unknown to all but a few of the negotiators at the United Nations Conference on International Organization in San Francisco who were debating the place to be assigned to disarmament in the Charter. The new weapon became generally known only when it was used against Japan with scant warning in midsummer at the very time when governments were taking steps to adhere to the Charter.

This ironic juxtaposition of events partly explains why disarmament is mentioned as though only in passing in Article 11 of the UN Charter where the General Assembly is given authority to

> consider the general principles of cooperation in the maintenance of international

---

[3] Department of State *Bulletin*, February 8, 1965 (Vol. 52, No. 1337), p. 187.

[4] See, for example, the summary of the general debate of the nineteenth General Assembly in *UN Monthly Chronicle*, January 1965 (Vol. 2, No. 1), pp. 37–104. Admittedly, statements for the record of this sort do not provide a precise measurement either of governmental concern or of UN influence in disarmament.

peace and security, including the principles governing disarmament and the regulation of armaments, and . . . [to] make recommendations with regard to such
principles to the Members or to the Security Council or to both.

A more important reason for this apparent lack of interest in disarmament,
however, was the paramount concern to organize international power by
mobilizing national military contingents to be placed at the "disposal" of the
Security Council. Where the Covenant of the League of Nations had specified
in Article 8, paragraph 1, that

the maintenance of peace requires the reduction of national armaments to the
lowest point consistent with national safety and the enforcement by common
action of international obligations

the UN Charter emphasizes "regulation" rather than "reduction" and says
nothing about "national safety." This change was entirely consistent with the
new theory of world order in which the major powers, owing to their special
responsibilities and authority as Security Council members, for all practical
purposes were empowered to maintain international peace by determining
when aggression occurred and by punishing the offender.

The powers that were to become the permanent members of the Security
Council practically wrote their own ticket. They had agreed without too
much difficulty at Dumbarton Oaks that the mobilization of armed force in
support of the UN Charter should have priority over disarmament. This point
was also pretty generally accepted by the lesser powers at San Francisco. But
the latters' efforts to restrict the authority and influence of the permanent Security Council members, first, by attacks on the extent of their veto privileges,
and, secondly, by efforts to increase the General Assembly's authority in matters involving peace and security, were harbingers of things to come. Those
at the San Francisco Conference, however, agreed with the Sponsoring Governments that the General Assembly should be limited to the consideration
of "principles governing disarmament" while the Security Council was specifically to "be responsible for formulating, with the assistance of the Military
Staff Committee . . . plans . . . for the regulation of armaments."[5] Similarly
the Military Staff Committee was assigned the duty of advising and assisting
the Security Council on "military requirements" for the maintenance of international peace and security, "the regulation of armaments, and *possible* disarmament."[6] However, with the advent of the "absolute" weapon, priorities
changed abruptly even before the Assembly held its first meeting.

[5] Article 26 of the UN Charter.
[6] Article 47, paragraph 1, of the UN Charter. Italics added.

Implications of Major Proposals for the United Nations[7]

From the outset the role of the United Nations as a control organization has been at issue in disarmament negotiations. The Baruch Plan of June 1946, presented by the United States to the UN Atomic Energy Commission, included a proposal to establish by treaty an International Atomic Development Authority to own, operate, manage, and license all facilities for the production of atomic energy. To insure that atomic energy would be used solely for peaceful purposes the Authority was to have freedom to carry on inspections on a continual basis in all countries and was to manage its affairs by majority vote. By insisting that violations of the new control agreement should be met by "swift condign" punishment unhampered by the Security Council veto, Bernard M. Baruch was saying in effect that the security and disarmament provisions of the Charter were obsolete before they were tried. All states would be disarmed as far as atomic weapons were to be concerned, and a single world authority would have the only atomic potential. The United States, however, would not be required to disarm until the Authority's control mechanism was in full operation with the result that its atomic advantage over the Soviet Union would be preserved until the international monopoly was established. Other governments in effect were asked to accept the "sacred trust" which President Harry S. Truman declared the United States would hold for all mankind until international controls had been established. The proposed Authority was thus to receive information from the United States in a series of "stages" of which only the last would include both control over atomic weapons and the secret data pertaining to them.

Had the United States not been so preoccupied with the actual role of United Nations bodies in atomic energy control, it would not have been necessary for Bernard Baruch to stress with such emphasis the veto issue in the UN Atomic Energy Commission. While there was to be no formal amendment of the Charter itself, a new threat to mankind was held to demand a new body with unprecedented authority to be specified in a new treaty. Similarly, any serious breach of the treaty would be such an unprecedented threat to the peace as to require immediate punishment. Because this would not be forthcoming if enforcement action by the Security Council could be thwarted by the veto, the proposed treaty would modify the Security Council voting formula on matters arising as a result of breaches of the treaty. The United States, in short, sought to retain the United Nations while at the same time

[7] Acknowledgment is made to the following major sources: *The International Control of Atomic Energy: Growth of a Policy* (Department of State Publication 2702) (Washington, D.C: U.S. Government Printing Office, 1946); Bernhard G. Bechhoefer, *Postwar Negotiations for Arms Control* (Washington, D.C.: Brookings Institution, 1961); Lawrence S. Finkelstein, "The United Nations and Organizations for the Control of Armaments," *International Organization,* Winter 1962 (Vol. 16, No. 1), pp. 1–19; and Lincoln P. Bloomfield, *The Politics of Arms Control: Troika, Veto and International Institutions* (Special Study Group, Memorandum No. 3) (Washington, D.C., October 6, 1961).

urging the establishment of what in effect was limited world government to enforce atomic disarmament. While the Charter's enforcement provisions were to stand as they were, a new treaty would have effectively altered Article 27 in atomic energy matters.

The Soviet Union chose to stand by the original Charter and its unanimity principle. Soviet Ambassador Andrei Gromyko countered with two proposals that were diametrically opposed to the United States position. Two conventions were to come into force simultaneously, one to outlaw the production and use of atomic weapons and the other to organize the work of the UN Atomic Energy Commission to facilitate the exchange of scientific information for peaceful purposes. Arms control was to be enforced primarily by *national* governments under the general supervisory powers of an International Control Commission which would have the right to conduct only limited and "periodic" inspection of declared plants and facilities. The Soviet proposals would have had the effect of disarming the United States before an effective control system had been established by requiring the prior destruction of nuclear stockpiles. The enforcement of control measures, moreover, was to be decided only by agreement of the Security Council's permanent members.

Hard lines were quickly drawn. The United States could rely on a majority sufficient to substitute the General Assembly for the Security Council in peacekeeping and enforcement and to maintain support for its view that disarmament could come about only as a consequence of effective international arms control. Despite this support, however, the United States and its allies faced a dilemma in this early period. On the one hand, they sought to maintain what came increasingly to be an artificial separation between "conventional armaments" and "weapons of mass destruction" to justify the Assembly's endorsement of the Baruch Plan for the international control of atomic energy, while, on the other hand, they sought to implement the Charter's preatomic provisions for conventional armaments regulation and peacekeeping forces. The Soviet Union, in contrast, urged a general reduction of all armaments and the prohibition of the manufacture and use of atomic weapons. The result was a compromise in the form of a resolution on the "Principles Governing the General Regulation and Reduction of Armaments" carried unanimously in the 1946 General Assembly. The Security Council was instructed to seek practical measures to reduce and regulate armaments, to expedite the work of the UN Atomic Energy Commission in controlling atomic weapons, and to provide armed forces under Article 43 of the Charter. The resolution in addition urged the withdrawal of armed forces from territories beyond national frontiers.[8] Most important for the relationship of United Nations bodies to armaments control organization was the seeming agreement on

[8] General Assembly Resolution 41 (I), December 14, 1946.

the principle that an international control system, including regulation, inspection, and reduction of conventional armaments, with special organs to enforce the system, should be established within the Security Council's framework. This agreement on principles, however, could not paper over the fundamental disagreement between the Western powers and the Soviet bloc. The former continued to insist on a control system including inspection and verification before they were ready to countenance major steps toward disarmament while the latter pressed for prior outlawing of atomic weapons and reduction of *all* weapons without effective international control by means of inspection. The relationship between these points of view to the balance of military forces in the East-West struggle need not be elaborated here. Suffice it to say that the concern of each side to gain military advantage over the other through disarmament negotiations has prevented the implementation of these principles in a twenty-year period. Although the Security Council followed the Assembly's mandate by establishing a UN Commission for Conventional Armaments in February 1947 consisting of the governments represented on the Council, no progress was made since the membership was divided 9–2 on the fundamental issues involved.

A New Initiative

By 1951 the pro-West majority softened the emphasis on the Baruch Plan with the result that disarmament negotiations became concerned with less radical departures from the Charter. The United States, the United Kingdom, and France, the principal NATO parties, at that time careful to move together in defense and disarmament strategy in both NATO and the United Nations, proposed at the sixth session of the General Assembly a plan for the regulation, limitation, and balanced reduction of *all* armed forces and armaments.

There were good reasons for a new initiative. Disarmament discussions, such as they were, had ceased when the Soviet Union refused to participate in meetings with the Nationalist Chinese after the establishment of the Peoples' Republic (Communist China) on the mainland in 1949. The United States' monopoly of atomic weapons ended in September of the same year when President Truman announced that the Soviet Union had succeeded in setting off its own atomic fireworks. The Korean War began nine months later and, although "limited," soon gave rise to apprehensions and war-weariness especially in Europe where rearmament threatened to wipe out economic recovery which was gathering momentum under the Marshall Plan. The end of the United States' monopoly had made the Baruch Plan irrelevant. A World Congress of Partisans of Peace in Stockholm contributed to a sizable popular movement to "ban the bomb." The next moves were destined to be somewhat closer to the original Charter conception of armaments regulation and collective security due in part to the fact that the Soviet Union had increased its bargaining power.

The first step was the establishment of the Disarmament Commission by the sixth General Assembly in 1952 by a vote of 42 in favor, 5 opposed, with 7 abstentions, which, in effect, consolidated the UN Atomic Energy Commission and the UN Commission for Conventional Armaments. Like the UN Atomic Energy Commission, the new body included in its membership all the Security Council members plus Canada. It was directed to prepare a draft treaty for Security Council and Assembly approval for the regulation, limitation, and balanced reduction of all armed forces and all armaments, for the elimination of all weapons adaptable to mass destruction, and for effective international control to insure the prohibition of atomic weapons and the use of atomic energy for peaceful purposes only. However, progressive and continuing *disclosure* and *verification* of all armed forces and all armaments, including atomic armaments, remained as a first and indispensable step in the new disarmament program, a provision that presumably provoked the five negative votes of the Soviet bloc.

The second step was the readiness of the Soviet Union and the Western allies to negotiate the following year as members of the five-power Subcommittee of the Disarmament Commission where there was less temptation to play to the galleries and more opportunity for serious negotiating. This development came about as the result of a suggestion incorporated in a resolution of the eighth General Assembly in 1953 that the Disarmament Commission study the desirability of establishing a "sub-committee consisting of representatives of the Powers principally involved," which was to work in private to make recommendations for the solution of disarmament problems and particularly the issue of control. The French representative has been singled out for particular credit in this sensible effort to return to the spirit of the Charter's basic principle.[9] Difficulties to come, however, were foreshadowed when the Soviet Union abstained in the vote on the resolution which otherwise carried unanimously. The principal difficulty was Communist China. When the Western states suggested that the members of the Subcommittee should be the Soviet Union, the United States, the United Kingdom, France, and Canada, the Soviet Union acquiesced only after urging unsuccessfully the addition of Czechoslovakia, India, and Communist China. The inclusion of the latter was totally unacceptable to the United States and was to continue to remain so for many years to come. In time the exclusion of Communist China would lend an air of unreality to any discussions that seemed to be seriously concerned with disarmament. In 1953, however, it could perhaps

[9] Bechhoefer, p. 209. The resolution in question is General Assembly Resolution 715 (VIII), November 28, 1953.

be argued that neither Chinese government was "principally involved" in disarmament matters.

That disagreement on substantive matters continued despite the subcommittee device is clear from the fact that throughout its life until the final deadlock and adjournment in 1957, the two sides were unable to resolve their major differences on how to implement the objectives listed in repetitive Assembly resolutions. The Western majority continued to emphasize "verification" and "inspection" as elements of a control system that was to be fully operative before any prohibition of atomic weapons was to be put into effect. The Soviet Union, after receding from its initial position that atomic weapons should be banned first and controls established second, remained adamant on another point: that there must be no interference "in the domestic affairs of states" by an international control organ. With no agreement either on the control measures to be established or on means of enforcement in the event of violation of such measures, there could be little specific discussion of the relationship of control organs to the United Nations.

Collective Enforcement Versus Freedom of Action

Lawrence S. Finkelstein has stressed the point that two principles of arms control and disarmament enforcement have been in competition from the beginning: collective enforcement by the United Nations or some other international body on the one hand, and resumed freedom of national action in the event of information indicating the breach of a control treaty on the other hand.[10] This point had already been at issue when Mr. Baruch chose to emphasize the abolition of the veto whereas a previous United States study, the Acheson-Lilienthal Report, which had served as a "foundation" for the Baruch proposals, had stressed the point that violations of an atomic energy control agreement would provide a period of time as a margin of safety during which states would be free to take whatever measures, individual or collective, that seemed necessary for their safety. By emphasizing freedom of national action rather than international sanctions, after the disclosure of a break in an arms control treaty, the control problem becomes simplified and the relationship of control organs to the Organization becomes less important. It was the principle of resumed freedom of action, coupled with the essential scientific achievement of national inspection or self-inspection of nuclear testing throughout the world, which made possible the partial test-ban treaty in 1963. On the evidence of the 1965 test episode in the Soviet Union the principal international control element was an information flow and its correct interpretation by the governments involved. The scientific contribution to the political problem of arms control has been to devise at least the beginning of a control technology that may be acceptable in the current stage of interna-

[10] Finkelstein, *International Organization*, Vol. 16, No. 1, p. 7.

tional relations in which the major governments continue to resist supranational institutions. The implied sanction in such a control system is national
action which a state party to an arms control treaty is free to follow once it
has detected a violation. It may, of course, protest the violation in an international forum such as the General Assembly in order to gain support for and
legitimization of its national enforcement and defense measures, as the United
States sought to do in the Cuban confrontation of 1962.

Given the nature of the proposals before it, the Disarmament Commission
and its five-member Subcommittee could make little progress toward agreement between 1953 and 1957. At no time was it possible to demonstrate a compensating gain in international control to make up for the freedom of action
that would have been lost by acceptance of a control arrangement. Rather
extreme proposals for the cessation of weapons tests, the elimination of nuclear stockpiles, the termination of nuclear production, and "open skies" over
agreed inspection zones to eliminate "surprise attacks" were calculated constantly in terms of politico-military advantage. This was particularly the case
with "disengagement proposals" relating to a zone of limited armaments in
Central Europe with nuclear armaments specifically prohibited, proposals
that had for their objective not general disarmament but the continued nuclear disarmament of Germany and the withdrawal of United States military
power from Europe.

The UN was moved to the forefront in a closely related set of negotiations,
however, dealing with the control of the peaceful uses of atomic energy. In
1953 United States President Dwight D. Eisenhower presented an "atoms for
peace proposal" before the General Assembly in which he suggested that cooperation in the peaceful uses of atomic energy could contribute to the prevention of atomic energy for military purposes. Subsequent negotiations
under United Nations auspices led to the establishment of the International
Atomic Energy Agency (IAEA) in 1957.

Disarmament and Peacekeeping

In retrospect it is clear that the five governments were negotiating under
a major handicap throughout the entire four-year period. The United Nations
security system was obviously inadequate. Because the second attempt to establish a universal collective security system had failed to meet the major demands thrust upon it, regional security arrangements had become necessary.
The result was that disengagement proposals ran afoul of the obvious importance of NATO and the Warsaw Pact in maintaining both a European
and a world military balance. The United Nations could make only a modest
contribution in checking the Suez fiasco which may well have confirmed the
British and French governments in their intentions to develop nuclear forces

of their own. As with the League experience, disarmament once again seemed impossible to achieve without a dependable collective security system.

Although the inadequacy of the collective security system had been obvious from the day the Charter came into force, a new factor in world politics, however, has served to maintain disarmament as a national goal. Nuclear capacity to "overkill" has brought safety to no nation and maintaining the "balance of terror" has hindered the pursuit of national goals such as economic development. Statements by the heads of government of even the nuclear powers to the effect that war had become "unthinkable" and that no nation was safe from a nuclear holocaust seem to have been made with serious intent to negotiate arms control proposals and not solely for propaganda effect. Weapons became so destructive during the 1950's that a safeguarded arms control agreement contained the possibility of providing greater national safety by stabilizing the balance of terror. Yet arms control negotiations isolated from discussion of the pacific settlement of disputes and international peacekeeping proved futile just as they had in the League. This line of thought brought governments back to the problem of peacekeeping which already had been linked closely to armaments regulation in the Charter.

On February 18, 1960, Secretary of State Christian A. Herter outlined before the National Press Club what was to be the theme of the subsequent United States' Proposals for General and Complete Disarmament. The purpose of negotiations would be

> to cut national armed forces and armaments further and to build up international peacekeeping machinery, to the point where aggression will be deterred by international rather than national force.

He went on to relate disarmament to a conception of world order. The United States would seek "to create universally accepted rules of law . . . backed by a world court and by effective means of enforcement—that is, by international armed force." He continued his discussion of a world disarmed of national forces with the statement that "a useful framework and a considerable body of experience already exists in the United Nations."[11]

The United States statement was a rejoinder to a Soviet proposal made by Premier Nikita Khrushchev to the General Assembly during the previous September which also had urged "general and complete disarmament."[12] Whether to call a bluff or for substantive intent, the United States was emphasizing the circumstances that were essential to make this possible. Where the Soviet leader had emphasized the horrors of war and new opportunities for economic development following disarmament, he had scarcely mentioned the United Nations. He chose to stress partial measures such as an "atom-free"

[11] Department of State *Bulletin*, March 7, 1960 (Vol. 42, No. 1080), pp. 354–357.
[12] General Assembly *Official Records* (14th session), pp. 36–37. The specific proposals are in UN Document A/4219.

zone in Central Europe, the abolition of military bases in foreign states, and the conclusion of a nonaggression pact between the members of NATO and the Warsaw Treaty Organization rather than the buildup of a United Nations peacekeeping capacity. The United States rejoinder was that general disarmament was impossible unless the UN had the capacity to keep the peace.

Western and Soviet differences on the role and responsibilities to be assigned to the United Nations began to narrow slightly after this point. Following Secretary Herter's statement, the four nuclear powers (France, the United Kingdom, the United States, and the Soviet Union) convened the Conference of the Ten-Nation Committee on Disarmament on the basis of East-West parity. Western proposals to this Conference emphasized that a disarmed world required stengthened international peacekeeping machinery and control organizations in the UN. Soviet proposals began also to emphasize the necessity of measures to preserve peace and security "in accordance with the Charter of the United Nations" so that an international police force composed of national units would be "at the disposal of the Security Council."

The McCloy-Zorin agreement, presented to the Assembly on September 20, 1961, as a "Joint Statement of Agreed Principles for Disarmament Negotiations," came a year later after the Ten-Nation Conference had been disrupted by the U-2 incident and the resulting collapse of the Paris "summit" meeting. The seriousness of these events was underscored by a rash of Assembly resolutions following an address by President John F. Kennedy setting forth once again proposals to achieve general and complete disarmament. The McCloy-Zorin agreement included another element: reliable procedures for the peaceful settlement of disputes as well as effective arrangements for the maintenance of peace in accordance with the principles of the UN Charter. States were to be obligated "to place at the disposal of the United Nations agreed manpower necessary for an international peace force to be equipped with agreed types of armaments." Such a force was to ensure "that the United Nations can effectively deter or suppress any threat or use of arms in violation of the purposes and principles of the United Nations."[13]

The Conference of the Eighteen-Nation Disarmament Committee at Geneva, as an expanded version of the Ten-Nation Conference to accommodate the influence of nonaligned nations, has sought to implement the McCloy-Zorin agreement. In an "Outline of Basic Provisions of a Treaty on General and Complete Disarmament in a Peaceful World," submitted in April 1962 and amended in August 1963, the United States has urged the development of "arrangements" for the establishment of a United Nations Peace Force after a reduction of weapons specified in Stage I and to take effect in Stage II. By Stage III of arms reduction the parties to the Treaty would progressively strengthen the United Nations Peace Force established in Stage II

[13] Department of State *Bulletin*, October 9, 1961 (Vol. 45, No. 1163), p. 589.

until it had sufficient armed forces and armaments so that no state could challenge it.[14]

The Soviet Union, in turn, submitted a draft "Treaty on General and Complete Disarmament Under Strict International Control" to the General Assembly in September 1962 and added amendments as late as February 1964 following discussion in the Conference of the Eighteen-Nation Disarmament Committee, which under Article 37 would obligate all parties to the Treaty to "conclude agreements with the Security Council" for the provision of "armed forces, assistance and facilities."[15] Where the United States draft contemplated various ways of achieving a United Nations Peace Force, including "the experience of the United Nations" as well as the "feasibility of concluding promptly the agreements envisaged in Article 43," the Soviet Union stayed closer to the Charter. The Soviet proposals specify in Article 18, paragraph 2, that national forces designated for the United Nations "shall form part of the national armed forces of the States concerned and shall be stationed within their territories." It would appear that before all the contemplated forces could actually be available to the United Nations in time of need, the veto must be hurdled in the Security Council, and the governments concerned must agree to release their troops. When the forces were actually being used by the Security Council, moreover, it is clear that they would be under the command of a "troika" since the command would be

> composed of representatives of the three principal groups of States existing in the world, each to be represented equally with decisions to require the assent of all three groups.

The difference between the two proposals would appear to be both basic and familiar. In stressing previous United Nations experience with peacekeeping, the United States as well as those Members which have already taken steps to designate part of their armed forces as international police forces have indicated they are ready to build on the lessons gained by the United Nations forces in Egypt and in the Congo which were enabled to operate outside the veto. The Soviet Union, on the other hand, continues to emphasize unanimity and has extended its skepticism of the impartiality of international administration to the command of the United Nations forces. France has refused to pay for the troops in the Congo for closely related reasons.

The Problem of a Control Organization

Proposals for test bans and disarmament since 1958 have included consideration of proposed control organs but have been obscure on the relationship of such organs to the United Nations itself. A contemplated control organi-

---

[14] Department of State *Bulletin*, October 16, 1961 (Vol. 45, No. 1164), p. 654.
[15] *Current Disarmament Proposals as of March 1, 1964* (New York: World Law Fund, 1964).

zation to supervise a comprehensive nuclear test ban was evidently expected
to enter into an "appropriate relationship with the United Nations" rather
than to be an integral body of the Organization. When the comprehensive
effort was abandoned, the partial test ban was enabled to sidestep this issue,
as already noted, owing to the acceptability of its self-enforcing features.

Both proposals under consideration at the Conference of the Eighteen-Nation Committee on Disarmament provide for the establishment of an International Disarmament Organization (IDO), similarly conceived with similar
structures and with functions consisting principally of inspection and verification. Differences appear in the manner by which IDO will reach decisions
and relate to the United Nations. The Soviet draft prescribes in Articles 41
and 42 that both the General Conference and the Control Council of IDO
will reach decisions on procedural matters by a simple majority vote and on
substantive matters by a two-thirds majority. The United States draft says
nothing about voting in IDO in Part B of Stage I, but in Part H of Stage II
and in Part I of Stage III the determination of whether each stage has been
carried out is to "be made by affirmative vote of two-thirds of the members
of the Control Council, including at least the United States and the Union
of Soviet Socialist Republics." There is a further stipulation that IDO and
its inspectors "have unrestricted access without veto to all places as necessary
for the purposes of effective verification."

As in the case of the proposed United Nations forces, the differences in the
two proposals with respect to the relationship of IDO to the United Nations
would appear to be crucial. Both drafts indicate unmistakably that the new
body is to be established within the framework of the United Nations. The
Soviet draft requires IDO to report to the General Assembly and the Security
Council much in the manner of a specialized agency reporting to the Assembly and the Economic and Social Council (ECOSOC). In the event of a violation of the disarmament treaty the Soviet version specified in Article 40:

> All questions connected with the safeguarding of international peace and security
> which may arise in the course of the implementation of the present Treaty, in-
> cluding preventive and enforcement measures, shall be decided by the Security
> Council in conformity with its powers under the United Nations Charter.

From this it is quite evident that states (Members of the Organization), and
not the Organization itself, are to be the effective centers of enforcement decision making, that the control agreement will or will not appear to provide
adequate safeguards to the extent that its obligations are self-enforcing rather
than enforceable by an international institution, and that the control organization is to be closely linked to the United Nations.

The United States draft is less specific on the relationship question. In
Paragraph G(4) the General Conference is to approve agreements "between

the IDO and the United Nations and other international organizations" implying that the Organization's relationship to the United Nations may not necessarily be more important than its relations with other bodies. The Security Council is mentioned only in connection with the peaceful settlement of disputes. In the matter of enforcement, an intriguing paragraph, H (4) in Stage I, specifies that the parties to the Treaty would

> agree to support measures strengthening the structures, authority, and operation of the United Nations so as to improve its capability to maintain international peace and security.

Evidently, the United States values flexibility and chose to emphasize the possibility of strengthening the United Nations by Charter amendment or otherwise while the Soviet Union opposes change.

A separate but related difference that reflects opposing conceptions of international administration is to be found in comparing the provisions of the two treaties which relate to the staff. The Soviet draft specified in Article 2, paragraph 4, that IDO, like the UN Command, is to be the familiar "troika," with its staff "recruited internationally and in such a way as to ensure the adequate representation of all three groups of States existing in the world." In the United States version IDO would have as early as Stage I an Administrator to manage it under the direction of the Control Council which would have authority, staff, and finances adequate to ensure effective and impartial implementation of IDO's function.

After twenty years it seems obvious that the Soviet Union and the United States remain far apart in their conception of what sort of international institutions best serve their interests in disarmament and peace enforcement. It would be quite incorrect, however, to lay the disarmament impasse on the doorsteps of these two powers alone. The France of Charles de Gaulle also takes a strict constructionist view of the Charter, and certainly there can be no general disarmament without the cooperation and support of Communist China. Meanwhile experiences with Article 19 and the United Nations Conference on Trade and Development (UNCTAD) in Geneva can hardly fail to influence United States thinking on the role of the United Nations in disarmament. The first experience suggests the danger of pushing major powers to a point of diminishing returns in pressing proposals that would change a voluntary agency into a compulsory one. The second implies that the confrontation between the rich and poor nations could well diminish the support the United States has enjoyed for twenty years in the General Assembly.

The UN as a Disarmament Forum

Although it is difficult to assess the role of the United Nations as a disarmament forum, there appear to be correlations, on the one hand, between the political orientation of the Organization's membership and the substance of disarmament proposals and, on the other hand, between the size of the Organization and the extent to which its principal organs, particularly the General Assembly, are used as negotiating forums. The establishment of an analytical framework to discover and test such correlations would be useful for the study of international organization and would also shed light on disarmament diplomacy. However, since a thorough study of this nature is beyond the scope of the present analysis, only a few general conclusions can be drawn from the rather obvious juxtapositions between the progress of disarmament negotiations and the size and composition of the General Assembly.

The Security Council may be quickly disposed of since it has played scarcely any role in disarmament discussions despite the Charter's mandate that it should formulate plans "for the establishment of a system for the regulation of armaments."[16] It was obviously intended to be active in formulating disarmaments agreements during the period of the UN Atomic Energy Commission and the first Disarmament Commission since its membership, Canada excepted, was made identical with these bodies. Had the major protagonists been able to compromise their differences, the Council would have been enabled thereby to play its assigned role by confirming the agreements already reached in the specially designated negotiating bodies. When no agreement was forthcoming, the Assembly began to encroach on Security Council territory as East and West sought to mobilize support for their equally intransigent positions. With the immediate danger of radioactive "fallout" from nuclear testing in the mid-1950's and the potential danger of a world holocaust should war begin, the Assembly became more involved as all nonnuclear states, particularly the nonaligned, sought to bring pressure on both East and West to curb the arms race. A closely related factor denigrating the Security Council in the second ten-year period of the United Nations has been the conviction of the non-Western states that its composition no longer represented their interests adequately.

The Secretariat has played a useful if inconspicuous role by providing services which have been drawn upon even by non–United Nations bodies such as the Eighteen-Nation Disarmament Committee. The Secretary-General has taken important initiatives on a number of occasions by suggesting how to influence the course of disarmament discussions. He pressed for the reestablishment of a United Nations negotiating forum when he suggested in 1958 that the General Assembly "might wish to define its attitude toward the results of the Conference of Experts and to consider the primary objective of balanced world-wide disarmament."[17]

---

[16] For a stronger indictment see Leland M. Goodrich, "The UN Security Council," *International Organization,* Summer 1958 (Vol. 12, No. 3), pp. 280–281.
[17] Bechhoefer, p. 457.

It is the Assembly, however, that has become the significant forum as both major and minor powers have sought to mobilize support for their points of view. Blocs have tended to loosen at times in disarmament debate as the confrontation between nuclear and nonnuclear powers has developed. For example, the United States and the Soviet Union both opposed a resolution sponsored by the nonaligned states in the sixteenth Assembly urging the nuclear powers to refrain from further tests pending the conclusion of a test-ban treaty. More typically, however, the two principal nuclear powers have sought to justify their opposing views. Changes in the political orientation of the Assembly's membership evidently afforded the Soviet Union an opportunity to seek support for its conception of international administration. With the massive increase in membership of nonaligned nations, principally African, beginning in 1960, the Soviet Union emphasized the "troika" principle in its proposals for the executive management of the International Disarmament Organization. The effect of this step, taken in conjunction with similar proposals for the Secretariat as a whole, has not only been to build another "control" into United Nations and disarmament organization decision making but also to appeal to neutral support in a manner consistent with the Soviet Union's anticolonial posture. This is not to say that the advantage always lies with one particular point of view. The application of the "troika" principle to the Secretariat, for example, was partially blocked by nonaligned Members. It is too early, however, to predict how the "troika" will fare in discussions pertaining to IDO.

The United States appears to have misjudged the political atmosphere in the Assembly on the disarmament question in 1957 when it sought to mobilize support against the Soviet Union after a deadlock in the five-nation Subcommittee. Twenty-four Members were enlisted as cosponsors of a United States resolution, and no effort was made to compromise with the Soviet Union which had submitted two counterproposals. While the latter were defeated at the price of 25 abstentions, the United States resolution carried only after repeated efforts by the Latin American states, India, Norway, and Pakistan to mediate between the nuclear powers and to urge the United States not to press for all or nothing. In their efforts to mobilize support, major powers have been confronted instead by Assembly pressures to compromise.

With respect to the size of the Organization, the history of disarmament since the Second World War suggests that the Assembly has often been thought to be too unwieldy a body for fruitful negotiations. Even at the start, the United Nations Atomic Energy Commission was accepted unanimously by the membership as an appropriate body for serious, continuing negotiations. The establishment of the UN Commission for Conventional Armaments in 1947 and the consolidated Commission for the Control of Armaments and Armed Forces in 1952 presumably reflected the same conviction. The most intense negotiations have taken place in even smaller and more appropriately composed bodies such as the five-member Subcommittee of the Disarmament Commission in the 1952–1957 period, the ten-nation Conference of Experts to Study the Possibility of Detecting Violations of a Possible Agreement on the Suspension of Nuclear Tests in 1958 and the tripartite discussions in Washington and Moscow on the partial test ban in 1963.

What appears to be significant with respect to the problem of size is that all arms control and disarmament negotiations were held in the United Nations bodies until the breakdown of discussions in the Disarmament Commission's Subcommittee in 1957. Since that time negotiations have been carried on principally in non-United Nations bodies, and the shift in the negotiating forum corresponded with the approximate doubling of United Nations membership that began in 1955. This increase in size has been due very largely to the increased representation of nonaligned states with the result that the United States and its Western allies have had more difficulty in gaining support for their position than was the case prior to 1957. This change became evident that year when the Soviet Union pressed demands that the Disarmament Commission be dissolved and replaced by a United Nations committee of the whole meeting in public or by a smaller body composed equally of Members from the Eastern and Western blocs. The United States opposed these suggestions until it became evident that its rigid position was becoming untenable. It then agreed to a compromise resolution to expand the Disarmament Commission to 25 members (26 when Canada is not sitting on the Security Council) introduced by Sweden, India, Japan, Canada, Paraguay, and Yugoslavia. The Soviet Union in turn was criticized when, not satisfied with this proposal for a negotiating forum, it would not participate in the Commission. What appears significant in these particular episodes of the twelfth Assembly is that the Soviet Union and the United States both appeared unreasonably intransigent to smaller nonnuclear powers, aligned and nonaligned alike.

The Assembly has been enabled to assume a mediating role owing partly to the fact that the UN's newer Members are more critical of the United States than the original Members. Of the 22 new Members in the 1955–1957 period, for example, thirteen have recognized Communist China. The Assembly has always had an active concern, however, and has passed resolutions on various aspects of arms control and disarmament in every session with the exception of the ill-fated nineteenth. The thirteenth Assembly was dubbed the Disarmament Assembly because the debate on the subject lasted for 27 days with a greater number of states participating in the drafting of resolutions than ever before. The sixteenth Assembly adopted a total of ten resolutions dealing with such matters as the cessation and elimination of nuclear tests, the denuclearization of Africa, the designation as illegal of all uses of nuclear and thermonuclear weapons, and the nonproliferation of nuclear weapons.

The effect of such vigor is to pressure the major powers to continue negotiations. Only France, owing to its preoccupation with becoming a full-fledged nuclear power, has remained largely impervious. Even when disarmament negotiations shift to non-United Nations bodies such as the Eighteen-Nation Disarmament Conference, however, reports of success or failure are demanded in the General Assembly. To say that Assembly pressure brought about the partial test ban would probably be to ascribe too much to its influence. When the three major nuclear powers felt that it was in their self-interest to accept such a ban, however, they had Assembly resolutions to legitimize their agreement. It may not be too much to assume that they welcomed this support in their respective differences with France and Communist China.

Conclusions

It is in a sense beside the point to ask whether disarmament negotiations are making progress. Whether they are or not, they will continue because nations' interests are perceived constantly in terms of war and peace. What is more, a forum as wide and visible as the General Assembly reinforces the place of disarmament discussions as a continuing feature of the international political landscape. Specific interests and foreign policy goals are sought in the United Nations through disarmament policy. This state of affairs applies to lesser powers as well as to the Great Powers, if to a lesser degree. India, Canada, and Yugoslavia, to take but three examples, have been influential in disarmament matters at one time or another and have utilized the United Nations to mobilize support for their points of view. Indeed, with the increasingly "dysfunctional" character of massively destructive weapons, a premium is necessarily placed on disarmament diplomacy as a continuing international process.

Another straw in the wind indicates that the two major nuclear powers may both be moving back toward the original United Nations notion of collective security. While continuing to insist, perhaps beyond the bounds of prudence, that the cost of peacekeeping forces were expenses of the Organization which the Members were obligated to bear in amounts determined by the General Assembly, the United States nonetheless indicated its readiness to utilize the Security Council to a greater extent for the future mobilization of international forces.[18] It is too early at the time of writing to know whether this change of emphasis will be reflected in the United States position at the Eighteen-Nation Disarmament Conference scheduled for resumption at Geneva in the spring of 1965. A more serious roadblock, of course, is the nonparticipation of France and Communist China either in the Eighteen-Nation Conference or, along with Cuba, in the partial nuclear test ban.

[18] *The New York Times,* November 11, 1964, p. 1.

Efforts to make the United Nations or UN-related bodies the center of action for armaments control or for disarmament negotiations have been fraught with difficulties. The General Assembly is too unwieldy for serious negotiations. The concept and authority of the United Nations itself as an international organization are now too much the subjects of controversy for it to be able to monopolize disarmament discussions or armaments control. On the other hand, the Organization cannot avoid being heavily involved no matter how great the efforts to curb its role. For one thing, progress toward disarmament depends heavily on concurrent progress toward an international legal order. No international disarmament organization of itself can make the peace by transforming the nature of international relations. While progress toward disarmament can theoretically and perhaps practically hasten the approach of an international "community," disarmament, like the community itself, appears to be more the result than the cause of achievements in other areas of pressing concern such as the settlement of outstanding political differences by the major powers and the achievement of human rights and economic development.

The United Nations will continue to be involved for another reason. Disarmament is seldom considered as an isolated problem. Disarmament policies are linked closely with other political strategies the implementation of which is sought frequently in the General Assembly owing to the broad scope of its concerns and the size of its membership. This may well explain why the Soviet Union seeks a full-scale public debate on disarmament by the entire UN membership prior to the resumption of "private" discussions in the Eighteen-Nation Disarmament Conference in Geneva at a time when the United States is in the quagmire of "counterinsurgency" in Vietnam.

Finally, the most tenable conclusion to be drawn from twenty years' experience is that disarmament discussions have been fruitful in limiting the armaments race to the extent that they adhere to the Charter principle of big-power unanimity. Admittedly, this is scant comfort in the quest for peace.

Colonialism, Political Development, and the UN

RUPERT EMERSON

THE United Nations two decades after San Francisco is a very different body from the one which its creators fashioned, and it is a reasonable presumption that there were none or virtually none who presided over its creation who foresaw even dimly what it would become in the short span of twenty years. In particular, few could have believed at that time that the tidal wave of anticolonialism would sweep so drastically over the domains of the imperial powers and leave behind in its wake an organization so largely populated by the new Asian and African states which emerged from the deluge. It is also one of the significant elements in the situation that few could have imagined that the process of decolonization could be carried through with so little needed in the way of violent struggle by the colonial peoples and so much conceded in peaceful acquiescence by their colonial masters. One of the world's great revolutions has been accomplished with a minimum of revolutionary action and sacrifice.

Nothing more dramatically illustrates what has happened to the UN in this context than a bare recital of the figures showing the changing membership of the Organization. At the end of 1945, among the 51 states which were then Members of the UN, the Middle East contributed six, Africa four (including Egypt), and Asia only three. A decade later, at the end of 1955, 25 new Members had been added but a dozen of them were European states; nine more states represented largely the first great sweep of anticolonialism in Asia; three were added to the Middle East quota; but only Libya had joined the meager African ranks. The next decade was marked by an unparalleled eruption of new states, rising from the ruins of colonialism, which took place primarily in Africa but reached into other parts of the world as well. In 1965 the total

RUPERT EMERSON, an honorary member of the Board of Editors of *International Organization*, is Professor of Government and Research Associate, Center for International Affairs, Harvard University.

120

UN membership had soared to 114, to which Africa no longer contributed four or five states but 35, while the Asian Members had risen to fifteen, and the Middle Eastern to eleven. The number of ex-colonial Members was further swelled by the appearance as independent states of Jamaica and Trinidad in the Caribbean. Of the colonies which have come to independence only Western Samoa has not sought UN membership, preferring to remain associated with New Zealand on a voluntary basis for the present. A variety of morals can be drawn from these facts and figures, and some will be sought in succeeding pages. One which can be pointed out immediately is that for an important range of issues concerned with colonialism—to be defined in the UN context for most practical purposes as white rule imposed on nonwhite, or non-European, peoples overseas—it is now possible to count on an overwhelming anticolonial majority when the Communist states are added to the ex-colonial Members and their sympathizers from Latin America and elsewhere.

This radical change in the balance of membership has pushed the dominant opinion in the UN far over into the anticolonial column. From its earliest days the UN has had more of a leaning in this direction than its predecessor, the League. Apart from the mandates system—a mildly modified form of colonialism under international supervision which contained no necessary presumption of independence—the League scarcely busied itself at all with colonial issues. By the time the UN Charter came to be written, however, it was no longer possible to pass colonial issues by in silence; in Asia and the Middle East the revolt against colonialism was in full swing, and in Southeast Asia the overthrow of the colonial governments by the Japanese had sapped the foundations of Western imperial control. The Charter, in consequence, acknowledged the principle of equal rights and self-determination of peoples among its purposes; markedly tightened up the mandates system under the new heading of trusteeship; and established a set of principles and obligations in relation to all non-self-governing territories which gradually opened the door to a demand for international accountability on the part of all the colonial powers.

The UN was from the outset concerned with probems of colonialism, but the nature and intensity of its concern changed radically as the years went by. In the early days the colonial powers and their allies and associates retained a very strong position in the UN, but in the later days, as the membership statistics demonstrate, the forces of anticolonialism had in very large part taken over. The nature of the UN's concern changed as the old elite of the international order gave way to the new immigration.

This transition was from a somewhat peripheral UN interest in colonial matters, which were seen as guarded from prying international eyes by the protective mantle of domestic jurisdiction, to the absorption of a major share of the UN's energies in an anticolonial crusade which took for granted that such matters were in the international public domain. The earlier assumption that each colonial power should at its own discretion and in an unhurried way lead its dependent peoples to well-being and self-government gave way to the proposition that colonialism was an intolerable and illegitimate abuse to be done away with as speedily as possible by the international community. Where the Charter provided that the administering authorities should insure that trust territories played their part in the maintenance of international peace and security, the conviction now spread that the continued existence of any dependency by itself created a threat to peace and security.

THE CHARTER AND THE OPENING YEARS

Revealing light is thrown on the state of mind which prevailed at San Francisco by a comment made just after the United Nations Conference on International Organization by Huntington Gilchrist, who had served as a Conference staff member and had also worked in the Mandates Section of the League Secretariat. Discussing the drafting of Article 73(b) of the Charter, he remarked:

> Independence was not mentioned as a goal, for the simple reason that no colonial power except the United States looks upon it as a normal and natural outcome of colonial status—and it must be remembered that the Conference was a conference of governments and not of dependent peoples.[1]

To this he added that the innovation of requiring reports from the states administering non-self-governing territories was far from giving the UN "the authority to meddle in colonial affairs," although the reports would no doubt be made public and might be discussed in appropriate international bodies. The crystal ball available to even the best informed in 1945 did not disclose that the UN was shortly to fall into the hands of the ex-dependent peoples and that the authority to "meddle" in colonial affairs would not only be asserted but exercised on a grand scale.

At San Francisco and in the first years of the UN the anticolonial pressure does not appear to have been intense. The United States, which had given the matter considerable attention in its wartime planning for the future international organization, was interested in seeing provision made for more responsible and progressive colonial management and for an extension of international supervision, but it was a long way from contending for a radical and immediate attack upon colonialism. If, on the one hand, it was in the process of granting to the Philippines the independence which it had promised, it was, on the other, embroiled in its domestic inability to decide under what, if

[1] Huntington Gilchrist, "Colonial Questions at the San Francisco Conference," *The American Political Science Review*, October 1945 (Vol. 39, No. 5), p. 987. He suggested, however, that at least potential independence must be included in the pledge to develop free political institutions.

any, international auspices it would take over the Japanese-mandated islands. Moreover, it had an eye on Okinawa and other Japanese islands, which have, in fact, continued to linger in its possession up to the present day.

The Soviet Union, less inhibited in the expression of radical sentiments, seemed at the time not to be particularly interested in colonial questions and obviously had at home and on its frontiers appalling problems of reconstruction and reorientation. It was also taking over the Kuriles and southern Sakhalin from Japan with no hint of trusteeship, and it had indicated an interest in falling heir to Italy in Libya. At San Francisco the Soviet delegates spoke for independence for colonial peoples and wanted a tightening up of the control procedures, but they spoke in muted tones. Nikita Khrushchev was not to pound his shoe for a number of years to come.

For the rest, it was no doubt asking too much to expect the colonial powers to acquiesce cheerfully in the dismemberment of their empires or the impairment of their control over them at the end of a long and exhausting war in which the dependencies had in one or another fashion played a part and were now counted on to assist in recovery. The United Kingdom, France, and the Netherlands were aware that a new day had dawned, but they hoped it would not be too drastically new. There is no evidence that Belgium recognized that any significant change was necessary in its paternalistic management and exploitation of the Congo. The British were hostile to the formula that independence should be established as the normal goal for all colonies, and, although they acknowledged advance toward self-government as desirable, they preferred to place their emphasis on development and welfare, leaving any serious political overhaul to some later time when the social and economic foundations of the colonies were firmly established. In company with the other colonial powers they looked with no love on international instruments of control or supervision, and proposed instead the creation of advisory regional bodies, unconcerned with political matters, on the model of the Caribbean Commission. The French, characteristically, were moving toward some sort of a union or federation which would link their overseas territories intimately with the metropole, in part in implementation of their assimilationist principles and in part to ward off what later came to be known as Balkanization and to which their own *loi cadre* of 1956 markedly contributed. The Netherlands, for its part, had proclaimed early in the war the need for a cooperative reform of the relationships within its empire. It found, however, that the task of reconstructing the prewar system was both painful and difficult when the time came to seek a reconciliation with the nationalists who at the end of the war had taken over in Java, Sumatra, and elsewhere, proclaiming the independence of the Republic of Indonesia.

The controversies in the colonial sphere which heatedly occupied the UN's attention in the early and formative years seem innocuous enough compared with what was to come later, but cumulatively they acted as a series of wedges to pry the door wider and wider open. Emil Sady is presumably correct in his implication that at San Francisco there was no misunderstanding as to the minimal character of the obligations undertaken by the administering states under Article 73 or of the fact that no supervisory machinery was provided for dependencies other than those under trusteeship.[2] The unavailing effort of the colonial powers was to establish their claim that Chapter XI of the Charter was a declaration (as it was expressly labeled) made by each Member separately which endowed the UN with no jurisdiction to intervene in what they regarded as still their private colonial affairs. In their eyes what was necessary was scrupulous attention to a strict interpretation of Article 73: To be sure, it laid down general norms for enlightened colonial administration, but it omitted mention of independence; it called for no reports on political conditions;[3] and the reports, already subject to limitation by security and constitutional considerations, were only to be transmitted to the Secretary-General for information purposes.

On the other side, the anticolonialists worked busily to establish for all non-self-governing territories requirements and machineries which would be effective counterparts of those which the Charter had laid down for the trust territories. The first significant step in this direction was the creation at the first session of the Assembly of a temporary *ad hoc* committee to look into various matters connected with the information submitted under Article 73(e). Despite the protest of the colonial powers that it constituted an abuse of the Assembly's powers, the Committee on Information, always somewhat nominally on a temporary basis, was continued in existence until it was ultimately replaced in 1963 by a more powerful body which had no scruples about attempting to assert virtually unlimited jurisdiction in the colonial sphere. Its mere existence was an unpleasant reminder to the administering authorities that a growing contingent of Members of the UN claimed a right habitually to look over their shoulders and supervise them, but the powers of the Committee were very limited. Like the Trusteeship Council, although with a different mix, it was made up of an equal number of administering and non-administering countries which tended to inhibit action and, as the anticolonialists saw it, to equate their righteous cause with the patent evils of colonialism; but recourse to the Assembly was, of course, possible when issues arose which appeared to warrant it. Since the Committee was not ordinarily in possession of political information and was debarred by its ground rules from making

---

[2] Emil J. Sady, *The United Nations and Dependent Peoples* (Washington, D.C: Brookings Institution, 1956), p. 24.

[3] The nearest approach to a legally acceptable ground for the repeated request that the colonial powers submit reports on political conditions was that since they were committed by Article 73(b) to develop self-government and take other political steps, the Assembly could rightfully demand that it be kept informed as to what was being done.

recommendations in relation to particular territories, political matters were dealt with by the Assembly itself and its Fourth (Trusteeship) Committee except in the restricted number of cases which went to the Security Council. Unlike the Trusteeship Council, the Committee on Information was not equipped with the power to receive petitions or hear petitioners, to send out visiting missions, or to probe into and make recommendations about the policies, programs, and institutions adopted in the large number of non-self-governing territories with which it was concerned. Although how much effective significance its deliberations had is open to question, the Committee was drawn into highly controversial spheres when it was called upon to examine the factors to be taken into account in determining whether territories were non-self-governing or had moved into higher spheres and to make recommendations concerning the decisions of states to stop transmitting information.

The role of the Committee on Information was sharply limited and in its early years the Assembly was not dominated by anticolonial forces, but, as time went on, UN majorities in move after move created precedents which encroached upon what the colonial powers firmly asserted to be matters embraced within their domestic jurisdiction. As in other spheres of UN activity the result was frequently a clash between resolutions adopted by the Assembly and the readiness of the states directly affected to acknowledge the validity of the Assembly's concern and to heed its advisory admonitions. Since the machinery for the enforcement of such resolutions was nonexistent, or virtually so, it was all too easy to arrive at a state of affairs in which resolutions were merely ignored by those to whom they were addressed. A typical case of this sort arose from the repeated assertion of the Assembly that it had the authority to lay down the general rules governing a determination as to whether a territory was or was not self-governing and to apply these to particular cases where information was or was no longer being transmitted. The most striking, and least acceptable, example has been the intransigent insistence of Portugal that it possesses no non-self-governing territories and that its far-flung pieces are all equal parts of a single country.

For the colonial powers it added insult to injury that they often found themselves under attack by countries whose domestic regimes they held, not without some justice, to be more oppressive and less liberal, democratic, and efficient than the colonial situations which were being castigated. It was in part in response to the inequity represented by such attacks that the so-called "Belgian thesis" was unavailingly launched to seek to broaden out the application of Chapter XI to bring under its protection not only the colonial peoples but all others who were substantively not self-governing.

The Contribution of the UN Prior to 1960

It is a cumbersome but not particularly difficult problem to survey wha
the various organs of the UN have said and done about colonialism, sel
determination, and the rise of new states. It is far more difficult to arrive at
balanced and objective judgment as to what the specific contributions of th
UN have been and to seek to answer such "iffy" questions as what differenc
it would have made in the flow of events if the UN had not been in existenc
Even the opening up of presently unavailable governmental files and th
reading of perhaps still unwritten memoirs and apologias will furnish n
decisive answer because of such intangible elements as the atmosphere whic
the UN created at different times and under different circumstances and th
effect of anticipated reactions on the part of the UN which invited or in
hibited certain actions or attitudes.

It is sounder to assume a lesser rather than a greater role for the UN i
the massive contemporary sweep of decolonization. That role has surely no
been negligible and it has grown, or at least has grown much bolder, as th
years have rolled by; but the anticolonial drive was well under way befor
the UN came into existence and most of the actions which have been take
to translate non-self-governing territories into independent states have ha
no direct link whatsoever to the UN save in the sense that they had UN bles
ing as exemplified most notably after the fact in the speedy acceptance of th
new states as Members. Even in several of the specific cases in which UN
intervention of some sort took place, it is by no means easy to establish tha
the resolutions which were adopted and the negotiations which were carrie
on had any marked effect on the outcome. To pick one somewhat at ran
dom, could a clear case be established that the evolution of Algeria's affair
was substantively influenced by the UN's debates and determinations?

The UN was operating in an atmosphere of mounting anticolonialisr
which it certainly did not create but to which it equally certainly contributec
It is not far off the mark to see the UN as rather reflecting the trend of opir
ion in the world than itself very decisively influencing it, and a good inde
of the change which was taking place is to be found in the drastic shift i
membership in the second decade of the UN's existence. In all the earlic
years the colonial powers were able to ward off such efforts to dictate thei
policies as the setting of target dates for independence. In 1960, followin
the inrush of African states, the Assembly adopted unanimously the impo
tant Declaration on the Granting of Independence to Colonial Countries an
Peoples which called for immediate steps to transfer all powers to the peopk
of trust and non-self-governing territories; and from that time forward the A
sembly and the committee which it established to see to the implementation c
the Declaration were engaged in issuing a series of directives to the coloni;

powers instructing them as to the steps to be taken in securing prompt freedom for their remaining dependencies.

With the exception of its involvement in Indonesia, in the withdrawal of French and British troops from Syria and Lebanon, and in the Palestine turmoil surrounding the birth of Israel, the UN took no part in the first rounds of the process of decolonization which had such great importance in establishing the precedents for similar action elsewhere. In fact, its intervention was neither invoked nor necessary in most of the later cases of transition from colonial status to independence. At least until after 1960 it was really only the stickier situations which brought the UN into the picture. Thus, the independence of the Philippines, India, Pakistan, Burma, and Ceylon was achieved without reference of any kind to the UN, and the same was true at a later stage for Malaya, Ghana, Nigeria, and the whole array of sub-Saharan territories which had been under French rule. The most singular failure on the part of the UN to have any share in the proceedings was presented by the long and bloody warfare in Vietnam, the first phase of which ended in 1954 in the independence of that country, although divided in two, and of neighboring Cambodia and Laos. On no ground of principle is it possible to distinguish the Indochinese situation from the Indonesian one, which was a UN concern from the outset. Even in the Indonesian case, however, it might be open to question whether the final outcome would have been significantly different if the UN had been as absent from the scene as it was in Vietnam and the Geneva Conference of 1954 which put a temporary end to that conflict. UN concern with the attainment of independence by Tunisia and Morocco was minimal but was more extensive in the longer drawn-out agony of Algeria.

In keeping with the difference in their status it was naturally the trust territories which received the most intensive UN supervision and whose move to independence was most closely supervised by the Organization. With the exception of Palestine, into whose troubled affairs the UN was inevitably drawn, the A mandates of the Middle East had won independence before it became necessary for the UN to concern itself with them. At the other extreme, South West Africa, which South Africa refused to transmute into a trusteeship, has remained a constant source of anxiety, activity, and frustration for the UN. In the African and other trust territories the UN exercised substantially the full range of the powers with which it was endowed by the Charter and kept itself intimately informed as to their affairs although radical attacks upon their administration and prospects tended to be blocked by the makeup of the Trusteeship Council. All save tiny Nauru, the United States' strategic trusteeship in the Pacific, and the still primitive Australian-run New Guinea have received independence and, except for Western Samoa, whose amicable departure from

formal New Zealand tutelage had been well prepared, at a date earlier than
had been at all expected.

Despite the open invitation voluntarily to place other territories under the
trusteeship system, the only addition was the former Italian Somaliland which
was placed under Italian tutelage for a fixed period of ten years. No special
problems attended the independence of Tanganyika, but it is worthy of remark that in the whole sweep of decolonization the only territories in which
self-determination was accomplished through a formal consultation of the
people by plebiscite were British Togoland and the British Cameroons.[4] Both
of these territories, be it noted, opted for a solution other than straightforward
independence, leaving an inescapable sense of doubt as to whether other peoples in Asia and Africa might not have chosen different destinies than those
assigned to them if they had been given the chance.

In a quite different vein, it seems apparent that none of the colonial peoples found the supposedly more enlightened and progressive system of trusteeship preferable to their unilateral attachment to a single colonial power.
None of the Asian or African nationalists have spoken up in favor of supervision by the Trusteeship Council. It is, of course, possible that some elements
in Angola or Mozambique would have made such a choice if their voices
could have been heard, but the great bulk of the available evidence indicates
that while trusteeship looked good to external critics of colonialism, the colonial peoples themselves preferred to deal directly with their imperial overlords,
and the latter certainly displayed no eagerness to internationalize their colonial responsibilities. As a result, both sides preferred to live with the evils they
knew rather than to risk those of a new scheme of things.

Through the combined labors of the Assembly, the Trusteeship Council,
the Committee on Information, and other special bodies a mass of information was built up concerning the world's dependencies, and principles were
gradually worked out in terms of which colonial situations and problems
could be judged. The relevant sections of the Secretariat were both well informed on colonial matters and, behind the scenes, inclined to lend their
support to the anticolonialists. From the beginning and until the more radical
turn in 1960, perhaps the most hotly debated issue concerned the classification of territories as non-self-governing or, alternatively, as being out from
under the mild supervision afforded by Article 73. What was at stake was
less the relatively harmless nuisance of compiling an array of material to be
sent to the Secretary-General than the principle that the "private" colonial
possessions of the powers were open to public international scrutiny and that

---

[4] In a number of colonies, elections or other forms of popular consultation were held prior to independence which gave people an opportunity to express their opinions, but these were organized and run
by the responsible colonial government. One to which attention might particularly be called was the
referendum on the De Gaulle Constitution in October 1958 which gave the French colonies an opportunity to opt out by voting "no" and which was utilized for that purpose by Guinea.

the Assembly majority had the right to reach its own conclusion as to the status of particular territories, overruling, if necessary, the official determination of status made by the administering authority.

THE ALL-OUT ATTACK ON COLONIALISM SINCE 1960

The year 1960 marked the decisive swing away from the continued toleration of colonialism in the UN.[5] From the multiplicity of happenings in that busy year, two distinctive events, each of which had many repercussions, may be singled out. One was the admission to UN membership of seventeen ex-colonial states, all of them African except for Cyprus. Among them were not only by far the most populous of the African states, Nigeria, but also Belgium's Congo which from almost the opening days of its independence has imposed unique burdens on the UN. The other outstanding event of the year was the passage on December 14 by the General Assembly of Resolution 1514(XV), the Declaration on the Granting of Independence to Colonial Countries and Peoples. On the basis of this Declaration, which can without too gross exaggeration be taken as almost an amendment of the Charter, a drastic extension of the anticolonial activities of the UN has been undertaken, including the establishment of the Special Committee on Colonial Independence to pursue and harass the colonial powers in relation to their remaining dependent territories.[6]

The representation of Africa in the UN, after a decade's lack of motion after 1945, began to rise with the admission of Libya in 1955 and three other North African states, including the Sudan, in 1956. The independence of Ghana in 1957, promptly followed by its UN membership, is usually taken as the watershed which marks Africa's breach with colonialism. With the single exception of Guinea, which found itself grievously in the bad graces of General de Gaulle because of its "no" vote in the 1958 constitutional plebiscite, no French-speaking African state south of the Sahara had found its way to independence until the grand sweep of 1960 when no less than thirteen French colonies or trusteeships were voted into the UN as independent states, accompanied by the Congo (Leopoldville), Somalia, and Nigeria.

[5] For a statistical examination of anticolonialism and the corresponding decline of pro-colonial sentiment as reflected in Assembly voting in the first sixteen sessions, see Edward T. Rowe, "The Emerging Anti-Colonial Consensus in the United Nations," *The Journal of Conflict Resolution,* September 1964 (Vol. 8, No. 3), pp. 209–230. Breaking these sessions down into eight sets of two each—the first and second, third and fourth, etc.—and rating roll-call votes in terms of their anticolonial or pro-colonial character, he presents a tabulation in which the highest anticolonial vote of a set of sessions rises fairly steadily from 38.6 percent of the membership in the first two sessions to a peak of 79.8 percent in the fifteenth and sixteenth sessions (1960–1961), whereas the lowest anticolonial (or highest pro-colonial) vote declines in the same period from 47.4 percent to 1.9 percent.

[6] See Rupert Emerson, *Self-Determination Revisited in the Era of Decolonization* (Occasional Papers in International Affairs, No. 9) (Cambridge, Mass: Center for International Affairs, Harvard University, December 1964).

Save perhaps in the sense of having created a general atmosphere conducive to the overthrow of colonialism, the small role played by the UN in the proceedings may be easily illustrated by two comments. It was evident to any informed observer that the Congo was singularly ill-prepared to take over the management of its own affairs. Although the Belgians had laid foundations on which self-government might in some future time be built, they had created virtually nothing either in the way of cadres of experienced Congolese or of institutions fitted to the needs of a new African government. Here, it might utopianly be thought, was an open invitation to inventiveness on the part of the UN to seek to meet in advance what had from the outset a threatening look, perhaps by making use of the trusteeship provisions which, among other things, allowed the UN itself to become the administering authority. But the UN was in no way consulted before the fact of independence, nor did it have any jurisdiction to intervene until the speedy outbreak of trouble forced a long-continued and in many ways unsatisfactory and frustrating intervention in the affairs of a state which shortly became a UN Member and hence could no longer be treated overtly as anyone's ward.

Another African example of a quite different variety is furnished by the contrast between Nigeria and the congeries of states which emerged from the French colonial empire. In the Nigerian case, the United Kingdom, through the devices of federalism and otherwise, held together in a single state, and hence as a single Member of the UN, a substantially larger number of people than those embraced in all of French Africa. In the latter instance, however, due to the working of the *loi cadre,* to French manipulations in Paris and in the field, and to the rivalries of African political leaders, the two preexisting federations of French West and Equatorial Africa, which France had reported on as units to the UN under Article 73, were broken down into their twelve component parts. To these were added the two trust territories of Togo and Cameroun and Madagascar. In brief, the smaller number of heirs of the French colonial empire in sub-Saharan Africa emerged as fifteen states, many of them with little hope of strength and vitality, and endowed with fifteen votes to overwhelm the single vote of their Nigerian colleague. It is obvious that such decisions and outcomes must have a significant bearing on the future of the UN, but it had no claim to be consulted or to take action at any stage prior to its extending a greeting to its newly sovereign Members.

What one is to make of the multiplication of the number of small Members of the UN is obviously a matter on which there can be wide divergences in judgment, but it is my own opinion on a variety of counts, including the well-being of both the peoples involved and the Organization itself, that it is undesirable to crowd the UN benches in this fashion. Regrettably, despite the fact that it is an expensive matter in both men and money, membership in the UN tends to be self-perpetuating and self-strengthening, as against the creation of unions or federations, because it gives the country, or, more particularly, its political leaders, an opportunity to make their appearance on the world stage and to join in pronouncements and decisions on global destiny.

A consideration of a quite different order is that the membership of all the former colonial territories as well as such noncolonial neighbors as Liberia, Saudi Arabia, Afghanistan, and Thailand furnishes an incomparable opportunity for the delegates of these states to meet, to compare notes, and to work out common lines of action. Although each ordinarily remains free to speak and to vote on UN measures as it sees fit, the ability to function as a bloc, especially in matters relating to colonialism, is of real importance. For the African states, occupying a vast continent still sparsely equipped with means of transport and communication but with strong pretensions toward pan-African solidarity, it is peculiarly a boon to be able to maintain the kind of continuous contact which UN membership offers.

The other major event of what has been called, because of the influx of new states, the African year of the UN was the passage of the Declaration on Colonial Independence by a formally unanimous vote but with the noteworthy abstention of nine states, including the United States, the United Kingdom, France, Belgium, and Australia. The immediate starting point for this Declaration was a Soviet request, laid before the Assembly by no less a personage than Nikita Khrushchev himself, for the adoption of a declaration demanding immediate freedom for all non-self-governing countries. A more moderate and less precipitate substitute declaration, sponsored by 43 Asian and African Members and carried through to victory by acclaim, based itself on the ardent desire of the peoples of the world for "the end of colonialism in all its manifestations," echoing the condemnation first broadcast to the world at Bandung in 1955. In its major provisions this Declaration: 1) ruled that the subjection of peoples to alien subjugation is contrary to the Charter; 2) recognized the right of all peoples to self-determination; 3) denied that inadequacy of preparation could ever be a pretext for delaying independence; 4) called for an end of all repressive measures directed against dependent peoples; 5) sought immediate steps to transfer all powers to the people of territories not yet independent; and 6) held incompatible with the Charter any attempt to disrupt the national unity and territorial integrity of a country. In brief, colonialism was stripped of its legitimacy and the self-determination of colonial peoples substituted for it, with a further guarantee of their independent integrity once freedom was achieved.

The outlawing of colonialism on the triple grounds that it denied fundamental human rights, was contrary to the Charter, and impeded the promotion of world peace gave the ever growing contingent of anticolonialists every opportunity they could ask for to carry the war into the enemy camp, but always with the highly important reservation that the limitations which hedged in the ability of UN organs to act and to compel action on the part of states could not be substantially affected by a General Assembly resolution. Colonialism might be outlawed, but no quantity of UN resolutions could force Portugal to acknowledge that its territories were non-self-governing and must therefore be reported on, compel South Africa to change its ways in relation to *apartheid* or South West Africa, or make the United Kingdom admit a UN mission of investigation to Aden or order Southern Rhodesia to democratize its constitution. The result was in part a stalemate. The stalemate was by no means complete, however, because the anticolonial forces gained in confidence and strength as they went along. Both the Secretariat and such "neutralists" as there were in this controversy moved increasingly toward an overt acceptance of anticolonialism, and the colonial powers no longer responded with the same united defensiveness since, with the exception of Portugal and to a lesser degree of Spain, they had already abandoned so many of their holdings and positions as to make continued controversy on the old lines unprofitable. The UN could no more enforce its anticolonial decisions after 1960 than before, but both the atmosphere and the facts of the case had undergone radical change.

The proliferation of committees dealing with one or another aspect of the colonial problem indicated the extent of the Assembly's interest, if not the tidiness and coherence of its organization, and the Security Council was also drawn in from time to time. In addition to the Trusteeship Council, the Assembly's own Fourth Committee, and the Committee on Information, there were committees dealing with South Africa's *apartheid* policies, with South West Africa, and with territories under Portuguese administration. The chosen instrument for the colonial problem in the large, however, was the Special Committee,[7] first endowed with seventeen and then 24 members, which was established late in 1961 to oversee and to speed the implementation of the 1960 Declaration on Colonial Independence. The zeal and vitality with which the Special Committee pursued its purpose has led to its taking over the labors of other committees, including, in 1963, the functions of the Committee on Information. This action, embodied in Resolution 1970(XVIII) of December 16, 1963, was justified on the ground that

> all United Nations activities concerning Non-Self-Governing Territories should now be co-ordinated and consolidated, with a view to the immediate ending of colonialism,

thus also bringing the trust territories within the domain of the Special Committee.[8]

[7] The impressive full title of this body is the Special Committee on the Situation with Regard to the Implementation of the Declaration on the Granting of Independence to Colonial Countries and Peoples.
[8] See *Yearbook of the United Nations, 1963* (United Nations: Office of Public Information, 1965), p. 443.

Perhaps the most significant feature of the Special Committee was its composition which, differing radically from the balance between administering and nonadministering members in the Trusteeship Council and the Committee on Information, more nearly resembled its parent body, the Assembly itself. Thus, in 1963 the Special Committee had a balanced membership only in the sense that twelve of its 24 members were Asian or African, but four more, including the Soviet Union, were drawn from the Communist world, which could be counted on for full anticolonial sympathy, and three were drawn from Latin America. Only five members represented the West—the United States, the United Kingdom, Italy, Denmark, and Australia—and they were obviously in a hopeless minority when they chose to challenge the anticolonial steamroller.

The whole purpose of the establishment of the Special Committee was to throw the full weight of the UN behind the complete and prompt application of the 1960 Declaration, but, as has been seen, its powers were necessarily limited despite the evident intent of the majority from the outset to make it an action body which would deal directly with the colonial powers and their management of particular dependencies. In the resolution setting it up, the Committee was requested to examine the implementation of the Declaration and to suggest how it might be promoted. To this end, in a sonorous but imprecise paragraph, the Committee was directed by Resolution 1654(XVI) of November 27, 1961:

> To carry out its task by employment of all means which it will have at its disposal within the framework of the procedures and facilities which it shall adopt for the proper discharge of its functions.

In 1962, "noting with profound regret" the large number of cases in which the Declaration had not been implemented, the Assembly by Resolution 1810(XVII) of December 17 enlarged the Special Committee and invited it to propose specific measures for the speedy and total application of the Declaration to all territories which had not yet attained independence.[9] In addition, it was to take to the Security Council any developments in the colonial sphere which might threaten international peace and security.

Given the wide sweep of the decolonization which had already taken place, the territories with which the Special Committee and other UN bodies have dealt since 1960 have in almost all instances involved special problems of one sort or another which explained why they had not already been removed from the non-self-governing category. A Special Committee document of October 1963[10] set out a provisional list of no less than 64 territories in which

---

[9] One effect of the use of the term "independence" in this resolution was to enable the Committee to continue to belabor the United Kingdom concerning Southern Rhodesia, a territory commanding much UN attention, which the United Kingdom has claimed is self-governing and hence beyond the range of corrective British action but which had not become independent.

[10] UN Document A/5446, Annex I.

it was held the Declaration had not yet been implemented. Of these, 40 were British, for the most part little islands scattered about the face of the globe, representing the days when Britain was an indefatigable collector of scraps of empire. It should be noted that no Soviet-controlled territory has been listed or investigated by the Special Committee, nor have any of the still quasi-colonial attachments of France, including French Somaliland.

In a rough way the territories involved can be broken down into three or four major categories, although there are some—such, for example, as Hong Kong—whose circumstances are unique and defy any general classification.

The first and least troublesome category embraced colonies which were in fact already explicitly moving toward independence—Kenya, Nyasaland, Northern Rhodesia, Zanzibar—and where all that was necessary was for the Committee to make sure that the United Kingdom lived up to its announced intentions. A somewhat more difficult problem, of much the same order, concerned the three High Commission Territories of Basutoland, Bechuanaland, and Swaziland where advance to self-government and probable independence was affected by the fact that they fell within the orbit of South Africa. Special circumstances also complicated the situation of British Guiana where the British were no doubt as sincere in asserting their desire to get out as they were elsewhere but where racial conflict and the threat of a Communist takeover inhibited action and, it is asserted, brought the United States into the picture in an effort to prevent the emergence of another Cuba.

Problems of still greater difficulty confronted the UN in its efforts to deal with the white-dominated and in considerable part white-settled countries of southern Africa: the large Portuguese territories of Angola and Mozambique; Southern Rhodesia, still firmly in the grip of a white minority and only tenuously linked to the United Kingdom; and South West Africa over which South Africa had no intention of relinquishing its control. Two other large territories which had only made a tentative start toward self-government were Australian-administered Papua and New Guinea, where at an earlier stage it would have been appropriate to plead the still primitive character of the bulk of the inhabitants, a contention now expressly ruled out by the 1960 Declaration.

The most puzzling feature of the bulk of the remainder of the territories in whose destiny the UN has become involved was how to determine what constituted a sensible and viable solution for a widely variegated assortment of dependencies whose one common factor was the smallness of their population. By the terms of the Declaration, by subsequent pronouncements of UN bodies, and by the native bent of the majority of the UN's Members, the inclination has been very strong to insist that independence was the only answer, although earlier Assembly resolutions had accepted the idea that a dependency could achieve a respectable status of full self-government not only through independence but also through other forms of association on an equal basis with the metropolitan or some other country.[11] On the face of it, it is open to serious doubt whether it is in the best interest of either the peoples concerned or of the world at large that such territories as the United States' Virgin Islands or New Zealand's Cook Islands or Australia's Christmas Island should become sovereign members of international society. Abhorrent as the thought may be to the more ardent anticolonialists, it can also not be left out of account that there are occasional instances in which continued association with the metropolitan power on appropriate terms is more acceptable to the people of a territory than is independence. One such case, always available for international dispute, appears clearly to be that of Puerto Rico where general public sentiment, insofar as there is dissatisfaction with the present commonwealth status, prefers statehood in the United States to independence despite the clamor of a small body of nationalists. A case which seems to reduce the matter to absurdity is that of the trust territory of Nauru, the exhaustion of whose phosphate deposits will force evacuation of the island in the not distant future and for whose less than 5,000 people the Soviet Union has demanded full and sovereign independence.

If a single case may be selected somewhat at random to illustrate the Special Committee's mode of action and the forthrightness of its recommendations, it might center on the resolution adopted on June 23, 1964, deploring the United Kingdom's failure to grant independence to British Guiana or even to set a date for it.[12] The divisions within the Committee are indicated by the fact that eighteen members voted for the resolution, while the United Kingdom, the United States, and Australia opposed it, and Italy, Denmark, and Venezuela abstained. Reaffirming the inalienable right of the people of British Guiana to independence, the resolution called upon the United Kingdom to fix the date for independence without delay, asked that all political prisoners and detainees be released and that the state of emergency be ended, and appealed to the political leaders and others to take immediate steps for harmony and peace. Responding to the request of several of its members that constitutional experts be sent to the territory to assist in drafting a constitution, the Special Committee established a subcommittee of good offices to visit Guiana and to take any necessary steps to implement the resolutions adopted in relation to the territory. But the United Kingdom promptly protested that its long-established attitude toward UN visits to British territories made it impossible to agree to a visit by the subcommittee. In all the circumstances it must be a wide-open question whether the Committee's prodding on Guiana has had any significant effect on the United Kingdom's attitudes or actions, but at the least London must be amply aware of the outcry in the UN which any retrograde step would produce.

[11] See, for example, General Assembly Resolution 742 (VIII) of November 27, 1953, which lists "factors indicative of the attainment of independence or of other separate systems of self-government."

[12] See UN Monthly Chronicle, July 1964 (Vol. 1, No. 3), pp. 35–43. The text of the resolution is given on p. 35. It is also contained in UN Document A/AC.109/86.

FUTURE PROSPECTS

It is unhappily plausible to assume that perhaps the most difficult and frustrating phases of the decolonization program still lie ahead. If any appreciable quantities of goodwill and intelligence are available, it should be possible to deal with the problem of the disposition of the many little leftover bits and pieces of empire without stirring up significant international controversy, although it is also true that various of them, such as the United States' Trust Territory of the Pacific Islands, Gibraltar, or Brunei, could very handily be used by anyone interested in so doing to stir up trouble. The two major spheres, however, that seem likely to challenge the ability of the UN to manage them are the discovery and implementation of acceptable solutions for the countries of southern Africa and the advancement of political, economic, and social development.

The record to date of the ending of colonialism for the great majority of those who had been subjected to alien rule has been a mixture of surprisingly peaceful transition to independence, as in the case of all the French sub-Saharan colonies, and of bitter colonial wars, as in Algeria and Indochina. In some instances the UN has been involved and in others it has either been wholly an outsider or has played only an incidental or tangential role. Two special cases involving the use or the threat of force in which the UN was involved in very different fashions were the Indian seizure of Goa and the transfer to Indonesia of West Irian. The case of Goa is a peculiarly striking illustration of the proposition, generally accepted by the UN majority, that all colonialism is illegitimate and that the use of force to overthrow it is therefore justified.

The degree to which the UN may become entangled in the actual working out of the problems of southern Africa is impossible to determine at this point, but it has become more and more deeply concerned with them as the years have gone by. From the opening days of the Organization, South Africa has been on the UN docket in relation to the treatment of Indians, the *apartheid* question, and the status and disposition of South West Africa. Pressure has constantly grown to force the country, through boycotts and possible sanctions, to institute reforms of a democratic and egalitarian nature fitted to a period in which the dominant call has been for liberation through self-determination, but the Afrikaner government has shown no inclination to give way at any point. There are many who look to the forthcoming International Court decision on South West Africa in the case brought by Ethiopia and Liberia in the hope that it may furnish an opening wedge for action in relation not only to that country but to South Africa as well.

The Portuguese, who appear for the time being to have successfully contained the revolt in Angola but are now also under attack in Mozambique, have likewise given no indication that they are prepared to make any significant concessions on the basic issue of acknowledging that the inhabitants of their several territories have a right to self-determination. It is, however, difficult to conceive that they can hold out very long against the internal disaffections and the pressures of the countries of the Organization of African Unity (OAU) and most of the rest of the world in the UN. Similarly, Southern Rhodesia, despite its present refusal to move toward racial integration at more than a snail's pace, seems sure to be swept into the currents of the winds of change. South Africa, with its population of more than 3,000,000 whites, its advanced and prosperous economy, and its strong military forces, gives every promise of being the hardest nut to crack, but it is always possible that violence might break out in any segment of southern Africa, presenting the UN with some exceedingly difficult choices. The presumption must be that pressure by the UN on the southern African countries will increase, but it is not easy to see how a winning combination of forces can be brought into being.

The greatest positive contribution which the UN and the specialized agencies can make is in the broad and vital sphere of development—a sphere to which an immense amount of attention has already been devoted, even though the gap between the advanced and the underdeveloped has widened rather than narrowed in the two postwar decades of the development drive. Until independence was achieved, responsibility rested with the colonial powers, and the international agencies were restricted in their access to the non-self-governing territories. After independence the gates were open for technical assistance, financial aid, and other programs, but the resources of the UN and its associated bodies were inevitably too limited to make possible any full-scale attack upon the monumental problems with which the new countries and, through them, the entire world have been confronted. Whether the issue be posed in terms of peacekeeping through the elimination of injustice and causes of friction, of rounding out mankind's economic potential, or of a humanitarian recognition that internationally as well as domestically the rich must come to the aid of the poor and attack the causes of poverty, there can be no doubt that development will be a major concern of the UN for a long time to come. The new Members of the UN are highly unlikely to let the rest of the world forget what they see as its obligation to them, an obligation derived in part from the sins and extortions of imperialism for which recompense must be made.

A particularly grievous need of all the new countries, varying greatly in scale among them, is the shortage in trained and expert manpower for administrative and other purposes. A bold new program was proposed by Secretary-General Hammarskjöld in 1956 when he pointed out that

> nations emerging from long foreign rule generally lack an independent administrative tradition and a social structure within which it is easy to build up a class of national administrators.

He suggested that the gap might be filled by the creation of a new international career service of men and women prepared to work in the underdeveloped countries as public officials integrated into the national administrations.[13] As he pointed out, this kind of service would be distinguished from the usual technical assistance programs in that, instead of merely giving advice, it was expected that the new style officials would serve in an executive capacity in the governments to which they were seconded. After making its way through the UN's machinery, the Secretary-General's plan found modest support in Assembly Resolution 1256 (XIII) of November 14, 1958, which won general approval although the Soviet Union and some others decried the idea that international officials should be assigned operating posts in national governments. In more recent years, under the UN program for the provision of Operational, Executive, and Administrative Personnel (OPEX), this has been continued and somewhat expanded, provision being made for some 75–85 posts a year. OPEX, of course, is merely one phase of the multifaceted attack on the problem of underdevelopment which has been carried on by the UN and its associated agencies, with a greater or less degree of coordination with the bilateral programs of a number of countries. A quite different approach was reflected in the creation of the economic commissions for Asia, Africa, and Latin America.

Much the greatest single venture in furnishing aid, or, more broadly in seeking to prevent a country from disintegrating into ruin, was the UN Operation in the Congo (ONUC), which had its marked successes as well as its failures but which has little prospect of being repeated elsewhere for a variety of political and financial reasons. An even less likely prospect is that there should be resort at this late date to either a multistate or a direct UN trusteeship as a means of bringing peoples to a point where it is reasonable to hope that they can run their affairs without danger of disaster or of slipping back into colonial dependence. Such a proposal was put forward for Korea at the end of the war to ease the transition from Japanese rule to independence, but nothing came of it. In the case of West Irian the UN takeover was a brief and tentative caretaker operation rather than serious tutelage, even though a persuasive argument might have been made for the desirability of tutelage under disinterested auspices. The areas which would be most likely to profit from such treatment in the foreseeable future are South West Africa and the Portuguese colonies because of their wholly inadequate experience in self-government. In the aftermath of the Congo, however, such a proposal seems to lack reality, save in the improbable event that the permanent members of the Security Council can agree on a common positive program. It is, indeed, quite possible that other countries, already UN Members, will draft into periods

[13] See the Secretary-General's speech of May 30, 1956, at McGill University in *United Nations Review*, July 1956 (Vol. 3, No. 1), p. 12. He further referred to this scheme in the *Introduction to the Annual Report of the Secretary-General on the Work of the Organization, 16 June 1955–15 June 1956* (General Assembly *Official Records* [11th session], Supplement No. 1A), p. 5.

of threatening decay when some established form of international supervision might be invaluable, but the existence of international machinery effectively available to deal with such problems is probably more dubious now than it was at earlier stages in the UN's history. In view of the fact that independence has already come to so many of the colonial peoples, it becomes, perhaps, merely an academic matter to suggest that if inadequacy of preparedness can no longer serve as a ground for delaying independence, the need will be all the greater to extend assistance to those who achieve it unprepared.

Reflecting on the experience of Egypt, Lord Cromer concluded that international institutions were formidable checks to action and that administrative internationalism tended to create administrative impotence:

> Any action often involves a presumed advantage accorded to some rival nation, and it is a principle of internationalism, which is scornfully rejected in theory but too often recognized as a guide for practical action, that it is better to do nothing, even though evil may ensue, than to allow good to be done at the expense of furthering the interests, or of exalting the reputation of an international rival.[14]

Great changes have taken place on the international scene since Lord Cromer's day, but international rivalries persist, as do their inhibiting effects on international action. Despite the fact that all states profess their adherence to the cause of development, it has been impossible to establish it as an enterprise to which all would jointly contribute and in which all would share. The international unity without which the UN is clearly incapable of dealing with so crucial a challenge has given way instead to cleavages and rivalries, including those within the third world itself, which impose sharp limits on the ability of the UN to act. Even when the Cold War has been taken into account, only part of the story has been told because neither of the blocs has been able to maintain coherent unity. With the shifting circumstances the West has come to be divided within itself, and the Soviet-Chinese rupture has led to further defections in the ranks of the satellites. Lord Cromer would recognize the paralysis which sometimes ensues as the different categories of rivals suspiciously eye each other.

Except for a handful of the toughest cases, the work of decolonization has been very largely achieved, at least in the sense of securing formal independence. What is left to be done is the very large order of attempting to ensure that those who have been liberated have some measure of continued operating access to the modern world. The UN has immense tasks before it, but it still remains to be proved that the structure of the international society will allow it to accomplish them.

---

[14] *Modern Egypt* (London: Macmillan and Co., Ltd., 1908), Vol. II, p. 304.

The United Nations and Human Rights

LOUIS HENKIN

SOME writing about the UN may suggest that there are those who conceive of the elephant that is the United Nations largely in terms of its human rights programs. The allusion to the fabled task of the blind men is not intended to impugn the vision of those who concentrate on that significant United Nations activity. The United Nations is a multifaceted and incongruous body, and the broadest view would not permit seeing it whole and in detail at the same time. Aware of the inevitable distortion that concentration brings, I would on this occasion look at this particular limb, hoping not to lose sight of the fact that it is part of a living if strange beast in a real world.

HUMAN RIGHTS IN THE UN SCHEME

Human rights would occupy a significant chapter in any story of the United Nations. Their place in the original conception of the United Nations is underlined in the Charter: Faith in human rights is "reaffirmed" in the preamble; Article 1 proclaims international cooperation to promote human rights as one of the purposes of the United Nations; Articles 55 and 56 make the achievement of universal respect for human rights one of the few explicit undertakings of United Nations membership; both the General Assembly and the Economic and Social Council (ECOSOC) are charged to make recommendations to promote human rights (Articles 13 and 62); and a human rights commission is the only subsidiary organ expressly ordained (Article 68). Human rights have figured prominently in the activities of the United Nations since its creation. In every session they have preoccupied one of the major committees of the General Assembly, and every year the Economic and Social Council has struggled with the subject. The Commission on Human Rights has had a singular history among United Nations bodies of continuous, difficult, and creditable activity. Human rights have also been of special con-

LOUIS HENKIN is Professor of Law, Columbia University.

cern to nongovernmental organizations accredited to the United Nations, and numerous works have been written on the international protection of human rights.

The results of this labor have been described elsewhere, and most of them are well-known. A place of honor, surely, belongs to the Universal Declaration of Human Rights prepared by the Human Rights Commission under the chairmanship of Mrs. Eleanor Roosevelt and unanimously approved by the General Assembly in 1948. The Commission for many years has labored to prepare a number of additional draft covenants on human rights, and we are now in sight of the end of the process with their approval by the General Assembly. The Assembly has recently approved the Declaration of the Rights of the Child (1959) and the Declaration on the Elimination of All Forms of Racial Discrimination (1963); other draft declarations will soon be presented for adoption. The General Assembly itself has sponsored a number of human rights conventions, beginning with the Convention on the Prevention and Punishment of the Crime of Genocide of 1948, some of which are now in force. In addition to recurrent exhortations by the General Assembly in support of human rights generally, there have been a number of resolutions on specific human rights issues, from condemnations of violations in the Soviet Union (1948) to the current campaign against *apartheid* in the Republic of South Africa.

There are, too, the small, important, undramatic activities every year and every day—the preparation of the annual *Yearbook on Human Rights,* the programs of national reports, studies, advisory services, fellowships, and seminars. These represent efforts by the Assembly, ECOSOC, the Human Rights Commission and its Subcommission on the Prevention of Discrimination and the Protection of Minorities, the Commission on the Status of Women, and—not least—the Secretariat; in addition, the specialized agencies, particularly the International Labor Organization (ILO) and the United Nations Educational, Scientific and Cultural Organization (UNESCO), have had important human rights programs in their respective domains and have also cooperated in the programs of the United Nations. One might even define human rights activities to include the postwar resettlement work of the International Refugee Organization (IRO) and the continuing efforts of the UN High Commissioner for Refugees (UNHCR) to assure their rehabilitation after resettlement.

While the record of the United Nations is clear, what that record means is less clear. One may seek meaning in terms of the United Nations itself. Why has it done what it has done? Why has it left undone what it might have done? One may seek meaning in the purpose of all this activity—in the impact of the United Nations and its programs on the individual rights of individual human beings in every country of the world.

What Has Been Achieved

It is agreeable on a ceremonial occasion to assert that twenty years of United Nations activity have been important in promoting the cause of human rights.

The achievements are modest, subtle, gradual. Foremost, the existence of the United Nations, the language of the Charter and its dissemination among all peoples, the adoption and invocation of the Declaration, and mountains of documents and years of discussions have made human rights a subject of international concern and indelibly established human rights in the aspirations of peoples, even in the consciences of governments. Governments may continue to claim that how they treat their own inhabitants is of concern to them alone; increasingly it is a losing claim with little hope that it can prevail in politics if not in law. The international concern with human rights has international consequences spilling back into national behavior. The political organs of the United Nations hardly refrain from discussing any human rights issue which any Member puts on the agenda, whether forced labor in the Soviet Union or the treatment of Buddhists in Vietnam. And though obviously impossible to prove, one may assert, with whatever confidence, that the existence of the General Assembly, ECOSOC, and the Human Rights Commission with the ever present threat of investigation and criticism helps to deter governments from blatant violations. No doubt, too, new international concern with human rights influences the judgments of international institutions, even, perhaps, when the International Court of Justice concludes that it has jurisdiction to judge the human rights policies of the Republic of South Africa under its mandate in South West Africa.

Of special significance is the Universal Declaration of Human Rights. Its unanimous authority and high prestige have been frequently invoked in criticism or exhortation of nations. The Declaration is reflected in the draft covenants which, after many difficult years, the General Assembly will soon urge upon nations in the hope that legal obligation will add to other influences to improve the behavior of governments toward minorities and individuals. More subtly, but perhaps more surely, the Declaration has permeated international life and influenced national institutions. By subtle processes, it may even be acquiring some yet uncertain status in international law. Whatever its legal quality, the Declaration has set a standard by which national behavior can be measured and to which nations can aspire. The Declaration has helped to give contour and content to the generalities of the Charter, reflecting the spirit and the needs of the day.

It is instructive to compare the provisions of the Declaration with those of an eighteenth century bill of rights. Built on traditions of British liberty and the philosophy of Locke, the United States Bill of Rights was wholly a charter of limitations, rooted in the view that "that government governs best which governs least." The Declaration reflects other philosophies, other needs. It too is concerned with what government should not do *to* the individual; it is concerned at least as much with what government should do *for* the individual. Taking contemporary notions of the purposes of government, the Declaration focused and refined them for use in national and international life. Its influence, if it cannot be measured, can readily be traced. The Declaration is reflected in new constitutions of new nations. It is invoked by many, in or out of the United Nations, who seek to exhort or press governments to raise their standards of behavior even toward their own citizens. The Declaration—with the Charter and the United Nations institution—may perhaps be credited also with influencing nations with similar political goals and more developed traditions of freedom and welfare to build legal obligations and institutions for the protection and promotion of human rights, as in the Convention for the Protection of Human Rights and Fundamental Freedoms (1950) and the European Court of Human Rights.

Finally, the United Nations may be credited with at least one specific and major advance. White racism is dying, and the United Nations has been a major instrument in its inevitable demise. As national policy, discrimination on the basis of race or color is no longer tolerated by the international community. Indeed, no nation would admit to such a policy, even to deny that it is the business of other nations or of the United Nations. South African *apartheid* is not an exception. The South African government vehemently denies that *apartheid* discriminates against the black population. The United Nations, in turn, is vehement in its condemnation of *apartheid* and is seriously considering sanctions against it. Other countries, too, must take account of the attitudes of nations concentrated in the United Nations. Even the United States Civil Rights Act of 1964 owes its existence in some measure to the subtle influences of United Nations concern to end racial discrimination.

NATIONAL BEHAVIOR IN TODAY'S WORLD

It would be agreeable to be able to say also that now, thanks to the existence, efforts, or influence of the United Nations, there is wide and growing respect for human rights. Unfortunately, even the most sympathetic observation does not warrant such a cheerful conclusion. If this is disappointing, disappointment may reflect unwarranted expectations. Even during the postwar international honeymoon, optimism about national respect for human rights was not solidly founded. There was no widespread and eager domestic commitment by nations to enhance the human rights of their citizens. Surely there was no rush, for example, to write human rights into international law and give them whatever influence law can bring to bear on the behavior of nations. The adoption of the United Nations Charter, with its numerous references to human rights, did not reflect determination to establish forthwith a new age in human rights. The Charter fathers, it should be recalled, did not build high. The generalities of the Charter were hopes, not undertakings, not even programs. In fact, these Charter provisions seem hardly to have troubled the most tyrannical of governments among the original signatories. One cannot even assume that the adoption of the Charter entailed a resolve by Member nations to change or mend their ways. There is little evidence, too, that nations which later adhered to the Charter took more seriously its purposes, exhortations, and pledges of cooperation to promote human rights or recognized that these were in any way relevant to their domestic affairs or to their treatment of individuals, minorities, or even majorities. The unanimous vote for the Universal Declaration and the extended, earnest, sincere debates on the draft international covenants on human rights in the Commission, ECOSOC, or the Assembly have not reflected the domestic policies of nations.

With the end of war, observance of human rights was required of defeated nations in the peace treaties. The victors were not subject to similar obligations. That these provisions were imposed on the vanquished gave them the character of punishment, of "reparations." They were not the responsibility of free nations generally. Their quality as punishment inevitably made them resented, nor could they survive the fate of the treaties as a whole when they later fell casualty to the political realignments of the Cold War.

Twenty years after World War II one cannot say that in most countries the rights of individuals are duly respected or even that they stand measurably higher than in 1945. While nations have asserted the dependence of international peace and security on national observance of human rights, while they have proclaimed the interdependence and indivisibility of human rights throughout the world, nations have also insisted that their treatment of their citizens are their concern. The relation of human rights to peace was visible in retrospect to the conquerors of Hitler and to the victims of Hitler's Germany. Some may see it today in regard to *apartheid* in South Africa or wherever white governments violate rights of colored groups in circumstances redolent of colonialism. Some may be ready to see it more broadly in the failings of other nations as well. Few appear prepared to build a kingdom of rights with beams taken from their own eye. Many have adhered to some human rights conventions, but it might be suggested that they have agreed to outlaw only what no longer exists for them, e.g., slavery, or what they cannot conceive of as relevant to them, e.g., genocide. Even for these conventions they have not agreed to serious measures for their enforcement.

If these attitudes are disappointing, they should bring no surprise. The fate of human rights around the world reflects inevitably the major influences of our time. Human rights fare well where there are traditions of freedom, stable political institutions, economic well-being, ethnic and cultural homogeneity or concord, and freedom from external fears and foreign crises. These conditions prevail in some countries in varying degree. In others, however, there are forces which discourage human rights. Ours is an age of revolution: Revolutions are not conducive to respect for human rights, and class revolutions or colonial revolutions in particular leave an aftermath of repression. Ours is the day of newly independent nations, jealous of their "sovereignty" and hardly amenable to international direction in their internal affairs. The rights of the individual are not yet high on their own list of domestic values and aspirations. The human rights behavior of other nations, too—except where colonialism or race is involved—is not high on their list of concerns; they are particularly unconcerned where repression is the fruit or concomitant of revolution.

The new nations—and many old ones—are eager to leap into a new technological age. For many of them the drive for development uncovers the conflicting values and cruel dilemmas which are subsumed under "human rights" in our times. In many countries, concentration on rapid industrialization and economic development appears to call for rigidly planned and controlled economies which may indeed enhance the economic and perhaps the social rights of a people. But at least in countries lacking traditions of political rights, concentration on development brings temptations of totalitarianism, including totalitarian political mobilization not conducive to free political rights and institutions. These differing attitudes of different nations to different human values have found expression in the drafting of the human rights covenants. They contributed to a bifurcation in the drafting effort, resulting in two draft covenants, a covenant on civil and political rights and one on economic, social, and cultural rights. This separation was perhaps designed to permit different handling by members of the international community; it makes it possible, of course, for a nation to adhere to one covenant and not the other. Unhappily, for many nations the two covenants may reflect an apparently inevitable choice.

Ours, too, is the age of ideological conflict. Even in times of "coexistence" Communism has entailed a closed society and has not proved itself able to afford substantial freedom. Surely there was little hope for liberal treatment of the person when totalitarian ideology found itself in the Cold War. Under Joseph Stalin, all now admit, repression in the Soviet Union was the order of life. Even aliens, long protected by international law, could not expect justice and other human rights, there or in other Communist countries. And, in war, even Cold War, the most enlightened nations too may succumb to panic; the still fresh memory of Senator Joseph R. McCarthy reminds us of dangers to individual rights in the United States. The Cold War, on the other hand, occasioned those particular advances in human rights reflected in asylum and the assimilation of refugees. It produced a notable and special advance when, in Korea, with the approval of the General Assembly, the principle of voluntary repatriation of prisoners was accepted and given effect.

Local or regional political controversies have also had their unhappy effects. Religious wars in India and Pakistan have left many dead or homeless. Tribal wars in Africa have unleashed massacres and new floods of refugees. The politics of the Middle East have for years kept hundreds of thousands of Arabs in camps instead of providing for their settlement, and no resolution is in sight.

National behavior on human rights has reflected internal tensions and international forces. Our time has seen the first universal effort, largely through the United Nations, to establish the rights of the individual. Our time has also seen the revolutionary forces, the competing values, the ideological conflict, and the international pressures that hamper progress in human rights.

POLITICS AND HUMAN RIGHTS IN THE UN

Political and economic revolution, domestic instability, international tension, Cold War—these have inhibited the growth of human rights in many parts of the world. Inevitably, these same forces shaped the United Nations and guided its politics and programs and its human rights activities no less than its other preoccupations.

The relevance to human rights of the political character of the United Nations appeared, of course, even in San Francisco and is reflected in the compromises of the Charter. Idealistic goals are enshrined as purposes of the United Nations, and Members undertake to cooperate in their promotion. Political realities and national reluctances are protected by lack of definiteness and definition, by hortatory phrases instead of commitment, by the ultimate availability of "domestic jurisdiction" to dilute obligation and bar scrutiny.

In regard to human rights as elsewhere, the United Nations began early to reveal the *données* of our international society: nations equal in their "sovereignty" and legal status, but unequal in power, wealth, political stability, technological development, social and educational advancement, and traditions and values of freedom and individual rights. Human rights were the domain and responsibility of the General Assembly where all nations had equal voice if not equal influence. But human rights meant something very different in Saudi Arabia, Stalinist Russia, Denmark, or Pakistan. Members could only agree on selected human rights in selected political situations, for example, in dependent areas, not in their own societies. Ultimately, the influence of the Assembly came to be reflected in what could command its temporary majorities.

But Assembly majorities reflect the interdependence of international relations, international issues, and the political character of United Nations diplomacy. Nations which presume to judge the behavior of others in regard to human rights perform a delicate political act affecting relations with that country and with others, in and out of the United Nations, and inviting retaliation. Nations will not lightly risk their good relations with other nations or jeopardize the solidarity of "blocs" or other political groupings for the sake of a principle of human rights or the welfare of some individual in a foreign land.

The human rights activities of the United Nations began to feel, too, the impact of the major forces of our time: the nuclear revolution, the ideological conflict, the irresistible stirring of dependent peoples, and the leap to industrial development. The nuclear revolution has not had a direct impact on the United Nations human rights record. It has of course been indirectly relevant through its effect on the East-West struggle. In the long run it may have the paramount influence, for radical technological transformations will remake societies and their attitudes toward the individual and his rights.

Immediately, perhaps the greatest influence, unfortunately, has been that of the Cold War. The early "discovery" that nations did not have common political interests in the world, and therefore in the United Nations, applied to human rights as well as to international peace and stability. Human rights proved not a common interest but a political football. Except for the early drafting of the Declaration, the Cold War inevitably turned United Nations activity from cooperation in promoting human rights to exploitation of human rights issues for Cold War purposes. Overwhelming majorities, at Western behest, properly condemned forced labor in the Soviet Union, but in immediate import at least the Assembly's action could only be a political attack on the Soviet Union, not a plausible, hopeful effort to terminate forced labor there. Similarly, condemnations of the Soviet assault on Hungary and its citizenry had political motives; they did not offer much hope of ending individual repression there. Fabricated germ warfare charges against the United States obviously did not purpose to promote any human rights.

The political context of UN activities could not be escaped in the Human Rights Commission, surely not when the Assembly considered what the Commission produced. The drafting of covenants continued, but it was soon revealed that nations were not equally prepared to assume obligations or to assume the same obligations, even less to have them implemented and enforced. The political climate in which the covenants were drafted meant that nations were not cooperating to attempt to achieve common, higher standards or to achieve a covenant which might command maximum adherence; they were competing in the image of themselves they sought to project and in efforts to embarrass others. The shattered harmony of the postwar world engendered attitudes and a vocabulary of Cold War not conducive to agreement or cooperation. Attitudes of cooperation in enlightened self-interest—

where it may have existed—soured early and, for example, in the United States, gave way to defensive nationalism. With the Korean War, cooperation with the Soviet Union on anything seemed ludicrous. International institutions came to be judged by whether they could be used to advantage in the Cold War. The "threat" of international cooperation outside or above the Cold War fired sentiment for the Bricker Amendment to amend the United States Constitution in ways designed primarily to deprive the United States of power to adhere to covenants like that on genocide or projected ones on human rights. The Eisenhower Administration helped defeat the Bricker Amendment but, having won the battle, gave away its fruits by renouncing the use of treaties for international legislation to establish common standards and specifically by abjuring for the United States any intention to adhere to the human rights covenants. Later, with some détente, President John F. Kennedy began to reverse this policy by seeking consent of the United States Senate to ratification of three treaties—the Convention on Slavery, the Convention concerning the Abolition of Forced Labor, and the Convention on the Political Rights of Women. Although none of these would add to the protections presently afforded in the United States, it remains to be seen whether the United States Senate will consent. It remains to be seen, too, whether the new policy will be extended by the Johnson Administration to treaties that reach further, that increase the domain of rights even in the United States, and that modify and extend laws of the federal government or of the individual states.

The other major phenomenon of contemporary international society, the struggle to end colonialism, also swallowed up the original purpose of cooperation for promotion of human rights. The gradual elimination of dependent areas and their admission to the UN meant an ever increasing Assembly majority with some agreed attitudes, particularly a determination to extirpate the remnants of white colonialism and white discrimination. These attitudes impinged on the human rights program as well. Of course, they assured the sharpest scrutiny of human rights in dependent areas. Administering powers could not claim "domestic jurisdiction," and inhabitants of these areas had ready champions. But it was a championship of anticolonialism, designed to accelerate "self-determination." It was not an assertion of general standards which other nations, including the champions, were prepared to accept in their own countries. Even the attacks on South African *apartheid*, whether in South West Africa or in South Africa itself, were attacks on white governance of blacks, on racism of colonial flavor, rather than on general violations of human rights. Nations were not ready to admit investigation, scrutiny, criticism, or discussion of the treatment of their own citizens. Discussion of accusations was resisted, of course, by the accused nations; but other nations, too, were reluctant to press charges. All might agree to charge colonial powers; few would agree to intervene in the domestic affairs of other nations lest their relations with the accused nation be jeopardized and lest, too, their own treatment of minorities, opposition parties, political dissidents, foreign tribesmen, or even white settlers also become a proper subject for international intervention. It is not yet clear, for example, whether in the United Nations the abhorrence of racial discrimination will apply to discrimination against whites by black majorities. Clearly, to some governments the fate of white hostages in the Congo (Leopoldville) was not a primary concern and did not justify United States–Belgian "intervention" to save them.

Anticolonialism, like the Cold War, also pervaded the Human Rights Commission and colored the human rights covenants. The United States, having announced that it would not adhere to any covenant, sacrificed effective influence and a role in the drafting; it also antagonized the other members and played into the hands of those who wished to use the Commission's activities for other purposes, sometimes to attack the West. Inevitably, the dominant influence went to nations who in their own societies sacrificed political rights for other goals, including economic rights. The anticolonial atmosphere of the Assembly and the increasing and confident majorities of "new nations" led to the injection of anticolonial issues into the human rights covenants. Self-determination was added to the roster of human rights as an additional weapon against colonialism although there was no suggestion that this was a right of the individual, that the individual could claim it against an unrepresentative government, or that minorities could invoke it to support secession. Similar motivations impelled the suggestion that there was also a human right of "economic self-determination," the right of a "people" to control its economy and its natural resources. Again, immediately, the rights alleged seemed to promise little to individuals. They are of major importance and they may ultimately bring great benefits to many individuals. Their injection into the human rights covenants could only hamper progress on the covenants and reduce further the likelihood of adherence by important nations. Human rights was being used as a political weapon against colonialism or economic imperialism, not to enhance the rights of all persons against all governments.

CHALLENGES AND PROSPECTS

The behavior of nations in regard to human rights has not been distinguished even since 1945. The United Nations has sown for days ahead; it has achieved more than might have been expected, less than might have been hoped. Its efforts have been hampered by sovereign states jealous of their "domestic jurisdiction" and diverted by the Cold War and the supervening struggles to destroy colonialism and to achieve economic development. The prospects—say, for the next twenty years—are uncertain, not hopeless. Their fate will depend on what happens elsewhere in the life of nations.

The most serious danger to individual rights could come from war, including aggravated Cold War; in many nations there are also obstacles to enjoyment of human rights in continuing instability, danger of internal wars, intervention and counterintervention, insurrection, and subversion.

The principal hope for human rights lies in continuing international peace, in reduced international tensions, in internal stability, in developing political institutions, and in rising standards of living. For the most part, human rights can only be promoted indirectly, by promoting welfare in national societies and a peaceful, cooperative international society in which human rights can strike root and grow.

Directed and dedicated programs, in and out of the United Nations, can contribute to that growth. Given the basic conditions that make observance of human rights possible, there can be meaningful influence of nations on each other and of the UN on all. For observance of rights, like their violation, is contagious. Closed societies are increasingly difficult to keep closed and even curtains of iron prove permeable to news and ideas, particularly in this day of revolutionized communications. Even governments that suppress individual rights feel compelled to pay them the homage of hypocrisy, and those who preach, even if they do not yet practice, inevitably keep alive the aspirations and hopes and demands of their citizens. Peoples demand rights which others enjoy; governments are pressed to accord rights which others grant. All governments, moreover, seek friendship and political influence, whether in the United Nations or in ideological or regional groupings; instability and repression at home are not conducive to continued influence and leadership, whether in Africa or in the Communist Bloc. The threat of complaint and criticism—in the United Nations, in a regional organization, before organizations like the International Commission of Jurists, or in the world press—is a deterrent of significance.

Increasing interest in exchange, whether cultural or commercial, will exert its influence: The human rights of aliens are in substantial measure protected by international law and are the concern of their governments; countries interested in tourism or in visiting investors will be careful of their rights. And today, visitors do not come readily where there is domestic repression, nor can the rights of citizens for long lag behind rights accorded to strangers.

It is not suggested that the progress of human rights in the next twenty years will be easy or rapid. Nor can one be confident that UN efforts will be generally welcomed and supported. In some respects and in some countries, the state of human rights, indeed, may be better than that sought by organized efforts to promote them. Many nations are prepared to do more than they will commit themselves to do; the United States is not the only nation which has high standards of human rights but is not eager to make the treatment of its inhabitants the business of other nations or of the United Nations.

They are particularly reluctant to do so when they have fear, warranted or not, that other nations may abuse such commitments for base and baseless political attacks.

In other countries, where United Nations efforts are sorely needed, the facts of national and international life which have been suggested may continue to depress standards and deter cooperation to raise them. One cannot be sanguine that meaningful agreements will receive general adherence in the coming years. Nations prepared to adhere to agreements to observe rights will still be reluctant to agree on effective machinery to assure compliance. Surely, it would be surprising if nations began readily to complain of human rights violations by other countries, except in special circumstances like those we have seen: where violations are based on race and smack of white colonialism, as in South Africa; or where the complaint is a weapon in political warfare (as in complaints by Western countries of forced labor in the Soviet Union); or where the complaining state has some special interest and seeks support for its diplomatic efforts (as in the case in 1948 of the Russian wives of Chileans). Nor will all nations agree to accord a right to complain or to investigate to an international body, whether to a commission or an international "Attorney General."

These are not arguments against proceeding with covenants on human rights or against any particular means for enforcing their provisions. The existence of covenants will compel nations at least to consider adherence, will generate forces to induce adherence, and will influence behavior even by nations which do not adhere. Stable, enlightened nations with traditions of freedom might well adopt such covenants to show the way which others might be persuaded to follow. Surely the countries of Western Europe have shown that among like-minded nations agreement is possible even on enforcement measures and that the arrangements will not be abused and will exert their influence, however uncertain. And while, in general, insistence on rigorous enforcement machinery should not become an obstacle to adherence to the covenants, the existence of some responsible body concerned to look over the shoulder of nations will influence some of them in some measure—even countries which may not formally adhere to international covenants.

It may be time also to reexamine the program of United Nations activities to assure that they reflect the new United Nations and the new world of nations. Some UN programs may lend themselves to a society of 120 nations: the *Yearbook on Human Rights,* reports, studies, seminars, and services do their work drop by drop, routinely, undramatically, and—hopefully—irresistibly. The influence of law—for example, through the covenants—is uncertain. Universal law is almost impossible to achieve in a universe of 120 nations. Covenants adhered to by a few, by a minority, may even dilute the authority of the Declaration; surely, they will not enjoy the influence that comes with general approval. In any event covenants will be launched.

It may now be time to implement and supplement this program with other approaches. It may be time, for example, for the UN actively to seek decentralization, to promote and encourage regional and group agreements and, even more important, regional and group enforcement. It may be necessary to have special programs, perhaps even special agreements, promoting particular rights which have greater urgency and which would respond to special treatment in different areas.

The role of the Assembly in human rights problems also deserves reexamination, perhaps as part of a new look at the Assembly in all its activities. General Assembly consideration of particular cases means, inevitably, political consideration of acts and of issues. It will not build norms of "neutral principle," generally applicable and responsibly, evenhandedly applied. The prospect of political discussion of an issue will not deter and may even encourage violation by those who are confident of approval or condonation by majorities, whether because of their power, or wealth, or poverty, or geography, or previous condition of dependency, or other political influence.

It is time to explore new inducements to comply. It may be that in some cases achieving compliance is urgent and "sanctions" seem the only method which might induce compliance; many nations seem to believe that to be true about South African *apartheid* although economic sanctions have not frequently succeeded and have been difficult to maintain because they also "punish" those who impose them as well as third states. In some cases, condemnation by UN resolution or the threat of such condemnation might have some effect.

For the most part, inducements to comply will have to be more subtle and indirect. There is usually more influence in alert scrutiny by impartial groups interested in advancing human rights than in political embarrassment of one nation or another. And if withdrawal or abstention by the United Nations will promote compliance with obligations and observance of rights, let the United Nations withhold its hand. The United Nations needs no special role or credit in human rights. Its purposes will be achieved if human rights are respected apart from anything it does. The leadership of the more enlightened will set the example. The decentralization of human rights activity, I have suggested, will, perhaps with assistance, support, and services by the UN, create pressures for compliance to which some nations at least will be more responsive.

Above all, the UN can contribute to human rights by contributing to general human welfare. The promotion of human rights as a purpose of the UN depends on other purposes of the United Nations. Progress in human rights will be accomplished only if and to the extent that other purposes of the UN are achieved. As with these other purposes, the UN itself can only exert an influence, limited by the political forces of our time.

If. peace can be maintained, international stability enhanced, nations left alone to work out their destiny, the economic and social development of nations assisted by those who have more, then the rights of individual human beings will have a chance to flourish, and the UN can play a role in speeding the process, to increase these rights, to make these rights count.

The Court and the Judicial Process

SHABTAI ROSENNE

A POINT of departure for considering the evolution of the judicial function in the United Nations system can be found in three interrelated decisions of principle incorporated in the UN Charter itself, of which the Statute of the International Court of Justice (ICJ) forms an integral part.

The first of these decisions of principle was that while the Members of the United Nations have taken upon themselves the negative obligation to refrain from the use or threat of force in their international relations, save in conformity with the Charter, they assumed no positive obligations with respect to the employment of any particular means of pacific settlement for any given type of dispute. More specifically, insofar as relates to recourse to the principal judicial organ of the Organization, they did not, as was the case with the League of Nations, undertake as a matter of principle to submit so-called justiciable disputes, according to some abstract and *a priori* definition, to either judicial settlement or arbitration. This is embodied in Articles 2, 33, and 36 of the Charter. The latter provision also emphasizes the political character of the preliminary decision of "justiciability," of whether to have recourse to judicial settlement in any concrete case.

The second decision of principle was that, save where the Security Council is taking enforcement measures with respect to threats to the peace, breaches of the peace, and acts of aggression under Chapter VII (Articles 39–51) of the Charter, the machineries of the Charter would be at the disposal of states— Members or non-Members—on a voluntary basis. This finds expression in the powers of recommendation given to the General Assembly in Articles 10–12 and 14 and to the Security Council in Articles 36–38. A similar thought lies behind Article 36 of the Statute of the Court which represents a compromise between those who desired to see some form of compulsory jurisdiction and those who thought that since the Statute was to be integrated with

SHABTAI ROSENNE is Legal Adviser in the Ministry of Foreign Affairs of Israel, a member of Israel's delegation to the United Nations, and a member of the International Law Commission.

the Charter, any form of compulsory jurisdiction would be inconsistent with the basic structure of the United Nations as a whole.

The third decision of principle was to terminate the Permanent Court of International Justice as it had existed between the two World Wars and to establish the present International Court of Justice as one of the principal organs and the principal judicial organ of the United Nations.

ATTITUDES AT THE TIME OF SAN FRANCISCO

These decisions are all compromises, whether between different approaches inside any single country or between the positions of the different powers themselves. Like all compromises, the detailed provisions of the UN Charter and the ICJ Statute lend themselves to differing and not always reconcilable interpretations. The records of the United Nations Conference on International Organization at San Francisco and the commentaries to the legislatures before ratification of the Charter are full of expressions of intent that the achievements of the interwar period in the realm of international adjudication should be preserved and that the role of the Court should be expanded. At the Conference itself, it was authoritatively stated in the report of Committee IV/1 (Judicial Organization, International Court of Justice) that the establishment of the Court as a principal organ was evidence of a firm intention that it should play an important role in the new Organization.[1] Yet the question must be asked whether the language of the Charter is not rather a screen for fundamental and perhaps unbridgeable differences than a declaration of common purpose. The longer-term impulses behind the attitudes of the powers no doubt influenced the San Francisco negotiations as they have the evolution of the judicial function since.

Of the Sponsoring Governments, the United Kingdom displayed the most interest in an international court as an effective institution for the pacific settlement of international disputes. As far back as 1943 Prime Minister Winston Churchill instructed the British representatives to press for the revival of the Court in connection with the reestablishment after the war of an international political organization.[2] The refusal of the United States Senate as late as 1935 to accept the Statute of the Permanent Court after it had been revised to meet the United States point of view imposed a measure of caution on that government even though the Administration had expressed itself, for instance, in Cordell Hull's statement of July 23, 1942,[3] as favorable to the reestablishment of the international judicial organ after the war. There is little evidence to

---

[1] *Documents of the United Nations Conference on International Organization, San Francisco, 1945* (New York: United Nations Information Organization, 1945), Vol. 13, p. 381.

[2] Winston Churchill, *The Second World War*, Vol. 5: *Closing the Ring* (London: Cassell & Co. Ltd., 1952), p. 251.

[3] Department of State *Bulletin*, July 25, 1942 (Vol. 7, No. 161), p. 645.

show that in the Soviet Union international adjudication held any prominent place in official thinking about postwar international organization. Indeed, Soviet insistence on great-power hegemony and unanimity in the Security Council as the main prop for the maintenance of international peace is hardly compatible with acceptance of the idea that an international judicial organ could play any significant role in the pacific settlement of international disputes. If the Soviet delegations at Dumbarton Oaks and San Francisco went along with the proposals concerning the Court, it is probable that they did so out of recognition that others wished them rather than out of any conviction that the Soviet Union itself would in the foreseeable future be likely to be a willing party in international litigation and would see in the Court an instrument for the furtherance of its own diplomatic aims.

Looking back, with the advantage of hindsight, over the twenty-year period that has elapsed since San Francisco, this somber background may be taken to place in correct perspective the bright picture painted by the rapporteur of Committee IV/1. The International Court of Justice commenced its existence under quite different auguries than those of the Permanent Court after World War I.

JUDICIAL SETTLEMENT UNDER THE CHARTER

The Charter, contrary to the Covenant of the League of Nations, is not tied in with any peace settlement. Arbitration and judicial settlement are excluded from the Peace Treaties of 1947, the policing of which, moreover, is not left to the major powers collectively in the Security Council except as part of their general responsibilities for the maintenance of international peace and the prevention of aggression. This, coupled with the renunciation of the use or threat of force, has the practical consequence that arbitration and judicial settlement by the International Court appear not as an alternative to an imposed decision or one brought about by force but as an alternative to other forms of political action which may not necessarily lead to a decision in the positive sense, for instance, repeated discussion in the political organs. These organs themselves have shown no inclination to deflect the political discussion into legal channels and there is no handle for discreet diplomatic action aimed at persuading the parties to a dispute to submit it to arbitration or judicial settlement.

The voluntarist basis of the contentious jurisdiction of the International Court is not merely a matter of legal theory but of political reality as well. Furthermore, experience seems to have shown that today arbitration or judicial settlement is not a particularly attractive alternative to political discussion. Partly, no doubt, this is because in the nature of diplomacy a formal and binding decision will usually be regarded as less satisfactory than either an agreed solution or no solution at all. As Wilfred Jenks has recently pointed out, in many cases the alternative is no longer arbitration on the one hand or war or other forcible measures of redress on the other, but adjudication or arbitration on the one hand or stalemate on the other.[4]

But deeper reasons can be seen in the absence of unanimity among the permanent members of the Security Council. This is an important factor hampering the positive settlement of many disputes. It is therefore no coincidence that beside the decline in the number of cases submitted to the Court (49 in all since 1946) there has been an even steeper decline in the recourse to arbitration machineries. One of the achievements of the Permanent Court was that it disposed of a number of disputes which, had they been allowed to fester, might have led to serious complications.[5] But as far as the United Nations is concerned, there appears to be no strong aversion to allowing many disputes to smolder indefinitely in the absence of any agreed basis of settlement acceptable to the parties concerned and to the major powers. Dangerous though those disputes may be, their perpetuation is preferred for the time being, while reliance is placed on extraordinary measures (frequently outside the framework of the United Nations) to prevent them from getting out of hand or to restore a precarious balance in cases of emergency.

In the United Nations, while the former unanimity rule is abolished and parties whose interests are specially affected have the right to participate in the Security Council, they do not have the right to vote as they did in the League of Nations. There is a great deal of difference between the pacific settlement of a dispute when the parties have a vote and when they do not, and this procedural change alone is enough to hamper the employment of the judicial process within UN dispute-settlement patterns.

The unwillingness of the United Nations to make use of the "rapporteur system" and the temptation to push resolutions through by majority rule have hampered the chances of a discreet exploration of the probability of a fruitful recourse to arbitration or judicial settlement as an agreed, or at least acceptable, outcome of the consideration of the matter by the organ in question. This can be substantiated by a perusal of the General Assembly and Security Council debates in which the possibility of recourse to the Court has been broached, only to be rejected.[6]

One consequence of these procedures has been the high degree of politization and publicity given to decisions to have recourse to the Court, which have in the past usually been taken as dispassionately and discreetly as possible, as is still the case for normal reference of bilateral disputes to the Court.

[4] C. Wilfred Jenks, *The Prospects of International Adjudication* (London: Stevens & Sons Limited, 1964), p. 104.

[5] Manley O. Hudson, *International Tribunals, Past and Future* (Washington, D.C: Carnegie Endowment for International Peace and Brookings Institution, 1944), p. 239.

[6] For a partial list, see Shabtai Rosenne, *The Law and Practice of the International Court* (Leyden: A. W. Sythoff, 1965), pp. 664–666 (General Assembly) and pp. 667–669 (Security Council).

The employment of the judicial function as the consummation of a political discussion has thus become a highly political concept. This is the very antithesis of the traditional approach to the nature of the international judicial function as well as to the underlying conditions in which it can operate satisfactorily.

Two recent instances illustrate this development. The first is seen in the procedural treatment of the question of the status of the German-speaking element in the Province of Bolzano (Bozen) during the fifteenth (1960) and sixteenth (1961) sessions of the General Assembly when the issue of whether arbitration or judicial settlement could be envisaged as a practical outcome of the debate, satisfactory to the two states concerned. This was in fact settled by the decision to allocate the agenda item to the Special Political Committee and not to the Sixth (Legal) Committee.[7] The second instance, which is even more striking, is the Cuban proposal, discussed in the 992nd–998th meetings of the Security Council (March 14–23, 1962), to request an advisory opinion on a number of questions connected with the Punte del Este Meeting of Consultation of the Ministers of Foreign Affairs of the American States and relating to the expulsion of Cuba from the Organization of American States (OAS). The proposed request for the advisory opinion constituted the point of departure for the debate. The published records indicate that the debate was conducted in excessively political terms with little attempt to explore whether there were "legal questions" which might appropriately—in terms of dispute settlement—form the subject of a request for an advisory opinion.

THE CONCEPT AND USE OF ADVISORY COMPETENCE

Three features are seen as the most prominent indicators of the changes in the nature of the judicial function that have become apparent since 1945. The first is the new direction given by the General Assembly to the use of the advisory competence of the Court and the Court's reaction to this. The second is the development by states of the conception of the partial settlement of disputes through the preliminary objection procedure of the Court. The third is the uncertain political and even legal status of the postadjudicative stage, an aspect which has made itself felt in contentious cases but which is most prominent and more intransigent in advisory cases. This latter aspect is only of indirect concern to the Court itself.

The introduction of the concept of the advisory opinion into the practice and procedure of the Permanent Court of International Justice alongside the traditional contentious usages was one of the most controversial innovations of the founders of the League of Nations and of the Permanent Court.

[7] See the discussion of the General Committee in General Assembly *Official Records . . . General Committee* (15th session), pp. 2–4, 7.

The abolition of the unanimity rule in the United Nations has, as far as the employment of the advisory competence is concerned, enabled requests for advisory opinions to be adopted despite opposition, carried even to the length of negative votes, in the requesting organ. Indeed, of the ten requests for advisory opinions adopted by the General Assembly since 1946, only one was adopted "unanimously" (i.e., with no negative vote).[8] In one instance, two of the permanent members of the Security Council voted against a proposal in the General Assembly to request an advisory opinion—a request which nonetheless was adopted.[9]

In comparison with the practice of the League Council (the Assembly, although authorized, never requested an advisory opinion), this is a revolutionary development. For despite certain theoretical doubts as to whether a request was substantive or procedural (in which event it would have been formally exempt from the unanimity rule), the League Council in fact refrained from requesting advisory opinions if it was satisfied that there was opposition to the request. Moreover, there is ground for thinking that the consensual basis of the contentious jurisdiction itself is the application of an even broader underlying principle. This is to the effect that all the activities of an international tribunal should rest upon some measure of consent by the states immediately affected by the outcome of the judicial activity that the tribunal should so act.

The International Court has reacted to this new practice of the United Nations in an interesting way. On the one hand, it has been careful to retain as a principle the doctrine of the *Eastern Carelia Case*[10] that the existence of advisory competence should not permit surreptitious introduction of compulsory forms of judicial settlement. It has also developed a new doctrine of the duty of the Court, as a principal organ of the United Nations, to participate in the activities of the Organization and to cooperate with the other principal organs and indeed with the specialized agencies in the attainment of the purposes of the Organization. This has led the Court to the position that only compelling reasons should induce it to refrain from giving an opinion.[11]

The result has been a considerable accentuation of the Court's discretionary power to give an advisory opinion. This extends both to the question of whether it should accede to the request at all and to the whole procedure by which the issues would be presented to the Court and the opinion rendered. Although since 1945 there has not yet been any instance in which the Court has carried its discretion to the extent of refraining from giving a requested opinion, it is believed that these developments must increase the uncertainty

[8] For details, see Rosenne, p. 664.
[9] General Assembly Resolution 1731 (XVI), December 20, 1961, requesting the advisory opinion in the case *Certain Expenses of the United Nations (Article 17, paragraph 2, of the Charter).*
[10] *Publications of the Permanent Court of International Justice* (1923), Series B, No. 5.
[11] Discussed more fully in Rosenne, pp. 708–718.

implicit in recourse to an adjudicative organ because for governments the decision to attempt to invoke the advisory process by means of a diplomatic operation through an appropriate organ nowadays not only presents itself as a choice simply between "winning" or "losing" the case, but it also involves the consideration of whether the Court will deal with the case at all, with all the attendant complications should it decide not to do so.

While it is not easy to separate cause and effect, it is a fact that all these factors taken together have led to the evolution of new concepts of the employment of the advisory competence and new ideas regarding the nature of the advisory opinion itself. Except for the case *Interpretation of Peace Treaties with Bulgaria, Hungary and Romania* (1950)—in which the "respondent" governments, not being Members of the United Nations, could not participate in the deliberations of the General Assembly—the advisory competence has not been employed as part of the procedure for the pacific settlement of international disputes as had been the experience of most of the advisory cases brought before the Permanent Court. In fact, of the 27 instances to which footnote 6 above refers, in which proposals to request advisory opinions were not adopted by the General Assembly or the Security Council, no less than eighteen related to concrete disputes or situations and the remainder to broad issues of interpretation (sometimes, however, with concrete disputes or situations as the *arrière-plan*).

It has been employed for the elucidation of a series of major issues of constitutional interpretation and for the clarification of several major legal questions troubling the international community. Whatever conflicts of interests underlay the introduction of these items on the agenda of the General Assembly, they nevertheless could be presented to the Court and treated by it not as concrete disputes between two or more states but as more generalized legal questions. In its early years and before the full import of the constitutional changes of the UN Charter over the Covenant of the League had made themselves felt, the Court's reaction was to seek to attain a high level of abstraction in its advisory opinions, sometimes to the extent of passing completely over the factual background which led to the question being put to it.

This approach had the disadvantage of neither giving to the majority of the General Assembly the practical guidance it had sought nor gaining the confidence of the political opposition (as in the first *Conditions of Admission of a State to Membership in the United Nations* [*Article 4 of the Charter*] case of 1948). But the advisory opinion of July 20, 1962, in the *Certain Expenses of the United Nations (Article 17, paragraph 2, of the Charter)* case, with its insistence on treating the case as a concrete one so as to give the General Assembly some practical guidance, indicates a change on the part of the Court and a less timorous attitude toward the fundamental problems of the Organization of which it is the principal judicial organ. The Court has shown commendable courage in dealing with this type of case and in not allowing other, partly experimental, traditions appropriate to the entirely different institutional framework of the League of Nations to hamper the development of its own organic personality as the judicial organ of the United Nations.

The end of this development of the advisory competence is certainly not yet in sight. Many politicians and jurists feel that the increasing politization of the preadjudicative decison-making process needs to be tempered by an even greater measure of judicial caution than was displayed by the Permanent Court in the *Eastern Carelia Case*. Nevertheless, it is believed that the present Court has been careful to preserve that principle for the type of case in which it was itself formulated, i.e., an advisory opinion requested on a legal question connected with a concrete dispute or situation pending between two or more states without their consent; and that what it has done, correctly interpreting the Charter (it is submitted), is not to extend the limits of that principle where the legal question does not encompass such a dispute or situation. The practice today is that the advisory competence of the present Court has evolved into a completely independent branch of judicial activity, with its own principles and its own rules which are not necessarily the principles and rules which lie at the basis of the contentious jurisdiction (although, of course, with an interaction between them which is inherent in the Court's judicial character).

From the long-term point of view, this may be regarded as the most significant contribution of the Court itself to the evolution of the judicial technique, for it opens the way to new developments which in due course may be applied to different types of international legal problems. At the same time it would be misleading not to recall that this evolution has not won for itself general political approval, and indeed some quarters hold serious reservations toward it. This, too, has had its effect. In the nature of things, the invocation of the judicial process is sporadic and spasmodic, and at the best of times it is a complex diplomatic operation. The fact that, in the twenty years of the functioning of the United Nations, only twelve requests for advisory opinions in all (ten by the General Assembly and one each by two of the specialized agencies) have been adopted, many of them under conditions of high political controversy, has made it difficult to place these developments in clear perspective, and if the Court has firmly enunciated the guiding principles which govern its activities in this sphere, it has had little opportunity to apply them with any degree of consistency. It is no accident that in the important Special Committee on Principles of International Law Concerning Friendly Relations and Cooperation Among States, which recently met at Mexico City, there was no consensus on a proposition that attention should be given to making greater use of the advisory opinion, both to develop United Nations law and to settle disputes between states.[12] Perhaps it was a mistake to put the two aspects into

[12] UN Document A/5746, paragraph 183.

a single proposition because they do not stand on an equal footing, and it is more in connection with the former that this evolution has taken place and that the real difficulties are found.

Development of the Preliminary Objection Procedure

If the assumption is correct that the diplomatic temperament prefers negotiation and partial settlement to formal decision, there is in the nature of things an element of incompatibility between the diplomatic approach, with its proper insistence on negotiation as the point of departure and agreement as the point of arrival, and the very process of "decision" which is the intended objective of the invocation of the judicial process in a contentious case. Furthermore, as already stated, in many cases a formal and binding decision such as issues from a judgment of the International Court is frequently an unattractive alternative to other diplomatic processes, including those mentioned specifically in Article 33 of the Charter. This factor is reflected to an increasing degree in the judicial experience of the last twenty years. That something like this may have been instinctively realized almost from the beginning of the activities of the Permanent Court may be seen in the extremely wide scope which the Permanent Court gave to its competence to decide any dispute as to whether it had jurisdiction in a concrete case and in the parallel development of the "preliminary objection" as a recognized form of judicial procedure.[13]

Apparently breaking free of all analogies from the patterns of domestic litigation, this competence has been revealed in the experience of the last twenty years under the Court as containing a number of elements which together make it possible for a contentious case to take place without leading to a "decision" in the sense of the formal disposition of the concrete dispute. On the other hand, such a partial decision, by disposing of a number of issues even if only in a tentative way, can lay the basis for the renewal of negotiations which had previously reached a deadlock whether on the ground of genuine differences of opinion as to what the law dictated, for delicate reasons of national prestige, or even for reasons embedded in domestic politics. Furthermore, there are signs that this can be done without too much probing into facts, a process which can easily lead to pejorative assertions in the pleadings and which, in turn, would not be conducive to a diplomatic settlement of the dispute. While leaving unimpaired the basic conception of the preliminary objection as an interlocutory procedure designed for the elucidation of the single question of whether the Court has jurisdiction in the concrete case, i.e., whether the two parties are under the legal obligation to accept the decision of the Court in that case (which may frequently be a highly technical and even narrow point), states have shown an increasing tendency to

---

[13] See Rosenne, pp. 437–468.

submit "preliminary objections" of considerable complexity and of broad scope so that the argument on them before the Court will in effect embrace the whole of the legal components of the dispute, albeit in a preliminary and possibly procedural way. This also has a certain diplomatic advantage since the prestige of a government may be less heavily engaged if the case is lost on a "preliminary" ground than if it is lost on the merits.

Since 1946 the present Court has delivered 28 judgments, of which fourteen were judgments on preliminary objections; and of those fourteen judgments, the Court found that it could not deal with the case, for one reason or another, in seven instances. In only one of those seven instances did the party which won on the procedural point find itself the substantive winner of the dispute in the sense that the judgment on the preliminary question effectively settled the dispute in its favor (the *Nottebohm Case* [*Liechtenstein* v. *Guatemala*] [1955]). Even here, the judgment, devoted to the ostensibly technical question of the admissibility of the dispute (after pleadings which covered the whole of the merits), in fact declared the legal position of the two parties without imposing any obligations on either of them. In five cases—the *Anglo-Iranian Oil Co. Case (United Kingdom* v. *Iran)* (1952), the *Case of the Monetary Gold Removed from Rome in 1943 (Italy* v. *France, United Kingdom of Great Britain and Northern Ireland and United States of America)* (1954), the *Case of Certain Norwegian Loans (France* v. *Norway)* (1957), the *Interhandel Case (Switzerland* v. *United States of America)* (1959), and the *Aerial Incident of 27 July 1955 (Israel* v. *Bulgaria; United States of America* v. *Bulgaria; United Kingdom* v. *Bulgaria)* case (1959)—the judgment declaring that the Court was without jurisdiction or (in the *Interhandel Case)* that the case was inadmissible, sometimes on a narrow technical ground, sometimes on grounds more substantial and closer to the real dispute, merely laid the basis for a renewal of diplomatic negotiations leading to the ultimate negotiated settlement of the dispute. In the seventh case, the *Case Concerning the Northern Cameroons (Cameroon* v. *United Kingdom)* (1963), the formal decision of the Court that it could not adjudicate on the case was reached after a careful analysis of a number of hypotheses favorable to the applicant, an unusual exercise of judicial reasoning designed to meet the curious circumstance that the Court was being asked to decide a "moot" case (in the American sense). It seems that the underlying political tension was reasonably assuaged by this example of the judicial function which permitted the Court to indicate its views on the merits but in a very indirect way.

Now the significant feature of all these judgments, by which the Court treated the dispute "once removed," so to speak, from its original formulation, is that the confrontation of the parties in the Court through the process of pleading permitted the dispute (except, in some of these cases, controverted issues of fact on which discussion and decision might well have exacerbated the political tensions) to be fully aired in Court even when, on technical grounds, the judgment is limited to the minimum necessary to establish the inability of the Court to deal with the merits of the case. This is certainly not the original conception of a "preliminary objection," and at first glance one might think that the prevalence of this practice may lead to abuses of the Court's procedure. For its part, the Court has not discouraged this form of judicial settlement, while at the same time taking great pains to protect both itself and the litigants against abuse of legal procedures. It has done that by developing firm guiding principles with regard to the technical aspects of the law governing its own jurisdiction and leaving the discretionary element which the International Court, like every higher tribunal, possesses to the areas less given to precise formulation, such as the questions of "admissibility." In this respect there are signs of strongly held views on judicial policy which has supplied the Court's jurisprudence with a marked element of consistency (in parts going back to the Permanent Court). This may be found, for example, in its approach to difficult questions raised by the so-called objections *ratione temporis* (a type of issue, the implications of time on the jurisdiction of the Court, rarely encountered in domestic litigation), or the problems posed by pleas of "domestic jurisdiction," whether in the traditional "objective" form or in the newer "subjective" form introduced by the so-called Connally Amendment.[14]

In general, the Court seems to have shown great concern to shield from undesirable influences the underlying stability of the law governing its own jurisdiction, and some of its decisions on these aspects have been reached with a surprisingly high degree of unanimity. What has to be balanced in this type of case is not only the right of the applicant state that the case proceed to final judgment unless the Court is shown to be without jurisdiction or unless the inadmissibility of the case be established and the right of the respondent state that these aspects be judicially determined before it pleads to the merits; but these two incompatible rights themselves also have to be weighed against the very character of the Court as a judicial tribunal. The Court itself is the exclusive guardian of the integrity of the judicial function.

Dispassionate examination of this aspect of the Court's activities and of the response of states to it will show, it is believed, that the Court has discharged this delicate task with a high measure of success. The key for this can be found in the oft repeated observation (first made by the Permanent Court in 1929) that the judicial settlement of international disputes is simply an alternative to direct and friendly settlement and that the Court must cooperate in the settlement of disputes, one of the main aims of the United Nations. The Court has shown great adaptability to changing circumstances in the furtherance of this aim. This development of the "preliminary objection" processes may

---

[14] See Rosenne, pp. 393–399.

legitimately be regarded as its latest contribution to dispute-settlement procedures.

The fact that no less than 50 percent of the judgments rendered by the Court since 1946 have formally been judgments on preliminary objections (as compared with about 30 percent of the judgments rendered by the Permanent Court during the whole period of its existence) has led many observers to the belief that the main judicial activity of the Court has been directed toward establishing merely whether or not it has jurisdiction. Further, it has too frequently been asserted that the Court has not been bold enough in assuming jurisdiction in contested cases. But clearly, this is a gross oversimplification of the significance of these judgments and even more so of the significance of the pleadings which accompany them.

In only two cases was the preliminary objection directed exclusively to the question whether the necessary consents to the exercise of jurisdiction had in fact been given, and in both of them the Court assumed jurisdiction. In the first, *The Corfu Channel Case* (1948), the existence of that consent was so obvious from the record of the earlier discussion in the Security Council that one is sometimes tempted to wonder why the objection was raised in the first place. In the second, the *Case Concerning Temple of Preah Vihear (Cambodia* v. *Thailand)* (1961), the litigation took place against a background of deteriorating relations between Cambodia and Thailand, between whom, indeed, diplomatic relations had been severed. That situation had led to some discreet diplomacy by the Secretary-General of the United Nations, and one may suppose that the later reference of the case to the Court was an outcome of the improvement which followed those good offices. However, as there was no public record of this, there may have been some general advantage in having the jurisdiction of the Court formally established before proceeding to the merits of the case. These and other cases also show that the Court is slow to permit objections based on mere artificialities and forced constructions to stand in the way of its jurisdiction if it is reasonably satisfied that a genuine obligation to accept the jurisdiction exists.

However, these broad, and in our view beneficial, developments in the scope of the judicial practice and its adaptation in its substantive aspects to a marked trend in the practice and needs of states, have not been accompanied by any formal changes in the Court's procedure. This is particularly noticeable in connection with this modification in the role of the preliminary objection although the stagnancy of the Rules of Court goes much further. The present Rules of Court were adopted in 1946, and they are for the most part merely a reproduction of the final edition of the Rules of Court of the Permanent Court, issued in 1936. Although a new provision (Article 70) inserted into the Statute of the Court in 1945 gives the Court a power of initiative to propose amendments to that instrument, and *a fortiori* the Court pos-

sesses a similar power as regards the Rules of Court which it itself promul-
gates, there is no indication of any official attempt to analyze whether these
texts, which are reasonably satisfactory as far as they go, meet all the needs
of contemporary dispute settlement by a judicial organ or whether the time
has not come to investigate the possibility and the desirability of introducing
new concepts and new procedures. Other contemporary international tribunals
not operating within the framework of the United Nations system have done
this, and many possible openings are explored by Dr. Jenks in his work cited
above. It may be a sign of excessive conservatism, not matched in its substantive work, that the Court is the only international organ today working on
rules of procedure drawn up before the Second World War.

QUESTIONS RELATING TO THE POSTADJUDICATIVE PHASE OF CASES

Indications are to be found of serious uncertainties in matters pertaining to
the postadjudicative phase of a case. The United Nations has witnessed a phenomenon which the League did not experience, namely, the nonimplementa-
tion of a judgment (especially, but not exclusively, the final judgment in *The
Corfu Channel Case*) and the refusal of states to act in accordance with the
legal position as stated in an advisory opinion.

For contentious cases, those who drafted the Charter correctly perceived
that it was not the business of the Court itself to ensure the execution of its
decisions.[15] They therefore gave ultimate competence to the Security Council
(Article 94 of the Charter). The efficacy of that approach depends upon the
general standing of the Security Council and its ability to take action in the
concrete case. For advisory cases in general, however, the position was left open;
and as far as advisory opinions dealing with the interpretation of the Charter
were concerned, the position was left in an even more obscure state owing to
the ambiguities of the declaration on the interpretation of the Charter adopted
by the Conference.[16] This declaration seems to imply that if an interpretation
made by any organ—and the Court is an organ of the United Nations—is not
generally acceptable, it will be without binding force. This uncertainty has
led to the ineluctable situation in which, while every advisory opinion requested by the General Assembly has subsequently been adopted by it in one
form or another,[17] states dissatisfied with the conclusions of the opinion have
frequently (but not invariably) refused to comport themselves in accordance
with the law as found by the Court. The outstanding examples of this—there
are others—are seen in the attitude of South Africa toward the advisory opinion of 1950 on the *International Status of South-West Africa* and in the atti-

---

[15] *Documents of the United Nations Conference on International Organization, San Francisco, 1945*
(New York: United Nations Information Organization, 1945), Vol. 14, p. 853.

[16] *Ibid.*, Vol. 13, p. 709.

[17] For particulars, see Rosenne, pp. 748–754.

tude of the states concerned to the advisory opinion given in the same year in the *Peace Treaties* case. Nor is this all. The General Assembly itself, after a lapse of time, did not find such conduct to disqualify various states from admission into the United Nations. It may well be true, as is sometimes argued, that one must distinguish between the determination of the law at a particular point of time and the operation of long-term historical forces.[18] A distinction of that nature can usefully explain away particular cases where the operation of these long-term historical forces can be clearly identified. But it supplies no answer to the major issues of principle which this phenomenon itself poses. Nor does it in any way soften the generally detrimental impact of this undesirable development on the standing of the Court in diplomatic circles.

The origins of this state of affairs can be found in three factors at least. One lies in the fundamentally different, if not contradictory, approaches of the different powers to the very nature of the judicial function within the framework of the United Nations, manifested at San Francisco and repeated many times since. This leads to discordant views both as to when recourse to the judicial function is appropriate and as to the responsibilities of the competent political organs and of the powers represented on them when they are faced with the necessity of deciding on political action upon receipt of a judicial pronouncement. This latter aspect has arisen, somewhat obliquely, in the Security Council when it was faced in 1951 with a complaint of the failure of Iran to implement certain interim measures indicated by the Court in the *Anglo-Iranian Oil Co. Case*. Even if there are important technical differences between a judgment, an advisory opinion, and an indication of interim measures, the marked indecision of the Security Council and, above all, the disagreements between its five permanent members are discouraging for the development of a positive role for the Court within the United Nations system.

The second factor has its seat in the unclear status of resolutions of the General Assembly. If in principle a resolution of the General Assembly has the diplomatic status of a recommendation which states are not legally obliged to accept, can it be any different as regards a resolution signifying the General Assembly's acceptance of an advisory opinion? This is one of the underlying issues of the crisis of the nineteenth session of the General Assembly, and it may well be that on the outcome of current negotiations will depend the future ability of the Court to play an important role in the interpretation of the Charter and its application. The roots of the third factor are buried in the new procedure of the United Nations, with its abolition of the unanimity rule for requesting opinions. If a request for an advisory opinion can be

---

[18] Jenks, p. 665.

adopted over the opposition of states, how can those states be afterward held to be obliged by the contents of an advisory opinion?

These are distasteful developments. They indicate serious structural weaknesses of the United Nations constitutional texts, and in retrospect it seems that some of the advisory opinions, which related to highly controversial situations, were put to the Court with excessive enthusiasm and without sufficient regard either for the long-term historical forces molding the evolution of that situation or for these structural weaknesses.

There is no doubt now that the absence of formal legal rules determining the legal consequences in terms of permissible conduct for states arising out of a judicial pronouncement cast in the form of an advisory opinion is a serious drawback to the effective use of the advisory procedure. It is, moreover, a possible source of detriment to the general standing of the Court in the sense that the General Assembly has hitherto shown insufficient inclination to draw practical consequences from a refusal by states to comport themselves in accordance with the legal position established in an advisory opinion. But that is a question of the general constitutional law of the international organization, and it seems that the necessary clarification will only be obtained when the constitutional principles can be more firmly drawn than they are at present. Until then, it may be hoped that recourse to the advisory competence will be limited to those situations (and they are many) in which the legal factors predominate over the political and where the immediate controversy is not too strident so as to drown out the echoes of the long-term historical forces; and that attempts to seek judicial settlement of a dispute or situation composed primarily of political facets, over the heads of unwilling states, will be avoided.

Lag in the Growth of the Judicial Role

The founders of the United Nations took the position that as far as the political and economic organs of the international community were concerned they were free to embark upon a complete reconstruction without being held too closely to the institutional patterns and established practices of the League of Nations. On that basis they completely remodeled the General Assembly and the Security Council in comparison with the principal parallel organs of the League. As far as the Court was concerned, their approach was the exact opposite. Although the Statute of the Court underwent more concentrated, expert examination prior to San Francisco than the provisions of the Charter, the general tendency of this examination was a conservative one in the sense of retaining the existing structure, subject to such minor modifications and adjustments as experience dictated. Then the political decision was taken to transfer the Court, lock, stock, and barrel, into the framework of the United Nations. But no real attempt was made at the time to investigate whether this formal integration of the Court in the United Nations, in place of the looser attachment of the Permanent Court with the League, was fully coordinated. The San Francisco Conference itself, fragmented into four virtually independent commissions, did not go at all deeply into the fundamental question of the relations between the different organs of the United Nations (a matter on which the Court has made a major, even if sporadic, contribution in various of its advisory and contentious pronouncements which have dealt with the interpretation of the Charter on this particular point). The upshot is that the Court appears completely uncoordinated with the United Nations. It suffers from the disadvantage that by being formally tied into the United Nations, its prestige, at least in political circles, has become inextricably bound up with the general standing of the Organization, sharing its ups and downs, while on the substantive side both states in many cases and the Security Council and the General Assembly are inclined to overlook not only its status as a principal organ but also the fact that by virtue of the Charter only the Security Council and the Court, but not the General Assembly, have formal dispute-settling powers. It is in respect of this complete functional distance between the Court and the United Nations that the expectations of the San Francisco Conference regarding the Court's role in the settlement of international disputes are seen to have been misplaced.

There is now general recognition, at least in Western circles and probably in wider circles of jurists, that the affairs of the Court have not developed as anticipated in 1945. This finds outward expression in such aspects as the statistical decline in the number of cases, both contentious and advisory, submitted to the Court; in the meager quantity of acceptances of the so-called compulsory jurisdiction of the Court under Article 36, paragraph 2, of its Statute; and in the difficulties of obtaining agreement to the insertion of compromissory clauses into general multilateral conventions, whether or not concluded under the auspices of the United Nations, conferring jurisdiction on the Court over disputes relating to the interpretation or application of the treaty.[19]

To these more formal aspects has to be added the growing discontent of a large number of Members of the United Nations with the composition of the Court which, according to that view, does not assure the representation, in the body as a whole, of the main forms of civilization and of the principal legal systems of the world (Article 9 of the ICJ Statute). This discontent has been heard as an undercurrent ever since 1946. In the view of some observers it has been aggravated by the introduction into the Statute of 1945 of the system of partial elections of five members of the Court every third year. This is seen to have intensified the political and psychological factors of this char-

---

[19] Shabtai Rosenne, "On the Non-Use of the Advisory Competence of the International Court of Justice," *British Year Book of International Law, 1963* (London: Oxford University Press, 1964), Vol. 39, pp. 6–8, 22–23.

acter. Recently, this dissatisfaction has come more and more into the open, being now articulated frankly in the Sixth Committee of the General Assembly, in the International Law Commission, and lastly in the important Special Committee on Principles of International Law Concerning Friendly Relations and Cooperation Among States.[20] This may provide sufficient justification for a small, but unconditional, increase in the number of the judges.

The widening gap between the membership of the United Nations and the Court is vividly demonstrated by the fact that in 1947 political sentiment favorable to the notion of international adjudication was in a strong enough parliamentary position to secure the passage in the General Assembly of a resolution[21] calling for greater use of the International Court, both on its contentious and on its advisory side, even though this had little if any practical effect. Since 1960, when the question was discussed in the Sixth Committee, no Member has yet found it opportune to submit a draft resolution on the question, and at Mexico City no consensus could be attained even on the desirability of encouraging recourse to the Court as a normal dispute-settlement procedure.[22]

OVERALL CONTRIBUTIONS OF THE COURT

With all the obstacles which the foregoing survey has shown, it remains to say that in its substantive work, the Court has made a significant contribution to the settlement of major political disputes. This applies both to disputes of prime political significance—*The Corfu Channel Case* (1949), the *Asylum Case (Colombia/Peru)* (1950), the *Fisheries Case (United Kingdom* v. *Norway)* (1951), the *Anglo-Iranian Oil Co. Case* (1952), the *Case Concerning Right of Passage over Indian Territory (Portugal* v. *India)* (1960), the *Case Concerning the Arbitral Award Made by the King of Spain on 23 December 1906 (Honduras* v. *Nicaragua)* (1960), and the *Temple of Preah Vihear Case* (1962) are illustrations—and to disputes touching on major aspects of international economic relations. This aspect is illustrated by two cases involving issues of economic warfare and arising out of the Second World War, the *Nottebohm Case* (1955) and the *Interhandel Case* (1959), and two cases regarding international economic relations in general, the *Case Concerning Rights of Nationals of the United States of America in Morocco (France* v. *United States of America)* (1952) and the pending *Case Concerning Barcelona Traction, Light and Power Company Limited (Belgium* v. *Spain)*. In addition, the Court has also dealt with a number of disputes which were not themselves a cause of major tension, irritating though they may have been to the powers concerned.

[20] UN Document A/5746, paragraphs 191–193.
[21] General Assembly Resolution 171 (II), November 14, 1947.
[22] UN Document A/5746, paragraphs 166–178.

In general, the impression is formed that if one were to subtract from the statistics of the Permanent Court all those cases which had their origin in some provision of the 1919 peace settlement, one would find that not only has the contentious business of the International Court increased quantitatively but that the scope of the issues which it has been asked to settle is much broader and the legal problems much more weighty and varied. It is sometimes said that much of the work of the Permanent Court was concerned with problems of treaty interpretation. Be that as it may, treaty interpretation is not really a prominent part of the work of the present Court which has, in fact, encompassed a great many of the fundamental problems of contemporary international law and relations.

In this respect, the dispute-settlement processes of the International Court and the exposition of legal principles which is a part of it have had a forward reach going far beyond the immediate dispute. For example, the judgment in the Anglo-Norwegian *Fisheries Case,* which at the time was taken in many circles as almost revolutionary in its boldness, within a few years became accepted and, indeed, constitutes a thesis for the codification of the law of the sea completed under the auspices of the United Nations in 1958; and that codification in turn has formed the underlying basis for the concrete settlement of a significant number of bilateral, and even regional, fisheries disputes in different parts of the world. The *Anglo-Iranian Oil Co. Case* and the subsequent settlement of that particular dispute, even though the Court's judgment did not go into some of the major issues of the international validity of nationalization measures, has become an important element in the general development of contemporary views on the legal problems created by measures of nationalization. The Court's "judgment of Solomon" in the *Right of Passage Case* certainly facilitated the process of decolonization in the Indian subcontinent, and a careful study of the impact of that judgment may show that the Court here made a major contribution to the peaceful continuation of the process of decolonization in other parts of the world. The currently pending *South West Africa Cases (Ethiopia* v. *South Africa; Liberia* v. *South Africa),* already preceded by three advisory opinions (1950, 1955, and 1956) and a far-reaching judgment on the preliminary objections (1962), will give the Court an opportunity to pronounce itself on some of the major tensions prevalent in several organs of the United Nations, including the Security Council and the General Assembly. Virtually all of these cases have constituted a greater or less danger to peace. In all of them, the reference to the Court removed that particular threat.

If the disputes which have been referred to the Court are not as many as one would like to have seen, one must remember that mere statistics can never be taken as the real guide to the function which the Court is performing in the international society. The general significance of the disputes which have come before the Court and in many cases the circumstances in which they were brought are better indications of the measure of the Court's contribution to the pacific settlement of disputes.

The general picture, nevertheless, is not encouraging and indicates some general malaise not yet fully diagnosed. It is not disparaging to the International Court, nor to any other international tribunal, to stress that the judicial settlement of international disputes is a political function. The framers of the 1945 documents showed a wise appreciation of this and reached a number of conclusions of a general, organic character. On the other hand, it seems now that several of the more important consequences of their decisions have, in fact, not necessarily been adequate to fit the Court for the tasks which it is called upon to perform in the vastly changed international society. That, it is suggested, is the aspect to which those who are conscious of the need for a strong and effective international judicial arm should now devote their attention.

The United Nations and the Role of Law

LEO GROSS

LEGAL controversy within the United Nations has resulted from the confrontation of the Organization's purposes with the specific rules set forth in the Charter for their implementation. Two sections of the Charter stand out as having produced yet unresolved legal tangles: One is the provision relating to the maintenance of international peace and security through effective collective action; the other is the group of provisions relating to self-determination and human rights. The Cold War and the attempts of the Great Powers to use the UN to attain or defend their policy objectives have shaped the attitude of Members toward the law and the role of law in the more clearly political activities of the UN. Consequently, politico-legal controversy has arisen with respect to the allocation of competences and powers between the General Assembly and the Security Council, the manner of operation of these two bodies, and the distribution of responsibility for "enforcement action" between the UN and regional organizations.

In addition, controversy has developed between Members anxious to implement speedily the purposes relating to human rights and racial equality or nondiscrimination and Members resisting such policies as impinging on domestic jurisdiction. The clash between the commitment of the Organization to the promotion of human rights and the sweeping reservation in Article 2, paragraph 7, has also shaped in large measure the attitude of Members with respect to the role of law in this area of UN activities. For these differences in interpretation did not remain restricted to issues relating directly to human rights, as in the South African questions, but came soon to embrace other issues as well, such as self-determination and control over natural resources—in fact, all aspects of colonialism including economic development.

LEO GROSS, a member of the Board of Editors of *International Organization,* is Professor of International Law and Organization, Fletcher School of Law and Diplomacy, and Visiting Professor of Government, Harvard University.

These problems, however, except for a few general remarks in the following section, must remain outside the scope of the present analysis, which is concerned with the deliberate efforts of the United Nations to contribute to the development and codification of international law. The world Organization has attempted to fulfill this task directly through resolutions, declarations, and draft conventions and indirectly through the International Law Commission. This is a vast and challenging area which this study will try to describe briefly.

THE CHARTER AND LIVING LAW

With respect to the general problem of the role of law in the United Nations, some theoretical observations may be made. It has been argued that the United Nations is essentially a political and dynamic institution and therefore cannot be held to a strict observance of the law. To this writer such a view is not persuasive. There is no contradiction between the essentially political character of the United Nations as an international institution and its obligation to respect applicable rules. As the International Court of Justice said in the first membership case:

> The political character of an organ cannot release it from the observance of the treaty provisions established by the Charter when they constitute limitations on its powers or criteria for its judgment. To ascertain whether an organ has freedom of choice for its decisions, reference must be made to the terms of its constitution.[1]

The Charter is not exclusively or even predominantly concerned with purposes; as well as setting forth the objectives of the United Nations, it formulates principles and even detailed rules with respect to the manner in which the Organization's goals can be achieved. Certainly, the UN can best attain its aims by respecting the law, by acting so as to give effect to its purposes and principles and yet not breach its Charter in any way.[2]

The United Nations is indeed a political and dynamic institution, but it does not follow, as sometimes suggested, that it operates in a politico-legal vacuum. Politically it operates within the system of sovereign states competing and cooperating; legally it operates within the framework of the Charter. Rules of interpretation are abundant, and a skillful interpreter can easily "prove" the compatibility of almost any resolution with the applicable rules.[3] It should not be forgotten, however, that the often quoted San Francisco state-

---

[1] *Admission of a State to the United Nations (Charter, Article 4), Advisory Opinion of May 28, 1948: I.C.J. Reports 1948*, p. 64.

[2] See the joint dissenting opinion of Judges J. Basdevant, B. Winiarski, Sir Arnold D. McNair, and John E. Read in *ibid.*, pp. 85, 92.

[3] Leo Gross, "Problems of International Adjudication and Compliance with International Law: Some Simple Solutions," *The American Journal of International Law*, January 1965 (Vol. 59, No. 1), pp. 48–59.

ment on interpretation which declares that each organ of the UN "will interpret such parts of the Charter as are applicable to its particular functions" also says:

> It is to be understood, of course, that if an interpretation made by any organ of the Organization or by a committee of jurists is *not generally acceptable* it will be *without binding force*. In such circumstances, or in cases where it is desired to establish an authoritative interpretation as a precedent for the future, it may be necessary to embody the interpretation in an amendment to the Charter.[4]

Since amendments are hard to come by, particularly when they would impose further limitations upon the sovereignty of the Members,[5] the first sentence quoted should be regarded as the correct statement of principle: The organs of the United Nations have no power of authoritative interpretation except, of course, where finality attaches to their decisions, as in the cases of Assembly resolutions admitting states to membership or Security Council action to which Article 25 applies.[6] As a consequence, it follows as a working rule that for an interpretation to acquire binding force it must be "generally acceptable." This condition may be regrettable, but those who wish to disregard it will have either to change the state system or trust that through such extralegal methods as diplomatic pressure the dissenting Members will be brought to acquiesce. Bowing to such pressure does not, however, necessarily signify a change in the Member's legal position. Resolutions of both the General Assembly and the Security Council need not be legally binding in order to be effective; they may be effective even though their legality is doubtful. The Charter, however, probably reflects the maximum rather than the minimum of consensus that could have been reached at San Francisco. Going beyond the San Francisco consensus has proved extremely difficult although, as in the instance of decolonization, not impossible. Decolonization, however, was far more the result of political forces, not necessarily connected with the UN, than of the acceptance of increased legal authority for the UN.

It has also been argued that the United Nations is a "living" institution and that the Charter is more like a constitution than an ordinary treaty. According to this view, allowance must be made for change and adaptation of the

[4] Report of the Rapporteur of Committee IV/2 (Judicial Organization, Legal Problems) to Commission IV (Judicial Organization), Document 933, June 12, 1945, in *Documents of the United Nations Conference on International Organization, San Francisco, 1945* (New York: United Nations Information Organization, 1945), Vol. 13, p. 710. Italics added.

[5] By Resolution 1991 (XVIII) of December 17, 1963, the General Assembly, in accordance with Article 108, adopted amendments to the Charter providing for an increase in membership of the Security Council from eleven to fifteen and an increase in the requisite majority from seven to nine; the membership of the Economic and Social Council (ECOSOC) would be enlarged from eighteen to 27. These amendments, if entered into force, will change the "balancing power" between various groups of Members but will not impose new obligations upon the Members.

[6] D. H. N. Johnson, "The Effect of Resolutions of the General Assembly of the United Nations," *British Year Book of International Law, 1955–1956* (London: Oxford University Press, 1957), Vol. 32, pp. 97–123.

law, and the possibility should be recognized of the growth of a "common law" arising from the practice of the organs in applying, adjusting, modifying, supplementing, and even supplanting provisions of the Charter.[7] This approach to the Charter goes back to the earliest years of the UN[8] and has come to be used as an instrument for fulfilling a variety of aims. It has been sustained by a desire, even a sense of duty, on the part of many UN Members to reach out for solutions or some manifestation of authority unhampered by "legalistic" considerations; a feeling that the law was inadequate for the task at hand; a general distrust of international law by some Members; a sense of frustration over the abuse of the veto and a corresponding determination to prevent the extension of the veto by refusing to admit a sort of "absentee ballot" in the Security Council, or a financial veto in the Assembly, or any kind of veto in the operation of regional organizations; and a determination to eliminate all vestiges of colonialism.

Like the liberal interpretation of the Charter, however, the successful use of the so-called "common law" and even of customary international law requires broad acceptance of the resulting legal formulas—practice alone will not suffice. As Judge Sir Percy Spender put it, "Unless it is of a peaceful, uniform and undisputed character accepted by all current Members . . . ," practice has no probative value.[9] While, as noted above, each organ has the right to interpret the Charter, "the majority has no power to extend, alter or disregard the Charter."[10] To be sure, those who regard practice, pure and simple, as a source of the "common law" of the United Nations may draw comfort from the opinion of the Court in the *Expenses* case to the extent that it relied on practice[11] without the qualification suggested by Judge Spender. But the melancholy proceedings at the nineteenth session of the General Assembly and its failure either to apply Article 19 or to find a solution acceptable to all should dampen the faith of the more exuberant interpreters in the ability of the United Nations to operate without a broad consensus. The truth of the matter is that in 1964–1965 the United Nations was not yet ready to implement this

[7] One example of this kind of evolution is the practice of the General Assembly of electing two Members for one nonpermanent seat on the Security Council in disregard of the "mandatory" provision of Article 23, paragraph 2. Another is the general long-standing practice of taking lightly the "mandatory" provision in Article 23, paragraph 1, that in electing nonpermanent members due regard should especially be paid "in the first instance to the contribution of Members of the United Nations to the maintenance of international peace and security. . . . " One wonders whether the Members which participate in these elections believe they are acting in accordance with the "good faith" principle in Article 2, paragraph 2.

[8] Benjamin V. Cohen has pointed out that on October 30, 1946, the United States representative, Warren R. Austin, declared in the General Assembly: "Under the broad and flexible construction of the Charter which the United States wishes to develop, we foresee a great and expanding area of operations for the General Assembly." (*The United Nations: Constitutional Developments, Growth and Possibilities* [Cambridge, Mass: Harvard University Press, 1961], p. 16.)

[9] *Certain Expenses of the United Nations (Article 17, paragraph 2, of the Charter), Advisory Opinion of 20 July 1962: I.C.J. Reports 1962*, p. 195.

[10] *Ibid.*, p. 197.

[11] *Ibid.*, p. 160.

forward-looking advisory opinion of the Court. The minority in opposition was small and determined. Its ranks would, however, soon swell to include all the economically developed Members[12] if the Assembly were to include in the budget of the Organization an item of, say, $5 billion for economic development, surely a major purpose of the United Nations, and assess those Members accordingly. Pursuant to the advisory opinion this could be regarded as a "reasonable" exercise of the powers recognized by the Court to be vested in the General Assembly.

What has been said about practice as a source of the "common law" of the United Nations applies in principle to the alleged growth of customary international law. Strictly speaking, there is an aggravating factor. Even if the time element is excluded from consideration, according to prevailing doctrine consistent and uniform practice must be supplemented by its acceptance as law. Proof of such acceptance is extremely difficult and, in the absence of a judgment by a commonly accepted authority, almost always a matter of controversy. No doubt certain practices have developed in the United Nations, but have they been accepted as law? The mere fact that Members support by their vote certain resolutions does not necessarily imply that they do it out of a sense of legal obligation rather than in a spirit of accommodation nor even that they regard the resolution as constitutional. Members are responsive to certain moods and pressures, and the Organization itself can become an outstanding "pressure group" defying the application of the legal yardstick. As Judge Spender pointed out, the majority rule which prevails in the Assembly and the Council "may enable action to be taken which is beyond power" but when legal considerations are invoked, "*de facto* extension of the Charter must be disregarded."[13] In short, the growth of customary international law within the framework of the Charter is not excluded, but assertions that such growth has occurred should be treated with caution unless there is reliable evidence that there is not merely consensus as to practice but that this practice has become a matter of law.

LAW AS AN OBJECTIVE OF THE UN SYSTEM

From the beginning of its existence the United Nations has been concerned with the development of international law. The Covenant of the League of Nations, in its preamble, declared that the High Contracting Parties intended to promote international peace and security "by the firm establishment of the understandings of international law as the actual rule of conduct among

[12] The distinction between "economically less developed countries" which includes all Members other than 26 listed by name has been made by the General Assembly in recent resolutions relating to the financing of the UN Operation in the Congo (ONUC) and the UN Emergency Force (UNEF). See, for instance, Resolutions 1885 (XVIII) of October 18, 1963, and 1983 (XVIII) of December 17, 1963.

[13] *I.C.J. Reports 1962*, p. 197.

Governments. . . ." The Charter, on the other hand, refrained from committing the United Nations to such an objective, which after the cataclysm of the
Second World War may have struck its founders as premature. A more cautious attitude seemed to be indicated. It was reflected in the preamble and in
Article 13, paragraph 1(a), of the Charter. The preamble recognized that conditions had to be established under which respect for international law could
be maintained. Article 13, paragraph 1(a), directed the Assembly to initiate
studies and make recommendations for the purpose of "encouraging the progressive development of international law and its codification." This task the
Assembly has discharged in a variety of ways, directly or through one of its
subordinate committees or commissions, principally the International Law
Commission. In addition to the Assembly, the contribution to the development of law of other principal organs, namely, the Economic and Social
Council (ECOSOC), the Secretary-General, the United Nations Administrative Tribunal, and the International Court of Justice, should be noted.

Rather than taking up separately the contributions made by these agencies,
this analysis will attempt to make some generalizations regarding the objectives pursued by the General Assembly. Throughout the years the Assembly
may be said to have tried, first, to revitalize international law and to deal with
the fundamentals of a new international legal order. Secondly, it has contributed to the development and codification of traditional law and, thirdly, to the
formulation of principles in areas not yet governed by international law. In
order to achieve or promote these objectives the Assembly has proceeded
pragmatically, using a variety of media, including the International Law Commission or *ad hoc* committees or conferences, and has embodied the results
in conventions or resolutions. A few selected examples will illustrate the pertinent activities of the United Nations.

Within the third field of its endeavors, the General Assembly, by Resolution 1962 (XVIII) of December 13, 1963, adopted the "Declaration of Legal
Principles Governing the Activities of States in the Exploration and Use of
Outer Space" and by Resolution 1963 (XVIII) of the same day formulated
the legal principles involved in "International co-operation in the peaceful
uses of outer space."[14] These basic resolutions in a new field of concern to
Members emanated from the Committee on the Peaceful Uses of Outer Space
which was established by the Assembly and which reported to the First (Political and Security) and not the Sixth (Legal) Committee. The legal significance of these resolutions in the formulation of international law will be discussed later. Insofar as Resolution 1962 (XVIII) is concerned, it proposed no
further steps. By contrast, Resolution 1963 (XVIII) recommended that consideration should be given "to incorporating in international agreement form"

[14] The Assembly dealt in Resolutions 1802 (XVII) of December 14, 1962, 1721 (XVI) of December
20, 1961, and 1472 (XIV) of December 12, 1959, with the problem of the peaceful uses of outer space.

legal principles governing the exploration and use of outer space. The Assembly considered, then, that these principles needed, in order to become fully binding, to be incorporated in a treaty, the classic medium of international legislation. The same medium was considered, in the same resolution, necessary for formulating principles concerning liability for damage caused by objects launched into outer space and assistance to and return of astronauts and space vehicles. The Assembly's Committee on the Peaceful Uses of Outer Space was charged with the necessary preparatory work. Resolutions 1721 D (XVI) of December 20, 1961, and 1802 IV (XVII) of December 14, 1962, on satellite communications have already been implemented by the "Agreement Establishing Interim Arrangements for a Global Commercial Communication Satellite System" of July 24, 1964, which entered into force on August 20, 1964.[15]

The Work and Contributions of the International Law Commission

For purposes of codification and progressive development of international law the Assembly has relied chiefly on the International Law Commission, an autonomous body established by Resolution 174 (II) of November 21, 1947, which incorporates the Statute of the Commission. Originally composed of fifteen and since 1962 of 25 experts[16] elected by the Assembly in their individual capacities, the Commission has become representative of the membership and of the world's principal legal systems. The Commission's members serve only part-time, which has its drawbacks—the inevitably slow pace of its work—as well as its advantages—to wit the availability of first-rate lawyers who could not accept a full-time appointment. It seems to be the fact that although the members serve in their individual capacity and therefore independently of governments, an increasingly large number, now about two-thirds, nevertheless hold official positions.

The Commission's Statute, like Article 13, paragraph 1(a), of the Charter, distinguishes between codification and progressive development.[17] In practice, however, the distinction has become blurred, and "a single consolidated pro-

---

[15] *United States Treaties and Other International Acts Series,* No. 5646 (Washington, D.C: U.S. Government Printing Office, 1964). See also, James Simsarian, "Interim Arrangements for a Global Commercial Satellite System," *The American Journal of International Law,* April 1965 (Vol. 59, No. 2), pp. 344–351.

[16] Membership was increased to 21 by General Assembly Resolution 1103 (VI) of December 18, 1956, and to 25 by General Assembly Resolution 1647 (XVI) of November 6, 1961.

[17] Article 15 of the Statute reads as follows:

> In the following articles the expression "progressive development of international law" is used for convenience as meaning the preparation of draft conventions on subjects which have not yet been regulated by international law or in regard to which the law has not yet been sufficiently developed in the practice of States. Similarly, the expression "codification of international law" is used for convenience as meaning the more precise formulation and systematization of rules of international law in fields where there already has been extensive state practice, precedent, and doctrine.

cedure has been made applicable to both types of work."[18] This practice did not affect the provision in the Statute stating that the General Assembly and other agencies, but not the Commission, had the power to initiate projects which were wholly or predominantly concerned with progressive development.

The Commission during its first ten sessions concluded work on sixteen projects.[19] Since then it has completed the draft articles on consular intercourse and immunities[20] and finished the last section of its draft on the law of treaties,[21] which it has now submitted to governments for their observations. The completion of this draft constitutes a major achievement in view of the significance of treaties in interstate relations. The Commission will at a later stage, presumably after reexamination of all the draft articles in the light of the observations received from the governments, consider whether the three parts of the law of treaties should be amalgamated to form a single draft convention or whether they should be embodied in a series of related conventions.[22] The Commission's program of work provides for completion of the study of the law of treaties and of special missions[23] and for work on the question of relations between states and intergovernmental organizations, in that order. The Commission then will deal with questions of succession of states and governments and state responsibility.[24]

Of the topics studied by the Commission several have been submitted to international conferences and cast in the form of regular conventions open for signature and notification. The United Nations Conference on the Law of the Sea, held in Geneva in 1958, adopted four conventions on the law of the sea and an Optional Protocol on Compulsory Settlement of Disputes. The Conference failed to agree on the width of the territorial sea, a matter on which the Commission has refrained from submitting a proposal.[25] The second Geneva

[18] Shabtai Rosenne, "The International Law Commission," *British Year Book of International Law, 1960* (London: Oxford University Press, 1961), Vol. 36, p. 142.

[19] 1) Draft declaration on rights and duties of states; 2) ways and means for making the evidence of customary international law more readily available; 3) formulation of the Nuremberg Principles; 4) question of international criminal jurisdiction; 5) draft code of offenses against the peace and security of mankind; 6) question of defining aggression; 7) reservations to multilateral conventions; 8) draft on arbitral procedure; 9) draft convention on the elimination of future statelessness; 10) draft convention on the reduction of future statelessness; 11–14) draft convention on the law of the sea, comprising territorial waters, the high seas, fishing and conservation of the living resources of the high seas, and the continental shelf; 15) draft on diplomatic intercourse and immunities; and 16) revision of 1958 draft on arbitral procedure. (*Yearbook of the International Law Commission, 1958* [UN Document A/CN.4/SER.A/1958/Add.1], Vol. II, p. 109, footnotes 39 and 40.)

[20] General Assembly *Official Records* (16th session), Supplement No. 9, p. 2.

[21] General Assembly *Official Records* (19th session), Supplement No. 9, p. 7.

[22] *Ibid.*, p. 9.

[23] At its 1964 session the Commission adopted sixteen draft articles on the subject of special missions. (*Ibid.*, pp. 98–142.)

[24] *Ibid.*, p. 143.

[25] The Commission had also omitted articles on the question of access to the sea of landlocked states. This subject was, after a preliminary conference convened by the Swiss government, part of the agenda of the Geneva Conference.

Conference on the Law of the Sea, which met in 1960, again failed to reach agreement on this extremely controversial question by a very narrow margin.[26] The United Nations Conference on Diplomatic Intercourse and Immunities of 1961 adopted the Vienna Convention on Diplomatic Relations, and the United Nations Conference on Consular Relations of 1963 adopted the Vienna Convention on Consular Relations.[27] The 1959 United Nations Conference on the Elimination or Reduction of Future Statelessness which considered the Commission's draft conventions on the elimination of future statelessness and on the reduction of future statelessness adjourned without accomplishing its task (although the 1961 New York Conference did adopt the Convention on the Reduction of Statelessness). No action has been taken so far by the Assembly with respect to the draft code of offenses against the peace and security of mankind. The 1953 draft on arbitral procedure was not acceptable to the General Assembly largely for two reasons: first, because the Assembly deemed that the Commission

> had exceeded its terms of reference by giving *preponderance* to its desire to promote the development of international law instead of concentrating on its *primary* task, [*i.e.*] the codification of custom

and secondly, because it was felt "the Commission's draft would distort traditional arbitration practice, making it into a quasi-compulsory jurisdictional procedure."[28] The Commission at its tenth session adopted a set of model draft articles from which, in the words of the rapporteur, Professor Georges Scelle, *"every trace of obligation has been eliminated."*[29] This draft did not, however, fare better than the first, as the Assembly merely took note of it.[30] The rapporteur probably came close to the truth when he analyzed the reasons for the negative attitude of governments as follows:

> As the number of States Members of the United Nations increases, so the majority hostile to the Commission's draft seems bound to increase, for the more recently the new Members have acquired their sovereignty the greater will be their desire to maintain it whole and entire.[31]

This resolution must have been a personal disappointment to the rapporteur who had devoted his life to the promotion of the rule of law. The episode is merely one more evidence of the intractability of the environment.

The report of the Commission on reservations to multilateral conventions[32]

[26] See Arthur H. Dean, "The Second Geneva Conference on the Law of the Sea: The Fight for Freedom of the Seas," *The American Journal of International Law,* October 1960 (Vol. 54, No. 4), pp. 751–789.

[27] At both Conferences optional protocols on acquisition of nationality and compulsory settlement of disputes were also adopted.

[28] *Yearbook of the International Law Commission, 1958,* Vol. II, p. 80.

[29] *Ibid.,* p. 3. Italics added.

[30] General Assembly Resolution 1262 (XIII) of November 14, 1958.

[31] *Yearbook of the International Law Commission, 1958,* Vol. II, p. 2.

[32] General Assembly *Official Records* (6th session), Special Supplement No. 9, pp. 2–8.

was adopted by the General Assembly in Resolution 598 (VI) of January 12, 1951. The Assembly recommended that organs of the United Nations, specialized agencies, and states

> should, in the course of preparing multilateral conventions, consider the insertion therein of provisions relating to the admissibility or nonadmissibility of reservations and to the effect to be attributed to them.

None of the conventions resulting from the work of the Commission contains such provisions.

The Commission's draft declaration on rights and duties of states was deemed by the Assembly

> a notable and substantial contribution towards the progressive development of international law and its codification and as such commends it to the continuing attention of the Member States and of jurists of all nations.[33]

The work of the Commission on the Nuremberg principles and the draft code of offenses against the peace and security of mankind will be discussed later.

There has been a good deal of controversy about the work of the Commission and the desirability of codifying international law. The principal target of complaints has been the slowness of its progress.[34] The Commission has been sensitive to this criticism and in defense it has pointed out that the record was far from discouraging. The Commission noted that for the first ten years it presented on the average one completed piece of work to the Assembly each year; it responded to several requests of the Assembly which did not call for draft articles but only for a report or opinion; the quality of the work was more important than the rate of speed with which it was turned out; and finally, at a time when

> the whole of international law and international relations was now going through a period of adjustment . . . speed was not necessarily the most important consideration.[35]

The Commission, in order to work more efficiently, has in recent years established a drafting committee to which have been referred

> not merely pure drafting points, but also points of substance which the full Commission had been unable to resolve, or which seemed likely to give rise to unduly protracted discussion.[36]

[33] General Assembly Resolution 375 (IV) of December 6, 1949.

[34] See the debate on the work of the Commission in the Sixth Committee at the fifteenth session in General Assembly *Official Records . . . Sixth Committee* (15th session, Part I), pp. 9–115. H. Lauterpacht expressed the view that the work of codification would require several generations in his "Codification and Development of International Law," *The American Journal of International Law,* January 1955 (Vol. 49, No. 1), p. 42. J. Robinson found the balance sheet of the Commission discouraging in "The Metamorphosis of the United Nations," *Recueil des Cours de l'Académie de Droit International,* 1958 (Leyden: A. W. Sythoff, 1959), Vol. II, p. 575.

[35] *Yearbook of the International Law Commission, 1958,* Vol. II, pp. 109–110.

[36] *Ibid.,* p. 108.

Private meetings of this sort have been immensely useful in expediting agreement. The Commission has also extended its regular annual session, held short winter sessions in 1962 and 1963, and has proposed to hold a four-week winter session in 1966 in order to complete its current program of work before the expiration of its term of office in 1966.[37] But delays attributable to such political factors as the Cold War and the emergence of new states[38] are beyond the control of the Commission and may in fact have been less potent in the work of the Commission in the last few years than is sometimes assumed. The crucial test for the Commission will come in connection with the codification of the law of state succession and responsibility of states.

In spite of what, in the present view, must be regarded as an impressive record of achievement, the question is still open of how effective the work of the Commission will be. A good though not conclusive gauge for measuring this is the progress in ratifying the conventions mentioned above. The conventions resulting from the recent Vienna Conferences may not offer an adequate test although the Convention on Diplomatic Relations received 33 ratifications as of November 1964, that is, within three years.[39] By January 1, 1965, that is, after a lapse of close to seven years, the various Geneva conventions had been ratified by numbers ranging between fourteen and 29 states.[40] Conventions which fail to receive a substantial number of ratifications may not be heralds of new or even more precise law, but they may still be potent enough to unsettle what previously passed for established though uncertain customary rules of international law. This could be so in spite of the fact that all of the conventions have been approved by two-thirds majorities at the Geneva and Vienna Conferences and that virtually all the then existing states participated in them with the notable exception of Communist China. Thus, the new states, which sometimes express the view that traditional customary international law has developed without their collaboration and fails to reflect their interests and aspirations, have had an opportunity to participate in the codification of large portions of the law.[41] The pessimists

[37] General Assembly *Official Records* (19th session), Supplement No. 9, p. 51, paragraphs 37, 38.

[38] Rosenne, *British Year Book of International Law, 1960*, Vol. 36, pp. 155-156.

[39] UN Document ST/LEG/SER.A/213, p. 19. The Convention came into force on April 24, 1964 (UN Document ST/LEG/SER.A/208, p. 14).

[40] The Convention on the Territorial Sea and the Contiguous Zone was ratified by 23 states including the Soviet Union, the United Kingdom, and the United States; the Convention on the High Seas by 29 states including the same Great Powers; the Convention on Fishing and Conservation of the Living Resources of the High Seas by fourteen states including the United Kingdom and the United States; and the Convention on the Continental Shelf by 24 states including the Soviet Union, the United Kingdom, and the United States. (*Treaties in Force: A List of Treaties and Other International Agreements of the United States in Force on January 1, 1965* [Department of State Publication 7817] [Washington, D.C: U.S. Government Printing Office, 1965], p. 263). The Optional Protocol of Signature concerning the Compulsory Settlement of Disputes received only one ratification (Haiti)! (UN Document ST/LEG/3, Rev.1, pp. 26–28.)

[41] A substantial number of recently emerged states ratified the conventions mentioned above. See also Rosenne, *British Year Book of International Law, 1960*, Vol. 36, p. 159.

may yet be right,[42] but the progress achieved so far cannot be regarded as less than encouraging although some sticky problems still lie ahead.

Formulating the Bases of a New Legal Order

The activities of the Assembly relating to the fundamentals of a new international legal order cover a very wide field and are difficult to survey and even more difficult to evaluate. A beginning might be made with the interest of the Assembly in formulating in an up-to-date fashion the basic principles of such an order. In accordance with this aim, the Assembly requested and the Commission drafted the declaration on the rights and duties of states mentioned above. In fourteen articles the Commission set out some principles already contained in the Charter, e.g., in Article 2, paragraphs 2 and 5, and Article 51, as well as some principles which have frequently been referred to as fundamental rights of states. These included the rights to independence, jurisdiction, and equality, and some duties, such as the duty to refrain from intervention, fomenting civil strife, resorting to war as an instrument of national policy, and, as corollary thereto, recognizing any territorial acquisition in violation of the prohibition. Finally, Article 14 stated the duty to act in accordance with international law and "the principle that the sovereignty of each State is subject to the supremacy of international law."[43] Obviously the drafting was open to criticism as were some of the proposed articles.[44] The last mentioned article was attacked as a reactionary attempt to enslave certain states. And yet, if there is to be a viable "new international order," which the preamble of the resolution proclaims as already established, it is difficult to see how this principle could be excluded. As for the rest, some ground rules need to be established and accepted if there is to be any meaningful order among states at all. Be that as it may, the Assembly's request to governments for comments and suggestions on the draft articles and any further action went unheeded, and in 1951 the Assembly postponed the matter until a majority of Members had transmitted their replies.[45]

The attempt at a wholesale reconstruction of the underpinnings of the new order was then discontinued in favor of a piecemeal approach in the course of which a number of related projects were undertaken which will be discussed presently. The Assembly, however, was to be led back to the consideration of fundamentals in consequence of a Soviet proposal to consider principles of peaceful coexistence. The term "peaceful coexistence" being anathema to the free-world segment of the United Nations membership, General Assem-

---

[42] For a reserved opinion, see Julius Stone, "On the Vocation of the International Law Commission," *Columbia Law Review,* January 1957 (Vol. 57, No. 1), pp. 16–51.

[43] General Assembly Resolution 375 (IV) of December 6, 1949.

[44] Hans Kelsen, "The Draft Declaration on Rights and Duties of States," *The American Journal of International Law,* April 1950 (Vol. 44, No. 2), pp. 259–276.

[45] General Assembly Resolution 596 (VI), December 7, 1951.

bly Resolution 1815 (XVII) of December 18, 1962, bears the properly sanitized title "Consideration of principles of international law concerning friendly relations and co-operation among States in accordance with the Charter of the United Nations." The preamble is long and full of reaffirmations of certain statements which have become current in discussions within United Nations organs. The resolution recognized "the paramount importance, in the progressive development of international law and in the promotion of the rule of law among nations" of seven principles already embodied in the Charter,[46] resolved, pursuant to Article 13 of the Charter, to study these principles and decided to place four of these principles, (a), (b), (c), and (f), on the agenda of its eighteenth session. At that session the Assembly adopted Resolution 1966 (XVIII) on December 16, 1963, and decided to entrust the study of these principles to a Special Committee on Principles of International Law Concerning Friendly Relations and Cooperation Among States, to be appointed by the President.[47] Thus, the Assembly decided to bypass the International Law Commission and to work with a political committee. To be sure, the Special Committee was to be representative of the principal legal systems, it would be based on the principle of equitable geographic distribution, and Members were invited to appoint jurists as their representatives.

The Special Committee was fully aware of the importance of its task. It considered the four principles as constituting "cornerstones of peaceful relations among States" and as going "to the very root of peaceful relations among States." As to the wisdom of undertaking the task assigned to it, the Committee was divided. On the one hand, some members thought it was necessary to bring the Charter principles up to date by taking into account "the evolution that had occurred in international law during the past twenty years, both in the practice of States and of the United Nations." On the other hand some members

> expressed doubts about the utility of hasty declarations or statements which proclaimed in a non-binding fashion principles already binding upon States under the Charter

and were of the opinion that failures on the part of the United Nations "had not been due to lack of clarity of Charter principles . . . but to the fact that

---

[46] To wit: (a) This principle is identic with Article 2(4); (b) this is identic with Article 2(3); (c) "The duty not to intervene in matters within the domestic jurisdiction of any State, in accordance with the Charter"; (d) "The duty of States to co-operate with one another in accordance with the Charter"; (e) "The principle of equal rights and self-determination of peoples"; (f) "The principle of sovereign equality of States"; and (g) "The principle that States shall fulfil in good faith the obligations assumed by them in accordance with the Charter." By General Assembly Resolution 1966 (XVIII) it was decided to place principles (d), (e), and (g) on the agenda of the nineteenth session, which was, however, paralyzed by the controversy over the application of Article 19 of the Charter.

[47] General Assembly *Official Records* (18th session), Supplement No. 15, p. 70. The President appointed 27 Members to serve on the Special Committee, including a small number of new states. As Cameroun was unable to attend, the Special Committee, which met at Mexico City from August 27 to October 2, 1964, consisted of 26 members.

certain States were not resolved to support any international system of law."
As to the procedure to be followed it was said that

> resolutions of the General Assembly did not in themselves constitute international
> law, but they might represent an important step in the process of making inter-
> national law

and that "the most important element in the process of evolving international
law was universality." The Special Committee's function then was seen as
ascertaining "the area in which there was a consensus among delegations."[48]

The results of the Special Committee's labors were perhaps necessarily and
predictably disappointing. On the first three principles no consensus was
reached,[49] and the Special Committee achieved unanimity only on the principle
of equality. The agreed statement contained the four points already accepted
at the San Francisco Conference[50] and these additional understandings: Each
state has the duty to respect the personality of other states, and each state has
the right freely to choose and develop its political, social, economic, and cultural systems.[51]

Thus, the second attempt of the United Nations to formulate more precisely
some basic principles of the international legal order largely miscarried, so
far at any rate. Once again the high hopes in some quarters that a fresh approach by a body on which developing states were adequately represented
offered "an opportunity to rethink problems and to establish rules which can
be utilized to eliminate the cause of tensions and of threats to the peace"[52]
have been dashed. The elimination of tensions may well be the basic precondition. But this is a task for high-level statesmen and not for jurists.

RESPONSIBILITY OF INDIVIDUALS FOR ACTS CONTRARY TO INTERNATIONAL LAW

In another effort to infuse new principles into the old international order,
the Assembly was concerned with the formulation of individual and criminal
responsibility of individuals for acts contrary to international law. Various
tribunals both national and international, notably the International Military
Tribunal in Nuremberg, have recognized such responsibility. The General
Assembly, by Resolution 95 (I) of December 11, 1946, affirmed "the principles
of international law recognized by the Charter of the Nürnberg Tribunal

---

[48] Report of the Special Committee on Principles of International Law Concerning Friendly Relations
and Cooperation Among States (UN Document A/5746, November 16, 1964), pp. 15–18.

[49] *Ibid.*, pp. 60, 67, 104, 141.

[50] Document 944, *Documents of the United Nations Conference on International Organization, San
Francisco, 1945* (New York: United Nations Information Organization, 1945), Vol. 6, p. 457, and
Vol. 1, p. 614.

[51] Report of the Special Committee, UN Document A/5746, p. 163, paragraph 339.

[52] John N. Hazard, "New Personalities to Create New Law," *The American Journal of International
Law,* October 1964 (Vol. 58, No. 4), p. 959. For a recent study of coexistence, see Edward McWhinney,
" 'Peaceful Coexistence' and Soviet-Western International Law," *The American Journal of International
Law,* October 1962 (Vol. 56, No. 4), pp. 951–970.

and the judgment of the Tribunal." At the same time the Assembly instructed the Committee on the Codification of International Law, the forerunner of the International Law Commission,

> to treat as a matter of primary importance plans for the formulation, in the context of a general codification of offences against the peace and security of mankind, or of an International Criminal Code,

of those principles.[53] In another resolution the Assembly affirmed that genocide, as defined therein,

> is a crime under international law which the civilized world condemns, and for the commission of which principals and accomplices—whether private individuals, public officials or statesmen, . . .—are punishable.

It directed the Economic and Social Council to study the preparation of a draft convention on genocide.[54] The stage was thus set for a major effort at lawmaking in a relatively uncharted and highly controversial field.

The Economic and Social Council produced and the Assembly adopted in due course the Convention on the Prevention and Punishment of the Crime of Genocide.[55] This entered into force on January 12, 1951, and was ratified by a large number of states. It is surely a landmark in the legal protection of national, ethnic, racial, and religious groups and therefore of individuals belonging to such groups. As stated in the preamble, the object of the Convention is "to liberate mankind from such an odious scourge." Whether this has been achieved may be doubtful. The efficiency of enforcement by national tribunals is open to question, and the international penal tribunal referred to in Article VI of the Convention has not been established. But by Resolution 260 B (III) of December 9, 1948, the Assembly requested the International Law Commission to study "the desirability and possibility of establishing an international judicial organ for the trial of persons charged with genocide or other crimes."

The Commission was divided but decided by a majority vote that the establishment of an international criminal jurisdiction was both desirable and possible. In the rapporteur's view, "the rule of law in the community of States could only be ensured" by such a jurisdiction vested with power to try and punish persons "who disturbed international public order."[56] The Assembly established a committee[57] which submitted a draft statute for an International

---

[53] Resolution 95 (I), contained in UN Document A/64/Add.1, p. 188.

[54] General Assembly Resolution 96 (I), December 11, 1946 contained in *ibid.,* p. 189.

[55] General Assembly Resolution 260 A (III) of December 9, 1948. For an analysis, see Josef L. Kunz, "The United Nations Convention on Genocide," *The American Journal of International Law,* October 1949 (Vol. 43, No. 4), p. 738.

[56] General Assembly *Official Records* (5th session), Supplement No. 12, paragraphs 135, 140. The Assembly in Resolution 260 B (III) referred to the above and requested the International Law Commission to pay attention to the possibility of establishing a criminal chamber in the existing International Court of Justice; the Commission expressed no view on the subject.

[57] General Assembly Resolution 489 (V) of December 12, 1950.

Criminal Court in 1951.[58] Like the Commission, this committee was divided on both the desirability and possibility of establishing such a court.[59]

In the meantime the International Law Commission pursued the formulation of the substantive law to be applied by the proposed Criminal Court or another tribunal. It adopted the text of the Nuremberg principles without, however, expressing an opinion on whether or not "the principles contained in the Charter [of the International Military Tribunal] and judgment constituted principles of international law." It was thought to be precluded from doing so by the affirmation of those principles in General Assembly Resolution 95 (I).[60] The Commission then took up work on the draft code of offenses against the peace and security of mankind. It submitted a draft to the sixth session of the Assembly,[61] but the Assembly failed to take it up either at that or the seventh session. The Commission then, in the light of comments received from governments, completed its task at its sixth session and submitted the draft code to the Assembly.[62] The draft code included the Nuremberg principles and the provisions of the Genocide Convention, as well as additional offenses and a makeshift open-ended definition of aggression.[63]

THE PROBLEM OF DEFINING AGGRESSION

It may be recalled that in 1950 the Assembly had referred to the Commission a Soviet proposal concerning a definition of aggression.[64] The Commission, however, did not furnish a separate definition of aggression but included it in the draft code of offenses.[65] The Assembly was not satisfied with this approach. It considered a definition "possible and desirable, with a view to ensuring international peace and security and to developing international criminal law" and decided to study the matter itself at the seventh session.[66] At that session it established a special committee of fifteen members for this purpose.[67] The special committee met in 1953 and submitted a report which was discussed at the ninth session of the Assembly.[68] At this session the Assembly decided to reconstitute the special committee and instructed it to

[58] UN Document A/AC.48/4.

[59] See Quincy Wright, "Proposal for an International Criminal Court," *The American Journal of International Law*, January 1952 (Vol. 46, No. 1), pp. 60–72, and Yuen-li Liang, "Notes on Legal Questions concerning the United Nations," *ibid.*, pp. 73–88.

[60] General Assembly *Official Records* (5th session), Supplement No. 12, Part III, paragraph 96.

[61] General Assembly *Official Records* (6th session), Supplement No. 9, p. 10.

[62] General Assembly *Official Records* (9th session), Supplement No. 9, Chapter III, pp. 9–12.

[63] To wit, Article 2, paragraph 1, states:

Any act of aggression, including the employment by the authorities of a State of armed force against another State for any purpose other than national or collective self-defence or in pursuance of a decision or recommendation of a competent organ of the United Nations.

[64] General Assembly Resolution 378 B (V) of November 17, 1950.

[65] General Assembly *Official Records* (9th session), Supplement No. 9. See footnote 63 above.

[66] General Assembly Resolution 599 (VI) of January 31, 1952.

[67] General Assembly Resolution 688 (VII) of December 20, 1952.

[68] General Assembly *Official Records* (9th session), Supplement No. 11.

report to the eleventh session.[69] At the same time the Assembly decided to postpone further consideration of the draft code and of the question of an international criminal jurisdiction in order to be able to take these matters up together with the question of defining aggression.[70] Consideration of the three questions was again postponed in 1957;[71] the committee on the question of defining aggression met in 1965 but without result.

Thus ended another attempt to remedy some of the weaknesses of the international legal order. There is obviously room for different views as to the immediate importance of the draft code and a definition of aggression.[72] They may not be the most urgent tasks confronting the United Nations and even if they were—and the Assembly must have thought the tasks at least worthwhile—they may not have been feasible in the current state of international affairs. Certainly the decision to search for a definition of aggression and other serious breaches of international law is eminently political. Any addition to the law of the United Nations would necessarily be in the nature of a serious limitation on the freedom of action of the Members. Such limitations may seem undesirable unless and until the United Nations becomes capable of providing effective security and effective procedures for the peaceful settlement of disputes.

The fate of the Commission's draft on arbitral procedure and the nonuse of the International Court of Justice by both the United Nations and its Members bear eloquent testimony to the fact that neither the Organization nor its Members are prepared to entrust matters of vital concern to them to such depoliticized procedures. The decision to depoliticize such matters is itself a political decision. The question of security has become closely linked with the issue of arms control and disarmament, the achievement of which is not yet in sight. The momentum for a radical transformation of the international legal order, which impelled the Assembly to tackle the definition of aggression in the context of the draft code, has been lost. As a result of the Cold War and the ever present threat of thermonuclear destruction, the search for security through fundamental reforms of a structural character gave way to the search for security through more readily available and familiar patterns. In such familiar surroundings insecurity seems to have become bearable.

---

[69] General Assembly Resolution 895 (IX) of December 4, 1954. For the report of the 1956 session of the Special Committee on the Question of Defining Aggression, October 8–November 9, 1956, see UN Document A/AC.77/L.13.

[70] General Assembly Resolutions 897 (IX) of December 4, 1954, and 898 (IX) of December 14, 1954.

[71] General Assembly Resolutions 1181 (XII) of November 29, 1957, and 1186 (XII) and 1187 (XII) December 11, 1957.

[72] See Julius Stone, *Aggression and World Order. A Critique of United Nations Theories of Aggression* (London: Stevens & Sons Limited, 1958).

FORMULATING THE BASES OF A NEW SOCIO-ECONOMIC ORDER

The Assembly's concern for the advancement of a new international political and socio-economic order has taken the form primarily of passing resolutions, sometimes solemnly called "declarations." The following come readil
to mind as they surely constitute landmarks in this line of endeavor: th
Universal Declaration of Human Rights (General Assembly Resolution 217 /
[III] of December 10, 1948), the Declaration on the Granting of Independence to Colonial Countries and Peoples (Resolution 1514 [XV] of Decembe
14, 1960), the Declaration on the Elimination of All Forms of Racial Discrimi
nation (Resolution 1904 [XVIII] of November 20, 1963), and Resolution 180
(XVII) of December 14, 1962, on "Permanent sovereignty over natural re
sources." In a sense these resolutions are concerned with the same or closel
related matters that were involved in the more formal procedures discusse
above. Thus, the Universal Declaration is concerned with the rights of in
dividuals which may be regarded as a counterpart to the duties implicitl
assumed in the draft code of offenses against the peace and security of man
kind. The resolution on permanent sovereignty, like the draft declaration o
rights and duties of states, is concerned with an "inalienable right" of states.
The Declaration on Colonialism is concerned as is the Declaration on Racia
Discrimination with fundamental human rights and the former, in additior
proclaims an "inalienable right" of peoples.[74]

It would be extremely difficult to provide a representative sample of th
efforts of the Assembly to promote economic development. Reference may b
made to the 1964 United Nations Conference on Trade and Developmer
(UNCTAD) which in a sense capped the concern of the United Nations wit
the developing nations and brought into focus some of the guiding principle
The Conference adopted fifteen general principles and thirteen special principles by very large majorities with the United States as the lone dissenter wit
respect to some of them. They range from relatively innocuous statemen
often made before in other forums in the same or similar formulation[75]
controversial ones on which the future economic relations between differer
socio-economic systems and between developing and developed countrie

---

[73] In the preamble the Assembly speaks of "the recognition of the inalienable right of all States free
to dispose of their natural wealth and resources in accordance with their national interests."

[74] In the preamble of General Assembly Resolution 1514 (XV) the Assembly expresses the convi
tion "that all peoples have an inalienable right to complete freedom, the exercise of their sovereign
and the integrity of their national territory."

[75] E.g., General Principle One:
   Economic relations between countries, including trade relations, shall be based on respect for t
   principle of sovereign equality of States, self-determination of peoples, and non-interference
   the internal affairs of other countries.

This was adopted by 113 in favor, 1 against (United States), with 2 abstentions. (Proceedings of t
United Nations Conference on Trade and Development, Geneva, 23 March–16 July 1964, Vol. I: Fir
Act and Report [UN Document E/CONF.46/141, Vol. I], p. 18.)

should be based.[76] The principles in their entirety disclose an intent to formulate a Magna Charta for economic relations with a bias frankly in favor of the developing countries.[77]

UN Resolutions as a Source of Law

The resort to the medium of resolutions as a vehicle for the progressive development of international law does not imply that the United Nations has abandoned the medium of the treaty or convention, or in more colloquial terms that the formulation of "hard" law (treaty) has been set aside in favor of "soft" law (resolution or declaration). The United Nations is pragmatic about its choice of media, and sometimes "soft" law is only considered a precursor of "hard" law. Thus, in the field of human rights, pending the completion of the covenants on human rights, the General Assembly adopted several conventions on some specific subjects such as slavery, political rights of women, and consent to marriage.[78] On the other hand, the Assembly adopted the Declaration on the Elimination of All Forms of Racial Discrimination and at the same time requested the Economic and Social Council to give "absolute priority" to the preparation of a draft convention on the same subject.[79]

There are differences of opinion on the significance or role of resolutions or declarations of the General Assembly as sources of international law. It may be observed first of all that where the Assembly has chosen a two-stage approval—first a declaration or resolution, followed by a convention—it has drawn a distinction between the traditional and accepted source of legal obligation, the convention, and the novel and controversial form, the resolution

[76] Thus General Principle Four reads in part:

All countries pledge themselves . . . to help promote, in developing countries, a rate of growth consistent with the need to bring about a substantial and steady increase in average incomes, in order to narrow the gap between the standard of living in developing countries and that in developed countries.

The vote on this was 98 in favor, 1 opposed (United States), with 17 abstentions. (Ibid.)

[77] For a concise summary and evaluation, see Oscar Schachter, "Legal Problems" in Richard N. Swift (ed.), Annual Review of United Nations Affairs, 1963–1964 (Dobbs Ferry, N.Y: Oceana Publications, 1965), pp. 125–127.

[78] Supplementary Convention on the Abolition of Slavery, the Slave Trade, and Practices Similar to Slavery of September 4, 1956 (UN Document E/CONF.24/23 or UN Sales No. 57.XIV.2) (the Convention came into force on April 30, 1959, upon the deposit of the second ratification; by July 1963, 49 states were parties); Convention on the Political Rights of Women of 1953, to which 39 states are parties; and Convention on Consent to Marriage, Minimum Age for Marriage and Registration of Marriages (General Assembly Resolution 1763 A [XVII] of November 7, 1962). On the current state of the work of the United Nations on human rights, see Myres S. McDougal and Gerhard Bebr, "Human Rights in the United Nations," The American Journal of International Law, July 1964 (Vol. 58, No. 3), pp. 603–641; and Richard B. Bilder, "The International Promotion of Human Rights: A Current Assessment," ibid., pp. 728–734.

[79] General Assembly Resolutions 1904 (XVIII) and 1906 (XVIII) of November 20, 1963. It may be noted that the Assembly has been preparing a draft declaration on the right of asylum and a draft declaration and draft convention on freedom of information (General Assembly Resolutions 1839 [XVII] and 1840 [XVII] of December 19, 1962).

or declaration. The distinction is of vital significance and, it is submitted, should be maintained.

This is not to suggest that the traditional sources of international law should not be kept under continuous review and that their adequacy need not be tested in the light of contemporary developments. There is room for a number of intermediate positions between the two extremes: At one pole of a continuum is the proposition that the General Assembly has a legislative or quasi-legislative function,[80] and at the other pole is the proposition that resolutions of the Assembly are legally not binding. The former view assumes and must assume that where the Assembly adopts resolutions such as those relating to human rights, self-determination, etc., it is merely elaborating principles already accepted as binding by the Members; and, in turn, it assumes further that the Assembly has the power of authentic and binding interpretation.[81] As was pointed out earlier, this view has not been generally accepted,[82] and it is doubtful whether it would be desirable to accept it. The latter position adheres to the original conception of the Assembly as a deliberative body endowed with limited powers and certainly, by design and not by omission, not endowed with legislative prerogatives. The two-stage approach followed by the Assembly and mentioned earlier is a clear and incontrovertible evidence that the Assembly shares this view of its own powers.

The significance of the resolutions of the Assembly is primarily political. Many are designed to give direction to the Members and the Organization as well. Some resolutions, such as those dealing with outer space, may derive especial significance from the fact that they represent the consensus of the two powers which have a virtual duopoly in that virginal field.[83] Where there is or is claimed to be law, as, for instance, with respect to compensation for the expropriation of property owned by aliens, a resolution of the Assembly, such as that on "Permanent sovereignty over natural resources" may have sufficient force to create or increase uncertainty as to the claimed law without being sufficiently persuasive to create a new rule. In this particular case the international standard according to which the state taking such measures must pay "prompt, adequate and effective" compensation has been under attack for so long and by so substantial a number of states that it could be fairly doubted whether that standard ever was or still is a rule of customary international law. This being so, the resolution of the Assembly proposing merely "appro-

[80] Jorge Castañeda, "The Underdeveloped Nations and the Development of International Law," International Organization, Winter 1961 (Vol. 15, No. 1), pp. 38–48.

[81] Ibid., p. 47; and Manfred Lachs, "The Law in and of the United Nations," Indian Journal of International Law, 1960–1961 (Vol. I), p. 438.

[82] See pp. 549–550 above for Mexico City statement of the Special Committee on Principles of International Law Concerning Friendly Relations and Cooperation Among States.

[83] See Oliver J. Lissitzyn's remarks in Swift, p. 128. Additional factors are the absence of a competing doctrine or consensus.

priate compensation"[84] may be deemed to have administered the *coup de grâce* to the alleged international standard. This conclusion is based not on any assumption of the resolution's having an obligatory character. It may be based more simply on the traditional concept of customary international law according to which a rule requires practice and the *opinio juris,* that is, the manifestation of conviction that the practice has been accepted as binding or obligatory. The debates in the Assembly stretching over a period of years would indicate that this conviction was lacking, that there was no supporting consensus.[85] Thus, as a convenient index for determining the existence or absence of consensus, the debates in the Assembly and the resolutions which it adopts may serve a useful purpose. But consensus without state practice is not productive of a rule of law.

There is a long way from the birth of an idea to its consummation in a rule of law, be it conventional or customary. Resolutions of the Assembly purporting to be of a lawmaking character are certainly "an important link in the continuing process of development and formulation of new principles of international law."[86] It has been suggested that the traditional statement of sources of international law in Article 38 of the Statute of the International Court of Justice and the distinction between binding and nonbinding sources "was becoming increasingly irrelevant and unrealistic."[87] This is perhaps too extreme a view, although it may serve a useful purpose to reexamine Article 38, which had been part of the Statute of the Permanent Court of International Justice and was adopted in 1945 without change in the Statute of the new Court, and perhaps to arrange for a reexamining of the sources of international law generally by a committee of governments.[88] Until this is done, however, it may be proper to regard debates in and resolutions of the General Assembly not so much as sources but, in the words of Article 38, paragraph 1(d), of the Statute "as a subsidiary means for the determination of rules of law." They might rank with, or even ahead of, "the teachings of the most highly qualified publicists" but below judicial decisions.

To close this analysis on a slightly ironical note: The Sixth Committee held a far-ranging debate in which it frequently expressed dissatisfaction with the state of international law, its own modest role in the United Na-

---

[84] Operative paragraph 4 of General Assembly Resolution 1803 (XVII) of December 14, 1962.

[85] In the *Sabbatino* case the United States Supreme Court held that consensus was lacking for the old standard and referred specifically to the long-standing opposition of the Communist countries, the declared opposition of many new countries, and the actual practice of states which accepted less than full compensation. (*Banco Nacional de Cuba* v. *Sabbatino,* in *United States Reports* [Washington, D.C: U.S. Government Printing Office, 1964], Vol. 376, pp. 398 ff.)

[86] Wolfgang Friedmann, *The Changing Structure of International Law* (New York: Columbia University Press, 1964), p. 139.

[87] Lissitzyn, in Swift, p. 127.

[88] This proposal was made by Mr. Castañeda "in order to take into account numerous resolutions and decisions produced by a vast array of international organizations." (General Assembly *Official Records . . . Sixth Committee* [15th session], November 9, 1960, p. 79, paragraph 13.)

tions, the slow progress of the work of the International Law Commission, and its near starvation in having had referred to it only three out of about 90 items on the agenda of the General Assembly; it noted the attitude of new states toward traditional international law which, having grown up without their participation, has failed to reflect their interests; yet finally, it adopted unanimously a Ukrainian amendment to the pending draft resolution which called for the "strict and undeviating observance [of international law] by all Governments."[89]

Conclusion

There will be no disposition to quarrel with the estimate that while

> since the Second World War remarkable advances have been made in virtually every sector of international organization . . . there has been no comparable advance in international adjudication.[90]

To this may be added the almost pathetic appeal made in the International Court of Justice by the President, Judge Sir Percy Spender, on the opening of its hearings on the merits of the *South West Africa Cases* in 1965:

> This unique and permanently constituted judicial means of implementing a vital Charter purpose stands ever ready at the service of the members of the world community.[91]

This reminder could not be more timely as there will be only one case left on the Court's general list after the judgment in these cases. Important and substantial as have been the contributions of the Court in adjudicating contentious cases, these or the advisory opinions will not be discussed herein inasmuch as they are dealt with elsewhere in this volume.[92]

One observation, looking to the future, may be submitted. As the UN gains in stature and comes increasingly to play a significant part in international affairs, disputes of a legal character may well arise between it and its Members. Article 34, paragraph 1, of the Court's Statute which states that "only states may be parties in cases before the Court" may have been fully justified in 1920 when it was drafted and the League of Nations was quite new. It cannot be foreseen what expansion international organization will

---

[89] *Ibid.*, p. 115. The full text of the preambular paragraph in which the Ukrainian amendment was incorporated reads as follows:

> Considering that the conditions prevailing in the world today give increased importance to the role of international law—and its strict and undeviating observance by all Governments—in strengthening international peace, developing friendly and co-operative relations among nations, settling disputes by peaceful means and advancing economic and social progress throughout the world.

(General Assembly Resolution 1505 [XV] of December 12, 1960.)

[90] C. Wilfred Jenks, *The Prospects of International Adjudication* (Dobbs Ferry, N.Y: Oceana Publications, 1964), p. 1.

[91] ICJ Communiqué No. 65/3, March 15, 1965.

[92] See Shabtai Rosenne, "The Court and the Judicial Process," above in this volume.

take in the years to come. Today this provision has become an anachronism pure and simple and should be removed. The United Nations, at least, "at present the supreme type of international organization" as the Court said in the *Reparation* case,[93] should no longer be denied active and passive capacity in contentious cases. To confer this capacity on the United Nations will require the solution of many incidental problems such as which organ of the United Nations should have the capacity to institute proceedings,[94] but these problems are not beyond the ingenuity of lawyers.

The United Nations started out in an uncharted political situation. Settlements have been made in some areas. But other parts of the political map of the world remain only provisionally marked out. The ideological conflict has lost little of its virulence, and periods of "thaw" and "freeze" have alternated. Deeply felt emotions over the last but hard remnants of colonialism and racial discrimination have characterized the debates of the Assembly almost since the beginning. The rapid increase in the membership has made the United Nations more nearly universal and representative of the international society; it has also made it rather more unwieldy. The forum for the annual discussion of the arms race, while it has shifted from the Assembly to the Eighteen-Nation Committee on Disarmament in Geneva, continues to cast a shadow over the Organization. In these circumstances the wonder is that the United Nations has been able to accomplish as much as it has in promoting the growth of law and in laying the socio-economic as well as the political foundations for further growth.

Yet it may be fair to suggest that more could be done in using the standard of law in the day-to-day work of the United Nations. There is virtue in promoting solutions by accommodation or compromise rather than on the basis of law if that serves the purpose.[95] But which and how many disputes, one may ask legitimately, have been actually settled in this fashion? To be sure, the hostilities in Indonesia, Kashmir, Palestine, and Suez have been effectively brought under control, but have any of the underlying disputes—Indonesia, apart, which was a special case—been settled? This is not to imply that they could or would have been settled by the resort to law or to the Court. But perhaps they might have been brought nearer to a settlement. The same observation might be made for matters such as the question of Indians in South Africa or *apartheid*. There was a risk inevitably in referring a situation involving Article 2, paragraph 7, of the Charter to the Court for an advisory opinion, but even if the Court had denied the competence of the General Assembly the result would not have been disastrous as without it the Assembly failed

[93] *Reparation for Injuries Suffered in the Service of the United Nations, Advisory Opinion: I.C.J. Reports 1949,* p. 179.

[94] Jenks, pp. 210 ff.

[95] Oscar Schachter, "The Quasi-Judicial Rôle of the Security Council and the General Assembly," *The American Journal of International Law,* October 1964 (Vol. 58, No. 4), pp. 960–965.

anyhow to make any headway. Moreover, it is not unreasonable for a Member which claims that its vital interests are affected to ask that the legal issue of competence be judicially clarified. This is said without reference to any particular dispute or situation and without reference to any particular Member or Members.

The experience of the first two decades has demonstrated that the United Nations, particularly the General Assembly, has frequently through its far-ranging activities affected vital interests of the Members and no doubt may increasingly do so in the next decade. Accordingly it stands to reason that some means, some procedure, will have to be provided to resolve conflicts. A Member that desires to have legal issues clarified should be afforded an opportunity to have them so clarified by the advisory procedure of the Court. It may not be unreasonable to expect, as a counterpart, that the Member as well as the requesting organ agree in advance to abide by the advisory opinion. There are ways and means for the United Nations to protect itself against abuse, against purely obstructionist proposals to refer a host of questions to the Court. Moreover, the Court itself can be relied upon to insist upon the integrity of the judicial function.

One need not naïvely expect that a judicial clarification of questions of competence or similar legal issues will set all conflicts at rest as legal issues rarely comprise the whole controversy. But it may be expected that, without departing from the advisory opinion, the Member and the United Nations or the Members concerned will be able to move ahead on the political level where interests can be composed and conciliated. What seems to be required in the years to come is that both the Organization and the Members free themselves from a certain antijudicial bias which seems to have been prominent in the first two decades of the United Nations and that resort to legal arguments be not confined merely to the debates.

Law can and should play a more vigorous part in resolving legal controversies without contesting the role which politics must inevitably play in the activities of the United Nations. But it is simply not enough to brush aside the law on the ground that the issue in question is also political. No doubt this will be so in most cases which arise in the United Nations but if all legal issues have political angles, so have political issues a legal angle.

As the President of the International Court, Judge Sir Percy Spender, said recently:

> It is, of course, self-evident that all disputes between nations are not susceptible of resolution by judicial means. It is, however, equally evident that the functions of this Court may be invoked more frequently than they are, if not in final settlement of all the issues in disputes between nations, at least, on the judicial level, in clarification of certain issues involved, so rendering disputes more amenable to complete and final settlement. It is to be observed that the Charter enjoins the

settlement, by peaceful means, of disputes the continuance of which is likely to endanger the maintenance of international peace and security, and lays it down that legal disputes between States should be referred, as a general rule, to this Court to be dealt with in accordance with international law.[96]

Just as an advisory opinion will rarely empty a controversy of all its contents, so a judgment will not necessarily set at rest all the underlying political or socio-economic issues. Parties may be more willing to compromise their interests than their legal stands. The risk is, of course, unavoidable that a judgment or an advisory opinion may stiffen a party's position with respect to the underlying conflicts of interest. This risk is unavoidable. It requires a political decision to depoliticize a dispute or parts of it just as it requires a political decision to politicize the whole of the dispute.

[96] ICJ Communiqué No. 65/3, March 15, 1965, p. 3.

The Furtherance of Economic Development

ROY BLOUGH

IN 1961 the General Assembly declared the 1960's to be the UN Development Decade and called for intensified efforts to accelerate progress toward self-sustaining growth.[1] During 1965, designated International Cooperation Year,[2] the United Nations is to take stock of the progress made thus far. Next to peace and security, which are preconditions for progress in all fields, international cooperation to promote economic and social development of the less developed countries now holds the highest priority for United Nations action.

Economic development was not regarded by the major powers as the most important goal of international cooperation when the Charter was drafted. The Soviet Union considered international economic cooperation to be irrelevant for economic development, an interference with national sovereignty, and a manifestation of Western imperialism. The United States and the United Kingdom considered the major economic problems to be the reconstruction of Europe, the restoration of a viable international economy with stable currencies and freer trade, and the avoidance of a repetition of the Great Depression. The less developed countries, however, beginning with the wartime conferences on postwar problems, pressed for effective international machinery to accelerate their economic development through provision of financial assistance and adoption of trade policies favorable to their industrialization.

The only provision of the Charter that refers directly to economic development is Article 55, which states among other objectives that "the United Na-

ROY BLOUGH, a member of the Board of Editors of *International Organization,* is Professor of International Business, Columbia University.

[1] General Assembly Resolution 1710 (XVI), December 19, 1961.
[2] General Assembly Resolution 1907 (XVIII), November 21, 1963.

tions shall promote higher standards of living, full employment, and conditions of economic and social progress and development. . . . " This language obviously is very general and covers a broad range of economic and social objectives. The Charter specifies certain structural and procedural matters but it does not confer on the United Nations authority to require any government to do anything in the economic field; action there clearly rests on a foundation of cooperation.

THE INSTITUTIONAL FRAMEWORK

The major institution provided by the UN Charter to promote economic and social objectives is the Economic and Social Council (ECOSOC). Although ECOSOC was declared to be one of the six principal organs, it is, however, subordinate to the authority of the General Assembly, which elects its eighteen members, votes and controls its budget, and approves or disapproves its actions and recommendations.

It was not intended that the United Nations itself should carry the whole burden of international economic cooperation. This responsibility is shared with the specialized agencies. Some of these, such as the Universal Postal Union (UPU) and the International Labor Organization (ILO), antedated the United Nations by decades. Others, such as the Food and Agriculture Organization (FAO), the International Bank for Reconstruction and Development (IBRD), and the International Monetary Fund (IMF) grew out of conferences held during the war. Others emerged in the early postwar years.

While none of the specialized agencies was concerned solely with economic development, the activities of all had some degree of relevance to it. Each agency's program necessarily was only a fragment of a total approach to economic development, and the different programs inevitably overlapped in some respects. The founders of the United Nations presumably wanted the specialized agencies to be coordinated with one another and with the United Nations, for Article 63 of the Charter directs ECOSOC to enter into agreements with them and to

> coordinate the activities of the specialized agencies through consultation with and recommendations to such agencies and through recommendations to the General Assembly and to the Members of the United Nations.

If coordination was really expected, however, "consultation" and "recommendation" were inadequate prerogatives for dealing with agencies each of which had its own governing body, its own budget, its own program, and its own philosophy.

Article 68 of the Charter instructed ECOSOC to

> set up commissions in economic and social fields and for the promotion of human rights, and such other commissions as may be required for the performance of its functions.

In the economic field these functional commissions have been for various reasons less than a success in the long run. For example, in the creation of the major Economic and Employment Commission it was assumed that the technical aspects of maintaining employment and economic stability could be separated from the political aspects and that the Member States would be represented on the Commission by professional and technical people. In practice, the political problems were basic, the representation was political in character, and the Commission functioned as a lower-level version of ECOSOC. It accordingly lost its reason for being and was terminated. Only the Statistical Commission, among the economic commissions, remains strong and healthy, undoubtedly because in this area there is a technical body of knowledge of a relatively unified character that can be separated from political questions. The work of the functional commissions, however, was not abandoned but was carried on with increased effectiveness by the Secretariat, by *ad hoc* committees of experts, and by special conferences.

Studies made immediately after the establishment of the United Nations led to the conclusion that an effective approach to the problems of most immediate concern to the Member countries required the establishment of regional organizations. Accordingly, in 1948 and 1949 the Economic Commission for Europe (ECE), the Economic Commission for Latin America (ECLA), and the Economic Commission for Asia and the Far East (ECAFE) were established. These were intergovernmental political organs with membership drawn primarily from the region although they included a few associate members from the outside. Their terms of reference were specified by ECOSOC, their budgets were voted by the General Assembly and financed by the United Nations, and their secretariats were under the general direction of the Secretary-General.

The regional commissions expanded and grew in importance. Member countries of the different commissions have from time to time informally cooperated in an effort to expand commission budgets and to shift functions, power, and the administration of funds from the center to the regions. An economic commission for the Middle East was found not to be practicable because of the hostility between the Arab nations and Israel. After considerable resistance by the United States and the former colonial powers, the Economic Commission for Africa (ECA) was established in 1959.

The history of the United Nations has been marked by the establishment from time to time of various institutions, both *ad hoc* and permanent, to meet situations as they arose. The more important of these institutions will be mentioned in the course of the discussion in the following sections.

The Broad Range of UN Activities

The United Nations and its affiliated institutions are engaged in so many activities related to economic development that the impression is one of bewildering profusion. It would be difficult to visualize any field of study or action significant for economic development in which the United Nations or an affiliated institution does not have at least a finger. Perhaps the point can be sufficiently illustrated with an abbreviated list: economic and social theories of economic development, and theory and practice of development planning; science and technology; land tenure, taxation, and budgeting; improvement of public administration; economic "infrastructure" of harbors, airports, transportation, and communication facilities, electric power and other public utilities; industrial development; health, housing, education, "community development," and other aspects of social development; population; vocational training of workers, labor organizations, cooperatives, improvements of labor, and social security laws; regional river development; and agriculture, fishing, forestry, mining, and manufacturing.

To attempt to deal in the few pages that follow with all or even a considerable fraction of the items mentioned might be more confusing than enlightening. At the risk of oversimplification, discussion will be concentrated on the dialogue through which ideas were developed and shaped into action programs to promote economic development and on some of the steps in the evolution of the major types of programs.

The Economic Development Dialogue

One of the more successful activities of the United Nations has been the achievement of a continuing international dialogue on the problems of economic development and the methods by which it can be promoted. The principal forums in which the dialogue has been carried on are ECOSOC and the Second (Economic and Financial) Committee of the General Assembly. Others are the meetings of the regional commissions and various special conferences.

It is universally recognized that the principal responsibility for promoting the economic development of a country lies with the country itself. International cooperation is an aid to and not a substitute for national action. International economic cooperation is easier to achieve than political cooperation because the national interests of different countries are less difficult to harmonize in economic than in political matters. International economic cooperation can provide not only the negative benefits of avoiding conflict but also the positive benefits of increasing welfare for all countries.

But conflict over sharing the benefits among the cooperating countries is al-

ways present. With respect to economic development, a conflict of views between the more developed and the less developed countries was evident even
before the United Nations was established. The cleavage was not over the
desirability of economic development, which was accepted doctrine, but over
the urgency of the problem of underdevelopment, its causes, and the ways and
means of alleviating it. The industrially advanced countries tended to believe
that the policies to which they attributed their development and prosperity
would have the same results in the less developed countries; the less developed countries insisted on faster progress and more positive international assistance; and the Soviet Union argued that each nation by following the Communist pattern could develop itself.

In the forums of the United Nations system, the underdeveloped countries
have emphasized their national aspirations, brought up their needs for economic development again and again, and pressed to secure favorable action.
The industrially advanced countries have been similarly active in the debate.
Some of their proposals would advance economic development in the less
developed countries. For the most part, however, the industrial countries regrettably but inevitably have found themselves in a defensive posture, resisting
the demands of the less developed countries which, just as inevitably, have
seemed insatiable.

An integral aspect of the dialogue has been research, using that word in
the broad sense of increasing knowledge and understanding, as distinguished
from mere dissemination. Without the continued addition of new knowledge,
debate rapidly becomes sterile. Research also is necessary if the action programs
that result from the dialogue are to be increasingly effective.

In practice, debate and research have been mutually supporting. The dialogues carried on within the policy-making organs disclose gaps in knowledge
that must be filled if intelligent policy decisions are to be made. The policy-
making bodies therefore give instructions for appropriate studies to be made.
The information developed by such studies often discloses the presence of
problems and issues not previously recognized. Moreover, the research programs of the various secretariats include not only these special studies but also
continuing programs of information collection, analysis, and publication that
are deemed necessary for the work of the policy-making organ. Thus, the
policy-making organs and the secretariats interact in the initiation of research
projects and the development of research programs.

Most of the UN research is, by nature, policy oriented or operations
oriented, although some is sufficiently fundamental to be considered basic
research. In addition to the research carried on by the secretariats of the various branches of the United Nations system, highly effective use has been
made of special study groups and conferences. Frequently, experts in the
field are commissioned to prepare papers which are discussed at a conference.

The original questions are answered or clarified, problems are disclosed, and new research assignments are made. One use to which the research and conference techniques just described have been put is the development of manuals setting out principles, procedures, and methods of operation for the use of Member countries. An example is the *Manual for Programme and Performance Budgeting* developed by the Fiscal and Financial Branch of the Secretariat's Department of Economic and Social Affairs.

The impact of the dialogue and research functions of the United Nations has been very great. In the author's opinion, these UN activities have been a major influence in the shift of attention by economists generally to the field of economic development and in the growth of sophistication regarding the requirements for economic development and ways and means of promoting it.

METHODS OF PROMOTING ECONOMIC DEVELOPMENT

The specific measures taken by the United Nations to promote economic development are innumerable, but they can be largely comprised within the headings of national policies, technical cooperation, financial aid, and trade policy. While activities in these categories have proceeded simultaneously, they will be discussed in the order mentioned.

National Policies

Much of the dialogue and research in the United Nations has been devoted to finding the national policies that countries might follow to promote their own development. The Soviet Union, of course, has denigrated all methods of economic development except Communism; other countries generally agree that economic development is not a simple process and that many elements must be present to bring it about expeditiously. There are, however, substantial differences of opinion on the relative importance of international assistance and of action by the country seeking development. The less developed countries have emphasized their lack of capital and the importance of enlarging their supplies of foreign exchange through grants, loans, and favorable trade policies. The developed Western countries have stressed the need for stable government, competent and honest administration, "fair" treatment of foreign investment, better distribution of the tax burden, land policies to encourage production, etc. The less developed countries find such reforms difficult to achieve quickly, and in many cases the groups in political control find them quite unacceptable because of their probable consequences for the domestic structure of power and wealth. Other proposals are rejected by the poorer countries because they represent a threat to their sovereignty. For example, in response to suggestions that they create inducements to foreign investment, the less developed nations have insisted on their inalienable right of sover-

eignty over natural resources and freedom to nationalize industries, and they
have requested that foreign businesses behave in what they regard as a responsible manner.

A second aspect of national policy on which the developed and less developed countries have disagreed is the priority to be placed on the promotion
of different industries. The less developed countries have placed very heavy
emphasis on manufacturing, even promoting, through protective policies, financial subsidies, or government ownership, industries to which the country
was not well suited; and they have been prone to invest heavily in "showcase"
industries such as steel mills and international airlines. The developed countries have condemned these policies and have emphasized the need for giving
priority to agriculture, education, and other "basic" factors ahead of manufacturing. The less developed countries have attributed this position to a selfish
interest in markets for manufactured products.

Elaboration of the arguments employed in the dialogue would take us somewhat afield. It can be said, however, that while the dialogue and the research,
plus experience, have not eliminated the points of difference, both the developed countries and the less developed countries have been substantially enlightened, and there seems to be a greater consensus than there was in earlier
years.

Technical Cooperation

In the early years, United Nations activities were largely limited to discussion
and research. While studying and discussing the problems was a necessary stage,
there was a growing feeling in the Secretariat and among governments that
the UN should be doing more, that it was not enough to make recommendations for national action, and that positive international action was necessary.
However, in the economic field the United Nations not only had no power to
enforce national action, but it had very little money for programs of international action.

A subject on which there was general agreement was the need of the less
developed countries for better technology. Not surprisingly, the method of
promoting economic development on which there was the least disagreement
between the Western developed countries and the less developed countries
was the international transfer of technology through "technical assistance,"
or, somewhat more accurately and less invidiously, technical cooperation. The
United Nations and most of the specialized agencies had small appropriations
for technical assistance, but in almost every case they were completely inadequate.

A major step toward practical action was the adoption in 1950 of the Expanded Program of Technical Assistance (EPTA). EPTA funds were to be
supplied by voluntary contributions and allocated for use in the technical as-

sistance programs of the United Nations and the specialized agencies, not including the International Monetary Fund and the International Bank, which had their own sources of funds. The responsibility for the overall supervision and approval of the Program was vested in the Technical Assistance Committee (TAC) of ECOSOC. Responsibility for planning and coordination was given to the Technical Assistance Board (TAB), which was to consist of representatives of the United Nations and the participating specialized agencies.

The magnitude of activities under EPTA is determined by the size of contributions. The Program has been limited by the policy of the United States to contribute only a certain percentage of the total (now about 40 percent) and by the amounts that other countries have been prepared to give. In effect, however, since the United States has always pledged a larger sum than other members were prepared to match on the specified basis, the limiting factor has been the contributions of other countries. The position of the United States has been that for it to contribute a larger percentage of the total would destroy the international character of the Program. The United States' contributions under bilateral programs have been much larger than its contributions to the technical assistance programs of the UN and the specialized agencies.

Technical assistance is given only to countries which request it. The operations have taken various forms but predominantly have consisted of supplying experts in technical fields who help local counterparts to start or carry on programs, train local personnel in the best methods for a particular task, and, hopefully, eventually withdraw and leave the project entirely in national hands as a going concern. In some cases such training of local personnel for various jobs in the national government is all that is required; in other cases technical assistance has taken the form of expert advice to governments, for example, on tax, land, or monetary policy.

In yet other instances technical assistance has meant the supplying of foreign experts to perform some activity which the country is unable to do for itself, such as a study of fishing resources, a survey of mineral resources, or the planning of a harbor or other public work. This type of project, which relates to a specific "preinvestment" task and not a continuing program, has been a particular emphasis of another UN program—the United Nations Special Fund. The Fund began operations on January 1, 1959, and, like EPTA, is financed by voluntary contributions; the General Assembly set $150 million a year as the immediate goal, a goal which has not yet been reached.

The Special Fund carries on surveys regarding national resources, assists in the formation of national development plans, does research on the feasibility of specific projects, and engages in the development of trained manpower. It has financed institutes for economic and social planning in each of the regional commissions except ECE. The institute at Santiago, Chile, was established in 1962, and those at Dakar and Bangkok in 1964. These institutes give courses in economic development, carry on research, and help countries with their economic and social planning.

Applications for Special Fund financing of projects are made to the Managing Director, who passes along to the Governing Council those projects which he considers worthy. He also decides which of the specialized agencies (including the United Nations as a specialized agency for this purpose) will be the executing agency. More than 80 percent of the funds are currently being administered by three agencies, FAO, the United Nations Educational, Scientific and Cultural Organization (UNESCO), and the UN.[3] The specialized agency in turn decides how to execute the project, whether by its own staff or through private contractors. In practice, the Managing Director of the Special Fund has been in a position to act more independently than has TAB in the determination of priorities, the allocation of funds, and the promotion of an integrated program.

To meet the needs of developing countries for governmental personnel to carry on activities for which there are no local qualified persons, Secretary-General Hammarskjöld in 1956 proposed the creation of an International Administrative Service, which would in effect be a career service under international responsibility. This was considered too revolutionary, and a stopgap program, the provision of Operational, Executive, and Administrative Personnel (OPEX) for developing countries, was created in 1958. Prior to 1964 the cost of OPEX was met from United Nations funds; now the cost is met by the agency in whose sector of work the administrator is engaged. About 100 posts in all fields are being carried under this program.

A recent development with respect to training is the establishment of a United Nations Training and Research Institute.[4] Its major purpose is to train personnel from the developing countries for service with the United Nations and the specialized agencies or with national administrations. Forty-eight countries are supporting the Institute through voluntary contributions; the anticipated budget is about $1.5 million.

Doubts have been increasing over the years whether the unmodified capital-intensive technology of the industrial world is appropriate for the less developed countries. To move immediately to the automated processes of the new industrialism, it is contended, would not only require capital far beyond that which could be provided or absorbed but also would leave large numbers of permanently unemployed. The UN Conference on the Application of Science and Technology for the Benefit of the Less Developed Areas (UNCSAT), held in Geneva in February 1963, gave impetus to the need to create new technologies tailored to the special conditions of particular regions and,

[3] *Yearbook of the United Nations, 1963* (United Nations: Office of Public Information, 1965), p. 181.
[4] General Assembly Resolution 1934 (XVIII), December 11, 1963.

in particular, more labor intensive than the technologies developed in the industrial nations. Philippe de Seynes, Undersecretary for Economic and Social Affairs, has expressed this new responsibility of the United Nations as being

> that of facilitating the birth and development of an indigenous technology with which to correct or compensate for the accidents of geology or climate, of helping countries, which still lack them, to obtain minimum scientific facilities . . . of encouraging the modern spirit of science and technology . . . and of preparing the institutional changes which this development requires.[5]

Experience has shown that this is not a matter which private enterprise can be expected to undertake, at least without leadership; it is a matter for collective action. How much can be accomplished is impossible to forecast, but clearly the idea opens up a field of action of great significance.

Increasing the Flow of Capital

Once the loans for the reconstruction of Europe were completed, all the resources of the International Bank for Reconstruction and Development became available for financing economic development. The amounts involved seemed small to the developing countries, which also considered the "hardloan" policy of the Bank unsuited to their needs and disliked the fact that their influence on the Bank was limited by its system of weighted voting.

As early as 1949 the less developed countries started pressing in ECOSOC and the General Assembly for the creation of a United Nations capital fund to be used for financing economic development. In 1951, the General Assembly called on ECOSOC to submit a detailed plan for such a fund. The United States opposed this move on the ground that it could not support such a fund during the fighting in Korea. In 1953, after the end of the hostilities, President Dwight D. Eisenhower, speaking before the General Assembly, tied participation by the United States in a UN capital fund, known as the Special United Nations Fund for Economic Development (SUNFED), to savings to be realized from multilateral disarmament—for all practical purposes an indefinite postponement. Other capital-supplying countries also opposed SUNFED, while the less developed countries continued to push for its establishment. The Soviet Union in 1955 shifted from its original opposition and became a supporter.

In view of the substantial amounts of capital which the United States was making available in bilateral aid, its argument that heavy armaments expenses made impossible its participation in SUNFED convinced few if any representatives of other countries. A more plausible explanation was retrospectively presented in 1964 by Richard N. Gardner, United States Deputy Assistant Secretary of State for International Organization Affairs:

[5] UN Document A/C.2/L.722, September 27, 1963.

The United States opposed the creation of SUNFED . . . and currently opposes the creation of a capital development fund by the General Assembly, precisely because large amounts of capital aid would be dispersed under circumstances that would not assure the promotion of U.S. foreign-policy objectives. It is not merely that large amounts of aid might be given to Communist countries; it is also that the standards essential to the successful application of external aid would not be likely to be maintained.[6]

The resistance of the United States delayed but did not prevent an approach by the General Assembly toward definitive action on SUNFED. Perhaps the first tangible result was the reversal in 1956 of the earlier opposition of the United States to the establishment of the International Finance Corporation (IFC) as an affiliate of the International Bank. A second result was the United States proposal in 1957 of a "Special Projects Fund"—the Special Fund referred to above. This was interpreted as a United States alternative to SUN-FED, although the United States claimed otherwise.

Still another indirect result of the pressure of underdeveloped countries for larger capital funds was the approval by the United Nations and the establishment in 1960 of the International Development Association (IDA) as a "soft-loan" affiliate of the International Bank. IDA reflected not only a further development of the position of the United States but also a substantial shift of opinion on the part of Bank officials, who during the earlier SUNFED debates had indicated opposition to soft loans on the ground that they would impair the integrity of the Bank's "hard loans."[7] Still other institutions for expanding capital flow that can be attributed to UN debates are the recently formed African Development Bank and the prospective Asian Development Bank. Nevertheless, many UN Members are still urging the formation of a capital fund which would be an organ of the United Nations.

Capital flows to less developed countries also take the form of private foreign investment. Some of this is channeled through the international institutions. IFC is designed to help finance private projects, and the International Bank gets most of its loanable funds from the private capital market. However, almost all of the Bank's loans go to government projects since the government of the country must guarantee loans to private borrowers.

The UN has also sought through studies and resolutions to promote international direct private investment in less developed countries. At the same time, resolutions reaffirming national rights over foreign investment have been a source of disquiet. Debates in the United Nations regarding the obligations of host governments to private investors have been frequent and vari-

---

[6] Richard N. Gardner, *In Pursuit of World Order* (New York: Frederick A. Praeger, 1964), pp. 120–121.

[7] The Bank's loans are "hard" only in a relative sense; the Bank borrows funds on the market at lower than commercial rates because of the guarantees implicit in the unpaid subscriptions of the member governments.

ous resolutions have been passed. In one of these, the "Declaration on permanent sovereignty over natural resources" of December 1962,[8] host governments recognize obligations to abide by international law with respect to private foreign investment. The International Bank in 1964 offered its services to conciliate or arbitrate investment disputes. Other agencies such as the General Agreement on Tariffs and Trade (GATT) and the IMF have helped improve the "investment climate," while much of the International Bank's investment and that of other agencies has gone to develop the economic underpinnings necessary for an enlarged flow of private investment.

Trade Policy

The historical tradition of trade negotiations of industrial countries is that trade barriers should be lowered mutually on a reciprocal basis. Lowering trade barriers benefits all countries, it is argued, by promoting international specialization and exchange. The method of negotiated reciprocal reductions diminishes balance-of-payments problems and apportions the benefits between the countries, if not always fairly, at least on an agreed basis.

The less developed countries, however, have long argued that two kinds of general changes from this tradition were necessary to make possible the acceleration of their economic development. First, they ask that their products be allowed to enter the developed countries without the imposition of customs duties, internal taxes, or other penalties, or at least that such restrictions on imports be progressively decreased. This, it is urged, is necessary to increase the foreign exchange earnings of the less developed countries to finance the purchase of capital equipment and other requirements of economic development. Second, these countries also ask for the right to restrict their own imports to the extent they deem to be necessary for the protection and promotion of their infant manufacturing industries.

The inherently different positions of the more developed and the less developed countries were evident before the United Nations was established and have affected its activities throughout the two decades of its experience. By 1965 it could be said in general that the view of the less developed countries had finally been publicly accepted in principle by the more developed countries but that the practical application of the principle was as yet only in its early stages.

The first substantial trade policy effort of the United Nations with respect to economic development was the United Nations Conference on Trade and Employment, convened pursuant to a resolution of ECOSOC[9] at its first session in the spring of 1946. This resolution was initiated by the United States, and proposals previously formulated by the United States constituted the orig-

---

[8] General Assembly Resolution 1803 (XVII), December 14, 1962.
[9] ECOSOC Resolution 13 (I), February 18, 1946.

inal agenda of the Preparatory Committee. These proposals were not directed mainly at the problem of economic development, although it was argued that they would promote it as a consequence of trade liberalization. The promotion of industrialization was considered by the United States to be a function of ECOSOC and the International Bank and not of the International Trade Organization (ITO) which it was hoped would be established. The less developed countries, however, insisted that the Havana Charter of ITO should contain affirmative proposals to promote industrialization, including the provision of credit and capital, technical assistance, and freedom for the less developed countries to impose restrictions on imports. Eventually a chapter on economic development was included in the Havana Charter. It provided for the waiving for the less developed countries, under certain circumstances, of the general prohibition against the use of quantitative restrictions on imports. ITO was not given any financial or operational responsibilities with respect to economic development, but members were to cooperate with ECOSOC and other intergovernmental organizations on economic development.

The Havana Charter dealt with almost every conceivable aspect of international trade relations. Perhaps because of this broad scope, which included regulation of restrictive business practices, provisions for the negotiation of international commodity agreements, and responsibilities for maintaining full employment, as well as the special provisions for the less developed countries, the Havana Charter failed of approval by the United States Senate and was abandoned.

In the meantime a tariff-negotiating session in Geneva resulted in the founding of GATT in 1947. The Agreement not only provided for the reduction of tariffs, chiefly among the industrial countries, but it also included many of the rules of the Havana Charter against trade discrimination and subsidization. It did not, however, incorporate the exceptions for the less developed countries. When the Havana Charter failed, GATT remained, meeting many of the needs of the industrial trading countries but not satisfying the less developed countries, which proposed another world trade conference to correct its deficiencies. In 1953, after the death of Joseph Stalin, the Soviet Union also began pushing for a world trade conference and a new trade organization. The United States and other industrialized countries opposed the calling of such a conference.

The pressure in the United Nations led to the formation in 1954 of the Commission on International Commodity Trade (CICT), which was established to study and make recommendations for stabilizing and improving the terms of trade of the less developed countries. The United States refused to accept membership on the Commission, although it became a member some years later after the language of the resolution had been modified. CICT studied many aspects of the international commodity problem, and its general approach to a solution was that of international commodity agreements for specific commodities. The United States had initially rejected this approach but began to relax its opposition about 1960. It became increasingly clear to everyone, however, that the problems of the primary-producing countries were not going to be satisfactorily solved through such agreements.

In 1955, the GATT Contracting Parties adopted provisions which granted exemptions to less developed countries from some of the GATT rules. The less developed countries began to join GATT, and by 1964 the membership had grown to include 62 full members and thirteen other countries related by less than full membership. Since the United Nations recognizes only 26 countries as being developed, it appears that GATT has become an institution of the less developed as well as the more developed countries.

In 1963, most GATT countries, with the notable exception of members of the European Economic Community (EEC), adopted a Program of Action that called for the reduction or elimination of quantitative restrictions, tariffs, and internal taxes on products of the less developed countries. In February 1965 the Contracting Parties signed a new chapter on trade and economic development that went far in the direction of accepting the economic arguments and trade principles for which the less developed countries had been contending. It was specifically stated, for example, that

> the developed contracting parties do not expect reciprocity for commitments made by them in trade negotiations to reduce or remove tariffs and other barriers to the trade of less-developed contracting parties.[10]

The commitments of the new chapter did not go quite as far as the language of the Program of Action; for example, no reference was made to abolishing all customs duties and other trade barriers on tropical agricultural products. Moreover, the language provides exceptions for "compelling reasons." Nevertheless, the chapter represents a major advance for the less developed countries, and the machinery for what might be called "persuasive enforcement" may be expected to bring at least gradual progress in opening freer markets to their products.

Prior to these developments in GATT, and surely not unrelated to them, the pressures for a United Nations conference on trade resulted in a General Assembly resolution in 1962 calling for the convening of the United Nations Conference on Trade and Development (UNCTAD) in 1964.[11] The Geneva Conference had 2,000 delegates from 119 countries and lasted nearly three months (March–June). The Secretary-General of the Conference was Dr. Raúl Prebisch (Argentina), who had recently retired from the post of Executive Secretary of ECLA, where he had long been a powerful influence in de-

---

[10] General Agreement on Tariffs and Trade, Protocol, February 1965, Part IV, Article XXXVI, paragraph 8.

[11] General Assembly Resolution 1785 (XVII), December 8, 1962.

veloping theoretical foundations and political pressures on behalf of the less developed countries. He pointed out that if the 5 percent annual growth target of the UN Development Decade was to be fulfilled there would be an estimated gap in the foreign exchange requirements of the less developed countries amounting to $20 billion a year and that, even with as much as $10 billion of inflow of foreign public and private capital, an increase of $10 billion in net exports by the less developed countries would be necessary.

Numerous methods by which this trade gap might be overcome were discussed, including: elimination of all protection and other restrictions on the importation by industrialized countries of primary products; tariff preferences for the manufactures and semimanufactures of the less developed countries; permission for less developed countries to subsidize their exports; commodity agreements; compensatory financing in years when foreign exchange earnings were low; reduction in the cost of shipping and insurance; easing of the servicing charges on foreign debts; agreement to special regional trade arrangements among the less developed countries; and the establishment of a new trade organization. Little real agreement was reached between the less developed countries and the industrially advanced countries. It was significant, however, that 77 less developed countries joined forces for the first time in history to assert their claims and enhance their bargaining power. The principal tangible outcome was the establishment of UNCTAD on a continuing basis as an arm of the General Assembly to meet periodically, with provision for a 55-member Trade and Development Board to operate between regular sessions of the Conference, as well as a secretariat to service UNCTAD and its subsidiaries.

An interesting development of the 1964 Geneva Conference was the failure of the Soviet Union to play an important role. That country had been one of the strongest proponents of a world trade conference and many had feared that it would succeed in joining forces with the less developed countries for at least a propaganda victory. In the event, however, it developed that to whatever extent the Soviet Union may be effective in making trade agreements with specific less developed countries, it was in no position to increase substantially its purchase of primary products from the less developed countries as a whole.

IMPRESSIONS OF PERFORMANCE AND OUTLOOK

The variety of the UN's activities, the complexity of its structure, and the difficulty of understanding from the outside the actual relationships that exist among its various parts give its fight against economic underdevelopment a resemblance to a large, complex military operation; it is not feasible to evaluate the overall results because of the numerous separate engagements. All that will be ventured here is to suggest a few tentative impressions regarding the answers to three questions: 1) What progress has been made in economic development? 2) Have the Member countries made appropriate use of the United Nations system? 3) How has the system performed?

Progress in Economic Development

In terms of growth of per capita income there has been on the whole limited progress. Generalizations are likely to be misleading, since substantial growth has been experienced in some countries, little if any in others. Population increase has absorbed much of the gain and poses a continuing threat. In some countries per capita food supply has increased little, if any. The industrial countries have grown in general more rapidly than have the less developed, so that the "income gap" has probably widened rather than narrowed.

On the positive side, there has certainly been a great increase in the recognition that the problem of economic development threatens the peace and security of all countries and that industrialized countries must be prepared to make temporary sacrifices to solve it. The advances in knowledge about the development process have been great, and a very large and lively literature has sprung into being. A structure of international and national institutions exists, ready for more vigorous use.

The fact that the economic development problem obviously has not been solved is bound to be interpreted in some quarters as a demonstration of United Nations failure. Peoples in the grip of a great imperative are impatient; two decades—a moment in history—seem a long time. Frustrated people look around for another institution in the hopes that it may be more quickly successful. The effort now under way to create a United Nations specialized agency for industrial development may reflect this attitude.[12]

Use of the UN System by Member Countries

Only a small fraction of financial aid from industrial to less developed countries goes through the UN system. In 1957–1958, for example, out of $3.0 billion in grants and net loans, $2.6 billion were bilateral and $0.4 billion were multilateral.[13] In 1963, the industrial countries of the Organization for Economic Cooperation and Development (OECD) contributed a total of $6.0 billion to less developed countries and multilateral agencies; of this total $0.2 billion went to the UN technical assistance and relief agencies, $0.2 billion to International Bank and IDA capital subscriptions, $4.0 billion to bilateral grants and grant-like contributions, and $1.7 billion to bilateral lending; thus

---

[12] See UN Document A/5826, December 4, 1964.
[13] Paul G. Hoffman, *One Hundred Countries, One and One Quarter Billion People: How to Speed Their Economic Growth—and Ours—in the 1960's* (Washington, D.C: Albert D. and Mary Lasker Foundation, 1960), p. 26.

one-sixteenth of the contributions went to agencies of the UN system.[14] While the figures given are not entirely comparable, the story of nonuse of the UN is clear.

The unwillingness to use the United Nations as a channel for financial aid is undoubtedly due for the most part to the belief that bilateral aid can better promote a country's foreign policy and to the desire to concentrate aid in particular countries. There also have been concerns related to the Cold War, which may be diminishing, and to the growing voting strength of the less developed countries, which is not. The principle of "one state, one vote" enables the less developed countries numerically to dominate the General Assembly and most other bodies of the United Nations and the specialized agencies. This voting power is not matched by military strength or economic power. The industrial minority owns the great bulk of the world's productive resources and constitutes its major market for both primary products and manufactures.

Several possible results could come out of this anomalous situation. First, the less developed countries may use their majority to pass resolutions promulgating their principles and views of economics and calling on the industrialized countries to implement the resolutions through national policies and through financial contributions to the work of the Organization. If the cleavages of opinion and interest between the industrial and the less developed countries are deep, the result may be a stalemate in which the industrialized countries simply refuse to implement the resolutions but continue the dialogue, or the final end may be the collapse of the Organization. The failure of SUNFED and the use, instead, of the International Bank and IDA reflect the unwillingness of the industrialized countries to use the United Nations. The fact that OECD has become very active in the economic development field gives the industrialized countries a possible channel for multilateral action in which the less developed countries have no vote.

Second, the less developed countries can restrain themselves and vote only those resolutions that the industrialized countries will accept. There have been many occasions when the less developed countries in the General Assembly did not force the issue on a resolution because they could not get the support of the industrialized countries. Perhaps most of these occasions occurred in the days when the less developed countries could not muster a sufficient majority and preferred a weak resolution to none at all. Today, the restraint is showing up in the form of what is called "conciliation." The word "conciliation" describes the process whereby consultation on an issue continues until a result is reached that is acceptable to all of the major power groups. For example, in conversation a UN official has referred to the lack of firm rules in

[14] *The Flow of Financial Resources to Less-Developed Countries, 1956–1963* (Paris: OECD, 1964), pp. 18, 155, 159.

the new GATT chapter on "trade and development" as being the result of the conciliation process. The UNCTAD Trade and Development Board has adopted "conciliation" as one of its procedures.[15]

The major hope for the success of conciliation is that it may be in effect "collective bargaining" rather than simply conciliation. If all that is going to happen is that opposing views are compromised to the point that everyone agrees, the resulting resolutions might well be meaningless. If, however, both sides are in a position to withhold from each other favorable action of importance, a continuing process of collective bargaining can optimize the benefits to the various parties in the negotiation. The results need not be static; with the passage of time new arrangements could be found which would be mutually acceptable.

The temptation to the industrial countries to bypass the United Nations in favor of an organization they control, such as OECD, should not be underestimated. To bypass the United Nations in this way, however, would involve a major hazard, that of the loss of cooperation. In an organization controlled entirely by the industrialized countries, it would be difficult to avoid the odor of charity, of the gracious gratuity by a wealthy donor to an impecunious recipient. Such a relationship is no longer acceptable. Cooperation of equals promoting a common cause has gone too far to be abandoned. The conciliation procedure, involving as it must the recognition by the less developed countries that neither they nor the industrialized countries should dictate, may prove to be a major advance.

Performance of the UN System

Space does not permit more than a few comments about the performance of the United Nations in promoting economic development. Recently an officer of one of the UN bodies, when asked whether the United Nations had gone to the heart of the development problem, responded, "We're still on the fringes of the fringes." While this was probably intended as an exaggeration for dramatic effect, it seems uncomfortably close to the truth. Economic development is going to be a long and slow process. Yet, it is the belief of the present writer that more has been done to promote economic development per dollar of expenditure by the United Nations as an organization and by the whole system of UN institutions than by public funds spent in other ways. This can be said with some assurance because of the relatively small amounts that Member governments have been willing to channel through the UN.

The UN has been consistently and validly criticized for its failure to achieve an overall, integrated, adequately coordinated program of economic develop-

---

[15] For strong support of the use of conciliation, as well as an informative survey of the work of the 1964 UNCTAD, see Henry Bloch, *The Challenge of the World Trade Conference* (New York: School of International Affairs, Columbia University, 1964–1965).

ment, to permit a joint attack on problems for which no one agency has either jurisdiction or funds, and to concentrate effort on purposes of the highest priority. Year after year ECOSOC and the General Assembly renew their criticism of poor coordination, although what they seem to expect is unrealistic in view of the power structure. There no doubt has been progress,[16] but whether this will continue or be overwhelmed by centrifugal forces is not clear to the present writer. Experience demonstrates that the Member governments cannot be counted on to bring about coordination.

In the present political context the best hope for effective coordination appears to be the channeling of an increasing proportion of funds through the centralized procedures of the Special Fund. The proposed merger of the Special Fund and EPTA, now under consideration, may eventually lead to this result, but there is danger that the pressure of the less developed countries for greater assurance of funds and fewer restrictions on their use will result in retrogression rather than progress in this respect.

As a final point it should be noted that the UN system, and especially the UN itself, has not successfully brought the dynamism of private entrepreneurship to bear in promoting economic development. Resolutions on the subject are not lacking, but operational methods of bringing together international civil servants, governmental officials, and local businessmen into effective cooperation are another matter. Some way should be found to do this, since in the long run most of the economic developing will have to be done by private business if it is going to be done at all.

---

[16] See later in this volume, Walter R. Sharp, "The Administration of United Nations Operational Programs."

The Administration of United Nations Operational Programs

WALTER R. SHARP

THIS discussion purports to review some of the more significant developments that have marked the management of UN operational programs during recent years. The emphasis of the commentary is on the highlights of field administration since 1960 when the research for the present writer's more extensive study on this subject was completed.[1]

THE GROWTH OF UN FIELD ACTIVITIES

The emergence of the United Nations as an operational instrumentality, managing a worldwide field establishment, has been one of the unanticipated consequences of the San Francisco Charter system. Notwithstanding the broad character of the economic and social mandate contained in Chapters IX and X of the UN Charter, there is little evidence that extensive field programs under the aegis of the UN itself were then envisaged. The United Nations Relief and Rehabilitation Administration (UNRRA), well under way in 1945, was designed to meet what was thought by most to be only a temporary situation. Nor was the other far-flung "field" agency, the International Refugee Organization (IRO), expected to form a permanent part of the machinery of the Organization.

Even though the text of the Charter includes no direct reference to the establishment of field programs, the terms of its permissive and hortatory provisions in the economic, social, and health and welfare domain can easily be construed as authority to inaugurate programs of direct technical aid to Member States.[2] As early as 1948, two steps taken by the Organization heralded

WALTER R. SHARP, a member of the Board of Editors of *International Organization,* is Professor of Political Science, Yale University, and a consultant to the United Nations specialized agencies.

[1] See Walter R. Sharp, *Field Administration in the United Nations System: The Conduct of International Economic and Social Programs* (New York: Frederick A. Praeger, 1961).

[2] There are, of course, limited precedents for field action in the experience of the League of Nations.

what was to be a long, steady expansion of operational activities over the next decade and a half. The first move was a series of General Assembly resolutions authorizing modest programs of assistance in the fields of economic development, social welfare, and public administration financed from the UN regular budget. The other step was the decision to set up regional economic commissions of the Economic and Social Council (ECOSOC)—one for Europe, another for Asia and the Far East, and a third for Latin America.[3] In different ways these bodies, but in particular the Economic Commission for Asia and the Far East (ECAFE) and the Economic Commission for Latin America (ECLA), helped to shift policy formulation in the economic and social field from New York to the regions and thus to pave the way for initiatives aimed at aiding the weaker and less developed states and dependent territories of each region in their efforts to absorb modern technology and raise living standards.

In the meantime, a new pattern for field activity in this functional domain took form in the shape of the UN Children's Fund (UNICEF). Set up originally to "utilize some of the residual funds of UNRRA for work that, with the anticipated termination of the agency, threatened to come to a stop,"[4] UNICEF responded to such a powerful humanitarian appeal that it was continued by the General Assembly on a year-to-year basis until 1953 and then given permanent status. UNICEF represented an innovation primarily in terms of the method of its financing by voluntary contributions in lieu of budgetary assessments. It thus enjoys the distinction of being the oldest of the UN voluntary programs as well as the most popular.

It was, however, the institution of the Expanded Program of Technical Assistance (EPTA) in 1950 that was to provide the principal impetus for the use of the voluntary principle for fund raising to support continuing operational programs.[5] This method offered a convenient way by which certain nations, chiefly the economically advanced states of the West, could launch a new program without waiting for participation by the Communist Bloc. No state was bound to contribute any fixed amount; conversely, it could increase its contributions to a level well beyond its regular budget quota any time it wished without being committed to any set percentage in the years ahead.

After 1950, with the large influx of new Member States from Asia and Africa, a drive for constantly expanding UN approved aid for their development punctuated the annual debates in ECOSOC and the General Assembly. The long controversial discussion over the Special UN Fund for Economic

[3] It was not until ten years later (1958) that the Economic Commission for Africa (ECA) was established.

[4] Robert E. Asher and others, *The United Nations and Economic and Social Co-operation* (Washington, D.C: Brookings Institution, 1957), p. 58.

[5] For a detailed treatment of the financing of the voluntary programs, see John G. Stoessinger and others, *Financing the United Nations System* (Washington, D.C: Brookings Institution, 1964), Chapter 8.

Development (SUNFED) proposal eventually resulted in a compromise that led to the establishment of the UN Special Fund in 1958, designed as a program for larger-scale technical assistance projects than EPTA could, or did, provide and aimed at strengthening countries in their efforts to obtain capital investment funds from outside sources.

In 1959 the General Assembly authorized the program for the provision of Operational, Executive, and Administrative Personnel (OPEX) to developing countries. OPEX provides trained technicians and administrators for temporary appointment to the civil services of requesting governments. The governments pay them in "base" salaries the amount they would receive if they were "citizen" civil servants, and the UN supplements such compensation as necessary to bring the total up to the level a UN technical assistance expert would receive for comparable service in an advisory capacity. OPEX was originally handled by the UN Division for Public Administration out of regular budget funds, but authorization has recently been given for EPTA to include "operational" posts within approved "country programs," while at least two of the specialized agencies, the World Health Organization (WHO) and the UN Educational, Scientific and Cultural Organization (UNESCO), now use some of their regular budget resources to finance comparable appointments within each agency's functional ambit.

Space does not permit more than the mere mention of a number of other voluntary programs. These have included the United Nations Relief and Works Agency for Palestine Refugees in the Near East (UNRWA),[6] the various refugee activities administered by the UN High Commissioner for Refugees (UNHCR) with the UN Refugee Fund and the proceeds raised by the World Refugee Year in 1959.[7] There is also the World Food Program (WFP) run jointly by the UN and the Food and Agriculture Organization (FAO) with its experimental three-year effort to provide agricultural surpluses to food-deficient peoples to assist in economic development. Finally, there is a modest amount of technical aid that can be provided under the regular budgets of certain of the specialized agencies—WHO and UNESCO principally, but also the International Labor Organization (ILO), the International Atomic Energy Agency (IAEA), and FAO. Except for IAEA, these have all developed permanent networks of field offices to facilitate the management of their operational activities.

[6] *Ibid.,* p. 201.
[7] Another special voluntary operation, begun in 1950, was the UN Korean Reconstruction Agency (UNKRA) which planned and managed rehabilitation, relief, and refugee work in South Korea. The work of the Agency, dependent mainly on the United States for financial support, was absorbed into the United States' unilateral military and economic aid program for Korea in 1958.

CURRENT DIMENSIONS OF OPERATIONAL PROGRAMS

The development and expansion of operational programs of a nonpolitical character have proceeded over the years without being noticeably affected by the political, constitutional, or financial vicissitudes of the UN itself. Indeed, it might almost be said that as the political and security status of the UN has become strained, its activity in the domain of economic and social policy has thrived. The large influx of new Members from the developing world has tended to shift the UN's functional focus to the Afro-Asian (and Latin American) states. It is their claims for aid and services that have confronted the industrialized states each year, with increasing insistence, in ECOSOC and the committees of the General Assembly. Even though the campaign for a United Nations capital development fund has so far not attained success, its impact on the proposal to set up the Special Fund to finance preinvestment operations obviously was important.

Before undertaking to assess the kinds of problems to which the management of the cluster of operational programs has given and still gives rise, it may be illuminating to scan quantitatively their current dimensions.[8] By using monetary expenditure as one index and the involvement of personnel as the other, one can delineate a fairly distinct picture of the extent of operational programs both in the aggregate and in comparison with other UN activities.

On the monetary side the total expenditure for field programs has increased more rapidly during the past fifteen years than have the regular budgets of the UN and its affiliated agencies. By 1960, field program expenditures had attained equality in amount with the aggregate regular budgets for the whole UN family of agencies (excluding major peacekeeping outlays). Since then, the former type of expenditure has gradually pulled ahead of the latter. The situation for 1963–1964 is summarized in approximate totals below:[9]

Category	$ Million
UN Regular Budget (1964)	$101.0
Regular Budgets of Specialized Agencies and IAEA (1964)	112.0
Total	$213.0

[8] The International Bank for Reconstruction and Development (IBRD) and the International Monetary Fund (IMF) also engage in technical assistance activities on a limited scale, some of them in conjunction with loan applications. These activities are financed from the revenues of the two institutions.

[9] The figures listed here were derived from a variety of official UN documents, some covering the year 1964, and others only the year 1963, in view of the fact that certain annual reports for 1964 were not available when this commentary was drafted (March 1965).

Category	$ Million
Special Fund (1964 Estimated Income)	$ 85.6
EPTA (1964 Estimated Income)	51.6
UNRWA (1963 Expenditures)	37.0
UNICEF (1963 Expenditures)	39.0
Congo Fund (1963 Expenditures)	11.7
UNHCR (Special Voluntary Programs)	6.0
WFP (Approved Projects, January 1963–November 1964)	52.0
Total	$283.0

The excess of expenditure for operational activities over regular budget outlays is in actuality substantially greater than these figures suggest since some
$30 million of regular budget funds are earmarked for field projects, thus
bringing the aggregate up to roughly $313 million, in comparison with a net
of about $183 million for all other UN system functions except peacekeeping.

Yet even this does not give an entirely realistic picture. Administrative outlays for the maintenance of field offices may for the most part properly be
charged to operational program costs. Thus, the annual budgets of the three
UN regional commissions located outside Europe (amounting for 1964 to
nearly $9 million) plus the costs of running the network of regional and coun-
try offices of the major specialized agencies constitute a further element in the
aggregate outlays for field program operations.[10]

A second indicator of the size of such operations is the use of manpower.
Of the total civilian personnel now employed by the UN family of agencies,
in the neighborhood of three-fourths are concerned with economic and social
matters while close to one-half have field duty assignments, some on the staffs
of field offices but the major fraction serving as "project" technicians (including OPEX appointees), covering an ever widening range of functional subject
matter. Statistical data showing precise totals by categories are not readily
available, but the table on the next page provides a rough breakdown.[11]

If we subtract the totals for the regional commission staffs and the regular
budget technical assistance experts (2,661) from the established post total
(14,205), the resulting figure of 11,544 covers nonoperational program person-

[10] It is virtually impossible, without painstaking inquiry at agency headquarters, to construct reliable
estimates of the costs of running field offices since many staff members divide their time between "office"
and "project" duty.

[11] The totals in this table are drawn from budgetary documents and agency and program reports for
1963 and 1964. The table does not include personnel assigned to the 48 UN Information Centers (323
in 1964) within the "operational" program category even though the emphasis at the centers located
in developing countries is on the publicizing of economic and social development activities.

Number of Established Posts (1964)	
United Nations (Headquarters and Field)	5,539
Specialized Agencies (Including IAEA)	8,666
Total	14,205
Personnel on Operational Programs	
Staffs of ECA, ECAFE, and ECLA (1964)	1,000
Technical Assistance Experts Financed by Regular Budgets	1,661
EPTA (Field, 1963)	3,037
Special Fund (Field, 1964)	1,523
EPTA Plus Special Fund (Headquarters and Field)	1,595
UNICEF (Headquarters and Field, 1964)	519
UNRWA (1963)	180
Congo Civilian Operations (1963)	631
Total	10,146

nel plus staff assigned to field office duty and staff at UN and agency head-quarters who devote varying portions of their time to research, analysis, briefing, and other backstopping functions relating to operational program requirements. It is therefore a fair estimate to say that the duties of UN system civilian personnel (all types) are about evenly divided between operational and nonoperational program activities.

Problems: Program Making

The most difficult problems in terms of program making, within the proliferation of operational functions, have quite naturally appeared in the two major programs that involve the UN and the specialized agencies in continuing cooperative situations, namely, EPTA and the Special Fund. EPTA takes the recipient country as the unit for program formulation, while the Special Fund builds its program around projects without any very close regard for the way in which its resources are distributed by countries. By and large, however, both programs face pressures from governments for as large a share of the technical assistance "pie" as possible. In the case of EPTA, it has not seemed possible to devise any acceptable formula for allocating available resources "objectively." During recent years, moreover, the expansion of UN and agency membership, especially from Africa, has had the effect of multiplying the total number of field projects to more than 2,000 now under way concurrently in some 130 countries and dependent territories.[12] Efforts to elim-

[12] In 1958, by comparison, there were only 1,300 EPTA projects.

inate or consolidate "tiny" projects of only a few weeks' or a few months' duration have not met with very much success.

On the other hand, some progress has been made toward planning country programs for a longer period than one year. In 1959 the Technical Assistance Committee (TAC) decided to shift to a biennial basis for EPTA programming in the hope that such a change would

> permit a more thorough appraisal of proposed projects and also provide more time for the recruitment of suitable experts and the ordering of supplies and equipment.[13]

In addition, it was subsequently decided to introduce so-called "project" pro-. gramming by asking governments to stipulate the requirements of projects from their beginning through to their expected termination. Projects planned for longer than two years were to be designated as "long-term" projects since they would have to be carried over into the next biennial budgetary period for the completion of their financing.

Biennial programming, although still favored in principle, has not yielded unmixed benefits. First, there has been a tendency for projects to pile up during the first year of the biennium. Second, projects planned not to start until the second year have been subject to so much change in the meantime as to become almost unrecognizable in many instances. This situation has necessitated frequent transfers of fund allocations from one project to another, not always after adequate analysis of the merits of the proposed project alterations.

As regards the so-called "long-term" projects, the results have also been somewhat disappointing. During the first biennium (1963–1964) in which this program procedure was employed, nearly 40 percent of all projects fell within the long-term category, but for the 1965–1966 program the number dropped to less than 34 percent.[14] The probable reason for this decline is believed to be that governments prefer not to commit themselves as to the precise details of project construction for longer than two years since they know that they can always apply for project extensions within the target of their country program for the following biennium.

The Technical Assistance Board (TAB) Resident Representative now plays a much more influential role in the shaping of country programs than during earlier years. This change stems in part from the general upgrading of the status and role of the Resident Representative since he took on the responsibility for directing Special Fund program operations within the areas constituting his territorial jurisdiction, usually a single country but occasionally a regional cluster of countries. A second and only slightly less important reason

---

[13] Sharp, p. 409.
[14] UN Document E/3995.

is that the new countries have had so little experience in national development planning and are so lacking in effective planning machinery and personnel that they are prone to look to the Resident Representative for extensive program advice. In the third place, the recent abolition of agency "subtotals" in EPTA country programming has given the Resident Representative more freedom for maneuver in suggesting adjustments in the proposed program with respect to the shares of the participating UN organizations.[15]

Programming procedures under the Special Fund are geared directly to projects, each considered on its own merits in terms of preinvestment value.[16] From its initial phase the Special Fund headquarters staff has insisted that a thorough examination of all project requests be carried out. Increasingly, the technical expertise of the UN Headquarters staff is being supplemented by advice from the agency that will presumably be asked to execute the project if approved. In addition, the Resident Representative is drawn into the process at the country level through consultations with the appropriate officials of the requesting government. Nowadays, the larger volume of Special Fund operations (larger than those of EPTA) in most countries means that the Resident Representative actually has to devote more of his time to the former than to the latter program.

A second significant difference between Special Fund and EPTA program making is that Special Fund projects are both substantially larger in monetary dimensions and longer in duration. The average monetary allocation for the 485 projects approved by the Special Fund down to January 1965 has been nearly a million dollars, with some projects running over twice this figure. Special Fund projects average about four years in duration. The Special Fund has been much more successful than EPTA in requiring governments to develop in advance detailed plans of project operations and in forcing them to contribute a specified amount toward the local costs of each project. Thus, for the cumulative total of the 485 projects mentioned above, government contributions have aggregated something over $600 million, in comparison with around $400 million from the Special Fund's own resources, resulting in an impact of more than a billion dollars since the Special Fund began operations in 1959.[17] Approximately two-fifths of the Special Fund's projects thus far approved have consisted of resource surveys and feasibility studies; another two-fifths, technical education and training projects; and the remaining fifth, the development of applied research institutes.

Discussion of programming by the Special Fund affords a convenient point

[15] Even so, the participating agencies still compete to a considerable extent for their "shares." In this connection, they now submit to governments "lists of suggestions" which some governments heed and others disregard. The actual distribution of project funds among agencies has not changed materially.
[16] For a detailed analysis of Special Fund operations, see Ronald A. Manzer, "The United Nations Special Fund," *International Organization*, Autumn 1964 (Vol. 18, No. 4), pp. 766–789.
[17] Special Fund Press Release 3045, January 14, 1965.

at which to call attention to two interesting trends in the evolution of program machinery during recent years. One of these trends has been in the direction of greater centralization in the interagency sense; the other has brought about considerable decentralization in the geographic sense inside the UN itself. The Special Fund represents the furthest degree of centralization of policy control yet adopted for a major UN operational program involving the participation of the specialized agencies as instruments of execution. This centralization was effected by establishing a single Managing Director subject to one central body, the Governing Council, for policy guidance and budgetary control. Elected by ECOSOC, the Governing Council of 24 members is divided equally between the developed and the developing countries. As the organ of intergovernmental control over the Special Fund, it has tended to defer to the vigorous leadership displayed by the Managing Director, who has acquired a broad degree of independence in handling Special Fund affairs.

The status of the Executive Chairman of TAB is fairly narrowly circumscribed by the important role of TAB itself as an intersecretariat body on which each of the specialized agencies has a direct voice, if not a veto power. Over the years the Executive Chairman has, by skillful and astute manipulation, been able to exert a steadily wider control over TAB's program decisions. Despite this indirect kind of *de facto* centralization, however, most of the specialized agencies tend to cling to TAB as their means of preventing UN "domination" of EPTA.

This issue has come to the fore since 1962 in connection with various schemes for merging EPTA and the Special Fund. Advocates of the merger proposals have made much of the advantages that would accrue from simplifying contacts with recipient governments, from administrative economies that might be realized, and from arrangements that should promote fuller consistency as between the two programs. ECOSOC in 1964 recommended approval by the General Assembly of a partial merger which would combine EPTA and the Special Fund into a "UN Development Program" under a single intergovernmental control body, a Governing Council, on the order of the existing Special Fund Council and would replace TAB by an Interagency Consultative Board with only advisory functions.[18] The consolidated program would be managed by an Administrator together, for the time being at least, with a Coadministrator, an arrangement obviously designed to protect the positions of the present Managing Director of the Special Fund and the Executive Chairman of TAB.

This merger plan stipulates that the "special characteristics" of the two prede-

---

[18] ECOSOC Resolution 1020 (XXXVII), August 11, 1964. The "voteless" nineteenth session of the General Assembly took no action on this recommendation, but it is generally assumed that it will eventually be approved.

cessor programs are to be preserved. This provision reflects the strong predilection of the newer and least developed countries for the EPTA "country
program" pattern under which they believe they may confidently count on
a predetermined slice of the technical assistance pie each year and exercise
fuller freedom in establishing project priorities than under the Special Fund.
In the context of the proposed combined program, it is also not unlikely that
the specialized agencies may attempt to utilize the new Interagency Consultative Board with a view to protecting their own program "interests." Certain
broader implications of the merger will be noted in the concluding section.

The second recent trend in the administration of the UN's own technical
assistance operations is one that reflects the growing force of regionalism
within the Organization. Here the focuses of decentralization are the three regional economic commissions serving Latin America, Asia, and Africa respectively. The General Assembly, at its 1961 session, adopted two complementary
resolutions, one of which authorized the "Decentralization of the economic
and social activities of the United Nations and the strengthening of the
regional economic commissions," and the second of which recommended,
inter alia, the establishment of regional "economic development and planning
institutes" under the auspices of these commissions.[19] In the implementation
of these resolutions, steps have since been taken to enlarge the staffs of the
regional commission secretariats; to establish within them "technical assistance
co-ordination units"; to greatly increase the number of roving regional advisers attached to the commission staffs so as to facilitate more direct relations
with the governments of the region on program needs and planning; and to
devolve upon the commission secretariats considerable authority to initiate
and supervise regional projects.[20]

According to informed opinion at UN Headquarters, these measures have
caused a number of administrative complications. With their expanded staffs,
the commission secretariats now tend to regard themselves almost as "interagency" bodies. Despite efforts to bring the Resident Representatives (of TAB
and the Special Fund) into closer relations with the commission secretariats
through periodic meetings of the two groups, the regional advisers appear
not infrequently to bypass the Resident Representatives through their contacts
with governments on country program matters, and it is claimed that they
sometimes try to impose a "regional" line in conflict with the UN Headquarters position on general program policy. Being on the spot, the regional
adviser can often make a decisive impact on the views of national ministries
while the New York Headquarters can exert its influence only by remote

---

[19] General Assembly Resolutions 1709 and 1708 (XVI), December 19, 1961, respectively. See W. R.
Malinowski, "Centralization and Decentralization in the United Nations Economic and Social Activities," *International Organization,* Summer 1962 (Vol. 16, No. 3), pp. 521–541, for a comprehensive
account of the background of this action.
[20] UN Document A/5584, October 30, 1963.

control. It perhaps is hardly surprising that the Executive Secretaries of the regional commissions should seek to enhance their own position and status within the UN system hierarchy by promoting regional values and regional policies.

Probably the most effective and most highly regarded work of the regional commission bureaucracies is their role in advising on plans for regional economic cooperation, particularly in the case of Latin America. To assist in furthering this type of activity, three regional planning and development institutes financed by the Special Fund are now going concerns at Santiago (linked with ECLA), at Bangkok (linked with ECAFE), and at Dakar (linked with ECA). These institutes for training and research bid fair to become valuable instruments for strengthening regional educational and technological resources in the development domain. The Mekong River project, associated with ECAFE, constitutes a strikingly successful example of combined multilateral and bilateral financing of a large-scale cooperative international development undertaking.

As they grow in operational experience and quality of staff, the regional commission secretariats should be able to realize more fully their potentialities as regional instruments. Already the secretariats of ECLA and ECAFE are showing considerable sophistication in their behavior. ECA apparently has not yet had time fully to find itself. Basically, however, regionalism in operational program making may weaken the overall integrity of UN system aid to development, including adequacy of financing, if it is allowed to proceed much further even if administrative crossed wires are eliminated.

PROBLEMS: MANPOWER

A second important category of problems in the management of UN operational programs lies in the recruitment and utilization of field personnel. No matter how admirably balanced the structure and process of programming may be, the ultimate test of a program lies in the quality and dedication of the people who serve it as technical advisers, teachers, demonstrators, administrators, and institution builders out in the field. As the size of the major programs has grown, the task of recruiting suitable field staffs has increasingly taxed the ingenuity of personnel officers.

Three factors have contributed to their difficulties: First, a much tighter labor market has emerged during recent years in terms of levels of compensation for professional and technical work in national civil services, universities, and industry through most of the economically advanced countries of North America and Europe compared with UN salary scales. Second, there has been a considerable decline in the drawing power of UN agency employment as a result of political setbacks suffered by the UN, particularly since

1960. In the third place, the growing insistence of the developing nations upon a wider geographic distribution of field experts has added to the task of finding adequately trained and experienced personnel in various subject-matter specialities.

In considering how these factors are being confronted, it should be observed that the personnel "crisis" in the operational programs is not as acute as for established posts in the regular secretariats. Recruiting for field assignments of limited duration does not involve the offering of permanent career prospects while it appears to be possible to "manipulate" the salary system somewhat more freely for such appointments than for career posts. Also, geographic distribution does not have to be applied in accordance with any rigid formula such as that employed for the central secretariats.[21] But the difficulties vary only in degree.

For example, there are now certain professional fields where shortages of available personnel are particularly severe the world over. These include various branches of engineering, hydrogeology, agronomy, forestry, and the soil sciences—fields drawn upon especially for projects financed by the Special Fund with FAO and the UN as executing agencies. As a partial solution to this problem, these two agencies have recently resorted to the device of "subcontracting" projects to private consulting firms. By June 1964, 128 such subcontracts valued at $28 million, had been awarded to 88 firms in twenty countries (including twenty firms in the United States, 26 in France, and twenty in the United Kingdom). Four of these arrangements took the form of international consortia.[22] Although to some extent private firms have to tap the same reservoir of expertise for field teams as the UN agencies themselves, the former are able to provide unusually favorable rates of compensation and other special inducements. They also tend to have greater flexibility in regard to the assignment of, for example, engineers for short periods overseas and their rotation within the firm's own range of projects. A further advantage is derived from the relative homogeneity of such teams through the members' having worked together previously. Where this situation obtains, a private firm is often able to get a project off the ground and even to carry it to completion more quickly than can an international public organization.

Clearly, use of the subcontracting device must remain limited. Already certain governments are said to have objected on the ground that "private capitalism" is thus getting its foot directly into the UN technical assistance door. Hence, the various UN organizations must rely for the most part on their own direct efforts to attract qualified candidates. Although none of these organizations has developed any formal field recruitment machinery, in large part

[21] In 1964, 238 out of 1,523 experts on duty with projects financed by the Special Fund were nationals of countries receiving Special Fund assistance.

[22] UN Document SF/L.112, December 3, 1964. Yugoslavia was the only Communist country represented in the list of firms.

because of lack of budgetary support, they do make extensive use of the network of UN system field offices for interviewing and confidential reporting services. The regional commission secretariats and Resident Representatives' offices are drawn upon for screening applicants from Latin America, Asia, and Africa. The weakness in this arrangement is that few if any of these field officials are trained personnel technicians; being busy operators, moreover, they often do not have the time to take the interviewing chore as seriously as it ought to be.

Within the UN itself, its Technical Assistance Recruitment Service (TARS), although handicapped by inadequate professional staff, does manage from time to time to send pairs of staff representatives on "talent-fishing" trips across the United States to major universities, institutes, laboratories, and meetings of national professional associations. Since President Lyndon B. Johnson's memorandum to the heads of executive departments in August 1964 on the provision of United States personnel for international organizations, the United States government itself has become more active in helping TARS and the UN generally in their recruitment problems; one member of the United States mission in New York, for example, has been assigned to give special attention to the problem.

In Western Europe, Israel, Syria, the United Arab Republic, India, Pakistan, and Japan, national committees have been set up by the governments to aid in recruiting national personnel for the UN, along with their own bilateral programs. Most of these committees have been provided with permanent staffs; accordingly, they are now being utilized quite intensively by TARS (as well as by the specialized agencies). In Latin America, ECLA has received a controlled delegation of authority to recruit within the region for specified projects.

One significant development within the past few years has been the changed attitude of the Soviet government regarding the provision of Soviet nationals. Not only does the Soviet Union now permit the UN to interview on Soviet territory as many as five candidates for a given post and to indicate its choice, but the nominee is in some cases allowed to accept a term of as much as three–five years on the UN staff. This less rigid attitude has made it possible for TARS to send recruitment teams to the Soviet Union.[23] Candidates thus proposed by TARS may ordinarily accept appointments with no strings attached although the demand for Soviet experts for EPTA and Special Fund projects still remains decidedly small.

The effect of the lag of UN salary levels behind those for comparable outside work in North America and Western Europe has reportedly been mixed. On the one hand, it has frequently become necessary to offer higher initial

[23] The Director of TARS himself was about to set out for Moscow for the first time when interviewed by the writer in New York (March 1965).

salary rates to applicants for UN posts than would be warranted by the duties performed by persons of similar qualifications and experience already on the UN payroll. On the other hand, in certain highly technical (especially engineering) specialities from which personnel must be recruited, it is claimed that the disparity between UN and private industrial levels of compensation tends to produce a kind of automatic preselection; persons motivated primarily by material considerations—"the money grabbers," to employ a term used in the writer's presence by one UN personnel official—are ruled out by what amounts to a prescreening situation. How this affects the quality of men recruited for such responsible posts as managers of Special Fund projects should be deserving of systematic study.

United States readers will be interested to learn of the marked stimulus given by the Peace Corps experiment to the provision of youthful field personnel to the UN, with no cost to the Organization, by various Western European governments, notably the Scandinavian countries, West Germany, and Belgium. These young men and women, officially designated as "associate experts," who numbered about 60 in 1964, are expected to increase to around 150 for the current year. They are, as a rule, assigned to project teams under the direction of the team chief. Rarely are they allowed to work as isolated individuals. Their record has on the whole been excellent, some of them eventually being promoted to higher posts on the UN payroll.

One further question concerning personnel suggests itself. Has there been over the years any discernible trend toward longer tenure of service for project staffs? While no published statistics on this point are available, there seems to be little doubt that field experts now on the average remain longer in UN (or specialized agency) employment than was true during the first decade of EPTA. Two-year program planning by TAB makes it easier to continue the stay of experts for the full program period, and in the case of the "long-term" projects somewhat longer. Special Fund projects permit the engagement of personnel for even more extended periods. In both programs an appreciable proportion of project experts is offered assignments on a succession of projects.[24] But it would be stretching the facts to contend that international technical assistance work is likely soon, if ever, to offer anything like permanent careers.

The point at which there has been the most distinct tenure trend during recent years is in the post of Resident Representative. A 1963 study showed that of 58 Resident Representatives then on duty, as many as eight had served ten years or over, while another thirteen had been from five to nine years on the job although not necessarily at the same location.[25] Most Resident Representatives now stay at the same post for three or four years. In part, this trend

---

[24] A limited number of technical assistance experts, after experience in the field, apply for appointment to UN Secretariat established posts. Some of them are reported to have made excellent officials.
[25] UN Document E/TAC/L.326, December 17, 1963.

reflects the advantage of keeping a man on a given country assignment long enough to master the complexities of handling the very much greater volume and variety of program operations than marked the period prior to the advent of the Special Fund; in part, also, it is probably an index of the higher over-all quality of appointees to this key post in the UN system field establishment.

Problems: Program Execution and Evaluation

The execution of field programs cannot be entirely separated from program making, for the two processes in practice tend to overlap and rightly so. In essence, effective program execution involves the coordination of secretariat operations at the center, effective communication between headquarters and the field, and the maintenance of field machinery which will both facilitate project execution and ensure interagency cooperation insofar as this may be necessary.

On all three of these counts, encouraging progress has marked the period since 1960. The working relations of the UN and agency secretariats now involve much closer consultation on project arrangements than during the previous decade. This consultation takes place in a variety of ways, e.g., by written and telephonic communication, through informal intersecretariat working parties, through subsidiary bodies set up by the Administrative Committee on Coordination (ACC) to deal with such cross-agency functional areas as urbanization, water resources, community development, education and training, and social welfare, and through the assignment of liaison officers by one agency to the secretariat of a sister agency.[26]

In 1962 the headquarters staff of the Special Fund inaugurated the practice of annually sending a team of its senior officers to each special agency headquarters to conduct with agency officials a review of the problems and difficulties that have arisen in executing Special Fund projects during the preceding year. At FAO headquarters, for instance, the review team has spent as much as ten days going over the situation, country by country, with as many as 75-100 FAO staff officers in attendance at a series of joint meetings. The consequences of this face-to-face discussion, according to the Special Fund directorate, have been markedly beneficial, resulting in distinctly prompter implementation of field projects by the executing agencies concerned.

One of the unanticipated byproducts of adding Special Fund project operations to the operational burden of the agency secretariats has been a diminution of interagency rivalry as regards technical assistance programs generally. There is now much less tendency for agencies to try to carve out wider areas

[26] To cite a slightly different type of arrangement, a joint division was recently set up by FAO with IAEA in Vienna to advise on the agricultural activities of common concern to the two organizations. Also, WHO, FAO, and IAEA have agreed to exchange liaison officers in order to promote closer coordination in common borderline action. (UN Document A/5859, January 25, 1965.)

of jurisdiction and to define functional boundaries competitively—if only because the major agencies have almost more than they can handle by way of field activity.[27] Concomitantly, arrangements for cooperating on joint projects in the field have become more common than during the earlier years of EPTA.

A recent interesting example of interagency cooperation is that involving FAO and the International Bank for Reconstruction and Development (IBRD). The novel feature here is that the International Bank has agreed to help finance various agricultural projects for economic development for which FAO is to provide the execution and supervision. It is proposed to send some 25 joint missions to the field for general survey and project appraisal purposes. The Bank has assigned a liaison officer to Rome to assist FAO in carrying out the program.[28]

With respect to headquarters-field relationships, the general atmosphere has noticeably improved during recent years. Not only are the lines of communication less prone to become tangled (with the possible exception of the relations between the regional commission staffs, Resident Representatives, and New York, referred to earlier), but the attitudes of headquarters and field staffs toward each other are considerably more understanding and tolerant than was formerly the case. This changed psychology appears to be due in large part to the more extensive interchange of staff between headquarters and the field. Today the majority of middle- and upper-grade officers in the TAB and Special Fund headquarters secretariats have had previous field experience; similarly, with the staff of the Bureau of Technical Assistance Operations in the Department of Economic and Social Affairs. It is now not exceptional for a senior UN official at New York to be tapped for assignment as a Resident Representative. Being sent to the field is no longer looked upon "as being consigned to Siberia!" A comparable change, judging from personal inquiry made by the author at various specialized agency headquarters during 1963, seems to be taking place in most of the other agencies.

Along with this improved psychological context has come at least some strengthening of arrangements for inspection and reporting. Field trips by senior headquarters staff appear to be more intelligently planned, and they occur somewhat more frequently than formerly. While the quality of project reporting still varies tremendously, the confidential appraisals submitted by Resident Representatives on Special Fund projects and on the performance of OPEX appointees, for example, are said to be extremely frank and objective. Generally speaking, project reports are now subject to more thorough analysis at headquarters than they used to be, the results being employed in

---

[27] For a more detailed study of interagency relationships in the context of the role of ECOSOC and ACC, see the writer's chapter "Program Coordination and the Economic and Social Council" in a forthcoming Syracuse University volume under the general editorship of Gerard J. Mangone.

[28] UN Document A/5859.

connection with future project planning and the briefing of future experts.

As intimated earlier, the growth in volume of field program operations that has occurred since the inauguration of the Special Fund has led to a substantial expansion of the field establishment maintained by the UN and, to a lesser extent, also by the principal specialized agencies. A second factor in this situation has of course been the marked increase in the number of UN Member countries located in the underdeveloped regions.

For United Nations-sponsored programs, the following field offices were in operation in 1964:[29]

Regional Commission Secretariats	3
Plus Suboffices in Africa and Latin America	4
UN Economic and Social Affairs Office at Beirut	1
Resident Representatives of TAB/Directors of Special Fund Programs	73
Lesser Offices for TAB/Special Fund Liaison Officers and Correspondents	8
UNICEF: Regional Offices	6
Other (Smaller) Offices	28
UNRWA: Head Office at Beirut	1
Field Offices	7
UNHCR: Branch Offices	16
Total	147

As for the major specialized agencies, there has been some proliferation of "subregional" offices, chiefly in Africa, accompanied by a countertendency to liquidate small "country" offices where the Resident Representative's staff facilities are sufficiently large to handle the local administrative services required for agency project personnel on duty in the country.

The keystone of the UN field structure is the office of the Resident Representative. Except in eight instances, where a group of small countries constitutes its jurisdiction, this office is organized on a single country basis. Within the past five years there has been a conscious effort to convert this into a kind of across-the-board coordinating office, at least *de facto* (since the separate "autonomies" of the specialized agencies must still be given official recognition). In 1961, ACC laid down ten principles designed for the guidance of the Resident Representative and the agencies with a view to expediting this evolution. One result of this action was to encourage certain of the specialized agencies to request the Resident Representative to act for them as their "country representative" although this arrangement does not preclude the maintenance of an agency "mission chief" in countries in which the agency's tech-

29 In addition, there were 48 UN Information Centers.

nical assistance project work is of substantial dimensions. Where this is the situation, he serves as technical adviser to the Resident Representative in his agency's functional field.

Equally significant has been the strengthening of the Resident Representative's office staff and facilities. By 1964, at 63 out of 73 locations he had been provided with a senior Deputy Resident Representative, while in 35 places there was an Assistant Resident Representative for Program and in 46 an Assistant Resident Representative for Administration. Including locally recruited personnel, the total staff assigned to Resident Representative offices amounted to over 1,200, with an average per office of seventeen.[30] The annual cost of maintaining this office network, which now exceeds $6 million, is shared by EPTA and the Special Fund—in 1964 on a 55–45 ratio. For 1965, however, with the dollar total of Special Fund operations in the field exceeding that of EPTA for the first time, the supporting budget is to be divided between the two programs proportionately. By agreement and advance central clearance, the Resident Representative is subject to direction from both the Executive Chairman of TAB and the Managing Director of the Special Fund—an administrative anomaly which appears to work without friction because of the excellent personal relations of these two program heads.

As part of the overall attempt to rationalize field machinery, there has recently been some spotty progress toward the interagency consolidation of field office premises in perhaps a dozen of the larger centers.[31] The realization of this objective will involve tedious negotiation with host governments as well as among the UN agencies concerned. Without large-scale financial assistance from the host countries, the outlook for rapid advancement in this direction is not bright since the tight financial position of the UN itself makes it unlikely that the General Assembly will vote funds for the construction of buildings for field purposes.[32]

The expanding role of the Resident Representative raises the question whether the overall load now falling on his shoulders may not be too much for one man. The reply usually given is that with the additional professional staff now at his disposal he should be able to command his job provided he knows how and when to delegate responsibility to his subordinates. Various central officials are of the firm opinion that the general quality of Resident Representatives has improved during recent years, due among other things to the higher levels of pay now being offered.[33] One official who had had

[30] These figures are taken from UN Document E/TAC/149, October 30, 1964.

[31] For details, see UN Document A/5807.

[32] One specialized agency, WHO, has, however, financed the construction of a modern edifice to house its regional office in Manila.

[33] Of the 73 Resident Representatives in office in 1964, 25 were at the D-2 and 32 at the D-1 salary level. (UN Document E/TAC/149.) There is said to be a special difficulty in finding able Resident Representative candidates for Latin America because of the paucity of otherwise qualified men who can speak Spanish.

experience in the field himself thought, however, that there had been little change in the caliber of the Resident Representatives. In his view, appointees with a predominantly political or diplomatic background did not make the best Resident Representatives; a combination of national and international administrative experience was usually more likely to provide the kind of capacity needed to plan, organize, and manage the functions of the Resident Representative's office.

There appears to be little support in TAB or Special Fund circles for the proposal to endow the Resident Representative with authority to represent the Secretary-General in a diplomatic capacity. Any such action, except in highly exceptional and limited circumstances (e.g., the Congo [Leopoldville]), would, it is feared, tend to entangle the economic and social programs in local politics; nor would the specialized agencies look with equanimity on any plan to provide the Resident Representative with a diplomatic hat.

However this may be, the Resident Representatives are being increasingly given the opportunity to exchange views on their own experience. Regional meetings of Resident Representatives, which are now convened more frequently than in the early years of EPTA, afford a means of airing grievances, both among themselves and with representatives of headquarters. A general conclave on a world scale of Resident Representatives is projected for the current year.

The larger problem of program evaluation is one that has plagued TAB and agency officials ever since the initial years of EPTA. Resolution after resolution in ECOSOC has, by way of ACC, exhorted program bureaucracies to undertake systematic appraisals of the impact of technical assistance activity on the economic progress of the recipient nations.[34] They have been rather disappointing. Two difficulties help to explain why: 1) The techniques and tools of evaluation now available leave much to be desired; and 2) the peripheral role played by UN system aid in the totality of aid programs available for economic development makes it very difficult to differentiate and measure the impact of UN operations alone. There is a further subtle factor inherent in the tendency of certain officials to remain blind to the weaknesses of programs for which they themselves have been responsible; elimination of this element of subjectivity is not easy. Trained teams of social scientists drawn from outside sources might provide more objective evaluations if allowed to pursue their inquiries in complete independence. UN officialdom, however, has always looked askance at any such arrangement.

The other aspect of evaluation presents fewer complications. This relates to program performance in terms of costs and operational targets. Here somewhat more progress, even though it is also spotty, has been registered. Cur-

---

[34] The most recent of this succession of resolutions was ECOSOC Resolution 1042 (XXXVII), August 15, 1964.

rently, for instance, administrative performance studies of EPTA are being carried out in a sample of countries by small teams each consisting of an economist, a headquarters administrator, and a field official. Part of the procedure of these teams is to sit down with government officials and discuss problems and difficulties "off the record" in the hope that the latter will be willing to talk freely. Something beyond mere description may emerge from this undertaking if it is conducted with skill and insight.

Five years ago the present writer made the observation that "international organizations of the UN type might take a firmer line with beneficiary governments concerning project carry-through."[35] Nothing that has happened since then would lead him to modify this statement. Its reference was primarily to projects involving translation into national legislative policy and/or administrative action but not requiring any considerable capital financing. The potentialities of applying subtle pressure on governments to act on well-conceived project recommendations have by no means been exhausted. It may be that the shift in majority voting power in the UN to the developing countries themselves is inducing timidity in certain types of operating officials.

A special effort is being made in connection with the Special Fund's operations to assist governments in finding sources of investment capital. An investment advisory service was recently made available from the Special Fund's headquarters to governments on request.[36] Partly by reason of this service, the Special Fund was able to report by the end of 1964 that as a consequence of sixteen feasibility projects then completed and costing the Special Fund only $16 million to carry out, there had been $780 million of capital investment from domestic and international sources.[37] The management of the Special Fund likes to regard this as an encouraging sign that the Fund's rationale is really working.

THE YEARS AHEAD

The foregoing survey has attempted to highlight some of the more significant trends in the management of UN operational programs during the past half decade. To risk a generalization, these trends tend to confirm the view that within the political and legislative restrictions in which it has to function, the UN's administrative leadership is continuing to display intelligent initiative, resourcefulness, and ingenuity in handling program development. At the same time it should be said that the complex, dispersed, multiagency structure of the larger programs necessitates highly involved bureaucratic procedures governing program making and implementation. Increasingly, major donor governments are manifesting concern over what some of them, in par-

[35] Sharp, *Field Administration in the United Nations System*, p. 549.
[36] A similar service is also maintained by the International Bank in Washington.
[37] UN Document SF/L.112, December 3, 1964.

ticular, the United States, charge is productive of unjustifiably high overhead costs, along with confusion and frustration on the part of recipient governments as they grope their way through a labyrinth of sources of assistance (including the specialized agencies' own offerings and a variety of bilateral programs).

It is against this background that the pending merger of EPTA and the Special Fund should be weighed. As indicated earlier, this merger is only a partial one, applying chiefly to intergovernmental policy control which would be unified. The management of the two programs is already a joint affair in all but name. What if anything, then, is likely to happen to the substantive character of the two programs? While prediction is hazardous, there is reason to expect that sooner or later a *rapprochement* in program content will take place, especially with respect to Special Fund and EPTA "long-term" projects. An effort will probably be made to introduce more flexibility into country programming, allowing more freedom to the program management to allocate program resources in accordance with national development needs in terms of agreed objective criteria. Ultimately, the distinction in the two original programs may disappear. The Resident Representative's title will presumably be changed to "Representative of the United Nations Development Program" while his role status is likely to be further enhanced.

If this evolution occurs, the UN system should be in a tidier operational position to assume the management of capital development resources.[38] Whether such resources are ever turned over to the UN will depend mainly on the willingness of the major donor countries to utilize a globally political system, in addition to the Western-oriented World Bank complex, for the dispensing of capital investment funds. This writer would be disposed to argue that, from the administrative standpoint at least, the UN could handle this responsibility as honestly and efficiently as the United States government now handles its bilateral aid program or even as the World Bank and IDA have been doing with their own loan operations.

This is not to say, however, that there are not ways by which the UN might further improve its standards of program formulation and implementation. In concluding this survey the writer would like to reiterate one such recommendation he has put forward elsewhere, namely, that a small but high-level administrative unit, staffed on an interagency basis, be set up under the general aegis of ACC to conduct continuing program audits, analyses, and appraisals covering all the participating agencies.[39] Such a unit should not be given any direct administrative responsibilities. One of its functions would

[38] In this connection, the Secretary-General upon instruction from ECOSOC has made a study of how the present Special Fund might itself take over capital development functions. (UN Document E/3947, July 15, 1964.)

[39] See the writer's chapter in the forthcoming Syracuse University volume mentioned above for a fuller exposition of this proposal.

be to spot emerging developmental possibilities arising from the impact of science and technology and to suggest future program strategy with regard thereto. While it would have no power to impose a "master plan" on the operating organizations, it should be able gradually to exert a substantial impact on the proposals of management to program-governing bodies and, in particular, to facilitate the tasks of interagency program integration through ACC and ECOSOC.

In international no less than in national or local administration, staff arms of central management have a crucial role to play. Examination of the experience of the UN family of agencies reveals a tendency to minimize or insufficiently to provide financial support for general budget, personnel, and program-planning units. There are now some signs that more adequate recognition may be accorded to such units in the future. This trend should eventually pay dividends in strengthened administrative performance.

Outer Space and International Cooperation

On October 4, 1957, when *Sputnik I* was successfully orbited, it was popular to say that mankind had entered a new age—the Age of Space. If this was not just hyperbole, perhaps we are entitled to make a few judgments about the Space Age as it moves toward the end of its first decade. For, even from this short a perspective, the Space Age sharply illustrates the portentous conflict in our time between the forces of neonationalism and, for want of a better word, internationalism.

Few areas of competitive activity so dramatize the contemporary struggle among nations for power and prestige as does outer space. This has been the case in the genesis of the space programs, in every stage of their technical growth, and in their great political meaning. To be sure, the first earth satellite experiments were conducted under the banner of the International Geophysical Year (IGY). But the booster rockets that made it possible for the Soviet Union to be spectacularly first under that banner were originally developed to hurl an intercontinental ballistic missile across vast distances on earth. In 1965, still to all practical intents the monopoly of the two superpowers, space preempts a growing portion of both their budgets and scientific efforts. The United States spends about $7\frac{1}{2}$ percent of the national budget on space, more than on any cluster of domestic programs. Even more startling evidence of the steadily increasing commitment to the claims of the space race is the fact that almost all of the 30,000 or so engineers and scientists that entered research in the United States last year were absorbed into space-related activities.

President John F. Kennedy in May 1961 defined the goal of the United States as "landing a man on the moon and returning him safely to earth" during this decade. The time has arrived, he said, "for this nation to take a

LINCOLN P. BLOOMFIELD, a member of the Board of Editors of *International Organization*, is Professor of Political Science and a senior staff member of the Center for International Studies, Massachusetts Institute of Technology.

clearly leading role in space achievement which, in many ways, may hold the key to our future on earth."[1] President Lyndon B. Johnson has described his goal as that of making the United States the world's number one space-faring nation.

As for the Soviet Union, although former Premier Nikita Khrushchev may have denied in 1963 that his country was in a race to the moon, it is noteworthy that the combined Soviet military and space budget continued to climb, that the Soviets did not respond to the United States offer of a jointly planned moon shot, and that Soviet space technology has become increasingly sophisticated and complex, specifically in the techniques of maneuver and rendezvous in space which have potential military significance. The heroic welcome for Soviet cosmonauts and their treatment as new folk heroes, the unqualifiedly military complexion of the Soviet Union's space program, and the payload of the Soviet Union's pioneering hard moon landing in September 1959[2] all indicate the high regard in which the Soviets hold their space effort.

As Western Europe resumes its place on the world scene as a potent mover of events, it too enters the space race. The European Launcher Development Organization (ELDO) and the European Space Research Organization (ESRO), Europe's joint space agencies, are now paced by Eurospace, a combination of more than a hundred European commercial firms seeking significant shares in the lucrative space equipment business. After flirting with the notion of an independent, competitive satellite communications organization of their own, the European countries have now made satisfactory arrangements with the United States Communications Satellite Corporation (Comsat), the United States' quasi-private instrument for space communications. But substantial space programs are under way in Europe, as much, one surmises, for prestige reasons as for any other.

A possible future significance of space, which we overlook at our potential peril, is as a new *place d'armes,* a sort of strategic suburb of earth to which the Cold War has already expanded and from which, as visualized by at least some military strategists, a hot war could be fought. Both superpowers have agreed in a 1963 United Nations resolution to abstain from placing nuclear weapons in orbit around the earth.[3] But both are also reportedly at work developing, among other things, manned space platforms, a fundamental first step in establishing a controllable and potentially versatile military presence in space. Information about military technology in space is highly classified, but whether through genuine fear of United States progress or as a smoke screen for their own militarization of space the Soviets have recently made such significant statements as this one:

---

[1] *The New York Times,* May 26, 1961.

[2] It consisted of multiple metal fragments bearing the hammer and sickle emblem and etched with the Cyrillic characters "CCCP," which scattered on impact, plus a foot-long Soviet flag.

[3] General Assembly Resolution 1884 (XVIII), October 17, 1963.

The Soviet Union, which is resolutely opposed to the utilization of outer space for military purposes, cannot ignore all these preparations of the American imperialists and is forced to adopt corresponding measures in order to safeguard its security against an attack through outer space. It is no secret that the technical basis for the launching of earth satellites and spaceships is the ballistic missile and its guidance system. Such complex, perfected technical equipment . . . is in the possession of the Soviet Union.[4]

If we allow our imaginations to wander, then, to the darkest prospects for the future, we can envisage the day, not too far off, when the Great Powers have positioned secretly launched weapons systems in outer space. The consequences would surely be that each power would be trying fiercely to preempt the other's satellites, tension on earth would be greatly heightened, hostile action threatened on the ground—in short, all the direst consequences of an all-out struggle for prestige, power, and ever more exclusive sovereignty and secrecy in heaven as it is on earth. This then would be outer space as one more arena for virulent forms of nationalism, powerfully reinforced by the clash of ideologies. From all this can only come increased hostility, growing suspicions, ever greater militarism, and, perhaps in the end, World War III. (The optimists who see competition in space as a desirable kind of surrogate for conflict on earth must be mistaken as long as one of the superpowers remains devoted, however qualifiedly, to the downfall of the other.)

The other side of the space race is the reverse of the first in spirit and outlook and grows out of technological—but not necessarily political—reality. If anything makes nonsense of national boundaries, however useful and meaningful they may be in other ways, it is the earth satellite, orbiting every 90 minutes or so over different countries, transiting their boundaries without passports, travel documents, customs inspection, or even permission. Still more mocking of the narrow provincial spirit on earth is the flight outward to the moon, to Mars, to deep space. One of the favorite dialogues in contemporary science fiction has to do with the perspective by which observers view the exclusive barriers erected by men and their petty earthly quarrels when earth is seen from a great distance. From this perspective one is, at least in theory, entitled to deduce the self-evident norm of internationalism—at a minimum cooperation, at a maximum integration.

Both aspects of space—as an arena for the conflict of national ambitions and as a nation-transcending challenge to the skills and knowledge of mankind—both of these "faces of space" represent reality. Neither alone explains the full nature of the political problems involved in space cooperation nor

[4] V. Larionov, "Kosmos i strategiya," *Krasnaya Zvezda,* (March 21, 1963, p. 3. See also V. D. Sokolovskii, *Soviet Military Strategy,* translated and edited by Herbert S. Dinerstein and others (Englewood Cliffs, N.J.: Prentice-Hall, 1963), p. 427. Retired United States Air Force Chief of Staff Curtis E. LeMay recently wrote that "many of the techniques the Soviet Union has developed so far point strongly toward a military space effort." (*The New York Times,* March 26, 1965.)

indicates with any reliability the avenues of policy that are actually open to the responsible countries with space potential. And neither alone completely describes the prospects we can legitimately envisage when we ask ourselves whether there is to be real cooperation—or real conflict—in space in the time ahead.

TECHNOLOGICAL ADVANCE AND POLITICAL CONFLICT

In thus seeking to set forth an appropriate background for a discussion of international cooperation, one recognizes the extraordinarily high degree of political content that is superimposed on "neutral" technology. One of the enduring clichés of the Space Age speaks of the gap between technical progress and political arrangements for mastering that progress to the benefit and enrichment of mankind rather than for his possibly accelerated destruction. In 1961 the United States representative to the United Nations may have been too pessimistic when he conceded that:

> Unhappily this astounding progress in space science has not been matched by comparable progress in international cooperation. In the race of history, social invention continues to lag behind scientific invention.[5]

But Ambassador Adlai Stevenson may have been overly sanguine when two years later he said:

> In outer space . . . our sense of social responsibility and our capacity for social invention are not doing too badly in response to the challenge laid down by the inventions of our scientists.[6]

The truth of the matter is that while the growth of technology tends to proceed along a fairly uniform curve—though sometimes at an exponential rate—the political curve is characteristically irregular, faltering, sometimes cyclical, and not at all predictable. In turn the capacity for political invention is irregular because it is a function of the changing dynamics of international political life.

Specifically, it is not possible to chart with any depth of understanding the progress of international cooperation on outer space without specific reference to the state of Soviet–United States relations at any given time. Mr. Stevenson's 1961 statement was made in a frosty atmosphere engendered, after a period of relative thaw, by a renewed Soviet hard line, exemplified in intensified threats to Berlin culminating in the erection of the Wall, the stealthily prepared breach of the three-year moratorium on nuclear testing, and the boasts of terror weapons that accompanied it. His 1963 statement surely reflected the warming trend resulting when, after the 1962 Cuban missile adventure had failed, reality had at least temporarily returned to Soviet strategic

---

[5] Statement in the First (Political and Security) Committee (United States Delegation to the General Assembly, Press Release 3875, December 4, 1961).

[6] Department of State *Bulletin*, December 30, 1963 (Vol. 49, No. 1279), p. 1011.

thinking and détente, reinforced by the steadily mounting costs of space and defense, was in the air again. If 1963 was a vintage year in terms of limited agreements about both arms and space, it was because both the United States President and the Soviet Premier had committed themselves to policies of relative restraint in international relations, strategically supported by mutual deterrence that made it politically possible, at least at the time, to fend off pressures for more bellicose policies on both sides.

The political curve can thus lag behind the technological curve and be un-affected by apparent moral and intellectual imperatives that people believe they discern in the march of science. But it can just as well speed up and carry social invention along with it at a surprising clip, given the will and the pro-pitious congruence of political and strategic forces. The key variable may be the pressure of technology on politics. But its operational force depends on the drawing of relevant political conclusions—not always a self-evident process.

What *is* unmistakable is the pace of technology. In 1958 the United States successfully orbited five earth satellites; in 1964, 73. In December 1963, with the launching of *Tiros 8* from Cape Kennedy, it became possible for every point in the inhabited world to have access to "instant weather" pictures in a "local" area of 900,000 square miles, read out through a slow-scan technique that makes it possible to acquire a ground receiver for as little as $32,000.

Progress in space communications is even better-known. The United States *Telstar, Relay,* and *Syncom* satellites have brought space home to millions of viewers of the Japanese Olympics, Churchill's funeral, and less serious matters. The synchronous satellite, with its capacity to appear to hover over the equator and thus remain stationary in relation to its earthly audiences, has the poten-tial to revolutionize communications, education, and propaganda. The *Early Bird* satellite, launched over the Atlantic in April 1965 with telephone and television channels, is the forerunner of a basic operational system to be de-ployed in 1966 that will provide telephone, telegraphy, high-speed data, fac-simile, and television communications services on a global and nondiscrimina-tory basis. The Soviets for their part launched a communications satellite, *Molniya I,* in late April 1965.

It will be some time before one can make the predicted ten-cent overseas phone call via satellites. But they can soon link together countries in Africa that have traditionally been "wired" directly to European capitals and can even permit such countries as Brazil to bypass some stages of conventional internal, wired communications by linking remote areas within the country through the use of a few ground stations and satellites. The British writer Arthur C. Clarke, no mean prophet of the Space Age so far, has written:

> It may be no exaggeration to say that priority in establishing the satellite com-munication system may determine whether, fifty years from now, Russian or

English is the main language of mankind. The TV satellite is mightier than the ICBM, and intercontinental TV may indeed be the ultimate weapon.[7]

Satellite science is teaching men more than they ever dreamed about the nature of space, solar "weather," conditions on the surfaces of the planets, and the real visage of the planet earth. But even here there are important military implications. The *Secor* system, like the earlier *Anna* and *Transit,* not only aids scientists in determining the exact size and shape of the earth but also helps to pinpoint targets by improving the exact navigation of *Polaris* and other weapons delivery systems. The Soviet Union and the United States are making faster progress toward reaching the moon than toward making arrangements to coordinate their findings or to ensure against hostile acts from emplacements in near space or on celestial bodies such as the moon. If life exists on Mars or Jupiter we are by no means yet guaranteed against the prospect that the first one to reach one of these planets might fatally contaminate it—or that we as a society of nations are spiritually and socially prepared to apply the golden rule to "them" any more than we apply it to each other.

CRITERIA FOR INTERNATIONAL COOPERATION IN SPACE

Against this background we can now examine the steps that have actually been taken, in and out of the United Nations, in the direction of cooperation. To assess these steps, however, we are handicapped by the lack of appropriate criteria. The same problem exists in seeking to judge the relative success or failure of the United Nations itself. For example, it is not uncommon to hear the UN deprecated because it has failed to prevent the Great Powers from acting in undesirable ways. But by this standard the UN must invariably fail since it was not designed to enforce its will on the Great Powers. One *can,* however, legitimately expect the UN to seek to moderate great-power relationships and to provide marginal influences in cases of direct confrontations between them. When it fails to do so, it is legitimately open to criticism.

In the same way, one must identify realistic—yet challenging—standards by which to judge the comparative success or failure of international cooperation in outer space, especially in terms of the performance of the United Nations and its related agencies. Of course, if we identify as the prime standard of measurement the "internationalization" of all outer space activities, we will have stacked the deck hopelessly—and unrealistically—against an intelligible finding.

The objective of keeping space immune from conflict appears unrealistic unless one can also eliminate the political warfare that underlies it. As long as that continues, space will represent a race for prestige and for strategic superiority. The time may be coming when political conflict on earth will have

[7] Arthur C. Clarke, *Profiles of the Future* (New York: Harper & Row, 1962), p. 190.

abated to the point where space can be labeled as truly out of bounds. But it is hardly a fair test of international action today. To carry out an effective ban against the military use of space would require successful action in the realms of disarmament, inspection, verification, sanctions, and enforcement measures—elusive goals not limited to the context of space and in the absence of which the powers struggle to provide for their own security.

What then *can* legitimately be set forth as reasonable and realistic desiderata for international cooperation in space, enabling us to evaluate the role and prospects of the available means of such cooperation, notably the United Nations?

First, given the assumed continuation of political conflict between leading nations, it is both desirable and reasonable to seek to achieve a maximum of cooperation in every aspect of space activity, while not expecting the conflict to cease or the leading nations to abandon prestige or power as fundamental goals.

Second, given the unlikelihood of enforceable international law under present international political circumstances, we should expect a maximum effort to draw up practical functional rules of conduct in and concerning space, rules that it is clearly in the interest of all to have established and obeyed. To the extent possible the quest should also be pressed to establish broad principles of national conduct that can become "law" through custom or international covenant.

Third, one can legitimately ask for the creation of the appropriate international machinery to do those jobs which nations agree to delegate to it and, in addition, for the optimum utilization of existing international organizational machinery.

Fourth, a special exception to the highly constrained political framework we have postulated here, it is in our own and in the common interest to seek a maximum of arms control in the realm of space. Hopefully, we should find movement toward this goal easier than the attainment of arms control on earth because space is as yet unmilitarized. Nonetheless, negotiations on space take place within the larger reality that inhibits agreements involving significant inspections of sensitive military installations, especially if it is proposed that such inspections include undeclared facilities or are to be made at random.

United Nations Efforts

Bearing in mind the counterpoint supplied to the theme of international cooperation by the shifting music of the continuing great-power struggle, we can summarize the record of United Nations activity in a way that brings to the fore some provisional answers to the questions raised.

The United Nations was not slow to take up its duties regarding the new dimension of space, although there was little real sense of what those duties in fact were. The thirteenth General Assembly on December 13, 1958, established an eighteen-member *Ad Hoc* Committee on the Peaceful Uses of Outer Space. The composition of the Committee not surprisingly emphasized the relatively developed countries most likely to be involved in space; the Soviet Union, perhaps also not surprisingly, boycotted its activities. Trouble first arose in negotiations over the Committee's creation when the Soviets sought to tie the issue of space to the strategic issue that above all others preoccupied them—the elimination of all foreign (i.e., United States) bases. After dropping this, they brought up the issue of "parity" that was to take form in the various troika proposals; even in 1958 the Soviets had decided that their new preeminence called for greater recognition than was accorded by three Communist-held seats out of eighteen. The issue was not resolved to their satisfaction, and the Committee went ahead without the Soviet Union, Poland, and Czechoslovakia. Presumably as an expression of their nonalignment, India and the United Arab Republic also declined to take part as long as the Soviets maintained their boycott. Dividing itself into two committees of the whole, one legal and one technical, the abbreviated Committee held 25 meetings in all.

The Committee's consideration of the subject was rather cautious and conservative, inhibited both by the absence of several members and, some felt, by a lack of positive direction on the part of the United States. The final report, adopted on June 25, 1959, by the thirteen states that remained, nonetheless represented the first concerted intergovernmental assault at the political level on outer space as an international problem area.[8]

The Committee ruled out at the start any comprehensive legal code that would impose a rigid framework on a subject not yet well understood. Instead, in responding to the Assembly's request to report on "the nature of legal problems which may arise in the carrying out of programmes to explore outer space," the Committee identified the following as questions calling for "priority" treatment: 1) freedom of exploration and use in outer space; 2) liability for injury or damage caused by space vehicles; 3) allocation of radio frequencies; 4) avoidance of interference between space vehicles and aircraft; 5) identification and registration of space vehicles and coordination of launchings; and 6) legal problems involved in the reentry and landing of space vehicles.

The Committee designated as a "nonpriority" question the favorite of international lawyers up to that time—the matter of where outer space begins and sovereign airspace ends. Discerning "no consensus" here, the Committee believed an international agreement would be "premature," but it did suggest that a range might be set with the "boundary" neither so low as to interfere with

---

[8] UN Document A/4141.

existing aviation nor so high as to impede exploration.[9] As other nonpriority questions the Committee listed protection of public health and safety, safeguards against contamination (which has become more recently a genuine priority item for biologists), questions relating to exploration of celestial bodies, and avoidance of interference among space vehicles. Many of these items, in both categories, became the subject of later action.

In responding to the Assembly's other major request, the Committee reported that it saw the need for international agreements on a range of practical functional questions. These included the use of radio frequencies in space, termination of radio transmission at the end of a satellite's useful life, destruction of spent satellites, reentry and recovery of manned vehicles, return of equipment, identification of origin, and the contamination problem.

The Committee was particularly cautious in approaching the question of new institutional machinery or international controls. It posed as the "crucial question . . . how international cooperation in the peaceful uses of outer space should be fostered." It considered the possibility of establishing a special advisory group to the Secretary-General or a special United Nations body charged with keeping under review the cooperative arrangements of international scientific organizations, specialized agencies, and states. It concluded, however, that it was "inappropriate at the present time to establish any autonomous inter-governmental organization" or to "ask any existing autonomous inter-governmental organization to undertake overall responsibility." Its technical committee, however, reported the desirability of a "suitable Centre related to the United Nations that can act as a focal point for international cooperation" and the Committee therefore recommended that the Secretary-General establish a "small expert unit" within the Secretariat for this purpose.[10]

At the fourteenth General Assembly that autumn, the outer space issue was debated, and this time, thanks to successful negotiations between the principal nations, a resolution was unanimously passed, making no reference whatever to the *Ad Hoc* Committee but in effect enlarging it to reflect a modified version of "parity" (twelve Western or pro-Western states, seven Soviet bloc states, and five neutrals) and rechristening it the Committee on the Peaceful Uses of Outer Space.[11]

The fall of 1961 was a highpoint in the UN's effort to meet its responsibilities in the space field. On the basis of proposals outlined by President Kennedy in his speech to the Assembly on September 25, 1961, the Assembly passed a resolution which established basic principles of conduct in space that

[9] The question has been newly raised by a Soviet writer in *Nedelia*, the weekly supplement of *Izvestia*, March 20, 1965.
[10] UN Document A/4141.
[11] General Assembly Resolution 1472 (XIV), December 12, 1959.

stand today as the closest thing to common law on the subject. One preambular paragraph is worth quoting:

> Believing that the exploration and use of outer space should be only for the betterment of mankind and to the benefit of States irrespective of the stage of their economic or scientific development. . . . [12]

The resolution recommended to states for their "guidance" the principles that international law, including the UN Charter, applied to outer space and the celestial bodies and that the latter were free for exploration and use by all in conformity with international law and not subject to national appropriation. The resolution called on the Secretary-General to set up a public registry of launchings; it encouraged the plans of the International Telecommunication Union (ITU) to foster the development of global communication satellite systems, and similarly the efforts of the World Meteorological Organization (WMO) with respect to weather satellite activities; finally, it increased the Committee's membership to 28.

In March of the following year a dialogue began between the leaders of the two space powers that ultimately yielded some modest steps of direct co-operation. In a letter to Premier Khrushchev, President Kennedy suggested a number of joint activities including establishment of an early operational weather satellite system, radio tracking stations on each other's territories, co-operation in mapping the earth's magnetic fields, testing of communications by satellites, and exchange of information on space medicine and on manned and unmanned space explorations. Premier Khrushchev replied favorably on all but the tracking stations proposal.

The same month the newly reconstituted UN Committee met, this time with all in attendance. Over the next month the technical subcommittee and its legal counterpart met in Geneva. In these discussions the Committee recommended: 1) further steps to facilitate exchange of information; 2) support for international programs such as the International Year of the Quiet Sun and the World Magnetic Survey; 3) increased national participation in international programs established by the Committee on Space Research (COSPAR) of the International Council of Scientific Unions (ICSU) for synoptic rocket and polar cap experiments; 4) United Nations Educational, Scientific and Cultural Organization (UNESCO) fellowships to assist scientific and technical training; and 5) the establishment of sounding rocket facilities under UN sponsorship, an interesting action for which India volunteered.

It was in the legal subcommittee that ideology and political conflict caused disagreements, some of which persist to the present time. The major points of disagreement were five: 1) the Soviet desire to prohibit "war propaganda," which quickly brought up two unresolvable issues—the question of what

[12] General Assembly Resolution 1721 (XVI), December 20, 1961.

constitutes "peaceful uses" of space and the question of disarmament itself; 2) the Soviet desire for prior agreement (i.e., a veto) on any measure that might affect another country's use of space (the United States believed that COSPAR's Consultative Committee was an adequate forum for prior discussion and questioned how much prior agreement there should be); 3) the Soviet insistence on "states" as the only agents in space—a crack at the evolving Comsat concept in the United States; 4) the Soviet desire to condemn what it called "intelligence gathering" from space (clearly aimed at United States reconnaissance satellites); and 5) the principles governing the use of space and the form of instruments to be used in setting them forth.

Aside from the substantive issues the Committee was to wrestle with for the next two years, an institutional development of high potential significance emerged in the voting procedures agreed to in the Committee. This provided for preliminary informal consultations among all participants until such time when unanimous agreement on a given issue was reached. Thereafter, the consensus of the Committee was recorded by acclamation and without voting. (The potential utility of such a "sense of the meeting" substitute for formal voting was demonstrated in an ironic fashion several years later when the deadlocked nineteenth Assembly resorted to informal polling followed by "voteless" voting by acclamation in order to accomplish its minimum business in the face of the threat of confrontation over Article 19.)

The counterpoint of superpower relationships accompanied the Committee's work externally as well as dominating it within. Talks between two leading government scientists (the Deputy Administrator of the United States National Aeronautics and Space Administration [NASA], Dr. Hugh Dryden, and Anatoly A. Blagonravov, Chairman of the Space Commission of the Soviet Academy of Sciences) began, talks that have continued since. This period also saw the uncommonly heated United States Senate debate leading to establishment of Comsat. And in July 1962 the age of space communications commenced in fact with the orbiting of the first active repeater satellite—*Telstar I*. Finally, the Cuban missile crisis in the fall of 1962 can be seen as a turning point in Soviet–United States relations, followed as it was by a renewed thaw.

In the period that followed, negotiations intensified on some of the specifics of space law and control. In New York in April and May 1963 the legal subcommittee saw a considerable narrowing of the central differences, accompanied, however, by continued Soviet refusal to record agreement on some items without accord on all. In addition, the United States charged the Soviets with failing to report six space launchings to the UN registry. Conceivably, this was a counter to a Soviet complaint, joined to a considerable extent by many scientific leaders, against unilateral United States orbiting of a band of copper needles (Project Westford) that might interfere with astronomical observation although as it turned out, it did not.

LIMITED PROGRESS TOWARD INTERNATIONAL AGREEMENT, 1963–1964

Despite continued differences it was nonetheless a period of renewed détente, capped by the "hot line" agreement, the agreement not to orbit nuclear weapons, and the signing of the limited test-ban treaty which, *inter alia,* prohibited the testing of nuclear weapons in outer space.

On August 22, 1963, the United States and the Soviet Union reported to the UN a number of agreements on cooperative space ventures.[13] These included a coordinated weather satellite program, joint experiments with communications using a passive reflector satellite *(Echo II),* and joint contributions of satellite data to the World Magnetic Survey to be conducted in 1965. Their memorandum also announced the scheduled establishment by early 1964 of a full-time telecommunications link between Washington and Moscow for transmission of cloud photographs and other data from experimental meteorological satellites operated by each country.

In October and November 1963 an event of great importance for the development of space communications took place. The ITU Extraordinary Administrative Radio Conference, called to make allocations of radio frequencies for space communications, upped the proportion of the table of frequency allocations available for outer space from about one percent (1959) to about 15 percent. This represented a surprisingly large allocation to communication satellites of 2,725 megacycles (2,000 of which were contained in the United States proposal), sufficient through the late 1970's when, it is estimated, two-thirds of the world's communications will be via satellite. The allocation is sufficient to handle 500 television programs or 300,000 telephone calls simultaneously. The Conference cleared the frequencies necessary for meteorological and navigation satellite communications and, of particular interest to radio astronomers listening for signs of intelligence in space, the crucial "hydrogen band" after the Soviets dropped their reservations.

Another milestone in the same period was the General Assembly resolution of October 17, 1963, welcoming expressions by the United States and the Soviet Union of their intention not to station in outer space any objects carrying nuclear weapons or other kinds of weapons of mass destruction, and calling on all states to refrain from stationing such weapons in outer space.[14] Although the unofficial agreement did not provide for inspection, it nevertheless was of high potential significance since technological progress could eventually be expected to permit unilateral rendezvous and "eyeball" investigations for violations.

Shortly thereafter, in November, the UN Committee agreed on a draft "Declaration of Legal Principles Governing the Activities of States in the Ex-

[13] UN Document A/5482.
[14] General Assembly Resolution 1884 (XVIII).

ploration and Use of Outer Space." This incorporated the principles previously approved by the Assembly in December 1961. On the points of previous major disagreement, it asserted that an earlier Assembly resolution condemning propaganda threatening peace was applicable to space; urged states to undertake "appropriate international consultation" when they have reason to believe their activities might cause potentially harmful interference with the activities of other states; agreed that states would bear international responsibility for national activities in space, whether by governmental or nongovernmental agencies; stated that states should regard astronauts as "envoys of mankind in outer space" and should give them all possible assistance; and made no mention of the espionage issue.[15]

A further step in international cooperation in space took place when in January 1964 a group of six scientists visited the Thumba International Equatorial Sounding Rocket Launching Facility, a cooperative enterprise of India, France, and the United States. The group unanimously recommended that the facility be given UN sponsorship.

When the legal subcommittee met in March 1964 to consider proposals and draft agreements on liability for damage caused by space objects and on assistance to and return of astronauts and space vehicles, it was against a background of increasingly practical issues. Differences on all these issues were not resolved, but the outlook was moderately promising for continued negotiation. Both the Soviet and United States drafts on the question of assistance and return, for example, declared that a state should use every means at its disposal to assist astronauts in distress. The Soviets, however, insisted that the launching country had the exclusive right to carry out unassistedly any search on the high seas and wanted to restrict the return of space vehicles to cases where they were launched "for peaceful purposes" and officially announced.

On July 23, 1964, culminating a surprisingly successful conference in Washington called by the United States to bring other nations into the Comsat enterprise, eighteen nations and the Vatican completed agreements on the international ownership and management of the global communications satellite system being developed by the United States. When the sixth session of the UN Committee met in October and the results of the Washington conference were reported, the Soviet Union and its satellites were not unexpectedly critical. They called the agreements inconsistent with the agreed principles that satellite communications should be available to the world on a global and nondiscriminatory basis and that states bear international responsibility for activities in outer space. The Soviet Union said that the agreements bypassed the UN and ITU, that they were drafted with monetary profit as an objective, and that the provision for weighted voting in the agreements was

[15] These principles were embodied in General Assembly Resolutions 1962 and 1963 (XVIII), December 13, 1963.

incompatible with the principle of sovereign equality. In reply, the United States said that the agreements remained open for signature or accession by any state member of ITU, that all states would have access to the system whether or not they became parties to the agreements, and that only governments could sign and accede. Although voting was to be weighted according to the proportionate investment of each signatory, it was provided that in enumerated major decisions significance was also to be given to the number of states assenting.

ROLE OF THE SPECIALIZED AGENCIES

So far we have been discussing the United Nations in its basic political role, to which legal and technical themes are important but clearly subordinate. But for the principal operational activities reflecting international cooperation in space, one must look to other agencies in the UN family. Indeed, the recommendations of the Committee on the Peaceful Uses of Outer Space

> are designed to facilitate and promote international cooperation by supplementing and supporting the activities of existing organizations and by focusing attention on areas where action is necessary.[16]

Two of the specialized agencies, ITU and WMO, have been the most involved in the actual control of space activities.

ITU is responsible for the international coordination and rational use of all forms of telecommunication, by land, submarine cable, and radio; all its constituent bodies have in the normal course of their activities a role to play in the field of space communications. Mention has been made of the 1963 Extraordinary Administrative Radio Conference when radio frequency bands for space radio communication purposes were allocated. The Conference decided that the same distress signals used by ships and aircraft should also be used by spacecraft and set aside the frequency of 20,000 kilocycles for this purpose. One can hope that ITU's performance in the Space Age has conformed to the Conference's criterion

> that the utilization and exploitation of the frequency spectrum for space communication be subject to international agreements based on principles of justice and equity permitting the use and sharing of allocated frequency bands in the mutual interest of all nations.

WMO, in pursuit of its normal tasks regarding the atmospheric sciences, has necessarily become involved in space-related activities and has been mentioned in virtually all the General Assembly's resolutions on space. Its tasks have included the application of meteorology to weather prediction, the development of international atmospheric observation and telecommunication networks, and the promotion of research. It has also aided new or developing

---

[16] UN Document A/AC.105/L.12.

countries in their effort to establish or improve meteorological services, to promote research, and create training institutes.

The fourth World Meteorological Congress, held in Geneva in April 1963, created a high-level WMO advisory committee to consider principal research problems in the atmospheric sciences, ways of promoting meteorology, and methods of ensuring the availability of data. The Congress endorsed the concept of a "World Weather Watch" aimed ultimately at integrating national and international meteorological activities; it initially designated Moscow and Washington as world centers for data processing and envisaged a future third center in the southern hemisphere. In general, WMO has admirably fulfilled its new responsibilities, showing a capacity to adapt and create, as well as successfully involving the most disparate countries in the World Weather Watch.

Other UN agencies are also participating in space-related activities in lesser ways. UNESCO has sponsored scientific meetings relating to space and supported studies of the prospects offered by space communication for increasing the range and scope of mass media and promoting a free flow of information, the spread of education, and a wider cultural exchange. The World Health Organization (WHO) is in the process of defining its tasks in the study of cosmic biology, genetics, and radiation, the physiology and psychology of man in space, and environmental contamination from the transfer of chemical and biological agents to and from the earth. The International Civil Aviation Organization (ICAO) made a recommendation to the ITU Conference on telecommunication support for the operation of spacecraft and the use of earth satellites for communicating with aircraft. And the International Atomic Energy Agency (IAEA) has been concerned with the use of nuclear power for propulsion.

International cooperation is not exclusively an intergovernmental responsibility, and there has been a substantial division of labor between the UN system and other forms of relationships. A nongovernmental organization, the International Council of Scientific Unions, has probably overseen more tangible cooperation than any other single international body. COSPAR, its Committee on Space Research which was established in October 1958 to continue the international cooperation in space research undertaken during the International Geophysical Year, is an interdisciplinary scientific committee with the objective of furthering international scientific investigation using rockets or rocket-propelled vehicles. Much of the impetus to scientific learning through space exploration grew out of the International Geophysical Year, and through COSPAR the IGY pattern of cooperation has been extended. COSPAR has not been immune from Cold War rivalries and incorporates in its procedures what some scientists deplore as a sort of great-power "veto." In the main, however, it has proceeded effectively in bringing together scientists from the countries most concerned with space to work on problems of astrophysics, the atmospheric sciences, the life sciences, and other categories of scientific research.

REGIONAL AND OTHER EFFORTS

The one geographical region of the world that has organized itself for joint participation in space activities has been Western Europe (plus Australia). ELDO, the European Launcher Development Organization, aims at the development and construction of space-vehicle launchers and their equipment. The objective of its initial program, to be completed by 1966, is the design, development, and construction of a space vehicle launcher consisting of three stages carrying a satellite test vehicle. The first stage will be the British *Blue Streak* rocket, the second a French *Coralie,* and the third a West German rocket; the hybrid will be named *Europa I.* The test vehicle will be Italian; the Netherlands will develop the long-range telemetry links, including associated ground equipment; Belgium will develop and construct equipment for the downrange guidance stations; Australia will provide range and support facilities for trial firings of the first stage and the complete launcher; and development firing of the second stage will be at Colomb-Béchar, Algeria.

Alongside ELDO is ESRO, the European Space Research Organization, designed to further the training of European specialists in space technology, promote exchange of scientific and technical information, and provide national research groups with launching facilities. The first two sounding rocket experiments were carried out in July 1964, and two small satellites, *Esro I* and *Esro II,* will be launched by NASA in or about 1967. Also planned are a European Space Technology Center (ESTEC), a computing center at Darmstadt, and an institute in Italy to undertake pioneer research concerning physical and chemical processes in space.

The Inter-American Committee on Space Research, established in November 1960 to promote space research and assist in the creation of national bodies to encourage and coordinate space-related activities in Latin American countries, has not yet actually gone beyond the planning stage.

No account of international cooperation in space would be complete without at least passing reference to what is undoubtedly the most lively area of joint action and active participation on the part of a large number of countries—the United States' bilateral programs. *Ariel,* the first international satellite, was conceived, designed, and instrumented by British scientists and engineered and launched by NASA in April 1962. Other United States–United Kingdom and United States–Canadian joint satellites have been orbited, and future joint launchings are planned with Italy, France, and ESRO.

Reference has been made to the agreements reached by the United States in July 1964 with eighteen other nations for the establishment of interim arrangements for a global communications satellite system. In response to invitations by NASA and the United States Weather Bureau, the weather services of 41 countries have participated in an international program of ground observation synchronized with passes of the *Tiros* satellite. In experiments using sounding rockets for high altitude research, the United States divides responsibility with at least thirteen other nations for rockets, experiments, and ground facilities, and each country finances its own share of the work. Experimenters from 23 countries will observe and measure NASA's ionospheric beacon satellite. It is interesting to note that seven foreign proposals have been chosen in preference to those put forward by the United States for experiments to be performed in the United States' "flying observatory" satellites. Finally, United States-negotiated worldwide facilities for ground tracking, data acquisition, and command services for its manned flight program are furnished and operated by or in cooperation with seventeen other nations.

Summing Up the Record

How then can we sum up this record in terms of our desiderata? Is space cooperation just one more damaging example of the trend, discerned by Erich Fromm, "toward a world of impotent men directed by virile machines"? Or are those involved succeeding, in the words of Dean Rusk, in "occupying the horizons of their responsibilities"?

First, one emerges with a strong sense that, within the formidable constraints imposed by the Cold War, the amount of actual cooperation that has been achieved through a combination of United Nations, specialized agency, nongovernmental, and bilateral relationships has probably been about as great as the traffic will in fact bear.

Second, some rule making has been undertaken, both at the level of general principles and in terms of detailed rules, particularly in the highly practical matters of ownership of satellites, responsibility for damages incurred, and rescue and return of both astronauts and their vehicles. Regulations are most precise and binding with respect to the allocation of radio frequencies. One must continue to remember that the amount of agreed law will necessarily follow consensus on political objectives and suffer in effectiveness from the lack of procedures for punishing violations of international law. But it may not be wholly without meaning that soon after the sortie into space of Soviet cosmonaut Colonel A. Leonov a Soviet commentator wrote that it posed "for the first time" problems of citizenship, legal status, and ownership; he concluded that "it is time to begin to settle these."[17]

Third, maximum use has undoubtedly been made of the existing specialized agencies, particularly recently as they have sought to adjust to new and unforeseen responsibilities. One need only visit the computer room of ITU in

[17] *Nedelia*, March 20, 1965.

Geneva to sense the strides that it and other "old-line" agencies have taken in this regard. Likewise, the UN's administrative structure has been adapted to service the agencies in their space-related activities as well as the General Assembly's Committee on the Peaceful Uses of Outer Space. A small unit, the outer space affairs group, exists in the Secretariat to assist the Committee; in addition, there are an interdepartmental working party on space (which has reportedly not been very effective) and a special interagency working group under the Administrative Committee on Coordination (ACC) for consultation and correlation on space matters between the UN and the specialized agencies; the latter has now gotten off the ground and is reported to be working well.

Although I have in the past urged that the UN establish a separate agency to administer space-related activities, I believe that what is now required is rather a single office within the Secretariat that can functionally combine the several interests involved without the excessively political emphasis of the present unit under the Department of Political and Security Council Affairs. Even under the existing machinery there is ample opportunity for the exercise of imagination and energy in helping to steer the Space Age into further constructive channels of cooperation. One interesting suggestion that was made by two staff members of the Massachusetts Institute of Technology combines scientific, technical, and political desiderata in a recommendation for an international space vehicle launching facility. It would be located in the Australian-administered trust territory of New Guinea (New Ireland is the site recommended) and would provide additional needed launching facilities, proximity to the equator, accessibility to sea transport for heavy booster rockets, and a relatively uniform climate—all in an area politically free of historical great-power vested interests.[18] This proposal deserves further study.

Finally, in the realm of arms control, which could ultimately prove to be the most important aspect of international cooperation in space, some modest steps have been taken through the ban on weapons tests in outer space and the agreement not to orbit nuclear weapons. The latter, particularly, is handicapped by lack of inspection and verification procedures; as has been emphasized throughout, arms control in space suffers from its intimate connection to earthbound arms control. It may, however, offer some special prospects growing out of the relative newness of outer space and the consequent common interest in demilitarizing it, much as Antarctica was demilitarized and in effect internationalized by the 1959 Antarctic Treaty.

It is possible that even without formal international agreements the technology of rendezvous and inspection by satellite will proceed unilaterally to the point where technical means will be at hand *de facto* for a scheme of

[18] Joel B. Searcy and Philip K. Chapman, *A Proposal for a New Space Launching Facility* (Lexington, Mass., April 1964, multilithed).

international verification, unplanned though it may be. The Soviet Union's revelation, after years of denouncing the United States reconnaissance satellite program as "espionage," that it too has a "spy in the sky"[19] conveys important implications for moving toward a more open world which many feel is the precondition to reliable arms control agreements. The further suggestion that this sort of space observation could be legitimatized as a substitute for unilateral aircraft flights through sovereign airspace[20] makes it seem more possible than before to envisage serious negotiations, in the first instance between the space superpowers, about a regime of international cooperation in space dealing with the paramount questions of security and prevention of surprise attack. Such agreements, either concerning space itself or using space as a means of bypassing the inspection deadlock on the ground, could justify everything nations have invested so far in the Space Age.

[19] Interview of former Premier Khrushchev by former United States Senator William H. Benton, reported in *The New York Times*, May 30, 1964.

[20] *Ibid.* According to Drew Middleton, Mr. Khrushchev suggested that space photography had eliminated the necessity for reconnaissance flights over Cuba.

The Secretariat: Retrospect and Prospect

CHARLES WINCHMORE

By the Charter of the United Nations the Secretariat is established as one of the six principal organs of the United Nations. The Secretary-General is designated "the chief administrative officer," not—be it noted—of the Secretariat but of the Organization. The Secretariat comprises the Secretary-General together with the staff appointed by him. The two institutions, the Secretariat and the Secretary-General, may well be regarded as distinct but inseparable—distinct in that the Charter confers in Articles 98 and 99 certain functions and powers specifically on the Secretary-General; inseparable in that the Secretariat is a unitary institution, organized on a functional basis, the members of which are "subject to the authority of the Secretary-General" and "responsible to him in the exercise of their functions."[1]

Perhaps the experience of two decades has served to accentuate rather than to diminish the distinctiveness of the two institutions. In particular, the office of Secretary-General has been shaped by the character of its three successive incumbents, and more especially by the outstanding achievements of the second Secretary-General, Dag Hammarskjöld. His own description of the post as a "one-man 'executive'" (the term employed by him in his address at Chicago in May 1960) marked a climax in the mounting prestige of the office. On many occasions it is the office of Secretary-General, rather than the Secretariat, which has been referred to as the sixth principal organ of the United Nations and with considerable justification since, to use again Dag Hammarskjöld's words, "he is the only elected officer in principle representing all members," and since his authority extends over the Secretariat as a whole. Nevertheless, it is not without significance that the Charter ascribed the quality of "principal organ" to the Secretariat rather than exclusively to its chief administrative officer.

CHARLES WINCHMORE is a former Research Scholar, Royal Institute of International Affairs.

[1] Staff Regulation 1.2.

EVOLVING ROLES OF THE SECRETARIAT AND SECRETARY-GENERAL

The functions of the Secretariat have a less dramatic quality than the role of the Secretary-General and, though this is perhaps debatable, have shown a lesser capacity of dynamic development. Yet undoubtedly the scope of the Secretariat's work has also undergone a remarkable expansion, partly as a reflection of the activities of the Secretary-General but also as a response to the need of the nations of the world to pursue through international institutions certain common social and economic, and even political, objectives. It is timely to reflect on this experience and to seek to ascertain to what extent the achievements of the two decades are merely eccentricities of history, destined to leave no permanent mark on the world's political development, or to what extent they have laid a basis which affords further opportunities of constructive growth.

It may be regarded as to some extent inherent in the circumstances of the Organization in the first decades of its development that the distance between the two institutions, the Secretariat and the Secretary-General, has tended to increase with the passage of the years. It necessarily fell to Trygve Lie to grapple with the initial administrative problems of the Secretariat—the financial structure, terms of employment, and similar questions. In large measure these initial administrative problems had been successfully dealt with by the end of the first Secretary-General's tenure of office. On assuming his position as Secretary-General, Mr. Hammarskjöld envisaged perhaps that his contribution would be primarily administrative, more especially in the social and economic field, and he undertook at the outset an overhaul of the structure of the Secretariat. Nevertheless, the main problems of personnel and finance had been largely settled by 1953. The post of Assistant Secretary-General for Administration and Finance was allowed to lapse with the retirement of Byron Price, partly on the grounds that only a residuum of administrative problems remained to be dealt with, problems which should not demand more than about an hour a day on the part of the Secretary-General and which involved decisions which he should be and would be in a position to take himself. But in the second decade of the life of the United Nations, the office of Secretary-General became with remarkable rapidity the focal point of international activities of a relatively novel character. The crisis of October 1956 gave rise to the circumstances in which political forces needed the Secretary-General as their catalytic agent, and the experience he then gained proved applicable also in later crises. The new political duties of the office necessarily had a primary claim on the attention of the Secretary-General, and to some extent his increasingly close relations with governments and delegations were achieved at the price of greater remoteness from the generality of the Secretariat. He himself realized that this was so, and it is significant that his last speech, on September 8, 1961, was a speech to his own staff. Undoubtedly, if the Secretariat is to maintain a lively sense of unity, it is essential for any Secretary-General to ensure that his office functions as a center from which the sense of purpose and dedication permeates the entire staff.

This consideration is the more important in that the fissiparous tendencies in an international secretariat are undoubtedly more marked than in any national civil service. Within a national civil service, men and women are brought together as public officials who have been reared in a common cultural background and who, by reason of their experience, pay homage to institutions which symbolize the unity of their political community. An international civil service has no such "natural" basis on which to operate. It is essentially an institution derived from an exclusively rational recognition of the need for its existence. Within it men and women work together who, brought from the four quarters of the globe, are of the most diverse cultures and are bound together by little but their common humanity and their commitment to the ideals of the institution which they serve. For these reasons the administrative structure of an international secretariat is necessarily somewhat fragile. In many respects the relationships within an international secretariat are diplomatic rather than administrative—diplomatic in that cooperation depends rather on persistent recourse to the arts of persuasion than on continuous exercise of the power of command. This generalization holds perhaps with regard to any administrative structure, but most of all with respect to an international secretariat.

Moreover, many of the members of the international secretariat who joined in the early years became civil servants at a time when they had already mapped out for themselves a quite different professional career. The international civil service is still too recent an innovation for many men and women to have engaged in it as the vocation of a lifetime and so to have become wholly molded to its quite special exigencies. Those who join it become for the most part exiles, living in circumstances alien to them. Hence the disintegrative tendencies in an international secretariat are strong. Conscious effort is required to develop the corporate spirit capable of absorbing into itself the energies of the individual members of the Secretariat and of imparting to them a sense of "belonging" in order to compensate in some measure for their alienation from their own natural background. This infusion of a common sense of purpose requires a conscious and tireless effort, and in the development of this common purpose the leadership of the Secretary-General is vital. In the absence of such leadership each department, even each division or section, may tend to become a segregated area in itself, taking its character to only too great an extent from the qualities of its head. So too the secretariat of each agency remains largely particularized, its character deriving in part from its special sphere of work but reflecting also the qualities of its first principal administrator. The unification of the international secretariats—and even coordination between agencies within a common system—remains largely a task of the future. The obstacles which lie in the path of any such achievement are formidable. Perhaps what is remarkable about international secretariats is not that at times they may display some inefficiency in the utilization of their resources of manpower; what is remarkable is that this artificial structure works at all. It is indeed a testimony to the adaptability of the human mind.

CONCEPTIONS OF AN INTERNATIONAL SECRETARIAT

For these reasons it would seem crucial that the Charter itself stipulated that the necessity of securing the highest standards of efficiency, competence, and integrity was to be the paramount consideration in the employment of the staff and in the determination of the conditions of service; and that the Charter designated the responsibilities of the Secretary-General and his staff to be of an "exclusively international character," which the Members of the United Nations are committed to respect. The Staff Regulations approved by the Assembly and the Staff Rules promulgated by the Secretary-General represent the effort over two decades to translate into detailed terms these general stipulations of the Charter. They are not and cannot be rules of a trade union nature devised to protect the vested interests of the employees of the United Nations; they constitute rather a deliberate judgment, developed over two decades of experience, as to the essential conditions required for the maintenance of a secretariat characterized by "efficiency, competence, and integrity." Protection of the interests of the members of the Secretariat finds a place in those rules insofar as such protection is essential to ensure that those members may devote themselves wholeheartedly and exclusively to the service of the Organization. At a time when the very character of the international secretariat is under attack by those who would in effect replace it by seconded governmental officials, the anchorage of the existing system in the stipulations of the Charter itself should be kept prominently in mind.

The Preparatory Commission of the United Nations reported that it was essential that the bulk of the staff should consist of persons who would make their career in the Secretariat since insofar as members of the staff remained dependent on national administrations for their future, they could not be expected to subordinate the national interests of their countries to the international interest. The principle of a career staff is therefore embedded in the detailed stipulations of the Staff Regulations and Rules: the conditions of appointment providing for probationary appointments leading to "indefinite appointment," the arrangements for affording reasonable prospects of promotion within the service, and the safeguards against wrongful termination. Emphasis on the career character of the staff necessarily leads to a certain rigidity in its composition, inseparable from the expectation that the normal staff member will devote some 35 years to the service. The necessity to adapt the composition of the staff to the expanding membership of the United Nations has led since 1960 on the one hand to greater emphasis on nationality in matters of recruitment and on the other hand to the more extensive use of the fixed-term contract as a means of ensuring greater flexibility in composition. The problem of recent years has been whether efficiency, in the sense of the recruitment of the best man for the post, can be reconciled with the requirement of recruitment with a view to the improvement of geographic distribution and whether greater recourse to the fixed-term contract might detract from the career character of the staff and tend to erode the sense of exclusive devotion to the interests of the Organization. The General Assembly has asserted that no incompatibility arises between the obligations of efficiency, competence, and integrity on the one hand and the requirements of geographic distribution on the other. Undoubtedly, in the long run, these dual objectives can be served and an efficient secretariat of appropriate national composition achieved.

At the same time the temptation must be withstood to regard the international character of the Secretariat as synonymous with its multinational character. The wide distribution of nationalities within the Secretariat may contribute to its international character, but it is not and cannot be the decisive factor. The Secretariat must remain international in the sense in which science is international—not by reason of the diffusion of scientists among the many nationalities of the world but by reason of their commitment to purposes of universal validity.

In fact, the concept of the international civil servant would seem not only to have withstood with considerable success the strains placed upon it during the two decades which have elapsed but also to have been given sharper definition and embodied in more precise institutional form as the years have passed. The tensions which resulted from the engagement of a high proportion of the UN staff on temporary indefinite contracts in the first years were surmounted in 1952 when, as a result of the survey of the staff by the Walters Selection Committee for the Review of Staff Members on Temporary Appointments, the proportion of staff on permanent contract was raised to 70 percent. Though concessions were made to the United States government in 1953 in relation to Secretariat members of United States nationality, concessions such as the introduction of a procedure for clearance of United States nationals on recruitment, the permission of United States governmental agencies to conduct their inquiries within the premises of the UN itself, and the dismissal of staff members who refused to testify before a United States Federal Grand Jury, the more extreme pressures of the United States government were in the end successfully resisted. Staff members were enabled to test the legality of their dismissal before the Administrative Tribunal, and the independence of the Tribunal in the award of damages was vindicated by the International Court of Justice. So too the pressures arising from the increase of membership since 1960 and from advocacy of a changed basis for the Secretariat have not been permitted to subvert the fundamental character of the Secretariat. The adjustment of the composition of the Secretariat in response to the demands for more equitable geographic distribution has proceeded gradually as vacancies have arisen to permit the new recruitment to take place. It is true that greater use has come to be made of the fixed-term contract, notably as a basis for the engagement of officials seconded from government service or as a means of recruiting for a defined period persons with qualifications and experience not to be found within the staff itself. Yet while the recruitment of outsiders on fixed-term contract at the higher levels may have lessened somewhat the prospects of promotion of the career staff, the principle of promotion, as distinct from recruitment, has not been allowed to be affected by considerations of geographic distribution, and the prospects of promotion appear in fact to have remained reasonably good. The International Civil Service Advisory Board (ICSAB) has established a standard definition of the obligations of the international civil servant; and the Board itself has recently been reorganized and strengthened in order that it may make further contributions to the reinforcement of the concept of the service.

If the international civil service has thus resisted the strains placed upon it, some credit for this performance may be attributed to the efforts of the staff itself and to the means which have been established to enable the staff to make its own constructive contribution to the shaping of the service. The Staff Council of the UN Staff Association, which was established through the spontaneous action of the staff in the first instance, was duly recognized by the General Assembly in 1952 as the means of ensuring continuous contact between the staff and the Secretary-General. The Council is entitled to be consulted on questions relating to staff welfare, including policy on such matters as appointments and promotions, and to make proposals to the Secretary-General on such questions. The position taken by the UN Staff Council was undoubtedly a factor in checking the degree to which the pressures exercised by the United States government upon the UN Secretariat in 1950–1953 were permitted to give rise to deviations from established Secretariat practices. The staff associations of the various international organizations are linked together in the Federation of International Civil Servants, which brings together the principal staff representatives for consultation on common problems. While consultation between the Secretary-General and the Staff Council is confined to general problems of policy, considerable progress has also been made in the second decade in associating staff representatives in the work of both administrative and semijudicial bodies within the Secretariat. These provisions with regard to staff participation in problems of administration have served to ensure greater harmony between the Secretary-General and his staff in the second decade of the Secretariat's history than in the first decade, though opinions may vary as to whether the staff has seized the opportunity to make as continuous and constructive a contribution to the shaping of an international secretariat as these provisions make possible.

It has seemed desirable to draw attention, no matter how summarily, to the progress made in the past two decades in the formulation of rules and the establishment of institutions to govern the effective functioning of the international civil service. For the significance of advances in the realm of international administration can only too readily be minimized or even overlooked. The contentious political problems which come before international institutions, whether problems of long standing, such as disarmament or the control of nuclear weapons, or evanescent problems such as the Congo (Leopoldville), tend to overshadow in public attention the far less dramatic developments in international administration. Yet, in the long run, the world's success in dealing with its major political problems is likely to depend on the establishment and maintenance of sound and effective practices of an administrative character on an international scale. Political agreements may come to be concluded to deal with problems of armaments and nuclear weapons and other matters which need to be regulated on a global scale; but the smooth implementation of such agreements must depend in no small measure on the establishment of conditions which enable international officials to work smoothly, effectively, and loyally together.

Compared with national institutions, international institutions still remain fragile and inchoate. The arena of world politics is for the most part concerned with the clash of national purposes. Yet the concept of an international civil service has proved to be a concept of increasingly expanded application in the past twenty years. Indeed, it may be held that, in the transference of the concept from the framework of the League of Nations to that of the United Nations, the concept imperceptibly underwent a revolutionary transformation. For the League was, by the terms of the Covenant, essentially an instrument in the hands of its members. The United Nations is, by the terms of the Charter, committed to the pursuit of certain "Purposes and Principles." These principles are not static; they have been developed in Assembly declarations. Whereas the essential quality of the League Secretariat might well be regarded as neutrality between the policies of its members, the international character of the United Nations Secretariat must depend in large measure on its positive commitment to the Purposes and Principles which govern the Organization itself.

Such considerations warrant the conclusion that the concept of the international civil service has been given more precise expression in the last two decades. The justification of the international secretariat must depend in the long run on its ability to serve purposes which can be discharged neither by any national civil service nor by a service composed of civil servants seconded from their national governments. The international civil servant is called upon to display qualities of mind and character, and indeed of intellect, which are inseparable from his calling and which are likely to be developed only as a result of long acclimatization to the service of an international organization. The national civil servant is likely to be conscious of a defined framework of policy within which he works and to be committed to pursue that policy with a certain rigor and insistence. The intellectual qualities and outlook which he is expected to display are likely to be those developed within the university in his own country at which he has been trained. The international civil servant on the other hand is likely to find that even his professional training needs to be readapted to the special requirements of the international organization in whose employ he finds himself. Rarely will he find himself working within a clearly defined framework of policy, and his concern must be to serve the interests of the Organization while avoiding offense to the susceptibilities of Member States. While caution and discretion necessarily mark his approach to any problem, he must be ever alert to detect these opportunities for advancing the common aims which arise, often in seemingly adverse circumstances, and he must display resourcefulness in working toward the achievement of desired objectives.

The Expanding Role of the Secretariat

In appraising the role of the international secretariat, the generalization might be advanced that the effective contribution of the Secretariat to the work of the United Nations in any sphere of activity will vary directly with the degree to which a common purpose can be developed between the Member States. It is indeed a function of the Secretariat to translate into precise form the often inchoate elements of cooperation which can be discerned between the Members of the Organization. Secondly, the greater the degree to which agreement exists as to appropriate technical means for pursuing the common purpose, the greater will be the degree to which work is delegated to the Secretariat. Because these two conditions are to some degree fulfilled in the sphere of social and economic activity, the role of the Secretariat in social and economic matters is greater and more firmly based than in the political sphere. But perhaps the most novel extension of the concept of the international secretariat in the past decade has been the involvement of the military profession in peacekeeping activities under the direction of the Secretary-General.

These three aspects—social and economic, military, and political—may be briefly reviewed to illustrate the expanding application of the concept of the international civil service.

The Social and Economic Sphere

In a statement to the Economic and Social Council (ECOSOC) meeting at ministerial level on July 11, 1960, Secretary-General Hammarskjöld made the following brief summation of the development of the United Nations: "Born as an instrument for mutilateral diplomacy, the United Nations has grown into an operational agency of significant dimensions." This growth took place in the first instance with regard to the work of the Organization in social and economic matters and in technical assistance, for in these areas of activity the preconditions for the expansion of Secretariat activities, viz., community of purpose among governments and widespread agreement on techniques, were found to exist.

The common objective has been provided by the general acceptance of responsibility for the economic development of underdeveloped countries. Throughout the two decades, the economic activities of the United Nations and of the specialized agencies have tended to focus increasingly on this aspect, and the United Nations and its agencies have provided a ready instrument in the service of this end. They have constituted the only universal agency in which countries with widely differing political institutions and at different stages of economic development could discuss and initiate collective action. Such collective action has been made possible through the broadness of the provisions of the Charter on the subject of the promotion of economic and social cooperation.

The predominant form of action has been aid which, in social and economic development and in public administration, has taken the form of the provision of experts, the granting of fellowships, and the organization of study groups and training centers. Activities of this nature have come to be regarded as appropriately conducted within the framework of the international civil service. Aid, commenced modestly in 1947 in a sporadic manner for a short time, was administered at the outset within the previously existing United Nations framework of staff and budget. Under the impetus of President Harry S. Truman's Point Four speech in 1949, aid activities came to be placed on a systematic basis. The first major program of an operational nature to be undertaken on a long-term basis by the United Nations and its related agencies was inaugurated in 1950 as the Expanded Program of Technical Assistance (EPTA). Eight years later the operational programs of the United Nations were extended by the establishment of the Special Fund designed to provide support for preinvestment projects.

The enlarged role of the United Nations and its agencies in matters of economic development has brought about the establishment of new institutions to deal with problems of coordination and the reorientation of existing institutions toward the goal of integrated development. The Technical Assistance

Board (TAB) was established as the coordinating agency for the activities of the United Nations and its agencies, and within each agency and the UN Secretariat itself an expansion and reorganization of activities have taken place. The Bureau of Technical Assistance Operations (TAO) has been established as the operative branch of the Secretariat in matters of technical assistance, while the Special Fund program has necessitated the establishment of the Office of Special Fund Operations to which is assigned responsibility for the implementation of those Special Fund projects for which the United Nations is designated as the executive agent.

The focusing of economic and social work on the goal of integrated development has resulted in a significant change in the nature of the work of the Secretariat. The emphasis has come to be placed less on activities dealing uniquely with fact-finding, codification, and other forms of research, and rather more on operational programs which serve directly the purpose of integrated development. This shift of emphasis has necessarily resulted in organizational changes. A Center for Industrial Development and a Division of Resources and Transport have been established to deal to an increasing extent with matters of an operational character; similarly, programs of a social nature, as in human rights, have been reoriented toward programs of an operational nature, including advisory services; and international action in the field of housing has been developed. Various branches of the Secretariat (the relevant substantive departments, the Office of Personnel, and the Office of General Services) are called upon to provide services in support of technical assistance and Special Fund operations.

This development has been facilitated insofar as issues that were initially regarded as primarily political have been transformed into activities of a predominantly technical character, accepted by governments as appropriate functions for international civil servants. Officials of the Secretariat have been called upon more and more to assist in the formulation of programs, the determination of priorities, and the most effective types of aid to be given. Activities of this character are a far cry from research and servicing activities in the narrow sense. It remains true, nevertheless, that the influence of the Secretariat in these matters has been mainly indirect, taking the form of recommendations to governments. At the same time it is significant that heads of agencies themselves have, in their addresses to organs of the United Nations, taken a lead in recommending policies or warning against certain courses of action.

In matters of technical assistance the Secretariat has exercised its influence in the form of recommendations to governments. But the record of twenty years would be incomplete without at least passing reference to those instances in which international civil servants have assumed more direct responsibility for governmental processes. That responsibility was most complete in the case of the United Nations Temporary Executive Authority (UNTEA) for

West Irian, which was provisionally placed under the authority of an Administrator appointed by and responsible to Secretary-General U Thant for the
purpose of effecting the transfer of the area from Netherlands to Indonesian
sovereignty. Such a venture in international administration in the fullest sense
of the term may well prove to be unique—the product of special political
circumstances in which the transient control of the territory by the United
Nations averted the menace of conflict between the two states directly involved. As in all such situations of crisis, expedition in the recruitment of the
necessary corps of administrators was essential to the success of the operation;
and such expedition was in large measure made possible by the experience
gained earlier in the recruitment of experts for purposes of technical assistance.
A venture of hardly less political significance but more directly the outcome
of previous United Nations efforts in the area of technical assistance was the
civilian operations of the United Nations Operation in the Congo (ONUC)
within which the United Nations and the specialized agencies joined in a
unified administrative structure for the purpose of maintaining in working
order the social, economic, and administrative structure of the new state.

The Military Sphere

It is hardly to be expected that this expansion in the realm of the economist
could be or would be matched in the sphere of activity normally falling within the purview of the military profession. The precaution with which the
drafters of the Charter approached the problem of the involvement of the
military profession in the activities of international political organization is
exemplified by the text of the Charter itself. It was realized that the collaboration of the military profession in the working of the Organization might well
be a condition of its success. This line of reasoning was one factor in the inclusion in the Charter itself of provisions relating to the Military Staff Committee. Yet the Military Staff Committee has remained a somewhat anomalous
body among United Nations organs. The Charter specified in Article 47 that
it should be composed "of the Chiefs of Staff" of the permanent members
of the Security Council or their representatives. Its peculiar status is reflected
in the organization of its secretariat which functions under the direction of
the Principal Secretary of the Committee, a post which is held in successive
months in rotation by a member of the constituent delegations. It is significant also that no solution was arrived at in the Charter as to the command
of armed forces to be placed at the disposal of the Security Council; the provision was simply included that this question was to be worked out subsequently. Since the agreements called for by Article 43 have not been concluded, the question of command has necessarily remained in abeyance.

The failure to implement Chapter VII of the Charter has made it necessary
for the United Nations to supplement its resources for the maintenance of

peace by the establishment, on the one hand, of the United Nations Field Service on a permanent basis and, on the other hand, of special peacekeeping forces such as the UN Emergency Force (UNEF) and ONUC on an *ad hoc* basis. The former, established in 1956 by Secretary-General Hammarskjöld, was integrated within the framework of the Secretariat itself, while the relation of the ONUC forces to the Secretariat is somewhat more problematic.

The United Nations Field Service was the outgrowth of the request by the UN Mediator for Palestine to send 50 armed guards to assist the military observers in the supervision of the truce in Palestine. In responding to this request, the Secretary-General justified his action by reference to Article 97 of the Charter. The Special Committee on a United Nations Guard, set up by the General Assembly in 1949 to examine the Secretary-General's proposal for a United Nations Guard, reported that his revised proposal for a Field Service "was not an international military force" but "would in fact amount to a systematization of the regular functions of the Secretariat." The Field Service has since played a supremely important role in the provision of technical services for United Nations missions. The Special Committee concluded that Article 97 of the Charter provided the Secretary-General with full authority for the establishment of such a unit.

The relation of United Nations peacekeeping forces to the institution of the Secretariat cannot be stated in any such clear-cut manner as in the case of the Field Service. Yet there is good reason to consider to what degree these forces constitute an outgrowth of the Secretariat. Only the barest outline of the relationship can be indicated here since proper consideration of the status and character of each force would call for detailed scrutiny of the terms of the relevant resolutions of the Security Council or General Assembly. A few general observations must suffice at this point.

The organization of these forces has in each instance been entrusted to the Secretary-General. The commander has operated under the guidance and instructions of the Secretary-General. While in the case of UNEF the commander functioned as the principal agent of the Secretary-General in the area of operations, in the case of ONUC the leadership of the force was separate from the role of the principal representative of the United Nations appointed by the Secretary-General. The regulations for the forces which defined their international character have been derived, *mutatis mutandis,* from the Staff Regulations which govern the Secretariat—the obligation imposed on members to discharge their functions and to regulate their conduct with the interest of the United Nations only in view; to receive instructions only from the UN commander and the chain of command designated by him; and to exercise the utmost discretion in all matters relating to their duties and functions. Directives to the United Nations forces have been derived from the "Principles and Purposes" of the United Nations and from the texts of the relevant resolutions of the principal organs. In such respects the position of the United Nations forces may be considered as at least analogous to that of the Secretariat. Soldiers from the armed forces of Member States, serving under the UN flag, though still subject to national discipline, have thus gained experience in applying "the arts of war to the infinitely subtle and difficult problem of maintaining the peace."[2]

The Political Sphere

In dealing with the functions of the Secretariat in the political sphere, attention has been concentrated mainly on the role of the Secretary-General. It is not the intention to repeat here what has already been said in numerous articles and books. Indeed, Dag Hammarskjöld himself expounded his own conception of the functions of the United Nations and of the role of the Secretary-General with such fullness and clarity that a commentator can do little but quote extensively from the numerous reports and addresses produced in the few years of his tenure of the office. Attention will be paid rather to the broad context within which the political work of the Secretariat is conducted.

It is particularly in the realm of political activity that the distinction between the Secretary-General and the Secretariat, alluded to at the outset, has become most marked. It is a matter of common knowledge that in national governments the office of the prime minister, under the direction of the prime minister himself, not infrequently assumes the predominant role in the formulation and conduct of foreign policy, especially in circumstances of national crisis, with the consequence of relegating the foreign office to a quite secondary role. In an international secretariat, within which it is far more difficult to maintain coherence of views than in a national government, the tendency of the Secretary-General to retain the direction of political matters in his own hands and to discharge his obligations through collaborators well-known to him and especially chosen by him is necessarily even more marked. In large measure it is a condition of his personal ability to retain the confidence of governments in his conduct of policy. One consequence has been that the Secretary-General has discharged the political duties entrusted to him to a far less degree through the ordinary machinery of the Secretariat in political matters than in other matters. Indeed, in the Committee of Experts on the Review of the Activities and Organization of the Secretariat, which had been appointed in 1960, the representative of the Soviet Union insistently asserted that the Department of Political and Security Council Affairs, which has normally had a Soviet citizen at its head, had not been permitted to play the part assigned to it in the organization of the Secretariat.

[2] Brian E. Urquhart, "United Nations Peace Forces and the Changing United Nations" in Lincoln P. Bloomfield and others, *International Military Forces: The Question of Peacekeeping in an Armed and Disarming World* (Boston: Little, Brown and Company, 1964), p. 137.

Attention may be drawn to another factor which has vitally affected the role of the Secretariat in political matters—the establishment of the permanent delegations of the Member States in New York. The permanent delegations constitute in effect an institution of the United Nations which was not provided for by the Charter but which has grown up as a byproduct of the General Assembly and of the continuity of conference arrangements at Headquarters. When the Security Council was first organized, it was apparent that members of the Security Council would need to maintain at Headquarters permanent representatives, and indeed alternates, in order that the Council might be able to fulfill the requirement of the Charter that it be so organized as to be able to function continuously. No constitutional arrangement made it essential for the generality of Members of the United Nations to maintain permanent delegations at Headquarters. It may be recalled that, during the period of the League, the Secretariat had rather discouraged the establishment of permanent delegations in Geneva, since it was desired to maintain direct relations between the Secretariat and governments. Moreover, since the Council of the League met intermittently in Geneva, it fell to the Secretariat to undertake the preparatory work necessary for meetings of the Council. Much political work which would otherwise need to be undertaken by the UN Secretariat is now carried on by direct consultations between the delegations themselves. To a large extent the effectiveness of the United Nations must depend indeed on the reports sent by permanent representatives to their governments and on the influence which these reports may have in shaping the policies of these governments. Though the permanent delegations are collectively of the greatest importance in the functioning of the United Nations, they have, unlike the Secretariat, no corporate organization of their own. It has become an essential function of the Secretary-General himself to act as a channel for communication and for consultation between delegations. As Andrew Cordier, the Executive Assistant to the first two Secretaries-General, has pointed out, the Secretary-General is in a position, through the instrumentality of the permanent representatives, to discuss alternative approaches to problems before the United Nations and to ensure that his own views are placed before governments. There has thus devolved on the Secretary-General a considerable share of responsibility in the formulation of any consensus of views among delegations on specific issues under consideration.[3] The Secretary-General has thus become in a very real sense the "chief administrative officer of the Organization."

The special relationship of the Secretary-General to the delegations is perhaps most clearly evidenced by the establishment of the Advisory Committee on UNEF and the later Advisory Committee on the Congo. They constitute

[3] See Andrew Cordier, "The Role of the Secretary-General" in Richard N. Swift (ed.), *Annual Review of United Nations Affairs, 1960–1961* (Dobbs Ferry, N.Y: Oceana Publications, 1962), pp. 1–14.

the most defined institutional response to a problem of which the late Secretary-General was acutely conscious—the need to "find constitutional means and techniques to assist him in so far as possible in reducing the elements of purely personal judgment." The Secretary-General strove to ensure that his personal judgment should to the utmost degree be of a constitutional character; and, as many writers have pointed out, to this end he excelled in deriving lines of political action from the Principles and Purposes of the Charter. Even so, he urgently needed a means of testing his own conclusions as the responsible executive against the advice and judgment of those who were in a position to build up and maintain a consensus of support for his activities within the political organs of the United Nations. For this purpose he needed an institutionalized mode of consultation, which he found in the Advisory Committees. They were in a sense anomalous bodies: composed of the representatives of delegations, external to the Secretariat, yet sitting under the chairmanship of the Secretary-General who sought to formulate the conclusions to be derived from the discussion.

The establishment of permanent delegations has exercised considerable influence on the role of the highest officials of the Secretariat. In 1946 it was envisaged that the Assistant Secretaries-General would have, as one of their functions, the maintenance of liaison with governments of the areas from which they originated. This function, though still of some importance, has declined in significance. Changes have in consequence been effected, though these changes have also been motivated by reasons arising from the administration of the Secretariat itself. The designation of Assistant Secretary-General for the heads of Departments was dropped at the outset of Dag Hammarskjöld's term of office and was replaced by that of Undersecretary to emphasize the essentially administrative responsibilities of these officials. The Departments were reduced to three in number—Political and Security Council Affairs, Trusteeship, and Social and Economic Affairs; other major units came to be designated as "Offices." The question of the political significance of the senior posts has, however, remained a recurring theme throughout the discussion of the higher organization of the Secretariat. The Secretary-General pointed out in his 1953 report on the structure of the Secretariat that it was the original intention that the Assistant Secretaries-General should constitute a group of officials

> broadly representative of the Member nations, on the highest responsible level, who, in addition to being heads of departments, would serve the Secretary-General in a representative capacity with individual Member countries and groups of countries.[4]

The reorganization of 1954 might be regarded as having brought this position

[4] UN Document A/2554.

to an end; but from time to time the question of the specifically political responsibilities of the Secretary-General's senior advisers has recurred. It assumed special prominence at the time of the election of the present Secretary-General who, on assuming office, undertook to consult with certain principal advisers "individually, collectively, or otherwise" as the occasion should demand.

One enduring modification introduced by Dag Hammarskjöld has proved to be the creation of the posts of Undersecretary for Special Political Affairs. The broader suggestion made by him in June 1961, in response to the recommendations of the Committee of Experts, for the appointment of five Assistant Secretaries-General to advise the Secretary-General on political problems was not in the end implemented, though the post of Undersecretary-General for General Assembly Affairs was established as an outcome of those suggestions.

The question as to what extent the Secretary-General can develop within the normal structure of the Secretariat the facilities for policy advice in the discharge of his political responsibilities will doubtless continue to be explored. Experienced political advisers within the Secretariat should be in a position to remain broadly familiar with the policies of Member States. They should be in a position to convey to the Secretary-General a knowledge of the political preoccupations, which are not infrequently of a domestic character, emotionally charged attitudes, and the calculated political interests which sway governments in the conduct of their policies. Because of their habituation to the work of an international organization, they are more likely to be in a position to advise the Secretary-General in these respects with clarity and in a disciplined manner than are the members of permanent delegations. Their advice should be the more usable by the Secretary-General in being free from the elements of pressure and urgency which necessarily attend the presentation of representatives of governments. These means of advice should be developed to the utmost. But there are inbuilt limitations to the advice received by the Secretary-General from within his own staff. As international civil servants, they cannot be in constant communication with governments, as are permanent representatives. They are unacquainted with the more confidential considerations which enter into the formulation of government policy. They may be precluded from assessing the varying degrees of urgency in the different elements of government policy. They will remain largely unaware of those points on which governmental policy is adamant and of those areas where some elements of flexibility remain. In short, their quality as international civil servants is achieved at the cost of ceasing to act as the tentacles of Member governments, and it is precisely with these tentacles that the Secretary-General must remain in touch. The conclusion would seem to follow that one important line of advance within the United Nations will continue to be the institutionalization of the channels of communication between the Secretary-General and the permanent delegations. What may be contemplated, if the United Nations is to consolidate its strength as an organization, is that the permanent delegations will be increasingly integrated within the framework of the United Nations.

To stress this point should not be regarded as detracting from the significance of the work of the career service in political matters but rather to delineate its area of expertise as distinct from that of members of the permanent delegations. It is not necessary to stress the indispensable character of what may be termed the administrative services rendered by the Secretariat, the services essential to the conduct of meetings in a manner acceptable to all delegations involved. Such services may range over matters such as the rendering of advice on procedural problems, the drafting of committee reports, or the preparation of United Nations documentation of an official and public character. The impartial character of such work is ensured only by the disciplined training of officers committed exclusively to the service of the Organization. Nor is it necessary to stress the need for the continuous preparation within the Secretariat itself of advisory political documentation bearing on problems before the United Nations or on political activities in which the United Nations is involved. Within the Secretariat no less than in a foreign office, the assignment of officers to such work is a precondition of the formulation of any coherent line of political action. Little doubt can be entertained that, as the political responsibilities of the United Nations expand, the arrangements for "policy planning" will need to be strengthened and consolidated. In situations in which the utilization of emergency peacekeeping forces is called for, the problem of their political direction and control emerges as one of the key problems in their successful functioning.

Such developments mainly concern the Headquarters staff. But perhaps even greater emphasis should be laid on the vital contribution made by the career officers sent out from Headquarters to undertake political responsibilities "in the field," whether in connection with committees of investigation or mediation or with representative duties on behalf of the Secretary-General, as in the Congo (Leopoldville). The success of United Nations activities in such circumstances depends in rather greater measure on the skill and wisdom of the Secretariat members assigned to such tasks than it does in the case of functions exercised at Headquarters. Especially with regard to the Congo it would be difficult to overestimate the contribution made by career staff members of all ranks sent out to perform functions of a relatively unprecedented character. Such situations can be seen to have called for a combination of resourcefulness and self-restraint linked with a deep knowledge of and dedication to the special purposes of the Organization, qualities which are most likely to be displayed by those who have committed themselves fully to the international service. The view may perhaps be advanced that the progress of the international secretariat can be measured by the degree to which the higher—and even the highest posts—in a representative capacity under the Secretary-General come to be filled from within the service rather than by the *ad hoc* appointment of eminent persons from outside the Secretariat. The possibility of rising to posts involving the discharge of public international responsibilities of the highest order is likely to be an essential condition of the recruitment and retention within the career service of men and women of outstanding ability.

Conclusion

The preceding observations constitute no more than a sketch of the development of the Secretariat in the past twenty years. It should however suffice to indicate that the conception of an international secretariat has developed far since the initial decision of Sir Eric Drummond that the League Secretariat should consist of civil servants whose obligations were exclusively obligations toward the League itself. The innovation introduced in 1920 has proved to be a device of far-reaching implications. The concern to create a body whose characteristic would be impartiality as between the conflicting purposes of states has given rise to an international group whose thought and objectives must go well beyond the limited notion of impartiality. They must endeavor to translate into practical terms the broad objectives whose realization is to be sought if the world is to live together in peace and cooperation. As the range of human problems in the social, economic, and political area increases, as it becomes increasingly urgent that these problems be pursued effectively on a global scale and in the interests of the human race, so the significance of an international secretariat must grow correspondingly.

III. The United Nations and Its Members

The United States and the United Nations

H. FIELD HAVILAND, JR.

THE United States was the principal architect and builder of the United Nations, and the great mass of the American people welcomed the new edifice with enthusiasm and high—perhaps too high—hopes for a new world. Now, two decades and many crises later, United States opinion is wiser and more ambivalent. A large majority of the public still gives general support to the United Nations, but its enthusiasm is tempered by experience, and a vociferous minority holds views ranging from biting criticism to total rejection.

The majority, and governmental, view is expressed by President Lyndon B. Johnson when he says, "We support the United Nations as the best instrument yet devised to promote the peace of the world and to promote the well-being of mankind."[1] But millions in the minority are closer to the critical attitude voiced by former Senator Barry Goldwater:

> The United Nations . . . is, at best, a secondary instrument of international accord. It is useful to the West now for a special reason: it provides a forum in which to discuss Communist violations of the Charter. If we will not so use it, its usefulness should be questioned in our Congress, where the most responsible decision regarding our membership can be made.[2]

Despite the gap between these views, they both reflect a general United States recognition of the important fact that the United Nations, unlike the League of Nations, has become too prominent a force in world affairs to be ignored and that it is a significant current in the general tide toward increased intermingling of national societies.

H. FIELD HAVILAND, JR., a member of the Board of Editors of *International Organization*, is Director of Foreign Policy Studies, The Brookings Institution, Washington, D.C.

[1] White House Press Release, "Remarks of The President to the United Nations General Assembly," December 17, 1963.
[2] "My Proposals for a 'Can-Win' Foreign Policy," *Life*, January 17, 1964.

The present analysis looks through United States glasses at the record of the United Nations in relation to the original aspirations, weighed on the scales of United States interests, and draws conclusions for future United States policy toward the United Nations. Because of the broad range of United Nations activities, the analysis is selective, concentrating on two main concerns: peacekeeping and developmental assistance.

UNITED STATES INTERESTS AND THE UNITED NATIONS

The basic objectives that have motivated United States support of the United Nations system from the beginning have been simply stated by President Johnson:

> The United States wants to see . . . war end. . . .The United States wants to cooperate with all the members of this organization to conquer everywhere the ancient enemies of mankind—hunger, and disease and ignorance. The United States wants sanity, and security, and peace for all. . . . [3]

The key to the original United States strategy was its determination to improve upon the League of Nations in two fundamental ways. One approach was to do everything possible to achieve collaboration among the Great Powers as the cornerstone of the peacekeeping system; the instrument for this collaboration would be the Security Council. The other concern was to strengthen the Organization's economic and social programs as the best long-range means of preventing future wars. While these aims foreshadowed heavy international commitments for the United States, they were considered essential for a world environment conducive to the security and well-being of the United States. This double strategy forged a new tool, combining the sword and the plowshare.

These broad objectives were written into the purposes and principles of the United Nations Charter:

> 1. To maintain international peace and security . . . ; 2. To develop friendly relations among nations based on respect for the principle of equal rights and self-determination of peoples . . . ; 3. To achieve international cooperation in solving international problems of an economic, social, cultural, or humanitarian character . . . ; and 4. To be a center for harmonizing the actions of nations in the attainment of these common ends.

It is in terms of these objectives, framed in large measure by the United States, that the record of the past two decades is appraised as a basis for considering future United States policy toward the United Nations.

---

[3] White House Press Release, "Remarks of The President to the United Nations General Assembly," December 17, 1963.

Controlling and Resolving Conflicts

Whoever would counsel the United States on its future policy concerning the role of the United Nations in maintaining world peace should be well schooled in the lessons of the past, judged not by abstract ideals but in terms of the feasible alternatives that were available and measured by the yardstick of United States national interests. The following paragraphs briefly review this experience according to major categories of conflict situations and major functions performed by the United Nations. The categories that seem most useful analytically are: 1) Cold War situations involving direct confrontation between the principal Communist and non-Communist powers; 2) conflicts between major non-Communist powers and developing states, flowing largely from the liquidation of colonial relationships; and 3) conflicts primarily between developing states with little great-power involvement. The chief functions reviewed are: inquiry and analysis, measures to subdue violence, peaceful settlement of issues, and development assistance to complement the other functions.

Cold War Conflicts

The first group of United Nations experiences to be appraised is the Cold War category. Controversies arising under this category have been dominated by direct and serious conflict between the major Communist and non-Communist powers. Because the interests of the United States have been vitally affected by such disputes, it has felt compelled to resort to the United Nations, whenever feasible, to maximize support for its own strategy and to confound the enemy. But because of the intense hostility and massive power involved in Cold War situations, it has been difficult for the United States to mobilize clear and strong support for its position in these cases within the United Nations except when the policies endorsed by the United States were accepted as unmistakably valid by at least two-thirds of the Member States and when those states felt sufficiently motivated and able to give the requisite substantive and material assistance. For these reasons, it has been assumed from the beginning that this kind of dispute would pose an acutely grave, perhaps intractable, challenge for the United Nations, and many observers have declared that the Organization cannot make a useful contribution in such situations and should avoid them.

Despite these difficulties, the United States and a large majority of the other Member States have considered it advantageous to use the United Nations as a major instrumentality for dealing with some of the most dangerous Cold War conflicts, chiefly those concerning Greece, Korea, Hungary, and the Cuban missile crisis. The conditions affecting United Nations involvement in such situations were sufficiently favorable to enable the Organization to make substantial contributions in most of these cases. At the same time, it is important to recall that the United States, as well as other countries, did not consider the United Nations climate sufficiently propitious to make significant use of the Organization to deal with other Cold War situations concerning the major postwar peace treaties, Germany, Taiwan, and Indochina.

The outstanding aspect of the UN's performance in this category of conflicts in relation to United States interests is the effectiveness of the Organization in focusing a strong mutilateral spotlight of inquiry and analysis on such problems. The most intensive and organized efforts along these lines were undertaken in the Greek, Korean, and Hungarian cases, involving the utilization of special agents, but even the less rigorous treatment given the Cuban missile situation proved therapeutic. Hampering this function has been the extraordinary difficulty of piercing the barriers erected by Communist-controlled societies against the outside world. This was a major impediment in all of the most serious situations—Greece, Korea, Hungary, and Cuba. Even in these instances, however, the United Nations gained revealing information from a variety of sources and exposed it to the searching gaze of a worldwide audience.

The peaceful settlement function is usually of little avail, however, without some compelling pressure to encourage its use. The most perilous and difficult pressure to exert is some form of military action, usually with the double purpose of suppressing violence and supporting pacific alternatives. In the three situations involving serious hostilities (Greece, Korea, and Hungary) the United Nations established special agencies to observe and report, although never gaining direct access to Communist-controlled territory, and mounted a major military and embargo operation, dominated by the United States, in Korea. The latter action represented the most ambitious use made by the UN of military as well as political and economic measures and, after serious fumbling, this operation was effective in repulsing the North Korean invasion. In the Cuban missile crisis, where massive force threatened, the United Nations mounted no direct operational action other than political initiatives, but it gave implicit backing to United States countervailing military maneuvers which supported the diplomatic offensive. The principal limitations impeding the use of United Nations force were the difficulties of gaining access to Communist-controlled areas; the problem of mobilizing sudden, voluntary, multinational operations; and the lack of bold, clear political guidance from the principal political forums of the United Nations.

Beyond inquiry and compulsion, what contribution did the United Nations make in moving toward a definitive settlement of the issues? This is the key function of reconciliation: the creative exploration of feasible alternatives, patient and sensitive negotiation, and the promotion of an environment conducive to agreement. It is not surprising that while one of the four Cold War ituations (Greece) was substantially alleviated, the United Nations played only a modest supporting part in achieving this progress. The dominant factors were the policies and resources of the major Communist and non-Communist powers, interacting largely outside the United Nations. There has been no definitive resolution of the issues in the more serious situations of Korea, Hungary, and Cuba. This is not to say that the United Nations has not had a significant impact on these problems, from a public airing of the issues to powerful military action (in the Korean case), but thus far these pressures have not been sufficient to achieve consensus among the major powers concerned. Yet these situations would probably have been even more inflamed without the United Nations contribution.

Putting out a fire is not enough without giving positive assistance to protect the structure against future conflagration. The United Nations has given such assistance in all of the Cold War situations involving serious hostilities— Greece, Korea, and Hungary. In the latter two cases, such aid was offered to both the Communists and non-Communists but managed to penetrate into the Communist fold only in the form of relief supplies to Hungary, initiated by a joint United Nations–Food and Agriculture Organization (FAO) mission. Reconstruction and development assistance to Greece was undertaken as part of the general aid efforts of the United Nations and the specialized agencies, beginning with a FAO mission in 1946. The most ambitious special rehabilitation program launched in any of these cases was organized for Korea in July 1950; it was ultimately administered by the United Nations Korean Reconstruction Agency (UNKRA) and dispensed aid valued at $149 million contributed by 39 countries. The United Nations helped to alleviate difficult refugee problems in all of these situations. Finally, the Organization assisted in strengthening the political as well as economic and social fabric in both Greece and Korea by, *inter alia,* encouraging democratic practices and training public officials. The chief obstacles were the familiar difficulty of piercing the Communist barriers, the paucity of resources available to the international programs, the difficulty of coordinating multilateral with other activities, and the inadequacy of indigenous arrangements to take advantage of the assistance.

What is the significance of all of this experience in relation to United States interests? The most noteworthy conclusion is that, even in this most difficult Cold War category, the United Nations, from the United States point of view, made significant contributions in four highly inflammable situations. It exposed all of the conflicts to intensive international inquiry. It sanctioned and mounted a large-scale military operation against the North Korean attack. It acted as an honest broker in the Cuban missile crisis. And it provided healing aid for Greece, Korea, and Hungary. The principal factors that encouraged United States support of United Nations action in these instances were: widespread agreement among the other United Nations Members with the objectives sought by the United States; acceptance of intervention under the United Nations flag in preference to other approaches; the effect of United Nations action in discouraging unilateral initiatives; and the sharing of political as well as material burdens involved in these enterprises. The principal weaknesses that hobbled these efforts were the inadequacy of access to Communist-controlled areas (Eastern Europe, North Korea, and Cuba); difficulties confronted by the United Nations in mobilizing and managing large-scale military forces; the absence of final settlements, except in the Greek case which was not significantly affected by United Nations action; and the lack of adequate comprehensive assistance programs. It should also be kept in mind that United Nations activity in these instances was reinforced by major bilateral efforts: substantial military and economic aid to Greece, Korea, and the Hungarian refugees and strong United States countermeasures against Cuba. At the same time, no other channels proved more effective than the United Nations in achieving a final resolution of the issues.

In other major Cold War conflicts, chiefly those concerning the principal postwar peace treaties, Germany, the China-Taiwan dispute, and Indochina, the United Nations played no significant role. United States policy makers were in large measure responsible for this inactivity because they believed, probably correctly, that it would have been difficult to generate sufficient collaboration among the membership in favor of the policies pursued by the United States in these areas. In the most explosive situations (Germany, Taiwan, and Indochina) the basic United States strategy was firm opposition to Communist expansion backed by strong military and economic assistance. The bulk of the United Nations membership was not prepared to give substantial support to this approach. The situation was further aggravated by the persistent United States opposition to the seating of Communist China in the United Nations, an attitude which has become increasingly unrealistic and unpopular. At the same time, as the United States has become more interested in the possibility of negotiating its way out of South Vietnam, it has given more attention and encouragement to the special strengths of the United Nations in facilitating communication across political barriers and in helping to arrange and police a cessation of hostilities.

North-South Issues

The second and largest category of disputes dealt with by the United Nations has had to do with tensions between major Western powers and the developing countries, many of which conflicts have risen out of the liquidation of colonial relationships. While most of these situations have provided fertile soil for some Communist cultivation, Communism has not been the dominant issue, and these questions cannot be thought of as major factors in the Cold War. Hence, their separation from the first category discussed above.

The cases included in this analysis, in rough chronological order, concern: Indonesia, South Africa's *apartheid* policy, North Africa (Tunis, Morocco, and Algeria), Guatemala, the Suez Canal, the Congo (Leopoldville), Goa, the Portuguese African territories, and West Irian. Other situations were discussed briefly in the United Nations but involved no significant United Nations effort; many others never found their way onto the United Nations agenda.

The United States has been especially schizophrenic in this category—torn between its close allies among the Western colonial powers and the new nations emerging from dependency. The basic United States objectives, which can never be very precise and which are often in conflict among themselves as well as with other purposes, have been to make the transition from dependence to independence as orderly as possible, to facilitate an equitable resolution of the conflicting interests of the parties, and to assist the healthy long-range development of the new nations. While the United States has rarely taken the initiative in bringing such disputes to the United Nations— others have been all too eager to play that role—the United States has often looked upon the Organization as a useful instrument to further the above objectives, especially to moderate the views of the anticolonial zealots while urging the colonial powers to bend with the wind.

Only in the Suez Canal and the Congo (Leopoldville) situations has the United States led the parade in urging United Nations action. In the first case, after inept United States maneuvering helped to precipitate the crisis, the United States was outraged by the surprise Israeli-Franco-British intervention and felt that it had no choice but to resort to the United Nations to extricate its allies from an untenable position. In the Congo, the United States decided that the United Nations was the best instrumentality for constructive intervention to help ease the withdrawal of the Belgians, establish more viable internal conditions, and fend off disruptive external influences. Unhappily, opposition from certain quarters, chiefly the Communist states and France, and the unrealistic effort, led by the United States, to force compulsory financial support of such operations resulted in the premature withdrawal of the United Nations military presence as well as the discouragement of other peace-keeping efforts.

In the case of Latin American disputes, the United States has generally discouraged resort to the United Nations in favor of channels restricted to American states, free of extremist opposition, and especially sensitive to United States influence. Only in the Cuban missile crisis did the United States accept United Nations intervention because it seemed capable both of adding substantial support to the United States position and of strongly influencing Soviet policy.

Reviewing the United Nations performance in the nine cases listed above, all of the situations but those concerning Goa and Guatemala were exposed to searching inquiry and discussion within the United Nations framework. There were several reasons why these two exceptions escaped intensive scrutiny. Goa seemed of relatively minor importance, and there was widespread endorsement of India's action among the emerging states. The United States managed to persuade enough Members to leave whatever multilateral attention was given to the Guatemala case to the Organization of American States (OAS). And conclusive unilateral action was taken quickly in both instances. While the Organization accomplished most of its intensive analysis of the seven other problems via the Secretary-General and his staff, special agencies were established by either the Security Council or the General Assembly to supplement these efforts in five instances: Indonesia, South Africa, Suez, the Portuguese African territories, and West Irian. Although access to these situations was easier than in the Communist-controlled areas, there was still much resistance to United Nations intervention by some of the parties to these disputes, not only by Western states, such as South Africa and Portugal, but by some of the emerging countries, such as Indonesia, Egypt, and India.

In the six situations afflicted by some degree of violence, the United Nations injected military personnel under its control to help enforce peace in three cases: Indonesia, the Suez Canal, and the Congo (Leopoldville). The Congo was the scene of the most ambitious intervention involving as many as 20,000 military personnel at any one time, contributed by 34 countries, and requiring a total expenditure of $402 million as of June 1964. The United Nations was a major force not only in discouraging external interference but in dampening civil strife and helping to construct a more viable state. While the United Nations made some progress in these efforts, serious problems remained when the Organization terminated its military operation in June 1964. The Suez operation was easier because Egypt was a more effective state than the Congo and because a relatively stable and pacific situation was established as a framework for the UN's surveillance role which was performed by a force of 6,000 military personnel drawn from ten Member States. The smallest operation was the supervision by as many as 55 United Nations military observers of the cessation of hostilities in Indonesia in 1949.

In these three cases, there was strong support among the great majority of the Members for the introduction of UN military missions and many of the contending states were relatively receptive to such intervention in preference to other alternatives. The major obstacles to UN intervention were the tensions prevailing among the antagonists, the internal strife in the Congo, the difficulty of providing clear and strong political guidance and support for such operations within the United Nations, and the inadequate military organization and resources available to the United Nations. No United Nations military presence was introduced in the other three situations involving violence: North Africa, Guatemala, and Goa. Major Western powers as well as other states resisted the consideration of such action in all three cases, and all of the major issues at stake were finally settled by forces operating outside the United Nations.

In its peacemaking role, the Organization was the principal sponsor of mediatory efforts in six of the nine situations in this category: Indonesia, South Africa, the Suez Canal, the Congo, West Irian, and the Portuguese African territories. In four of these situations (Indonesia, South Africa, West Irian, and the Portuguese dependencies) the United Nations created special agents, either commissions or individual mediators, and in the Indonesian and West Irian disputes, United States officials played prominent roles. In all of these cases, the Secretary-General and his staff were important factors in guiding events, and in the most explosive situations (the Suez Canal and the Congo) the Secretary-General was the key mediator. In three cases (Indonesia, the Suez Canal, and West Irian) effective settlement of the issues submitted to the United Nations was achieved. No comparable progress has yet material-ized in the other three conflicts in which the Organization was influential (South Africa, the Congo, and the Portuguese dependencies), problems which are exacerbated by extremely rigid attitudes on the part of South Africa and Portugal and by the civil strife in the Congo. In the three situations in which the United Nations played a less prominent role, France and the United States opposed major United Nations intervention in North Africa and Guatemala respectively, and India adopted a similar attitude regarding Goa. On the whole, the United Nations was notably more successful in exercising its peace-keeping influence in this category of North-South issues than in the Cold War situations discussed above, playing an important role in two-thirds of the cases and contributing significantly toward final settlements in half of these. It was least successful where one or more of the parties resolutely re-sisted its intervention or where, as in the Congo, there existed no viable state with which to deal.

To inject developmental assistance as part of the cure for these ailing situa-tions, the United Nations created special programs in three of the nine cases: the Suez Canal, the Congo, and West Irian. In the first instance, the effort was directed mainly toward reopening and developing the Suez Canal under a United Nations mission financed by a loan of $11 million contributed by eleven countries. The loan was rapidly repaid from charges levied against Canal traffic. In the Congo, a major relief and rehabilitation operation was launched as a constructive concomitant of the military effort, involving an expenditure of $40 million. During West Irian's transition from dependence upon the Netherlands to incorporation with Indonesia, the United Nations exercised a limited tutelary role by directly administering that territory from October 1962 to May 1963 through the UN Temporary Executive Authority (UNTEA). In the other cases, the United Nations contributed aid as part of its general developmental programs, striving not only to improve material conditions but to nourish more efficient and democratic government. The principal impediments to these efforts have been the paucity of resources available to the United Nations, the inadequacy of current developmental strategy, especially for political advancement, and the resistance of the developing societies to external influence.

Evaluating the entire experience in this second category of North-South issues in relation to United States objectives, the record is somewhat better than in the Cold War category, due largely to more effective access to and collaboration with the parties involved; the difference, however, is not absolute, only relative. In the nine cases considered, the United Nations can be said to have made a substantial contribution toward the general purposes pursued by the United States (orderly transition to independence, equitable resolution of conflicting interests, and long-range development of the emerging nations) in four of the situations: Indonesia, North Africa, the Suez Canal, and the Congo. In all of these instances, the United Nations was a useful factor in helping to extricate the dominant Western powers from untenable situations in formerly dependent territories, in facilitating a settlement of the main issues, and in beginning to build the foundations for more viable future development. While the United States and other countries attempted to use the United Nations to pursue the same goals in the Portuguese African territories and West Irian and to deal with the related *apartheid* problem in South Africa, little progress was achieved, due primarily to the extremely rigid opposition of the three major countries concerned: Portugal, Indonesia, and South Africa. Effective settlements of the Guatemalan and Goan issues were accomplished, but the United Nations played only a peripheral role in these cases. In the former situation, the United States gave its backing to what it considered the preferable group in a civil conflict, but it rightly assumed that it would be difficult to win support for this position in the United Nations.

In terms of functions performed, United Nations inquiry made a major contribution in seven of the nine cases considered, but not in Goa or Guatemala. In the six situations afflicted by significant violence, the United Nations exerted an important pacifying influence in three cases (Indonesia, the Suez Canal, and the Congo) but not in North Africa, Goa, or Guatemala. In six of the nine situations, the United Nations made significant mediatory contributions concerning Indonesia, South Africa, the Suez Canal, the Congo, West Irian, and the Portuguese African dependencies, but not in North Africa, Goa, or Guatemala. In only three of the nine cases were special aid programs introduced in conjunction with the peacemaking measures (in the Suez Canal, the Congo, and West Irian) but additional aid was rendered, benefiting most of these situations as part of regular United Nations assistance efforts.

Thus, the United Nations was of important utility in relation to most of the functions performed in a majority of these situations. The Organization worked best where there was clear and strong consensus in the United Nations on the issues and where there was readiness on the part of the principal countries concerned to engage in at least minimal collaboration with the United Nations. In comparison with other available channels, bilateral or multilateral, the United Nations had the special advantage of being more acceptable as an agency of inquiry, peacekeeping, and mediation than any single state or small group of states because of its comprehensive membership embracing the broadest spectrum of cultures, ideologies, and interests. The Organization facilitates the broadest sharing of political, military, and economic burdens involved in such enterprises. Even in this category, however, the United Nations is hobbled by conflicting policies and governmental resistance that can be just as intense as in the Cold War category, by restricted access to the areas concerned, and by the serious weaknesses and vast needs of the emerging countries with which the United Nations is ill-equipped to cope.

Disputes Between Developing States

The third category of disputes can be characterized as arising primarily out of tensions between the developing nations. While both the Cold War and North-South disputes have cast their shadows over these situations, they have not dominated them, and it is probable that these upheavals would have erupted even in the absence of the other factors. The major cases included in this category, again in approximate chronological sequence, are: Palestine, Kashmir, Cyprus, Lebanon, and Yemen.

While neither the United States nor its major Western allies have been direct parties to these disputes, except the United Kingdom in the Palestine and Cyprus cases, United States interests have been involved and often on more than one side of a dispute. The United States has been torn between its Jewish and Arab connections in the Palestine case, between its Indian and Pakistani associations in the Kashmir situation, between the Greeks and the Turks in Cyprus, and between Lebanon and the United Arab Republic in the Lebanese case. Its concern with Yemen has been more tenuous. The basic United States objectives in the bulk of these situations have been to dampen the conflagration before it could expand to dangerous proportions, to protect the interests of its friends, and to prevent its enemies from catching any fish in these troubled waters. The United States played a leading role in encouraging United Nations intervention in these situations because of the Organization's special advantages discussed in relation to the two previous categories.

In reviewing the performance of the United Nations in this category, it is noteworthy that gathering and winnowing the relevant facts were a central function in all five of these situations. This effort was especially intensive in the first four cases (Palestine, Kashmir, Cyprus, and Lebanon) involving lengthy and exhaustive field investigations. Special agencies, including commissions and individuals, were created for this purpose, reinforcing the key role of the Secretary-General and his aides. Unlike the Cold War category, the United Nations had direct access to these areas and was able to make a contribution in clarifying the facts and analyzing the issues within a world-wide framework.

To abate violence and promote peaceful alternatives in the four situations in which there was serious armed conflict, the United Nations contributed observer missions to help supervise cease-fire agreements in Palestine, Kashmir, and Yemen, and a peacekeeping force to help restore peace in Cyprus. The first United Nations observer operation was begun in 1948, in large measure through the efforts of the United Nations Acting Mediator, Ralph Bunche, to oversee the truce established in Palestine. It ultimately numbered approximately 700. The other operations were more modest, involving as many as 42 military personnel in Kashmir, 600 in Lebanon, and 200 in Yemen. Despite their small size, however, the UN missions performed useful services in investigating and settling violations of the agreements that they were charged with overseeing. The Cyprus situation was more difficult because no viable cease-fire was established as a precondition for the United Nations observation function. The international force, which numbered as many as 6,000, contributed by nine countries, was injected as one factor to help achieve a cessation of hostilities, and it made a useful but not decisive contribution in that direction.

To help mend these broken situations, the United Nations applied conciliatory measures in all five disputes. The most intensive efforts were those of the commissions and mediators who grappled for long periods with the problems of Palestine, Kashmir, and Cyprus. The Secretary-General not only played a key role in these cases, but he and his personal representatives were the major figures in trying to heal the disputes concerning Lebanon and Yemen. While the United Nations helped to discourage hostilities in the first three situations, no final settlement was reached among the parties to these disputes. The lesser conflicts in Lebanon and Yemen were substantially settled, but the United Nations made little contribution in this respect.

The principal attempt to use positive economic and social assistance as an integral part of a broad strategy to heal such conflicts was the program to care for Palestine Arab refugees. This has involved an expenditure of $510 million to date in order to prepare these displaced persons for productive lives and to find new homes for them. Thus far, more than 160,000 refugees have found permanent havens, but approximately one million remain under the aegis of the United Nations Relief and Works Agency for Palestine Refugees in the Near East (UNRWA). Assistance efforts related to other disputes have been the program for the cooperative development of the Indus River for the benefit of India and Pakistan and the development program for the Middle East which was proposed in relation to the Lebanese crisis but which has not progressed significantly. Other aid has been offered as part of regular United Nations assistance programs.

Reviewing the record in this third category of conflicts among smaller states, it may be surprising to some to find that the United Nations record is not markedly better than in the previous category involving direct great-power intervention. Among the United Nations achievements from the United States point of view were the exposure of all five situations in this category to international scrutiny, the injection of an important United Nations peace-keeping presence in all four cases of serious violence (Palestine, Kashmir, Cyprus, and Lebanon), the exercise of an important mediatory influence in all five instances, and a large-scale aid effort to assist the Palestine refugees. On the other hand, the United States and other nations found it difficult to use the United Nations to mount a major military action because of conflicting interests among the Member States, the unsatisfactory equation of power and authority in the procedures of the Organization, and the difficulty of gaining adequate access to the areas concerned. Despite its mediatory contribution, the United Nations was unable to play a major role in achieving a final settlement in any of these disputes.

It is clear from this experience that weaker nations, such as India, Pakistan, and Cyprus, can be just as obdurate as the Great Powers in opposing United Nations ministrations. Nonetheless, United States policy favored the United Nations efforts as an important aid to United States objectives in all of the cases except the Lebanese situation. In that instance, the United States criticized the Organization's observation mission for not being as rigorous or as objective as it might have been; even in that case, however, in which the United States itself was not above reproach, the deficiencies of the United Nations operation caused no serious damage to United States interests.

Bases for Future Strategy

Turning from the past to the future, what are the fundamental objectives that should guide United States policy in the peacekeeping field, what basic assets does the United Nations have at its disposal to help meet these requirements, and what practical steps should be taken to reinforce those assets?

The underlying objectives of the United States are the same as those that motivated the creation of the United Nations peacekeeping role in the beginning and that were quoted earlier from the purposes of the United Nations Charter: to maintain international peace and security, to bring about the peaceful settlement of disputes, to promote friendly relations based on respect for human rights and fundamental freedoms, and to achieve cooperation in solving related economic and social problems. At the same time, it should be recognized that these objectives seldom mesh neatly but more frequently clash and that their reconciliation must be worked out according to the circumstances peculiar to each situation. Because, for example, the struggle for basic freedoms, including some degree of democratic government and economic equity, has often involved an element of violence, an absolute emphasis on peace and security can impose a straitjacket that may enforce an evil status quo against liberalizing progress. On the other hand, large-scale violence, executed with modern weapons, can trigger intolerable devastation. Thus, in seeking the objectives cited, the United States must within tolerable limits of friction strike a reasonable balance between stability and change.

Though the conflicts that are likely to confront these purposes will arise in different circumstances, they share certain general characteristics: a struggle for political influence, material gain, or ideological supremacy; and a resort to conflict rather than conciliation. For the foreseeable future, these disputes will continue to vary according to the kinds of adversaries and interests involved, as suggested in the three categories discussed above: major Communist and non-Communist states, great Western powers and former or present dependencies, and smaller non-Communist states. A fourth kind of conflict, present in most of the other three situations, is civil strife. While such conflict by itself is not normally considered appropriate for United Nations action, it can be a threat to international peace by interacting with forces outside a country.

Although these varying conditions affect the role of the United Nations in different ways, the differences are relative, not absolute. Contrary to some analyses, the United Nations can make and has made important contributions in all four categories. While Communist intransigence can seriously hamper United Nations access to Communist-controlled areas, we have seen that non-Communist countries, such as South Africa on the *apartheid* issue and India on Goa and Kashmir, can be equally obdurate.

The prime asset enjoyed by the United Nations in the peacekeeping field is the fact that most nations are more receptive to intervention by the United Nations than by any alternative agent, unilateral or multilateral. Whether it be great or small, the typical country is less suspicious of the United Nations than it is of any individual state or restricted group of states. The United Nations is not the monkey's paw of any small segment of its membership, not even the Great Powers, but it represents a balance of many different national interests. Its membership is the most comprehensive of any international organization and reflects the broadest spectrum of cultures and views. It is guided by the objectives of the Charter which have been accepted by all Member States. Its operational policies are openly negotiated and proclaimed, and they are administered by a Secretariat responsible to the full membership. All states have a voice in the decision-making process, even non-Members under certain circumstances, although admittedly some "are more equal than others." Should some countries consider certain United Nations decisions repugnant, they can find protection in the fact that most United Nations decisions have the legal force of only recommendations, although in practice they may exert strong influence, and that access to countries is normally subject to the consent of those states. As even the weaker states are becoming more able and inclined to resist external intervention, the relative acceptability of UN intervention in troubled situations will become increasingly valuable. The Organization is even able occasionally to surmount the seemingly impenetrable obstacles erected by the Communists against UN action, as, for example, with regard to the relief mission to Hungary in 1957.

There are further advantages to the United States in the broad, multilateral character of UN intervention: 1) The UN presence discourages independent unilateral initiatives, as in the Congo; 2) the political and material burdens of such enterprises are collectively shared; 3) multilateral sponsorship reinforces the credibility of the UN's fact-finding function; 4) negotiation is facilitated because the broad membership of the Organization links most nations of the world; and 5) developmental assistance can be harnessed with peacekeeping functions within the same framework. Although the increase in membership makes the decision-making process less easily manageable from the United States point of view, the United States voice has far greater impact than its single vote would suggest, and our review of past experience demonstrates that most of the United Nations peacekeeping operations have been consistent with the United States' interests. Even when there has been some divergence from those interests, it has not been seriously injurious. The difficulties the United States has experienced occasionally in persuading other countries to share certain policies and burdens, as in the Congo, are not an inherent or insurmountable barrier to United Nations action. The pragmatic system of vague mandates combined with considerable Secretariat maneuverability and voluntary rather than compulsory financing provides considerable leeway for effective action. Thus, the United States has found the United Nations to be a useful instrument, despite all of its limitations, for dealing with a substantial portion of major postwar conflicts of all kinds, not in deference to abstract ideals but in recognition of practical assets.

Recommendations for the Future

What can be done to strengthen United Nations peacekeeping capabilities? The underlying strategy should be two-pronged: to improve the United Nations system itself and to cultivate a more receptive environment.

At the root of the first task is the problem of achieving a better linking of power and authority within the United Nations apparatus. The Organization cannot function effectively if decisions requiring the use of certain resources are made without giving due weight to the views of those who must pay the piper. Granted, large-scale resources are not required for all peacekeeping enterprises, such as inquiry and negotiation or even modest operations, but the support of the more powerful states can reinforce even these functions, and their backing is essential to large-scale enterprises, especially of a military and economic nature.

True, both the Charter and present practice accept the need for and achieve some degree of balance between power and authority. Nonetheless, situations such as the Suez and Congo experiences have dramatized the desirability of improvement. Any recommendation for the future must take into account two polar extremes. One, institutionalized in the Security Council, would make all United Nations peacekeeping decisions subject to unanimity among the Great Powers. The other, institutionalized in the General Assembly, would permit peacekeeping activities to be undertaken in voluntary compliance with a two-thirds vote of the General Assembly, without necessarily conforming to the wishes of any of the Great Powers. Exclusive reliance on either of these alternatives is not an adequate response to the needs of the future. A third proposal, some form of weighted voting in the General Assembly, stumbles over the fact that no weighting formula has yet been discovered that could win the necessary votes to amend the Charter and that would leave the United States in a better position than it now enjoys.

The most viable strategy would seem to be to provide that peacekeeping proposals be initially considered by United Nations bodies and processes that would give special weight to the stronger states. In case of stalemate, however, such a strategy would leave open the possibility of consideration by the General Assembly with its more permissive procedures. Approaches which are already being explored would require all peacekeeping decisions to be submitted first to the Security Council or to a subcommittee of the General Assembly which would be weighted in favor of the more powerful states. Increasing the size and representativeness of the Security Council should make it a more useful element in the peacekeeping system. The Assembly committee might adopt some system of weighted voting without having to surmount the hurdle of Charter amendment. Should neither of these alternatives prove effective and should United Nations action seem both urgent and feasible, the matter could be considered by the full membership of the General Assembly according to the usual procedures. The fact that the latter approach might be used against the United States can be balanced by compensating considerations: the powerful influence exerted by the United States, the generally co-operative attitude of the preponderance of the membership toward United States policies, and the fact that General Assembly resolutions have the legal force only of recommendations.

Once the decision is made to engage the United Nations in a peacekeeping operation, it is important that it have immediately available the necessary organization and resources to act with optimum efficiency. Much needs to be done in this area both to provide a stronger continuing core capability that can mount a peacekeeping operation without having to build from scratch and to improve the complementary resources of the Member States that can nourish such an operation. Beginning at the top of the Secretariat pyramid, the Secretary-General needs more adequate top-level assistance to share his oppressive burden of general direction. This group should be equipped to deal with all aspects of the endeavor—not only short-term military and political tactics but long-term development assistance of a fundamental political as well as economic and social nature. It is also essential to continue to protect the integrity of the Secretariat as the agent of the entire membership.

Because it is neither desirable nor feasible for the United Nations to maintain a large standing body of military or political and economic personnel, comparable with the resources of better-endowed national states, the United Nations must act more as a ringmaster who can call upon various talents supplied by Member States according to the requirements of each situation. This requires advance earmarking; training and experience for appropriate personnel, political and economic as well as military; and advance planning, legislation, and organization. Among the several agencies that should concern themselves with these tasks, the new United Nations Institute for Training and Research should be able to make a major contribution toward these goals.

Where substantial resources are required, the control of money is decisive. The United Nations has suffered from a crisis in this area because of the failure of certain powers, notably the Communist countries and France, to accept as binding the assessments approved by the General Assembly to support the Suez and Congo operations. One path around this roadblock is the strategy, discussed above, of fostering a more realistic linking of power and authority in the decision-making process. At the same time, because it is desirable to keep open the option of action under a General Assembly resolution, it is necessary to continue to have available the alternative of voluntary financing without attempting binding assessments.

Finally, there is the goal of strengthening the impact of the United Nations by making the environment of national societies more receptive to the United Nations presence. The very act of improving the United Nations performance will help to improve the climate of opinion. But more should be done to develop understanding of and support for the peacekeeping role of the United Nations. This can be achieved through many channels that reach both public and private leaders as well as the general populace.

ECONOMIC, SOCIAL, AND POLITICAL DEVELOPMENT

While the United Nations quenches the flames of conflict with one hand, it uses its other hand of constructive long-term assistance to build more viable societies for tomorrow. No country has played a more consistent and vigorous role than the United States in promoting this positive strategy which was foreshadowed in the purposes of the United Nations Charter:

> To achieve international cooperation in solving international problems of an economic, social, cultural, or humanitarian character, and in promoting and encouraging respect for human rights and for fundamental freedoms. . . .

But this wing of the United Nations structure has developed quite differently from what was anticipated in the original blueprint. Not only are the developmental activities of the Organization far larger than originally expected, but they include substantial capital as well as technical assistance, they place greater emphasis on central United Nations planning and coordination in relation to the specialized agencies, they have spawned regional commissions responsive to special area interests, they have shifted the geographic focus from Europe toward the developing countries, they have fostered direct operational involvement in the recipient countries as well as participation in the more traditional and detached functions of study, debate, and advice, and they have fostered social and political as well as economic development. The following paragraphs review the assets and liabilities of this experience and draw conclusions for the future in relation to basic United States purposes.

Economic Development

The United Nations building effort has aimed at increasing material production to provide a more secure and agreeable life. While Europe was in the process of recovering from the war and as tensions in the less developed countries became more threatening, dramatized by the Communist victory on the Chinese mainland, the major Western powers, led largely by the United States, became more inclined to use the United Nations and the specialized agencies, among various instrumentalities, to help ease the tribulations of the developing nations. In addition to the individual programs of the specialized agencies, which currently total approximately $200 million a year, the Expanded Program of Technical Assistance (EPTA) and the Special Fund were established to supplement these efforts and to provide stronger central coordination. These two enterprises currently dispense approximately $100 million a year, the bulk of which is administered through the specialized agencies. To provide capital investment, the International Bank for Reconstruction and Development (IBRD) and its affiliates, the International Development Association (IDA) and the International Finance Corporation (IFC), have gradually increased their lending to the emerging countries to a current level of $1,171 million a year.

What have been the major strengths and weaknesses of these enterprises in relation to United States interests? The basic United States objectives have been to develop the economies of other countries not only to make them better partners in world commerce but to make them socially and politically more stable, progressive, and democratic. The international development programs have furthered these purposes by strengthening the fabric of international cooperation through multilateral collaboration, by broadening the range of concepts, skills, and resources essential for development, by facilitating external access to the developing countries which consider the multinational nature of the international agencies a shield against individual national interests, by achieving some modest progress, and by discouraging unilateral intervention, thus reducing the possibility of pitting one donor against another.

Among the limitations that hobble these efforts, perhaps the most fundamental is the fact that the typical nation-state, small as well as large, democratic as well as nondemocratic, is reluctant to channel any substantial portion of its wealth through an organization over which it does not have decisive control. Thus, while the United States has been friendly toward the International Bank, in which it has a strong voice, it has generally opposed a "soft capital" program under the United Nations, and it has not taken full advantage of the potential of the multilateral technical assistance program. United States resistance to the multilateral approach is exacerbated by the disparity in voting strength between the countries that seek assistance and those that have the wherewithal to provide it. Occasionally the parliamentary power of the "have-not" countries has been used to press the "have" countries beyond what they have considered to be reasonable limits, as in the case of the Special United Nations Fund for Economic Development (SUNFED) proposal and the UN Conference on Trade and Development (UNCTAD), with consequent repercussions. Moreover, the administrative performance of the system leaves much to be desired due to the anemic resources of the United Nations, its decentralized structure, and its multinational composition which requires concessions to the principle of geographic balance. Finally, because of the broad range of interests represented and the permissive nature of the decision-making process, it is difficult to mobilize the Organization to move with unity, vigor, and determination.

Trade Cooperation

The United States was in the vanguard of those that originally hoped to build into the United Nations structure a bold program of trade cooperation. But subsequent opposition within the United States prevented the establishment of the proposed International Trade Organization (ITO). The General

Agreement on Tariffs and Trade (GATT), based on principles which had been elaborated for the proposed ITO, became the major multilateral instrument for trade liberalization. Nearly 80 countries now participate in its work. Since 1947, GATT has sponsored five rounds of negotiations which have reduced tariff rates on tens of thousands of items, and a sixth round of negotiations is now in progress. As the balance of payments of the participating countries improved, the GATT prohibition against restrictions on imports has been implemented, further liberalizing trade. Disputes among individual countries, including the United States, have been negotiated and a Program of Action was adopted in 1963, with the active support of the United States, to improve the trade position of the less developed countries. The Agreement has been modified to take into consideration the special problems of developing countries.

The most significant recent innovation in the trade field was the establishment of the United Nations Conference on Trade and Development. During its first session in the spring of 1964, 77 developing states formed an unprecedentedly effective caucus to mobilize support for freer access to markets in the developed countries, through such devices as tariff preferences, expanded use of international agreements to stabilize the prices of primary commodities at remunerative prices, compensatory payments for export losses, reduction of export service costs, and establishment of an international mechanism to further these objectives.

The principal impediments to further liberalization of trade are domestic programs to protect agricultural production and prices, as well as the reluctance of all states to open their frontiers to the free movement of international commerce without limitation. The developing countries demand preferential treatment to compensate for their present lack of competitiveness due to their late arrival in the manufacturing field. The United States and other developed countries recognize and sympathize with the aspirations and needs of the developing countries but question the practicality or long-term value of some of their proposals. Moreover, they are not willing or able to agree to the massive transfer of resources advocated by many of the developing countries. Even among countries of roughly equivalent development, trade restrictions are uneven and militate against any simple formula for liberalization, such as the 50 percent reduction provided for by the United States Trade Expansion Act. UNCTAD provides an opportunity for a new start in the dialogue between developed and developing countries on these admittedly serious problems relating to development. While the United States has made substantial concessions favoring trade as well as development cooperation, the growing economic gap between the more and less developed countries calls for even bolder efforts to reduce this gap through more generous and coordinated trade and aid programs.

Social Development

An essential objective of United States policy, shared with other developed, democratic societies, is to balance the emphasis on production and trade with a concern for the distribution and application of resources in ways that will enrich the quality of life for all men. This latter aim can be labeled social development. The most comprehensive United Nations approach to this problem has taken the form of a series of general surveys of world social conditions. The United Nations Educational, Scientific and Cultural Organization (UNESCO) has fostered a far-ranging miscellany of educational and cultural enterprises although there has been a recent inclination, encouraged by the United States, to concentrate more on programs of practical utility to the developing nations. The United Nations itself, the World Health Organization (WHO), and the United Nations Children's Fund (UNICEF) have sponsored programs to combat the debilitating and demoralizing impact of illness and have taken cautious steps toward coping with the explosive population problem. The International Labor Organization (ILO) has not only continued its prewar efforts to establish norms of advanced working conditions but has striven increasingly to assist the emerging countries in mobilizing and training their labor forces. Other programs have dealt with community development, housing, migration, welfare services, and the status of women.

These efforts have benefited from the special advantages of the multilateral approach: the wide range of concepts, experience, and resources available; and the receptivity of host countries to international programs which are looked upon as relatively neutral. On the other hand, these endeavors have suffered from the frustrations of gargantuan appetites starved by midget budgets. The broad range of political, economic, and social systems represented in the membership has complicated the task of arriving at consensus on ends and means. Despite these afflictions, the United States has generally felt that the social programs, in which American ideas and resources have played leading roles, have made an important contribution to progress.

Political Development

At the core of modern advancement is the central role of government, the system of power that in most nations has the broadest support, jurisdiction, authority, and resources. No other institution exerts more crucial influence in determining the general course a society is to pursue. It is natural, therefore, that the United Nations has been called upon to help strengthen this aspect of national development. At the same time, this field, more than most, is mined with explosive difficulties. Nations are understandably resistant to external intervention in their political life, and the problems of fundamental political development in all its ramifications have not been as widely recognized or analyzed as the problems of economic and social development. Yet the United Nations has already done useful work in the area, more than many observers realize, and it is capable of doing more in the future.

The general mandate for this mission is contained in the Charter:

> To develop friendly relations among nations based on respect for the principles of equal rights and self-determination of peoples, and . . . to achieve international cooperation in . . . promoting and encouraging respect for human rights and for fundamental freedoms for all. . . .

The strongest steps in this direction have been taken in relation to dependent territories. The Organization has had the greatest authority to determine norms and oversee compliance with those norms in the trust territories, most of which have now attained independence. In the case of other non-self-governing territories, the Organization's power has been limited to inquiry, debate, and advice, but, even here, various measures to hasten and strengthen self-government have been influential, especially in connection with the 1960 Declaration on the Granting of Independence to Colonial Countries and Peoples and the establishment of the General Assembly committee to encourage compliance with the Declaration. In a few cases, the United Nations has been given a tutelary role to exercise a degree of direct administrative authority over a territory in order to prepare it for independence. This was done with regard to Somalia, Libya, and West Irian. In two cases of armed conflict in which United Nations forces were heavily involved, South Korea and the Congo (Leopoldville), the United Nations exercised similar administrative powers which influenced the basic political development of those areas.

A broader and less directly controlling effort relevant to all states has been the United Nations program to help define and protect basic human rights, including the civic rights of security of person, free speech and communication, self-government, free movement within and between states, asylum, nationality, and due process of law. Major elements in this endeavor have been the 1948 Universal Declaration of Human Rights and the subsequent draft conventions. A companion campaign has been the attempt, led chiefly by African and Asian countries, to compel South Africa to abandon its *apartheid* policy. Other efforts have focused on developing the basic concepts, institutions, processes, and skills necessary for modern democratic government. This work has centered around programs concerned with community development, civic education, the advancement of law, public administration, and the improvement of mass communications.

The principal United Nations achievements in this field have been to dramatize basic civic rights and to take some action, chiefly in dependent territories, to foster self-government. But progress in this area has been less satisfactory than in economic and social development. Attention has been focused too narrowly and simply on the quest for independence, and too little on building the necessary political infrastructure to make independence viable. While useful assistance has been given to improve public administration, not enough has been done to emphasize basic civic development in relation to education, leadership training, mass media, and community development.

The United States has played a leading role from the beginning in favoring the development of democratic concepts and institutions, including its example in the Philippines, Hawaii, and Puerto Rico. It has tried to strike a reasonable balance between the extremes of colonialism and anticolonialism, an effort which has often generated more criticism than praise. At the same time, the United States image in this field has been tarnished by some of its own domestic deficiencies, including the racial problem and the nationalistic and niggardly handling of its Trust Territory of the Pacific Islands. And the United States has failed to take full advantage of the potential of the United Nations to advance basic political development.

Recommendations for the Future

What does all of this developmental experience suggest for future United States policy? While the nature of such programs should and will alter according to changing concepts and circumstances, clearly the United States has a continuing interest in working through the United Nations as well as other instrumentalities to help close the gap between the rich and the poor. This is not an expression of pure altruism but of self-interest in mitigating a dangerous source of international conflict, just as the United States has found it necessary to pursue similar policies at home. Because the developing countries often resist bilateral programs tied closely to particular national interests, the United States should explore ways of making greater use of the United Nations for developmental purposes. This approach will broaden the range of wisdom and resources available for the task and should win more enthusiastic cooperation from the developing countries.

This means directing more capital as well as technical assistance through United Nations channels and coordinating these efforts with trade policy, including a more sympathetic response to the aspirations expressed through the United Nations Conference on Trade and Development. Finally, more needs to be done to strengthen the basic political systems of the emerging countries. At the same time, the United States can be expected to be more hospitable to this strategy if the developing countries can be persuaded to help resolve the constitutional crisis in this field similar to the one that exists in the security field. Here, too, a better balance should be achieved between resources and authority.

The Soviet Union and the United Nations

Philip E. Mosely

From its founding the United Nations has been a frequent source of puzzlement and embarrassment to Soviet policy makers. Given the reticence of Soviet statesmen, past and present, and the inaccessibility of Soviet diplomatic archives, we can only speculate about the expectations which were in the minds of Premier Joseph Stalin and Foreign Minister Vyacheslav Molotov when they gave their approval to the Moscow Four-Nation Declaration on General Security of October 1943, the first great-power commitment to the establishment of a new international organization. For United States policy makers, certainly, this unprecedented commitment, buttressed by the Vandenberg Resolution, marked an important change in their nation's perspective and purpose. It represented a new determination, even if a vaguely defined one, to cooperate with other nations in establishing and maintaining a better foundation for international peace and order. For the Soviet leaders, who were celebrating the grim liberation of Kiev in the midst of the Moscow Conference, there was probably little time, and certainly no leisure, to speculate about the possible congruence or incongruence of Soviet ambitions with the stabilizing and even static assumptions that underlay a revived and expanded peacekeeping league of states.

Early Assumptions About the UN

In establishing the United Nations, the leaders of the Soviet Union, like those of the United Kingdom and the United States, placed special stress on the role of the five Great, or potentially Great, Powers. The Big Five were not to be coerced by the new Organization or its lesser Members. On the other hand, it could provide them with a meeting ground where they could concert

Philip E. Mosely is Director of the Institute of European Studies, Columbia University.

their policies and from which they could, if in agreement, exert an irresistible leverage upon other states to accept their joint decisions. Viewed from this angle, the United Nations appeared to some of its founders as a means of perpetuating the wartime arrangements under which the three strongest powers had taken many major decisions jointly and had then imposed them on their weaker allies and on neutrals. Reduced to its bluntest form, this expectation of a shared hegemony implied that the Soviet Union and the United States would settle their own and others' disputes in secret negotiation and would then join in imposing their decisions upon other states through the medium of the United Nations. If this arrangement broke down, the veto would still protect the Soviet government, as well as each of the other four permanent members of the Security Council, against actions inimical to its interests or claims.

Judging others by their own basically optimistic assumptions about the nature of international politics, United States policy makers assumed that all nations would be or should be satisfied within their own borders. In the postwar world, the main problem for the Great Powers would be not the satisfaction or denial of vast new ambitions harbored by any one of them but rather the forestalling or containing of nationalist, territorial, or other disturbing impulses by smaller powers. They assumed that this desirable goal could best be achieved by a league or concert of major powers whose overriding interest would be in preventing new wars and assuaging any new conflicts.

Neither the fledgling United Nations nor United States policy thinking were prepared for the new upsurge of Soviet ideological and political expansionism that followed upon the surrender of Germany and Japan. Far from joining in behind-the-scenes deals to satisfy a major part of the new Soviet claims—for example, in Turkey and Greece, in Iran and Japan, and in the former Italian colonies—the United States, now a status quo power except for the former Japanese mandate and Okinawa, turned to the United Nations as an instrument for resisting Soviet purposes and achieving some of its own. Whatever illusions the Kremlin may have held about the perpetuation of the wartime pattern of two-power hegemony were quickly dispelled by the role of the United Nations in pressing for the removal of Soviet forces from northern Iran.

In one major respect, however, Soviet policy continued to reflect the wartime assumption of a two-power hegemony. That was expressed in the Kremlin's tendency to allow the United Nations to act effectively in questions which, in Stalin's view, did not impinge directly on Soviet interests. Thus, despite its spate of hostile propaganda, the Soviet Union did not prevent the United Nations from negotiating and supervising a truce in Palestine, working out a cease-fire in Kashmir, or establishing the independence of Indonesia.

This self-restraint may also have reflected another basic assumption of Stalin's postwar policy, for Stalin sought the expansion of direct Soviet power along the periphery of his new empire, while at the same time avoiding any direct involvement in problems that lay beyond the reach of Soviet military and political control. Finally, in contrast to United States policy which tended to pick and choose, pursuing some interests within the United Nations and others outside it, Soviet policy assumed by 1947 that it had nothing to gain by submitting any of its interests to that body or raising its prestige in any way.

The Korean War and the stalemate that arose from it gave a new orientation, one of cold fury, to Soviet policy toward the United Nations. The probability is strong that the Soviet government genuinely believed that its absence from the Security Council in June 1950 would prevent that body from responding to the United States and South Korean appeals. It can be argued that Soviet policy makers assumed that the United States government had no intention of opposing the Communist conquest of South Korea through the use of United States forces; in that case, resolutions of protest from the United Nations would soon be forgotten in the reality of a reunited and Communist-ruled Korea. Moscow's bewilderment was compounded by its futile return to the Security Council and by the transfer of important powers of decision to the General Assembly, which, in its eyes, was abetted by the illegally expanded role of the first Secretary-General, to whom the Kremlin vowed unrelenting hostility. In this same period, at the height of the Cold War, the Kremlin seemed to despise, more than before or afterward, the maneuvers and advantages of the new form of "parliamentary democracy" represented by the United Nations. It seemed content to record the seldom varying number of votes of the Soviet-led minority in the General Assembly and to ring up a long sequence of vetoes in the Security Council.

REAPPRAISAL: NEW CONCEPTS AND POLICIES

Even before Stalin's death in March 1953, Soviet policy had been moving into a new phase as it appraised the course of the Korean crisis. In 1950 and 1951, as so often, Moscow had misread the portents. Linking together the United States' willingness to fight for South Korea, the rapid expansion of United States nuclear power and of the Strategic Air Command, and the decision to build an effective North Atlantic Treaty Organization (NATO) force backed by strong United States land power in Europe, Stalin had become convinced that United States policy was preparing for an early and decisive showdown. Accordingly, in 1950–1952 he shifted even greater resources to military preparation, secretly mobilized another million men, and imposed similarly rigid burdens, economic and political, on his European satellites.

The Congressional hearings of April and May 1951, however, had given him a remarkably complete picture of the basically defensive United States strategy. The willingness of Washington to relax its military pressure in Korea during long and inconclusive cease-fire negotiations also convinced Moscow that it had overestimated the size and range of the immediate danger. The reappraisal which followed found expression in the new formulas which the Kremlin presented in October 1952 to the Nineteenth Communist Party Congress.

In his last political utterances, before that Congress, Stalin outlined a new line of Soviet policy, one which, with varying degrees of emphasis, has been pursued by his successors. He abandoned the two-camp ("socialism" and "imperialism") concept and proclaimed that world politics was now to be shaped by "three camps" through adding the grouping of the newly independent and uncommitted nations to the two traditional "camps." The final outcome of the struggle between the "socialist" and "imperialist" blocs would be decided by winning over the third or "peace camp" to the socialist bloc. At that stage the "imperialists," isolated in Western Europe and North America, would be deprived of their markets and investments in the less developed countries and would have no choice but to acknowledge the supremacy of Communism throughout the world.

Although Stalin had laid the groundwork for a more active policy, it was left to his successor to take its implementation in hand. In 1955 the Kremlin undertook the first of several reconciliations with Yugoslavia's President Josip Tito. In its search for "anti-imperialist" support against Stalin's threats and pressures, the Yugoslav Communists had enlisted the active sympathy and support of important leaders of the "third world," notably Prime Minister Jawaharlal Nehru of India and Egypt's President Gamal Abdel Nasser. In its search for a wider and more flexible role, Moscow was now concerned with removing the image of a Communist Great Power bullying a smaller one. In the same year the Soviet government paid the price of restoring Austria's independence in order to reopen direct contacts with the major powers of the West, as it was able to do at the first Geneva summit conference. Meanwhile, it had renounced several unprofitable legacies of the Stalin period, such as the naval and air base at Porkkala, Finland, and the Soviet claim to Turkish bases and territories.

The clear-cut battle lines of the Cold War era now gave way to new and more fluctuating alignments, as in the Suez crisis in 1956 in which Soviet and United States pressures combined to call a halt to the Israeli-Franco-British action against Egypt. By 1956 the Soviet programs for nuclear weapons and advanced delivery systems had reached a point which allowed Moscow to brandish new and horrendous threats against many of its opponents. Finally, Stalin's successors could now abandon his sole emphasis on expansion along the periphery, a policy that had been brought to an unproductive halt in Europe by NATO and in Asia by the Korean War. They could now press Soviet interests and influence in more remote and more promising areas. Arms deliveries and economic development programs, launched in 1955, paid the sincere tribute of imitation to Western policies and rapidly opened a wide range of new contacts to Soviet policy.

Parallel to this new worldwide role, Soviet policy in the United Nations was undergoing important adjustments. Many newly independent countries had long resented the Soviet veto on enlarging the membership of the United Nations. This feeling was now assuaged by the Soviet acceptance of a "package deal" that omitted the seating of Communist China. In place of Trygve Lie, whom it had boycotted so rigorously, the Soviet government joined with the other major powers in the selection of Dag Hammarskjöld as Secretary-General. While it refused all financial responsibilities, the Soviet government either voted for or abstained on several questions of enlarging the peacekeeping role of the United Nations. After denouncing the increasingly effective technical assistance programs of the United Nations as a camouflage for imperialist exploitation, the Soviet Union now offered contributions of its own. Indeed, it has often complained that Soviet appropriations, which are limited to use in rubles, have not been put to full use.

Above all, Soviet policy found it easy and profitable to take its place on the extreme "anticolonialist" wing of the rapid movement of national independence in which the United Nations played such an important role. No ex-colonial spokesman could outshout the Soviet orators in their zeal for the most rapid conferring of sovereignty on each and every non-self-governing territory outside the Soviet empire. Since United States policy was genuinely though moderately in favor of decolonialization wherever conditions seemed somewhat propitious, the United Nations was more effective in this than in many of its other efforts, and the Soviet claim to primary credit for this massive movement to statehood has received more widespread credence than it actually deserves.

In its efforts to profit by the rapid advance of decolonialization, Soviet policy had many assets. Its reputation for anti-imperialism was of long standing, and it had no overseas colonies to let go; the story of the spread of Russian and, later, of Soviet power over non-Russian peoples was ancient history and therefore of no interest to the new nations for whom history seemed to begin between 1945 and 1960. For each new postcolonial regime, it has been almost a point of pride to establish relations with the Soviet Union and to secure either a substantial or a token grant of Soviet credits. A new nation often feels truly unaligned only when it enlists economic support from both East and West.

Exaggerating both the condition of Russia before 1917 as an "underdeveloped" country and its remarkable economic achievements since then, the Kremlin has offered the Soviet model of development as an alternative, indeed, a highly desirable alternative, to the more moderate precepts offered by the industrial countries of the West. Above all, having no responsibility and no interest in assuring a peaceful and orderly transition to independence, the Soviet spokesmen have been free to capitalize on the exaggerated expectations of the new postcolonial leaderships and on their impatience. The surprising thing is that with all these advantages the Soviet Union has so far failed to win any completely reliable clients among the many new states.

REACTIONS TO SETBACK

The competition, foreshadowed by Stalin, for the political allegiance of the newly independent countries came to a head in the Congo (Leopoldville) crisis of 1960 and the following years. When a quick moving and substantial Soviet effort to gain a leading position in Patrice Lumumba's Congo was frustrated by internal Congolese politics and then by the United Nations peacekeeping operations, Nikita Khrushchev's fury knew no bounds. Perhaps the Soviet reaction to this setback would have been somewhat less violent if Premier Khrushchev had been sheltered by the Kremlin walls rather than exposed, as he was in New York, to the blasts of the worldwide communications networks.

Soviet resentment over the interposition of resources and trained manpower, which were assembled and directed by the Secretary-General acting under resolutions of the Security Council, brought to a head the latent quandary of Soviet anti-imperialist policy. Should Soviet policy seek to make immediate political gains, to establish client-regimes of its own in the aftermath of colonial empires? Or should it follow a long and slow path, giving the new nationalisms time, according to Marxist-Leninist predictions, to prove their inadequacy, thus preparing the ground for a later and slower buildup of Communist or pro-Communist forces? The main measure of the disappointment and resentment that Soviet policy makers felt over their failure to make concrete political conquests in the process of decolonization is the fierceness with which they reacted to their failure in the Congo.

This reaction has taken two main directions. The first was Mr. Khrushchev's demand for the tripartite division of the office and responsibilities of the Secretary-General by assigning an equal voice to each of the "three camps" of Soviet political mythology: the industrial countries of the West, the "socialist" bloc, and the developing countries. Underestimating the political acumen of the leaders of the "new" states, as Soviet spokesmen so often do, Premier Khrushchev made a strong play to form, on this issue, a united front of the newly developing and Communist Bloc countries. When he failed to secure sufficient support among the former, Mr. Khrushchev tacitly dropped his campaign to take direct revenge on the United Nations for its role in the Congo.

A quieter but more effective counteraction has been the Soviet refusal, backed for different reasons by France and several other Member States, to refuse to pay any part of the peacekeeping budget of the United Nations. At the nineteenth session of the General Assembly, the financial veto reduced the United Nations to a state of suspended animation. In an effort to persuade the Soviet Union to pay some part of the accumulated arrears, the United States negotiated with it over possible terms for restoring the decisive role of the Security Council. Alternatively, it was agreed tacitly, as in the Cyprus action, that future support for peacekeeping actions would have to be provided on a voluntary basis by those states that chose to support them. Thus, in one way or the other, the Soviet Union has come close to establishing its own view of the proper limitations on United Nations action as a binding and general rule to govern the scope of that action in the future. The very success of the United Nations in interposing its moral and political prestige in the Palestine, Suez, and Congo conflicts had drawn down on it the wrath of the Kremlin. And the Soviet success in giving effect to that wrath, by weakening the capacity of the United Nations to act, increases the chances that a conflict arising anywhere in the world may lead to a bipolar confrontation, with its immeasurable risks for world peace.

The Dilemmas of Coexistence

The adamant refusal by the Soviet Union to accept the extension of the responsibilities assumed by the General Assembly and the Secretary-General runs counter to another theme of Soviet policy, that of "peaceful coexistence" which it correctly presents as the only reasonable policy in the nuclear age. The most serious and least manageable danger to peace arises from the crucial role of nuclear power. Despite the development of smaller nuclear capabilities (by the United Kingdom, France, and Communist China), only the United States and the Soviet Union possess awesome forces of almost instantaneous destruction, forces so tremendous that their use can annihilate the lives and the future of hundreds of millions of people. Indeed, either one can render the northern hemisphere practically uninhabitable. In this unstable and unprecedented situation, it is true, the two strongest powers have shown a considerable but not completely trustworthy sense of responsibility; nevertheless, the factors supporting the continuation of peace, or at least of nondestruction, remain perilously fragile.

In this situation the vitality of the United Nations is a matter of extreme importance to all nations, not least to the two great nuclear powers. The United Nations, at the least, offers a continuing center of contact and exchange of views. In an age of push-button reaction to threats, which may be misunderstood as easily as they may be correctly interpreted, it is even more important than it was in the prenuclear age that the two greatest powers remain in continuous contact in order to measure each other's intentions quickly and reliably. Reportedly, the "hot line" between Washington and Moscow has never been used for such exchanges; the setting of the United Nations, together with the embassies in Washington and Moscow, provides an always open channel of communication.

In a broader sense, the operations of the United Nations offer the principal channel by which all the other nations can make their views heard and may make their contributions to preserving peace. Virtue and wisdom are not synonymous with the possession of nuclear power, and all nations have, or should have, an opportunity both to assert their interest in their own survival and to present their ideas and offer their services for that purpose. Any weakening of the peacekeeping functions of the United Nations restricts the possible role and reduces the prospects of survival for all nations. Any such process curtails the options available for political wisdom and ingenuity, and constricts the prospects of prolonged "coexistence."

The policies of both great nuclear powers have displayed a continuing friction between their asserted will to "coexist" without nuclear war and their attitudes toward the peacekeeping function of the United Nations. Yet, because the clash is sharper between the theoretical devotion of the Soviet government to "coexistence" and its hostility, in practice, to granting any positive role to the United Nations, the conflict appears more clearly within its policy than in United States policy. If the Soviet government wishes genuinely to strengthen the prospects for "coexistence" or "cosurvival," it should logically be seeking ways to reinforce the usefulness of the United Nations, even in cases where it disagrees with its specific programs and actions.

In practice, however, "coexistence" as a concept and a policy has had a checkered history in Soviet thinking. Its content, while varying a great deal over time, also shows certain constants. One of those constants is the assertion that "coexistence" does not mean the preservation of the status quo. The final stage of coexistence, the Kremlin insists, must be the worldwide triumph of Communism and, with that, the disappearance of all other social and political systems. Furthermore, this triumph cannot be assured by waiting for the automatic processes of "history" to run their course. It must be promoted actively by Communist parties, both by those that exercise political and strategic power and by those that are seeking to come to power.

Within this basically dynamic, rather than static, Soviet concept of coexistence, however, some significant variations in emphasis can be traced. By 1955, for example, at the summit conference in Geneva, coexistence implied to the Soviet leaders a tacit agreement on the part of the West to respect the status quo in Central Europe, while leaving the Soviets free to seek new influence and, if possible, preponderant influence in Egypt and perhaps in the Middle East as a whole. After November 1958 "coexistence" was redefined to justify the Soviet demand for the surrender, at once or by stages, of the Western enclave of West Berlin. After 1960 the term was again redefined to justify the establishment of a political and strategic protectorate over Fidel Castro's Cuba. And, in the Soviet view, it was fully compatible with its attempt in 1962 to move from a defensive to an offensive position in Cuba with the installation of medium-range missiles.

The great difficulty which arises for the rest of the world from the Soviet use, or misuse, of the notion of "coexistence" is that it has no stable policy content. It means at any one time whatever the Soviet leadership says it means. This varying content of the term is reflected in Soviet policy in the United Nations. At any given time it seems concerned to place the maximum of constraints on the freedom of action of other powers, while avoiding or averting any United Nations actions that might place restrictions on its own freedom of maneuver. In this, Soviet policy is certainly not alone. But what is remarkable is the very clear gap between its professed support for "coexistence" and its hostility to the one almost worldwide body that can, potentially, do most to assure a more stable coexistence in fact.

Soviet thinking about the content of "coexistence" has, in some respects, been undergoing a slow evolution. For one thing, it is much less optimistic today than it was in 1957 about the immediate political value of its great nuclear-missile power. Between the displaying of its intercontinental missiles in September 1957 and the Cuban missile crisis in October 1962, the Soviet leaders seemed confident that their possession of a powerful nuclear deterrent had actually neutralized the United States system of power and that the way was now open to achieve a rapid and decisive expansion of Soviet power and influence. Like the United States, but with some lag, the Soviet policy makers have gradually discovered that this new form of power has serious limitations. It is too destructive to be used for any purpose except to deter a direct threat to national survival. Its possession by one, two, or more powers does not lead other nations to abandon their own values and purposes. Other states continue to act as if that power could never be used, and thus they frustrate many of the purposes of the nuclear powers. The acquisition of this understanding by the Soviet leadership has been a painful one, for it implies, logically, the subordination of ideological goals to the avoidance of nuclear holocaust. As the Soviet government has tried to make clear to its rivals in Peking, "One cannot build Communism among radioactive ruins."

If it is necessary in the interests of survival to hold great-power conflicts short of the use of nuclear power, then other forms of conflict must also be subjected to stringent review. Is it possible for "wars of national liberation" to be aided by outside forces without bringing on a confrontation, and eventually a nuclear confrontation, between the two greatest powers? After asserting, as it still does today, its support for "wars of national liberation," defined in its own terms, the Kremlin has increasingly pointed out the dangers that can arise from the involvement of one or both major powers in such conflicts. Naturally, it applies this warning to the United States' involvement in Vietnam, but it also turns it implicitly into a warning to Communist China against the worldwide risks that can arise from its own possible intervention in this conflict.

THE SINO-SOVIET CONFLICT

The changing Soviet definition of the content of "coexistence" is both a cause and a consequence of its estrangement from Communist China. In 1957 Mao Tse-tung shared Nikita Khrushchev's exhilaration over the Soviet acquisition of a long-range, nuclear-missile deterrent. Like Premier Khrushchev, he foresaw many new political and territorial gains arising from this major shift in the balance of world power. Whether naïvely or not, Mao Tse-tung assumed that the Soviet deterrent would be made available to Communist China to help it in the pursuit of its own ambitions of hegemony. The split between Moscow and Peking can properly be dated from the Quemoy-Matsu crisis of 1958 when Mao discovered that Soviet strategic backing had definite and restrictive strings attached to it.

One of Peking's major accusations against what Mao calls the "modern revisionists" in the Kremlin is that they are more concerned with seeking their own survival, and for that purpose in working out compromises with the "imperialists," than they are with fulfilling their revolutionary duty of promoting the spread of Communism. Thus, in a truly remarkable development of the revolutionary dialectic, Moscow finds itself attacked with great political violence from its own "Left" at a time when its own strong but more calculating urge to expand has been contained with both success and caution by those whom it regards as "imperialist warmongers." In this paradoxical dilemma, Soviet policy makers should logically give more thought and perhaps more support to the role of the United Nations in order to strengthen their own position in this precarious equilibrium. Whether they will at some stage do so is another question. To that question of questions, their rigid ideology gives one answer, while their political interests, which are now affected by events and risks that may arise anywhere in the world, give quite another.

The Chinese Communist challenge to the Soviet role in world politics is a sweeping one. Peking denounces the Soviet leadership for allegedly placing the economic development and modest prosperity of its own country ahead of its "internationalist" duty. It raises the specter of racialist hatred against the Soviet policy makers and tries artificially to conjure up a racial solidarity between itself and all nonwhite peoples. It asserts that the poor and developing countries are on the verge of sweeping upheavals that will bring "true Marxist-Leninist" forces into power and will sweep both "imperialists" and "revisionists" into the "dustbin of history." In contrast, Moscow has repeatedly placed its political and economic support behind nationalist and reformist leaderships in the developing countries. It has encouraged them to assert their independence of the Western powers rather than to rush into adventures that might disrupt their progress toward a genuine freedom of action. And it has emphasized on numerous occasions that the revolutionary will to power is not enough and that the "new" countries must develop their economic, social, and political strength before they can begin to build "socialism."

Advantages in Strengthening the United Nations

In this new and unforeseen competition on two fronts, Soviet policy should logically discover many advantages in strengthening the United Nations. The internationally managed and supported development programs of the United Nations offer valuable advice and modest assistance to a great many of the developing nations. They are greatly prized by most of these countries, even though bilateral assistance programs are far more massive. If the Soviet leadership believes that the outcome of the competition between political systems will eventually be decided by their performances in the economic field, it should give much stronger support to that type of international program which is politically most acceptable to the developing countries.

If effective agreements can be achieved on arms control and limitation of armaments either qualitatively or geographically, this will, in the end, require a more active role by the United Nations. It is through that body that the desire of all nations for stronger assurance of survival and the hope of shifting substantial resources from armaments to economic development are most clearly expressed. At present the United Nations is not equipped to take an active role in negotiating or enforcing agreements in the armaments field. Yet those governments that have participated in the eighteen-nation disarmament negotiations in Geneva have gradually come to recognize that mere wishes and slogans are useless without a clear understanding of the technological and strategic factors involved in the control and limitation of armaments. It is conceivable that the nonnuclear Members of the United Nations will at some stage be better equipped than they are now to facilitate the conclusion of workable arms agreements and to inspect their enforcement. If the Soviet Union is genuinely interested in assuring permanent and effective limitations on the use and availability of nuclear and other forces, it is logically in its interest to help the United Nations strengthen its capacity eventually to play an active role in this field.

Finally, the Soviet Union faces a serious choice in the crucial field of peace-keeping. If peace is an overriding necessity for mankind, regardless of the diverse regimes under which its various members live, then the strengthening of the peacekeeping ability of the United Nations is equally necessary for the Great Powers even if that function runs counter to this or that specific interest of one or another of them. It is shortsighted for any of the Great Powers to weaken or dismantle the only machinery so far available that can, as demonstrated in the recent past, interpose the general interest of peace between the particular interests or ambitions of the major contestants.

If coexistence in its more general, non-Communist sense has a permanent place in the Kremlin's hierarchy of values, its policy makers must bring themselves to rethink the place of the United Nations in their overall policy. If they genuinely believe that the world will be reshaped by a prolonged peaceful competition between varying systems, they should conclude that it is in the Soviet Union's long-range interest to protect and strengthen the only international body that, in practice, has demonstrated its ability to interpose the general will for peace between the conflicting purposes of the Great Powers and to express the aspiration of most nations for holding that competition within limits short of war. If they wish to strengthen the ability of the newly independent countries to participate, usefully for themselves and constructively for peace and development, in the shaping of world politics, they should seek to strengthen the United Nations through which the new nations are best able to achieve this goal. If the Soviet leaders genuinely believe in coexistence as a long-range policy, they should give thought to rebuilding the prestige and the ability to act of the only major international instrument of coexistence.

The Commonwealth and the United Nations

GEOFFREY L. GOODWIN

THE British Commonwealth of Nations and the United Nations have today at least one thing in common, namely, that each faces a crisis so serious as to threaten its very survival. Nor are the reasons for the crises so very different. In part they stem from the nature of the two institutions. Both are associations of sovereign states, each one of which views the Commonwealth or United Nations relationship as only one strand—and only rarely the most important strand—in a complex and variegated web of relationships.

On a smaller scale than the United Nations, the Commonwealth also embraces peoples of many races, creeds, and traditions and states of every size, all of which have their own particular ambitions and interests. Like the United Nations, the Commonwealth mirrors both what divides and what unites. Again in the aftermath of empire, both the United Nations and the Commonwealth are finding it difficult to assimilate and accommodate a rapidly expanding membership. In twenty years the membership of the United Nations has grown from 51 to 114; the Commonwealth from the six present at San Francisco to the current 21, all Members of the United Nations. Both are perplexed by the related task of reconciling the perennial facts of power with the new stock of ideas injected by the Asian and African powers. In the United Nations real power still resides primarily with the Great Powers, the permanent members of the Security Council. The Afro-Asian states understandably exhibit their voting power in the Assembly to propagate their ideas on colonialism, racism, or economic aid; yet, however reluctant they may be to acknowledge it, the fact remains that only the Great Powers can effectively translate these ideas into practice.

GEOFFREY L. GOODWIN is Professor of Political Science, The London School of Economics and Political Science.

With the growth in diplomatic resources and status of other Commonwealth members, the United Kingdom has become far less of a shield and a magnet than in the past; but it is still to a significant extent *primus inter pares*. Ideas about the future pattern of relationships may lay chief stress on the parity of all rather than on the primacy of one. But in practice within the Commonwealth it is still chiefly to the United Kingdom that most other members—and particularly the newly independent members—look for assistance and advice. The discrepancy between the power of the few and the ambitions of the many frequently produces a sense of tension in both the United Nations and the Commonwealth. This may occasionally serve as an invigorating irritant, but it is not calculated to ease the path of cooperation. Finally, in that both purport to transcend geographical bounds and regional groupings, both face the risk of being torn apart by the growth of regional ties if such ties come to be seen as excluding rather than supplementing the wider-ranging relationship that they have to offer.

The differences are obvious enough. Unlike the United Nations, the Commonwealth has no written constitution, no complicated institutional structure: "Like Topsy it just grew." And it grew, of course, out of an imperial heritage. The Commonwealth "is not a club but an historical phenomenon. Countries do not join it; they are born into it."[1] Indeed, to some of its critics the Commonweath is little more than a vestigial remnant of empire, able, like the Holy Roman Empire, to evoke loyalty long after the power to command it has vanished but incapable of materially influencing the course of world events —like, some might say, the Cheshire cat whose grin survived his physical disappearance.

The Loosening of Commonwealth Ties

Even if such pessimism be discounted, the loosening or snapping of the ties of empire, a certain draining away of power and influence from the center, and the assertion by the members of the Commonwealth—and not least by the newly independent members—of their full sovereign status makes it virtually impossible not only for the Commonwealth ever to speak with a single voice[2] but also to claim that the relationships between its members are of a very special character, that they are indeed not really "foreign" relations. In the past, common allegiance to the Crown was the basis of a doctrine, expounded, it is true, mainly by the United Kingdom, that

> those relations between countries of the Commonwealth which, if subsisting between any one of them and foreign countries, or between foreign countries,

[1] John Holmes, "The Impact on the Commonwealth of the Emergence of Africa," *International Organization*, Spring 1962 (Vol. 16, No. 2), p. 298.
[2] There are rare exceptions, such as the declarations of the Commonwealth Prime Ministers on Korea in January 1951 or on disarmament in March 1961.

would be regarded as international relations governed by international law, were neither international relations nor governed by international law.[3]

This *inter se* doctrine, that is, the notion that the relationships between the members of the Commonwealth were or ought to be different from ordinary international relationships, was never fully accepted even in the days of the League of Nations. Nevertheless, intra-Commonwealth disputes were then generally treated as if they did not fall into quite the same category as ordinary disputes between sovereign states. The doctrine has not entirely lapsed. Certain Commonwealth countries (the United Kingdom, Australia, Canada, and New Zealand) have accepted the optional clause (Article 36 [2]) of the Statute of the International Court of Justice with a reservation, *inter alia,* of

> disputes with the Government of any other country which is a Member of the British Commonwealth of Nations, all of which disputes shall be settled in such manner as the Parties have agreed or shall agree.[4]

Until 1961 the United Kingdom voted against resolutions calling upon South Africa to revise its *apartheid* policies partly on the grounds that United Kingdom policy was "not to intervene in the internal administrative problems of members of the Commonwealth."[5] In 1964 the decision to retain, for the time being, the separate identity of the Commonwealth Relations Office was defended on the grounds that it would be "quite wrong to treat [Commonwealth] countries as if they were not in a special position, to treat them in the same way as foreign countries."[6] Yet there can be little doubt that this *inter se* doctrine is now chiefly of historical interest and that in this respect as in many others the last twenty years have seen the steady assimilation of the relations of Commonwealth members *inter se* to those of international politics generally. One result is that intra-Commonwealth disputes are no longer amenable to Commonwealth mediation. Indeed, in order to preserve as much cohesion and intimacy as possible, members usually sedulously avoid touching upon such disputes in Commonwealth meetings. Instead, they are referred to the United Nations where the embarrassment of having to take sides may be less acute.

This assimilation of Commonwealth relations to ordinary international relations might seem to reduce the already rather intangible ties of the Commonwealth to invisible gossamer. Not surprisingly, it has made it increasingly difficult for other countries to accord to the Commonwealth the kind of recognition that more specifically regional groupings (e.g., Latin America,

---

[3] James E. S. Fawcett, *The British Commonwealth in International Law* (Stevens Library of World Affairs, No. 61) (London: Stevens & Sons Limited, 1963), p. 144.

[4] International Court of Justice, *Yearbook 1958–1959* (Leyden: A. W. Sythoff, 1959), p. 226.

[5] James E. S. Fawcett, "The Commonwealth in the United Nations," *Journal of Commonwealth Political Studies,* May 1962 (Vol. 1, No. 2), p. 127.

[6] United Kingdom, *Parliamentary Debates* (Lords), April 7, 1964 (Vol. 257, No. 47), col. 116.

Africa, and Western and Eastern Europe) can command. This is well illustrated by the fate of the "Commonwealth" seat on the Security Council. In 1944 the United Kingdom was unsuccessful in pressing for some kind of semipermanent representation on the Security Council for "middle powers" (a category which it was assumed would include more than one Commonwealth country). But it did insist, successfully, that the nonpermanent membership of the Council should be set at six to allow for a seat for a Commonwealth country. The existence of this "Commonwealth" seat was confirmed in the so-called "gentleman's agreement" of 1946 on the allocation of the nonpermanent seats on the Security Council. Recognition of the Commonwealth claim was both a tribute to the contribution of Commonwealth countries to the United Nations victory in World War II and a reflection of the fact that many Commonwealth members did not fit into the specifically regional groups to which the other nonpermanent seats were then allotted. Formal recognition of the Commonwealth was reaffirmed as late as 1957 when the General Assembly provided for Commonwealth (in addition to United Kingdom) representation on its General Committee.

In the expansion of the Council to fifteen seats as was recommended by the Assembly in 1963 to allow more equitable representation for the growing Afro-Asian membership, ten nonpermanent members would be elected on the following basis: five from African and Asian states, two from Latin American states, one from Eastern European states, and two from Western European and "other states." As soon as the permanent members have ratified the consequential amendments to the Charter (as required under Article 108) the Commonwealth seat as such will disappear. All that will remain will be the oblique reference to the Commonwealth in the euphemism "other states" to which, with Western Europe, two of the nonpermanent seats are allotted. Its disappearance, together with the disappearance in 1963 of any reference to the Commonwealth as a group with a right to be represented in the Assembly's General Committee, will mark both the general belief that the Commonwealth is no longer a sufficiently coherent grouping to continue to merit special recognition and the prior attachment of many Commonwealth members to their own particular regional grouping. This is not to say that Commonwealth countries will not continue to be well represented on the various organs and committees of the United Nations, but, in the future, geographical location rather than the Commonwealth connection will almost certainly be the determining factor.

THE COMMONWEALTH NEXUS

Nevertheless, the passing of the *inter se* doctrine and the disappearance of the Commonwealth seat on the Security Council and the General Committee

of the Assembly have not been matched by a complete atrophy of the rather
special relations between Commonwealth members at the United Nations. It
is true that the Commonwealth does not form a group or caucus in quite the
same way as do, for instance, the African or Latin American states; and it is
only very exceptionally that there emerges a "Commonwealth line" on an
issue before the United Nations. But the Commonwealth nexus at the United
Nations is still of real significance. The mere fact that all members of the
Commonwealth are permanently represented at the United Nations enables
a great deal of business, and not only United Nations business, to be trans-
acted there. The importance of this representation is particularly marked for
the smaller, newly independent members which lack the resources for representation on any scale and whose contacts with other countries—even with
other Commonwealth countries—can often best be made at the United Nations.

Moreover, although by 1964 the regular meetings of the Commonwealth
high commissioners in London with the Secretary of State for Commonwealth
Relations had ceased as had the regular meetings of Commonwealth ambassadors in Washington, Commonwealth delegates to the United Nations continue to meet fairly regularly, often biweekly during sessions of the General
Assembly and less frequently between sessions. Meetings are usually limited
to a small number of delegates from each member. At one time the United
Kingdom representative was normally in the chair. Since 1963, however, the
chairmanship each month rotates alphabetically though a member of the
United Kingdom delegation (usually the senior Commonwealth Relations
Office representative) still acts as secretary. All those present can converse
fluently in English and to an appreciable extent they still share a more empirical and pragmatic mode of thought than is the norm among United Nations Members. This makes for a degree of intimacy and frankness in the
discussion which is said to be lacking in the meetings of most other groups,
especially the Afro-Asian group. The intention of the discussions is not, of
course, to arrive at a consensus. The Commonwealth, consisting as it does of
colonial and anticolonialist powers, of economic "haves" and economic "have-
nots," of alliance-committed and nonaligned countries, would only very exceptionally find it possible to do so. Nor do the meetings any longer serve as an
occasion for reaching agreement on candidates for Commonwealth representation in the various organs and committees of the United Nations.

Nevertheless, participation in the meetings is of particular value to newly
independent members of the Commonwealth who, in this smaller, informal
setting, can learn more easily about how United Nations affairs are conducted
and, indeed, about the peculiarities and idiosyncrasies of their fellow members.
In public, some Commonwealth delegates will seem preoccupied with asserting their recently acquired national identity and with appearing no less vocif-

erous than their African and Asian colleagues in criticizing their former colonial masters,

> a position that may make the Commonwealth not only appear to be more di-
> vided than it really is, but which may also lead it to become just a shade more
> divided than it was before.[7]

In private, however (and especially since the departure of South Africa), most
Commonwealth members appear ready to discuss their differences in a more
friendly and less suspicious spirit.

Moreover, the formal meetings are probably less important in maintaining
the significance of the Commonwealth nexus at the United Nations than the
constant informal discussions between members of Commonwealth delegations. These contacts, at every level and both between and during formal meetings, are especially valuable when less politically charged issues are under debate and delegates' instructions (if they exist at all) leave them greater latitude
for negotiation. At all levels the belief that relations between Commonwealth
representatives should be particularly easy and informal persists. It is sustained
by the frequent personal friendships between delegation members, many of
whom have either attended a Commonwealth (usually a British or British-
type) university or have been attached to a Commonwealth post or delegation
for diplomatic training. These friendships are carefully nurtured by the older
Commonwealth members. Occasionally they may strike an onlooker as a trifle
brittle and artificial. But it is by no means unusual to find a genuine mutual
regard which helps to ease the more formal diplomatic exchanges.

It is difficult to assess the precise significance of these Commonwealth ties
at the United Nations. Clearly, cooperation and consultation are closer between the older members than within the Commonwealth as a whole. In this
respect there is, in a real sense, an "inner" and an "outer" circle of membership. Moreover, although colonial issues are raised, sometimes on British initiative, at other times by other Commonwealth members, there is a strong
disinclination to discuss intra-Commonwealth disputes (e.g., Kashmir) or to
raise other issues (e.g., economic sanctions against South Africa) on which
members of the Commonwealth are known to be deeply divided. Intemperate
and heated exchanges are thereby avoided, but at the cost of depriving the
meetings of much of their significance, particularly in the eyes of those African Commonwealth countries who may have valued the occasion chiefly as
an opportunity to bring pressure to bear on the senior members.

Given the great diversity of interests represented and the fact that for most
members the Commonwealth connection is not the most central, it is to be
expected that the Commonwealth meetings will normally be concerned more

---

[7] See Thomas B. Millar, "The Commonwealth and the United Nations," *International Organization*,
Autumn 1962 (Vol. 16, No. 4), p. 743.

with the tactics of presentation than with the substance of individual policies. Nevertheless, this distinction should not be pressed too far. The Asian and African members of the Commonwealth have probably come (after the brief postindependence honeymoon period is over) to attach less importance to the meetings than does the United Kingdom, which sees in them a means of enhancing its diplomatic influence at the United Nations. They appear to view these meetings benevolently, chiefly as a public affirmation of a relationship which they still wish to preserve but which they generally regard as of rather lower priority than their relationship within the African or Asian groupings. Yet the very diversity of Commonwealth membership can be a source of strength. Commonwealth links cut across regional groupings, racial antipathies, and economic divisions. As a result, Commonwealth meetings mirror fairly accurately (the Soviet orbit apart) the multifarious forces and pressures at work within the United Nations. Conversely, there is often an "indirect radiation of Commonwealth thinking ('influence' would perhaps be too strong a word) throughout the United Nations."[8]

In short, the Commonwealth

> association is not a vote changer, it is a harmoniser. It breeds understanding and respect amid disagreement. It helps blur the lines and blunt the edges of difference between the blocs.[9]

This is no small service and it may not be too optimistic to forecast that the larger the membership of the United Nations itself becomes, the more important will this smaller, more intimate representative cross section of powers become.

THE UNITED NATIONS' IMPACT ON THE COMMONWEALTH

In turning to the actual content of the policies of Commonwealth members at the United Nations, two closely interrelated questions arise. The first is whether the United Nations itself has had a marked impact upon Commonwealth relationships, either by easing tensions or by exacerbating strains. The second is whether the members of the Commonwealth, by virtue of their shared traditions, experiences, and relationships, have been able to make a special contribution to the functioning of the United Nations.

The United Nations' impact on Commonwealth relationships has varied greatly. It has on several occasions served individual members of the Commonwealth well by providing a repository for their unresolved problems. The United Kingdom has in this respect been the main beneficiary. In the case of Palestine, the United Nations served as a convenient depository for a problem which had defeated all British efforts for a settlement. In Cyprus, the United Kingdom has more recently been able to invoke United Nations help in assist-

---

[8] *The Spectator*, May 15, 1964.
[9] Millar, *International Organization*, Vol. 16, No. 4, p. 745.

ing the Cypriot government to contain communal strife which might have sparked external intervention. The United Nations eased the United Kingdom's withdrawal from the folly of Suez in November 1956 and from Jordan in 1958. By thus helping to "pick British chestnuts out of the fire," the United Nations has made a not insignificant contribution to the survival of the Commonwealth itself. More directly, it has provided the natural respository for several intra-Commonwealth disputes; and it may well be, as Inis Claude observes, that the friendly atmosphere in most Commonweath gatherings "is largely dependent upon the possibility of diverting gusts of interfilial animosity to the United Nations."[10] Outstanding examples are the disputes between Pakistan and India over Kashmir and over the Indus River waters and the dispute over the status of Indians in South Africa.

It is true that the major reasons for the early cessation of fighting in Kashmir in 1948 were that the chances of a quick decision had passed and that both countries were anxious to avoid an all-out war. Furthermore, the armed forces on both sides were commanded by British generals who were instrumental in securing a cease-fire. Since then, the Kashmir dispute has not only grievously poisoned all India-Pakistan relationships but it has also been a source of such bitter dispute before the Security Council that, as the United Kingdom has found to its cost, to appear to favor one side's case is automatically to provoke sharp criticism from the other. The United Nations has been no more successful than the Commonwealth in reaching toward a solution. But it could be claimed that the presence of the United Nations Military Observer Group along the partition line has helped to ease tension by reducing incidents to a minimum and by preventing those incidents which do still occur from assuming alarming proportions. It is a modest, but not insignificant, contribution to preventing an armed conflict which could be no less disastrous for the Commonwealth than it would be for the whole of southern Asia.

In the case of the Indus River waters dispute, the United Nations, or more properly speaking the International Bank for Reconstruction and Development (IBRD), has played a major part in securing a settlement. The prolonged efforts of Sir Charles Iliff, Vice President of the International Bank, were finally successful with the signature of the agreement in September 1960 which provided for large-scale irrigation works and an allocation of the waters on an agreed basis between the two countries. The agreement is not proving easy to implement, but it has at least eased another serious source of tension between the two countries.

In the dispute about the status of Indians in South Africa, successive South African governments have remained impervious to criticism from the United Nations; in any case this particular dispute has in effect become submerged

[10] Inis L. Claude, Jr., *Swords into Plowshares: The Problems and Progress of International Organization* (2nd ed.; New York: Random House, 1959), p. 122.

in the wider question of the policies of *apartheid* in South Africa. It is here that the United Nations' most direct impact on Commonwealth relations is to be found. The criticism expressed at the United Nations of the South African government's racial policies was a major factor in terminating South Africa's membership in the Commonwealth. At first, most of the older members of the Commonwealth shared the position of the United Kingdom government both that Commonwealth countries should not interfere in each other's internal affairs and that since these racial policies fell essentially within the domestic jurisdiction of the South African government, it was improper for them to be discussed, at least in particular terms, at the United Nations. However, this was a minority voice which could not stem the mounting international indignation against *apartheid*. Condemnation by the United Nations probably rallied wider "white" support in South Africa behind the government, thus militating against any modification of the policies. But the United Nations' concern effectively internationalized the issue and made it impossible for Commonwealth leaders to ignore it when they met.

By 1960 it was clear that the African and Asian members or potential members of the Commonwealth were determined to secure either a reversal of the policies of *apartheid* or the exclusion of South Africa from the Commonwealth; failure to achieve one or the other of these objectives would place their membership in the Commonwealth in jeopardy. Matters came to a head in the meeting of the Prime Ministers of the Commonwealth in March 1961 when the issue arose in the context of an inquiry from Dr. Hendrik Verwoerd whether South Africa on becoming a Republic would be accepted as a member of the Commonwealth. It was at this Commonwealth Prime Ministers' conference that the principle was enunciated by Canadian Prime Minister John Diefenbaker, though naturally with the strong support of the Asian and African Prime Ministers, that a multiracial Commonwealth must be based on the principle of racial nondiscrimination.[11] The South African government's policies were clearly inconsistent with this basic principle.

On becoming a Republic, South Africa ceased to be a member of the Commonwealth. Subsequently, the United Kingdom reversed its position that racial policies in South Africa were matters essentially within that country's domestic jurisdiction and it supported resolutions condemning policies of *apartheid*. But the United Kingdom has deprecated attempts to treat the South African government as an international pariah to be cut off from all contact with the international community, whether by expulsion from the United Nations or through economic and diplomatic sanctions. The rising clamor from the Afro-Asian states (including those of the Commonwealth) for such sanctions (which only the United Kingdom and the United States are in a

---

[11] See Peter Harnelly, "Canada, South Africa, and the Commonwealth 1960–61," *Journal of Commonwealth Political Studies*, November 1963 (Vol. 2, No. 1), p. 39.

position to make effective) and the possibility that, if the International Court of Justice were to decide against South Africa on the issue of the exercise of its mandate over South West Africa, such a decision might be seized upon as providing legitimate grounds for United Nations intervention in South West Africa suggest that the United Nations may soon stir up some very troubled waters which the Commonwealth in its present form may find the utmost difficulty in navigating successfully.

A further source of strain on the Commonwealth nexus at the United Nations is Afro-Asian pressure to remove the last vestiges of colonialism in Portuguese Africa and, more particularly, to secure recognition of the rights of the black African majority in Southern Rhodesia. The often bitter anti-colonial pressure in the General Assembly, in which India and Ghana have often taken the lead, has already given rise to acute resentment in the United Kingdom and has forced the United Kingdom frequently to take its stand at the United Nations with its Western European neighbors rather than with its Commonwealth colleagues. Criticism about the timing or manner of the granting of independence is to be expected, and, in general, differences have been marginal and specific rather than general and fundamental. United Nations pressure, by accelerating the pace of decolonization, may also prove in the long run to have contributed to a more viable Commonwealth relationship. But some of the criticisms appear to have been based on an almost pathological suspicion of British motives or to have been designed primarily to curry favor with the more irresponsible elements at home and in Africa and Asia generally. Irritation in the United Kingdom at this torrent of criticism is itself often a trifle querulous and it usually ignores the marked forbearance shown by Asian Commonwealth colleagues in regard to British policies in the 1950's in Malaya, Kenya, and Cyprus. But the activities of several Commonwealth countries in the anticolonial outcry at the United Nations have been one of the sources of disillusion—and not only in the United Kingdom—with the Commonwealth.[12]

United Nations pressure, because of the support it elicited from several Commonwealth countries, was a significant factor, however, in persuading the United Kingdom to accept the dissolution of the Central African Federation in 1963 and to accord independence in 1964 to both Nyasaland (Malawi) and Northern Rhodesia (Zambia), while withholding it from a Southern Rhodesia dominated by a white minority regime. United Kingdom governments (whether Conservative or Labor) may deny United Nations competence in these matters but they have often shown an odd habit of subsequently keeping pretty close to United Nations recommendations. In a real sense, when British Prime Minister Harold Wilson on October 27, 1964, cautioned the

---

[12] A disillusion which was deepened by the Indian use of force in Goa and by the withering away of parliamentary democratic forms of government in several Commonwealth countries.

Southern Rhodesian government against any unilateral declaration of independence and stated that the United Kingdom had "a solemn duty to be satisfied that, before granting independence, it would be acceptable to the people of the country as a whole," his warning was both a response to this pressure and a clear recognition that the Labor Government—like its predecessor—considers it more important to retain the goodwill of other members of the Commonwealth than to take the easy way out by acceding to Southern Rhodesian pressure. Yet to deny Southern Rhodesia immediate independence is one thing; to secure recognition of the rights of a disunited and ineptly led black African majority is another.

United Nations pressure has already exacerbated the situation in Southern Rhodesia through contributing to the overthrow of the more moderate government of Sir Edgar Whitehead (by rallying support behind Rhodesian Front leaders intent on maintaining white supremacy). United Nations admonitions and exhortations which imply either that the United Kingdom can, if it but showed sufficient determination, still control political developments in Southern Rhodesia or that it should, if necessary, be prepared to use force to do so portray an abysmal misunderstanding of the present situation and are almost bound, if persisted in, to give rise to much mutual irritation among Commonwealth members. Nor should it be forgotten that their very vulnerability to the repercussions of overhasty action may make Southern Rhodesia's African Commonwealth neighbors little less critical than the United Kingdom of some of their more hotheaded colleagues. But in these matters, common sense seems at a discount and United Nations pressure again threatens to build up a storm center for the Commonwealth.

A possible reply to the first question, therefore, is that the United Nations has been of assistance both to the Commonwealth as a whole, by assuming responsibility for various intra-Commonwealth disputes, and to individual members of the Commonwealth, by enabling them either to unload unwanted responsibilities onto the United Nations or to muster, as in the case of Malaysia's confrontation with Indonesia, wider diplomatic support through the United Nations. But against this must be set the possibility that United Nations polemics have helped to fan race hatred, to slam the door on all hopes of "partnership" in Southern Rhodesia, and to consolidate Dr. Verwoerd's power in South Africa. If this be so, the baneful consequences for a multiracial Commonwealth are obvious enough.

THE COMMONWEALTH'S CONTRIBUTION TO THE UNITED NATIONS

That the Commonwealth itself has been responsible for the addition of some peculiarly difficult problems among the many with which the United Nations has been faced can hardly be denied. To offset this, can it be claimed that the

Commonwealth, as a result of the special bonds between its members, has been able to make a special contribution to the work of the United Nations? Three aspects will be considered here. The first is the mediatory role of Commonwealth members; the second is their contribution to United Nations security and peacekeeping operations; and the third (which can only very lightly be touched upon) is their contribution to the efforts of the United Nations and its specialized agencies to narrow the gap between the economic "haves" and "have-nots."

The Commonwealth by its very composition and its range of affiliations is particularly well equipped to strengthen the United Nations' potentialities as a center for mediation and conciliation. The older Commonwealth members have generally shared the United Kingdom's stress on the Organization as a "center for harmonizing the actions of nations." Among the "middle" powers which have played a particularly valuable mediatory role are several Commonwealth countries, for example, Canada, India, and Nigeria, while such individual delegates as Chief S. O. Adebo (Nigeria), Lester Pearson (Canada), V. K. Krishna Menon (India), and Alex Quaison-Sackey (Ghana) testify to the fund of negotiating skill to be found within the Commonwealth circle.

The Commonwealth links proved particularly valuable during the Korean War. Clement Attlee (then the British Prime Minister) in his discussions with President Harry S. Truman in Washington in December 1950 was greatly strengthened by the Commonwealth support he received. Both Western and Asian Commonwealth countries warmly welcomed concurrent Indian initiatives at the United Nations to secure a cessation of hostilities; and the Commonwealth Prime Ministers at their conference in January 1951 were able to agree on a set of principles to serve as a basis for a cease-fire in Korea. At this time India was able to report authoritatively on Chinese attitudes and Canada and the United Kingdom were well placed to make sure Commonwealth views were not disregarded in Washington, despite the distinct coolness with which they were often received. Toward the end of 1952 the Indian delegation at the United Nations was instrumental in devising the formula on the prisoners-of-war issue which led in the following spring to the resumption of the armistice negotiations. And it was India which provided the chairman and the custodian force for the Neutral Nations Repatriation Commission. Throughout proceedings at the United Nations on the Korean issue, the main pressure for the coercion of the aggressor came from the United States, the efforts at conciliation from the Commonwealth. In securing an agreed resolution on the prisoners-of-war issue, the Indian delegation

> played the leading part. But they could not have got [the resolution] through without the wholehearted support of Mr. Eden and of their other Commonwealth partners. From first to last, the intimate daily co-operation of the Commonwealth

delegations was a decisive factor in gathering information, in forming opinion, and in mobilising a majority in the Assembly.[13]

This period saw the high-water mark of Commonwealth collaboration with Commonwealth statesmen, such as Anthony Eden (United Kingdom), Lester Pearson (Canada), Sir Percy Spender (Australia), Mrs. Vijaya Lakshmi Pandit (India), and V. K. Krishna Menon (India), working closely and successfully together.

With the growing stature of its Asian members and the widening circle of African membership, these Commonwealth ties have become of diminishing significance. But the Congo crisis showed that the Commonwealth nexus can still provide something of a bridge, both in the United Nations and in the world outside, between the different diplomatic groupings in the non-Communist world. Through their Commonwealth contacts individual members may often be in a stronger position to bring that "touch of healing"— to use Jawaharlal Nehru's happy phrase—to the antagonisms of intercontinental relations.

It is, however, in the second category, namely, their contribution to United Nations security and peacekeeping operations, that the Commonwealth countries have made a contribution probably second only to that of the United States. In the Korean War, Australia, Canada, New Zealand, and the United Kingdom contributed ground forces to form the First Commonwealth Division.[14] The same countries, together with South Africa, sent air and sea units; and India sent a field ambulance unit (which was part of the Commonwealth Division).

Lester Pearson's part in securing the formation of the United Nations Emergency Force (UNEF) during the Suez crisis is well-known. Mr. Krishna Menon, whose belated arrival in New York was "one of the fortunate accidents of history,"[15] was less helpful, but he was able to relieve President Gamal Abdel Nasser (United Arab Republic) of some of his suspicions regarding Canada's contributions to UNEF. Of the eight members of the Commonwealth, only two (Australia and South Africa) made no offer of men and material to the Force; a Canadian, Major General E. L. M. Burns, was appointed UNEF's Commander; Canada and India (despite viewing the project of resorting to an international police force with the greatest suspicion) provided the two largest components of the Force; and four of the seven members of the Advisory Committee on UNEF were from the Commonwealth.[16]

[13] Philip Noel Baker, "Korea, the Commonwealth and World Peace," *New Commonwealth*, August 31, 1953 (Vol. 26, No. 5), p. 217.

[14] C. N. Barclay, *The First Commonwealth Division: The Story of British Commonwealth Land Forces in Korea* (London: Gale and Polden, 1954).

[15] John Holmes, "The United Nations in the Congo," *International Journal* (Toronto), Winter 1960–1961 (Vol. 16, No. 1), p, 14.

[16] See James Eayrs (ed.), *The Commonwealth and Suez: A Documentary Survey* (London: Oxford University Press, 1964), p. 287.

The Commonwealth's role in the UN Operation in the Congo (ONUC) was less dramatic, but Canada again contributed invaluable (bilingual) signal units. The Indian Gurkha Brigade payed a vital role in Katanga. Ceylon, Ghana, Malaya, Nigeria, and the Sudan also at one time or another contributed contingents. The police forces from Ghana, and later Nigeria, were instrumental in restoring a semblance of order in Leopoldville itself. And many prominent citizens of Commonwealth countries served as military and political servants of the United Nations, for example, Rajeshwar Dayal (India), Robert K. A. Gardiner (Ghana), C. V. Narasimhan (India), Brigadier General I. J. Rikhye (India), George Ivan Smith (Australia), and Brian E. Urquhart (United Kingdom), to mention only a few.

This is not to underrate the contribution of many other countries, especially the United States, in logistic and financial support. Nor is it meant to play down the often sharp differences that arose between the Commonwealth countries, particularly between the United Kingdom and Ghana, over the actual conduct of United Nations policies. Nevertheless, the United Kingdom's acute misgivings over the propriety of using force to end the secession of Katanga did not inhibit it from contributing substantially both money and material to the Congo operation as a whole. Ghana's public attitudes might at times have seemed rather flamboyant and unnecessarily self-assertive, but what was more striking was the moderation of actual Ghanaian policies, whether in urging restraint on the Congo's Prime Minister Patrice Lumumba, in cooperating with the more conservative Tunisia, or in refusing to follow the lead of the other Casablanca powers in withdrawing its contingent. Rival ambitions and conflicts of interest and personality over the Congo at times placed a strain on Commonwealth relations, but not to the extent of jeopardizing much practical day-to-day cooperation both at Headquarters and in the field.

In West Irian, Pakistan provided the 1,000-man military contingent in support of the United Nations Temporary Executive Authority (UNTEA), while the UN Peacekeeping Force in Cyprus (UNFICYP) includes troops from Canada and the United Kingdom, in addition to those from Ireland, Finland, Denmark, Austria, and Sweden. Australia and New Zealand are among the five countries that have sent civilian police. General P. S. Gyani, the Commander of the Force for its first three months, and his successor, General K. S. Thimayya, come from India. The United Kingdom, Cyprus, and Nigeria have made voluntary contributions toward the cost of UNFICYP.

This is an impressive record by any standard, which both confirms the genuine attachment of most Commonwealth countries to the United Nations and the benefits which arise from the persistence of a common language and a more or less common military tradition among the commanders of Commonwealth forces. This positive desire, with the possible exception of Australia and India, to retain and strengthen the United Nations peacekeeping potentiality has been reflected more recently in a number of ways. For instance, the skillful guidance of Mr. Quaison-Sackey as President of the General Assembly and the initiatives of Lord Caradon, the Minister of State at the Foreign Office who now leads the United Kingdom delegation, were instrumental in avoiding a showdown on the issue of the financing of United Nations peacekeeping operations and in securing the Assembly's agreement to the setting up of a committee of 33 which will assist the President of the General Assembly and the Secretary-General in the search for an acceptable solution of *all* the problems of peacekeeping. The Canadian government has been sponsoring informal discussions between those countries that have intimated their willingness in principle to earmark national contingents for United Nations use. And Foreign Secretary Michael Stewart on February 23, 1965, announced the United Kingdom's willingness,

> *subject to our national commitments,* . . . [to] help provide logistic backing for a United Nations force of up to six infantry battalions. This could include, for example, short-range aircraft, engineering and signal troops, and ambulance, ordnance and motor transport units. *If it were desirable,* suitable units of these categories would be ear-marked for use as available.[17]

The Government, he said, "also hope to take a share in providing long-range aircraft for the transport of peace-keeping forces." The commitment (as the added italics show) was subject to a number of conditions, but it was, at least, "a timely gesture of encouragement."[18]

In the economic field, the Commonwealth by its very composition is well placed to help narrow the differences of approach and attitude between the "richer" and "poorer" countries at the United Nations. It is true that the major Commonwealth initiatives have been taken outside the United Nations in, for instance, the initiation of the Colombo Plan in 1950 and the Special Commonwealth African Assistance Plan in 1960. Moreover, in 1962–1963 only about 7 percent of the United Kingdom's aid was channeled through multilateral agencies whereas 40 percent of the bilateral aid went to colonial territories and 43 percent to the independent Commonwealth countries.[19] In terms, therefore, of the United Kingdom's (and most other Commonwealth donor countries') aid effort, the United Nations agencies play an important but only marginal role. Yet, for most of the developing countries in the Commonwealth, the United Nations' role figures little less significantly than the aid programs of the United States and the United Kingdom. That it is one which they would like to see strengthened has been made clear at the meetings of

[17] For the Foreign Secretary's statement, see United Kingdom, *Parliamentary Debates* (Commons), February 23, 1965 (Vol. 707, No. 63), cols. 234–236.
[18] *The Economist,* February 27, 1965 (Vol. 214, No. 6340), p. 875.
[19] See *Aid to Developing Countries* (Cmnd. 2147) (London: Her Majesty's Stationery Office, September 1963), p. 15, for the figures for the geographical distribution of British aid from which these percentages are derived.

Commonwealth trade and finance ministers in the Commonwealth Economic Consultative Council which provide an opportunity for reaching some kind of consensus preparatory to the meetings of the various United Nations agencies, e.g., the International Bank for Reconstruction and Development and the General Agreement on Tariffs and Trade (GATT). At the 1964 meeting a fair consensus is also said to have emerged on the issues to be discussed at the United Nations Conference on Trade and Development (UNCTAD). At the Geneva Conference itself the United Kingdom delegate (Edward Heath) was able to enunciate ten key points for the multilateral reduction of trade barriers which both reflected this consensus and contrasted favorably with the more negative approach of the United States and the insistence on the merits of regional economic groupings of French spokesmen. In the final hectic scramble to achieve some measure of agreement between the industrialized countries and the 77 developing countries, the Commonwealth connections were invaluable.

In the United Nations, Commonwealth delegates played a helpful part in the designation of the 1960's as the United Nations Development Decade.[20] Although the United Kingdom's balance-of-payments position does not at present permit an appreciable increase in its aid effort, the British Labor Government has pledged an increase in its contribution to the combined Expanded Program of Technical Assistance (EPTA) and the Special Fund from £3,500,000 in 1964 to £4,200,000 in 1965 and it has constituted a Ministry of Overseas Development to further the British economic aid effort. This effort is in total overshadowed by the United States' economic assistance and, relative to gross national product (GNP), it does not compare favorably with French aid. But it is on a scale which exceeds that of the whole Soviet orbit and within the United Nations complex it is second only to that of the United States.[21] Moreover, although the claims of the Commonwealth links and the United Nations system may occasionally appear to conflict, generally speaking, the two are seen as complementary and not as competitive (as is generally the French conception of relations between United Nations trade and development activities and those of the six-member European Economic Community [EEC] and its eighteen African associate members).

THE FUTURE?

In 1945–1946 many people in the United Kingdom and elsewhere in the British Commonwealth of Nations looked upon the United Nations as the

20 Although the initiative came from Paul Hoffman and the main backing from President John F. Kennedy.

21 This is not, of course, to overlook the heavy drawings by the United Kingdom on the International Monetary Fund (IMF). For details of aid figures, see *The Flow of Financial Resources to Less-Developed Countries, 1956–1963* (Paris: Organization for Economic Cooperation and Development, 1964).

first tentative step on the road to world government which would in due course absorb the Commonwealth. When the divisions of the Cold War threatened to tear the United Nations asunder, the Commonwealth came to be compared favorably with the United Nations as an example of intergovernmental cooperation which had worked and still worked—even though how and why it worked was for most people something of a puzzle. Gunnar Myrdal was not alone when he wrote in 1956 (just before the Suez crisis) that against a background of a divided world in which so many attempts at cooperative endeavor had proved such a dismal failure:

> The British Commonwealth stands out as a non-geographical grouping of independent nations with a common history, joined together by a considerable social sense of solidarity and in many instances by political allegiance to the symbol of the Crown. In spite of many centrifugal forces, tensions, and internal conflicts it remains a reality which is asymmetric, vague and shifting but nevertheless of considerable practical importance.[22]

Since then, the Commonwealth has continued to serve as a framework for the peaceable demise of the British Empire. That the process has been "accomplished with a minimum of violence and an unprecedented amount of goodwill is cause for the whole world to be gratified."[23] It is now nearing completion, however, and the ties which, though "light as air, are as strong as links of iron"[24] threaten to evaporate into thin air.

The United Kingdom's flirtation with the "Six" in 1961–1962, the British Immigration Act of 1962, the magnetic pull of United States military and economic power, the attractions of regional ties for the Commonwealth's African members, and the probability of heightened tensions at the United Nations between Commonwealth members over the future of South Africa suggest that the Commonwealth will be hard put to survive in its present form as a continuing "concert of convenience." Certainly, it is difficult to discern a capability for future growth comparable to that to be found in the European Communities. Yet, like the United Nations, the Commonwealth has shown remarkable resilience under pressure and a capacity for adaptation to changing circumstances which may yet confound the skeptics. Rather than a mere conglomeration of regional blocs or hegemonic spheres, both stand for a conception of the world as a true "comity of nations" which their peoples can ill afford to discard.

---

[22] Gunnar Myrdal, *An International Economy: Problems and Prospects* (London: Routledge and Kegan Paul, 1956), pp. 7–8.

[23] Holmes, *International Organization*, Vol. 16, No. 2, p. 301.

[24] Edmund Burke, *Speeches and Letters on American Affairs* (London: J. M. Dent [Everyman's Library], 1956), p. 189.

France and the United Nations

J.-B. Duroselle

When French Foreign Minister Aristide Briand proposed in 1929 to establish "a sort of federal bond" between the European members of the League of Nations, these states numbered 27 out of a total membership of 60. Today the United Nations has a membership of 114 states of which 23 are European. Of these 23 states, seven are popular democracies. (The Soviet Union, a special case, is not included in this calculation.) There remain sixteen countries extending in the form of a crescent from Finland to Ireland to France and from Portugal to Turkey which are part of the "free" or "Western world." The conclusion is obvious. The League of Nations was dominated by Europeans who furthermore controlled a large part of the overseas world in the form of colonies, protectorates, and mandates. The United Nations, where the major influence, linked to power, is exerted by the United States and the Soviet Union, is dominated by non-Europeans. This non-European domination—political, psychological, and moral—is the fundamental phenomenon, and it is the subject of this study.

We cannot understand European reactions with regard to the UN unless we take this terse fact into consideration. Europe is no longer the center. Thus, a number of European states—the United Kingdom, the Netherlands, Belgium, Italy, Spain, Portugal, and France—have had to adopt, in more or less long-term phases, a *defensive* attitude which has not failed to influence considerably the reactions of their public opinions and the policies of their governments with regard to the UN.

Among these countries, we will concentrate primarily on France. Aside from the United Kingdom, no other country has experienced so profoundly the transition from a preponderant position to one of being dominated. No other country figured so long as "the accused." And surely nowhere else have the reactions been more bitter or more angry.

J.-B. Duroselle is Professor at the Sorbonne. He directs the Commission Franco-Américaine d'Echanges universitaires.

BACKGROUND

The League of Nations as established in 1919 was not what France desired. Constituted as it was, it never appeared to the French government to be adequate to assure *collective security*. But the League of Nations was a great hope; if it could be strengthened, peace would be assured. Edouard Herriot, Joseph Paul-Boncour, and all those who were ardent defenders of the League —the socialist Albert Thomas in the International Labor Organization (ILO), the syndicalist Léon Jouhaux, the military expert General Réquin, and later Léon Blum himself—all lived with this vain hope. Collective or traditional, security was not assured. Twenty years later France faced defeat, Nazi occupation, and suffering.

The prospect of a new organization gave rise to new hopes. Not recognized *de jure* by the major allies until October 23, 1944, the provisional government of France, it is understandable, was not invited to Dumbarton Oaks. However, in Chapter VI of the Dumbarton Oaks Proposals, where the Security Council is discussed, provision was made for a permanent seat for each of the four Great Powers "and, in due course," for France. Although France at the time was weak, devastated, and able to carry little weight in the alliance, its rights were preserved for the future. Nevertheless, General Charles de Gaulle, who directed the provisional government until January 19, 1946, was not satisfied. He obviously preferred a more traditional form of security; he demanded the dismemberment of Germany. In Moscow on December 10, 1944, the General signed the Treaty of Alliance and Mutual Assistance Between the Governments of France and the Union of Soviet Socialist Republics creating a Franco-Soviet alliance in the old tradition of the Franco-Russian alliance of 1892. He tolerated with difficulty the fact that France was not invited to join the three Great Powers at Yalta.

On February 23, 1945, having agreed to participate in the UN Conference on International Organization at San Francisco, France announced that it would accept the title of "inviting power" but demanded certain modifications of the invitation process. The four signatories of Dumbarton Oaks did not accept these amendments, and on March 6 France retracted its decision to become an inviting power, declaring, however, that it was "firmly attached to the principle of collective security." The amendments prescribed by the French government on March 23 were not vastly significant. However, one of them is interesting. An idea of Léon Bourgeois at the Paris Peace Conference, it concerns an international military force:

> The national contingents of all forces stationed in appropriate security zones, or whose stationing would be permanently prepared, in case of need, should be permanently at the disposal of the Security Council.

Notwithstanding, on March 27 the Consultative Assembly, having heard Foreign Minister Georges Bidault, unanimously voted an agenda in which it would "approve in its entirety the project of Dumbarton Oaks and rely on the government to improve it."

At San Francisco the role of the French delegation was not a brilliant one. We have the impression that France, aware of its weakness, largely left to others the duty of perfecting the Organization while it was satisfied with defending "its rights." France was greatly pleased when French was declared to be one of the working languages. On June 21, based on a British proposal, the formula "the four inviting powers and France" was replaced by the alphabetical enumeration of the five permanent members of the Security Council. If not an "inviting power," France thus was in effect a Sponsoring Government. Considering its weakness, France had reason to be satisfied. Collective security appeared more assured than at the time of the League. Moreover, certain "French ideas," long opposed by the Anglo-Saxons, were taken up again and included in the UN Charter, particularly that of an international general staff. The French as a whole were not dissatisfied, but, in view of their profound disappointment in the League, they preferred to see the United Nations at work before making a judgment. As for General de Gaulle, the UN held a secondary place in his views on foreign policy.

THE BEGINNING, 1945–1950

The trial period that France and the rest of Europe awaited came about during the first five years. For France, with the departure of General de Gaulle and the advent of the Fourth Republic, it was a period of reconstruction to which the Marshall Plan gave a decisive impetus. It was also a period of government instability. However, the same Foreign Minister, Georges Bidault, remained almost constantly in power until July 1948, and his successor, Robert Schuman, held the post of Foreign Minister until December 1952. Both were Christian Democrats.

With the exception of the Socialists, the presidents of the Council of Ministers before the Korean War either did not even take the trouble to mention the UN in their programs or, if they did, it was only hastily and with an obvious lack of interest.

In signing the Franco-Soviet pact of December 10, 1944, General de Gaulle and Georges Bidault had manifestly decided on an "independent" policy, one of balance between the East and the West. However, until the beginning of 1947, despite gathering clouds, one could not yet speak of two "blocs" or of the "Cold War." To play the role of mediator in the developing quarrel appeared to be the inclination of France. Moreover, the Potsdam Conference— to which France was not invited—created a special organism to which France

belonged: the "Council of Foreign Ministers." This had as its purpose the
settlement of problems that had arisen out of the war. The UN was not responsible for peace treaties, and the negotiation of treaties—fruitless for Germany and Austria but relatively successful for the "Axis satellites"—was the
chief business thoughout 1946. The essential problem for France was the
future status of Germany. France desired the dismemberment of Germany.
Not having obtained this, France responded by refusing to adhere to a British
and United States plan to fuse the three Western occupation zones. Preoccupation with the German problem relegated the UN to a secondary role in
French policy.

With the beginning of the Indochinese War in December 1946, France was
forced to abandon its "independent" or "mediator" position which had produced nothing but disillusionment. In May 1947, Communist ministers were
excluded from the government, and during the last meetings of the Council of
Foreign Ministers in Moscow (March–April 1947) and in London (November–December 1947) France drew nearer to the United States and the United
Kingdom. It is scarcely necessary to recall here that the year 1947 saw the
formation of the two "blocs" with the advent of General George C. Marshall
in the United States Department of State, the "Truman Doctrine," and the
creation of the Communist Information Bureau (Cominform).

From 1948 to 1950 all else was dominated by anxiety over possible Soviet
aggression at a time when Western Europe was practically disarmed. "Neutralism" was now out of the question. France abandoned its isolated position
in Germany (London Accord, June 1948), allied itself with its European
neighbors, and with them sought an alliance with the United States. The
North Atlantic Treaty Organization (NATO) was substituted for the United
Nations as an assurance of security. Public opinion was well aware that lack
of confidence in the United Nations was the essential reason for the North
Atlantic Treaty, and it was said in vain that the new Treaty was merely a
regional agreement within the framework of the UN (Article 51). The Security Council veto prevented peacekeeping action against each of the "Great
Powers" and, when a minor state was likely to be a "client" of a Great Power,
even prevented it in cases involving minor powers.

In sum, the French did no more than verify the self-evident, although perhaps with more bitterness than other people of the West because of the hopes
they had nurtured. Edouard Herriot, the same man who in 1924 had proposed the Geneva Protocol, wrote in the preface of René Mayer's *Le pacte de
l'Atlantique, paix ou guerre?*:[1]

> Like so many human beings I believed that the Charter of the United Nations
> would finally bring us collective security. For the time being at least, I have had
> to give up this hope.

[1] For the original text in French, see René Mayer, *Le pacte de l'Atlantique, paix ou guerre?* (Paris:
Editions du Grand Siècle, 1949), pp. xi–xv.

It was all the fault of the Soviet Union which refused to "be a part of universal concord," the same Soviet Union to whose membership in the League Mr. Herriot had contributed.

> I think for my part . . . that a universal organization for security would be preferable to the present NATO organization. Collective security has always been a French proposition, and I upheld it constantly in the League of Nations.

The United States did not belong to that organization, but "this time it is the Americans who have warned us and who have offered us collective defense. . . . No other act does them more honor."

Resignation to a necessity, but to an imperative necessity, was the dominant tone of the ratification debates that took place from July 22 to July 26 in the French National Assembly, where only Communists and some pacifists refused to endorse the Treaty. It was approved by a vote of 395–189. That these sentiments were shared by the other European allies was remarked by René Mayer in his discourse of July 22, 1949.[2]

> We arrive . . . at the end of an illusion. We were compelled to sign this act, . . . as a result of the disappointments we have experienced. . . . It has become almost a banality to recall that the Security Council has been little by little seized with a gradual paralysis, [and] that the organs that the Charter constituted in its service, particularly the international general staff which, with the Security Council, was supposed to prepare to use the international force provided for by the Charter, have been swallowed up in indefinite discussions little by little. . . .

During this period France was present and active in the United Nations but never played a role of primary importance. To enter into the historical detail of this activity would be too involved, but the general aspect must be described. We can distinguish two categories of action, one *positive,* the other, concerning certain aspects of the colonial question, *defensive.*

Among the *positive* actions the first was the proposition made on January 17, 1946, by Georges Bidault, with the support of the Constituent Assembly, to break off diplomatic relations with General Francisco Franco's Spain. At the first Assembly of the United Nations in London at the beginning of 1946 France upheld the Panamanian project to exclude Spain from the United Nations. The executions which had taken place in Spain in February had stirred up violent reactions, and France closed its frontiers and demanded of the United States and the United Kingdom a common action which those countries accepted to undertake on March 5. The result was a common declaration hostile to General Franco. In submitting the Spanish question to the Security Council, France supported Poland. Later, when the Assembly considered the Spanish problem, France supported more stringent measures than the General Assembly was prepared to take.

[2] For the text of the entire discourse in French, see *ibid.*, pp. 97–131.

Among other *positive* actions can be included France's participation in the discussions on Iran, Greece, and disarmament. Between the United States proposals for disarmament with veto-free control and the Soviet thesis of control by the Security Council where the Soviet Union had veto power, the French representatives, Alexandre Parodi, and then Guy de la Tournelle, tried in vain to work out a subtle compromise. As Mr. Parodi remarked on April 1, 1947:[3]

> France recognizes the justice of the British and American theories on universal reduction of armaments. But if one of the powers insists on complete security before going on to the question of disarmament, then disarmament will never be able to come about. France will attempt to maintain an equilibrium between the two theories. World security and world disarmament are on an equal footing.

The *defensive* action of France in the United Nations was prompted generally by the colonial problem. To be sure, since the Brazzaville Conference in 1944, the provisional government had decided to grant equality to colonial peoples on an individual basis. The government also wanted to transform the empire into a French Union with Overseas Territories and Associated States. The repression of the revolts in Algeria (1945) and in Madagascar (1946) demonstrated, however, that the principle of French sovereignty remained intact. Fundamentally, France was seeking a policy of assimilation. The proposed constitution of May 1946, recognizing the colonies' "right of secession," was rejected by referendum and the constitution adopted on October 13, 1946, did not grant this right.

The year 1946 saw the first attack in the UN on French "colonialism." In February of that year, France resisted a Syrian and Lebanese protest against the maintenance of French (and British) troops in the two countries. The French point of view, upheld by E. N. van Kleffens of the Netherlands, was that evacuation should be delayed for several months. A second issue was whether France would place its mandates of Togo and the Camerouns under the trusteeship system. Georges Bidault at first refused but finally yielded because the other mandatory powers, except South Africa, had decided to adopt the system of trusteeship.

Once these decisions were made, France, temporarily safe from attack in the UN (except from the Soviet bloc regarding the Indochinese War which began in December 1946), was occupied primarily with helping other colonial powers and in strengthening its own position. Thus, France consistently upheld the Netherlands in the Indonesian affair and favored an Italian trusteeship for Tripolitania, claiming for itself a trusteeship in Fezzan (Bevin-Sforza Compromise of May 9, 1949). When the Assembly refused to entrust Tripolitania to Italy, France declared itself hostile to the project that would shortly give independence to Libya; in the final vote, France abstained. Regarding

---

[3] *L'Année Politique* (Paris: Editions du Grand Siècle, 1947), p. 107.

Palestine, France voted against the plan favored by the Arab states for a federal Palestine and finally accepted the partition plan of November 29, 1947, vigorously advocating the internationalization of Jerusalem. France, moreover, accepted the UN's decision to entrust to the United States the strategic trusteeship of the former Japanese mandates in the Pacific. Finally, France used the United Nations, whose majority was pro-Western and therefore assured, to force Thailand to return to Laos and Cambodia the provinces annexed in 1940 with the help of the Japanese.

Even if the essential issue was the incapacity of the UN to maintain peace, France nevertheless did participate in the different activities of the Organization and, without playing a primary role, it did achieve some success.

France and the Anticolonial Assaults, 1950–1962

With the beginning of the Korean War, the history of the United Nations entered a new phase. As a result of the absence of the Soviet Union from the Security Council, the UN was able, for the first and perhaps the only time in its history, to undertake collective measures against an aggressor.

France's participation was of necessity modest because of the war in Indochina. The dominant factor of the period, however, was the anticolonial action of the UN against France, engaged as it was in the Indochinese War until 1954 and in the war in Algeria which had begun the same year. The massive arrival of new Members in 1955 resulting from the "package deal" served only to strengthen the anticolonial attitude, and the Suez crisis in 1956 aggravated the situation. From all these events we can only extricate the guiding lines.

France and the Korean War

France voted with the United States during the Security Council meetings of June and July 1950. There was, however, the question of how much aid France could bring to the common effort, and on this point France insisted on the fact that it was conducting the fight against the Communists on another front, and alone. France, nevertheless, sent a battalion of volunteers recruited for this purpose. The essential problem, however, remained that of increasing United States aid in Indochina.

Although the Indochinese conflict predated the opening of the Korean War, there can be no doubt that the latter stimulated the war in Indochina. In his famous statement of June 27 President Harry S. Truman announced:

> I have . . . directed acceleration in the furnishing of military assistance to the forces of France and the Associated States in Indochina and the dispatch of a military mission to provide close working relations with those forces.[4]

[4] Department of State *Bulletin*, July 3, 1950 (Vol. 23, No. 574), p. 5.

The Korean War had another indirect aspect of particular interest to France. It stimulated fear of Communist aggression while tying down substantial United States forces in the Far East. It is not surprising that under these circumstances the United States as early as July launched a proposal for German rearmament. In September, France alone vetoed the admission of West Germany into NATO and in October France proposed instead the Pleven Plan for the creation of a European army that would include West German units. The Pleven Plan, like the Schuman Plan of May 9, 1950 (for a coal and steel community), envisaged a form of supranational European institution. If this point is stressed here, it is because the *European* problem thus presented certainly roused the interest, emotion, and passion of the French people more than the *world* problem did. At this stage the idea of Europe contributed largely to turning the French away from the UN.

Generally speaking, French public opinion was not much in favor of aggravating the war in Korea. For this reason the news of President Truman's recall of General Douglas MacArthur was greeted with relief. Torn as it was by internal quarrels, more and more weary of the war in Indochina, and divided on the issue of a European army (the Treaty of Paris provided for the European Defense Community [EDC]), France lost a great deal of interest in the UN, and this in spite of the fact that the sixth session of the General Assembly was held in Paris at the end of 1951. This attitude is clearly seen in the "declarations of investiture" of the future presidents of the Council of Ministers during this period when nothing was said about the UN.

The First Anticolonial Attacks, 1952–1956

The concerted attacks against French colonial policy began in 1952 in the Assembly of the United Nations. In September of that year a Soviet veto prevented the acceptance by the Security Council of a French proposal to admit to the UN the Associated States of Indochina, Vietnam, Cambodia, and Laos. All other Members voted in favor.

That same year the Arab and Asian countries sought to call an extraordinary session of the UN to consider the Moroccan and Tunisian questions but failed to obtain the necessary support. The Arab nations then announced they would raise these questions in the regular session; they succeeded despite French protests. France declared that it would abstain from the discussions. The French Foreign Minister argued against the competence of the United Nations in such matters by reason of the protectorate relationship, adjuring the UN to avoid "a decision that would be disastrous to the member nations and to peace." An Arab-Asian proposal condemning French policy was countered by a Brazilian proposal expressing the hope that France and Tunisia might continue to negotiate. The first draft resolution[5] was defeated by 24

[5] UN Document A/C.1/736.

in favor, 26 opposed, with 7 abstentions, and the second was approved,[6] 45 votes in favor, 3 opposed, with 10 abstentions. Although this result constituted an "expression of confidence" in the French government, it was not a total success for France.

In 1953 the same scenario unfolded, with the Tunisian and Moroccan questions placed on the agenda. This time the French delegation did not protest but announced again that it would not participate in debates which, according to France, were contrary to the Charter of the United Nations. Instead of approving an Arab-Asian draft resolution[7] demanding independence after five years, the First (Political and Security) Committee adopted somewhat more moderate Latin American proposals.[8] Nevertheless, because of the two-thirds majority required in the Assembly, the proposals were defeated.

Important new developments occurred during 1954. The coming to power of Pierre Mendès-France on June 18 had two noteworthy effects: the conclusion of the armistice in Indochina, and the granting of internal autonomy to Tunisia. Undoubtedly, it was a question of a new state of mind, with the result that the Moroccan and Tunisian questions, proposed as usual by the Afro-Asian group, were placed so low on the agenda that they were not considered. On November 1, however, the Algerian War began, and the French government decided to resist.

The war in Algeria was to become, during eight years, the essential preoccupation of the French government and before long of French public opinion in general. Whereas only the professional army had fought in Indochina, conscripted soldiers were sent to Algeria. The length of military service was extended to 27 months. In an atmosphere of increasing economic prosperity the Algerian affair was a thorn in the side of the country. For the Frenchmen of Algeria—one million out of nine million inhabitants—the issue was a fundamental one, and passions were aroused. Furthermore, the Algerian War obliged France to recall the Sultan of Morocco and grant his country independence, and the same concession was shortly made to Tunisia.

The Afro-Asian group, no longer feeling compelled to introduce the Tunisian and Moroccan questions in the UN, proceeded instead to demand that the Algerian question be placed on the agenda. Although Algeria was legally a part of France, the Afro-Asians had the situation in hand because they could show that the Algerian question was a "colonial question," that France was pursuing a "policy of force," and that this constituted a "menace" to universal peace. Despite the support of France's usual allies and despite the heated protests of French representative Antoine Pinay, in 1955 the Algerian question was placed on the Assembly's agenda at the fifteenth session. The United

---

[6] General Assembly Resolution 611 (VII), December 17, 1952.
[7] UN Document A/C.1/L.60.
[8] UN Document A/C.1/L.61.

States voted against this action, but Greece, allied to France, voted for it. This decision had a considerable effect in France. The French delegation left the hall when the results of the vote were announced. Would France resign from the UN? No. The whole of the French delegation, however, was ordered no longer to participate in the sessions, and France decided to stop supplying the UN with information about its overseas territories.

This violent reaction alarmed many Members of the Organization, particularly those from Latin America. Following a proposal from Colombia, a motion was made (in accordance with Article 21 of the Charter) to retract the decision and remove the Algerian affair from the agenda. The Indian delegate, V. K. Krishna Menon, played a significant role as mediator and the First Committee decided that the "Assembly will not discuss the Algerian affair." The Arab countries were content to state that they would take up the question later on. For the time being, France had won and its delegation returned. For a time the affair was suspended. France was then able to participate in the vital decision concerning the admission *en bloc* of seventeen new Members.

Suez and Algeria, 1956–1958

In the following year tension between France and the Arab countries (Egypt, in particular) was aggravated to the point that military operations broke out. The occasion was the Suez affair, which largely contributed to estranging France from the United Nations.

It is to be recalled that whereas the British engaged in military operations with the aim of maintaining free passage in the Suez Canal, of which they were the principal users, France, for its part, was much more concerned about the war in Algeria. The President of the Council of Ministers, Guy Mollet, considered Colonel Gamal Abdel Nasser (the leader of the Arabs) to be a new Hitler whose fall would discourage the Algerian nationalists. It was, then, from the perspective of the Algerian War that France decided to resort to force.

It is known that following negotiations which need not be discussed here the United Kingdom and France decided in September 1956 to submit the Suez affair to the Security Council. Egypt, for its part, had also asked the Council to examine the situation. The Franco-British draft resolution[9] was in two parts: an enumeration of principles concerning the free use of the Suez Canal, and a proposal for international administration by an association of users. The first part was adopted unanimously.[10] The second part, however, was rejected by a Soviet veto. The Egyptian refusal to accept the association of users explains the Franco-British decision to resort to force. The pretext

[9] UN Document S/3671.
[10] Adopted as UN Document S/3675.

was supplied the night of October 29–30 by the invasion of Sinai by Israeli troops.

The Franco-British ultimatum was characterized by President Dwight D. Eisenhower as a "fatal blow to the United Nations." In the Security Council a United States draft resolution[11] calling for the withdrawal of Israeli forces and a Franco-British agreement not to resort to force was rejected by France and the United Kingdom, with Belgium and Australia abstaining. A Soviet "cease-fire" proposal[12] met with the same vetoes, with the United States and Belgium abstaining. The Security Council, unable to make a decision, supported a Yugoslav proposal[13] to convoke the General Assembly.

There the debates were bitter. A United States draft resolution calling for an end to hostilities was adopted by the enormous majority of 65 votes in favor, 5 opposed (the United Kingdom, France, Israel, New Zealand, and Australia), with 6 abstentions, including those of Belgium and Canada.[14] On November 4 a Canadian draft resolution calling for the creation of an international force was adopted by a vote of 57 in favor, none opposed, with 19 abstentions.[15]

Operations were not halted by these resolutions (the Franco-British parachute operation took place on November 5) but rather by the Soviet threat addressed the night of November 5 to France, the United Kingdom, and Israel. Vaguely threatened by a nuclear counterattack at a time when they were not certain of United States support, the French and British governments, with sharply divided public opinions, both gave orders to their troops to cease firing. On the same day a Soviet proposal[16] for armed support to the victim of the aggression was rejected by France, the United Kingdom, the United States, and Australia in the Security Council. In these circumstances the use of unilateral force could not be successful. The proposal for the international force was adopted, and when it arrived France, the United Kingdom, and Israel had to yield.

These dramatic events had significant consequences. In a sense they strengthened the UN, but in a sense only. Aside from all moral and legal questions, it was clear in the eyes of French public opinion that only the conjunctive action of the United States and the Soviet Union had caused the maneuver to fail. The best proof was that the Hungarian affair could not be resolved by the UN because, in this case, the United States and the Soviet Union disagreed with each other.

On the level of French public opinion, rancor against the UN assumed

[11] UN Document S/3710.
[12] UN Document S/3713/Rev.1.
[13] UN Document S/3719.
[14] General Assembly Resolution 997 (ES-I), November 2, 1956.
[15] General Assembly Resolution 998 (ES-I), November 4, 1956.
[16] UN Document S/3736.

alarming proportions. It was attacked violently in the foreign policy debates in the National Assembly in December 1956. "There are two weights and two measures, depending on whether it addresses its recommendations to democracies or to dictatorships," said Foreign Minister Christian Pineau. Robert Schuman, disturbed about the impotence and partiality of the UN, wanted to reform it but realized that such reform was not likely. The only solution was to reestablish close relations with the United States and develop the process of European unification.

The eighteen months that passed between the evacuation of Franco-British troops and the military coup d'état in Algeria on May 13, 1958, were marked by the aggravation of the Algerian affair and, with this, the worsening of the French domestic situation. France felt itself isolated in the world; this was manifested by the General Assembly resolution[17] of January 19, 1957, on Israel which was approved by 74 votes in favor, 2 opposed (France and Israel), with 2 abstentions. In the renewed debates on Algeria, France again denied the competence of the Organization to discuss the question but nevertheless participated in the discussions. An Afro-Asian motion proclaiming the right of self-determination for Algeria was defeated. The General Assembly expressed its sentiments in a synthesizing motion "expressing the hope that in a spirit of cooperation a peaceful, democratic and just solution will be found." For France it was only a partial success. The competence of the UN was reaffirmed; if France did not find a peaceful solution, the debates would begin again and under worse conditions. Once again the United States stood by France, but there were strong anticolonialist currents and this support was scarcely certain for the future.

Nevertheless, in December 1957 France profited from a sort of respite. To an Afro-Asian motion[18] "regretting" that the resolution[19] of February 15, 1957, had not been realized and "recognizing that the principle of self-determination is applicable to the Algerian people," mild amendments[20] were added. These, however, were approved by only 37 votes in favor (including the United States), and 36 opposed, with 7 abstentions, in the First Committee, while the draft resolution itself was not adopted due to a vote of 37 in favor, 37 opposed, with 6 abstentions. It would take very little for the new states, in growing numbers, to gain the advantage.

De Gaulle and the End of the Algerian War, 1958–1962

General de Gaulle was brought to power June 1, 1958, because with his prestige he appeared to be the only man capable of restoring the army to submission and thus of reestablishing a France threatened with disintegration by the

---

[17] General Assembly Resolution 1123 (XI), January 19, 1957.
[18] UN Document A/C.1/L.194.
[19] General Assembly Resolution 1012 (XI), February 15, 1957.
[20] UN Document A/C.1/L.196.

weakness and instability of the Fourth Republic. In February 1958 the militarists already had taken it upon themselves to bombard the Tunisian village of Sakhiet Sidi Youssef which led to a Tunisian complaint in the Security Council. In fact, these militarists wanted to prevent the *internationalization* of the Algerian problem. Certainly no French government wanted to leave the solution of the problem to the UN, though there was the possibility of using the "good offices" of Morocco or Tunisia or of the United States and the United Kingdom. However, the coming to power of General de Gaulle meant absolute refusal of any internationalization. The Algerian problem would be settled by France and Algeria alone.

To the surprise of almost everyone, however, General de Gaulle progressively revealed himself to be an advocate of self-determination for Algeria. The slowness of the process—it took almost four years—was in all probability caused by the necessity of taking the army in hand and by the French population of Algeria. The latter, at first enthusiastic because it believed the General to be a partisan of "French Algeria," became furious and disgusted when his plans and his implacable realism became apparent.

The United Nations thus moderated somewhat its annual attempt to force France to concede independence to Algeria without delay. It must be added that the General was astonishingly liberal where the other colonies, those of black Africa, were concerned. He emancipated them completely in two stages. By the referendum of September 30, 1958, they were given the right to choose either independence or association with France. Guinea alone took advantage of the opportunity to break all ties. The others chose to become autonomous states of the French Community. Full independence was accorded to them within a few months. The beginning of an evolution of prime importance was then witnessed which transformed France, until then "accused" by the *tiers monde,* into "popular" France, and so much the more popular as the General maintained his distance from the Western camp and especially from the United States. But in doing this, General de Gaulle, far from relying any longer on the United Nations, was pursuing a strictly nationalist policy, and this stirred up lively attacks in the UN when France tested its first atomic bombs in the Sahara.

During the year 1958, the Algerian question was again put on the agenda of the Assembly. France denied that the Assembly had competence. Through informal negotiation it managed to have the expression "provisional government of the Algerian Republic" withdrawn from the text of the Afro-Asian proposal. The text of the draft resolution[21] then recommended negotiations between the interested parties. By a close vote, 34 in favor, 19 opposed, with 28 abstentions, the draft failed to obtain the two-thirds majority in the Assembly. It is significant that the United States, which had voted against the pro-

[21] UN Document A/4075.

posal in the First Committee, *abstained* in the General Assembly, causing great disappointment in France.

The following year, General de Gaulle offered self-determination to Algeria and Foreign Minister Maurice Couve de Murville announced the independence of the Camerouns and Togo. The debate on Algeria then took place in a more relaxed atmosphere. The Tunisian delegate even paid his respects to the "prestigious head of the French state." Pakistan's motion[22] entreating the two interested parties to engage in negotiations failed to receive the necessary two-thirds majority in the Assembly.

In 1960 a draft resolution,[23] supporting the arguments of the Algerian nationalists, "*recognizes* the right of the Algerian people to self-determination and independence" and proposed a referendum organized by the United Nations. In the First Committee it was approved by 47 votes in favor, 20 opposed, with 28 abstentions, but the Assembly adopted a milder proposal.[24] It was the United States and the new French-speaking African states that made possible the rejection of a Cypriot amendment[25] according to which the Assembly would have *decided* that a referendum would be organized by the United Nations.

In 1961, the Algerian problem was placed on the agenda for the last time. An Afro-Asian proposal was approved by the Assembly by 62 votes in favor, none opposed, with 38 abstentions.[26] But this time the atmosphere was calm because people knew that negotiations were progressing. The Evian agreements were signed on March 19, 1962, and, after a referendum, Algeria became independent at the beginning of July.

Every year the debates on Algeria had stirred up a lively interest in France and simultaneously a growing hostility toward the Organization that General de Gaulle scornfully called "the machine." From 1956 on, the attitude of the French was one of indifference or hostility. A survey of public opinion concerning the question, "Do you think the UN has justified its existence?" gave the following results: yes, 23 percent; no, 37 percent; no opinion, 27 percent; and unaware of the existence of the UN, 13 percent.[27]

It was in this atmosphere of indifference, mockery, and hostility that the debates on disarmament took place. Let us sum up the position of France without entering into the details of the debates. Speaking in September 1958 before the General Assembly, Foreign Minister Couve de Murville said:

> The halting of tests is conceivable only within the framework of effective nuclear disarmament. . . . Those who do not at this moment possess this diabolical weap-

[22] UN Document A/L.276.
[23] UN Document A/C.1/L.265 and Add.1–3.
[24] General Assembly Resolution 1573 (XV), December 19, 1960.
[25] UN Document A/L.333.
[26] General Assembly Resolution 1724 (XVI), December 20, 1961.
[27] *Sondages* (Paris: Institut Français d'Opinion Publique, 1958), Nos. 1–2, p. 192.

on . . . would in fact forbid themselves to manufacture [it], . . . would forego possession of the elements of real defense and, consequently, would rely entirely on the nuclear powers for their own defense. Conversely, the powers that today possess nuclear weapons . . . would by no means pledge themselves to discontinue their manufacture.[28]

The results of this position are known. France refused to participate in the Geneva Conference of the Eighteen-Nation Committee on Disarmament, deciding instead to pursue the preparation of an atomic arsenal, regardless of the opposition of its allies or of the countries of the *tiers monde.*

Since it was known that France was preparing for a nuclear explosion in the Sahara, the African and Asian countries made a proposal in 1959 expressing the grave anxiety caused the Assembly by the intention of the French government to carry out nuclear tests and entreating France to refrain from going on with these tests. This draft resolution was adopted in the First Committee by a vote of 46 in favor, 26 opposed, with 10 abstentions.[29] The French delegate, Jules Moch, though little in favor of the creation of a French *force de frappe,* had declared that the text of the resolution was "scientifically erroneous" and "politically odious" and underlined its "offensively discriminatory nature toward his country." A number of those who voted for the resolution later did not object when the first Communist Chinese atomic bomb was exploded.

Of course General de Gaulle had no intention of taking this vote into consideration. As early as November 10 he declared that the UN had never censured the some 200 tests that had taken place, and he added, "I cannot view it as anything other than an arbitrary maneuver against my country." The resolution was a "bad quarrel picked with France."[30]

The first French nuclear explosion took place at Reggane, in the Sahara, on February 13, 1960. It should be noted that the African states were not unanimous in protesting; most of the French-speaking countries either approved or accepted without comment the French nuclear test. The commencement of the Congo affair was rapidly to turn attention away from the problem.

The Present and the Future, Since 1962

The position of France has evolved since 1962. It can certainly not be concealed that there is a bitter memory of the ten years during which France was constantly regarded as the culprit. On the other hand, favorable signs of

[28] For the text of this speech in its English version, see *Speeches and Press Conferences* (New York: French Embassy, Press and Information Division, September 25, 1958), No. 115, pp. 1–8.

[29] UN Document A/C.1/L.238/Rev.1.

[30] For the complete text of the second press conference in its English version, see *Major Addresses, Statements and Press Conferences of General Charles de Gaulle, May 18, 1958–January 31, 1964* (New York: French Embassy, Press and Information Division), pp. 57–70.

an evolution have appeared. A dozen new African states have shown on numerous occasions that they are ready to follow the main lines of French policy
because France granted them independence and is no longer a colonial power
in actual fact. That the French language is more widely used in the UN does
not fail to satisfy the national pride of the French people. On a number of
points—recognition of Communist China, admission of Communist China
to the UN, neutralization of Laos and Vietnam, aid to underdeveloped countries, the unconcealed desire to increase France's "independence" with regard
to the United States, and a sometimes "neutralist" attitude—France voices
the aspirations of a great many countries of the *tiers monde*. Henceforth it is
clear that France might use the UN as a "tribune" for its policy and that from
its former position of culprit France might reach that of leader.

Nevertheless, at least until 1964, General de Gaulle was profoundly hostile
to the Organization. It is worthwhile to study his opinion in some detail. The
basis of this attitude was most clearly delineated during his fourth press conference on April 11, 1961.[31] France did not favor sending a United Nations
force to the Congo (Leopoldville) and from the beginning refused to pay
its share of the expenses of this project. A journalist asked the General to
explain this refusal and "why France, . . . in a more general way, has for some
time shown such great reservations with regard to the U.N."

The reply is interesting. General de Gaulle recalled that he was one of the
founders of the UN. At the beginning the UN was based on the Security
Council "which was a sort of government"; the General Assembly, "a kind
of . . . parliament," was not legislative. There were

> about forty States which had been in existence for a long time. . . . It seems
> that all these procedures would enable the States to establish contact with each
> other, to examine world questions jointly and to promote peace while restricting
> demagogic activities.

Furthermore, the Charter "was designed to prevent the Organization from
interfering in the affairs of each State." The United Nations of today bears no
resemblance to that concept. The General Assembly "at the present time . . .
has assumed all powers." It includes the representatives of more than 100
states

> most of which, at least many of which, are improvised States and believe it their
> duty to stress grievances or demands with regard to the older nations, rather than
> elements of reason and progress. . . . So that now the meetings of the United
> Nations are no more than riotous and scandalous sessions where there is no way
> to organize an objective debate and which are filled with invectives and insults
> thrown out, especially by the Communists and those who are allied with them
> against the Western nations.

[31] *Ibid.*, pp. 113-126.

: intervenes in all subjects, and even with arms as in the Congo.

> The result is that it carries to the local scene its global incoherence, . . . and the individual partiality of each of the States. . . . France does not see how she can adopt any attitude toward the United, or disunited, Nations other than that of the greatest reserve. . . . She does not wish to contribute her men or her money to any present or future undertaking of this organization—or disorganization.

The General, feeling that he has the full support of French public opinion on this point, has scarcely changed his point of view from that date. Yet he has become more optimistic and less bitter. In 1964 he received Secretary-General U Thant with much amiability. When questioned by a journalist about the UN crisis at his eleventh press conference on February 4, 1965,[32] he returned to the reasoning cited above but with serenity, foreseeing the possibility of reform. The Charter of 1945, he said, "was reasonable." He approved of

> the meeting and confrontation . . . of almost all the world's nations in a kind of forum from which international public opinion could emerge and which, by virtue of the equality of all its members, conferred upon each of them, especially on those which had just acquired sovereignty and independence, a highly esteemed dignity.

The affairs of Korea, Suez, and Hungary and the abuse of the Soviet veto have caused the United Nations to deviate from its Charter. The rivalry of the two Great Powers has forced the Secretary-General "to set himself up as a superior and excessive authority." The General Assembly "arrogated to itself" in 1950 the right of decision regarding the use of force. To be sure, intervention in the Congo (Leopoldville) "has ceased thanks to the wisdom of the present Secretary-General." But the intervention was unlawful. Thus, the need for reform. "In the present circumstances, it is clearly necessary for Washington, Moscow, London, Peking and Paris to agree to return to the point of departure." And he suggested that the meeting take place in Geneva, thus excluding New York which is situated within the boundaries of one of the two Great Powers.

While in the last three years France has played only a modest and reserved role in the United Nations, it may be that an idea of great reform has matured in the mind of the General, a reform in which France would suddenly play an essential role. Moreover, it is not excluded that Secretary-General U Thant might support certain elements of such a reform, for his positions are very near to those of France on many questions, notably on the admission of Communist China to the UN and the neutralization of Southeast Asia. Certain observers, such as Philippe Ben in *Le Monde*, February 25, 1965, have gone

[32] For the text, see "President de Gaulle Holds Eleventh Press Conference," *Speeches and Press Conferences* (New York: French Embassy, Press and Information Division), No. 216, pp. 1–13.

as far as to say that "the positions of France and Mr. Thant are quite close."
The crisis of the nineteenth Assembly—which in fact had been forced to adjourn—has led him to state that,

> from this time . . . it seems evident that the Americans have lost the battle that
> they so imprudently began on the application of article 19 of the Charter "to
> defaulting countries."

There is, however, a great difference between the United States position
which until the present favored strengthening the General Assembly as the
initiator of security operations, and the Soviet and French positions which,
recognizing only the authority of the Security Council in this regard, prefer
to consider the Assembly simply as a great world forum. The Soviet Union
has never recognized the Uniting for Peace Resolution of 1950[33] which delegated broad powers to the Assembly. France did recognize it but does no
longer. General de Gaulle is not responsive to the idea that the "blue helmets"
are not a force of repression but a force of neutralization or pacification, according to the conception of Dag Hammarskjöld.

Since the position of France is being studied here, it will be interesting to
conclude by evaluating the positive contribution that France will bring to the
inevitable necessity of a reform of the UN, as well as the negative, indeed contradictory, aspects.

First, it appears that the wounds to French pride are healing and that
France is resolved no longer to isolate itself from the Organization. The two
texts of General de Gaulle cited above, one from 1961 and the other from
1965, clearly demonstrate the evolution that is taking place. We must understand the significance of ten years of incessant attacks. Jean Schwoebel writing
in *Le Monde*[34] does not hesitate to speak of the "bitterness of the United
States," which thus puts the United States in France's old position:

> It is no longer from the European states that the underdeveloped countries . . .
> demand a reckoning, it is from the United States itself, whose entire policy is
> contested. . . . Faced with this growing contestation . . . American faith in the
> UN begins to waver, and their good will in financial matters begins to weaken.
> The Americans are more and more reluctant since then to play the role of scoffed
> benefactors and to become the laughingstock of the world by constantly settling
> the accounts of an organization which each year provides it with more and more
> disappointments.

If the United States, then, is perhaps entering the bitter phase, France is
leaving it. From now on France will think of the role it can play. It will think
of the reorganization of the UN. On this point, France's support of the admission of Communist China appears essentially realistic. It is abnormal to

---

[33] General Assembly Resolution 377 (V), November 3, 1950.
[34] *Le Monde*, February 21–22, 1965, p. 2.

exclude 700 million men from an organization that aims to be worldwide. At the same time the Chinese creation of a "United Revolutionary Nations," as Prime Minister Chou En-lai proposed to Indonesian Foreign Minister Dr. Subandrio, must at all costs be avoided.

The contradictory element in the French attitude toward the United Nations is, on one hand, its desire to return power to the Security Council at the expense of the General Assembly and, on the other hand, its opposition to an international force.

On the first point, it is not difficult to show that the small and medium-sized nations which are not permanent members of the Security Council will never allow peace to rest in the hands of the five possessors of the nuclear weapon unless they are able to participate in the discussions. At a moment when France has won remarkable popularity among these states by resisting the "hegemony of Moscow and Washington," it is absurd to propose to them the hegemony of the Security Council. Is this the effect of French nationalism? Of General de Gaulle's "policy of grandeur"? Of nostalgia for the past? The fact remains that France cannot at the same time proclaim the equality of nations and demand a diminution of the powers of the General Assembly where those states are present and equal.

It is just as contradictory for the country of Léon Bourgeois to condemn with scorn the expeditionary forces of the UN by opposing their financing, whether it be a question of Suez, of the Congo, or of Cyprus. The idea of a permanent international force proposed by the small European states (Sweden, Denmark, the Netherlands, and Finland) should be popular in France. It is not a question of security by military sanctions but of the removal of danger by the establishment of a sort of "buffer." Certainly the use of this force, given the divisions of the world, will be delicate and difficult. But is it not one of the principal hopes that we can place in the UN?

As long as it remains obstinate on these points, France will not find in the UN, henceforth well-disposed toward it, the means to work toward world peace, which is the vocation and ambition of its citizens who are weary of too many wars and eager for a higher civilization.

Latin America and the United Nations

BRYCE WOOD AND MINERVA MORALES M.

READINESS FOR A NEW ORDER

WHEN the governments of the Latin American states were taking part in the negotiations leading to the founding of the UN, they could hardly have done so with nostalgic memories of the League of Nations. The League had provided no protection to the Caribbean countries from interventions by the United States, and, largely because of United States protests, it did not consider the Tacna-Arica and Costa Rica–Panama disputes in the early 1920's. Furthermore, Mexico had not been invited to join; Brazil withdrew in 1926; and Argentina and Peru took little part in League affairs. The organization was regarded as being run mainly for the benefit of European states with the aid of what Latin Americans called an "international bureaucracy," in which citizens from the southern hemisphere played minor roles. The United States was, of course, not a member, and both the reference to the Monroe Doctrine by name in Article 21 of the Covenant and the organization's practice of shunning any attempt to interfere in inter-American affairs against the wishes of the United States made the League in its first decade a remote and inefficacious institution to countries that were seriously concerned about domination by Washington.

Although two disputes that the American states found intractable were the subjects of action by the League of Nations in the 1930's, its interposition did not improve its reputation in the Americas. In these cases Latin American countries were the embarrassed recipients of two reprehensible "firsts" in the history of the League. Paraguay during the Chaco War was the first state to be regarded as an aggressor by the League and to be the object of sanctions. It withdrew from the League in 1935 at this affront to its national honor. In the Leticia conflict the prestige of Peru was barely saved when in 1933

BRYCE WOOD, a member of the Board of Editors, is a visiting Professor of Public Law and Government at Columbia University and Executive Associate of the Social Science Research Council, New York. Minerva Morales M. is Professor at the Centre de Estudios Internacionales, El Colegio de México, and a visiting scholar at the Institute of Latin American Studies, Columbia University.

the League's Administrative Commission for the Territory of Leticia, carrying out the first "police action" in the history of general international organizations, masked the reoccupation of Leticia by Colombian troops. The services of the League were unappreciated, however, and in the protocol terminating the dispute the League was ignored, while the two countries congratulated themselves on their "agreeable duty" to prevent conflicts because of their "historical, social and sentimental ties" as states of the "American community."

If Latin America's retrospective view of the League was aloof and even unfriendly, its view of the inter-American "system" as a device for maintaining peace, rhetoric apart, was that it was nearly useless. In the Chaco, at Leticia, and in the Marañón conflict between Ecuador and Peru in 1941–1942, the nonbelligerent American republics had neither prevented nor shortened open hostilities, and their long and painful attempts to achieve enduring peace settlements resulted, in the main, in the ratification of positions won by the military victors—Paraguay, Colombia, and Peru, respectively. The Latin American states, on the basis of their own recent diplomatic and military history, were therefore ready in 1945 to contemplate more efficient methods for the pacific settlement of their quarrels.

The policy of the United States in these three conflicts, which were the first serious breaches of intra-Latin American amity in half a century, exemplified both neutrality and objectivity. Thus, the Latin American governments had good reason to believe that the great influence of the United States would be exerted only to prevent conflicts or, as in the Leticia affair, to maintain the validity of established treaties and not to gain any advantage for itself. Further, in the decade of the 1930's the United States government developed and demonstrated a conscious and principled adherence to a new policy known as that of the "good neighbor." This policy, in practice and in formal legal statement, renounced "intervention" in the domestic and foreign affairs of other American states, and for several years Washington ceased trying to implement its preferences among presidential aspirants and governmental policies in the Caribbean states by its previously customary methods of influence and diplomatic pressures. In whatever way the term "intervention" may be construed in the inter-American protocols and declarations of this period, the fact was evident to all in 1945 that since January 1933 the United States government had not put troops ashore in any Latin American country for other than mutually acceptable measures of hemispheric defense. In addition, the protection given in this decade to North American enterprise in Latin American countries in cases of actual or threatened expropriation had been sufficiently moderate in manner to permit satisfactory intergovernmental or other arrangements to be achieved.

Finally, the generally effective wartime collaboration of the American states except Argentina had created a new warmth of sympathy and a new sense of confidence and ease of relationships. The financial and technical assistance provided by the United States to Latin American countries during World War II helped to enhance this modern "era of good feeling," which reached a high point in 1945.

With this background the Latin American governments were strongly disposed in 1945 both to establish new ways of keeping peace among themselves and to strengthen ties with the United States, whose "hegemony" was no longer feared as it had been in the 1920's. In addition, they were concerned about the great and growing power of the Soviet Union and the consequently anticipated stimulus to activities of Communist parties in America.

LATIN AMERICAN CONTRIBUTIONS TO SHAPING THE UN

These factors and a reaction against "great-power domination" on the part of the Latin American countries combined to evoke intense opposition in 1944 when the Dumbarton Oaks Proposals were unveiled by the United States, the United Kingdom, the Soviet Union, and China. The intensity of the Latin American response to the Proposals appears to have surprised the United States Department of State, which agreed to Latin American demands for an Inter-American Conference on Problems of War and Peace, which was held in Mexico City in February–March 1945. In the Act of Chapultepec resulting from the Conference the parties recommended the negotiation of an inter-American treaty to meet acts or threats of aggression as a

> regional arrangement for dealing with such matters relating to the maintenance of international peace and security as are appropriate for regional action in this Hemisphere.

Consequently, at the United Nations Conference on International Organization in the spring of 1945, the Latin American states were unanimous in demanding recognition in the Charter for a special jurisdiction for regional organizations in matters of peace and security. This was achieved principally through Article 51 of the Charter, but also through some changes in Chapter VIII, Section C, of the Dumbarton Oaks Proposals.

The Latin American countries were not alone in the campaign to give regional agencies more scope under the Charter. Nevertheless, they played such a prominent role in promoting the amendments to the Proposals that they should be credited at least with sharing responsibility as principal agents in the framing of Article 51 and the final form of Chapter VIII of the Charter.[1] Expressing their interests as minor powers, Latin American governments played leading parts, but with much less success, in efforts to broaden the role of the General Assembly, to extend the jurisdiction of the International Court

---

[1] Arthur H. Vandenberg, Jr. (ed.), *The Private Papers of Senator Vandenberg* (Boston: Houghton Mifflin, 1952), pp. 186–193, *passim*.

of Justice by way of the optional clause in Article 36 of its Statute, and to restrict the scope of the exception to "intervention" by the United Nations contained in Article 2, paragraph 7, of the Charter.

At Rio in 1947 and Bogotá in 1948 the American states equipped themselves in the Inter-American Treaty of Reciprocal Assistance (Rio Treaty) and in the Charter of the Organization of American States (OAS) with institutions and procedures for maintaining peace among themselves. The OAS has had a remarkably successful record among the Latin American states. Brief fighting has occurred in a number of cases, but it has been limited in duration by the application of collective peacekeeping efforts which had never been utilized before 1948 in American conflicts. For example, the prompt arrival of neutral observers at scenes of violence has been effective in quickly bringing to a stop fighting in the more than half-dozen armed clashes occurring around the Caribbean since the 1948 Costa Rica–Nicaragua affair. These actions have been taken quite apart from the United Nations, except for *pro forma* reporting under Article 54 of the Charter of measures adopted by the OAS. It may therefore be said that the Latin American objective expressed at Chapultepec has been attained through the operation of the American system for dealing with questions of peace that "are appropriate for regional action in this Hemisphere."

REGIONAL VERSUS UNIVERSAL PROCEDURES

The fencing off of an area of regional jurisdiction from that of the United Nations did not mean that the Latin American countries intended to limit their international activities to inter-American affairs. The fence they had built was a barrier only to outsiders, and even then, only when appropriate. Latin American governments soon demonstrated their determination to make the most of their membership in both the world and the regional organizations, not only in peace and security issues but even more notably in the economic and cultural spheres.

With respect to peace and security, Latin American countries have aired quarrels among themselves in the United Nations; taken disputes with the United States to the Security Council and General Assembly; and appealed decisions by OAS organs to the United Nations.

Disputes Between Latin American Republics

As an illustration of the first of these actions, an accusation was made in the General Assembly in September 1960 by José R. Chiriboga Villagómez, Foreign Minister of Ecuador, that Peru had committed aggression against Ecuador in 1941 and that Ecuador was the victim of an unjust settlement, reached with the approval of the other American states while Peruvian troops were occupying Ecuadoran territory in January 1942. These charges were vehemently countered by Victor Andrés Belaúnde, Peru's representative, and the United Nations took no formal notice of the exchange.[2] This was not a case in which fighting had recently occurred, but it served notice that Ecuador was intensely dissatisfied with the boundary and continued to refuse to complete its demarcation. Ecuador, however, apparently broke one of the informal rules of the game since it was the first Latin American state to bring to the attention of the United Nations a dispute with another Latin American country. Argentina, Brazil, Chile, and the United States were "guarantors" of the boundary settlement, and a motive for Ecuador's denunciation of Peru in the General Assembly was its probably well-founded conviction that it could get no satisfaction from the OAS.

United States–Latin American Disputes

Disputes with the United States have been appealed to the United Nations by Guatemala in 1953 and 1954[3] and by Cuba in 1960, 1961,[4] and later. In neither case were military forces of the United States directly involved, but it was generally considered that the United States government had, in the first instance, provided equipment to the successful invading forces of Colonel Carlos Castillo Armas and, in the second, had trained and equipped Cuban exiles for their unsuccessful invasion of Cuba in April 1961. These appeals demonstrated that Latin American countries did not regard the OAS as providing the most effective source of restraint on the exercise of military power by the United States, and they were the occasions for important declarations affecting the relations between regional agencies and the United Nations. Indeed, the question of regional-global relationships with respect to the use of force is the most important feature of Latin American contacts with the United Nations, and it is therefore given detailed consideration in this discussion.

The results of the appeals of Guatemala and Cuba to the United Nations were not satisfactory either to the appellants or to other Latin American governments. In the Guatemalan case, the Security Council first refused to refer the matter to the OAS and then declined to place a second Guatemalan complaint on its own agenda. Before further action could be taken by the United Nations or the OAS, Colonel Castillo Armas was in control of the country. The failure of the Security Council to act gave rise to serious criticisms by Latin American governments, which were repeated in the Cuban crises in 1961 and 1962. For example, the delegate of Ecuador stated in the General Assembly on October 1, 1954:

> We are members and staunch supporters of the Organization of American States, but we cannot by any means agree that it has exclusive jurisdiction in a dispute

---

[2] General Assembly *Official Records* (15th session), pp. 238–246.
[3] UN Documents S/2988 and S/3232.
[4] UN Documents A/4543 and A/4701.

such as the one I have just mentioned [Guatemala's appeal]. . . . We hope that there will be no more such negative decisions by the Council, lest the prestige of the Organization suffer and one of the fundamental objects of the Charter—protection against attack—become illusory or come too late.[5]

Similarly, the delegate of Uruguay stated on September 28, 1954, that his government considered that

the principles of the regional system and the safeguards which it offers cannot be invoked in order to prevent States from having direct and immediate access to the jurisdiction of the United Nations or to deprive them, no matter how temporarily, of the protection of the agencies of the world community. The legal protection afforded by both systems should be combined, never substituted for one another. . . . The delegation of Uruguay considers that any protest to the United Nations against aggression is entitled at least to a hearing.[6]

Finally, the representative of Argentina stated in the General Assembly on October 4, 1954:

The existence of regional agreements does not mean that they or the agencies created under them take precedence over the United Nations, or that the United Nations should refrain from discussing or endeavouring to settle problems submitted to it by a government representing a Member State. . . . To hold that the regional organization has exclusive jurisdiction would in our view lead to the absurd position that a State Member of the United Nations which was a party to a regional agreement would be at a disadvantage as compared with other States which for some reasons were not members of regional agencies. We cannot accept a legal argument that would involve a discriminatory situation in regard to the United Nations Charter, and which would make the security of a country depend on the special political characteristics and circumstances of regional arrangements.

The Argentine Republic cannot accept a view that might deprive it of the right, as a Member of the United Nations, to request the United Nations to consider or settle any international problems affecting it.[7]

These Latin American views were apparently shared by Secretary-General Dag Hammarskjöld, who, in his *Annual Report* for 1953–1954, stated:

The importance of regional arrangements in the maintenance of peace is fully recognized in the Charter and the appropriate use of such arrangements is encouraged. But in those cases where resort to such arrangements is chosen in the first instance, that choice should not be permitted to cast any doubt on the ultimate responsibility of the United Nations. Similarly, a policy giving full scope to the proper role of regional agencies can and should at the same time fully preserve the right of a Member nation to a hearing under the Charter.[8]

[5] General Assembly *Official Records* (9th session), p. 148.
[6] General Assembly *Official Records* (9th session), p. 98.
[7] General Assembly *Official Records* (9th session), p. 174.
[8] *Annual Report of the Secretary-General on the Work of the Organization, 1 July 1953–30 June 1954* (General Assembly *Official Records* [9th session], Supplement No. 1), p. xi.

When Cuba appealed to the United Nations in April 1961 on the occasion of the Bay of Pigs invasion, the General Assembly was in session. Previous Cuban complaints, made as early as October 1960, that the United States was planning an invasion of Cuba, had been referred to the Assembly's First (Political and Security) Committee, and the new appeal was considered there.

Draft resolutions more or less condemnatory of the United States were presented by Rumania, by Mexico, by Venezuela on behalf of six other Latin American states, and by the Soviet Union.[9] During the debate in the First Committee, the Mexican representative, Luis Padilla Nervo, referred approvingly to the above-quoted statements made in the debate following the Guatemalan affair. The draft resolution presented by his delegation stated:

> *Firmly believing* that the principle of non-intervention in internal affairs of any State imposes an obligation on Members of the United Nations to refrain from encouraging or promoting civil strife in other States,

all governments should ensure "that their territories and resources are not used to promote a civil war in Cuba," and they should both "put an immediate end to any activity that might result in further bloodshed" and seek a peaceful solution of the "present situation." The draft resolution made no reference whatever to the OAS, and this omission was unfavorably regarded by the United States delegation and some Latin American delegates who sponsored a less censorious text. The seven-power Latin American draft resolution referred to "the peaceful means of settlement established at the Seventh Meeting of Consultation of Foreign Ministers of the American Republics," and exhorted

> those Member States which belong to the Organization of American States to lend their assistance with a view to achieving a settlement by peaceful means in accordance with the Purposes and Principles of the Charter of the United Nations and the charter of the Organization of American States.[10]

In the First Committee the seven-power draft resolution was given voting priority and was adopted by a vote of 61 in favor, 27 opposed, with 10 abstentions. Mexico, Cuba, and the Soviet bloc voted against the draft resolution, and Ecuador and the Dominican Republic were among those abstaining. The Mexican draft resolution was adopted by the Committee by a vote of 42 in favor (including Mexico, Bolivia, Brazil, Chile, Cuba, and Ecuador), 31 opposed (including Argentina, Colombia, Costa Rica, El Salvador, Guatemala, Honduras, Panama, Paraguay, Peru, Uruguay, Venezuela, and the United States), with 25 abstentions. The Dominican Republic abstained, and Haiti did not take part in the voting.[11]

In the plenary session of the General Assembly the seven-power Latin Ameri-

9 UN Documents A/C.1/L.274, A/C.1/L.275, A/C.1/L.276, and A/C.1/277, respectively.
10 UN Document A/C.1/L.276.
11 General Assembly *Official Records . . . First Committee* (15th session), pp. 108–110.

can draft resolution was adopted by a vote of 59 in favor, 13 opposed, with 24 abstentions. Cuba voted against, and Mexico, the Dominican Republic, and Ecuador abstained; Haiti did not vote. Through an initiative on the part of Nigeria and the Sudan, however, specific reference to the Organization of American States was eliminated in the operative part of the resolution, and in General Assembly Resolution 1616 (XV), April 21, 1961, the Assembly did no more than exhort "all Member States to take such peaceful action as is open to them to remove existing tension." At the Assembly's 995th plenary meeting the Mexican draft resolution received a majority vote, but less than the two-thirds required for adoption. The vote was 41 in favor (including Mexico, Bolivia, Brazil, Chile, Cuba, and Ecuador), 35 opposed, with 20 abstentions. Except for the Dominican Republic, which abstained, and Haiti, which again did not put in an appearance, all the other Latin American delegations joined the United States in opposing the draft resolution.

No further action was taken at this time by the United Nations in view of the failure of the expedition and the evident lack of intent in Washington to encourage a new one. The incident, however, was the second major break in what before 1954 had been a nearly solid front of American states in favor of settling American quarrels within the OAS.

In this voting it was clear that the Latin American delegations were significantly divided. The existence of a "bloc" or "caucusing group" among the Latin American delegations to the United Nations has been examined elsewhere,[12] and no more than brief consideration is possible here. There are various ways of defining "blocs," and for some purposes it is sufficient to say that they are sets of states that show certain common voting patterns. For other purposes, the issue of policy may be relevant to the definition of a "bloc." Whether or not the delegations of states with common voting patterns hold meetings to concert policy does not necessarily determine whether the states form a bloc, as the usefulness of such meetings would depend primarily on the amount of discretion which the participant nations' foreign offices allow to their UN delegations. At any rate, in recent years the delegations of Latin American governments have rarely held meetings for the working out of common voting tactics on questions other than those related to personnel. When such matters are at stake as chairmanships of committees, seats on the International Court of Justice, and officerships of the General Assembly, delegations of Latin American countries, presumably provided with lists of names by their foreign offices, meet to agree upon candidates who will be solidly supported by the group. Otherwise, delegations usually vote without formal "Latin American" gatherings, although a substantial amount of informal, pre-

12 Thomas Hovet, Jr., *Bloc Politics in the United Nations* (Cambridge, Mass: Harvard University Press, 1960); and Margaret M. Ball, "Bloc Voting in the General Assembly," *International Organization*, February 1951 (Vol. 5, No. 1), pp. 3–31. These statements are also based on conversations with members of missions to the United Nations.

voting communication undoubtedly takes place. Similarly, it appears that the United States delegation does not hold meetings with Latin American delegates as a group but handles its problems of persuasion or dissuasion on a bilateral rather than a multilateral basis.

The intimate and secluded relationships between delegations and home governments are, of course, relevant to the matter of "bloc" voting, but it is exceedingly difficult to obtain information about them. Another relevant and perhaps even more inaccessible set of relationships is that of prevoting communications, if any, among Latin American ministries of foreign affairs. Common interests are more important than formal majority votes as determinative factors in Latin American voting regularities. Another element that should not be forgotten in this connection has been emphasized by Jorge Castañeda, a Mexican delegate to the United Nations:

> Often the basic criterion used by a small state for voting is the fear of antagonizing the great power to which it is linked. Frequently the proposals concerning important questions are voted on with regard to their origin and not to their intrinsic merits. This situation is well known and even admitted by the delegates of many small countries. Of the evils that afflict the United Nations, probably "satellitism" is one of those which has most delayed the political maturity of the Organization and contributed to damaging the moral authority of its decisions.[13]

The Guatemalan and Cuban cases showed that the United States government, which had had to be convinced at San Francisco of the merits of Article 51 and the amendments to Chapter VIII, had become more regional than the original regionalists.[14] As a result of the OAS, the United States government has been able to increase its influence in conflicts among Latin American states. The regional organization permits the United States to remind disputants of a relatively firm set of obligations, and it can successfully press for a quick, impartial investigation of a military situation. In cases where its own conduct is protested, the United States appears to consider that its interests will be better served if the forum for complaints is the Council of the OAS rather than either the Security Council or the General Assembly, where it would be exposed to the criticism of the Soviet Union and other unfriendly countries. In the OAS, its opponents do not have the support of non-American allies, and they probably are less bold in censuring the United States in the more direct confrontation of the regional body, where diplomatic pressures exerted by the United States can effectivey influence a large proportion of the total voting group. For example, it is questionable whether the Mexican gov-

---

[13] Jorge Castañeda, *Mexico and the United Nations* (New York: Manhattan Publishing Co., 1958), p. 147.

[14] See Vandenberg, pp. 186–193, *passim*. For a further description of the way Article 51 was adopted, see also Romain Yakemtchouk, *L'ONU: La Securité Régionale et le Problème du Régionalisme* (Paris: A. Pedone, 1955).

ernment would have taken as strong a leadership initiative in the OAS at the time of the Bay of Pigs affair as it did in the General Assembly.

Appeals to the UN from OAS Decisions

Latin American states have occasionally appealed decisions by OAS agencies to the Security Council. As a preface, it may be noted that the Soviet Union asked the Security Council in September 1960 to deny the validity of diplomatic and economic sanctions adopted against the Dominican Republic by a vote of 19–0 (with the Dominican Republic and Venezuela abstaining) by the Sixth Meeting of Consultation of Ministers of Foreign Affairs of the OAS at San José, Costa Rica. The request was based on the claim that the sanctions were "enforcement action," which, under Article 53 of the United Nations Charter, was not to be taken "by regional agencies without the authorization of the Security Council." The Soviet Union was supported in the discussions by other members, but the decision by the Council was to "take note" of the OAS action without making any judgment on its legitimacy.[15]

Presumably aware of this unpromising precedent, Cuba on March 19, 1962, asked that the Security Council request from the International Court of Justice an advisory opinion clarifying the competence of regional agencies to deal with pacific settlement of disputes and, particularly, to adopt "enforcement action." The Cuban draft resolution was aimed at the measures adopted against it at the Eighth Meeting of Consultation of the OAS held in January 1962 at Punta del Este, Uruguay. The only support for Cuba in the Security Council came from the Soviet Union and Rumania; Chile and Venezuela voted with the United States in a 7–2 majority; the United Arab Republic abstained; and Ghana was absent.[16]

It should be noted that, despite significant but by no means unanimous Latin American opposition to the policy of the United States in the Guatemalan and Cuban cases, there was unanimous support for President John F. Kennedy in his "quarantine" of Cuba in October 1962. During the missile crisis the United States requested support for its policy from the Council of the OAS. The members of the regional organization did not on this occasion ask that the great-power dispute be taken to the United Nations, and their support strengthened the position of the United States. The circumstances were regarded as entirely appropriate for the application of regional procedures—in this case, the Inter-American Treaty of Reciprocal Assistance of 1947.

In summary then, in cases of disputes between Latin American republics the nations involved, except Ecuador, have preferred the OAS over the UN as the agency of settlement. In cases where the United States has been accused of giving aid or encouragement to invasions of Latin American states, how-

[15] Security Council Official Records (15th year), 893rd–895th meetings, September 8–9, 1960.
[16] UN Document S/5095; and Security Council Official Records (17th year), 998th meeting, March 23, 1962.

ever, the attacked governments have preferred to take their appeals to the United Nations and not to the regional body. When these circumstances have occurred, the aggrieved government has received substantial support from several other Latin American states including Mexico. This type of situation was unforeseen in 1945, possibly because Latin America may well have hoped that the policy of nonintervention would be continued by the successors of Presidents Franklin D. Roosevelt and Harry S. Truman. In addition, Cuba has appealed to the United Nations against the sanctionative judgments of its fellow Americans assembled in the OAS; and, finally, during the principal great-power crisis in the history of the Americas, the Cuban missile affair of 1962, the Latin American countries, operating through the OAS, expressed solid support for the United States, and they also endorsed its policy in the United Nations.

There is thus little that is doctrinaire about the policies of the Latin American countries with respect to their regional ties and institutions. The word "regionalism" has not been in this discussion since the evidence does not suggest that there is, on the part of the Latin American countries, a principled commitment to handling American disputes at home despite the obligation to do so in Article 2 of the Rio Treaty and Article 39 of the UN Charter. Changing moods and interests, rather than treaty or theory, seem to inspire their policies.

THE ISSUE OF COLLECTIVE INTERVENTION

One of the most controversial issues in inter-American affairs at the present time is that of "collective intervention." As early as 1958 Mr. Castañeda claimed for a group of influential Mexicans that the aims of the Rio Treaty were being deformed. He said that enforcement measures were being used

> not for their fundamental purpose—which is to repel armed aggression or to serve as an instrument of collective security of the United Nations under the authority of the Security Council—but as a means to judge, condemn, and eventually overthrow the internal regimes of the states, to the extent that they do not meet with the approval of the majority of the American republics.[17]

In contrast, the United States Department of State as recently as September 1964 has declared that it favors the broadening of the scope of "collective action" in cases where

> repression, tyranny and brutality outrage the conscience of mankind. . . . The United States has never believed that collective action for such purposes is proscribed by the Charter of the Organization of American States; but if the majority of the member states are of a contrary opinion, then let us amend the Charter.[18]

[17] Castañeda, p. 187.
[18] *Foreign Affairs Outline No. 8—Democracy vs. Dictators in Latin America—How Can We Help?* (Department of State Publication 7729, Inter-American Series 90) (Washington, D.C: U.S. Government Printing Office, 1964).

Mr. Castañeda, however, has said that if the Rio Treaty were to be used "for intervention in the domestic affairs of the American States," Mexico should seriously consider the denunciation of the Treaty.[19]

The problem of the proper treatment of internal tyranny is a source of tension not only between Mexico, as representative of some Latin American countries on the one hand, and the United States and certain Latin American countries on the other, but also between the OAS and the United Nations. On this issue Mexico and its supporters insistently oppose "collective action" by the American republics and would consistently appeal to the United Nations in all cases that might undermine what Mr. Castañeda has called the "cornerstone of the inter-American system . . . intransigent non-intervention."

The Mexican government has refused to accept as binding on it the decision, approved by a 15–4 vote, of the Ninth Meeting of Consultation of Ministers of Foreign Affairs of the OAS in July 1964 that diplomatic and economic ties with Cuba should be broken. Bolivia, Chile, and Uruguay, the other states in the minority, decided later to act in accordance with the resolution, leaving Mexico as the only member country of the OAS that maintains relations with Cuba. Mexican sources have suggested that this difference of views about interpretation of the OAS Charter, the Rio Treaty, and Chapter VIII of the UN Charter might be referred to the International Court of Justice. The United States has not wished to take this question to the Court, any more than it desired to accept the similar Cuban proposal which has been mentioned earlier, apparently because it does not want any non-American body to issue authoritative interpretations of inter-American treaties. The Mexican government is alone among the American states in desiring a Court opinion on this issue, but the action itself is evidence of an enduring Latin American view that the United Nations is the principal and perhaps the only, albeit dim, hope for rectification of an unacceptable decision by the Organization of American States.

IMPORTANCE OF UN AGENCIES IN DEVELOPMENT

In the economic field the principal Latin American achievement in the United Nations was the establishment in 1948 of the Economic Commission for Latin America (ECLA). At that time the Pan American Union maintained a section on economic affairs, but it was under the direction of a United States citizen, and the plans of Latin American economists could be carried out neither in that setting nor through the Economic and Social Council of the OAS.

[19] Similar views have been expressed by another senior official in the Mexican Foreign Affairs Office, Antonio Gómez Robledo, in *La Seguridad Colectiva en el Continente Americano* (Mexico City: Universidad Nacional Autónoma de México, 1959) and also in "La crisis actual del sistema interamericano," *Foro Internacional,* July–September 1962 (Vol. 3, No. 1) and October–December 1962 (Vol. 3, No. 2).

The United Nations afforded to Latin America through ECLA the opportunity to escape from the constraining influence exerted by the United States in all of the American regional agencies. At the same time, the Latin American governments did not place themselves under a form of restraint by working in a body established under the United Nations. The formation of ECLA, which they effectively controlled, liberated them from United States domination, and they found it possible to operate within a heady atmosphere of collaboration in a freedom which they had never known before. It was in this atmosphere that Latin American economists have developed their well-known positions concerning the terms of trade, the need for import substitution in Latin American economies, and the development of Latin American cooperation on many fronts. ECLA has served as a university for the training of economists and others and for the dissemination of economic theories aimed at explaining and solving the economic problems of Latin America. ECLA has also served as a political force, notably in its effective promotion of the Latin American Free Trade Association (LAFTA) and the Central American Common Market (CACM).

The experience of Latin American countries with the United Nations Educational, Scientific and Cultural Organization (UNESCO) has had comparable results with their participation in ECLA. In the cultural as well as in the economic field, the United Nations has given to Latin Americans opportunities to develop initiatives which were not generated in the regional organization. In Santiago, Chile, the Latin American Faculty of Sociology (FLACSO) has offered training for students of social science throughout Latin America. The Regional Center for Fundamental Education in Latin America (CREFAL) in Patzcuaro, Mexico, is a notable example of the ways in which Latin American enterprise in United Nations agencies can produce enduring results. In this case, the presence of Jaime Torres Bodet as Director General of UNESCO was influential in the establishment of the institute, in which the OAS collaborated. The Latin American Center for Social Science Research (CENTRO) in Rio de Janeiro, founded through UNESCO, and maintained by the cooperation of Latin American governments, provides further evidence of the Latin American predilection for the development of educational institutions through the United Nations rather than through the Organization of American States.

Despite the long history of inter-American relations, only recently have there been established inter-American institutions that may come to display the thrust and vitality of the cultural agencies formed by the Latin American states since 1945 through UNESCO. An attempt to explain this contrast is beyond the scope of this discussion, but the fact that Latin Americans are able to control the United Nations creations, although they have not been in control of regional agencies, should not be minimized. A new trend may be emerging, however, that will give greater independence to Latin American states in developing subregional collective action of various types. For example, ministers of education of the five states concerned held the third regular meeting of the Cultural and Education Council of the Organization of Central American States in August 1964 in Managua, Nicaragua. This meeting implies that there is a subregional as well as a supraregional level of relationships which may offer to Latin American states a way of developing collaborative enterprises separate from the inter-American agencies in which the United States is represented. If time shows a trend toward Latin American integration, this tendency might well be the result of the escape hatch from the OAS offered by the agencies of the United Nations.

The establishment of economic, cultural, and educational alternatives to the institutions of the OAS makes reasonable Jorge Castañeda's question:

> Is Pan Americanism, that is, the permanent association of the United States and Latin America in a regional agency, the best possible solution to the necessity for a regional life in America?[20]

The negative implications of this question, however, are currently under attack through the varied initiatives of the Alliance for Progress. The Alliance may be developing new and more creative types of regional association that will in the near future compete effectively with the attractiveness of opportunities afforded by ECLA and UNESCO.

[20] Castañeda, p. 172.

The Asian Nations and the United Nations

ARTHUR LALL

IN terms of the opening phrase of the Charter of the United Nations—"We the peoples of the United Nations"—the dominant image which comes to mind is that of Asia. Though not all the countries of Asia are Members of the United Nations—notably Korea, Vietnam, and now Indonesia—the Asian peoples of the United Nations (including the Chinese) not only greatly exceed in numbers those from any of the other major areas of the world but considerably outnumber all the peoples from these areas taken together.[1]

Twenty-three Asian states are Members of the United Nations.[2] This numerical figure exceeds that of any other regional grouping except Africa, which now contributes 35 Member nations (including South Africa) and very soon will add a 36th state (Gambia). However, in terms of population, Asians outnumber Africans in the proportion of six to one.

The foregoing facts are relevant to an appreciation of the role of Asia in the United Nations over the last twenty years and the current feelings of Asian states and peoples regarding the Organization. Moreover, they have their place in any assessment of the universalist aspirations of the United Nations.

ASIA AND THE MAKING OF THE UNITED NATIONS

Asia did not play a large role on the international scene during the formative years of the United Nations. Of the 26 countries which originally signed

ARTHUR LALL, former permanent representative of India at the United Nations, is Lecturer in International Law, Cornell University.

[1] *Population and Vital Statistics Report: Data available as of 10 October 1964* (UN Document ST/-STAT/Ser.A/71).

[2] This figure includes Cyprus and Turkey, states which sit in the Afro-Asian group at the United Nations, and excludes Israel although that state is geographically in Asia.

the Declaration by United Nations at Washington, D.C., on January 1, 1942, only two were from Asia—China and India. By the spring of 1945 the number of Asian signatories was swelled by the modest addition of six states—Iran, the Philippines, and the four Arab states of Lebanon, Iraq, Saudi Arabia, and Syria. Consequently, no more than these eight states made up the Asian contingent at the San Francisco United Nations Conference on International Organization at which 50 states met in April 1945 to draw up the Charter of the United Nations. On the other hand, all twenty states from Latin America were present at the Conference; and of the fourteen Western European Members, eight were represented at San Francisco.

Nor is it irrelevant to observe that although, as a result of President Franklin D. Roosevelt's efforts, China was among the powers that sponsored the San Francisco Conference, only the United States, the United Kingdom, and the Soviet Union took part in the first, and by far the more important, of the two rounds of discussions at Dumbarton Oaks in 1944 prior to the convening of the San Francisco Conference. Moreover, China at that time was not only struggling against Japan but was not united internally. It was further along toward the cataclysmic changes which were to be completed before the end of the fifth decade of the twentieth century than was generally realized. In short, for a number of reasons China was not able to play its full potential role either in the preparatory phases or at the Charter Conference, although it did make a number of substantive contributions.

What of the other seven Asian participants at San Francisco? India was not yet independent. Indeed, India's national leaders, who were to come into *de facto* power about a year and a half later, were strongly opposed to the policies of the then British government of India. The Indian delegates to the San Francisco Conference and their British-appointed advisers neither had the support of nationalist India nor did they voice the opinions of that India. It was to these kinds of representatives that Winston Churchill referred when, justifying to his own government the case for the admission of the Ukrainian and Byelorussian Soviet Socialist Republics as separate Members of the United Nations, he wrote: "For us to have four or five members, six if India is included, when Russia has only one is asking a great deal of an Assembly of this kind."[3] Little wonder then that India's role at the San Francisco Conference turned out to be a minor one. The Indian delegation introduced only four proposals or amendments at the Conference, with which we might contrast the 29 proposals and amendments introduced by a more independent colleague state in the British system—Australia. That the Indian performance was disappointingly and disproportionately small is borne out further by the fact that Egypt, a state which had only recently emerged from protectorate status under the

---

[3] Winston S. Churchill, *Triumph and Tragedy* (New York: Bantam Books, 1962), p. 308.

United Kingdom, introduced as many as 25 proposals and amendments at the Conference.[4]

The Philippines, like India, was not independent at the time of the Conference, and its showing was on a par with India's, though the Philippine delegation did put forward a slightly larger number of proposals than did India.

The four Arab states at the Conference were not conspicuous participants. Saudi Arabia, which had the longest period of independence to its credit of any of the four, made not even a single proposal to the Conference. Iraq, Lebanon, and Syria had all been mandated territories. Though Iraq had gained its independence in 1932, its actions in the field of foreign policy and in some other respects were fettered by the terms of its treaty with the United Kingdom of June 30, 1930. As for Lebanon and Syria, French troops returned to these territories at the end of the war, and their presence there was the subject of a joint Syrian-Lebanese communication to the Secretary-General of the United Nations, dated February 4, 1946, bringing the situation to the attention of the Security Council under Article 34 of the Charter.[5] The presence of British and French troops was not desired by the governments of the Levantine states. Clearly, in these circumstances, these two small Arab states had been in no position during the previous summer at San Francisco to take much effective part in the deliberations of the Conference.

The remaining Asian state at the Conference, Iran, did make some interesting proposals stressing the importance of international law and suggesting that it be a fundamental purpose of the United Nations to safeguard the territorial integrity and independence of Member States. These proposals, however, were not accepted by the Conference.

The nature of the Asian situation in 1945 was by and large not such as to ensure an adequate expression of the attitudes of the by far most populous area of the world in the profoundly important task of the making of the law of the world Organization. Had Asia been in a state of quiescence, this fact might not have been of great consequence. But the fact was that Asia was in the throes of a great reawakening which would inevitably bring into focus its major problems, political as well as economic and social. If this increased realization of Asian problems had occurred before the calling of the Charter Conference instead of in the next four or five years, the concepts on which the UN was based and its structural makeup might have been more appropriate to the world as presently constituted. It might, moreover, have somewhat enhanced the capacity of the United Nations to engage itself successfully in the problems which were to arise in subsequent decades in Africa.

As it was, the Asian delegations at San Francisco made no more than 38 out

[4] *The United Nations Conference on International Organization: Selected Documents* (Department of State Publication 2490, Conference Series 83) (Washington, D.C: U.S. Government Printing Office, 1946), pp. 89–242.

[5] Security Council *Official Records* (1st year), Supplement No. 1, pp. 82–83.

of the 547 proposals and amendments which were submitted in respect to the Dumbarton Oaks Proposals. While the maintenance of international peace and security was obviously a matter of prime importance, and particularly in so large an area of the world as Asia, delegations from that continent submitted the paltry number of three proposals out of a total of 136 put forward by participants under this specific heading. All three Asian proposals, two from Iran and one from the Philippines, were rejected. One can envisage some of the effects on the United Nations if there had been strong Asian support, as there could have been in other circumstances, for the Iranian proposal that any threat to the territorial integrity or independence of a Member State should be regarded as constituting a threat to the maintenance of peace and international security.[6] If this concept had been explicitly accepted and included in the Charter, might it not have created a valuable and calming approach to many territorial problems, including some of the major problems of Central Europe, where the threat that force will be used to alter lines of territorial division gives rise to deep anxieties and fears of conflict? In Asia itself the effect on relations between India and China, Indonesia and Malaysia, Cambodia and Thailand, and other bilateral situations would have been a calming one. In the building of the Organization the interests of international peace and security were not furthered by the virtual absence of an effective and independent Asia at the San Francisco Conference.

Seven and a fraction of the 38 Asian amendments were accepted at San Francisco. Four of these made very peripheral changes in the Charter—they had to do with introducing the idea that the Economic and Social Council (ECOSOC) should extend its sphere of interest to cultural affairs. Only two Asian amendments of some substance were adopted. The first was a Chinese amendment which provided much of the content of Article 13, paragraph 1(a), of the Charter, which makes it incumbent on the General Assembly to initiate studies and make recommendations for the purpose of encouraging the progressive development of international law and its codification. We owe to this Chinese initiative the basis for the valuable work of the International Law Commission and of such legal conferences as those on the law of the sea and on diplomatic immunities and privileges.

The second interesting Asian amendment to be adopted came from India. It furnished the substance of the provision which has come so much to the fore these days—Article 19 of the Charter. Actually, the Indian proposal was simply that a country which was two years or more in arrears in the payment of its dues should not vote in elections held by the General Assembly. The idea was taken up and extended to fill the terms of the present phraseology of the Charter.

---

[6] *The United Nations Conference on International Organization: Selected Documents,* p. 175.

The Early Years of the United Nations

In spite of the very slight impact that Asia had on the making of the United Nations, membership in the Organization was a strong stimulus to the growth in international stature of some of the Asian states which became Members. That the relatively small and militarily weak Arab states of Syria and Lebanon could bring a complaint (the one to which we have briefly referred) against two of the five Great Powers of the United Nations, without assurance of any great-power support for their case, was in itself evidence of a new dispensation as far as Asia was concerned. Furthermore, on this occasion in the early history of the UN, the small powers of Asia came to realize that they could gain support for their causes from the Great Powers. The issue, ostensibly one that concerned the United Kingdom and France as far as the Great Powers were concerned, became one between the United States and the Soviet Union with both these leading powers playing roles directed partly, or so it seemed to the Asian states concerned, toward championing the underdog. In the course of giving expression to this then newly emerging role, the Soviet Union voted against a United States draft resolution and thereby cast the first veto in the Security Council.[7]

In this event lay the second lesson for the Asian states: While the crux of the growing dispute between the "European powers"—the Asians included both the United States and the Soviet Union in this grouping—was foreign to the Asians, nevertheless, this dispute could be used in order to further their own (Asian or national) ends. In other words, if the United Nations did not bring into being a wholly effective system of international security and peace, it did offer the services of great-power champions and in this way provided to the small powers a degree of international protection which they had hitherto lacked.

If the arrangements envisaged in Chapters VI and VII of the Charter had worked smoothly, it is possible that the fiats handed down by the Great Powers acting in concert might on occasion have been not only onerous but, in terms of Asian situations, arbitrary. Suppose, for example, great-power unanimity had resulted in the Security Council's taking the view that the Soviets had a right to maintain troops in Iranian Azerbaijan. This would have been very much to the detriment of an Asian state. Or, in the Syrian-Lebanese complaint, we might envisage great-power unanimity permitting British and French troops to remain in the Levant for an indeterminate period in the interests of international security—which would not have been incompatible with a Franco-British agreement of December 13, 1945. In replying to the charges of the Syrian and Lebanese delegations in the Security Council, the representatives of the United Kingdom and France both explained that

[7] Security Council *Official Records* (1st year), 23rd meeting, February 16, 1946, p. 367.

the agreement implied no intention on the part of their governments to keep troops in the Levant indefinitely and *in the absence of a discussion in the Security Council.*[8] It is easy to see that this formulation might raise apprehensions among the Asian states concerned that the Great Powers desired to direct the discussions in the Security Council so as to provide sanction for the continuance of British and French forces in their territories. It was in this view of the matter that the representatives of Syria and Lebanon requested that the phrase in the United States draft resolution which expressed "confidence . . . that negotiations to that end [the withdrawal of foreign troops from Syria and Lebanon] will be undertaken by the parties without delay . . . " should be amended to read "technical negotiations exclusively to that end will be undertaken by the parties without delay."[9] The statement of the representative of the United Kingdom[10] that he would not accept this amendment could not have relieved the fears of the two countries concerned.

The Soviets came to the assistance of the Asian parties by introducing three amendments to the United States draft resolution, including one in the sense of the amendment requested by Syria and Lebanon and refused by the United Kingdom. These amendments were defeated, and in response the Soviets voted against the United States proposal.[11]

The final outcome was not unpleasing to the Arab states involved. The United Kingdom and France kept their word to the Security Council that, though the United States resolution had been vetoed, they would abide by its terms. Within the next three months they reported to the Security Council that evacuation of their troops from Syrian and Lebanese territories was being completed. The evacuation was, in fact, completed as reported. Thus, the Asian states achieved the objective which they had sought in going to the Security Council. In addition, the wrangle in the Council between the Great Powers had given them the feeling that they had found a champion. Statements to this effect will, of course, not be found on the Security Council records, but they were voiced in private to friendly delegates.

This feeling, we should note, has been a continuing aspect in the attitudes of Asian and other countries toward the United Nations. In an unanticipated way the Security Council has become the guarantor of what a state might deem to be rights which an unfriendly neighbor was trying to wrest from it. Students and writers tend to allude to the vetoes of the Soviet Union as if they were merely expressions of selfish Soviet interests in the world. While it is, of course, clear that the Soviets would not call the veto into play unless they felt it furthered their own international position or interests, it is

---

[8] *Yearbook of the United Nations, 1946–47* (Lake Success, N.Y: United Nations Department of Public Information, 1947), p. 343. Italics added.

[9] *Ibid.*

[10] *Ibid.*

[11] *Ibid.*, p. 344.

well to remember that the Soviet veto has not always been cast directly to safeguard a Soviet position. The Soviets have used their veto power also in defense of the interests of other states, generally Asian or African states, when it has appeared that the other party to the dispute or situation before the Security Council could count on the support of other Great Powers in the Council. It is well to bear in mind that this is how many Asian states have viewed the exercise of the Soviet veto power. In short, to them the use of the veto has been not a manifestation of a Machiavellian Soviet policy aimed at frustrating efforts to bring order into a specific dangerous international situation but rather an insistence by the Soviets that the parties concerned must find the ways and means of agreeing in direct negotiations to resolve, or at any rate alleviate, the threatening situation in which they find themselves.

Of course, it was not only the Soviet veto which was available for this purpose. The Western side too could champion the states of Asia, and often did. The very first time the Security Council convened to transact business it was to entertain the request of Iran, made in its letter dated January 19, 1946, that the Council might investigate the situation created by the presence in Iran of Soviet troops and recommend appropriate terms of settlement.

Though the first resolution[12] adopted in that case was one introduced by the United Kingdom, amended by the Soviet Union, and unanimously accepted by the Council, in the later stages of the issue, during the Council's consideration of which the Soviet Union frequently absented itself, the United States was the main champion of Iran. Indeed, the United States' support went so far that at one stage, when Iran withdrew its complaint from the Security Council, the Western powers—minus France, which significantly sided with the Soviet Union—insisted on maintaining the issue on the agenda of the Council.[13] And, indeed, though Iran had withdrawn its complaint, it took advantage of this majority view to make subsequent reports to the Council regarding certain aspects of its relations with the Soviet Union.

A discussion of the lessons learned by the Asian countries during the early years of the United Nations does not, however, provide a complete view of the significance of those years in terms of Asian participation in the work of the Organization. We must further note a preoccupation with themselves to the exclusion of an interest in world problems, except insofar as those problems concerned the question of colonialism. It is true that from the very beginning the Indian and the Philippine delegations played a noteworthy role in the Fourth (Trusteeship) Committee of the General Assembly and had much to do with the setting up by the Assembly of the Committee on Information from Non-Self-Governing Territories. Furthermore, the Indian delegation at the first session of the General Assembly raised the matter of

[12] *Ibid.*, p. 329.
[13] *Ibid.*, pp. 334–335.

the treatment of people of Indian origin in the Union of South Africa and thereby sparked the most extended debate in United Nations history on the meaning and applicability of Article 2, paragraph 7, of the Charter. But this discussion of a most important Charter provision was incidental as far as India was concerned—India was raising a matter of direct interest to itself.

During the UN's early years there was practically no contribution from Asia on such questions as disarmament, the peaceful uses of atomic energy, the calling of international conferences by the Economic and Social Council, or even the enlargement of the Economic and Social Council. Their own affairs, colonial questions, and, as far as the Arabs were concerned, their relations with Israel practically constituted the whole domain of interest for the Asian nations in those years.

It is, of course, relevant that the natural leader of Asia had during these very years suffered a total eclipse as far as the United Nations was concerned. From the very beginning it was clear that China was not pulling its weight in the councils of the United Nations. Then came the revolutionary change in regime, and, whatever might have been their views as to which kind of government they would like to see in China, many of the Asian Members of the United Nations believed that the small group of Chinese on the island of Taiwan could not possibly speak effectively for China. The one Great Power in Asia, in terms of the United Nations Charter, became totally ineffective at Lake Success and thereafter on the East River. This fact left the Asian cause in the United Nations without its natural helmsman and must not be overlooked in assessing the part played by the Asian countries and their effectiveness.

THE EXPRESSION OF THE ASIAN VIEW AT THE UNITED NATIONS

As the fifth decade of this century turned into the sixth a combination of events and circumstances tended to broaden the Asian view at the United Nations. These included the Korean War, increasing awareness of the nature of the Cold War, an increase in the number of Asian UN Members, a degree of realization that the new technological age made it unrealistic to focus attention solely on national or regional issues, and an increased concern about economic well-being and the relevance of international action in this regard.

The Korean War directly involved Asia in the first major post-World War II armed struggle and brought the realization that some of the problems of the Asian continent were such that the Great Powers of other continents would get involved in them. The new situation thus differed from the interwar years when the advance of Japan into Manchuria and other parts of China did not lead non-Asian powers into the military involvement on the Asian continent. Now, however, it became clear that even "civil" wars might tend to become global. The fact that the United Nations had much to do with the articulation of this development meant that the states of Asia, like other states, had to realize that the terms of their membership in the Organization were not really compatible with a narrow view of international life, a confining of attention to questions of parochial interest.

At the United Nations itself we must take note of two important occurrences related to the Korean War. First, it led to the formation of the Afro-Asian group, and secondly, it was finally an Indian proposal in the General Assembly which solved the prisoners-of-war tangle which had been holding up the signing of an effective armistice to end the fighting in Korea.

Meanwhile, in spite of the interaction of the large number of vetoes cast by the Soviet Union on applications for membership together with the large degree of reluctance of the West to admit more Communist states, a trickle of new Member States gained admittance between 1946 and 1950; six of these nine were from Asia—Afghanistan, Burma, Indonesia, Pakistan, Thailand, and Yemen. Theoretically, this brought Asian membership to fourteen states. However, since the Korean War made it painfully clear that China was virtually unrepresented at the United Nations, the sixteen-nation Afro-Asian group did not include China when it first met. The group has never been able to correct this state of affairs because many of its members have felt that China continues to be virtually unrepresented at the United Nations. Thus, the Afro-Asian group initially consisted of the remaining Asian countries and the then three African countries in the United Nations—Egypt, Ethiopia, and Liberia. The group was not as cohesive as any of the other three regional groups at the United Nations—the Western European states which were nearly all members of the North Atlantic Treaty Organization (NATO), the Communist nations which, even before they had acceded to the Warsaw Treaty, had maintained a firmly united position at the United Nations, and the Latin American countries which with the United States had developed a stronger regional organization than existed in any other part of the world.

Nevertheless, the drawing together of the Asian countries and the three independent African states represented a growing awareness among the Asian states and their African neighbors that it was desirable and even necessary to meet together to discuss major world problems and not to confine their attention simply to the consideration of issues of direct concern to themselves. True, the group was most effective when it could take a common stand—on such issues as colonialism in general and on support in the United Nations for the Algerian cause. On the latter matter the group set up a standing committee under the chairmanship of the present Secretary-General, who was then the permanent representative of Burma. This committee kept the issue constantly under review, led delegations to the Secretary-General, brought facts to the notice of the Security Council to indicate that events in Algeria constituted a threat to international peace, and made informal representations to the other Great Powers at UN Headquarters.

The group did not set itself up in opposition to other groups. Indeed, in the matter of elections to the various United Nations bodies, it frequently parleyed with the representatives of other groups and reached agreement with them. Sometimes on issues such as the racial policies of South Africa it reached agreement with the Latin Americans as to strategy in the General Assembly. Another example of its nonexclusive character is furnished by the fact that in the autumn of 1955 it decided (it so happens on the initiative of the author) to invite Turkey to join the group. Some of the representatives argued that it would not be wise to bring into the group a country which was in NATO. My view was that this did not constitute a valid reason for the exclusion of Turkey, a country which had attended the Asian-African Conference at Bandung in April 1955. Since the group had to deal with members of NATO, it might lead to appreciation of the Afro-Asian point of view on various matters if a member of NATO were to receive these views firsthand. Ambassador Selim Sarper, later Foreign Minister of Turkey, was pleasantly surprised by the invitation which I conveyed to him and his government on behalf of the group. After consultation with his government, the invitation was accepted, and since then Turkey has sat in both the Afro-Asian group and the Western European group at the United Nations. Another case of overlapping membership is provided by Mongolia, which sits with the Afro-Asian group and with the Communist group of countries. This eclecticism has been possible because the group generally aims at the airing of issues rather than the formulation of common policies. Indeed, the group was conceived, in its initial stages, as a forum in which certain Asian states with a growing concern about such matters as international peacekeeping, disarmament, and economic imbalances could exhort the other Member nations from Asia and Africa to extend their interests to these fields.

ROLE OF THE NONALIGNED

A most important development flowed from these meetings. This was that many of the leading countries in the group began to tend toward an independent or nonaligned foreign policy—or neutralism as some writers, inaccurately, in the Asian-African view, have termed it. The showing of the Afro-Asian countries in the United Nations, particularly the leading part they played in supporting Egypt during the 1956 Suez crisis and their robust opposition to colonialism, impressed the new Members of the United Nations and was a factor in spreading the view that nonalignment was a policy that could best represent their own interests and predilections in international affairs. New countries launched upon the sea of international responsibility generally have tended to seek a course which they could chart without yielding, or seeming to yield, their recently achieved independence. The two sides to the Cold War could offer these new countries certain obvious inducements which could not be matched by the largely indigent nonaligned world. It was also common knowledge that, on the whole, those countries which had joined one bloc or the other in the Cold War had received more per capita aid than those that had remained nonaligned. But there were strong countervailing factors: The nonaligned countries had not been refused economic aid by either side; they had pressed hard in the United Nations on all issues connected with human rights, economic programs, and colonialism; and, finally, they had maintained an independence of the Great Powers. Whereas such autonomy seemed to be an appropriate fulfillment of national political independence, to join one side or the other appeared to be the acceptance of leadership from without.

It has been largely an Asian initiative at the United Nations, strongly supported by the United Arab Republic, that has spurred the spread of nonalignment. In the early fifties the nonaligned at the United Nations numbered a bare half-dozen states, but with the passage of time many states which appeared at first to be more disposed to one side or the other have joined the ranks of the nonaligned on most world issues. This has happened over the years in the cases of Ethiopia, Mexico, the Sudan, Ceylon, Laos, Cambodia, and some of the Latin American states; and it appears to be happening on a widening scale. According to *The New York Times* of March 14, 1965, when President Muhammad Ayub Khan returned earlier in the month from his trip to Communist China, this hitherto staunch and committed ally of the West "was hailed as the leading neutralist of Asia." There are press reports that Turkey is considering a neutral policy, and similar reports emanate from Thailand. Though reports are not easily available regarding the mood of Hanoi, it is sometimes reported, notably via France, that North Vietnam would be disposed to adopt a nonaligned position not unlike that of Yugoslavia. In any event, we have the fact that the mere half-dozen nonaligned countries of the early fifties became 25 states by September 1961 when the first Conference of Nonaligned Nations met at Belgrade and rose spectacularly to some 47 states when the second Conference was held at Cairo in October 1964.

The significance of the United Nations as a world forum has been great in influencing countries toward nonalignment. It is here, for example, that the Member States have heard the nonaligned delegations press for the banning of nuclear tests—a move made yearly by India since Prime Minister Jawaharlal Nehru first turned the attention of the United Nations to this issue in April 1954. This sort of move has caught the imagination of a growing number of countries and has won from them support and a consequent growth of the nonaligned approach. This particular nonaligned initiative reached its logical climax when, at the seventeenth session of the General Assembly, the non-

aligned countries—with a strong Asian infusion—submitted a draft resolution which flatly condemned all nuclear-weapons tests and suggested ways of
securing an agreement to end them. It was a measure of the matured strength
of nonalignment that the resolution[14] was adopted by a vote of 75 in favor, none
opposed, with 21 abstentions, in spite of the fact that both the Soviet Union, on
the one hand, and the United States, the United Kingdom, and France, on the
other, did not support it. The inclusion of non-Asian delegations among the
sponsors of this resolution meant that what had been an Asian initiative had
been espoused by an ever increasing number of states from practically all regions of the world.

No Asian diplomat at the United Nations would make much of the facts
that nonalignment at the United Nations, in general, and the particular move
for a test ban were originally Asian products. In diplomacy the emphasizing
of such matters would be counterproductive, but the objective student is
entitled to take note of these facts. Occasionally, however, a diplomat from
another continent will acknowledge these facts, as Ambassador Burudi Nab-
wera, the permanent representative of Kenya, did in a speech on May 1, 1964.
He said:

> It was not until after India had achieved independence, and this was after the
> second World War, that the policies of nonalignment or positive neutrality began
> to take shape. The credit for this radically new policy goes to Premier Nehru of
> India and his compatriots who thought it out carefully and gave it practical ex-
> pression on an international plane. Hitherto, neutrality had meant a withdrawal
> from the conflict. That is to say, those countries which regarded themselves as
> neutral were not prepared to make public pronouncements on the burning issues
> of the day. But since the advent of positive neutrality the situation has changed.
> Nehru argued, and this is the very core of positive neutralism as we know it
> today, that when there is an issue or a conflict we should examine its pros and
> cons. . . . [Today] practically all the African countries, under the Addis Ababa
> agreement, have declared themselves nonaligned. Many countries in Asia and
> some countries in Europe, the Caribbean and Latin America also belong to this
> group.[15]

To grasp how this happened we must go back to the starting point already
indicated—the decade which opened with the Korean War. War had come
to Asia, a war which seemed to contain the seeds of a possible global conflict
to be fought out on the soil of Asia. Moreover, this was a United Nations
war. These factors combined to create an attitude of vigilance on the part of
the Asian states, particularly those at the United Nations, and they felt it to
be their duty to try to explore all possible avenues of diplomatic effort. It
is not possible in this brief study to trace the course of the efforts launched

---

[14] General Assembly Resolution 1762 A (XVII), November 6, 1962.
[15] Text of statement obtained from the permanent mission of Kenya to the United Nations.

through Delhi, largely at the urging of the then permanent representative of India to the United Nations, Sir Benegal N. Rau, but it is worthwhile recollecting that the purpose of these efforts was so patently to try to bring about a cessation of the fighting that they gained a certain measure of support both in the West and in Communist China.

Eventually the point was reached when the fighting could stop, provided a formula could be found to deal with the question of the prisoners of war. It seemed that the Western powers and Communist China approached the issue from diametrically opposite points of view. To bridge the gap appeared impossible. The issue was a grave one. United States Secretary of State Dean Acheson and British Foreign Secretary Anthony Eden were both present at New York to take part in the debate on this issue at meetings of the First (Political and Security) Committee of the seventh session of the General Assembly. Andrei Vishinsky of the Soviet Union spoke for his country and apparently also for the absent Communist Chinese. He remained vehemently opposed to the Western point of view, and they remained solidly opposed to his. In these circumstances the West felt that the best that could be done was to offer the Assembly a draft resolution which would put the seal of United Nations approval on their position. Some twenty countries sponsored the Western draft resolution, and there was no doubt of a considerably larger than two-thirds majority vote in favor of the text since the Western allies alone constituted more than two-thirds of the Assembly which then comprised 60 Member States. The date for the vote had all but arrived.

At this stage India, through V. K. Krishna Menon, presented its plan for a solution of the seemingly unbridgeable gap. The scheme presented took into account Communist China's susceptibilities as India saw them, and, of course, it also sought to meet the Western position. The Indian plan seemed to furnish some of the magic which the moment demanded. Dean Acheson and Anthony Eden immediately signified their interest and agreed that the Indian draft resolution should have priority over their own text in the voting. Unfortunately, at that stage of the Cold War the clear support of one side meant the almost automatic opposition of the other. Mr. Vishinsky would have no part of the Indian plan, and he suggested that Peking would not either. The Soviet Union voted against the Indian proposal, but the West, the Asian states, and other nonaligned delegations supported it, and it was handsomely carried.[16] What is more, the Indian reading of Communist Chinese attitudes turned out to be more correct than that of the Soviet Union: The Chinese eventually signified their interest in the Indian formula which became the basis of the accepted plan for the settlement of the prisoners-of-war issue and brought about an end to the fighting in Korea. This whole incident was of profound significance. It marked the first fruits of Asian nonalignment at the

[16] General Assembly Resolution 610 (VII), December 3, 1952.

United Nations, one might almost say of "Asianism" at the United Nations because this was a move which neither those committed to the West nor those devoted to the Communist cause would have conceived. It came out of synthesizing attitudes which, at that time, one could hardly expect of two great opposing champions.

MOUNTING PARTICIPATION IN DISARMAMENT DISCUSSIONS

It was this success and the world factors which prompted the effort toward it that brought the Asians out of their parochialism at the United Nations and led to the focusing of part of their attention on world issues. Up to that time the debates on such subjects as disarmament had been debates between the two sides in the Cold War with minimal participation by other countries and the proposals put before the Assembly almost always were presented by the Cold War adversaries. From the eighth session of the General Assembly (1953) onward, however, this ceased to be the case. At its ninth session the Assembly, for the first time since 1946, reached unanimity on a resolution on the crucial subject of disarmament.[17] That resolution included ideas suggested by the Asian countries, and, furthermore, it transmitted to the Disarmament Commission a draft resolution on the subject which had been proposed by India and another draft which had been introduced by the delegations of Australia and the Philippines jointly.

Thereafter the Asian countries and some of their nonaligned friends came increasingly into the foreground of disarmament discussions at the United Nations. The next high point in their effort occurred in 1957 at the twelfth session of the General Assembly when a resolution sponsored by India and supported by a number of Asian countries drastically cut into the previous voting patterns of the Assembly. Though this draft resolution on the discontinuance of nuclear tests was defeated, the number of those states that voted in favor of it together with those that abstained on it exceeded those that opposed it.[18] From then on the Asian states and the growing number of those countries which were responding to what had been and largely continued to be an Asian initiative in the field of disarmament were a parliamentary force in the United Nations which had to be taken seriously. It was as a result of their stand that the fifteenth session of the General Assembly (1960) witnessed the extraordinary development that no substantive text on the subject of disarmament was put to the vote. There were as many as nine draft resolutions on the subject before the First Committee—a proliferation of texts which itself showed how great the interest of the Assembly had become in regard to this matter.

[17] General Assembly Resolution 808 (IX), November 4, 1954.
[18] UN Document A/L.232. The vote on November 19, 1957, was 24 in favor, 34 against, with 20 abstentions.

Most of these texts, however, sought to obtain from the Assembly its sanction for the position of one or the other of the major sides in the Cold War. A group of countries led by some Asian states and the United Arab Republic took the view that it would no longer serve the interests of disarmament or the fundamental purposes of the Charter for any partisan resolution to be adopted by the Assembly. Meanwhile Canada presented a procedural resolution which asked the First Committee to defer voting on eight of the nine texts and to proceed instead to adopt a draft[19] which stood in the name of Canada and eighteen other countries including a small fraction (three states) of the Asian membership of the Assembly. This was prima facie a brilliant tactical move on the part of Canada and one which previously would have been approved with a wide margin of votes to spare. Even in 1960 it was the calculation of the Canadian delegation and its numerous friends that this procedural device would be accepted by the Assembly.

At this point the Asians and their friends explained the futility of proceeding in a manner which would present the disarmament negotiators with a one-sided directive for their task. India introduced an oral amendment to the Canadian procedural text in the sense that the vote on all—rather than all but one—of the various proposals before the First Committee should be deferred. In this way, at least, an unbalanced directive to the negotiators would be avoided. The Indian motion came to the vote and was adopted by the First Committee,[20] an action indicative of the growing sophistication of the Assembly.

Meanwhile, the negotiators on disarmament were running into trouble. The Disarmament Commission's five-nation Subcommittee—itself partly the outcome of an Asian initiative in the Assembly—after struggling with the subject for several years and achieving no progress whatsoever in the form of tangible agreements, had ceased to function. Then in 1960 came the parity negotiations in which five Western powers and five Communist countries participated. But these rapidly collapsed. The two sides were unable any longer to exclude from the negotiations a body of nonaligned states, that is, of states which had come to espouse broadly the approach to international affairs first introduced to the United Nations by India and other Asian states. Thus, the Eighteen-Nation Disarmament Committee, which has been longer in near continuous session than any other disarmament negotiating body and which, unlike its predecessors, has to its credit some tangible successes in the field, represents in a sense the flowering from an Asian seed.

---

[19] UN Document A/C.1/L.255/Rev.1 and Rev.1/Add.1–5.
[20] General Assembly *Official Records* . . . *First Committee* (15th session), pp. 278–279, 283–284.

Contributions to Peacekeeping

We should take note of another flowering from the same Asian seed. This is the significant role of the nonaligned countries in many of the peacekeeping operations which the United Nations has conducted in recent years. Indeed, nonalignment in considerable measure facilitated the earliest major peacekeeping operations by providing sources which could ensure prima facie nonpartisan contingents for the situations concerned.

When the United Nations Emergency Force (UNEF) was assembled in 1956 following the Suez crisis, India furnished the largest national unit for service on the perimeter of the Gaza Strip. Indonesia was another Asian country which contributed forces to this operation. When peacekeeping operations had to be mounted in the Congo (Leopoldville), the Asian states of Ceylon, the then Federation of Malaya, India, Indonesia, and Pakistan all contributed forces. The Indian contingent was once again the largest, and Indonesia's was at one stage among the largest. Finally, it was a large Pakistani force which kept the peace in West Irian during the short interim period of United Nations control before the territory was handed over to the administration of Indonesia.

If we do no more in this study than to note rather than discuss extensively the role of the Asian states at the United Nations in the movement to terminate colonialism and to advance to independence the states in the trusteeship system, it is because this role is widely acknowledged. We have already drawn attention to the early efforts of the Philippines and India in these matters. Thereafter, and notably until the large influx of African Member States in 1960, the Asian states constituted the vanguard of opposition to the continuance of colonialism within the Fourth Committee of the General Assembly and the Trusteeship Council. It was they that concentrated on the accelerated termination of the trusteeship status of Tanganyika and thereby quickened the realization of independence in several states of East Africa.

Finally, the Special Committee on the Situation with Regard to the Implementation of the Declaration on the Granting of Independence to Colonial Countries and Peoples (Special Committee of Twenty-Four) counts among its membership the five Asian states of Cambodia, India, Iran, Iraq, and Syria. They cooperate closely with the seven African members of the Special Committee together with which they constitute half the Special Committee's membership and a most important section of its working strength.

Concern for Economic Development

Of developed material wealth Asia, with the exception of Japan, cannot boast. It is not surprising then that the Asian countries should have cosponsored the earliest effort of the General Assembly in 1950 to direct attention toward the need for increased flow of capital to the less developed world.[21] The concept of a special development fund took definite form, again largely through an Asian effort in which some other countries joined, in 1952 when the Assembly resolved to request ECOSOC to submit to the next session of the General Assembly

> a detailed plan for establishing, as soon as circumstances permit, a special fund for grants-in-aid and for low-interest, long-term loans to under-developed countries. . . . [22]

The detailed plan was to go into the size and composition of the special fund, its policies, conditions, and methods for making grants.

Thus, again largely as a result of an Asian initiative, a new idea was launched at the United Nations. From then on, the underdeveloped world was rallied by the efforts of India, Egypt, Indonesia, and soon by other less developed countries, such as Burma, Ceylon, Afghanistan, Mexico, Pakistan, Nepal, and Yugoslavia, to the long struggle with most of the highly developed countries on the establishment of a United Nations capital loan fund. As the Cold War rigidities hardened, the notion of a United Nations source of financial assistance, rather than bilateral assistance from the Great Powers, became increasingly attractive to the economically needy countries of Asia and the then small number of African Member States as well as some of the Latin American countries in the United Nations. In this way the recipient nations hoped to insulate themselves against even the suspicion of political strings attached to economic aid.

A typical effort by the Asian countries was a draft resolution requesting the *Ad Hoc* Committee on the Question of the Establishment of a Special United Nations Fund for Economic Development (SUNFED) to set forth the different forms of legal framework on which SUNFED might be established and to indicate the types of projects which could be programmed for a UN economic development fund. Introduced during the eleventh session in the Second (Economic and Financial) Committee, the draft was cosponsored by fifteen Asian countries, i.e., the entire Asian membership at that time except Japan (which as a developed country tended to side with the Great Powers in the long debate on the issue) and Iran (which became a sponsor before the draft was put to the vote). Initially combining with the cosponsors were a few Latin American nations, Greece, the Netherlands, Yugoslavia, and four African states. In the debate which followed, many other countries joined in the mainly Asian initiative, and the draft resolution was adopted unanimously both in the Second Committee and by the Assembly.[23]

---

[21] General Assembly Resolution 400 (V), November 20, 1950.
[22] General Assembly Resolution 520 (VI), January 12, 1952.
[23] General Assembly Resolution 1030 (XI), February 26, 1957.

At the next session of the General Assembly, India, in recognition of the part played by the Asian states in promoting the proposal for SUNFED, was asked to introduce an eleven-power draft resolution which sought to set up a UN economic development fund.[24] The highly developed countries stated that they would oppose the draft in the form in which it was submitted. They were adamant in the view that they could not agree to contribute to a fund which would make capital available to the less developed world through the United Nations until there had been some disarmament. They were, however, willing to contribute, through the United Nations, "seed money" which would assist the less developed countries to assess their economic resources and make surveys in connection with possible large-scale projects which could attract foreign capital to the extent necessary. As a compromise, the presently existing Special Fund, which makes funds available for preinvestment studies, was set up by a unanimously adopted resolution.[25] The effort in the United Nations to set up a capital development fund still goes on, however, and among those pressing for it are the Asian countries.

The 1963 declaration of the 75 developing countries on the then proposed United Nations Conference on Trade and Development (UNCTAD), which was welcomed in a resolution by the General Assembly,[26] bore the signatures of the representatives of all the Asian Members of the United Nations except Japan (which is not in the category of less developed countries) and China (because at present there is no unanimity among the developing countries as to the representation of China at the United Nations). As is well-known, the 75 less developed countries maintained their solidarity throughout the ensuing Geneva Conference in 1964 and played a determining role in the adoption of the *Final Act* of the Conference and of the numerous detailed recommendations annexed thereto.[27]

While these efforts in and through the United Nations continue to be made by the Asian countries to secure an increased flow of economic aid and better terms of trade, the countries concerned are too realistic to depend solely on them. They continue to accept aid and to attract capital from countries which are willing to make such assistance available bilaterally. Indeed, such assistance far exceeds what they have so far been able to obtain through the United Nations. Thus, in the year 1963 the net flow of direct long-term capital assistance to the developing countries from the United States, the United Kingdom, West Germany, and the Benelux countries amounted to $4,741 million, whereas the allocation of capital by these countries to international institutions (and through them to the developing countries) amounted to no more than

24 UN Document A/C.2/L.331.
25 General Assembly Resolution 1219 (XII), December 14, 1957.
26 General Assembly Resolution 1897 (XVIII), November 11, 1963.
27 *Final Act of the UN Conference on Trade and Development* (UN Document E/CONF.46/L.28).

$561 million.[28] Much of the direct aid went to Asian countries. Moreover, in the three-year period 1960–1962, about 55 percent of the long-term flow of capital from the capital-exporting countries went to thirteen developing countries, the share of India, Pakistan, South Korea, Indonesia, South Vietnam, and Taiwan amounting to 30 percent.[29] Of the remaining 45 percent of this capital flow, other Asian countries were among the major recipients. Asia receives a considerably higher percentage of the flow of long-term international capital which reaches the developing world than any other region, and the bulk of this is from outside the United Nations system.

DIVERSITY WITHIN ASIA

The impression must not be given by what has been said that all the Asian states are of one mind in the Assembly. On the contrary, the differences between them remain sharper than those in other regions such as Latin America or even Africa. There are cleavages between India and Pakistan, Malaysia and Indonesia, Thailand and Cambodia, and some Asian states, such as the Philippines, continue to oppose strongly the alteration of the representation of China. Furthermore, unlike Latin America and Africa, there is no regional organization where Asian states come together to discuss their affairs. Though Africa has many problems, the Organization of African Unity (OAU) might be able to deal with some of them and alleviate the circumstances created by others. Of the vitality of the inter-American system there can be no doubt. Asia is without any comparable arrangements, and its divisions are clearly apparent at the United Nations. Furthermore, though some viable adjustments of inter-Asian problems are undoubtedly possible, Asia is probably further away from any form of unity than all the other areas of the world. This being so, while one can discern certain largely Asian contributions to the United Nations, as we have been engaged in doing, it would be unrealistic to expect the emergence of a single Asian voice at the UN. This is not necessarily a disadvantage. Asia is historically a zone of much exchange of culture and mixing of races. It is natural that at the United Nations as elsewhere it should speak with many voices. This diversity is the wealth of Asia.

ASIAN PROSPECTS AT THE UNITED NATIONS

Of all the regions of the world, both in terms of power and demography, Asia is currently the least fully represented at the United Nations. The Americas, both North and South, are virtually entirely represented. Europe is fully represented except for Germany—and for the orderly development of peace-

---

[28] UN Document E/3917/Rev. 1, p. 18.
[29] *Ibid.*, p. 26.

ful relations in our world it is becoming increasingly necessary that steps be taken to end the exclusion of Germany from the Organization. Even Africa, the latest continent to come into its own, has greater representation than Asia. In terms of the people involved, unrepresented Asia exceeds the total populations of Africa and North and South America taken together or of Africa and Europe. While it is, of course, true that the United Nations is an association of states, the demographic factor has a bearing on the importance of the Organization and the allegiance it commands. The defection of Indonesia from the United Nations is to be explained in an important degree by the fact that a Communist China outside the United Nations is growing in power and prestige. The longer this large nonrepresentation of Asia in the United Nations continues, the greater the likelihood that there will be further defections from the Organization. Thus, if the United Nations is to reach its full measure of effectiveness and value in Asia, it must become much more effectively representative of the continent. This is a matter the resolving of which, in the interests of the United Nations and of the growth of an attitude of peaceful cooperation in the world in general, has now become one of very real urgency. Drift is likely to alienate the Organization from an increasing number of countries.

The interests of Asia in the United Nations boil down to problems of peace and security on the one hand (including the removal of the last vestiges of colonialism) and economic assistance and cooperation on the other. Social and cultural needs there are, but their fulfillment is not as closely dependent upon international cooperation.

The Cold War failed to drive either side out of the United Nations, and it is to be hoped that the present financial crisis will be equally unsuccessful in pushing matters to so dire a conclusion. In this connection, the efforts of the Asian and African countries are directed mainly toward keeping the Organization going and solving the financial issue within the framework of a functioning United Nations. In a sense this emphasis on the survival of the Organization resembles the stress laid in the opening phrase of Article 1 of the Charter on the maintenance of international peace and security. It was proposed at the 1945 Charter Conference that the notion of justice should be stated alongside of peace and security. This was not done because it was felt that the first duty was what we might call the preservation of the species. In the view of most Asian countries, the preservation of the Organization is of analogous importance.

But we are beginning to witness the incipient proliferation of the centers of macropower. It is difficult enough to keep two Great Powers and their supporters talking, but if there are soon to be four or even more powers possessing macrodestructive power and if two of them are not taking part in the dialogue of peace—partly because they feel they have too long been kept out

of such discussions—the strains on the processes of maintaining world order
will become much greater. Indeed, we could find ourselves back in the era
prior to the League of Nations when there were a number of Great Powers
all seeking to keep the balance of power by alliances and secret understandings.

Regression of this kind will not only poorly serve international purposes
in a nuclear world but might well bring us near the end of all national and
international purposes. Defections from the United Nations by Asian countries could develop a trend to such a state of affairs. Unfortunately, such defections are not unlikely unless the Great Powers, or more truly the powers in
all the various regions, pledge themselves again to make the United Nations a
vigorous reality. The neglect of the problems of Asia could cause irreparable
damage to the United Nations. Fortunately, this is not the desire or policy of
most Asian states, but they alone will not be able to steer the ship of the continent through the rising seas of international tensions.

The UN and Disimperialism in the Middle East

J. C. HUREWITZ

IN the first dozen years of the UN's existence Middle East disputes came before the Security Council and appeared on the agenda of the General Assembly with greater frequency than did disputes in any other region of the world. Thereafter the Middle East did not always occupy the center of the UN's peacekeeping stage. Yet as recent developments in the Arab-Israeli area and in Cyprus and Yemen disclose, the Middle East remains a region of deep restiveness that continues to threaten world peace and security. Every regular session of the General Assembly, except the first session in 1946, has considered Middle East items. Two special sessions dealt with the Palestine problem, and two emergency sessions handled the Suez and Lebanese crises. The Security Council has turned to the Palestine problem or its lineal descendant, the Arab-Israeli dispute, at approximately every sixth meeting.

A quick glance at the UN peacekeeping record reveals that the Security Council or the General Assembly or both have resorted to the use of an international force along the Israeli-Egyptian armistice line (since 1956) and on Cyprus (since 1964); maintained continuously (since 1948) in the Arab-Israeli area the UN Truce Supervision Organization (UNTSO) first as part of the truce arrangement and later as part of the armistice system; sent observer missions to Palestine, Lebanon, and Yemen; appointed mediators to Palestine and Cyprus; designated the Secretary-General to provide good offices in resolving the Suez crisis and to observe compliance with the Security Council's call for a cease-fire in the fighting between Tunisia and France in July 1961; and sent out a variety of commissions of inquiry, administration, and conciliation to various parts of the region.

J. C. HUREWITZ is Professor of Government, Columbia University.

Variables Conditioning the Place of the Middle East at the UN

Before an evaluation of the UN's intimate involvement in Middle East problems is attempted, it must be borne in mind that multiple variables are being dealt with. Unlike Asia, Africa, and Latin America, the Middle East as such never acquired an identifiable personality at the UN. For one thing, the Middle East does not fill a continent; instead it spills over two and splashes a third. For another, it has no stable definition, expanding and contracting for the occasion or for the convenience of a given diplomat or author.[1] Internally disunited, the Middle East, moreover, never formed a caucusing group at the UN.

On the eve of the UN Conference on International Organization at San Francisco, it is true, the Arab states created their own regional organization. The growing number of Arab League members that have been admitted to the UN have functioned as an interest group, surpassed in voting cohesiveness at the General Assembly only by the Soviet bloc.[2] Nevertheless, both inside and outside the UN, the Arab League states have quarreled vigorously with their non-Arab neighbors of the Middle East—invariably with Israel, but often with such Muslim states as Turkey, Iran, and Pakistan as well. It was the stubborn dispute with Israel in the context of the larger regional divisiveness that prevented the establishment of an economic commission for the Middle East, as envisaged by the General Assembly in 1947,[3] although such commissions came into being for Latin America, Europe, Africa, and Asia and the Far East.

It must also be remembered that the UN and the Middle East have changed measurably in the first two postwar decades. In the Middle East as well as in the rest of Asia and Africa, this was the period of disimperialism, a process to which, as will be seen, the UN contributed to no small degree. As states were born in the region at an average rate of one every seventeen months, they were admitted to membership in the UN. Thus, the Middle East also helped transform the General Assembly from an organ dominated by the Western powers into one progressively responsive to the wishes of the new states of Africa and Asia which now form a majority of the total UN membership.

Yet disimperialism started in the Middle East before the creation of the UN. After World War I, the Soviet Union and the United Kingdom failed to preserve their spheres of influence in Iran, and in 1927 King Ibn Sa'ud, having united most of the Arabian Peninsula under his sway, withdrew from the United Kingdom's Persian Gulf quasi-protectorate regime. In the British-

---

[1] The Middle East, as defined herein, stretches from Morocco to Afghanistan and Pakistan.

[2] Thomas Hovet, Jr., *Bloc Politics in the United Nations* (Cambridge, Mass: Harvard University Press, 1960), pp. 56–64 and Tables 13–18 on pp. 134–139.

[3] General Assembly Resolution 120 (II), October 31, 1947.

and French-mandated countries, nationalist demands for independence weakened the hold of the imperial powers. In Egypt, too, nationalist pressure persuaded the United Kingdom to terminate its protectorate as early as 1922. Moreover, Iraq and Egypt became members of the League of Nations in the next decade, although both countries were still tied to the British imperial system by preferential alliances which were chips off the old sphere-of-influence block but shaped to fit the new doctrine of self-determination.

At the San Francisco Conference in 1945 a majority of the thirteen Asian and African states were from the Middle East. Five (Egypt, Iran, Iraq, Lebanon, and Syria) still played host to alien troops. The high number of civilian casualties in the street fighting in Damascus between French imperial forces and Syrians late in May 1945 brought Syria's and Lebanon's claims to independence dramatically to the attention of the San Francisco conferees. As preferential allies of the United Kingdom, Egypt and Iraq had not lost their central status in the United Kingdom's Middle East empire. Though technically sovereign, Iran was still divided into Soviet and British zones of occupation. Turkey and Saudi Arabia alone among the UN's Middle East charter Members escaped billeting foreign garrisons in World War II. The states of the Middle East thus went to San Francisco on sufferance.

For all political intents and purposes, the Middle East at the close of World War II still constituted a projection of Europe. This was true not only of Turkey and Iran but also of Afghanistan, which, although sovereign, continued to serve as a buffer that kept the Soviet Union from touching the British Empire. During World War II the Anglo-Soviet occupation of Iran effectively sealed off Afghanistan from access by the Axis powers. Although Turkey held fast to neutrality until the summer of 1944, it was turning to the United Kingdom (and the United States) the following spring for support against Soviet claims to Turkish territory and bases.

South of the buffer the Arab lands of Asia fell solidly within the British sphere. Even in mandated Syria and Lebanon, after the British and the Free French had forcibly ejected the Vichy administration in 1941, the United Kingdom assumed basic responsibility for integrating the two Arab countries into the allied war effort and, as custodian of security, stationed British troops there for the duration of the war. In adjacent Northeast Africa the British sphere encompassed Egypt, the Sudan, and, after the expulsion of German and Italian troops in 1942–1943, most of Libya as well. The United Kingdom mobilized for the war effort this wide assortment of Asian and African territories in differing conditions of imperial dependence and, as a result, gave the region greater political, military, and economic unity than it had ever enjoyed before. As the reluctant wartime capital of the United Kingdom's Middle East empire, Cairo housed the British Middle East War Council which was chaired by a resident minister of the War Cabinet and which was com-

posed of the top political and the top military officer in each associated country. Although the War Council and its subordinate (United Kingdom–United
States) Supply Center disappeared before the end of 1945, the United Kingdom retained a unified Middle East Command with headquarters in Cairo.

Much smaller in scale but more tightly integrated even before 1939 was the
exclusive French sphere in Northwest Africa, with only a peripheral presence
of Spain in Morocco and an international enclave in the city of Tangier.
France administered Algeria after 1871 as if it were an extension of the me-
tropolis, cutting the country up into *départements* whose European residents
were represented in both houses of the national legislature in Paris. As protectorates, Tunisia and Morocco did not merit similar rights but were nevertheless treated as extensions of Algeria for French settlement.

THE PROCESS OF DISIMPERIALISM QUICKENS

After the war the process of disimperialism in the Middle East accelerated
under UN auspices or was spurred on by its actions. All mandates were formally terminated by 1948 and no trust territories were created in the region.
The only two proposals, one for a temporary trusteeship over Palestine and
the other for the projected international regime for Jerusalem, never saw the
light of day. Yet disimperialism was taking place not in an international
vacuum but under the influence of the Cold War. As British and French
power melted away, the United States and the Soviet Union directly confronted each other in the Middle East with increasing frequency. This un-
avoidably affected the actions taken by the UN in coping with the consequences of disimperialism in the region. For reasons that will be explored
below, the Soviet and Arab caucusing groups at the General Assembly often
found it mutually advantageous to vote on the same side in the concerted
anticolonial drive.

The UN helped contain imperialist expansion into the Middle East as early
as 1946 when the Soviet Union tried to absorb the buffer belt. The pressure
focused primarily on Turkey and Iran. In 1945 the Soviet Union demanded
districts in the northeastern part of Turkey and joint responsibility for defense of the Straits. The next year it sought to dismember Iran. Iran submitted
its complaint to the Security Council in January 1946, even before that organ
had drawn up provisional rules of procedure. Public discussion of the Soviet-
Iranian dispute in the UN embarrassed the Soviet Union and enabled the
United States to frustrate Moscow's purpose while avoiding resort to military
measures. The Turkish-Soviet quarrel, meanwhile, was settled outside the Organization.

In the decade that followed, the United Kingdom took its Middle East
imperial structure apart piece by piece. Without retention by the United King-

dom of political or military privilege, the mandate in Palestine, codominant authority in the Sudan, and the preferential alliance in Jordan came to an end. Also surrendered after an eight-year ordeal was the massive Suez base which had been the headquarters of the United Kingdom's Middle East Command. In the economic sphere, the United Kingdom accepted the nationalization of the Anglo-Iranian Oil Company's properties and exclusive concession in Iran and, in the final settlement, a minority status in an international consortium. After abandoning in 1946 its claims to a special position in Syria and Lebanon, France also gave full independence a decade later to its two North African protectorates, Morocco and Tunisia. Then, at the end of 1956, at the height of the Suez crisis, France and the United Kingdom reverted to gunboat diplomacy. Since by the exercise of the veto the United Kingdom and France were able to thwart effective action by the Security Council, the General Assembly was convened in emergency session under the Uniting for Peace Resolution. In consequence, the two European powers had to withdraw their troops, the United Kingdom lost its contingent right of return to the Suez base, and management of the Canal became exclusively Egyptian.

The contribution of the UN to disimperialism in the Middle East did not always take the form of preventive measures, as the unique case of Libya illustrates. After the Council of Foreign Ministers of France, the Soviet Union, the United Kingdom, and the United States had failed in 1948 to agree on the disposal of the former Italian colonies in Africa, the question came before the General Assembly in accordance with the terms of the Italian peace treaty. As one result, the Assembly in 1949 adopted a resolution calling for Libyan independence no later than January 1, 1952, and for UN assistance in drafting a constitution and establishing a government.[4]

THE PALESTINE AND SUEZ PROBLEMS

In Palestine, the process of disengagement proved especially sticky. The Jewish side adamantly refused to consider anything less than early independence for a Jewish state in an adequate area of the mandate. The Palestine Arabs and the independent Arab states, for their part, refused no less firmly to seek a negotiated settlement with the sponsors of a Jewish state. By the time the United Kingdom referred the problem to the first special session of the General Assembly in the spring of 1947, the mandatory power had exhausted efforts to reach an agreement outside the Organization. The General Assembly, with the endorsement of the United States and the Soviet Union, approved a proposal for the partition of Palestine. But after the Arab states tried forcibly to stop the execution of the scheme, the Security Council

<hr>

[4] Treaty of Peace with Italy, February 10, 1947, Article 23 and Annex XI; and General Assembly Resolution 289 A (IV), November 21, 1949.

brought the Palestine war to a halt and, through the UN Acting Mediator, assisted the parties to structure an armistice system in 1949. The General Assembly, moreover, placed the Palestine Arab refugees in its custody. Within the two principal UN organs at this time Soviet–United States hostility in the Cold War gathered momentum after the enunciation in the Truman Doctrine of the policy of checking Soviet expansion. While the Soviet Union seemed determined to ease the United Kingdom out of Palestine and keep the United States from moving in, the United States seemed equally determined to keep the Soviet Union from direct participation in any subsidiary organ created by the UN to deal with the dispute.

Between May 1947 and September 1949 the General Assembly and the Security and Trusteeship Councils established at different times no fewer than ten commissions to handle the several aspects of the Palestine problem.[5] The Soviet Union, however, did not sit on any of these bodies. But this could not be attributed to lack of Soviet interest. After agreeing at the first special session of the General Assembly to the creation of a special UN inquiry commission, the Soviet delegate insisted that the permanent members of the Security Council should assume

> together with the United Nations as a whole, the responsibility not only for final decisions . . . taken by our Organisation . . . but also for the preparation of these decisions.

In the end the Assembly upheld the United States position of excluding the permanent Council members from the eleven-state body.[6] In June 1948 Count Folke Bernadotte, the Palestine Mediator, requested Belgium, France, and the United States (whose consuls at Jerusalem constituted the Security Council's Truce Commission for Palestine) as well as his native Sweden to furnish military personnel as observers for what was to become the UN Truce Supervision Organization. The Soviet delegate argued that "the Soviet Union has grounds which are certainly no less cogent than those of the United States for including a small group of military observers." But a Soviet proposal that would have allowed all willing Security Council members, Syria apart, to appoint observers failed to muster the requisite votes. So too did later Soviet moves in the General Assembly and the Security Council to have all military observers recalled.[7]

[5] These commissions included: the United Nations Special Committee on Palestine (UNSCOP), the United Nations Palestine Commission, the Security Council Truce Commission for Palestine, the United Nations Special Municipal Commissioner for Jerusalem, the United Nations Mediator (and Acting Mediator) in Palestine, the United Nations Relief for Palestine Refugees (UNRPR), the United Nations Conciliation Commission for Palestine (UNCCP), the United Nations Truce Supervision Organization (UNTSO), the United Nations Economic Survey Mission for the Middle East, and the United Nations Relief and Works Agency for Palestine Refugees in the Near East (UNRWA).

[6] General Assembly *Official Records* (1st special session), Vol. 3, pp. 80–81, 132, 149–150.

[7] Security Council *Official Records* (3rd year), 314th meeting, June 7, 1948, p. 3; 317th meeting, June 10, 1948, p. 44; and 320th meeting, June 15, 1948, pp. 6–8, 11–13; and General Assembly *Official Records . . . First Committee* (3rd session, part II), Annexes, p. 75.

The UN enabled the United Kingdom to disengage itself from Palestine and subsequently kept alive an armistice system that was never intended to harden into permanence. The failure of the parties to reach a formal settlement, however, invited violations. Tensions rose on both sides of the armistice lines culminating in Israel's preemptive strike in Sinai in October 1956 followed by the French and British intervention at Suez. Israel was compelled to withdraw its military units from the Gaza Strip and from the Sinai Peninsula. The United Nations Emergency Force (UNEF), which the General Assembly at its emergency session brought into being partly to supervise the withdrawal, has to this day continued to patrol the Egyptian side of the armistice line and the Sinai littoral of the Gulf of 'Aqaba, thus shoring up the armistice system. Since then, remarkably few incidents have disturbed the Israeli-Egyptian frontier or Israeli shipping through 'Aqaba waters and the Straits of Tiràn leading to the Red Sea. The Palestine Arab refugees, too, have remained a charge of the international community, with the expenses being borne by voluntary contributions. The assessments for the support of UNEF represented one of the key elements in the dispute over UN finances at the nineteenth session of the General Assembly.

Dismantling the French and British Imperial Holdings

From the outset, the very consideration of an issue by or simply its reference to the Security Council or the General Assembly prodded a metropolitan power to early retirement from a dependency. France seemed to require such nudging. Syria and Lebanon presented a joint complaint to the Security Council in 1946 against the continued postwar presence of French (and British) troops on their soil. The Soviet Union vetoed as too weak a United States proposal expressing

> confidence that foreign troops in Syria and Lebanon will be withdrawn as soon as practicable, and that negotiations to that end will be undertaken by the parties without delay. . . . [8]

The two Western powers nonetheless reached an understanding in the spirit of the United States proposal for the prompt evacuation of their garrisons from the two Arab countries. Analogous was the later experience in North Africa. The General Assembly in 1952 expressed

> its confidence that . . . France will endeavour to further the effective development of the free institutions of the Tunisian people . . . [and] the hope that the parties will continue negotiations on an urgent basis with a view to bringing about self-government for Tunisians. . . .

France refused to participate in the discussion, the United States voted for

[8] Security Council *Official Records* (1st year), 22nd meeting, February 16, 1946, pp. 332–333.

the resolution, and the Soviet Union abstained on the ground that it was "clearly insufficient to ensure the observance of the legitimate rights of the Tunisian people. . . . "[9] Comparable were the positions of the three powers on a somewhat stronger resolution on Morocco at the same session.[10] The Assembly consideration of the questions hastened France's grant of independence to the two North African protectorates, particularly in view of the Muslim rebellion in Algeria that was threatening to get out of hand.

Even more negative was France's reaction to the General Assembly's review of the Algerian question in 1955. France simply boycotted the tenth session until the First (Political and Security) Committee suspended discussion of the item. While France later held to the contention that the issue was clearly one of domestic jurisdiction, it nevertheless agreed to the Assembly's placing the question on its agenda.[11] France finally negotiated the Evian accord of March 1962 directly with the Provisional Government of the Algerian Republic. Still the recurrent Assembly discussions served to remind France that the international community was watching closely the French handling of the Algerian insurrection.

The United Kingdom's experience in the Cyprus dispute followed roughly the same course although the United Kingdom never refused to take part in the Assembly discussion. Endorsing the Greek Cypriot demands for independence, Greece submitted the question to the General Assembly's ninth session in 1954 and annually thereafter.[12] The United Kingdom also framed the Zurich settlement in 1959 in direct exchanges with Greece, Turkey, and the Greek and Turkish communities on Cyprus. Furthermore, not all questions of British imperial retirement from the Middle East reached the United Nations, as, for example, the termination of the Anglo-Egyptian condominium in the Sudan and of the preferential alliances in Egypt, Iraq, and Jordan.

By December 1960 when the General Assembly approved the Declaration on the Granting of Independence to Colonial Countries and Peoples,[13] disimperialism had almost run its course in the Middle East. The Zurich agreement on Cyprus had gone into effect the preceding August, and the new insular republic had taken its seat in the Assembly the following month. Even General Charles de Gaulle's delayed-action diplomacy on Algeria had already reached

[9] General Assembly Resolution 611 (VII), December 17, 1952; and General Assembly *Official Records* (7th session), p. 381.

[10] General Assembly Resolution 612 (VII), December 19, 1952; and General Assembly *Official Records . . . First Committee* (7th session), pp. 291–292. See also General Assembly Resolutions 812 (IX) and 813 (IX) of December 17, 1954; and General Assembly *Official Records . . . First Committee* (9th session), pp. 534–535, 571–572.

[11] For the Assembly's action on the Algerian question at its eleventh, twelfth, fifteenth, and sixteenth sessions see, respectively, General Assembly Resolutions 1012 (XI), February 15, 1957; 1184 (XII), December 10, 1957; 1573 (XV), December 15, 1960; and 1724 (XVI), December 20, 1961.

[12] See, for example, General Assembly Resolutions 814 (IX), December 17, 1954; and 1287 (XIII), December 5, 1958.

[13] General Assembly Resolution 1514 (XV), December 14, 1960.

the stage at which the French President disclosed that the Muslims would be given the right of self-determination and that the dependency would be emancipated, as indeed occurred eighteen months later. Otherwise, all that remained of European imperial possessions was the string of British-protected sheikhdoms along the southern and eastern coasts of the Arabian Peninsula and the Spanish toehold at Ifni on Morocco's Atlantic coast. It was therefore not surprising that the major disputes in the Middle East that came to the attention of the UN thereafter were no longer disimperial but postimperial disputes, emanating from within the region.

THE RISE OF REGIONAL DISPUTES

Many of these problems, of course, were legacies of European imperialism. Thus, the states of the Fertile Crescent (Lebanon, Syria, Iraq, Jordan, and Israel) grew out of cartographic exercises in London and Paris during the middle years of World War I and of the interwar competition of the triumphant allies. Yet to attribute all boundary problems in this zone or, for that matter elsewhere in the Middle East, wholly to the machinations and rivalries of the European powers is to ignore the older and more durable inheritance from the antecedent Muslim states. Besides, once the imperial powers surrendered their dependencies in the postwar years, they ceased as a rule to be principal parties to the disputes that engaged the new states of the Middle East. What made the Suez crisis of 1956 so grave was precisely the impression it conveyed that the two major European states, lately the leading imperial powers in the region, were trying to slow down the disimperial process or even bring it altogether to a halt. More characteristic was the many-faceted quarrel that set the Arab states rigidly against Israel. Since 1949 the two sides have brought a wide variety of complaints to the Security Council and the General Assembly concerning the future status of Jerusalem, rights of passage through the Suez Canal, and use of water from an international river system, to say nothing of infractions of the armistice agreements. Extraregional powers, to be sure, were drawn into the constituent disputes that make up the Arab-Israeli problem. This was inescapable in the continuing Cold War.

By 1958 the UN's peacekeeping operations in the Middle East had, it was clear, become more regional than disimperial. This was amply attested to by the Lebanese, Iraqi, and Jordanian crises of that year. The military officers who staged the coup d'état that put an end to the Hashimite dynasty in Iraq and to the short-lived Arab Federation that united Iraq and Jordan were inspired by the military regime in Cairo. The civil war in Lebanon also resulted largely from intrigue conducted by the Syrians and the Egyptians who had recently merged their countries into the United Arab Republic. General Qasim's bumbling effort to annex Kuwait immediately after the United Kingdom gave up its protection of the principality in June 1961 could hardly be ascribed to extraregional causes. The British military buildup in Kuwait, at the invitation of the sheikh, discouraged Iraq from its proclaimed action but encouraged the other Arab states to replace British forces with Arab forces. Thus, by the summer's end the issue ranged Saudi Arabia and the United Arab Republic against Iraq. The admission of Kuwait to membership in the Arab League, moreover, led to Iraq's temporary boycott of the regional organization.

Even more conspicuously regional was the United Arab Republic–Saudi Arabia dispute in Yemen. The United Arab Republic intervened promptly after Yemeni rebels proclaimed the formation of a republic and endeavored to overthrow the Imamate and to impose their rule over the entire land. Because of the Yemeni republicans' lack of experience and resources, the United Arab Republic simply took over the conduct of the war and the administration of the republican regime. Saudi Arabia, for its part, with the cooperation of Jordan at the start, gave material aid to the royalist tribesmen who rallied to the Imam's cause. The Security Council in June 1963 set up a United Nations Yemen Observation Mission (UNYOM) to supervise the evacuation of foreign troops and the cessation of external military support to both sides in the civil war.[14] The only foreign troops in Yemen came from the United Arab Republic. Financed by the United Arab Republic and Saudi Arabia on two-month grants renewed over a period of fourteen months, UNYOM failed in its assignment. No troops were withdrawn except those under rotation, and the total number of United Arab Republic soldiers increased from 28,000 to 40,000. They rose to more than 50,000 following UNYOM's expiry in September 1964. Repercussions in the adjacent British-protected Federation of South Arabia entangled the United Kingdom in the hostilities. Yet it could hardly be claimed that the United Kingdom had instigated the civil war in Yemen.

Finally, the breakdown in December 1963 of the Zurich agreement on Cyprus precipitated between the Greek and Turkish Cypriot communities a menacing civil war in which Greece and Turkey as well as the United Kingdom became embroiled. Once again it was not the imperial power that was responsible for the hostilities, unless its lack of firmness as the crisis was taking shape may have encouraged the Cypriots to resort to fighting. Here also the measures adopted by the Security Council in 1964 proved inconclusive. Although the United Nations Peacekeeping Force in Cyprus (UNFICYP) arranged a cease-fire in August, the simultaneous efforts at political mediation yielded no productive results.

The postimperial problems of peacekeeping, if the recent Middle East experience is an accurate guide, manifestly differ in kind from the disimperial

[14] UN Document S/5330, June 11, 1963.

variety. But before the meaning of the difference is analyzed, we ought first to explore how and why disimperialism in the Middle East took the forms that it did at the UN and in the region. The problem of European imperialism in the Middle East twenty years ago, it must be remembered, was pre-eminently an Arab problem.

PROBLEMS OF ARAB IDENTIFICATION AND INFLUENCE

The Arab League was formed in 1945 to defend Arab rights and promote the cause of Arab political emancipation. A potent stimulus to the creation of the League was the desire to frame common Arab policies at the United Nations and to coordinate Arab tactics in their execution. The five Arab founding Members of the UN thus went to San Francisco as an interest group and from that time have constituted the only such group from the Middle East at the UN. As the record shows, the Arab League proved more effective than its authors could have anticipated or had reason to hope.

The Arab interest group, in fact, never flagged in dedication to its original purpose: the political liberation of all Arab countries from imperial domination, beginning with those states members of the Arab League and the UN that were still tied to European imperial systems and then turning to all the rest of the Arab countries that had not yet achieved self-government. All Arab governments did not necessarily support wholeheartedly the League's pressures for the termination of foreign military bases. Thus, the Hashimite monarchs of Iraq and Jordan in the first postwar decade found it profitable and convenient to continue permitting the United Kingdom to have access to such bases, an attitude largely sustained by dynastic quarrels among the Arab states. Tunisia, Morocco, and even Algeria in the second decade also found it useful for essentially the same reasons to continue close military cooperation with France. Despite such dynastic, sectional, and, recently, doctrinal clashes (socialist United Arab Republic, for instance, against "reactionary" Arab monarchies), which have often threatened to destroy the regional organization, the League nevertheless managed to hold together at the UN.

The Secretary-General of the Arab League, who has since 1950 enjoyed the status of an observer at the UN, presides over the daily meetings of the Arab caucusing group during sessions of the General Assembly. The Arab delegations also convene, as required, at other times to guide Arab League members sitting on UN councils. Moreover, the Arab delegations invited to meetings of their group in the 1950's spokesmen of Arab independence movements from such countries as Tunisia, Morocco, Algeria, and Oman. The Arab states took the initiative in organizing other Asian and African countries into a larger caucusing group for the purpose of conducting a common crusade against imperialism. By such alliances the Arabs won support in their bid for representation in the elective seats of the principal UN organs and in the elective offices of Assembly committees. Thus, an Arab state has almost always won the Security Council seat assigned to the Middle East by the gentleman's agreement of 1946. Similarly, Arab delegations have sat on the Trusteeship Council until 1961 and on the Economic and Social Council (ECOSOC) up until the present with only one interruption (1950–1951). In these bodies the Arab representatives were able to join with those from the rest of Asia and Africa to speed up the process of disimperialism.

Until the Asian-African Conference in Bandung in April 1955, the Arab states were the most cohesive cluster in the emergent Arab-Asian caucusing group. Up to that time the Middle East states in Asia that were Members of the UN represented a majority of the total from that continent, and of these a majority were Arab. After Bandung, although Egyptian President Gamal 'Abd al-Nasir (Gamal Abdel Nasser) moved into the position of leadership in the Arab League, he nevertheless had to yield primacy in the Afro-Asian group to Prime Minister Jawaharlal Nehru of India; and so too farther afield in the triumvirate of neutralist states formed with President Josip Tito's Yugoslavia, it was Prime Minister Nehru who provided the inspiration and the leadership. On the other hand, although the states of the Middle East lost their numerical command in Asian membership at the UN in 1956, the Arab states alone gained dominance among the African Members of the Organization. With the admission to membership of Libya in 1955 and of the Sudan, Tunisia, and Morocco in 1956, the number of African states was increased to eight, and of these, five were Arab. This enabled Egypt to dominate the African delegations for a half-dozen years and to take the lead in creating an African caucusing group which for most purposes at this time was also still linked with the Asian group to form a unit. With Egypt thus participating in several caucusing groups, its bargaining power within and beyond them was accordingly enhanced.

The postwar Arab League drive against Western imperialism coincided with the Soviet desire to eliminate Western bases and political interests throughout Asia and Africa, especially in the Middle East. More than that, nationalists in the Arab states, unlike those in Turkey and Iran, were emotionally conditioned to favor the Soviet Union in the Cold War, since the Russian empire had never pushed far enough into the Middle East to touch the Arab zone. Nevertheless, effective cooperation between the Arab and Soviet caucusing groups at the UN had to await the mid-1950's because the Soviet Union had endorsed the Palestine partition proposal in 1947. Only after the Soviet Union had given its unequivocal blessings in 1953 to the Arab position in the dispute with Israel did a practical basis appear for mutual support at the UN. There the Arab-Soviet *rapprochement* found flamboyant leadership in 'Abd al-Nasir, particularly after the conclusion of the Soviet-Egyptian arms deal in 1955. Arab-Soviet cooperation, it should be stressed, did not suggest that Egypt or any other Arab state was subordinating itself to the Soviet Union; much less was any of them going Communist. Those Arab countries that followed Egypt's lead in becoming Soviet clients, such as Syria, Iraq, and, most recently, Algeria, were thoroughly nationalist, as attested to by their suppression of the local Communist parties, at times even in the face of Soviet protests.

In this phase of the Cold War the United States, though handicapped in the search for a common purpose with the Arab caucusing group at the UN, nevertheless was able as a rule to win enough support in the General Assembly on vital issues to reach decisions it favored. In the eyes of Arab nationalists and therefore of the most powerful Arab delegations in the caucusing group, the United States throughout this period was guilty by association with the departing imperial powers. This was so even though the United States supported proposals for self-determination, except on occasions when such a stand might have proved unusually embarrassing to one of its major allies. Even then, however, the United States tended to abstain rather than cast a negative ballot. The Suez crisis provided the most dramatic example of United States opposition to imperialism, when it was made unmistakably clear to the United Kingdom and France that resort to force would not be countenanced. Yet because of the United States' alliances with the United Kingdom and France and its efforts to steer a middle course in the Arab-Israeli dispute, the United States could not make common cause with the Arab states at the UN. At best the United States was able from time to time to wean away from the dominant views of the caucusing group, collectively or severally, such states as Jordan, Lebanon, Libya, Morocco, Saudi Arabia, and Tunisia. Beyond the Arab zone in the Middle East, of course, the United States could more consistently attract support for its moves in the General Assembly and the other principal UN organs.

After the admission of the sixteen African states in 1960, the influence of the Arab countries in that continent began to wane. By the mid-1960's, the African states evinced their own preoccupations with regional disputes, external alliances, or the search for black African leadership. This made them less amenable to Arab leadership or less sympathetic to Arab interests, especially to Arab preoccupation with claims against Israel. Thus, at the eighteenth session of the General Assembly in 1963 the African and Asian delegations were lobbying for the enlargement of the Security Council and ECOSOC. In the discussions of the Special Political Committee, the Soviet delegate advocated that the Middle East be represented as one of the six geographic areas entitled to elective seats on these organs. Czechoslovakia and Poland in turn submitted an amendment to the 54-state joint draft resolution which would provide for a rotational presidency of the General Assembly among the same six regions.[15] In the two instances the Soviet caucusing group's proposals were not accepted. The Iraqi delegate in the same Committee stated on behalf of the other Arab delegations of Asia that the Arab League states were entitled to one of the five nonpermanent seats set aside for Asia and Africa under the projected enlargement of the Security Council. In objecting to the proposal, the Ivory Coast delegate declared that the Arab states of Africa were unquestionably African and that his delegation would recognize the apportionment of African seats to Arab states on that basis only. The agreement finally reached on the allocation of seats in the schemes for enlarging the Security Council and ECOSOC expressly omitted the Middle East as one of the regions. So also did the annex to the resolution on the election of the Assembly President, the seven Vice Presidents, and the seven Chairmen of the main committees.[16]

THE FUTURE FOR THE MIDDLE EAST AT THE UN

Thus, ironically, the Arab states, which had played such a significant role in organizing the movement at the UN for disimperialism and which in the process enjoyed commanding positions first in Asia and then in Africa, lost their paramountcy as they came to be outnumbered in each continent. The transformation of the General Assembly, it was clear, essentially reduced Arab influence at the UN as it had that of the Soviet Union and the United States to say nothing of Latin America.

At the close of the Organization's second decade the Middle East seemed to be losing its identity altogether at the UN. The Arab League appeared as unable, or perhaps as unwilling, as it had been at the start to collaborate for regional ends with the non-Arab countries of the Middle East. Yet the League also failed to accept the reality of the loss of its primacy among the Asian and African delegations. What is more, the Arab caucusing group continued to adhere to its original crusade against imperialism as if this were still the most vital issue, and it appeared to ignore the fact that the old quarrels with the imperial powers have been giving way, imperceptibly, to new quarrels among the successor regimes. Unless these outmoded views are abandoned, even the Arab states are likely to be absorbed for working purposes at the UN by the larger number of countries in Asia and Africa.

Finally, the essential differences between the disimperial and the postimperial disputes must be kept firmly in mind. The disimperial genre included not simply regional problems but international ones since these disputes involved permanent members of the Security Council as principal parties and invariably ran the risk of spreading the war once fighting broke out.

---

[15] General Assembly *Official Records . . . Special Political Committee* (18th session), p. 257, 275.

[16] General Assembly *Official Records . . . Special Political Committee* (18th session), pp. 271, 276, 286; and General Assembly Resolutions 1990 (XVIII) and 1991 (XVIII), December 17, 1963.

Extraregional powers, it is true, were still becoming entangled in the post-imperial disputes. The danger of escalation thus remained, even though it was less acute because the involvement of outside powers was for the most part indirect. The disimperial quarrels were often protracted, as they were in Egypt and Algeria, but in the end they were settled by the termination of the imperial presence. The postimperial quarrels as underlined by the Arab-Israeli dispute or even the disputes over Cyprus and Yemen may at times be open-ended, and, as such problems fester and multiply, their cumulative impact adds to international restiveness. Does this not suggest that the UN, in the third decade, ought to redouble its efforts to devise new means of handling the new problems?

Africa and the United Nations

JOHN KAREFA-SMART

At the beginning of its nineteenth session the General Assembly of the United Nations decided by acclamation that Alex Quaison-Sackey, the permanent representative of Ghana, should preside over the session. This was only the second time in eighteen years that this, the highest honor in the Organization, was accorded to a representative of an African state, and the first time that a Negro African was thus chosen.

In 1945, at the San Francisco Conference, the only African states that were independent and therefore could become Members of the new international body were—not counting South Africa—Egypt, Ethiopia, and Liberia. It was not until ten years later at the tenth session of the General Assembly that these three original African Members were joined by Libya. During the eleventh session Ghana, Morocco, the Sudan, and Tunisia were admitted to the UN, and almost two years later Guinea joined the small group of African countries. By the time Sierra Leone became the 100th Member of the United Nations in September 1961, there were already 24 African Member States,[1] and with the expected admission of Gambia before the close of the nineteenth session, the African states will number 35[2] out of a total membership of 115. This enormous increase in the African membership has been a result of the unprecedented dissolution of the French and British colonial empires— a process which was fully supported through various resolutions and through the pressure of debate by the United Nations. It is not surprising to find that the majority, if not all, of the African countries regard representation at the United Nations as their most important diplomatic assignment.

During the first fifteen years of the Organization, the twenty Latin American countries formed the largest single bloc in the UN. As a result, they were able to play an important role in mediating between the Great Powers and at the same time to win for themselves valuable concessions in elections to the

JOHN KAREFA-SMART, former Foreign Minister of Sierra Leone, is Assistant Director-General of the World Health Organization.

[1] South Africa is not included in this figure.
[2] South Africa is not included in this figure.

major UN bodies' important posts within the Organization. The African states during this same period had no such influence as a separate group. They, however, eventually joined forces with the Asian countries which, they felt, shared their interests in economic development, human rights, and the struggle against colonialism. Thus, especially after the first Asian-African Conference in Bandung, the African and Asian delegations began to meet together regularly at the United Nations. Whenever questions of "due regard to geographical distribution" arose at the UN, the Afro-Asian group was viewed unofficially as a unit.

The Rising Tide of African Influence

It was not long, however, until their rapidly increasing numbers led the African nations to seek to express themselves as a separate entity. Therefore, after the admission of the first large aggregation of newly independent countries, the African delegations began to meet together monthly at the UN. The group thus formed, which followed the familiar UN practice of having a rotating chairmanship, could not make binding decisions but met for the purposes of consultation and informal exchanges of views. It was given a formal identity by the Organization of African Unity (OAU) when, at the May 1963 Addis Ababa Conference, the heads of African states and governments adopted a resolution according it official status. At this Conference the African UN delegations were authorized to establish a secretariat and to cooperate with any other group that shared its objectives.

The African group has already begun to make its presence recognized and felt. In the past those African countries which were represented on the Security Council have occupied seats allocated by the San Francisco "gentleman's agreement" to the Middle East and the British Commonwealth. Now the African group is making a claim for representation on the Security Council in its own right, pointing out that the twenty Latin American countries have always had two seats, while the African group, now numbering more than 30, must compete for a single seat allocated to a non-African group or region. This African demand, of course, creates a problem that can only be resolved either by a change in the gentleman's agreement or a revision of the Charter to enlarge the Security Council. We will return to both of these possibilities later.

Importance of the UN to the African States

As has been noted above, each newly independent African country has immediately taken steps to be admitted to the United Nations. Membership in this Organization has come to be regarded in Africa, along with a new flag and a national anthem, as one of the visible signs of independence. But this is not all that the United Nations means to the new African states.

First, although they believe that certain provisions of the Charter should be revised to provide for the adequate representation of Africans on the principal UN bodies and even though the Charter was written and adopted while most of the African states were still colonial territories, the Africans nonetheless hold the Charter of the United Nations in the highest esteem. They feel that the Charter embodies their hopes for a world in which all nations, large and small, rich and poor, powerful and weak, will work together in peace and security and contribute, each according to its means, to the development of the whole world's resources and to the economic, social, and cultural betterment of all people and the preservation of freedom and human dignity.

Secondly, many African states owe their very independence to the emphasis which the United Nations has placed on the obligation of Members administering colonial or trust territories to develop self-government within them. In this sense the United Nations is the foster mother of all the former dependencies which have now attained independence and been admitted to the Organization.

Thirdly, the United Nations has met the needs of the African states in some quite definite ways. Without the United Nations, it would have been difficult for new nations, especially when they were at the same time weak and impoverished, to break into the closely knit diplomatic circles of the older states. In the same way as the League of Nations allowed the Emperor of Ethiopia to appeal to the community of nations against the Italian assault on his country's territorial integrity, so the United Nations has provided a forum in which African leaders, both heads of state and their accredited permanent representatives, could express their views on world problems and seek support in matters of special interest to their countries. The privilege of using this forum derives solely from membership in the Organization and does not depend on the size or power of the nation or of its diplomatic mission.

Furthermore, a speech before the General Assembly of the United Nations usually receives more coverage by all the modern media of communication, including television, radio, international press services, and specialized publications, than one given before any other assembly in the world. Since the United Nations also puts at the disposal of Member nations its own extensive facilities for reporting its proceedings in the countries of its Members, it serves a useful purpose in helping to build popular support at home for and approval of the role a country's leaders are playing on the international scene.

By bringing together within the environment of one building the representatives of Member countries with many opportunities for direct contact in the lobbies, dining rooms, and committee rooms, the United Nations also makes it possible for the Africans to exert concerted pressures on behalf of their aims. Often an idea originating with one delegation gains the support of other friendly delegations. It is then taken to the African group where after full discussion it may be translated into a draft resolution jointly sponsored by several, if not all, the African countries. Other regional groups are then approached, and group pressures are used in terms of promises of reciprocal support until a reasonable certainty is reached that a majority of votes can be marshaled to get the resolution adopted by the Assembly or the committee. In this way success has been achieved in getting the Assembly and its committees to pass resolutions on human rights, the speedy liquidation of colonialism, the peaceful settlement of disputes, and flagrant breaches of the principles of the Charter, as in the case of the resolutions against the *apartheid* policies of the South African government.

The most recent activity of the United Nations which was of special importance to the African states was the 1964 UN Conference on Trade and Development (UNCTAD) in Geneva. Without exception the African countries believe that if suitable trade arrangements are set up to remove the perpetual disadvantage that laissez-faire world trade imposes on the primary-producing countries, they would be able to enlarge and improve their economic capacity. They believe that the financial benefits that would thus accrue to the developing countries would place them in a position where they would need less direct financial and economic assistance. In other words, more trade, less aid. UNCTAD permitted the less developed countries to press this point of view on the wealthier nations.

There has not always been unanimity, however, among African Member States in discussions of problems which affect the African continent. An important example is the difference of opinion over the manner in which the peacekeeping forces of the United Nations in the Congo (Leopoldville) were organized and conducted. There were some who believed that the UN Operation in the Congo (ONUC) should have been recruited exclusively from African sources, that it was wrong and undesirable to bring armed forces from other continents. There were those who disagreed with the manner in which the operations were conducted, some feeling that the actions were at times directed principally against the nationalist movement and its leaders, exceeding the peacekeeping mission and taking sides in the political struggle of the Congolese people. And there were many who felt no longer able to justify the costs of the prolonged operation which had become an unjust burden upon their own development.

When, however, the Soviet Union used the occasion of the Congo debate at the UN to renew attacks on the late Secretary-General Dag Hammarskjöld, the African states supported the Secretary-General and thus demonstrated that their differences about the Congo operation did not mean that they did not appreciate that the UN presence in the Congo had undoubtedly saved that new country, and perhaps all of Africa, from other forms of foreign armed intervention.

It is not only from its function as a forum, however, that the African states have derived great benefit from the United Nations. Concrete results have been achieved otherwise, to the benefit of Member States, by special United Nations bodies and the specialized agencies.

The most widely publicized United Nations body in the field of rendering assistance has been the United Nations Children's Fund (UNICEF). There is no African country in which, in the interests of the general well-being of mothers and children, UNICEF has not supported health and social welfare programs with money, equipment, and supplies and with general support of the programs of other agencies. Similarly, the World Health Organization (WHO), the Food and Agriculture Organization (FAO), and the United Nations Educational, Scientific and Cultural Organization (UNESCO) have each, in their particular spheres, contributed materially, and always only on request, to programs of assistance in public health, agricultural development, improvement of nutrition, and general education. The projects sponsored and supported by these agencies not only help to relieve the national budgets of the African countries but by improving the general well-being of their inhabitants also contribute indirectly to universal goodwill and peace.

Although membership in the United Nations and its agencies carries financial obligations, in the case of most African countries the minimum assessment of less than one-twentieth of one percent of the total operating budget is negligible in comparison with the much larger sums of money which are spent on them by UN agencies involved in assistance projects. The Technical Assistance Board (TAB), the Expanded Program of Technical Assistance (EPTA), the Special Fund, the International Bank for Reconstruction and Development (IBRD), the International Development Association (IDA), the International Finance Corporation (IFC), and the International Monetary Fund (IMF) are all on the credit side in the balance sheet of the African states in their relations with the UN.

Of special interest to African Member States is the regional United Nations Economic Commission for Africa (ECA). Already some of the studies which have been initiated by ECA have pointed the way toward accelerated economic development, and the Development Training Institute in Dakar, Senegal, sponsored by ECA, is helping to meet the need in all African states for trained leadership. The fears that the Economic and Social Commission of the OAU (which comprises all the independent African states with the exception of South Africa) might duplicate or conflict with ECA have not materialized. Instead, ECA has placed all of its facilities at the disposal of the OAU and cooperated fully in the detailed preliminary studies which have led to the formation of the new African Development Bank.

Africa and the Great Powers

At the time when the African Members began to join the United Nations, the solidarity and cordiality which, toward the end of World War II, gave birth to the name "United Nations" had already given way to division. On the one side were the United States and the Western European countries which were later to become allied in the North Atlantic Treaty Organization (NATO), and on the other side were the Soviet Union and its Eastern European Communist allies. These two opposing groups faced each other with the greatest tension in a divided and occupied Germany, and more especially in Berlin.

The African states soon found that practically every question which appeared on the agenda of the General Assembly or of the various committees was discussed in terms of this East versus West alignment. When the African countries showed a particular interest in economic and social questions, in human rights, and in the work of the Trusteeship Council, they found that the East and the West vied with each other for the role of champion of the causes in which the Africans were interested. The realization that the United Nations was far from "united" and that the East and the West constituted two separate power blocs, each one competing to obtain the votes of the new Members, led to the early assumption by the African states—following the lead given by India—of a position of nonalignment with respect to the two contending groups.

Nonalignment as the African states use the term simply means a refusal to be committed in advance to giving support to one group or the other in discussions of international problems. It is not intended to mean neutrality. Once the opportunity has been given to listen to both sides of any given controversy and to examine the facts and the arguments, the African countries expect to, and nearly always do, decide on which side to cast their votes or to whom they will lend support. Such support, however, is *ad hoc;* it is intended to be limited to the matter in hand and does not imply support in other future controversies or disputes. Since this position of nonalignment is intended to safeguard freedom of action at all times, it requires the avoidance of bilateral treaties or other agreements by which the African states would bind themselves to one of the Great Powers.

An important reason for adhering to a policy of nonalignment, although it has not been explicitly expressed in formal declarations, is that the African states are generally not impressed with ideological considerations. Their problems of economic development and social welfare are so urgent that they prefer to put all their resources into efforts to solve these problems and to receive assistance from any source. They suspect that to become too deeply involved in ideological disputes and to commit their support to any one side would restrict their freedom to receive assistance wherever it can be found or is offered.

DISILLUSIONMENT WITH THE UNITED NATIONS

In spite of all the positive aspects of their membership in the United Nations, the African countries have also experienced a certain disillusionment with the United Nations in the following areas.

First, the continuation of the Cold War and the huge sums of money spent by the Great Powers in defense and armaments cause concern among the African countries. In general, they regard the Great Powers' refusal to conclude peace treaties with East and West Germany and the related question of self-determination and reunification for the German people as constant potential threats to the free exercise by all small countries of their rights. Even more alarming is the extension of the Cold War to the internal struggles in the Middle East, in the Congo (Leopoldville), and, with almost catastrophic results, in Cuba in 1962.

Secondly, the African nations have been distressed by the refusal of the Western powers to support in the Security Council strong economic measures against South Africa. This failure to back up with positive action the nearly 40 resolutions of the General Assembly against *apartheid* has led the African countries to lose faith in the UN's ability to bring about a just solution of questions which do not primarily affect the Great Powers. In the same way they view Portugal's intransigence, despite adverse world opinion, in refusing to grant self-determination to its African colonies as being sustained by the unwillingness of Portugal's NATO allies to offend that government.

A third perennial question in the United Nations, on which, despite disagreement as to the solution, there is universal concern, is the question of the participation of Communist China in the Organization. Most African governments seem to realize that the obvious solution of granting membership to both the "exile" government in Formosa and the *de facto* government on the Chinese mainland is equally unacceptable to both Chinas. Nevertheless, they wish to remove the feeling of impotence that has resulted from inconclusive struggles over procedural aspects of the subject rather than a direct confrontation. The need to bring a population of some 700 million people into the family of nations seems more important to most African countries than the question of which China should occupy the present seats in the United Nations and its committees and agencies.

Fourthly, there is the present deadlock over payments for the peacekeeping operations in the Middle East and the Congo (Leopoldville). Since the financial and constitutional aspects of this question have already been discussed at length,[3] it is unnecessary to go over this ground again. The African countries

[3] See Inis L. Claude, Jr., "The Political Framework of the United Nations' Financial Problems," *International Organization*, Autumn 1963 (Vol. 17, No. 4), pp. 831–859.

are principally concerned over the stubborn refusal of both the United States on the one hand and France and the Soviet Union on the other to accept compromise solutions to the problem. According to the Africans, compromise requires a willingness not to insist on constitutional arguments and specific interpretations of the Charter. The important question for the African nations is not which interpretation of the Charter is the correct one, but what can be done now to provide funds to meet current deficits and to guaranteë adequate financial support for future peacekeeping operations. It has been discouraging that one proposal after another put forward by a committee led by the permanent representative of an African country (Nigeria) has been rejected, resulting in repeated adjournments of the nineteenth session and finally the close of the session with no substantive accomplishments.

HOPE FOR ASSISTANCE ON MODERNIZATION

Generally speaking, the African countries place great hope in the UN as a channel through which the economic and social development which is necessary in order to accelerate progress toward modernization will take place. It was with this in mind that they hailed the declaration of a Development Decade by the UN with enthusiasm.

The three main categories into which African interest in the UN role in development falls are increased and more mutually advantageous trade; technical assistance for the development of education, health, and other social services; and the provision of capital for development purposes.

All African countries attached great importance to the Geneva Conference on Trade and Development. It is now hoped that future meetings of this body will help bring mutual benefits from increased trade between the developed and the developing countries. It is also hoped that the Economic Commission for Africa will be able to assist in furthering trade, investment opportunities, and economic collaboration among the countries themselves.

United Nations support in the struggle against disease, particularly in the control of epidemics, and UN assistance in teacher training—a recognized bottleneck in educational advance—have been major factors toward development. African nations would like to see larger contributions made to the various funds which are available to the Technical Assistance Board, as well as significant increases in the operating budgets of all the specialized agencies which are participating in the technical assistance effort.

African countries also realize that until their own financial resources are adequate for this purpose they will have to rely on the participation of external capital in their development programs. For a variety of reasons most of the countries would prefer to obtain this capital through UN agencies such as the World Bank rather than from individual countries through bi-

lateral agreements. They would therefore like to see much larger contributions to the World Bank and at the same time a simplification of the procedures for getting financial assistance from the Bank. Concurrently, they welcome the launching of the new African Development Bank as another instrumentality for mobilizing and channeling capital for development projects.

LOOKING TO THE FUTURE

The African countries have not lost confidence in the United Nations.
Whether or not the great faith they have in the Organization will be maintained depends, of course, on whether effective solutions are found to some
of the questions already raised.

African countries are convinced that the time has come to revise the Charter
of the United Nations with particular reference to the provisions for the size,
membership, functions, and powers of the Security Council. At the time when
the Charter came into effect there were 51 Members of the UN, and the
Charter provided for an eleven-member Security Council of which five were
to be permanent members with the power of veto. The election of the six nonpermanent members with "due regard to an equitable geographical distribution" was to be based on a gentleman's agreement that allocated two seats to
Latin America and one seat each to Western Europe, Eastern Europe, the
Middle East (including the four African Members), and the British Commonwealth. Since that time, however, the Organization has more than doubled
in size, and it seems both logical and fair that the Charter and the gentleman's agreement should be revised so that the Security Council would more
adequately represent the present membership. Furthermore, those sections of
the Charter which specify the membership of other organs should also be
amended to reflect the changed composition of the Organization. Both of
these matters have received attention and a resolution which provides for enlarging the Security Council and the Economic and Social Council (ECO-
SOC) has been adopted. The necessary amendments to the Charter will, however, become effective only if the required majority of Member States ratify
them before September 1965.

The African states would also like to see a reliable method adopted for the
financing of UN peacekeeping operations. Such a method should not depend
on the wishes of any one state or group of states. Whether the Security Council should be given the entire responsibility in this regard should be carefully
studied. A useful proposal supported by several African delegations is that
the General Assembly establish a permanent fund for peacekeeping operations
that would be under the control of the Security Council. All countries and
also any groups of citizens of Member countries, private foundations, and cor-
porations could contribute to the fund. An amount of money sufficient to meet

present obligations might be raised in this way, and the fund could be maintained by annual voluntary contributions or by a scale of assessments reflecting contributions to the regular budget.

Of particular interest to the African countries would be a clarification of the relationships between the United Nations and regional international organizations like the OAU. The Economic Commission for Africa could possibly be merged or more closely associated with the economic commissions of the OAU, thereby creating considerable savings in duplicated efforts and personnel. Such a development would also relieve the major UN organs from long hours of discussing matters of primary interest only to the countries of a given region. In this way also, less opportunity would be provided for the injection of extraneous ideological struggles into matters of practical local and regional significance.

African nations have become increasingly fearful that the Great Powers might wish to curtail the growing importance of the smaller countries by proposing a revision of the "one Member, one vote" provisions of the Charter along the lines of some "weighted voting" scheme that would reflect size, population, gross national income, or other material factors that would be disadvantageous to the African countries. Acceptance of this kind of voting system would, more rapidly than any threat the UN has thus far faced, destroy the belief in the equal rights of men and women and of nations large and small on which the United Nations Charter depends.

To conclude, it can be safely assumed that the consensus of opinion among the African countries is that the United Nations is here to stay. They believe that the world needs such a forum where, without fear, problems affecting peace and security of the whole world can be discussed and peaceful solutions sought. Collectively and individually the African countries need the United Nations and, although it may not be quite proper for them to say so themselves, they also believe that the United Nations needs them.

The Small States of Western Europe in the United Nations

ANNETTE BAKER FOX

ONLY six of the small states of Western or Western-oriented Europe participated in the United Nations Conference on International Organization at San Francisco. They were Belgium, the Netherlands, Greece, Norway, Luxembourg, and, after a struggle between the Soviet Union and its wartime allies, Denmark. Their participation followed, for the most part, the model of the "honorable, independent, disinterested small state": sober, responsible, speaking mainly when spoken to, but assiduously seeking out ways to make their voices heard in the alleviation of international conflict. True, they were there as part of the winning coalition in World War II and shared the hopes and expectations of the larger Western powers concerning the role of the United Nations. But they joined similar countries outside Europe, particularly Australia, Canada, and New Zealand, in helping to shape a UN Charter which in certain ways differed from the Dumbarton Oaks Proposals. The role of the General Assembly was, for example, enlarged, thus modifying the special position of the Great Powers, and the scope of the United Nations in economic and social fields was expanded.[1] The influence of the small states in Europe stemmed from the desire of the major Western allies, particularly the United States, to ensure the success of the enterprise by concessions to those whose participation would be necessary to make it a worthwhile undertaking.[2]

Their ranks were swelled within a year by two other states of similar char-

ANNETTE BAKER FOX is Research Associate, Institute of War and Peace Studies, Columbia University. The author gratefully acknowledges the assistance of Anna P. Schreiber, graduate student in the Department of Public Law and Government.

[1] Leland M. Goodrich, *The United Nations* (New York: Thomas Y. Crowell Company, 1959), pp. 26–27; and George de T. Glazebrook, "The Middle Powers in the United Nations System," *International Organization*, June 1947 (Vol. 1, No. 2), pp. 307–315, especially p. 310.
[2] William T. R. Fox, "The Super-Powers at San Francisco," *The Review of Politics*, January 1946 (Vol. 8, No. 1), pp. 121–122.

410

cter, Sweden and Iceland. But the remainder, most of whom were knocking on the doors with various degrees of impatience, had to wait until the "package deal" of 1955 for admission. Already in the 1940's, however, several of these outsiders belonged to some of the specialized agencies, which the Soviet Union at first tended to shun. By 1955 the world had altered in many radical ways, in part because of the way the United Nations itself had developed. The temporary exclusion of the applicants, however, symbolized within the United Nations one phase of the Cold War which had meanwhile developed. One pillar upon which the original concept of a world security organization had rested was thereby undermined, i.e., great-power harmony, a harmony which most of these particular small states regarded as vital to their own security.

THE CHANGING POLITICAL ENVIRONMENT

Before examining changes in the expectations and behavior of the small states during the twenty years of the United Nations, we should note the atypical experience of two states, Switzerland and Spain, which indicated shifts in the general political environment.

When the Charter was adopted, the collective security features were much on the minds of leaders who were reacting to the particular way in which World War II had developed. To the Swiss, who had escaped its scourge and attributed their good fortune to their steadfast devotion to neutrality, the provisions of the Charter seemed to endanger this most cherished constitutional principle.[3] When they observed the rapid development of the United Nations into a forum for great-power controversy, they remained content with avoiding such a dangerously compromising position as membership in the Organization. In some of its "nonpolitical" activities, however, the United Nations, as well as the specialized agencies, dealt with questions very close to the immediate economic or humanitarian interests of Switzerland, and in these activities the Swiss participated, even providing the official home for some of them. They went so far in 1964 as to make a financial contribution to the peacekeeping forces on Cyprus. They also participated (on invitation) in the Neutral Nations Supervisory Commission which was to supervise the Korean armistice. Switzerland, however, has only consultant status on the Economic Commission for Europe (ECE), where Eastern and Western Europe meet. Thus, through choice, the most famous neutral remains partly on the sidelines, along with one of the great contenders in World War II. Germany remains a spectator not through choice, but like Switzerland it is also only a marginal participant in certain United Nations activities.

[3] Jacques Freymond, "The Foreign Policy of Switzerland," in Joseph E. Black and Kenneth W. Thompson (ed.), *Foreign Policies in a World of Change* (New York: Harper & Row, 1963), pp. 149–171, especially p. 152.

Far different was the case of Spain even though it too sought no contact
with the United Nations, and it too had been a World War II "neutral." As
one of the first orders of business, the Organization set about to ensure (pursuant to a Potsdam agreement between the United Kingdom, the United
States, and the Soviet Union) that Spain would not enjoy any of the benefits
of membership. Beyond that, Members were to withdraw their top diplomatic
officials from Madrid.[4] This highly quixotic method of encouraging a revolution could not but hold General Francisco Franco even more firmly in his seat
of power. The favor granted the Soviet Union in 1946 was rapidly withdrawn
as hostility developed between it and the Western powers. The United States
began in 1950 to take the lead in reorienting policy toward Spain, whose
diplomatic isolation had already been somewhat reduced by a few Latin
American states. To be fair, this brief account should acknowledge that one or
two of the "model" small states played leading roles in making Spain a pariah
in United Nations debates.[5]

Another prominent neutral, Sweden, faced and conquered the apprehensions it had earlier shared with Switzerland when it chose to apply for membership in 1946, before the Cold War had begun to take an alarming turn.
Since joining, Sweden has become the "universal" neutral, quite distinct from
the later self-denominated "nonaligned" states. The United Nations has come
to rely on Sweden to play a genuinely mediatory role despite the Swedish
allegiance to Western values.[6] Citing Sweden as an example, Austria persuaded the Soviet Union to permit it to enter the United Nations on the same
basis of neutrality.

The Small States' Expectations and Behavior

All the powers mentioned so far, except Iceland, plus those which entered
in 1955 (Portugal, Finland, and Ireland) had participated in the League of
Nations. This experience, along with their differing fates in World War II,
colored their expectations or lack of expectations regarding the United Nations. They were thus differentiated by more than economic and social devel-

---

[4] Nuño Aguirre de Cárcer and Gonzalo Fernández de la Mora, "The Foreign Policy of Spain," in
ibid., pp. 199–222, especially p. 208.

[5] Belgium, in particular, but also Norway favored a break in diplomatic relations; Denmark and
Sweden, however, considered this to be intervention in Spain's domestic affairs and in any case of no
avail. In the Security Council the Netherlands expressed doubt concerning the constitutionality of actions within the "domestic jurisdiction" of Spain. All these states later joined those agreeable to weakening the adamant opposition to Spain.

[6] See *Sweden and the United Nations* (Report by a Special Study Group of the Swedish Institute of
International Affairs Prepared for the Carnegie Endowment for International Peace) (New York: Man-
hattan Publishing Company, 1956), especially pp. 68–109, 196–197; Brita Skottsberg Ahman, "Scandi-
navian Foreign Policy, Past and Present," in Henning Friis (ed.), *Scandinavia—Between East and West*
(Ithaca, N.Y: Cornell University Press, 1950), pp. 256–305, especially p. 292; and Herbert Tingsten,
"Issues in Swedish Foreign Policy." *Foreign Affairs*, April 1959 (Vol. 37, No. 3), p. 477.

opment and political stability from many of the new states in Asia and Africa. The European Members were aware of the demands the United Nations would make upon them as well as the demands they could make upon it, and they were not obsessed by the idea of national independence which they took for granted.[7]

The European small states, however, did in some respects resemble the newer Asian and African states, and even the Latin American states. Most particularly, the European states were seeking a larger, but not necessarily louder, voice in those international affairs which concerned them. Like the others they were also reluctant to acquiesce in great-power dominance of world politics, at least in its cruder manifestations. Much more than the new states, however, these European Members stressed the importance of the United Nations as an "instrument of the international rule of law."[8] They clung to the hope that the United Nations would contribute to their security, perhaps more indirectly than directly, perhaps by offering some protection from hostile powers with illegitimate claims.[9] They anticipated that the UN's economic and social activities would contribute to their welfare through stimulating cooperation in fields of interest to them, and they were ready to participate actively in these fields. Like the less developed small states, the small European nations were highly dependent upon foreign trade, but their concern was to maintain already relatively high living standards; few of them had further need of outside assistance by the late 1950's. Thus, their expectations from the United Nations in trade and aid were quite different from those of the non-European small countries. Here, as well as in the field of security, the small European states entertained few illusions about the potentialities of the United Nations and were much more conscious of its limitations. They especially differed from the newer small states in recognizing the "inner conflict" between the desire that the United Nations play a strong mediating role between powerful opponents and the possible disadvantages to them of participating actively in such endeavors.[10]

The unwillingness of the leaders of the European small states to project themselves into the great-power fray has had its corollary in their modest claims on fellow Members, of whom they ask only that they keep the peace

[7] See Hamilton Fish Armstrong, "U.N. on Trial," *Foreign Affairs*, April 1961 (Vol. 39, No. 3), p. 397.

[8] Per Haekkerup, "Scandinavia's Peace-Keeping Forces for the U.N.," *Foreign Affairs*, July 1964 (Vol. 42, No. 4), p. 675.

[9] Neutrals, lacking powerful allies, especially entertained these hopes. Bruno Kreisky, Austria's Foreign Minister, said:

> We also knew . . . we would derive international recognition [of our neutrality] from membership. Such recognition implied a measure of security which we could not have found elsewhere.

(*Foreign Affairs*, January 1959 [Vol. 37, No. 2], p. 274.) See also the remarks of Finland's President Urho Kekkonen along the same lines as noted by Max Jakobson, "Finland in the United Nations," in *Introduction to Finland, 1963* (Helsinki: Finland Ministry of Foreign Affairs, 1963), pp. 67-73.

[10] See Sven Henningsen, "The Foreign Policy of Denmark," in Black and Thompson, p. 101.

and respect each other's jurisdiction. The Spanish demand for Gibraltar is an exception. The Austrian complaint against Italy for not granting more autonomy to the German-speaking people of the South Tyrol (the Bolzano case) and Portugal's complaint against India because of its conquest of Goa are two of the infrequent efforts by European small states to assert a claim in the United Nations. As in several other instances, Greece does not fit well into the category of states being considered. It has taken more than one case to the United Nations; in the 1940's it complained of the threat to it from the Communist states of Yugoslavia, Bulgaria, and Albania, and, in the 1950's and 1960's, it brought up two phases of the Cyprus problem.

The Cyprus case does fit into a category of claims which have been made *against* several of the small European states, namely, decolonization. The Netherlands, Belgium, Spain, and Portugal have all been subjected to more or less painful attacks in the United Nations as "colonialist" powers; all vainly claimed "domestic jurisdiction" to protect themselves.

In the nonpolitical sphere the small European states have been ready consumers of some services of the United Nations and the specialized agencies. In the early postwar years all of them relied on the Food and Agriculture Organization (FAO) and the World Health Organization (WHO) to fulfill certain needs, for example, and the poorer states still are aided by such agencies. To take another example at random, Belgium sought help from the Intergovernmental Commission for European Migration (ICEM) in resettling Belgian refugees from the Congo (Leopoldville); the Belgian government did, however, help to finance the operation. In addition, ECE provides a unique meeting ground for states of Eastern and Western Europe which otherwise are quite isolated from each other despite some common economic problems.

PROBLEMS OF ALIGNMENT AND NONALIGNMENT

Of course, none of the small European states were immune from political pressures to line up in the United Nations with one or the other side in the East-West and North-South conflicts. In the case of the former conflict, this pressure was particularly uncomfortable for the neutral states; each solved it differently and in a way that reflected how vulnerable each particular state was to pressure from one or the other of the superpowers.

The common signs of alignment on an issue—votes and speeches—are very imperfect measures. The political significance of abstention has to be determined separately for each case, and speeches may be made for home consumption. Votes and speeches in a particular committee, in the General Assembly as a whole, and in the Security Council all have to be interpreted differently. By themselves they tell little about behind-the-scenes accommodation or the influence of particular personalities within specific delegations. Taking all this into account, let us briefly illustrate the ways in which small European states have behaved on issues resulting from these two major global controversies.

Greece's difficulties with its Communist neighbors, an early manifestation of the coming Cold War, were the occasion for several of the small Western European states to participate actively in the UN's deliberations on the Greek question and its subsequent action. Belgium, the Netherlands, Sweden, Norway, and even Iceland played a role, first in stressing the need for adequate information, and when this was supplied, in accepting the conclusions about what had happened as reported by the UN Special Committee on the Balkans (UNSCOB), which included a Netherlands member.

The Korean crisis put heavy demands upon Western-oriented states which were Members at the time, demands which included some contribution to the UN forces fighting the war. Among the European small states, four North Atlantic Treaty Organization (NATO) allies of the United States provided troops: Greece, the Netherlands, Belgium, and Luxembourg. Denmark, another NATO ally, generally approved of UN action in Korea but decided to limit itself to a nonmilitary contribution; it was still discussing the desirability of either a voluntary military contribution or a Scandinavian force when the armistice intervened. Within Sweden there was great controversy, which resulted in this neutral state's making no military contribution. Sweden did, however, engage in relief activities, and through its participation in the Neutral Nations Supervisory Commission and the Neutral Nations Repatriation Commission, Sweden contributed toward the termination of hostilities and the working out of a peaceful solution.

The actions of the Soviet Union in the Hungarian uprising of 1956 were very embarrassing to two of the neutrals, Austria and Finland, which had recently become Members of the United Nations and both of which bordered on the Communist Bloc. The other Western European small states, including Ireland, found it easy to express their indignation and to favor some innocuous steps to be taken by the Organization. Austria, closest Western neighbor to Hungary, sponsored not only a resolution to aid Hungarian refugees but also one calling on the Secretary-General to seek a solution. It joined all the other Western European small states in voting for a resolution calling for an end to the intervention, acceptance of UN observers, and withdrawal of troops. Finland, on the other hand, a nation which had been crippled in the war with the Soviet Union and left to its tender mercies in the late 1940's, found in abstention the only safe vote on resolutions condemning the Soviet actions. Although Finland did vote for giving aid to the refugees and sending UN observers to Hungary, the votes on condemning the Soviet Union put it in the company of Yugoslavia and a number of Asian and African states. The Finns remembered their own fate in the League of Nations in 1939 and found Hungary in a not dissimilar predicament.

Since 1956 the Finns have become somewhat bolder. They caucus with the Scandinavian group and have also secured a special membership in the European Free Trade Association (EFTA). When the Soviet Union's interests are directly at stake, however, Finland tends to abstain in a UN vote.

The seating of Communist China in the United Nations, a question which until the late 1950's tended to separate the Western- from the Eastern-oriented powers, has become less and less meaningful in this context as Communist China and the Soviet Union have grown increasingly hostile. Finland, Sweden, Norway, and Denmark, NATO members or no, have combined in recent years to favor Communist China's representation in the UN. They did so on the principle that participation in the United Nations should be universal.

On North-South issues the differences between the small European states become much more noticeable. The most intransigent is Portugal, impervious even to the urgings of its NATO allies.[11] Resisting Asian and African efforts to compel acknowledgment of some responsibility to the UN for its African territories, Portugal sometimes finds itself alone with South Africa, although sometimes France keeps it company, as occasionally so do Spain and Belgium, depending upon the context. After some urging, Spain has been fairly compliant and cooperative regarding its colonies in Africa.[12] After the series of unhappy experiences in the Congo (Leopoldville), Belgian leaders, even Socialists, have become embittered about the UN's activities in the colonial field. But they were not particularly helpful from the beginning, especially when they resisted pressures, probably quite legitimately, to enlarge on their "information regarding non-self-governing territories" to be submitted to the General Assembly. They ceased in 1953 to participate in the Committee on Information from Non-Self-Governing Territories.[13]

The Netherlands initially was more cooperative. Even after their experiences at the birth of Indonesia (when Belgium gave its ally much support) the Dutch did not turn their backs on UN activities in the colonial field. When Indonesia claimed West New Guinea for its own, threatening to use force to wrest it away, the Netherlands proposed making it a United Nations-administered territory until the Papuans learned to govern themselves. In one of the most unprincipled acts ever sanctioned by the United Nations, this territory was handed over to its would-be conquerors. The Dutch had to recognize the old rule that the United Nations does not offer much protection

---

[11] However, when the United States in late 1962 secured a Portuguese agreement to permit United Nations representatives to visit its colonies, the Asian-African opponents would not accept the proposed resolution; they declared that they already had enough information to condemn Portugal.

[12] René Pélessier, "Spain's Discreet Decolonization," *Foreign Affairs*, April 1965 (Vol. 43, No. 3), pp. 519-527.

[13] Harold Karan Jacobson, "ONUC's Civilian Operations: State-Preserving and State-Building," *World Politics*, October 1964 (Vol. 17, No. 1), pp. 75-107, especially p. 81.

when a question involves great-power conflicts and the new rule that on a North-South issue a majority can now outvote the Europeans.

Sweden and Denmark count themselves as anticolonial but have often endeavored to bring moderation into the extreme demands of the new states. Ireland also speaks up vigorously on colonialism. Norway is probably the most likely to vote with the ex-colonies, but it too has tried to play a mediating role, as in the case before the Security Council between Malaysia and Indonesia in 1964. None of these states, however, were tempted to try Yugoslavia's expression of anticolonialism by actively wooing the new countries. In the tangled history of the Congo (Leopoldville), where East-West issues tended to get mixed with North-South questions, the small Western allies, including Greece, tended to stand together or at least not to oppose each other; they were usually joined by the European neutrals.[14]

With respect to certain other issues before the UN of interest to the small European states, the problems of alignment and nonalignment do not intrude quite so insistently. This is, for example, true of disarmament questions in which these small powers often have an intense concern. Two neutrals, Sweden and Ireland, have taken a leading part in some proposals, especially those relating to proliferation; but even Norway, Denmark, and Iceland have participated actively in these questions, including the question of bans on nuclear tests, regardless of the position of their big ally. Finland has tended to leave the substance of agreements to the nuclear powers rather than to some majority consisting of nonnuclear powers.

Another subject of much interest to several of the small European states is human rights. In this field Denmark has played a noteworthy role, especially in raising questions as to whether some ardent proponents of human rights were not more interested in restricting them than in guaranteeing them. The neutrals especially like to compensate for their lack of activity in "political" or "security" questions by concentrating on social and economic problems, with regard to which they quite rightly believe they have much to contribute in terms of technical aid.[15]

On trade and aid questions, the European small states have found themselves in opposition, whether they willed it or not, to the underdeveloped countries, as was the case at the UN Conference on Trade and Development (UNCTAD) of 1964. On trade and aid issues, as with so many others, the small European states differ strikingly from less developed countries in their

[14] For some analyses of these alignments, see Hayward R. Alker, Jr., "Dimensions of Conflict in the General Assembly," The American Political Science Review, September 1964 (Vol. 58, No. 3), pp. 642-657; Thomas Hovet, Jr., Bloc Politics in the United Nations (Cambridge, Mass: Harvard University Press, 1960); Bruce M. Russett, Trends in World Politics (New York: Macmillan, 1965), especially pp. 67-105; and Arend Lijphart, "The Analysis of Bloc Voting in the General Assembly: A Critique and a Proposal," The American Political Science Review, December 1963 (Vol. 57, No. 4), pp. 902-917.

[15] Ireland, however, in 1962 opposed a proposal in the General Assembly's Second (Economic and Financial) Committee to extend aid in population control to overpopulated underdeveloped states.

views on how the United Nations should operate. The Europeans are likely to ask, "Why not use the existing agencies?" They do so for many reasons, not the least of which is that they are stronger in the organizations already formed.

THE SMALL STATES VIS-À-VIS THE UN

Throughout the twenty-year life of the United Nations, these European small states, unlike other small states and also unlike the superpowers, have shown a distaste for using the UN as a propaganda vehicle; they wish to see adopted only such resolutions as are likely to be put into effect. As the Finns have expressed it, the UN should be a physician to its troubled Members, not a judge; it should be an "instrument of negotiations rather than a tribunal whose majority rulings too often prove unenforceable."[16] These states have most often regularly avoided "talking big and acting small," as one Irish delegate once put it.[17] Their emphasis on the conciliatory function has caused them to mistrust resolutions which fix blame and cause more conflict than they settle.[18]

To perform a mediating role, the United Nations, in their view, should be open to all states, South Africa as well as Communist China. Some, and notably Sweden, have played a leading part in conciliatory actions such as those relating to the partition of Palestine and to other Middle East controversies. These states have been especially anxious to avoid conflicts which directly pit the Soviet Union against the United States and vice versa. They find no profit for themselves in playing off one superpower against the other. They have stressed the importance of exercising the fact-finding function of UN agencies before hasty conclusions were accepted. They usually have taken a conservative view when the scope of authority of one UN body or another is in question. They are likely to emphasize, as did Sweden in the Congo crisis, that UN peacekeeping operations should be limited to keeping order and preventing clashes and that the UN should seek to stay out of domestic conflicts. Although they did uphold the authority of Secretary-General Dag Hammarskjöld as he gradually but firmly enlarged his political role, they urged, as he did, the need for clear-cut instructions. To these states such actions as he took seemed to strengthen the United Nations.

Denmark, Norway, and others have sought to build up the Organization by authorizing it to undertake as many joint technical aid projects as were practicable. In the specialized agencies, the small European countries have tended in recent years toward emphasizing education and training projects. Their views have differed on the desirability of research being conducted

[16] Jakobson, in *Introduction to Finland, 1963,* p. 68; and Ralf Törngren, "The Neutrality of Finland," *Foreign Affairs,* July 1961 (Vol. 39, No. 4), p. 606.

[17] Conor Cruise O'Brien, *To Katanga and Back* (New York: Simon and Schuster, 1963), p. 15.

[18] Their views in the Bizerte case between Tunisia and France show this tendency especially clearly.

directly by agencies such as WHO; some prefer that the UN agencies simply stimulate or coordinate independent research. In the 1960's they had to remind overeager Members of the need to match desired projects with available resources. In this decade they have also been confronted in the economic and social agencies by political demands from the underdeveloped countries strongly backed by Communist Bloc members. For example, with respect to such questions as the Declaration on the Granting of Independence to Colonial Countries and Peoples, disarmament, and the expulsion of South Africa, the Western European small states resisted such demands as inappropriate and likely to harm the work of the agencies.

Despite their views on the limits to effective action by the United Nations, the Organization has occupied a very important place in the foreign policy of most of the small European states. The reasons vary from one state to another. Perhaps the common element is that UN membership permits them to be independent in several different ways, an independence which these states tend to emphasize.[19] For Norway and Denmark, members of NATO but states having strong neutralist groups among their citizens, activity in the UN serves to balance their heavy reliance on the United States-led alliance for their security. For Sweden and Finland the UN offers a way of expressing their separation from any great-power bloc. The Scandinavian states are a very cohesive group in the General Assembly; they regularly caucus together and often speak as one voice. Their solidarity permits them to demonstrate their independence when a majority favors a line they do not wish to follow. Probably more important to them, UN participation is one way of preserving the "Northern Balance" upon which they rely in their relations with the Soviet Union.

The Benelux countries, strongly united in economic matters, also find strength in their cohesion in the UN, including their ability to stand out against a voting majority. Among the small European states the one most conspicuously independent of any caucusing bloc is Ireland. An Irish delegate to the General Assembly has explained that a small state in its position would be among those "most sought after" because its votes could not be counted on beforehand.[20] This result is a source of national pride, thus satisfying one of the values small states find in the United Nations—more international respect.

It is important to consider not only what the small Western European states *gain* in their foreign policy objectives but also what they *give*. They have in the last decade furnished approximately a quarter of the experts carrying out

[19] These comments apply to membership in the United Nations. For Austria and Finland, otherwise quite isolated prior to their admission to the Organization, membership in the specialized agencies meant prized international contacts. In later years, after its selection as the seat of the International Atomic Energy Agency (IAEA), Vienna aspired to be another Geneva.

[20] O'Brien, pp. 25–26.

technical assistance programs (mostly in countries outside Europe).[21] Over half the 2,400 experts in the Expanded Program of Technical Assistance (EPTA) in 1958 came from Europe; and the Netherlands ranked after the United States, the United Kingdom, and France in the number supplied.[22] They have provided other kinds of expert assistance in their home territories, through training, demonstration, and research facilities, far out of proportion to their relative number in the various UN agencies. They have also made large financial contributions to EPTA and the Special Fund. Sweden, Denmark, Norway, and the Netherlands are among the only nine UN Members which, when voluntary contributions are added, have contributed a larger percentage of the total support for UN activities than their assessment ratios.[23] Denmark has supplied proportionally the largest amount of technical aid of any Member.[24] Norway and Finland were the first to subscribe to the UN bond issue in 1962.[25]

The Secretariat has also drawn heavily on experienced civil servants from these small European states, again out of proportion to their numbers. This is a situation well-known to the less experienced new Members and the Communist Bloc, which express their displeasure by pressures to offset the criteria of international loyalty, efficiency, competence, and integrity by demands for greater "geographical representation" in the administrative staff.[26] And, of course, two of the three Secretaries-General in the twenty-year period have come from European small states, Norway and Sweden.

The reputation for not being tightly under the control of a major power, above all, a superpower, has made contingents from these highly developed small states especially welcome for UN observation teams and peacekeeping forces. Finland, for example, has furnished personnel for the Kashmir, Laos, Lebanon, and UN Emergency Force (UNEF) operations; and the first Cyprus mediator in 1964 was Finnish Ambassador Sakari Tuomioja, who died in office. Also in UNEF were contingents from Denmark, Norway, Sweden, and Yugoslavia. Twenty-one countries sent men to Lebanon in 1958; they were supervised by a committee headed by a Norwegian officer and in-

---

[21] Based on figures from the annual reports of the Technical Assistance Board (TAB), the *Yearbook of the United Nations,* and the annual report of the Special Fund.

[22] Walter R. Sharp, *Field Administration in the United Nations System: The Conduct of International Social and Economic Programs* (New York: Frederick A. Praeger, 1961), p. 140.

[23] Norman J. Padelford, "Financial Crisis and the Future of the United Nations," *World Politics,* July 1963 (Vol. 15, No. 4), pp. 531–568, especially p. 536. These same countries provided a higher percentage of their gross national product than the United States or the United Kingdom. Together the small Western European states contributed a larger percentage of the total than the Soviet Union.

[24] Henningsen, in Black and Thompson, p. 99.

[25] Jakobson, in *Introduction to Finland, 1963,* pp. 72–73.

[26] See Leland M. Goodrich, "Geographical Distribution of the Staff of the UN Secretariat," *International Organization,* Summer 1962 (Vol. 16, No. 3), pp 465–482; Georges Langrod, *The International Civil Service: Its Origins, Its Nature, Its Evolution* (Dobbs Ferry, N.Y: Oceana Publications, 1963), pp. 96–98, 176, 187–188, 190, 248, 251; and Sydney D. Bailey, *The Secretariat of the United Nations* (New York: Carnegie Endowment for International Peace, 1962), pp. 82–86, 91, 96, 99.

cluded Danes, Finns, Irish, Dutch, Norwegians, Portuguese, and Swedes. The quickly assembled initial force for the UN Operation in the Congo (ONUC) included contingents from Sweden and Ireland. When ONUC expanded to 20,000, Austria, Denmark, Ireland, the Netherlands, Norway, and Sweden were among the 28 countries furnishing troops. Forces serving with the UN Peacekeeping Force in Cyprus (UNFICYP) have come from, *inter alia,* Finland, Sweden, Ireland, and Denmark, while Austria has supplied noncombatant personnel as well as personnel for the civilian police. Voluntary financial contributions made to the Cyprus peacekeeping operation have come from, among others, Austria, Denmark, Greece, the Netherlands, Norway, Sweden, and Switzerland (a non-Member). Three Scandinavian countries and Finland are establishing national military forces specifically to be kept ready for UN use on short notice.[27]

Despite the pressure for more representation from Asia and Africa, representatives from European countries, including the small states considered here, have continued to serve in a larger proportion of the important offices in the UN than their numbers in the Organization would indicate, but the figures are beginning to decline.[28] Except for 1960–1961, a representative of one of the small Western European states has sat on the Security Council throughout the twenty-year period. There is no way to assess in detail the influence these countries are known to exert in behind-the-scenes maneuvers. Despite the weight of their influence, however, the tendency in many organs of the UN is toward a "small replica" of the whole United Nations rather than a "selectively loaded" group.[29] This is less noticeable in agencies in which small Western European states have a dominant interest such as the International Bank for Reconstruction and Development (IBRD). Their subscriptions are about 10 percent of the total; almost all have borrowed from the Bank, and they have a number of members among the Bank's Executive Directors. The same is true for the Intergovernmental Maritime Consultative Organization (IMCO), established in 1958, in the offices of which Western European small states have had numerous representatives.

As the Western European small states have become a smaller and smaller minority in the greatly expanded UN, they have also been taking note of the opportunities for international cooperation in their own more homogeneous region, whether the region is considered to consist of Europe alone, Europe and North America, or, even more broadly, the industrialized "North," including Japan. Thus, they have been drawn to activities where their voices

---

[27] Haekkerup, *Foreign Affairs,* Vol. 42, No. 4, pp. 675–681.

[28] See Marshall R. Singer and Barton Sensenig III, "Elections within the United Nations: An Experimental Study Utilizing Statistical Analysis," *International Organization,* Autumn 1963 (Vol. 17, No. 4), pp. 901–925, especially pp. 919–920.

[29] See Catherine Senf Manno, "Problems and Trends in the Composition of Nonplenary UN Organs," *International Organization,* Winter 1965 (Vol. 19, No. 1), pp. 37–55.

carried further than in the very heterogeneous United Nations and where they have not been overshadowed by the new Afro-Asian majority.

In view of the contributions which the small states of Western Europe have made over the years, some of them unique to this group, any dimming of their voices in the United Nations represents a loss. As they did twenty years ago when the UN was created, the Great Powers may again find their active participation indispensable.

IV. Looking to the Future

Regionalism and the United Nations

FRANCIS O. WILCOX

OLD soldiers may "just fade away" as General Douglas MacArthur reminded us, but the controversy over the relative merits of regionalism and globalism in international organization will ever be with us. That question generated as much heat as any other issue at San Francisco in 1945 with the possible exception of the veto. In more recent years the inadequacies of the United Nations, the changing nature of the Cold War, the growth and expansion of regional organizations, the proliferation of nuclear weapons, and the continued shrinking of the universe have kept the heat of this controversy at a relatively high level.

At one extreme are those staunch supporters of regionalism who contend that regional arrangements are a natural outgrowth of international cooperation and desirable stepping-stones toward world organization. Those who defend this view argue that regional agencies are not only compatible with the United Nations but, in reality, constitute an indispensable element in its successful growth and functioning. At the other end of the spectrum are those who insist that some regional agencies are little more than old-fashioned military alliances that foment great-power rivalries, weaken the effectiveness of the United Nations, and undermine the principle of collective security.

The issue, of course, has its practical aspects. Many people in this country, convinced that state sovereignty must yield further ground if the world is to survive in a nuclear age, have supported the creation of an Atlantic Union or a Free World Federation. Still others, perhaps disillusioned by the relative weakness of the United Nations, have urged the development of a stronger Atlantic Community or a concert of the free nations. Although the problem does not necessarily involve making a choice between organizing the world on a regional or a global basis, it is by no means clear how such organizations would fit into

FRANCIS O. WILCOX, a member of the Board of Editors of *International Organization,* is Dean of the School of Advanced International Studies, The Johns Hopkins University. He has served as United States Assistant Secretary of State for International Organization Affairs.

the present world order and what their relations with the United Nations would be.

After twenty years of experience in the peace and security field, it seems pertinent to inquire again whether the goals of regional agencies like the North Atlantic Treaty Organization (NATO), the Arab League, and the Organization of African Unity (OAU) are in harmony with the objectives of the United Nations. Have the efforts of the regional agencies conflicted with the United Nations or have they effectively supplemented its work? To what extent has the balance between the two concepts, so carefully worked out at San Francisco, been changed? Is there any real inconsistency in our efforts to deal with peace and security problems through both regional and global organizations?

THE SAN FRANCISCO CONFERENCE

In 1943, during the early stages of planning for the postwar world, some of the leaders of the democratic countries placed a rather surprising amount of emphasis on the concept of regionalism. Winston Churchill, who apparently had misgivings about the establishment of a worldwide organization, urged the creation of a number of regional councils through which the great nations might exercise their leadership in the world. By the time the Dumbarton Oaks Conversations convened, however, the Great Powers agreed that the new world organization should be given clear and unchallenged authority to deal with the basic issues of war and peace. They also recognized, with less enthusiasm, the valuable collateral role that regional organizations might play. As a result, the Dumbarton Oaks Proposals rather grudgingly provided that nothing in the UN Charter should preclude the existence of regional agencies provided they were "consistent with the purposes and principles of the Organization." Such organizations might play a constructive role, the conferees conceded, in the settlement of local disputes "either on the initiative of the states concerned or by reference from the Security Council." Moreover, it was agreed that in certain circumstances, the Security Council might utilize regional agencies for enforcement action with the understanding that this could be done only when authorized by the Council.[1]

At the United Nations Conference on International Organization at San Francisco the constant emphasis on the veto brought the regional issue to a white heat. The Latin countries, not willing to give up what they already had for something not yet within their grasp, insisted that the veto must not be permitted to block regional action in the Americas. On the other hand, members of the United States delegation, although responsive to the entreaties of the other American republics, remained fearful that the United Nations would

---

[1] "Proposals for the Establishment of a General International Organization," Department of State *Bulletin,* October 8, 1944 (Vol. 11, No. 276), p. 372.

be fatally weakened if regional groupings of states were authorized to take action without going through the Security Council. As Senator Arthur Vandenberg put it, "The Monroe Doctrine is protected only if we kick the daylights out of the world organization."[2]

In the end, hope was tempered with reality as three fundamental concessions were made in the direction of regionalism. The first amendments to the Dumbarton Oaks Proposals were designed to encourage states involved in local disputes to utilize regional agencies in their attempts to work out an amicable adjustment before turning to the Security Council for help. The result of several language changes was to reaffirm the compatibility of the regional and global approaches to the peaceful settlement of disputes and to provide a viable formula under which the two systems might function in mutual harmony. Regional agencies, to be sure, were not given exclusive jurisdiction over regional disputes; but they were given elbowroom to deal with local disputes in the first instance, and the Security Council was even urged to encourage and facilitate such attempts. On the other hand, the Charter reserved the basic right of the Council to deal with *any* dispute, whether regional, interregional, or global in character, whenever it needed to do so to discharge its primary responsibility for the maintenance of peace.

A second set of amendments dealt with the problem created by the existence of mutual assistance pacts, like the Anglo-Soviet Treaty of 1942,[3] and their integration into the United Nations system. The Conference met this issue head on by inserting Article 53 into the Charter providing for the utilization, where appropriate, of regional arrangements by the Security Council for enforcement action. "But," declares Article 53,

> no enforcement action shall be taken under regional arrangements . . . without the authorization of the Security Council, with the exception of measures against any enemy state . . . or in regional arrangements directed against renewal of aggressive policy on the part of any such state. . . .

The intent here is clear; while prior authorization of the Council is normally required for regional enforcement action, that requirement is waived with respect to measures taken against the resurgence of aggression by former enemy states.

Finally, the most important amendment recognized the right of individual and collective self-defense against armed attack. This amendment (Article 51) admitted the right of Member States to defend themselves "until the Security Council has taken the measures necessary to maintain international peace and

---

[2] Arthur H. Vandenberg, Jr., *The Private Papers of Senator Vandenberg* (Boston: Houghton Mifflin, 1952), p. 188.

[3] Treaty of Alliance in the War against Hitlerite Germany and Her Associates in Europe and of Collaboration and Mutual Assistance Thereafter Concluded between the Union of Soviet Socialist Republics and the United Kingdom of Great Britain and Northern Ireland, signed at London, May 26, 1942.

security." In such an event, however, the defensive steps taken by Members were to be "immediately" reported to the Council and

> shall not in any way affect the authority and responsibility of the Security Council . . . to take at any time such action as it deems necessary . . . to maintain or restore international peace and security.

Although these language changes may be criticized by some as a bundle of ambiguous compromises, what the framers of the Charter intended to do is reasonably clear. They intended to establish a flexible framework within which existing and future regional agencies and the United Nations might function together harmoniously, the one lending support and encouragement to the other in their mutually complementary tasks. They intended to underline the primary role of the regional agencies in the settlement of local disputes, and they obviously wished to recognize the inherent right of states to defend themselves against armed attack, veto or no veto. They did not intend, however, to "kick the daylights out of the world organization" or to detract from its primary responsibility for the maintenance of world peace.

THE BALANCE BEGINS TO SHIFT

One interesting shift in the delicate balance established at San Francisco—which is often overlooked—is reflected in the provisions of the treaties that have been negotiated setting up the various regional arrangements.[4] At the outset many supporters of the UN had grave doubts about the wisdom of developing regional instrumentalities like the Inter-American Treaty of Reciprocal Assistance (Rio Treaty) and the North Atlantic Treaty for fear of detracting from the influence and prestige of the UN and impairing its effectiveness. To reassure the skeptics, the regional and other security arrangements concluded since 1947 have traditionally contained repeated references to the United Nations. The Rio Treaty, in addition to the preamble, carries such references in eight of its substantive articles. Five of the fourteen articles of the North Atlantic Treaty, again apart from the preamble, pay homage to the UN and its Charter.

The depth of this feeling of loyalty for the United Nations was clearly demonstrated in this country in 1948 at the time of the passage of the Vandenberg Resolution by the United States Senate. In retrospect it is worth noting that the Resolution was sold to the Senate and to the American people primarily as a constructive program for strengthening the United Nations. Very little was said at the time about the much more important fact that its provisions, in effect, gave the President a green light to negotiate the North Atlantic Treaty.

[4] See Norman J. Padelford, "Regional Organizations and the United Nations," *International Organization*, May 1954 (Vol. 8, No. 2), pp. 211 ff.

A year later, when the NATO pact came before the Senate for debate, the Committee on Foreign Relations reiterated its strong support for the United Nations. "The treaty is expressly subordinated to the purposes, principles, and provisions of the UN Charter," declared the Committee, "and is designed to foster those conditions of peace and stability in the world which are essential if the United Nations is to function successfully."[5] This protective interest in the United Nations continued in evidence at nearly every hearing conducted by the Committee on important foreign policy matters. Thus, in 1954, during the hearings on the Southeast Asia Collective Defense Treaty, Secretary of State John Foster Dulles made clear that the Treaty did not disturb in the slightest United States obligations under the United Nations. "I can say categorically," declared Mr. Dulles, "that in my opinion this neither adds one jot or tittle nor subtracts one jot or tittle, from our objective as expressed in the Charter of the United Nations."[6]

Despite these repeated acknowledgments of the responsibility of the UN with respect to world peace, the language of the regional agreements entered into by the United States and other countries has tended to become less specific in its reference to the United Nations. The Rio Treaty, concluded shortly after the San Francisco Conference, was closely geared to the peaceful settlement and enforcement machinery of the United Nations. It is true that the Treaty was based on Article 51 of the Charter which reiterates "the inherent right of individual or collective self-defense" against armed attack. But it is also tied specifically to Article 54 under which the Security Council must be kept informed of activities either planned or undertaken by regional agencies with respect to the maintenance of peace. In this fashion, the Rio Treaty recognizes Chapter VIII of the Charter which clearly subordinates regional enforcement activities to the overriding jurisdiction of the United Nations.[7]

Both the NATO pact and the Southeast Asia Treaty Organization (SEATO) pact conveniently neglect to establish any regional relationship or commitments of this kind. The North Atlantic Treaty refers only to Article 51 and requires only that any measures taken against an armed attack "shall immediately be reported to the Security Council." Such measures, according to the Treaty, are to be terminated when the Council has taken the steps necessary "to restore and maintain international peace and security." Since no mention is made of Articles 52–54 of the Charter, the presumption is to be drawn that its signatories did not consider NATO a regional arrangement in the strict sense of that term. The SEATO pact, concluded in 1954, reiterates the principle that collective defense arrangements do not alter the rights and obligations of the parties under the Charter or the responsibility of the UN

[5] U.S. Congress, Senate, *Senate Executive Report* 8, 81st Congress, 1st Session, 1949.

[6] U.S. Congress, Senate, *Senate Executive Report* 1, 84th Congress, 1st Session, 1955, p. 10.

[7] U.S. Congress, Senate, *Review of the United Nations Charter*, 83rd Congress, 2nd Session, 1954, Document 164, p. 204.

for the maintenance of peace. Unlike its predecessors, the Rio Treaty and the NATO pact, it does not refer to any particular article of the Charter. Like both the Rio Treaty and the North Atlantic Treaty, it does require that measures taken against a common danger should be immediately reported to the Security Council, but it does not require that such action cease in the event the Security Council is able to restore peace and security.[8]

The significance of these changes is obvious. As the Cold War intensified, the parties to the newer arrangements considered it desirable to avoid the burdensome limitations and restrictions found in the regional articles of the Charter. It can be argued, of course, that the significance is more symbolic than real. Yet from both a legal and a practical point of view the net effect is to reduce the reliance of the parties on the UN and to deemphasize the need for coordinating regional action with the United Nations. Rightly or wrongly, the emphasis is less on teamwork and more on independent action. The signatories are thus free to act in an emergency without the possible delays and handicaps imposed by the restrictive language of Chapter VIII.

In any event there is no doubt that these trends created considerable concern in UN circles. In the *Annual Report of the Secretary-General* issued in 1954, Dag Hammarskjöld called attention to important developments outside the United Nations—but inside its sphere of interest—which required serious consideration.

> To fail to use the United Nations machinery on those matters for which Governments have given to the Organization a special or primary responsibility under the Charter, or to improvise other arrangements without overriding practical and political reasons—to act thus may tend to weaken the position of the Organization and to reduce its influence and effectiveness, even when the ultimate purpose which it is intended to serve is a United Nations purpose.[9]

Mr. Hammarskjöld pointed out that appropriate use of regional arrangements in the maintenance of peace was recognized and encouraged by the Charter. Nevertheless, where states choose to resort to such arrangements in the first instance, he said, "that choice should not be permitted to cast any doubt on the ultimate responsibility of the United Nations."

This was only one of many appeals to reason issued by Mr. Hammarskjöld during his career, and it struck a responsive chord in the hearts of many people. He was enough of a realist to know that he could not—even if he so desired—stem the tide of collective defense pacts. But he also recognized the imperative need to strike a proper balance between the regional and world organizations. For unless Member States kept in mind their long-range inter-

---

[8] The Charter of the OAU, the newest of the regional agencies, places even less emphasis on the United Nations. For the text of the Charter, see Boutros-Ghali, Boutros, "The Addis Ababa Charter," *International Conciliation,* January 1964 (No. 546), pp. 53–62.

[9] *Annual Report of the Secretary-General on the Work of the Organization, 1 July 1953–30 June 1954* (General Assembly *Official Records* [9th session], Supplement No. 1), p. xi.

ests in building a strong and effective United Nations, they might be tempted, for short-run advantages, to turn to other organizations in particular situations, thus weakening the UN and damaging the cause of world peace. He did not tell the Member States that they should have no other gods before them; he merely reminded them in his inimitable Swedish-English where their primary loyalties must lie if they were ever to arrive at the promised land.

PEACEFUL SETTLEMENT OF DISPUTES

A second shift in the balance between the regional organizations and the United Nations stems from the fact that the regional agencies have been far less active in the peaceful settlement of disputes than the framers of the Charter anticipated. With the exception of the Organization of American States (OAS), and more recently the Organization of African Unity (OAU), these agencies apparently have not recognized activity in this field to be among their prime objectives. As a result it cannot be said that any clear-cut pattern of working relationships or any satisfactory division of labor between the regional organizations and the United Nations has been developed. Moreover, the regional agencies have not eased the burden of the United Nations very much by serving either as a shock absorber or as a court of first resort for the settlement of local disputes.

There would appear to be at least three basic reasons why most regional agencies have played only a limited role in the peaceful settlement process. The first obviously flows from the inability of the United Nations to create the kind of enforcement machinery contemplated in the Charter. Peaceful settlement has a very intimate relationship with collective measures to keep the peace. The certainty of punitive action against those who disturb the peace increases considerably the probability that states will resolve their differences by peaceful means. On the other hand, without the deterring impact of an effective sanctions system some states may be far more inclined to take the law into their own hands, ignoring or bypassing the peaceful settlement machinery that is available to them. One can only hazard a guess, but in all likelihood if the Security Council had been able to discharge effectively its responsibility for the maintenance of peace, many more disputes of a local character would have been settled at the regional level.

In the second place, we sometimes forget that regional defense organizations were not created for the purpose of resolving differences between their own members. In NATO, as in other organizations of the alliance type, the basis of consensus among its members does not normally extend to the peaceful resolution of disputes that are unrelated to its *external* function. As Secretary of State John Foster Dulles pointed out in 1956: "NATO has not been organized as a regional association, nor has it any policy or jurisdiction to deal with disputes as between the members."[10] One of NATO's strengths lies in the fact that it has a fairly limited and precise mission to perform—the collective defense of the NATO area against aggression. In the early years of the Organization it was believed that if this commitment were broadened so as to include the extra burden of settling regional disputes, the unity of purpose of NATO might suffer and the alliance subjected to undesirable stresses and strains.

Yet the link between friendly relations and cooperative action in the defense field is an obvious one and regional alliance members have been increasingly willing to admit a degree of joint responsibility in this regard. In 1956 the report of the "NATO Committee of Three Wise Men," the Foreign Ministers of Canada, Italy, and Norway, acknowledged that it was "of crucial importance" in the development of political cooperation in NATO to avoid serious intermember disputes and to settle them quickly whenever they occurred. As a result of their recommendations, NATO members not only reaffirmed their obligations to settle such disputes by peaceful means, but they also agreed to submit them to good offices procedures *within* NATO "before resorting to any other international agency."[11] Since that time NATO members have increased both the breadth and the depth of their consultations in their attempt to settle disputes before they arise and to work out common policies on problems of mutual interest.

The third and perhaps the most important reason most regional organizations do not play a significant role in the peaceful settlement of disputes stems from the serious limitations on their membership. How could the Central Treaty Organization (CENTO) or SEATO possibly serve as a helpful factor in resolving the sharp differences between Pakistan and Afghanistan or the Kashmir dispute between India and Pakistan as long as India and Afghanistan are nonmembers? How could the Arab League be expected to settle the Palestine refugee problem or deal satisfactorily with the border clashes between Israel and its neighbors as long as Israel is not a member? How could NATO assure jurisdiction over the dispute between Italy and Austria over South Tyrol in view of the Austrian policy of nonalignment? How could SEATO make a useful contribution to the peaceful settlement of the serious differences between Malaysia and Indonesia when neither country is a member?

The conclusions are obvious. It is no doubt true that the friendly relations that normally exist among the members of an alliance have had a certain prenatal effect in preventing potential disputes within the alliance from coming to the fore. But the fact remains that most of the difficult issues of the

---

[10] Department of State *Bulletin*, June 4, 1956 (Vol. 34, No. 884), pp. 925–926.

[11] "Non-Military Co-operation in NATO: Text of the Report of the Committee of Three," *NATO Letter*, January 1, 1957 (Vol. 5, Special Supplement to No. 1), p. 8.

postwar era—Algeria, Cyprus, West Irian, the Congo (Leopoldville), Cuba, Angola, Suez, and many more—have not been settled at the regional level but have found their way into the broader forum of the United Nations. Whether this situation is due primarily to the fact that some regional organizations are ill-equipped to perform the peaceful settlement function, whether it is due to the desire of some states to gain political and propaganda advantages by taking their cases to a world forum, or whether it is due to the obvious fact that the Cold War has tended to convert many local differences into worldwide issues, it does suggest that every effort should be made to strengthen the peacekeeping machinery of the United Nations.

As far as the settlement of African disputes is concerned, the OAU could perform a valuable service for the United Nations. This function may be of special importance in Africa, which is a hodgepodge of nations with many poorly drawn frontiers and built-in boundary disputes. During its short life the OAU has already offered constructive help in bringing several difficult disputes within manageable bounds. The first of these was the frontier controversy between Algeria and Morocco, which smoldered under an uneasy truce for a year and then threatened to develop into open warfare. Following the creation of a seven-member arbitration commission by the OAU Council of Ministers in November 1963, a cease-fire was negotiated with the help of Emperor Haile Selassie of Ethiopia and President Modibo Keita of Mali. The "spirit of Addis" was also instrumental in stimulating Mali and Mauritania to sign a frontier delimitation treaty in July 1963. Finally, the long-standing and bitter dispute between Ethiopia and Somalia was eased considerably in February 1964, following a special appeal by the OAU Council of Ministers.

From a legal point of view the relationship between the regional organizations and the United Nations in the peacemaking field remains basically unchanged. For the most part there has been little competition for jurisdiction although sharp controversies have arisen between the OAS and the United Nations in connection with several important disputes. The first occurred in 1954 when the government of Guatemala simultaneously requested the OAS and the Security Council to take the necessary steps to bring to an end the attacks launched against it by Nicaragua and Honduras. In submitting its case to the Security Council the Guatemalan government in effect bypassed the OAS, contending that it had a right under the UN Charter to appeal directly to the Council for help. The United States, supported by certain Latin American states, insisted that OAS members were obliged to submit such disputes initially to the OAS which functioned as a court of first appeal in the western hemisphere. After a long procedural wrangle the Security Council failed to adopt the agenda by a vote of 4 in favor, 5 opposed, with 2 abstentions, in effect turning the dispute over to the OAS for further consideration.

Although the arguments were heavily weighted on the legal side, the motives in the transfer were largely political. The United States, together with Honduras and Nicaragua, hoped to unseat the Guatemalan government and thus supported regional jurisdiction in order to keep the Security Council out of the controversy. In the end the United States got what it wanted because it had the votes. What is important to note, however, is that the Security Council did not admit the exclusive jurisdiction of the OAS, nor did it admit any lack of authority to deal with the matter. The United Kingdom representative stated the views of the majority of the Council's members when he said: "For the Security Council to divest itself of its ultimate responsibility would be gravely to prejudice the moral authority of the United Nations...."[12]

The controversy between Cuba and the United States tested the central issue in much the same way with much the same result. Does a state involved in a dispute have a right to exercise its preference and take the issue to the United Nations even though a regional organization may be dealing with the matter at the time? Cuba, in calling for a meeting of the Security Council in July 1960 to consider its complaint against the United States, insisted that it had such a right. The United States contended that Cuba was legally obligated by the Rio Treaty to take the matter *first* to the OAS; however, in any event, the Security Council ought not to take any action until the problem had been dealt with by the appropriate organ of the OAS.

In the end the Security Council, without denying its own competence, turned the problem over to the OAS. This was done for pragmatic reasons. The Latin American members of the Council, Argentina and Ecuador, argued that disputes of this kind should normally be resolved within the framework of regional organizations, but in no case should a Member be denied access to the United Nations. Subsequent debate in the Security Council and the General Assembly during later stages of the Cuban crisis tended to underline these general principles.

Two other cases are of interest in this connection. The first had to do with a dispute between the Dominican Republic and Haiti which was brought before the Security Council at Haiti's request in May 1963. The second had to do with a complaint filed by Panama against the United States in January 1964. In both these cases the complaining parties agreed that the Security Council should step aside and permit the OAS to work out a solution to the problems involved. Meanwhile, in accordance with the desires of the parties, the Council retained the cases on its agenda, thus maintaining a posture of watchful waiting as the OAS proceeded with its task. In no way did these cooperative ventures impair the right of OAS members to have access to the

[12] On these issues, see Inis L. Claude, Jr., "The OAS, the UN, and the United States," *International Conciliation*, March 1964 (No. 547), p. 27.

Security Council at any time; in no way did they challenge the jurisdiction or the competence of the United Nations.

Despite all this pulling and tugging, from a legal point of view the basic relationship between the United Nations and the regional organizations remains relatively unchanged. Practically, however, it is apparent that the United Nations has yielded some jurisdictional ground to the OAS. It is particularly interesting to note that in all these cases, even though they joined the United States in supporting regional action, a good many Latin American countries carefully safeguarded the right of OAS members to take their problems to the United Nations at any time.

COLLECTIVE ACTION

As far as enforcement action is concerned, the relationships between the United Nations and the regional organizations have undergone far-reaching and, in the eyes of some people, highly disturbing changes. By their words and their deeds the OAS, the OAU, the Arab League, and, to a lesser extent, collective defense organizations like NATO, CENTO, and SEATO have either disregarded the authority of the United Nations or have taken positive steps to avoid the controls over regional action contemplated by the Charter. In some cases political, economic, and even military sanctions have been applied without the approval of the Security Council; in other cases the necessity for reporting enforcement measures to the United Nations appears to have been overlooked or ignored. The result has been that the authority of the Council to coordinate or control the enforcement activities of regional agencies has been sadly diluted.

The economic boycott of Israel, which was instituted by the Arab League in line with its policy of strangling Israel economically, is a case in point. As is well-known, the boycott was designed to achieve its purpose in two ways: by preventing trade between Israel and the Arab world, and by blacklisting foreign companies and ships doing business with Israel. Regardless of the merits of the case—and the historical justification advanced by the Arab countries—the boycott certainly was not in keeping with the persistent efforts of the United Nations to improve relations between Israel and its neighbors nor was it ever submitted to the Security Council for formal approval.

It is in connection with the activities of the OAS, however, that the authority of the United Nations received its first formal challenge and its first formal setback. The matter initially came to a head at a meeting of the ministers of foreign affairs of the OAS in San José in 1960. At that meeting the foreign ministers condemned the Dominican Republic for intervention and aggression against Venezuela and voted to set in train a series of diplomatic and economic sanctions, including suspension of trade in arms, against the aggressor. Since these measures fell short of the use of armed force, the OAS *reported* the action to the Security Council but apparently did not consider it necessary to seek the approval of the Council for their application.[13]

But the Soviet Union, with one eye on the developing Cuban crisis, had other ideas. The Soviet representative requested a meeting of the Security Council and urged the Council to give its formal approval to the sanctions voted by the OAS against the Dominican Republic. In this fashion he sought to establish, for future reference, the authority of the United Nations to coordinate and control OAS enforcement measures. Said the Soviet representative:

> Without authorization from the Security Council, the taking of enforcement action by regional agencies would be contrary to the Charter of the United Nations.[14]

This is at least a debatable point. The United States' argument that Security Council approval should be limited to enforcement action that involves the use of military power and should not be required for the limited kind of political and economic sanctions the OAS invoked against the Dominican Republic certainly has some merit. Clearly it is within the power of *any* sovereign state—without violating the Charter—to sever diplomatic or economic relations or to interrupt its communications with another state. Why, then, should UN approval be necessary for the same kind of action undertaken by a few states individually or by a *group* of states acting together?

Admittedly this argument would have carried more weight in the Council if its historical roots had been more impressive. The fact is, however, that from 1943 on, considerable evidence had piled up to support the Soviet contention that economic and financial sanctions should be treated as enforcement measures under Article 53 and therefore subject to UN control.[15] In any event, the Council members rallied to the support of the United States and by a vote of 9 in favor, none opposed, with 2 abstentions, approved a resolution by which the Council merely "takes note" of the regional measures against the Dominican Republic. Whether support for the United States was based on pragmatic or legal grounds is not entirely clear. What is clear is that the Security Council by its action in this case gave considerable impetus to regional autonomy.

Still further impetus resulted from the Cuban crisis. When the OAS in 1962 voted to exclude Cuba from participation in the inter-American system and to apply certain economic sanctions, Cuba took its case to the Security Council, contending that without the Council's approval such measures were illegal. As might be expected, the United States based its position in part on

---

[13] See Manuel Canyes, *The Organization of American States and the United Nations* (Washington, D.C: Pan American Union, 1963), pp. 52 ff.

[14] Security Council *Official Records* (15th year), 893rd meeting, September 8, 1960, p. 4.

[15] See Claude, *International Conciliation*, No. 547, pp. 48 ff.

the precedent established in the Dominican case. But this time the central issue revolved not so much around the right of the OAS to apply enforcement measures under the Charter as it did around the general relationship between the UN and the regional agencies. Thus, the Soviet representative solemnly warned against the desirability of freeing regional organizations from the overall control of the Security Council and underlined the risks that were involved in arbitrary action in Africa, Asia, and Latin America if the regional agencies usurped the authority of the Council. For its part the United States just as solemnly warned against the deadening impact of the Soviet veto and the dilution of regional efforts on behalf of peace if they were subject to the direction and control of the Security Council. "The principal issue," said United States Ambassador Adlai E. Stevenson,

> is whether a regional organization . . . has the right to manage its own affairs and to defend itself against a foreign-dominated Government, or whether the Soviet Union is to be allowed to paralyze that organization's activities through the exercise of the veto power in this Council.[16]

Although the final votes were inconclusive, they seemed to substantiate the proposition that the United Nations, veto or no veto, should not be permitted to block regional enforcement activity of this kind.

One further step was taken in October 1962 at the height of the Cuban missile crisis. At that time the OAS Council approved a resolution calling upon its members to take certain measures, "including the use of armed force," in support of the course of action embarked upon earlier by the United States. This was a historic event; among other things it was the first time the OAS had approved the application of *military* sanctions. Under more normal circumstances this might have stirred up a jurisdictional battle of considerable proportions. On this occasion, however, the United States took its case to *both* the OAS and the UN, calling upon *both* organizations to help avert a possible nuclear conflict. It is important to note that the United States apparently did not assume that it was necessary to seek the approval of the Council under Article 53 for the action taken by the OAS. Rather, it based its case on the principle of regional autonomy and the right of the OAS to take effective action without interference from the United Nations. And although the Soviet representative once more raised his voice in protest, the compelling need for great-power cooperation became apparent. As a result, the jurisdictional quarrel faded into the background as the two organizations joined hands to help find a way out of the dilemma.

Significantly enough, in these cases before the OAS, the Soviet Union departed from its traditional conservative position with respect to the authority of international organization and assumed a new role as the great defender

---

[16] Security Council *Official Records* (17th year), 993rd meeting, March 15, 1962, p. 14.

of a strong and effective United Nations. The United States, on the other hand, in arguing for the jurisdiction of the OAS, has often found itself in the embarrassing position of opposing a vigorous and expansive role for the United Nations. This change in policy is obviously due to a determination on the part of the United States to avoid the desultory effect of the Soviet veto. It does not mean that the United States government has rejected the principle that the primary responsibility for world order should rest with the United Nations. It does mean that the precise relationships between regional and world organizations must be worked out in each case in the light of the policy considerations that are involved and the need for effective action.

Unlike the OAS, the OAU has not been involved in any jurisdictional squabbles with the UN in connection with collective measures. To the contrary, the African states have taken the lead in the United Nations in promoting and encouraging the use of collective action against the Republic of South Africa and Portugal in a whole series of resolutions going back to 1961. Meanwhile, in its efforts to rid the continent of colonialism, the OAU has itself approved many nonpeaceful measures against both South Africa and Portugal. At Addis Ababa in May 1963, the Summit Conference of Independent African States urged the severance of diplomatic and consular relations, a total economic boycott of the two countries, the creation of liberation armies in various African states, as well as the establishment of a special coordinating committee to help in the liberation of dependent African territories.[17] Also, at its Cairo meeting in July 1964, the OAU went beyond the United Nations resolutions regarding air and sea transport by calling for the denial of rights to *any* aircraft or ship en route to or coming from South Africa or Portugal.

It may be argued that these resolutions are couched in the form of recommendations and carry with them no binding obligations for the members of the OAU. Nevertheless, they have set in train a series of developments both within and outside Africa that could be of great importance. Persistent efforts have been made either to boycott Portugal's and South Africa's participation in or to expel them from various United Nations organs and agencies. Some of the more militant African countries are heavily engaged in training freedom fighters and saboteurs. The OAU's African Liberation Committee (Committee of Nine) has raised a sizable sum—against a budget of some $4,000,000 a year—much of which is being used for propaganda purposes in colonial areas. And a subcommittee made up of Algeria, Egypt, and Guinea has drafted proposals for military aid for the liberation movement.

Governments may differ, as they obviously do, over the precise meaning of "enforcement action" and whether the joint measures taken by the OAS and the OAU legally require the approval of the Security Council. The fact is,

[17] See Norman J. Padelford, "The Organization of African Unity," *International Organization*, Summer 1964 (Vol. 18, No. 3), pp. 521, 536–540.

however, that the United Nations has been jockeyed into a position of relative inferiority so that the ties between the regional agencies and the world Organization exist "at the practical pleasure" of the regional agencies.[18] As Ambassador Francis Plimpton of the United States stated the case on March 23, 1962, after the Security Council vote on the Cuban proposal: "By its action today, the Security Council has forthrightly, resolutely and decisively upheld the integrity and independence of regional organizations."[19]

UNITED STATES POLICY

During the 1950's, the United States was often accused of worrying too much about security and of suffering from what some critics called an acute case of "regional pactitis." From other quarters the United States was accused of being softheaded and sentimental and putting too much emphasis on a relatively weak and ineffective United Nations in a world where national power remains the determining factor. Despite these criticisms the United States has continued to put its eggs in both these baskets. There seems little likelihood that this policy will undergo any substantial change in the near future. United States leaders continue to believe that the country has an important role to play in an international community in which many states both large and small, together with regional groupings of various kinds and appropriate global international organization, can make constructive contributions to peace and world order. The long-range goal of the United States remains a worldwide community of free nations.

It is not difficult to compile an impressive list of limitations on regional action in the peace and security field. There are the built-in handicaps inherent in most regional organizations because of their limited mission and their restricted geographic and functional jurisdiction. They are simply not geared to deal with many important problems that demand solution in a complex world. Moreover, some regional agencies, the OAU and the Arab League among them, are torn by internal stresses and strains and lack that unity of purpose that is so essential for effective action. Some like SEATO and CENTO, as we have pointed out above, suffer from understandable but significant gaps in membership. And some are incapable of vigorous and effective action precisely because they lack vigorous and effective leadership. Even more important, for most of the agencies, is the preemptive influence of the Cold War, for it has transformed many regional problems into world problems by requiring that they be dealt with in a broader forum where both the United States and the Soviet Union are represented.

18 E. S. Furniss, Jr., "A Re-examination of Regional Arrangements," *Journal of International Affairs* (New York), May 1955 (Vol. 9, No. 2), p. 84.
19 Security Council *Official Records* (17th year), 998th meeting, March 23, 1962, p. 30.

Despite these limitations, from the point of view of the United States, regional defense arrangements have served a number of extremely useful purposes. In the first place, they served notice to the entire world that the United States and its allies openly recognized the serious nature of the Communist threat and stood ready to take common action to meet it. In the second place, they stimulated the efforts of the treaty states to help themselves and each other, thus encouraging a higher degree of unity and teamwork than would have been possible through simple bilateral arrangements. Moreover, from a political point of view they provided an acceptable method and organizational framework for the introduction of United States power and influence into various regions of the world where weakness and instability invited Communist aggression.

It is, of course, impossible to prove that the existence of arrangements like NATO, SEATO, and CENTO actually stemmed Communist aggressive designs against the non-Communist countries of Western Europe and of Asia. One can only speculate about what *might* have happened if such organizations had not been created. This much, however, is perfectly clear: The *threat* of Soviet aggression had so permeated Western European thinking by 1949 and had stimulated such a feeling of fear and insecurity that real progress toward political stability and economic growth became impossible. NATO dissipated this fear and, together with the Marshall Plan, ushered Europe into a period of development and prosperity unparalleled in modern times. The case for SEATO and CENTO may be somewhat less obvious. The fact that Mao Tse-tung and other Communist leaders have repeatedly denounced them, however, would suggest that they have served not only as an irritant but also as a brake upon the expansionist ambitions of the Communist powers.

Prior to the assassination of President John F. Kennedy, Administration leaders placed a good deal of emphasis upon the so-called "grand design" in which a developed and integrated Atlantic Community would serve as the central core of strength of a worldwide community of free nations. Although these terms were never very clearly defined, it was apparent that President Kennedy's hopes for a strengthened Atlantic Community were conditioned by a realization that the United States is a global power with heavy commitments in Asia, Africa, Latin America, the Middle East, and Europe. He realized, too, that any move on the part of the United States to confine its interests to Europe or to Latin America would gravely weaken United States foreign policy and undermine its role as a world power. Administration leaders therefore frequently referred to the important work of the OAS, SEATO, CENTO, and other evolving organizations of the new nations and considered them—together with the Atlantic Community—as the "potential components" of a worldwide community of free nations. This development, they believed, would also contribute to a "stronger and more effective United Nations" and thus to the building of a broader world order.[20]

Since President Lyndon B. Johnson took over the White House, more attention has been given to domestic matters and relatively little has been said about the grand design. Administration leaders appear to take a somewhat more pragmatic approach to a pluralistic world—a "world of great diversity with many centers of power and influence . . . coming into better focus."[21] They recognize, on the one hand, that a genuine world community is not within our grasp either now or in the foreseeable future. They also realize that regional organizations are unequipped to cope with many important problems which are global in character and which are only made more difficult by attempts to distort them or squeeze them into regional molds. Speaking in Washington on March 11, 1965, Ambassador Adlai E. Stevenson put it this way:

> For the foreseeable future we will have to pursue world peace and world order in a combination of ways: bilaterally, multilaterally, regionally, and through the U.N. There must be continuous flexibility about this. Each of these methods has its limitations, as well as advantages.[22]

From the United States point of view the Cuban missile crisis illustrates very well the constructive results that can flow from cooperative action between a regional organization and the United Nations. Certainly the timely support of the United States position by the OAS coupled with direct bilateral negotiations between the Soviet Union and the United States were instrumental in preventing the outbreak of hostilities that might have escalated into nuclear war. But equally helpful was the indispensable role of the United Nations. It afforded an essential world forum for the presentation of the United States' case, it made possible extremely valuable diplomatic contacts, and, last but by no means least, it made available the unique assistance of a highly qualified third party, Secretary-General U Thant. In this instance surely, regional action combined with global diplomacy and direct negotiations all helped materially in bringing about the desired results.

In this connection some supporters of the United Nations have vigorously criticized the United States for "bypassing" the Organization and urging the solution of disputes in other forums. This treatment, it is argued, tends to expose the weaknesses of the United Nations and downgrade its influence in the world community. Would it not be better to encourage its development and strengthen its capacity to cope with difficult situations by turning to it more often? How can we expect it to discharge its responsibilities if we deliberately ignore it and avoid its jurisdiction?

---

[20] See Francis O. Wilcox and H. Field Haviland, Jr. (ed.), *The Atlantic Community: Progress and Prospects* (New York: Frederick A. Praeger, 1963), pp. 186 ff.

[21] Speech of United States Secretary of State Dean Rusk, New York City, January 10, 1964.

[22] Speech before the Overseas Writers Club.

While these arguments have some merit, it seems to me they overlook two fundamental considerations. In the first place, the Charter does not urge Member States to dump all their problems on the UN doorstep; to the contrary, it enjoins them to make every effort to settle their disputes elsewhere, resorting to the United Nations only if other methods of peaceful settlement prove unsatisfactory. Secondly, it neither helps the cause of world peace nor strengthens the United Nations when we ask it to perform impossible tasks. In the field of diplomacy, practice does not necessarily make for perfection; clearly the Member States can do the United Nations more harm than good by overburdening it with difficult problems.

In facing this dilemma the United States has used a pragmatic approach in which each case is examined on its merits. In the light of available facts, where can a particular problem be dealt with most effectively—in the United Nations, in a regional context, or through the channels of bilateral diplomacy? Will debate in the United Nations tend to exacerbate the dispute or is there a reasonable chance that it will help facilitate settlement? Will such action further the objectives of United States policy—which include the strengthening of the United Nations—or will it hamper their achievement? Responding to questions like these, the United States strongly supported UN action in Iran, Greece, Suez, and the Congo (Leopoldville) and in the later stages of the crisis over Cyprus. The United States favored regional jurisdiction in the Guatemalan and Cuban cases and it opposed, for what appeared to be sound reasons, UN intervention during the early stages of the Algerian and Cyprus disputes. The Administration has been unwilling, at least until April 1965, to invoke UN assistance in Berlin and South Vietnam because it did not feel, in view of the unique nature of the controversies and the parties involved, that the United Nations could make any useful contribution to these differences.

It is a mistake to assume, as some people apparently do, that the United Nations is an end in itself. It is only a means, and only one of the means, through which the United States and other countries can work toward a more orderly world. True, we can do a real disservice to the cause of international organization by arbitrarily preventing it from dealing with serious matters that urgently cry for peaceful adjustment. At the same time we must recognize the practical limitations on its use. In a world where goodwill and sincerity of purpose are scarce commodities and where states may bring their problems to international organizations in order to gain political advantage rather than to seek a just settlement, it would be a mistake to impose too heavy a burden upon the United Nations unless we are sure the Great Powers stand ready to support it.

Toward the Future

The experience of the last twenty years suggests that it is easy to overemphasize the effectiveness of regional organizations in the peacemaking process. Physical proximity often breeds controversy and in many instances the people of a particular region are less well equipped than outsiders to settle their own differences. Indeed, where disputes are deep-seated and bitter, the objective approach, the neutral facilities, and the constructive encouragement of countries or organizations outside the region are sometimes more acceptable to the conflicting parties than the assistance proffered by neighboring states.

In making these observations, one can not deny the obvious advantages of regionalism. Clearly a smaller organization, such as the OAS or the OAU, which is restricted geographically to nations in relatively close proximity to each other, can create the kind of machinery its members need to cope with their common problems more effectively than a world organization. States located several thousand miles away from each other, separated by vast differences in historical background, culture, language, and political and economic interests, may find it difficult to appreciate as fully as they should the mutual problems that afford them a common basis for cooperative action. Even more important, most states have not accepted the idea that world peace is indivisible. Insofar as collective action to repel aggression is concerned, they are inclined to respond with far greater speed and vigor to a security threat in their own area than to a distant danger whose focal point is far from their own frontiers.

The advantages of a global approach toward peace and security are equally obvious and equally persuasive. It is extremely difficult, for example, to determine with any degree of precision the geographic confines of a region or to decide which states should logically belong to a regional organization. NATO, SEATO, CENTO, and even the OAS, with their curious mélange of members, offer ample proof for this observation. Moreover, even within a well-defined regional area, states sharing the same linguistic and cultural backgrounds may differ sharply with respect to ideology and political institutions. In a world torn by Cold War cleavages such differences place serious limitations upon the effectiveness of regional action.

But still more convincing in practice is the striking fact that world problems simply do not recognize regional boundary lines. Even problems that are local at the outset often spill over into other regions of the world and assume a significance all out of proportion to their original importance. This was certainly true of the controversy between Italy and Austria over the problem of South Tyrol which eventually found its way into the General Assembly. It was also true of the dispute over Cyprus which was localized for many months until it erupted and became a threat to world peace. It is particularly true of many problems that take on Cold War overtones and by that fact cut across regional frontiers.

The obvious fact is that neither the United Nations nor the regional agencies have functioned as effectively as we would like, particularly with respect to peaceful settlement. Indeed, as one writer reminds us, the list of armed conflicts that have taken place since World War II "is probably as large as during any comparable period in history."[23] Literally dozens of controversies simmer on in varying degrees of intensity, without being submitted to any of the regional agencies for consideration or settlement. And many dangerously explosive disputes—including Laos, Berlin, and South Vietnam—go on indefinitely without finding a place on the agenda of the United Nations. This reluctance of states to turn to established organs for help is undoubtedly due to a variety of factors, but it stems primarily from the realization by the states involved that in submitting their problems to a multilateral forum they lose a certain element of control over their solution.

Yet despite the plethora of unresolved disputes that plague the international community, we have managed to muddle through twenty years of UN history without plunging the world into nuclear war. To that extent the deterring power of some of our regional agencies coupled with the moral force and the peacekeeping activities of the United Nations have been successful. A good many serious crises, including more recent situations in Algeria, West Irian, Lebanon, the Suez, and Cuba, have been met and are fading into history. Moreover, most of the open conflicts that have arisen have been limited both in terms of the weapons used and in terms of their geographic scope. In no case have nuclear weapons been called upon; and in nearly every instance the conflicts have been kept within the borders of a single state. Most important is the fact that the two superpowers have at all times avoided becoming involved in direct hostilities against each other.

Whether primary credit for these successes should be accorded to the United Nations or the regional agencies may be debatable. What is not debatable is the obvious fact that few if any burning issues have been resolved at the regional level. It is equally clear that the United Nations has served as a court of last resort handling many of the tough problems that have proved too hot to handle elsewhere. At the same time, inasmuch as the United Nations has not had at its disposal the armed forces needed to keep the peace, most reasonable men would probably agree that regional organizations and alliances have made an invaluable contribution to world order.

Clearly such general organizations as the OAS, the Arab League, and probably the OAU will continue to have an important role to play on the world stage. The future of regional defense organizations like NATO, SEATO, and the Warsaw Treaty Organization will depend, to a large extent, upon the

[23] Evan Luard, *Peace and Opinion* (London: Oxford University Press, 1962), pp. 35–38.

intensity of the Cold War and the nature of the security threat to which member states are subjected in a changing world. United States Senator Wayne Morse of Oregon remarked in 1964 that "we cannot see the communist bloc in Europe break up, without seeing the real basis for the NATO organization disappear with it." This may be true in part; certainly if the threat which brings an alliance system into being should disappear, the need for the alliance falls away. It is far too early to judge, however, whether the Communist Bloc is, in fact, breaking up or whether we are merely witnessing the first stages in the crumbling of the monolithic structure of the Communist system. If the statements of the Johnson Administration in 1964 and early 1965 are any indication, the United States is not counting its chickens before they are hatched. In the present state of world affairs what is needed is not a dissolution of NATO but a redefinition of its goals and a redirection of its energies in the light of the changing needs of its members.

In this uncertain world one must be careful with predictions. Ten years ago this writer suggested that, in addition to the creation of a number of collective security pacts and the assumption of greater responsibility by the General Assembly for peacekeeping, there remained at least two lines of development that might take place with respect to the role of the UN in the peace and security field. First, there was the possibility that Soviet intransigence might stimulate the creation of new defense pacts with the added possibility that they might be linked together, thus building a worldwide interrelated defense system with at least a nominal relationship to the UN. Second, there was the possibility that the enforcement functions of the UN might be considered too difficult to achieve in a worldwide organization and that the UN might tend to confine its activities to the peaceful settlement of disputes.[24]

On these two points I yield as gracefully as I can to the verdict of history. As far as I am aware there have been no serious moves during the past few years toward the creation of new regional collective defense pacts. Nor do any such moves appear likely in the present climate of world politics. The pressures on both the aligned and nonaligned countries to enter into such arrangements have abated somewhat; not only because the Soviet Union has struck a more reasonable posture in its international relationships but also because the role of the nonaligned nations, as United States Secretary of State Dean Rusk has made clear, has taken on a new aura of respectability in the eyes of the free world.

As far as the second point is concerned, admittedly the influx of new Members has diluted somewhat the unity of purpose of the UN and diminished the collective determination of the Members to keep the peace. With over 100

[24] See Francis O. Wilcox and Carl M. Marcy, *Proposals for Changes in the United Nations* (Washington, D.C: Brookings Institution, 1955), p. 179.

Members and with the Great Powers divided, the UN is far less likely to act with speed and vigor than it was when the Western countries sat at the controls. In the circumstances, it has not proved possible to put vitality into the collective security provisions of the Charter. Even so, the response of the UN in the Suez, Lebanon, Cyprus, and Congo crises suggests that the Organization, with all its limitations, can make a vital contribution to peace in many situations which lie quite beyond the reach of regional organizations.

There remains the possibility—more theoretical than practical—that steps might be taken to integrate existing regional pacts more effectively into the peacekeeping machinery of the United Nations. A number of suggestions to this end have been made, both by the UN's Collective Measures Committee and by the Commission to Study the Organization of Peace, but they continue to languish in the archives of UN history.[25] Most of them, such as the proposal that the armed forces created in connection with collective defense pacts should also be made available to the UN in case of aggression anywhere, are clearly designed to extend the control of the UN over the enforcement activities of regional organizations. When the time comes to examine once again the problem of revitalizing the UN's peacekeeping machinery, these proposals warrant careful consideration.

Still another suggestion that merits consideration is the idea that a concert of the free nations should be developed so as to enable those countries with "a real community of common interests" to work more closely together not only in keeping the peace but in furthering their social, economic, and humanitarian goals. This proposal naturally has a strong appeal for those who are attracted by the vision of closer ties between the Atlantic Community countries. Whether it would be feasible, however, to utilize the NATO alliance as a "nucleus of machinery" for any such concert, as some have suggested, is certainly open to question.[26] Theoretically, of course, NATO membership could be enlarged but it is extremely doubtful that very many of the nonaligned countries could be persuaded to join an anti-Communist alliance of this nature. Moreover, many strong supporters of the Western alliance firmly believe that any extensive geographic or functional expansion of NATO's activities would only tend to weaken its unity of purpose and undermine its principal objective.[27]

Any concert of the free nations would also have to keep in mind the strong attachment of the new countries to the United Nations. If such a concert were created in large measure outside the United Nations—and Senator Fulbright

[25] See, for example, Commission to Study the Organization of Peace, *Regional Arrangements for Security and the United Nations,* Eighth Report and Papers Presented to the Commission (New York, June 1953), pp. 9–11, 33.

[26] J. W. Fulbright, "For a Concert of Free Nations," *Foreign Affairs,* October 1961 (Vol. 40, No. 1), pp. 1–4. See also Wilcox and Haviland, which was previously published as a special issue of *International Organization* (Summer 1963 [Vol. 17, No. 3]).

[27] See "Non-Military Co-operation in NATO: Text of the Report of the Committee of Three," *NATO Letter,* January 1, 1957 (Vol. 5, Special Supplement to No. 1).

suggested this might be necessary—it would not only displease the new countries, but it would also deny the fundamental premise that we are all living together in a constantly shrinking world community. Global problems require global treatment. If the countries of Asia and Africa have anything to say about it—and they will—these problems will have to be dealt with in the broader forum of the United Nations. Even if the quest of the free nations for unity should prove successful, from a political point of view they cannot afford to permit their support for the United Nations to languish.

Sir Oliver Franks once described regionalism as "a halfway house at a time when single nations are no longer viable and the world is not ready to become one."[28] The world is not much closer to unity today than it was a decade ago, and it is likely the community of nations will find it necessary to resort to halfway measures for a long time to come. But halfway measures are never enough. It is imperative, therefore, that any move to strengthen the regional approaches to peace should keep in focus the long-range goal of *world* order and the proper role of global institutions in achieving that objective.

As we have seen, during the first twenty years the original concept of encouraging regional organizations to function under the general guidance and control of the United Nations has suffered a severe setback. Although most regional agencies have not been interested in asserting their jurisdiction over local disputes, they have demonstrated their autonomy insofar as collective measures of an enforcement character are concerned. Nevertheless, it would appear just as unwise today as it was in 1945 to place too much reliance upon regional agencies chiefly because their mandates are so severely limited both from a geographic and a functional point of view. Moreover, regional organizations are not capable of bridging the gap between the East and West—or the North and South for that matter—nor are they able to transcend the Cold War in a search for a common ground for the solution of great-power differences.

This brings us back to the United Nations. If anything like a reasonable balance is to be maintained between the regional and the universal, the United Nations must be reshaped to meet the realities of a new era. What we have had, during the past nineteen years, is basically a free world peacekeeping mechanism with the United Nations providing the moral and legal support. This is no longer feasible. What we should do now is to strengthen the Organization, first, by building a greater sense of responsibility in UN decision making and, second, by developing a more universal basis of support for UN peacekeeping operations. Unless these things can be done, more and more states may feel compelled to pursue their national interests increasingly outside the United Nations system either by a greater use of regional machinery or through bilateral action of an objectionable kind.

---

[28] Quoted in a speech by Harlan Cleveland, "Reflections on the Pacific Community," Department of State *Bulletin,* April 22, 1963 (Vol. 48, No. 1243), p. 614.

The Concept of Community and the Future of the United Nations

RICHARD W. VAN WAGENEN

IT may be unthinkable, even unimaginable, that the United Nations could itself become a true "community" in the near future. It is *not* unthinkable that the UN may be pushing the present disarray a little closer to that goal. The popular press abounds with loose references to the "world community," but men who have thought deeply and hardheadedly about this prospect have also hinted in that direction, using various terms for the same thing. To quote only two, Lincoln P. Bloomfield calmly mentions "the universal society of which the United Nations is the forerunner"[1] and Richard N. Gardner believes that a "genuine world community is waiting to be born. . . ."[2]

In mid-1965 we are concerned on the surface with nothing more exalted than self-preservation. International Cooperation Year (ICY) dawned with the departure of the first Member ever to resign from the Organization, followed by the adjournment of a crippled General Assembly seeking to solve the greatest constitutional issue in the UN's history. Beneath the present political alignments, the world is in fact divided in a number of ways, as Secretary-General U Thant has pointed out: economically, racially, and ideologically.[3] Under these conditions the "concept of community" may seem to be a paradox.

RICHARD W. VAN WAGENEN, a member of the Board of Editors of *International Organization,* is Dean of the Graduate School and Professor of International Organization, The American University. He served as Director of the Center for Research on World Political Institutions, Princeton University, from 1950 to 1957 and as Special Assistant for Training, International Bank for Reconstruction and Development, from 1962 to 1964.

[1] *The United Nations and U.S. Foreign Policy: A New Look at the National Interest* (Boston: Little, Brown and Company, 1960), p. 233. He wisely warned that
> there is no evidence that purely "functional" interrelationships will lead by any natural or automatic process to political integration, or even that integration as such will eventually be the dominant trend.

(*Ibid.,* p. 230.)

[2] Richard N. Gardner, *In Pursuit of World Order* (New York: Frederick A. Praeger, 1964), p. 262.

[3] See U Thant's address to the Pacem in Terris Convocation, February 20, 1965 ("The UNITED NATIONS in a Changing World," *UN Monthly Chronicle,* March 1965 [Vol. 2, No. 3], pp. 41–46).

THREE APPROACHES TO INVESTIGATION

This paradox needs to be examined in the light of the most advanced analysis available. In this brief space we have a choice of three approaches, only two of which are realistic here. One is to apply unstructured judgment on a straightforward premise that whatever seems to "strengthen" the UN is community building and will generate further integration. This runs into problems of definition right away. Another is to apply the findings of research on integration in certain other international contexts by using rough judgment and ignoring the fact that conditions underlying and surrounding the research in those other contexts are different and might render application to the UN unreliable. The third is to develop a framework for the specific study of the integrative function of the UN system and then apply it to that system.

The last is the best, but it is impossible to accomplish in a short space. The first and second can be explored, the first very briefly because the wealth of concrete information and analysis in the preceding pages makes a longer treatment superfluous.

Looking at the record of the United Nations over the first twenty years and applying political judgment and common sense, we are likely to conclude that, on balance, the UN is a community-building institution. The line of reasoning is familiar. As the technology of transportation and other forms of communication squeeze the globe into a sphere that is a fraction of its former size, global institutions have been invented or have grown from regional functional institutions. They do not grow as fast as the need for them, but there is a new realization that many things which have to be done *cannot* be done on a less-than-global basis, among them the regulation of transport and communication, the control of outer space, the control of disease, and above all the control of massive armed conflict.

If the doctrine of functionalism is taken at face value, the next step is to reason that the performance of these tasks, especially the economic and social ones in which the UN is so deeply engaged, will strengthen the sense of community over wide areas. This will help to build institutions which in turn strengthen the consensus needed for political community. A benign spiral then carries that sense of community to a point where the institutions gradually grow strong enough to support enforceable law. Such authority, in turn, may be able to check war, the greatest of dangers to man at the present time. The UN is the nearest thing we have to a global political institution. Therefore, to strengthen the UN in structure and function is to provide community-building authority.

There is probably a sound basis for this line of reasoning, but it still represents only a belief. We find it persuasive in the light of the many activities, most of them successful, which have been carried on by the UN in its first two decades. The situation is suggested by Adlai Stevenson, who gives the UN a large share of the credit:

> The central trend of our times is the emergence of what, for lack of a better label, might be called a policy of cease-fire and peaceful change. I would suggest . . . that we may be approaching something close to a world consensus on such a policy. . . . Cease-fire and peaceful change may strike some as a curious way to describe a period so jammed by violence, by disorder, by quarrels among the nations—an era so lacking in law and order. But I do not speak wistfully; I speak from the record. It is precisely the fact that so much violence and so many quarrels *have not led to war* that puts a special mark on our times.[4]

Convinced as we may be, for reasons of good judgment and desperation in unequal parts, that the UN is most assuredly worth supporting, we are left with a question: Did the UN really have much to do with the development of "cease-fire and peaceful change" or would this progress have come anyhow, swept forward by the facts of life? Indeed, does this alleged progress really exist? As analysts, we are uneasy until we have explored the intellectual basis—at least the underlying definitions and concepts—of the favorable assumption through social science research.

PREMISES AND CONSIDERATIONS OF THEORY

In exploring the second approach, the first thing to note is that the concept of community is elusive and slippery. Any number of scholars, especially sociologists and political scientists, have tried to grip it. The variables involved are almost infinite. The concept is crucial at various levels from the village to the globe; understanding seems to vary inversely with the height of the level so that the international is the most opaque of all. We are not concerned with other levels except as theory developed for studying them is useful at the international level. We do not need to start, therefore, with a comprehensive framework.[5] Rather, we seek a theory which is limited in two respects: It speaks to the international level and it points to the minimal kind of community needed to maintain peace.

We are interested at this point in trying to learn how the existence and operation of the UN may contribute to its strength as an international peacekeeping agency. Is there any sign of UN "community building" as a basis

[4] Address at Princeton University, March 23, 1964, published in Andrew W. Cordier and Wilder Foote (ed.), *The Quest for Peace: The Dag Hammarskjöld Memorial Lectures* (New York: Columbia University Press, 1965), p. 57. For a differing estimate by another respected statesman, see Herbert Hoover in Raymond A. Moore, Jr. (ed.), *The United Nations Reconsidered* (Columbia: University of South Carolina Press, 1963), pp. 80–82. For a strong proposal for action on clearly functionalist lines but outside the UN, see the thoughtful speech, "Approaches to International Community," to have been delivered on March 6, 1965, at Pennsylvania State University by Senator J. W. Fulbright.

[5] Such as that of Philip Jacob and Henry Teune in the opening chapter of Philip E. Jacob and James V. Toscano (ed.), *The Integration of Political Communities* (Philadelphia, Penna: J. B. Lippincott Company, 1964).

for institutional strength? Is there any secular trend slanting upward or downward through the pointed peaks and rounded valleys of UN crises, from the Iranian case of 1946 to the constitutional crisis of 1965? Does the UN itself have anything positive to do with that trend?

As to the "minimal or maximal" issue, it is a reasonable question whether those parts of the preamble calling for relief from the "scourge of war" and for the establishment of "conditions under which justice and respect for the obligations arising from treaties and other sources of international law can be maintained" are more basic than those parts reaffirming "faith in fundamental human rights" and encouraging "social progress and better standards of life in larger freedom." It is almost a cliché to say that peace is not merely the absence of war. But the absence of war is itself a valid overriding objective. What is specifically prohibited in the Charter is the unilateral use of force except in self-defense; if this is achieved, at least the "security" aim of the term "international peace and security" is realized.

To state a value premise, we believe that the war-prevention objective is the more fundamental because progress in the other elements of human welfare is impossible without this prerequisite. Yet the old question remains unanswered: Is a high level of welfare—economic and social and political— itself a prerequisite to a community cohesive enough to support institutions for keeping the peace? We take the minimal position: that where the object is peaceful change, the whole list of prerequisite or companion values is not necessary.

This drives us to the concept of security-community and integration as defined and elaborated some years ago in exploring "expanding community" as a focus for research.[6]

> A *security-community* is considered to be a group which has become integrated, where *integration* is defined as the attainment of a sense of community, accompanied by formal or informal institutions and practices, sufficiently strong and widespread to assure peaceful change among members of a group with "reasonable" certainty over a "long" period of time.[7]

To avoid circularity, "sense of community" and "peaceful change" were further defined, leading to the necessity of handling also the classic legal and psychological problem of "authority."[8]

When applied to the UN, this set of definitions does not reveal the basis of authority for what the Organization does and the lack of authority for what it does not do. How can it push toward a security-community over as wide an area as possible? How can it promote the process of integration?[9] We are

[6] Richard W. Van Wagenen, *Research in the International Organization Field: Some Notes on a Possible Focus* (Princeton, N.J.: Center for Research on World Political Institutions, 1952).

[7] *Ibid.*, pp. 10–11.

[8] *Ibid.*

[9] The word is used to mean both the process and the condition.

referring to what has been called the "ultimate task":

> to convert the world into a pluralistic society marked by a high adjustment poten-
> tial—by the existence of component parts which are susceptible of regulation in
> their relationships with each other and with the whole, through the processes of
> political accommodation.[10]

We are thinking sociologically of

> the possibility that the level of organization in the world may be raised, so to
> speak, so that a more inclusive social system comes to incorporate the national
> States.[11]

This would be incorporation to the minimum extent needed for a security-
community, that is, for integration.

It is quite true, as a thoughtful scholar has put it, that

> the competition of states can be pursued by means short of violence but still far
> in excess of those used by even sharply opposed political parties which accept the
> basic constitutional order of a state.[12]

Yet it is the habit of this very pursuit short of violence that is the proximate
and perhaps the ultimate goal we seek. Even though Stanley Hoffmann is correct in separating for purposes of analysis two different phenomena, the relations between individuals or groups across national boundaries ("transnational
society") and competition and cooperation of states having no common authority above them,[13] the study of the integrative process seems to underlie
both.

In the most thorough and sophisticated analysis of the doctrine of functionalism so far in print, Ernst Haas defines integration in a way not inconsistent
with the definition we have just cited, provided both are used in the sense of
process and not of condition:

> If the present international scene is conceived of as a series of interacting and
> mingling national environments, and in terms of their participation in interna-
> tional organizations, then integration would describe the process of *increasing* the
> interaction and the mingling so as to obscure the boundaries between the system
> of international organizations and the environment provided by their nation-state
> members.[14]

This is a more limited use of the word, but consistent especially when we
note that Mr. Haas considers

[10] Inis L. Claude, Jr., *Power and International Relations* (New York: Random House, 1962), p. 284.

[11] Robert C. Angell, in *The Nature of Conflict* (Paris: United Nations Educational, Scientific and
Cultural Organization, 1957), p. 205.

[12] Stanley Hoffmann, "Discord in Community: The North Atlantic Area as a Partial International
System," *International Organization*, Summer 1963 (Vol. 17, No. 3), pp. 526–527.

[13] *Ibid.*, p. 525. There is room for disagreement that as a tool of analysis "the word *community* does
more harm than good. . . . "

[14] Ernst B. Haas, *Beyond the Nation-State: Functionalism and International Organization* (Stanford,
Calif: Stanford University Press, 1964), p. 29.

modern nation-states as communities whose basic consensus is restricted to agreement on the *procedure* for maintaining order and settling disputes among groups, for carrying out well-understood functions.[15]

We are dealing with the United Nations as an organization. Concerning the outcomes of organizations, Mr. Haas identifies three types of decision-making processes or, as he calls them, recurrent patterns of outcomes. The least demanding is accommodation on the basis of the minimum common denominator, pleasing only the least cooperative bargaining partner. The other two are more demanding and carry the participants farther along the path toward integration: accommodation by splitting the difference and accommodation "on the basis of deliberately or inadvertently upgrading the common interests of the parties." Mr. Haas believes that

> the proof of an organizational impact lies in the appearance of a new set of general interests that command respect among the members—in short, a new world task.

There are three specific indicators: institutional autonomy, authority ("grudging implementation bestowed on organizational acts"), and legitimacy. He believes that the position of the UN system could be summed up convincingly if the degree of its legitimacy could be specified.[16]

His pioneering studies exploring integration in the European setting are well-known.[17] It is quite a jump from a set of nuclear European politico-economic organizations to a single-purpose functional worldwide international organization (the International Labor Organization [ILO]) and from there to a general-purpose political organization (the UN). Ernst Haas' work lends encouragement to those who would like to make this second leap.

The other lead toward assessing the integrative possibilities of the UN comes from the indicators devised by Karl Deutsch[18] in order to apply the Princeton concept of integration and security-community[19] and to develop it for exploring the integration of the North Atlantic area.[20] Again there is a conceptual leap from the historical cases of integration to the North Atlantic area and from there to the UN.

In the Princeton study *dis*integrative conditions were not handled systematically except in the case of amalgamated security-communities in history[21]

---

[15] *Ibid.*, p. 39.   [16] *Ibid.*, pp. 111, 131–133.

[17] Especially *The Uniting of Europe* (Stanford, Calif: Stanford University Press, 1958) and *Consensus Formation in the Council of Europe* (Berkeley: University of California Press, 1960).

[18] *Political Community at the International Level: Problems of Definition and Measurement* (Garden City, N.Y: Doubleday, 1954).

[19] See p. 815 above.

[20] Karl W. Deutsch, Sidney A. Burrell, Robert A. Kann, Maurice Lee, Jr., Martin Lichterman, Raymond E. Lindgren, Francis L. Loewenheim, and Richard W. Van Wagenen, *Political Community and the North Atlantic Area: International Organization in the Light of Historical Experience* (Princeton, N.J.: Princeton University Press, 1957).

[21] Since the amalgamated security-community is beyond even the most visionary notions about the future of the UN, only those parts of the study found relevant to pluralistic security-communities will be applied here.

so that we are unable to explore by this means whether the UN may be promoting some unknown disintegrative conditions at the same time it may be promoting integrative ones. Another of the many complications is the

> essential difference between the relations among states (even peaceful and cooperative) that are not engaged in the process of integration toward "political community" in Haas' sense, and the relations among states that have joined (even partially) in such a process,

the main difference lying "in the conceptual framework suitable for the study of those two types of situations."[22]

We are concerned especially with functions that tend to *change* the system. As we have suggested elsewhere,

> the criterion which has been generally overlooked is not the substantive result but the consensus-forming result of these international operations. This consensus-forming outcome might be considered not merely a by-product, but instead the most important single result from the standpoint of understanding the process of integration.[23]

Assessing Progress Toward Security-Community

Our second approach was to apply judgment to the observable facts, illuminated by the dim light issuing from the criteria we have just introduced.

Obviously the UN system as a whole is not a security-community and perhaps it never will be. Some groups of its Members already constitute such communities. The United States and Canada provide the clearest example and there are many others. Some are at the other end of the scale, for example, Israel and Jordan. Most are in between. Does the UN system promote or deter the process of international integration among large groupings of at least its non-Communist membership?

Do the findings of the Princeton historical studies have any application here?

One of the three conditions that were found to be *essential but not sufficient* for attainment of a security-community was

> a compatibility of the main values held by the relevant strata of all the political units involved; and with this condition there sometimes had to be also a tacit agreement to deprive any remaining incompatible values of their political significance.[24]

What can be construed as main values and relevant strata is wide open as far as the UN system is concerned. Values such as democracy and constitutionalism do not have equivalent meanings among many of the Members or among

---

[22] Hoffmann, *International Organization*, Vol. 17, No. 3, p. 527.
[23] Van Wagenen, p. 43.
[24] Deutsch and others, p. 123.

the relevant strata of society within Member States although they do have equivalent meanings among a majority of the Members having at least a bare majority of the population represented in the UN. Such broad values as social rights and economic welfare have a wide acceptance although the meaning of the terms is not identical everywhere. Prestige and independence are certainly among the main values of a nation-state, but they need referents: prestige in the eyes of whom, and independence from whom?

Our question is narrower, however, in two ways: 1) Integration does not ask congruence, only compatibility; peaceful coexistence, if it is genuine and permanent, is sufficient to uphold a security-community. 2) The present situation is not so much our concern as whether the UN promotes for the future any closer compatibility of values or the defusing of incompatible ones.

It is a temptation to decide that one value, an overwhelming desire to settle conflicts by peaceful (nonphysical) means, is more basic than any other in assessing progress toward a security-community. But this has not been proven, either as to its validity or as to its embodiment in national policies. Only two of the larger Members of the UN in 1964 or 1965 were on record with a policy of first-strike military force against another Member—the United Arab Republic (and its allies) and Indonesia—and by the end of the year one had resigned its membership. Two other Members came close to outright war in 1964 and it is not certain that they will avoid battle over Cyprus in the future. The availability of a UN alternative on the ground, which was not the case when three major Members of the UN undertook in 1956 to settle another problem by physical means, may have made some difference. The most that can be said about this indicator at present is close to simple assertion: Most students and observers of the UN system would probably judge that major national values are rendered slightly more compatible by constant exposure to each other in the UN system.

The second condition found to be essential was mutual responsiveness: mutual sympathy or loyalties, trust and consideration, at least some identification in terms of self-images and interests, and ability to predict behavior—a process of social learning.[25] Is there really much doubt that this kind of learning goes on in the UN? Clearly the Organization serves as more than a magnifier of existing images, merely enhancing congruences and incongruities alike. It also helps to predict behavior. The perpetual attention to, communication of, and perception of needs are there, as is at least some identification in terms of self-images and interests. Constant communication is one of the advantages of parliamentary diplomacy most frequently celebrated.[26]

[25] *Ibid.*, p. 129.
[26] Outside the formal agenda the General Assembly has become the world's greatest switchboard for bilateral diplomacy. . . . In New York last fall, in a period of 11 days, I conferred with the foreign ministers or heads of government of 54 nations.
(United States Secretary of State Dean Rusk, in Cordier and Foote, p. 74, referring to the fall of 1963.)

Even mutual sympathy or loyalties and probably increased consideration come out of the continuous friendly and unfriendly contact among representatives of governments at UN Headquarters.[27] But "trust" is a bigger word. This can develop on the individual level and also between certain governments, but in its full sense we cannot say that it is widespread. Yet we are not thinking of its full sense but only whether the existence of the UN causes any more trust or any more distrust among its Members than is already there. Nobody knows, but our own judgment is that a skeptical trust is fostered among those who are ideologically permitted such an adventure. Robert Osgood has pointed out that the Festinger principle of cognitive dissonance may have an application at the international level:

> When people are made to keep on behaving in ways that are inconsistent with their actual attitudes (e.g., as if they really trusted each other), their attitudes tend to shift into line with their behaviors. . . . [28]

There is also the only partially confirmed proposition arising from Chadwick Alger's close observation of General Assembly delegates to the effect that personal contacts with officials from other nations temper conflict with these officials, open new channels of communication with other nations, and keep them open when they might otherwise become closed.[29] And how much permanent damage is avoided by depriving delegates of "opportunities for the solitary accumulation of anger"?[30]

The third condition found to be essential was

> a multiplicity of ranges of communication and transactions between the units involved, and also a fairly wide range of different functions and services, together with the organizations to carry them out.[31]

The same judgment applies to this criterion as to the one calling for mutual responsiveness. There seems little doubt that the operation of the far-flung UN system meets this condition even though these operations are spread very thinly among the myriad contacts already flourishing outside that system—messages, face-to-face contacts, and especially trade. The operations are certainly pervasive.[32] But the question remains whether these are keeping up

[27] "In many eyes, the personal relationships established at the UN have as much, if not greater, importance than the formal decisions which are reached." (John G. Hadwen and Johan Kaufmann, *How United Nations Decisions Are Made* [2nd rev. ed.; Dobbs Ferry, N.Y: Oceana Publications, 1962], p. 58.)

[28] "Suggestions for Winning the Real War with Communism," *The Journal of Conflict Resolution,* December 1959 (Vol. 3, No. 4), p. 321.

[29] Chadwick F. Alger, "United Nations Participation as a Learning Process," *Public Opinion Quarterly,* Fall 1963 (Vol. 27, No. 3), p. 425.

[30] Hadwen and Kaufmann, p. 52. The crowded elevator described by the authors to make this point could be enlarged symbolically to include UN Headquarters as a whole.

[31] Deutsch and others, p. 144.

[32] "We must recognize that there is a United Nations angle, presently or prospectively, to every major subject of foreign policy." (United States Assistant Secretary of State Harlan Cleveland, in Francis O. Wilcox and H. Field Haviland, Jr. [ed.], *The United States and the United Nations* [Baltimore, Md: The Johns Hopkins Press, 1961], p. 147.)

with the increasing number of participating people and units in the world. If not, the effect may be integrative but fail to be net integrative.

Of the eleven conditions that were found to be *helpful but not necessary* to integration, four are so irrelevant to the UN situation that they should be ignored.[33] Another is a nullity because neither it nor its opposite are taking place as a result of the UN system.[34] Space does not permit us more than to mention the other six. With regard to the two economic conditions,[35] the evidence is not conclusive. Another is military,[36] to the effect that for a considerable number of years war had to be "so unrespectable that it seemed fratricidal," a condition that we would judge to be closer to fulfillment because of the existence of the UN than it was before. The other three emphasize social communication of various forms.[37] Such evidence as we have, either through judgment about performance or through data such as Mr. Alger's,[38] gives the edge to the UN as making at least some net contribution toward integration.

To summarize, the most that can be said is that the UN system seems to promote some integrative conditions and to have an ambiguous effect on others.

Moving from indicators arising from the study of historical cases in limited geographical areas, we can ask what can be done with indicators arising from the study of a contemporary international organization performing a definite but limited function on an almost worldwide basis?

Those developed by Ernst Haas are of two kinds: 1) As to procedures, there should be a greater integrative effect as they move from minimum common denominator into accommodation by splitting the difference and still farther into upgrading the common interests of the parties. 2) If the result of the operations is increased autonomy, authority, or legitimacy for the organization, and especially legitimacy, there is an integrative effect.

Most decisions in the UN are doubtless of the "minimum common denominator" sort, with little compromise involved. These are found in many fields— gestures of condemnation against South Africa, the Kashmir dispute, a declaration of human rights in place of conventions, and the like. Most of these decisions are the ones that do not move from the corridors into the conference rooms because feelers have shown that an alternative has too little chance to survive. Compromise then takes the form of agreed inaction, sometimes quiet and sometimes noisy. Some of the noisy instances might be called the senatorial courtesy cases, where a matter that obviously concerns the UN is brought forward but laid aside after it is made clear that one Member would "take a

[33] Deutsch and others, pp. 133, 137, 139, 156.
[34] *Ibid.*, p. 158.
[35] *Ibid.*, pp. 141, 157.
[36] *Ibid.*, p. 155.
[37] *Ibid.*, pp. 148, 149, 151.
[38] Alger, *Public Opinion Quarterly*, Vol. 27, No. 3, especially pp. 422, 425.

walk" if pressed—the instances concerning Hyderabad, Goa, and Algeria, for example. Probably the greatest of these is the current constitutional crisis, where the will and wisdom to avoid confrontation on Article 19 have halted the General Assembly in its tracks. Even ILO, by far the most carefully studied agency in the UN system, usually operates on this basis of the minimum common denominator, according to Ernst Haas.[39]

There is ample evidence that the two more advanced procedures specified by Mr. Haas are also found frequently in the conduct of UN business. Compromising the final bargaining positions of Members is done each year when the budget tries to squeeze between the cutters and the spenders. It is also done in revising the scale of assessments and recently when the Committee of Experts on the Review of the Activities and Organization of the Secretariat revised the formula for geographical distribution of Secretariat members among the competing interests. The Secretary-General's mediation work, for example, the ground-breaking Beck-Friis mission to Cambodia and Thailand in 1959 and the mission to Laos later that year, might be considered in the third category, but to be conservative we can consider it here. The fact that these missions did not permanently solve the problems facing them (just as the mediation job in Cyprus has not yet succeeded) does not surprise those familiar with international politics or subtract much from the efficacy of such operations at the time. The "opting out" technique is an odd example of this procedure. By this we mean that the failure of certain members to buy UN bonds does not stop the sale of bonds to other Members, nor does the failure of some Members to pledge toward voluntarily supported programs such as the Expanded Program of Technical Assistance (EPTA) and the UN Children's Fund (UNICEF) veto those operations.

The third and most advanced procedure is naturally harder to identify in the UN context, but two or three kinds of operations seem to involve upgrading the common interests of the parties. One is international military force authorized by a worldwide body, a "new world task" of recent times. Despite their distinctly different purposes, the UN Emergency Force (UNEF), the UN Operation in the Congo (ONUC), and the UN Peacekeeping Force in Cyprus (UNFICYP) are good examples. These are not simply the implementation of an existing will to peace, but a little bit more. Another kind of operation in this category is economic planning and execution on a multinational scale, a task of large dimensions and poor coordination. Within the UN system the main agencies are the International Monetary Fund (IMF), the International Bank for Reconstruction and Development (IBRD) and its two affiliates, the other specialized agencies in the economic field, the Special Fund, EPTA, and the four regional economic commissions. Some of these operations mesh with each other, but that does not bring them very close to

---

[39] Haas, *Beyond the Nation-State*, p. 445.

such regional non-UN organizations as the Inter-American Development Bank (IDB) of the Organization of American States (OAS) or the Development Assistance Committee (DAC) of the Organization for Economic Cooperation and Development (OECD). It is debatable whether the more successful these organizations become the more strongly they will give economic support to an existing political nationalism and hence have a disintegrative effect from the standpoint of the community as a whole. Yet they tend more and more to coordinate their efforts and at least some of them realize that not every country needs a steel mill.[40] It is the national foreign aid programs that cater more to the desire for unwarranted self-sufficiency.

The personal factor may well be a strong catalyst leading toward an upgrading of common interests. One of Mr. Alger's conclusions was that "there is a remarkably extensive change being implemented in international society through the building of international organizations"[41] and that an

> international organization such as the United Nations also permits the development of an international "interest group" that coalesces around a common desire to develop and strengthen the organization.[42]

We must not mistake this interest group for the whole international community, but even UN Headquarters is not an island. The delegations to the General Assembly normally include over a hundred members of parliaments, several hundred foreign office officials, and a number of high-status private citizens. It is undoubtedly true that both irritations and tolerations are renewed annually at the General Assembly, but we think most observers would agree that the latter outrun the former.

The "community of functional specialists," as Leon N. Lindberg calls it, is another kind of interest group which can be seen in some of the UN's activities. He analyzed the ministers of agriculture and other national officials in the agricultural sector of the European Community.[43] The medical profession connected with the World Health Organization (WHO) also forms a transnational bond able to influence national policies through the ministries of health.

Turning to the factor of institutional autonomy mentioned by Mr. Haas, it may

---

[40] Two recent publications of the UN illustrate this emphasis upon transnational approaches: *Possibilities of Integrated Industrial Development in Central America* (UN Document E/CN.12/683/Rev.1); and *The Economic Development of Latin America in the Post-War Period* (UN Document E/CN.12/659/Rev.1). On the grand scale, the Mekong River program involves 25 countries within and outside the Economic Commission for Asia and the Far East (ECAFE) region plus twelve UN organs or units.

[41] Chadwick F. Alger, "Hypotheses on Relationships Between the Organization of International Society and International Order," *Proceedings of the American Society of International Law*, 57th annual meeting, Washington, D.C., April 25–27, 1963, p. 42.

[42] *Ibid.*, p. 45.

[43] "Decision Making and Integration in the European Community," *International Organization*, Winter 1965 (Vol. 19, No. 1), especially pp. 71–73; see also his interesting observations on penetration into national administrative structures (*ibid.*, pp. 73–74).

be noted first that the Secretary-General's authority has gone up and down.[44] Trygve Lie asserted more leadership than he is generally given credit for and achieved a considerable image of authority and autonomy before being turned upon by one of the major powers. Dag Hammarskjöld exhibited surefooted leadership, reaching a point where he was given political jobs to perform without specific instructions. This began with the United States flyers in Communist China (late 1954) and moved to the observation task in Lebanon (1958) and to the Congo operation in 1960. He went still further philosophically in his Oxford address shortly before his death.[45] It is doubtful that he would have been able to push that quite revolutionary stretching exercise, but his work may foreshadow a long-range trend in the direction of autonomy and authority if the Organization survives the present downdraft.

There is little doubt about the favorable effect of IBRD representatives and field missions in creating respect for the Bank, but the reluctance of staff members to advertise their connection with the UN makes it likely that no more than the outer rim of the Bank's halo touches the UN system as a whole. The halo seems to be stretching, however, as the Bank's new President brings the Bank closer to the UN and the other specialized agencies. Evidence of the influence of UN Resident Representatives is not scarce but has never been fully analyzed. As of 1964, their increasing utility has been noted, save in the task of country programming.[46] The impact of these 83 offices headed by either a Resident Representative or a Deputy, all engaged in economic and social activities of interest to the local population, varies from country to country and from situation to situation, but it is unknown in terms of their authority-building function. The same is true for Directors of UN Information Centers and indeed for the effect of the entire UN information program. However, in Gerard Mangone's judgment "all evidence seems to point to a proliferation of the responsibilities of the Resident Representative" and

> the patterns of United Nations activities over the next decades . . . will shift from temporary, sporadic, and voluntary programs to permanent, continuous, and regular operations.[47]

Other on-the-spot contacts with representatives of UN functions at present, such as International Atomic Energy Agency (IAEA) inspectors and technical assistance experts of various kinds, plebiscite administrators, truce ob-

---

[44] See Charles Winchmore, "The Secretariat: Retrospect and Prospect," earlier in this volume.

[45] He stated his belief that the Secretary-General could "resolve controversial questions on a truly international basis without obtaining the formal decision of the organs . . . ," since the

> principles of the Charter are . . . supplemented by the body of legal doctrine and precepts that have been accepted by States generally, and particularly as manifested in the resolutions of UN organs.

(*The International Civil Servant in Law and in Fact* [Oxford: Clarendon Press, 1961], pp. 24–25.)

[46] Gerard J. Mangone, *The United Nations Resident Representative: A Case of Administrative Institution-Building* (unpublished paper, 1964), pp. 27, 79.

[47] *Ibid.*, p. 97.

servers, officials of the program for the provision of Operational, Executive and Administrative Personnel (OPEX), and, in the future, arms control inspectors and outer space monitors cannot be judged to be integrative, disintegrative, or simply nonintegrative without closer study than anyone has yet given them.

The distinction Ernst Haas makes between authority and legitimacy is an important one from the standpoint of creating a real security-community,[48] yet one of these includes the other. It would be hard to imagine legitimacy without authority, but authority without legitimacy is commonplace.[49] If research could follow the suggestion Mr. Haas makes, we could learn something significant about integrative progress. He proposes that

> a rough measure of legitimacy can be provided by distilling from the historical material the situations in which member states invoke the purposes and principles of the UN to justify some item of national policy, such invocation being at the same time accompanied by an expansion of the global task.[50]

This index would be rough indeed, but if it sidestepped the trap of false cause-and-effect, it would be worth making. Citing UN principles might be more of a justification than a true motive for something which a Member government wanted to do, seeking legitimation from the UN in the same way that battling troops seek the legitimation of God for their cause. Yet the mere fact that the blessing is sought would tend to build up the legitimacy of the blesser.

To our mind, the international military forces that have been authorized by the UN for various kinds of peacekeeping purposes would be prime subjects of study. Next best would be three prospective new tasks: governing atomic energy for peaceful international use, controlling the uses of outer space by whatever means are invented, and controlling military arms by focusing on inspection.

We could speculate at length about the effect that contact with the operations of the UN has upon Member States' attitudes toward the authority or legitimacy of the system. What might be called empirical speculation is more reliable:

> Central organizations themselves, although limited in ability to make authoritative decisions, may play crucial roles in building . . . a social structure by the learning experiences they provide for those playing organizational roles, and by

---

[48] Legitimacy provides a presumption of "repetition or expansion of peaceful change procedures . . . ," whereas mere authority does not. (Haas, *Beyond the Nation-State*, p. 133.)

[49] For example, one would suppose that the UN Truce Supervision Organization (UNTSO) is a good case of at least some authority without legitimacy at present, asking again an old question: "What is the consensus-forming effect, not simply the immediate agreement-reaching effect, of the United Nations' mixed commissions in Palestine?" (Van Wagenen, p. 44.)

[50] Haas, *Beyond the Nation-State*, p. 133.

the new linkages they provide between formerly isolated roles in individual units.[51]

This is exemplified by the change that occurs in Senators and Congressmen who serve a session on the United States delegation to the General Assembly, as observed by Francis O. Wilcox when he was on Capitol Hill and later when he was United States Assistant Secretary of State. Legislators, returning with greater knowledge, were not transformed but were in every case changed in a direction more favorable to the UN. In committee discussions and elsewhere they enjoyed deference when UN matters came up; this helped to generate in them an especially responsible attitude toward the Organization and in turn either took the edge off prior hostile attitudes or sharpened already favorable ones.

The Escalation of Community

The conclusions are more suggestive than conclusive in response to our opening questions: Is there any sign of "community building"? Is there any secular trend slanting upward or downward? Does the UN itself have anything positive to do with that trend? While the UN undoubtedly does some distintegrative and many nonintegrative things, it also does many apparently integrative things in integrative ways. It is not too exuberant to say that the net direction seems to be integrative, tending toward the eventual building of a security-community broader than we have today.

There is no way to be sure of a security-community before time has delivered the pragmatic test. Yet it is likely that the work of the UN system and the personal contact which that work entails will help to grow more of what we have been calling pluralistic security-communities where they do not yet exist.[52] This conclusion, however, evades a crucial question: Is it more dangerous to have fewer and tighter communities on a less-than-global level than to leave things as they are? Also, we cannot forget that if evidence of a trend toward integration appears on the international political scene it is impossible to estimate how much credit is due to the UN system.

How can the integrative work of the UN be strengthened? Activities should be undertaken which build muscle without the danger of hernia. These are activities that lead to the expansion of tasks that are successfully handled and that appear to incrcase the authority and later the legitimacy of the UN system.

In practical terms, this means that within the margins of maneuver open to Members the UN should be given jobs to do which 1) are conspicuously related to the UN, 2) have a good chance of success in a technical or administrative sense, 3) involve the lives of many influential people in several signifi-

---

[51] Alger, *Public Opinion Quarterly*, Vol. 27, No. 3, p. 426.

[52] Perhaps in Central America, parts of the Indian subcontinent and Southeast Asia, or some of the Arab states, for example.

cant Member States, and 4) bring tangible rewards to Members, if possible including the prevention of expensive wars.

This simple formulation may seem self-evident enough in logic and unattainable enough in practice to invite concrete illustration. The most convincing examples are the normal activities of the specialized agencies, which are at present by no means conspicuous enough.[53] Greater use of the International Court of Justice would be helpful in cases where advisory opinions are certain to be accepted and where decisions are most likely to be executed. The field of human rights also offers an opportunity that may have been underrated.[54] Further practice is recommended in forming UN peacekeeping operations where they have a fair chance of being conspicuously successful in the eyes of many Members of the UN. Proposals for designating national contingents and for drafting logistical head starts and other plans are in this realm and have already begun. A greater use of UN observers is also indicated. Arms control and outer space lie before us. The bed of the sea in some parts of the world is pregnant with resources and awaits community action to prevent fighting over their ownership. Indeed, the subtle "side effects" coming out of *any* operation bear close watching.

This brief inquiry into the concept of community has not shown us what it means to the future of the UN, but it may have given us a better idea of how to investigate over the next twenty years. We started with three choices of approach: to apply informed judgment to known facts, to use informed judgment in applying to known facts the findings that come from research in different contexts at the international level, or to develop and apply a framework for studying the integrative function of the UN system specifically. After a dip into the second, we recommend the first and the third.

The first is constantly employed; it is of course the best we currently have as a guide to national foreign policy in the UN. The reviews of UN experience brought out earlier in this volume are first-class testimony that educated insight and common sense have not been unhorsed. But it is time for someone brave enough to attack through the third approach—a colossal job. There is a good chance that

> . . . the dry bones littered by the way
> May still point giants toward their golden prey.[55]

[53] As with the reporting of public affairs at any level, the monotony of the unexciting brings about the monopoly of the exciting.

[54] See especially, Percy E. Corbett, *The Individual and World Society* (Princeton, N.J: Center for Research on World Political Institutions, 1953), pp. 47–59; and Gardner, Chapter 10.

[55] Stephen Vincent Benét, *John Brown's Body* (New York: Holt, Rinehart and Winston, 1941), Invocation.

The Evolution of Rising Responsibility

HARLAN CLEVELAND

As the United Nations stands on the threshold of its third decade, every Member of the Organization will do well to think about the kind of UN it wants, for that is what may well be achieved.

The UN system as a whole has opportunities to serve mankind which are limited only by the capacity of its Members to work together and keep on working together.

REVOLUTION OF RISING EXPECTATIONS

A revolution of rising expectations has swept across the colonial world and doubled the count of national sovereignties. Men and women who fifteen years ago were students or revolutionaries, or both, are today in charge of their countries' governments—or have already given way to younger students and more effective revolutionaries.

The aspirations that have risen so fast were well described in the Charter of the United Nations as "better standards of life in larger freedom." How the passions of our time have been aroused by passionate versions of that sober and balanced phrase!

It is surely time, as Pope Paul VI has said, to "raise a dike" against the passions of men, for they threaten to swallow up in passionate indignities the natural dignity of individual men and women on the perverted theory that individuals belong to the state, rather than vice versa. Nationhood is heady stuff. Every nation and every national leader can be expected to overindulge once in a while. But continued overindulgence in nationalist emotion can lead to much senseless killing and to the death of common sense itself. The question about our world and the question about the UN in this International Cooperation Year (ICY) is this: Can we all graduate fast enough from the "revolution of rising expectations" to the "evolution of rising responsibility"?

HARLAN CLEVELAND is former Assistant Secretary of State for International Organization Affairs, United States Department of State.

The need for a rising standard of responsibility is most evident in the UN because the UN is a magnified mirror of the tensions and dilemmas of the world at large. As we look ahead to the UN's next twenty years, four kinds of issues stand out as most likely to threaten the peace—because they threaten to unstick the glue that holds the world community together.

One of these issues is the proliferation of nuclear weapons. Another is the growing practice of unsolicited intervention by nations in each other's internal affairs. A third problem is how the international community does something effective about internal human rights. And, finally, there is a constitutional question about the organization of the UN itself.

PROBLEM OF PROLIFERATION OF NUCLEAR WEAPONS

The world is face-to-face with a disturbing trauma. The advancement of science has made the instruments of murder and destruction so efficient that there is no alternative to peace. The nuclear powers have learned, or are learning, that their inconceivable power should only be used in the presence of almost inconceivable provocation. And now the prospect is that within the next few years half a dozen countries, or perhaps as many as ten or twelve, could readily develop their own nuclear weapons. They have the scientists, the industry, the imagination, and the will to do the job.

Nobody thinks such proliferation of nuclear weapons would make any sense, and it would certainly make life more complicated and dangerous. But it could happen. And the reason that it could happen is that there is no agreed machinery for making it unnecessary.

Ever since we offered to internationalize our nuclear know-how under the Baruch Plan, the United States has been looking for an acceptable way to prevent the spread of these weapons around the world. There has been a little progress—a ban on tests in the atmosphere, a UN resolution against putting bombs in orbit, a "hot line" to reduce the danger of war by accident or miscalculation. We will keep on working at disarmament, which is always more important than it is discouraging. But meanwhile something can surely be done to prevent a rapid decline in the prospects for any general disarmament at all.

That something is to obtain agreement that no further nations will develop their nuclear weapons capabilities. For in a world already oversupplied with destructive capacity, both the ease and the folly of further proliferation are evident to every person who is concerned with the preservation of the human species.

That the Chinese Communists poured resources and talent into building a bomb is sad and, in the long run, very dangerous. But the worst thing about the Chinese action is that it may be contagious. Peking's neighbors and

Peking's adversaries in world politics can hardly be expected to watch another nuclear power develop nearby without thinking hard about what this means for their own security. The world community must either stop the further growth of nuclear weaponry altogether—which is what we have been trying to do in the Geneva disarmament talks—or it must somehow give assurances to the nonnuclear countries against domination by those nations that can make and deliver wholesale destruction.

Here, in truth, is a problem for all the world—and all the world had better start treating it with the urgency it deserves.

THE ETHICS OF INTERVENTION

For the moment, we are all precariously protected from the largest war known to man by the nuclear confrontation called mutual deterrence. But the alternative to world war unhappily is not necessarily world peace. It can be a world full of small wars and near wars.

Here we have made some real progress in limiting the kinds of warfare that killed so many people and occupied so many citizens in times gone by. Nearly all nations have come to believe now that it is unfashionable to raise a flag, roll the drums, and march across an international frontier onto the territory of another nation. Looking back on the story of man, the outlawing of formal, advertised aggression is no mean accomplishment. There are plenty of boundary disputes left in the world—49 of them, if the United States Department of State's research is up-to-date. But there is a presumption against overt military operations in somebody else's country, and that is a step forward in the progress of civilization.

However, the very fact that formal invasions are unfashionable has led to a new practice: the more or less hidden intervention by nations in the internal politics of their neighbors. Most of the fighting and killing that goes on in Asia, in Africa, and in Latin America can be traced to outside intervention designed to overthrow governments by violent means.

In Asia, Africa, and Latin America nearly every country wants and needs the help of outsiders in achieving those "better standards of life in larger freedom" which are the goal of their rising expectations and the promise of their political independence. So outsiders are bound to be involved to some extent in their international affairs. The question therefore is: Under what restraints will the outsiders operate on the inside?

Over the years, more through the practice of nations than the teachings of scholars, we have developed a rough-and-ready ethic to guide this widespread practice of mutual involvement. When the legitimate government, the constituted authorities of a nation, asks for outside help as a sovereign act, an expression of their own independence, then the involvement of outsiders is all right. But when outsiders come in, without the permission of the national government, to help dissident insiders in an internal struggle for power, that is not all right; it is all wrong.

It is not an easy line to draw. The principle that outsiders should be invited, not crash the party, is far from an infallible guide to good conduct. Invitations can be forged, and the government officials who issue them can be bribed or seduced. But still, the principle of permission is the best ethic mankind has yet developed to prevent a reversion to imperialism and foreign domination.

If the principle is established that the outsiders, not the insiders, decide when intervention is right, the fragile fabric of nationhood will come apart at the seams in dozens of nations in Africa and elsewhere. Every nation has its dissidents, its internal struggle for power, its internal arguments about who should be in charge and how the country should be run. But if every internal rivalry is to become a Spanish Civil War with each faction drawing in other Africans and Great Powers from other continents, the history of independent Africa in this century will be bloody and shameful and the aspirations of Africa's wonderful peoples will be cruelly postponed into the 21st century. This is why the United States supported the UN Operation in the Congo (ONUC) and was sorry that it had to be withdrawn, its mission incomplete, because of the UN's financial difficulties. And that is why we oppose, and must continue to oppose, foreign intervention in the Congo (Leopoldville).

Promoting Individual Human Rights

The moment will come, I hope and believe, when the third great issue of the UN's next twenty years is how—and indeed whether—to bring to life the human rights provisions of the Charter.

It is not yet clear whether the national leaders in the world, either in the large countries or in the small ones, really mean to promote (as they have agreed in Article 55 of the Charter) the "universal respect for, and observance of, human rights and fundamental freedoms for all without distinction as to race, sex, language, or religion." Nor is it clear that the governments of the Members of the UN intend to take (as Article 56 enjoins them) "joint and separate action in cooperation with the Organization for the achievement of the purposes set forth in Article 55.

The words I have just quoted from the UN Charter are not very familiar ground to most Americans—or to the citizens of other countries, either. The reason is simple: This is the underdeveloped area of the Charter.

Part of the trouble, I suppose, is a confusion between nationhood and freedom. Self-determination, that noble goal through which a billion people emerged from foreign rule, was sometimes a racial as well as a national battle cry. Too often in the modern nationalist revolution—let us say it with all honesty—the promise of freedom was a promise of "separate but equal" status in the world. Thus, the leaders of most nations made it perfectly clear that they wanted the UN to protect the achievement of nationhood by pressing for the self-determination of groups and peoples. But there is a good deal of uncertainty as to how far we—and our fellow Members—want the UN to go in criticizing and correcting the ethical delinquencies of peoples once they have declared their national independence.

It is this uncertainty, this confusion between nationhood and freedom, this feeling that national and racial and ethnic groups, not individual men, women, and children, should be the beneficiaries of the continuing struggle for freedom, which in the longer run may prove to be the most divisive and troublesome threat to a viable world organization. Yet if the central question about freedom is man's humanity to man, the UN's relevance to our future will partly rest on what it does or neglects to do about individual human rights.

Despite the growing international concern, human rights are for the most part unreachable from outside the walls of sovereignty. Those walls are thick, but they are not opaque. Light can filter through. And the prestigious light from an international agency shining in the dark corners of national oppression may add a new dimension to the protection of human rights, just as the penetrating laser beam has added a new dimension to physical light.

The problem is how sharp beams of international light can be effectively poked into the world's darkest recesses of reaction and how those beams, once inside, can be focused and intensified until, like the laser ray, they burn out the malignancy of man's inhumanity to man.

But right here is a policy question for us. Americans need to consider whether, as the necessary price for shining the UN's searchlight on oppression elsewhere, they are prepared to have the UN turn its attention to the mote in our own eye.

The prospect need not fill us with alarm. Nothing the UN could do would much increase the candle power of public attention that already surrounds the scene wherever racial or religious discrimination is practiced by public agencies against the law, the Constitution, and the public policy of the United States. The UN is unlikely to reveal anything about the United States that is not already thoroughly in the public domain, courtesy of our own political debates, our own wire services, and our own television networks.

The United States, for its part, in 1963 reversed a ten-year record of inaction on international human rights declarations and conventions. At that time, President John F. Kennedy submitted to the Senate for advice and consent three multilateral conventions, the Conventions on Slavery, Forced Labor, and the Political Rights of Women. Also pending in the Senate is another important instrument, the Convention on the Prevention and Punishment of the

Crime of Genocide, the practice of ethnic extermination. The Administration continues to support ratification of these conventions. The United States should not stand aside from support of fundamental principles which the American people have long held among their most cherished national assets.

Over the years many ideas have been offered to make the UN's work in the field of human rights more meaningful. Among them have been suggestions for appointing rapporteurs; for setting up special *ad hoc* committees to take testimony and issue findings; for establishing a new position, a full-time human rights commissioner who would observe developments in this area and publish annual progress reports; and for other arrangements aimed at having the UN "do more" in this field of human relations.

The world community must search its conscience to decide whether the beneficial rays of public attention cannot be used to shed new light on those dimly lit sections of the Charter which proclaim "the dignity of the human person" and the "equal rights of men and women and of nations large and small."

This is not a pointless exercise unrelated to political reality. Under the klieg lights of world opinion, a nation's prestige is engaged; and since national power is not unrelated to national prestige, governments are influenced by world opinion—even though this is hard to prove because they seldom admit it.

The blended conscience of men of goodwill may wink at injustice in the dark, but when the lights are on, a good conscience must speak, or desert its possessor. No government anywhere is quite immune to the moral indignation of those—including its own citizens—who watch it at work. The increased moral illumination brought to bear by the combined conscience of nations need dazzle no one here at home, where we have long grown accustomed to the light. But the results could be startling in those areas of the world that still live mostly in the dark.

The International "Apportionment" Issue

While the General Assembly is sorting out the ethics of nuclear weapons, nonnuclear intervention, and international attention to human rights, a great constitutional issue will be increasingly discussed in the corridors of the UN and the chancelleries of the world. We might call it the international apportionment issue.

In the United Nations today there are two clearly discernible facts which nobody disputes but which are not easy to combine into one political system: on the one hand, the sovereign equality of nations, an immutable principle of the Charter; on the other hand, the uneven distribution of real power and real resources in the real world. Somehow the small number of large and powerful countries must come to terms with the sovereign equality of nations.

And somehow the small-country majority in the United Nations must come to terms with the minority of nations that make the UN not a debating society but an action agency for peace.

The most striking example of this constitutional issue is the Soviet claim that all peacekeeping matters should be handled solely in the Security Council. I think it fair to say that no non-Communist country in the world agrees with this extreme position. Peacekeeping is the UN's most important function, and it is clear that the membership at large intends to have something to do with that function.

But, on the other hand, the command and control of UN peacekeeping operations must provide an adequate voice for those nations which provide the troops and the airlift and the money to carry out UN decisions.

Thus, a compromise will have to be worked out somewhere in the mainstream between the view that wants to give the peacekeeping monopoly to the Security Council and the view that wants the General Assembly to be the main reliance of a turbulent world. I think that sooner or later a middle way will be found. Because there is no alternative to peace, there is also no alternative to workable peacekeeping machinery in this fragile and dangerous world. One way or another, this parliament of the world's peoples will have to defend the powers it has—as every parliamentary institution in the long history of free institutions has from time to time had to do in order to stay in business at all.

There are many ways in which the Security Council and the General Assembly can share the responsibility for keeping the peace. The search for the best way—that is to say, the way that can work in practice, however messy it may look in theory—may be the most important single thing happening in the UN during International Cooperation Year.

A World of Diversity

These four great issues (the spread of nuclear weapons, the ethics of intervention, the dilemma of human rights, and the reconciliation of resources with representation in the UN system) are major issues visibly ahead of us in UN affairs. On their outcome depends the success or failure of the primary aim of United States foreign policy—to help create a world safe for diversity.

The vision of a world of cultural pluralism, a world of independent nations following their own historical bent, diverse in social systems, economic orders, and political creeds, participating nonetheless in mutual enterprise based on consent, constructing by stages a new system of world order based on common interest, defending the human rights of individual men and women and children—this vision is anything but visionary.

The job of breathing life and substance into this vision, which is the task of peace, President Lyndon B. Johnson recently called "the assignment of the century."

Implications and Questions for the Future

Inis L. Claude, Jr.

Undertaking to write about the future of the United Nations may well be regarded as a risky if not a downright foolhardy enterprise, particularly in 1965, between the tragicomedy of the nineteenth General Assembly and the great uncertainty of the twentieth session. For many people, the question is whether the United Nations *has* a future, and for some of them this question is purely rhetorical. I think that it has, or that, at any rate, *general international organization* has a future. Whatever may happen to the United Nations, I find it difficult to conceive that the men who conduct the foreign relations of states will ever again consider that they can dispense with a comprehensive institutional mechanism or that they will, in the foreseeable future, contrive a global mechanism fundamentally different in character from the United Nations. Objectively, the operation of the international system requires an organizational framework virtually coextensive with the system; just as education requires schools and universities and medicine requires hospitals and clinics, so international relations require at least as much organizational apparatus as the United Nations system provides. Moreover, there is evidence that this objective need has penetrated the consciousness of most statesmen. The questions that they have asked about international organization in the last twenty years have not included the question of whether it is sensible to equip the international system with a general institutional structure.

In essaying a look into the future, one has a basic choice between prophecy and prediction, that is, between asserting unconditionally what one believes will happen and arguing in an "if this, then that" vein. The prophet may consult a teacup or a crystal ball or, more likely, his fears or hopes. Prediction, on the other hand, involves analysis rather than intuition; it is a matter of

Inis L. Claude, Jr., a member of the Board of Editors of *International Organization,* is Professor of Political Science, University of Michigan.

postulating causative chains, of attempting to demonstrate the different consequences of alternative combinations of factors and circumstances. This is the
business of the scientist; he tells us not that X will surely occur, but that X
will result if A and B come into play, while the addition of C would produce
Y instead, and the deletion of A would bring about Z.

A political scientist dealing with the future of the United Nations could
minimize his risk by adhering strictly to a predictive function. The allegation
that political science has scarcely achieved scientific stature very often rests
upon the misapprehension that science is concerned with and expert at prophecy rather than prediction, as I have defined these terms. In fact, political
science is capable of yielding some rough predictions, some reasonably confident answers to the question, "What will happen *if* . . . ?," and it shares with
other sciences the incapacity to function prophetically, to deal with the flat
question, "What will *happen*?"

The essential starting point of a discussion of the future of the United Nations is an analysis of its past and present, such as has been provided by my
colleagues in this symposium. One can develop an understanding of the trends
that have come into operation, project them into the future, and attempt to
assess their implications for the further evolution of the Organization. This
may be characterized as a predictive enterprise, and it will be my major task
herein.

But will the trends carry over into the future, or will they be stalled, or
reversed, or offset by new trends? What will happen to the momentum and
direction of change? Such questions as these inexorably intrude, and they
require the introduction of a prophetic element in our analysis. To project,
or, for that matter, to refuse to project, the trends of the past into the future
is in some sense to prophesy, to assume, or to assert something about the future that cannot really be known. Moreover, the task of projection is complicated by the fact that contradictory trends are to be found in the development
of the United Nations, and one therefore has to concern himself with the
issue of *which* trends are likely to prevail in the years that lie ahead.

The task of describing the future of the United Nations would be difficult
enough if one had only to cope with trends—with plotting the course along
which the ship of multistate will presumably be taken by the winds of international politics and the currents of institutional development. But this is only
the beginning of the problem, for the vessel is *manned,* crowded with sailors
and would-be navigators who tamper with the sails, the tiller, and the throttle
of the auxiliary motors—an ill-disciplined and even mutinous crew. The future of the United Nations is dependent not only upon the working of broad,
impersonal forces and tendencies but also upon the policies of many governments and the vagaries of numerous individuals. The general trend toward
universality is a part of the picture—but so are United States policy toward

Communist China and the secessionist whim of a Sukarno. Under these circumstances, the future of the Organization is most uncertain, and the responsible scholar is obliged to exhibit a corresponding lack of certitude in his analysis. At best, one can state possibilities and probabilities, taking some comfort from the fact that part of what is unknown about the future of the United Nations is unknowable, given the role of indeterminate factors in the shaping of that future.

THE MOVEMENT TOWARD UNIVERSALITY

The most prominent development in the history of the United Nations thus far has been the enlargement of the Organization's membership, the progressive movement toward universality. This deserves to be called the "key" tendency because it has opened the way for many of the most basic changes that have taken place in the nature and functioning of the Organization. The number and variety of independent political entities in the world have grown rapidly, and the membership rosters of the United Nations and most of the specialized agencies have been lengthened not only primarily in response to this phenomenon but also by the increasingly comprehensive inclusion of older states. The United Nations has tended to reflect the steady globalization of international relations.

This growth in the size and the heterogeneity of the Organization results from attitudes on both sides of the membership fence, for admission to membership requires application and approval. Movement toward universality is dependent upon the desires of non-Members to effect entry and upon the willingness of the requisite combination of existing Members to permit entry.

Postwar governments, with remarkably few exceptions, have demonstrated the urge to have their states attain, and retain, membership in the United Nations. Many states have doubtless been disappointed in the values derived from membership, and some have chafed at the defeats and frustrations that they have experienced within the world body, but only Indonesia has thus far defected. On the whole, statesmen have acted as if they regard membership in the United Nations as a significantly useful feature of national policy; the demand for universality has remained high.

From the other side, support for the principle of universality has developed so far as to break down almost completely the restrictive membership provisions incorporated in the Charter. Few states have adhered with complete consistency to this principle, as recurrent political battles over the exclusion or expulsion of states have indicated. However, the general position that maximum comprehensiveness is a value to be sought by the Organization has gained ascendancy and has received expression in the extraordinary proliferation of flagpoles in the United Nations Plaza.

Looking to the future, we may reasonably expect the continued operation of the "want in–let in" formula to produce an ever closer approximation of a literally global United Nations. Of course, Indonesia's example may be emulated; certainly, there are other states with longer and more impressive lists of grievances against the United Nations than Indonesia's. Moreover, there are Members against which large blocs of states have persistent grievances, and it is possible that the growing expulsionist mentality may prevail. However, there is no evidence yet that disaffection or disillusionment with the Organization or discord within it is likely to reverse the trend toward universalization; expansion seems more probable than shrinkage. The collective advantage of having and the national advantage of participating in a virtually universal forum appear still to command widespread acknowledgment.

There is every reason to assume that this commitment to the value of universality will eventually prevail over the policy, championed particularly by the United States, of excluding Communist China from participation in the United Nations. It is by no means clear on what precise terms the complex issues relating to the representation of China may be resolved, but the notion that the most populous country in the world is actually represented by the regime ensconced in Formosa is a transparent fiction, and the day must surely come when the mirror of the United Nations will reflect the political reality of Communist control of China. That reflection may create as much difficulty in and for the United Nations as the corresponding reality creates in and for the world of states. But the acceptance of this consequence will represent simply the reaffirmation of the Organization's fundamental premise: the proposition that the United Nations should seek to limit the disturbance of international relations caused by conflict between states and that it must acknowledge the limitations imposed upon its functioning by conflicts arising between Great Powers. The future value of the United Nations is dependent upon the degree to which it manages to cope with the problems posed by global political reality, not upon the degree to which it can contrive to evade those problems by maintaining an artificially restrictive definition of that reality.

In any case, the growth that has already occurred has implications for the United Nations which have not yet been fully realized in either the formal structure or the political processes of the Organization. Even if the United Nations should move no further toward or should slip somewhat away from the point of total inclusiveness, there are adjustments to the accomplished transformation of the cast of characters—as, for example, in the so-called North-South confrontation and the East-West rivalry—that remain to be completed. In short, there are trends that appear to project themselves into the future development of the Organization, unpaid installments of debts already contracted to change. In these matters, the burden of proof rests upon one who would deny the projection; only if the changes of the past were thoroughly undone would the adaptation of the United Nations to those changes be removed from the prospect.

CONTRIBUTIONS TO ECONOMIC DEVELOPMENT

First, I would cite the trend toward the concentration of the attention and resources of the United Nations upon economic and social matters and, within this area, upon the problems and aspirations of the underdeveloped states. This trend, which has moved upward without interruption from the beginning of the Organization, owes something to the persuasiveness of the functionalist theory of international organization but much more to the combination of the emergence of scores of new Member States from the wreckage of the colonial system and the competitive strategies developed by the great antagonists of the Cold War. The actual and potential beneficiaries of international programs designed to promote and assist economic development have acquired numerical predominance in the United Nations, and there is every reason to assume that their political demand for expanding such programs will continue to grow in intensity and effectiveness.

Whether the supply of political incentive to meet this demand will undergo corresponding growth is less certain. Financial support for United Nations activities in this field derives largely from the United States and its Western allies, and the issue of maintaining or increasing the level of support depends primarily upon the internal policy-making processes of those countries, notably the United States. The strength of the political demand for internationally channeled economic aid, expressed within the United Nations, can hardly fail to be influential but it is unlikely to be decisive in the formulation of policy by the United States and other Western countries. Even less can one expect this demand to convert the Soviet Union into a substantial backer of United Nations economic programs.

The future of financial support for United Nations technical assistance and development activities has come to be tied up with the controversy over the funding of peacekeeping operations. Ironically, the assertion by the General Assembly of an enlarged competence to require financial support for the Organization's peacekeeping operations has endangered the supply of voluntarily contributed funds for its economic and technical activities. Preoccupied with the issue of the costs of the UN Emergency Force (UNEF) and the UN Operation in the Congo (ONUC), the United States espoused a principle broad enough in its implications to suggest that the Assembly has authority to assess Members for support of economic activities. However, it is clear that the United States has no intention of accepting the implication of its position on the budgetary issue. In the battle over the liquidation of the peacekeeping debt, it has been United States policy to threaten reduction or withdrawal of voluntary support for economic programs rather than to proclaim willingness to accept obligations that might be voted by the Assembly. If and when the financial controversy is solved, it seems likely that the Assembly will emerge with a reduced rather than an expanded capacity to make binding budgetary demands upon states, and there is a real probability that the strife over this issue will prove to have weakened rather than strengthened the disposition of the crucial Members to accede to demands for enlarged voluntary contributions in support of more ambitious economic programs.

Even though the immediate prospects for securing the funds to sustain a substantially expanded United Nations program of economic development may be poor, the point remains that we must expect the demand for such a program to be expressed with increasing vigor and to become the dominant theme in United Nations debates. The would-be beneficiaries can dominate the politics of the United Nations even if they cannot decide the policies of the wealthier Member States. The Organization will serve as a channel through which constant pressure for more generous international assistance to developing states will be exercised.

Preventive Diplomacy

A second major feature of the development of the United Nations whose projection into the future deserves consideration is the emergence of the peace-keeping operational function known as preventive diplomacy. This development is rooted in the Cold War and the arms race, the thermonuclear revolution and mutual deterrence, and the increasing prominence in the United Nations of the new states, which in this instance are considered as uncommitted rather than as underdeveloped states. Preventive diplomacy involves the use of the Organization for politically impartial intervention into a troubled area peripheral to the Cold War, for the purpose of forestalling the competitive intrusion of the major Cold War antagonists. It represents a kind of "disengagement before the fact." Its feasibility depends in the first instance upon the motivation of the Great Powers to avoid a confrontation that might shift their relations from stalemate to showdown, secondly upon their confidence that the United Nations will function neutrally rather than in the interest of the opposing Cold War camp, and finally upon the willingness of the Member States least involved in Cold War alignments to serve as agents of the United Nations in carrying out this function. The latter two points emphasize the essentially *neutralist* character of preventive diplomacy; it is a neutralizing function, to be exercised as far as possible by states whose uncommittedness in the Cold War is matched by a commitment to making the United Nations an effective stabilizer of international relations in the era of the Cold War. The concept of preventive diplomacy requires the United Nations to stand as a collective embodiment of positive neutralism, with its neutralist—or most nearly neutralist—Members setting the tone of its policy and bearing the major responsibility for executing its functions in the realm of world politics. By and large, this means that the Members which are the primary consumers of United Nations economic benefits must serve as the primary producers of its political services. In principle, the Cold War makes preventive diplomacy necessary, and the existence of a substantial group of uncommitted Members of the United Nations makes it possible.

But *is* the exercise of preventive diplomacy a possible role for the United Nations in the future? The Organization has acquired considerable experience in the conduct of peacekeeping operations falling under this rubric, most notably, the ventures launched in the Middle East in 1956 and in the Congo (Leopoldville) in 1960. While these operations have gone far to demonstrate the potential values of preventive diplomacy, they have gone even further to indicate the dangers and difficulties of the involvement of the United Nations in this kind of political function. The parlous condition of the United Nations at the present moment punctuates, with an exclamation point, the proposition that preventive diplomacy has proved dangerous business for the Organization in the past and, with a question mark, the assertion that it can or should be the political business of the Organization in the future.

The financial crisis of the United Nations is in reality a political crisis, stemming from disagreements concerning, above all, the conduct of the Congo operation. That undertaking demonstrated the difficulty of reaching and maintaining agreement on the precise definition of the functions of a United Nations peacekeeping force in a concrete and highly complicated situation, the unfortunate effect of a lack of universal confidence in the political impartiality of the Organization's executive mechanism, and the danger faced by the Organization in conducting an operation from which a major power has withdrawn its consent. The demand, pressed by the United States, for application of the legal principle that Members refusing to meet their financial obligations should suffer the penalty prescribed in Article 19 of the Charter has collided head on with the political principle that no state can realistically be expected to lend support to actions which it regards as inimical to its interests. The resultant crisis has put the United Nations in a state of suspended animation, hung up between the pegs of financial insolvency and political dissolution.

It is a curious but promising fact that the most fundamental disagreement between the United States and the Soviet Union, the leading players in the game of "chicken" in Turtle Bay, relates not to the future but to the past utilization of the United Nations. Although the General Assembly has asserted its authority to bind Members to pay their designated shares of the costs of UNEF and ONUC, it has refrained from invoking that authority in more recent and less expensive peacekeeping operations and gives every indication of being disposed to avoid that invocation in the future. This appears to be entirely acceptable to the United States which, having won the

endorsement of the International Court of Justice and the General Assembly
for its claim that the Soviet Union and other delinquents are obligated to pay
past assessments decreed by the Assembly, has developed the capacity to contain its enthusiasm for projecting into the future the Assembly's competence
to tax Members for the support of major activities which they may oppose.
The United States is in the position of demanding that the Soviet Union and
others yield to a principle which, if not yet discarded, has already been marked
for discard. As for the future, all the major powers share an interest in devising a financial control arrangement compatible with their intention to let
national interests (as they conceive them), not international majorities, determine what activities they will support. The controversy over the debts of
the past has tended to obscure this basis for possible agreement upon a budgetary system for the future.

On the other hand, the handling of this controversy at the nineteenth session of the General Assembly tended to make clear the virtually unanimous
motivation of the Member States to preserve the viability of the Organization.
The threatened showdown over the application of Article 19 appeared to endanger the United Nations, regardless of how the decision might go; the
choice seemed to lie between precipitating the disaffection either of the Soviet
Union and its companions in financial delinquency or of the United States
and its partners in the campaign to enforce Article 19. The extraordinary
methods adopted to avoid this potentially disastrous showdown may have
damaged the dignity of the Organization, but they reflected a deep commitment, shared by every important group of Members, to the protection of the
integrity of the Organization. This demonstration of the strength of the incentive to give the United Nations a future and the fact that the major powers
are less sharply divided on the issue of future financial arrangements than
on the problem of liquidating the debts of the past mean that there is some
basis, beyond vague faith in the capacity of statesmen to muddle through, for
the hope that negotiation can open a way out of the present impasse.

At this point, it is far from clear whether it will be possible for the United
Nations to continue the development of its role as an agency of preventive
diplomacy. What is clear is that this is the only operational role available to
the United Nations in the realm of high politics and security. Under the political and military circumstances of our time, the United Nations cannot
function as the operating center of a collective security system; whatever active contribution it can make to the stabilization of international relations at
points of crisis must be made in its capacity as a neutralizer, a servant of the
common interest in preventing confrontations that might produce catastrophe.
The continuing need for preventive diplomacy is evident; its future possibility
remains uncertain.

Whatever happens in this respect, the United Nations will undoubtedly encounter frequent opportunities in the future, as in the past, to test its capability for promoting peaceful settlement of international disputes by the more conventional methods of investigation, mediation, conciliation, and the like. Whether or not the technique of preventive diplomacy is discarded, parliamentary diplomacy will continue to operate, and quiet diplomacy will offer important possibilities.

The role of the United Nations in facilitating peaceful settlement has been restricted by the intractability of the parties to some disputes, the disposition of states to exploit the possibilities of parliamentary victory in United Nations organs, and their unwillingness to expose their positions to the pressures of politically uncongenial majorities in those organs. Regional organizations, which have escaped the direction and control of the United Nations that was stipulated in the Charter, have been used to some degree not only as alternative agencies for promoting the solution of disputes but also as jurisdictional refuges, providing pretexts for keeping disputes out of UN hands. These political factors are likely to continue to inhibit the full development of the United Nations' potentiality for assisting in the settlement of disputes. Nevertheless, there are favorable indications: the widespread consciousness of the danger of permitting disputes to degenerate into military conflicts that might prove uncontrollable; the relaxation of the rigidities of Cold War alignment and confrontation; and the increasingly neutralist political tone of the United Nations.

These developments suggest that a growing number of issues may become negotiable in principle, that statesmen may tend to exhibit the greater flexibility required for successful negotiation, and that the United Nations, becoming less a Western instrument and more an agency recognized as the joint property of all significant groups of states, may develop a more generally acceptable mediatory role in serious negotiations. There are even some signs that the Security Council may be reinstated as a significant political organ and put to its originally intended use as an organ for joint action by the major powers when they are in agreement and, more importantly in the actual and probable circumstances of the political world, as a chamber for meaningful negotiation between the major powers when they find themselves in disagreement.

Collective Legitimization

The third major trend which is intimately related to the virtual universalization of the United Nations is the development by the Organization of a political function that I should describe as *collective legitimization*. By this I mean to suggest that the political organs of the United Nations, most notably the General Assembly, have come to be regarded and utilized by Member States as dispensers of impressively valuable international approval and disapproval of the claims, policies, and behavior of states. In both domestic and international politics, the quest for legitimacy is a persistent feature; if not to satisfy their consciences, then to buttress their positions, political leaders seek authoritative endorsement of the validity and propriety of their positions and denial of this accolade to their opponents. In both realms, fashions tend not only to become almost universal but also to change from time to time; principles of legitimacy and agents of legitimization attain general recognition but ultimately give way to successors.

In our generation, international organizations have gradually gained acknowledgment as custodians of the seals of approval and disapproval for international purposes. While other multilateral bodies have shared in this, the fact that the United Nations General Assembly has acquired a fair claim to global representativeness accounts for its attaining the status of supreme agent of collective legitimization. In a more settled period, the International Court of Justice might be a favored candidate for this role, but under contemporary circumstances statesmen are strongly inclined to give priority to a political rather than a judicial organ. They seek validation of their political status and actions for its political value, and they prefer to pursue this through the political processes of the Assembly.

The function of collective legitimization carries with it the reverse function of *de*legitimization. Statesmen may be as eager to secure the condemnation of positions opposed to theirs as to gain endorsement of their own. Moreover, they may in some instances count it a valuable achievement to avoid the collective denunciation of their positions. The Assembly has become a forum within which battles over collective approval, disapproval, and acquiescence are constantly—and often hotly—waged.

The cynic may ask if it matters whether or not the Assembly—or some other international body—formally resolves to approve or not to approve, to disapprove or not to disapprove, a state's policy or action. The lawyer may point out that such a resolution has no legal significance, and the realist may note that it has no effective force behind it. The answer is to be found in the fact that statesmen *act as if it matters;* their subjective attribution of significance to the expressed attitude of the requisite majority of the Assembly confers an objective significance upon the Assembly's resolution or irresolution. The exertions of the representatives of states in the United Nations to gain parliamentary victories and avoid defeats testify to the importance attached to the role of the Organization as a validator of positions in international relations, and such exertions tend to *give* weight to the judgments expressed by the Organization.

This is not to say that states are prepared to acknowledge, in principle, that the formal pronouncements of the General Assembly or any other international organ are invariably entitled to universal respect or to restrict themselves, in fact, to behavior that is approved or condoned by a collective body.

Far from it: The state that loses a battle in the Assembly is very likely to denigrate the fitness of that body for the legitimizing role—although the same state would be the first to extol the virtue and wisdom of the Assembly if it had won the battle for approval. Moreover, any Member of the United Nations may act in violation of positions espoused by the Assembly; Nikita Khrushchev's celebrated declaration of the Soviet Union's intent to defy resolutions contrary to its interests differed only in style and tone, not in spirit, from the standard position of Member States. However, states are more inclined to deny their violations than to proclaim them as acts of defiance, and the very fact that they make strenuous efforts to influence Assembly resolutions means that they are reluctant to go against the grain of majority sentiment in that body. It is clear that states regard conformity with the collective opinion of Members of the United Nations as a factor of some importance in international relations. Statesmen are not firmly committed to *respect* the United Nations in its role as custodian of collective legitimacy, but they are heavily involved in the effort to *utilize* the Organization in that role.

The performance of the function of collective legitimization promises to figure prominently in the future role of the United Nations, regardless of what happens in the development of its operational functions. In some sense, collective legitimization is a function exercised by default; the United Nations cannot effectively say, "Thou shalt," so it says, "Thou should"; it cannot say, "Thou must," so it says, "Thou may." It substitutes authorization for commandment and condemnation for prevention. There is every reason to suppose that states will continue the effort to reinforce their positions by seeking United Nations endorsement—and, in so doing, expose their policies to the risk of collective disapprobation. Insofar as collective approval or disapproval becomes a significant factor in the calculus of national policy, the United Nations may exercise a salutary influence upon international relations. While many would argue that respect for law is the ideal principle, I would say that states could do much worse than to acquire and exhibit a decent respect for the opinions of mankind, translated as respect for resolutions approved by representatives of a majority or more of their fellow members of international organizations.

On the other hand, collective legitimization by United Nations processes has its seamy side. As in all political bodies, strength of interest tends to prevail in the Assembly over clarity of principle or purity of judgment. Bias and arbitrariness may be expected to characterize some decisions of the Assembly in the future no less than they have in the past, and states should perhaps be advised that wisdom requires them to take Assembly resolutions into account, not that justice requires them to accord those resolutions full respect.

Moreover, the passion for using the United Nations as an instrument of collective legitimization involves the danger that the Organization may be put into the position of discouraging and inhibiting, rather than encouraging and facilitating, the process of accommodation among Member States. The conferment of collective approval or disapproval may be treated as a substitute for negotiation of differences, and it may contribute to a rigidification of positions that hinders meaningful negotiation. How to avoid this pitfall is an unsolved problem bequeathed by the past to the future.

Conclusions

We cannot be unconditionally certain that the United Nations has a future. We can only assert that there is a clear need for the Organization, a need that appears to be generally recognized, and that the Organization has developed a distinct usefulness, a usefulness that appears to be generally appreciated. The value of the United Nations for the future lies not in any prospect that it will become stronger but in the promise that it may become more useful, and useful in more varied respects, to statesmen who have the responsibility of conducting international relations in an era of unprecedented complexity and danger.

Statesmen will doubtless compete in the future, as they have in the past, for the capacity to use the United Nations as an instrument of national or bloc policy in political contests. The greatest potential value of the Organization lies, however, in its being used as an instrument of the whole body of states to promote the stabilization of international relations, the accommodation of divergent interests and aspirations, and the development of consensus and cooperation wherever possible. If the United Nations can serve to enhance the general orderliness of international relations, it will thereby make its greatest possible contribution to the national interests of every Member State.

DATE DUE